The Progressive Era

The Progressive Era

MURRAY N. ROTHBARD

EDITED BY
PATRICK NEWMAN

FOREWORD BY
JUDGE ANDREW P. NAPOLITANO

MISESINSTITUTE
AUBURN, ALABAMA

Mises Institute
518 West Magnolia Ave.
Auburn, Ala. 36832
mises.org

paperback edition: 978-1-61016-674-4
large print edition: 978-1-61016-675-1
epub: 978-1-61016-677-5

Contents

Chapter 14: The Federal Reserve as a Cartelization Device: The Early Years, 1913–1930 463

Chapter 15: Herbert Hoover and the Myth of Laissez-faire. 513

Foreword

When I was in my junior and senior years at Princeton studying history in the early 1970s, I became fascinated with the Progressive Era. It attracted me at a time when America rejected as profoundly as it did under Lincoln and the Radical Republicans and even under FDR, the libertarian first principles of the American Revolution.

To pursue this interest, I volunteered to take a course in the Graduate School, a procedure permitted for a few undergraduates at the time. The course was an advanced look at Progressive intellectual thought taught by Woodrow Wilson's biographer and hagiographer, Professor Arthur S. Link. The readings were all pro-Progressive as were all the other students in the class. We studied Professor Link's works and the claptrap by his colleague William E. Leuchtenberg.

In my search for a rational understanding of the Era — and for ammunition to use in the classroom where I was regularly beaten up — I asked Professor Link if any academic had made the argument effectively that the Progressives were power-hungry charlatans in the guise of noble businessmen, selfless politicians, and honest academics.

He told me of a young fellow named Rothbard, of whose work he had only heard, but had not read. This advice sent me to *Man, Economy, and State*, which I devoured; and my ideological odyssey was off to the races.

Like many of Rothbard's student admirers, I also devoured *For a New Liberty*, all four volumes of *Conceived in Liberty*, and *The Mystery of Banking*. As any student of human freedom in general or of the Austrian school specifically, knows, these must-reads are all a joy to read. And we also know that in those works and others, Rothbard established himself as the great interpreter of Ludwig von Mises.

While he was writing those books and lecturing nationally and producing many ground-breaking articles and essays on human freedom, he began to write discrete chapters of a book he would not live to publish on the Progressive Era.

One of his great young interpreters, Florida Southern College professor and Mises Fellow Patrick Newman, has picked up where our hero left off. Professor Newman is a brilliant interpreter of Rothbard. His assemblage of these heretofore unpublished chapters, and the vast notes he has added to them have produced a masterpiece that might actually have made Murray Rothbard blush.

Readers of *The Progressive Era* will carry away an overwhelming impression that history is "a comprehensive resurrection of the past." Rothbard was never satisfied with the presentation of a general thesis or the sketch of a historical period, which is why readers will find detailed accounts of an enormous number of people. Only a historian of Rothbard's immense intellectual energy and knowledge could have written what would become *The Progressive Era*.

Rothbard did not amass details merely to give readers a sense of the Progressive Era, from the 1880s to the 1920s. Rather, he uses these details to support a revolutionary new interpretation. Many people view the Progressives as reformers who fought against corruption and modernized our laws and institutions. Rothbard proves to the hilt that this common opinion is false.

The Progressives aimed to displace a 19th-century America that respected individual rights based on natural law. They claimed that natural law and a free economy were outmoded and unscientific ideas; and argued that through applying science to politics, they could replace a corrupt and stagnant old order with a State-ordered more prosperous and egalitarian one.

Rothbard dissents:

> Briefly, the thesis is that the rapid upsurge of statism in this period was propelled by a coalition of two broad

groups: (a) certain big business groups, anxious to replace a roughly *laissez-faire* economy by a new form of mercantilism, cartelized and controlled and subsidized by a strong government under their influence and control; and (b) newly burgeoning groups of intellectuals, technocrats, and professionals: economists, writers, engineers, planners, physicians, etc., anxious for power and lucrative employment at the hands of the State. Since America had been born in an antimonopoly tradition, it became important to put over the new system of cartelization as a "progressive" curbing of big business by a humanitarian government; intellectuals were relied on for this selling job. These two groups were inspired by Bismarck's creation of a monopolized welfare-warfare state in Prussia and Germany.

Rothbard constantly overturns accepted ideas as he argues for his interpretation. Most of us have heard of the furor early in the 20th century over conditions in the Chicago meat packing industry, set off by Upton Sinclair's novel *The Jungle*. Few people are aware, however, that Sinclair's sensationalism was fiction, in direct contradiction to what contemporary inspections of the meat packing plants revealed.

Rothbard goes much further. He shows how, beginning in the 1880s, the large meat packing plants lobbied for greater regulation themselves.

Unfortunately for the myth, [about *The Jungle's* influence] the drive for federal meat inspection actually began more than two decades earlier, and was launched mainly by the big meat packers themselves. The spur was the urge to penetrate the European market for meat, something which the large meat packers thought could be done if the government would certify the quality of meat, and thereby make American meat more highly rated abroad. Not coincidentally, as in all Colbertist mercantilist legislation over the centuries, a governmentally-coerced upgrading of quality would serve to cartelize: to lower production, restrict competition, and raise prices to the consumers.

Rothbard sees in postmillennial pietism a key to the entire Progressive Era. The postmillennials preached that Jesus would inaugurate His kingdom only after the world had been reformed, and they accordingly saw a religious mandate to institute the social reforms they favored.

Their influence was pervasive. For example, Rothbard draws an unexpected connection between their ideas and eugenics:

> One way of correcting the increasingly pro-Catholic demographics ... often promoted in the name of "science," was eugenics, an increasingly popular doctrine of the progressive movement. Broadly, eugenics may be defined as encouraging the breeding of the "fit" and discouraging the breeding of the "unfit," the criteria of "fitness" often coinciding with the cleavage between native, white Protestants and the foreign born or Catholics — or the white-black cleavage. In extreme cases, the unfit were to be coercively sterilized.

Theodore Roosevelt was the quintessential Progressive, and Rothbard shows in convincing fashion how his analytic framework helps explain that bizarre and flamboyant figure. Roosevelt was allied with the banking interests of the House of Morgan. His "trust busting" activities were very selective. Only the trusts opposed to Morgan control were in Roosevelt's crosshairs. He supported "good" trusts, i.e., ones allied with the Morgan interests. Besides his Morgan alliance, Roosevelt was dominated by a bellicosity of maniacal proportions. "All his life Theodore Roosevelt had thirsted for war — any war — and military glory."

War and the Progressives were natural allies. War brought centralized control of the economy, and this allowed the Progressives to put their plans into effect. Rothbard writes:

> The wartime collectivism also held forth a model to the nation's liberal intellectuals; for here was seemingly a system that replaced *laissez-faire* not by the rigors and class hatreds of proletarian Marxism, but by a new strong State, planning and organizing the economy in harmony with all leading economic groups. It was, not coincidentally, to be a neomercantilism, a "mixed economy," heavily staffed by these selfsame liberal intellectuals.
>
> And finally, both big business and the liberals saw in the wartime model a way to organize and integrate the often unruly labor force as a junior partner in the corporatist

system — a force to be disciplined by their own "responsible" leadership of the labor unions.

I have addressed only a few of the themes analyzed in this vast book. Readers have many insights in store for them, including the origin of the Federal Reserve System, Herbert Hoover's activities as a Progressive, and the role of the Rockefellers in promoting Social Security. Nor does Rothbard shy away from the constitutional implications in all this, planted by Roosevelt and nurtured by his personal enemy but ideological comrade Woodrow Wilson. Rothbard notes that, the War Between the States aside, the Madisonian model — the federal government may only lawfully do what the Constitution directly permits — prevailed in government from 1789 to the 1880s. After the Progressive Era, the Wilsonian model — the federal government may do whatever there is a political will to do except that which the Constitution expressly prohibits — continues to prevail up to the present day.

We owe the appearance of *The Progressive Era* to the masterful detective work and patient labor of the good and youthful Professor Newman. In his "Introduction," he tells the dramatic tale of how Rothbard's book was discovered and assembled; and he has planted many teasers for the Rothbardian gems to come.

Rothbard's posthumous masterpiece is the definitive book on the Progressives. Only Murray Rothbard, with his unique scholarship, penetrating intelligence, prodigious work ethic, infectious love of life, and indefatigable devotion to liberty, could have written this book. It will soon be the must read study of this dreadful time in our past.

ANDREW P. NAPOLITANO
Hampton Township, New Jersey

Author of *Theodore and Woodrow: How Two American Presidents Destroyed Constitutional Freedom*

August 2017

Introduction

by Patrick Newman

Murray Rothbard was a scholar of enormous erudition with many diverse research interests. He wrote about economic theory, economic history, history of economic thought, pure history, philosophy, political science, and popular culture. Indeed, David Gordon writes, "A person examining the books and articles of Murray Rothbard without prior acquaintance with their author could not help wondering whether five or six prolific scholars shared the name 'Murray Rothbard.'"[1] Among all of these disciplines, one area of research to which Rothbard devoted a significant portion of his academic career and utilized many of the above fields was late 19th and early 20th century United States history, particularly the period that is known as the Progressive Era (approximately from the late 1890s to the early 1920s).

The Progressive Era was one of the most, if not the most, significant periods in U.S. history. The country was transformed from a relatively *laissez-faire* economy with a minimal government into a heavily regulated economy governed by an interventionist state. Correspondingly, the ideology of public intellectuals, business, the citizenry, and political parties drastically changed and became more interventionist. For most historians, this was the period when the country was growing up, when it

---

[1]David Gordon, *The Essential Rothbard* (Auburn, AL: Mises Institute, 2007), p. 7.

realized that minimal government was not suited for a modern industrial economy, because it produced numerous social ills such as frequent business cycles, unemployment, monopolies, crippling deflation, poor quality products, and enormous economic inequality. For Rothbard, on the other hand, it was the turning point, the time when America abandoned its *laissez-faire* strengths for the welfare-warfare state, and thereby plunged headfirst into all of its destructive consequences in the 20th century.

It is well known that Rothbard was deeply interested in the Progressive Era and throughout his life wrote numerous papers on it. Less well known, if it is known at all, is that Rothbard had also partially written a full blown *book* on the period, starting with the railroad interventions of the 1860s to the National Civic Federation of the early 1900s. The book was written while Rothbard was heavily involved with the Cato Institute during the 1970s. While Rothbard never formally completed the book, he informally finished it by writing the remaining chapters as various essays which were published in the 1980s and 1990s. Justin Raimondo, Rothbard's only biographer, commented on the project in 2000:

> Rothbard's writings on the Progressive Era, which have never been put together in a single volume, are a rich vein of analysis that contemporary scholars, libertarian or whatever, would do well to mine. In a fascinating narrative that unfolds like the plot of a novel, Rothbard documents his thesis with the fascinating stories of the men, and especially the women, who led the Progressive movement: ministers, social workers, intellectuals, and other professional do-gooders, whose zeal to remake America in the image of an (often secularized) God was rooted in the theological vision in which humanity would be the agency that would establish the Kingdom of God on earth.[2]

It is the task of this volume, at long last, to combine the unfinished book and other essays and publish the complete Rothbardian history of the Progressive Era.

In 1962, at the age of 36, the young Murray Rothbard had already produced multiple classics in the Austrian and libertarian tradition. Some of

---

[2]Justin Raimondo, *An Enemy of the State: The Life of Murray N. Rothbard* (Amherst, NY: Prometheus Books, 2000), pp. 252–53.

these were of smaller scope in the form of a paper or monograph. Others were much larger and more ambitious, such as his comprehensive treatise on economics. The first two volumes were published in 1962 under the title *Man, Economy, and State,* the last volume on government intervention deemed too controversial, *Power and Market,* in 1970. Another was *America's Great Depression,* which came out a year later, an economic history that gave the authoritative Austrian interpretation of the United States' Roaring Twenties and Great Depression. In addition to both of these, he also wrote his dissertation, *The Panic of 1819,* under Joseph Dorfman, which he defended in 1956 and published in 1962.[3,4] If he had ended his career then, Rothbard would have already cemented his status as one of the foremost scholars in Austrian economics and libertarianism.

However, Rothbard did not end his career, and he was still eager to write prodigiously, especially on completely different topics. In a letter to Kenneth S. Templeton, Jr., an associate of the Volker Fund which provided the research grant for *Man, Economy, and State,* he wrote:

> I am also happy to have the opportunity to leave the realm of economic theory, for, with the books published and especially with *Man, Economy, and State,* I believe I have said whatever I have to say about economics, and am now eager to move on. I have a constitutional aversion to repeating myself and milking my previous stuff *ad infinitum* — which seems to be a way of life for so many scholars.[5]

---

[3]See Murray Rothbard, *Man, Economy, and State: A Treatise on Economic Principles,* 2 vols., (Princeton, NJ: D. Van Nostrand, 1962); *The Panic of 1819: Reactions and Policies* (New York: Columbia University Press, 1962); *America's Great Depression* (Princeton, NJ: D. Van Nostrand, 1963); *Power and Market: Government and the Economy* (Menlo Park, CA: Institute for Humane Studies, 1970).

[4]Commenting on this period, Joseph Stromberg wrote that Rothbard was always busy working on multiple major projects. Joseph Stromberg, "Introduction," in Murray Rothbard, *Man, Economy, and State, with Power and Market,* 1st ed., (Auburn, AL: Mises Institute, 2004), p. lxii. This would continue throughout his life.

[5]Rothbard to Templeton, November 19, 1962; quoted in Stromberg, "Introduction," p. lxxxii. Indeed, one can detect a shift in research interests around this time by looking at his book reviews written for internal circulation at the Volker Fund, published in Murray Rothbard, *Strictly Confidential: The Private Volker Fund Memos of Murray N. Rothbard,* David Gordon, ed. (Auburn, AL: Mises Institute, 2010). The reviews on economic works included in the volume dated mostly from 1959–60, while his reviews on history and foreign policy were from 1961–62. The latter were on a wide range of topics, from the

For the remainder of the 1960s, Rothbard would focus his energies on a number of different fields, including history, political philosophy, and popular libertarianism. Like before, he would work on many projects of varying sizes at the same time. His next major work was a history of the United States. In late 1962, through the auspices of Templeton, he received a grant from the Lilly Endowment that would last until 1966 to write a one volume text on American history from a libertarian perspective. He was to work with Leonard Liggio, a young historian Rothbard's junior who had developed a close connection with him in the 1950s.

Rothbard's major projects frequently took on a life of their own. *Man, Economy, and State* was originally supposed to be a textbook translation of his mentor Ludwig von Mises's *Human Action*; instead, after careful deliberation, Rothbard decided to transform it into a full blown treatise on economics.[6] The last work of his life, *An Austrian Perspective on the History of Economic Thought*, was originally supposed to be a small volume that provided the anti-Heilbroner alternative to economic thought from Adam Smith onward. It too became a massive two-volume work (the planned third volume was unfortunately never written) that spanned from the ancient Greek philosophers to Karl Marx.[7] And the current history project would not be published as a general overview of American history at all, but instead a five-volume work titled *Conceived in Liberty* which spanned from the founding of the American colonies to the United States Constitution.[8] Commenting on the evolution of the project in an inter-

---

American Revolution to Jacksonian America up to World War II. They demonstrate that Rothbard was well versed in historical method as well as current works. See also Sheldon Richman, "Commentator on Our Times: A Quest for the Historical Rothbard," in *Man, Economy, & Liberty: Essays in Honor of Murray N. Rothbard*, Walter Block and Llewellyn H. Rockwell, Jr., eds. (Auburn, AL: Mises Institute, 1988), pp. 361–69.

[6]Ludwig von Mises, *Human Action: A Treatise on Economics* (New Haven, CT: Yale University Press, 1949).

[7]Murray Rothbard, *An Austrian Perspective on the History of Economic Thought*, vol. 1: *Economic Thought Before Adam Smith* (Brookfield, VT: Edward Elgar, 1995); *An Austrian Perspective on the History of Economic Thought*, vol. 2: *Classical Economics* (Brookfield, VT: Edward Elgar, 1995).

[8]Murray Rothbard, *Conceived in Liberty*, vol. 1: *A New Land, A New People: The American Colonies in the Seventeenth Century* (New Rochelle, NY: Arlington House Publishers, 1975); *Conceived in Liberty*, vol. 2: *"Salutary Neglect": The American Colonies in the First Half of the Eighteenth Century* (New Rochelle, NY: Arlington House Publishers, 1975); *Conceived in Liberty*, vol. 3: *Advance to Revolution, 1760–1775* (New Rochelle, NY: Arlington House Publishers, 1976); *Conceived in Liberty*, vol. 4: *The Revolutionary War, 1775–1784* (New

view, which equally applies to his other work, Rothbard said "I don't chart this stuff in advance. I don't like to work that way. I go step by step and it keeps getting longer."[9]

The major theme of *Conceived in Liberty*, which also applied to his other historical work, was the idea of Liberty versus Power. Throughout history, there has been an eternal battle between those who wield the coercive power of the State apparatus, and those who wish to resist it. Throughout most of human history, to quote the famous words of Thomas Hobbes, life was "nasty, brutish and short." Tyrants of all stripes, emperors, kings, feudal barons, and warlords, subjugated the masses and ruled over them with an iron first. The dominant economic system of this *ancien régime* was mercantilism, where government subsidies and other forms of protectionism were granted to favored businesses and other special interests. Then suddenly, in Britain and the American colonies in the 17th and 18th centuries, this changed, and much different forms of government were created — ones that were more limited in scope and allowed for greater liberty. The American colonies in particular cast off the oppressive shackles of their royal governors, and then later the British government completely in the American Revolution, in favor of a far more limited government and *laissez-faire* economic system that the people directly controlled. The fight was not over however, as those fighting for liberty and limited government continually clashed with those wishing to expand the size of government in the 19th century.

How did this occur? How were the ideas of Liberty versus Power disseminated to the broad populace? Why, for so long, did the public stand the depredations of their rulers in the *ancien régime*? Why did they later revolt against this dispensation and fight for liberty? And fast forwarding

---

Rochelle, NY: Arlington House Publishers, 1979). The first two volumes were written with the assistance of Leonard Liggio, and Rothbard was the primary author. The fifth volume on the American Constitution was never published, it was handwritten and then dictated into an audio recorder, which was lost.

For more on the project, see Brian Doherty, *Radicals for Capitalism: A Freewheeling History of the Modern American Libertarian Movement* (New York: PublicAffairs, 2007), pp. 296, 339, 672; Leonard P. Liggio, "A Classical Liberal Life," in *I Chose Liberty: Autobiographies of Contemporary Libertarians,* Walter Block, ed. (Auburn, AL: Mises Institute, 2010), pp. 187–88; Murray Rothbard, "A Conversation with Murray N. Rothbard," in *Austrian Economics Newsletter* 11, no. 2 (Summer 1990): 3–4.

[9]Murray Rothbard, "A Conversation with Murray N. Rothbard," p. 4.

to the Progressive Era, why did the pendulum shift back to statism and acceptance of increased state rule?

The answers to all of these questions involve the role of ideology and intellectuals filtering these messages down to the public. Throughout history, there have been two types of intellectuals. The first are the court intellectuals, originally the priests and the clergymen. Their job was to convince the public of the righteousness and legitimacy of the ruler through religious means (such as "The King is Divine") and to truckle to his predations. In return for these necessary public relations, the court intellectuals were to receive their fair share of the pelf taken from the public. This relationship was the famous Alliance of Throne and Altar that existed throughout most of history in various forms. On the other hand, there are the radical and revolutionary intellectuals who were out to spread the message of liberty and fight against the coercive order. They were not in it for power or prestige but instead liberty and justice.

The principal transmission mechanism during the American Revolution was the natural rights theory of John Locke. While Locke's work provided the ultimate theoretical edifice, it was very abstract, and the message was instead distributed to the public through the much more popular and easier readings of *Cato's Letters*, written by John Trenchard and Thomas Gordon.[10] Here were the works that instilled in the public a radical libertarian ideology that emanated in various ways in subsequent years. The importance of intellectuals in filtering ideas to the public, statist or libertarian, would be a major theme of Rothbard's historical work.

Rothbard never did write a complete history of the United States, as originally intended, but he did subsequently concentrate on certain periods, particularly the late 19th and early 20th centuries, which included everything from the Progressive Era to World War I to the Great Depression.[11] The Progressive Era was the main catalyst behind later events, for

---

[10]Murray Rothbard, *Conceived in Liberty*, 4 vols. (Auburn, AL: Mises Institute, 2011), pp. xv–xvi, 1114–1120. Much of this analysis was published earlier in Murray Rothbard, "Economic Determinism, Ideology, and the American Revolution," in *Libertarian Forum* (November 1974): 4–7. For appreciative surveys of Rothbard's approach, see Gordon, *The Essential Rothbard*, pp. 55–61; Gerard Casey, *Murray Rothbard: Major Conservative and Libertarian Thinkers* (New York: Continuum, 2010), pp. 103–06.

[11]The closest Rothbard came to writing a detailed overview of American history in its entirety was a review written for the Volker Fund on an American history book. Severely critical, he wrote a review well over 100 pages extensively on each era (from colonial times to post-World War II), and documented all of the historical episodes that the authors needed

it provided the necessary framework that created the modern welfare-warfare state and increases in government power. In 1965, while heavily researching American history and writing *Conceived in Liberty*, in his seminal article "Left and Right: Prospects for Liberty" Rothbard had already laid out his general framework for understanding this transformation, using the historical work of Gabriel Kolko:

> In *The Triumph of Conservatism*, Kolko traces the origins of political capitalism in the "reforms" of the Progressive Era. ... Despite the wave of mergers and trusts formed around the turn of the century, Kolko reveals, the forces of competition on the free market rapidly vitiated and dissolved these attempts at stabilizing and perpetuating the economic power of big business interests. It was precisely in reaction to their impending defeat at the hands of the competitive storms of the market that big business turned, increasingly after the 1900s, to the federal government for aid and protection. In short, the intervention by the federal government was designed, not to curb big business monopoly for the sake of the public weal, but to create monopolies that big business (as well as trade associations of smaller business) had not been able to establish amidst the competitive gales of the free market ...
>
> Thus, Kolko shows that, beginning with Theodore Roosevelt's New Nationalism and culminating in Wilson's New Freedom, in industry after industry, for example, insurance, banking, meat, exports and business generally, regulations that present-day rightists think of as "socialistic" were not only uniformly hailed, but conceived and brought about by big businessmen. This was a conscious effort to fasten upon the economy a cement of subsidy, stabilization, and monopoly privilege.[12]

---

to revise their interpretations on or include in their work. Murray Rothbard, "Report on George B. DeHuszar and Thomas Hulbert Stevenson, *A History of the American Republic*, 2 vols.," in *Strictly Confidential*, Gordon, ed., pp. 86–188.

[12]Murray Rothbard, "Left and Right: The Prospects for Liberty," *Left and Right* 1, no. 1 (Spring 1965): 13–14.

Here Rothbard explains the central idea that big business, far from being *laissez-faire* ideologues, was interested in developing government regulations to actively hamper their competitors and help it cartelize in order to restrict supply and raise prices. He would extend this theme in two later essays he wrote shortly thereafter on the Progressive Era, "War Collectivism in World War I" and "Herbert Hoover and the Myth of Laissez-Faire."[13]

Kolko, along with the Chicago school economist George Stigler, espoused what later came to be labelled the "capture" theory of regulation. This theory states that regulation purportedly designed to curb business abuses is actually often "captured" by various businesses in order to enhance their own profits and weaken their competitors. In addition, in many cases the regulation is even promoted by the businesses themselves for this specific purpose. This is opposed to the "public interest" theory, which argues that regulation is designed for, and ultimately benefits, the general public, and the "bureaucratic" theory, which argues that regulations are enacted to empower various bureaucrats and government agencies. As will be seen below, Rothbard combined both the capture and bureaucratic theories in his historical narrative of the Progressive Era.[14] His narrative was intimately linked with his general historical method, which sought to understand the various motivations of special interests who lobby for government legislation.

---

[13]Murray Rothbard, "War Collectivism in World War I" and "Herbert Hoover and the Myth of Laissez-Faire," in *A New History of Leviathan*, Ronald Radosh and Murray Rothbard, eds. (New York: E.P. Dutton, 1972), pp. 66–110, 111–45.

[14]See Gabriel Kolko, *The Triumph of Conservatism* (Glencoe, IL: The Free Press, 1963); Gabriel Kolko, *Railroads and Regulation* (Princeton, NJ: Princeton University Press, 1965); George Stigler, "The Theory of Economic Regulation," *Bell Journal of Economics and Management* (Spring 1971). For a contextualization of Kolko's works in comparison with other contemporary historians and economists, see Robert L. Bradley Jr., *Capitalism at Work* (Salem, MA: M&M Scrivener Press, 2009), pp. 142–81. For a discussion of Kolko's works by various historians, including Kolko, see Otis L. Graham, Jr. ed., *From Roosevelt to Roosevelt: American Politics and Diplomacy, 1901–1941* (New York, 1971), pp. 70–109. See also Thomas K. McCraw, "Regulation in America: A Review Article," *The Business History Review* (Summer 1975): 159–83; Jack High, "Introduction: A Tale of Two Disciplines," in *Regulation: Economic Theory and History*, Jack High, ed. (Ann Arbor: University of Michigan Press, 1991); Robert L. Bradley, Jr. and Roger Donway, "Reconsidering Gabriel Kolko: A Half-Century Perspective," *Independent Review* (Spring 2013): 561–76; William D. Burt, "Gabriel Kolko's *Railroads and Regulation* at Fifty," *Railroad History* (Spring-Summer 2016): 23–45.

While Rothbard was Mises's foremost student in wielding the praxe-ological method to deduce a body of abstract economic theorems, he was also his foremost student in applying them to history and utilizing his thymological method, best described in *Theory and History*.[15] In contrast to praxeology, the science of human action, thymology is the science of understanding why humans act a certain way, or "psychologizing" their behavior (psychology understood in the common-sense definition). This historical method strives to answer the eternal question "Cui bono?" or, "Who Benefits?" from an action, particularly a change in government institutions. More specifically, the thymological method looks at both pecuniary and nonpecuniary (such as religious) motivations, and seeks to answer the question "*Who thinks they stand to benefit?*" The latter question emphasizes that not all results of a government intervention are intended, and that not all special interest groups who lobby for a regulation actually do benefit *ex post*. To answer the latter question, one needs to engage in a detailed historical understanding of the various actors involved and not just a statistical test, which is the usual approach of an economist.

Rothbard's use of the thymological method in his historical analy-sis is also closely related to his consistent application of the sociological law called "The Iron Law of Oligarchy." The law states that governments, politicians, and legislation are not controlled by democratic majorities or public opinion, but instead by a small entrenched group of individuals. This group contains a mix of big businesses, politicians, and bureaucrats who wield the state apparatus for their own benefit at the expense of the rest of society. Court intellectuals supply the necessary public relations in various ways, such as by arguing that the government is not controlled by a small elite or that certain government actions are necessary, in return for power and prestige. There is a close relationship between this law and the method in political science called "Power Elite analysis." Governments are controlled by well-established financial and political elites who pull the levers "behind the scenes," and government officials and bureaucrats often have many important links, including familial ties, with the busi-ness community that provide powerful motivations for explaining why they acted a certain way while in office. These approaches and Rothbard's consistent application of them have often been criticized as crank "con-spiracy theories," but it is important to note that proper use of them is

---

[15]Ludwig von Mises, *Theory and History: An Interpretation of Social and Economic Evolu-tion* (New Haven, CT: Yale University Press, 1957).

only an extension of Mises's thymological method, which seeks to understand human action and explain its motivations. Government officials do not fall from the sky without any prior connections to the political and business world, and they are just as self-interested as those in the private sector. There is a strong similarity between what is called "Public Choice analysis" and the thymological approach, although the two are not completely identical. The thymological method places more emphasis on engaging in pure historical work in understanding the motivations of acting individuals, as well as the fact that individuals often act in a certain way and expect to benefit but do not actually do so. In addition, Rothbard's particular application also places much more emphasis on the oligarchical and coercive aspects of State rule.[16]

As the late 1960s and early 1970s passed, Rothbard would not turn away from utilizing the thymological method in his scholarly work. On the contrary, he would continue to elaborate on the method in important popular articles, updating *Conceived in Liberty* for publication and publishing other historical papers, such as "The New Deal and the International Monetary System."[17] More importantly for our purposes here, Rothbard also began writing his book on the Progressive Era while affiliated with the Cato Institute.

---

[16]On Rothbard's historical studies and their connection with Mises's method, see the important work by Joseph T. Salerno, "Introduction," in Murray Rothbard, *A History of Money and Banking in the United States: The Colonial Era to World War II*, Joseph Salerno ed. (Auburn, AL: Mises Institute, 2005), pp. 7–43.

[17]Murray Rothbard, "The New Deal and the International Monetary System," in *Watershed of Empire: Essays on New Deal Foreign Policy,* Leonard Liggio and James Martin, eds. (Colorado Springs, CO: Ralph Myles, 1976), pp. 19–64. For examples of popular articles, see Murray Rothbard, "Only One Heartbeat Away," *Libertarian Forum* (September 1974): 5–7; "The Conspiracy Theory of History Revisited," *Reason* (April, 1974): 39–40. During the 1970s into the 1980s Rothbard also encouraged other scholars, including prominent Progressive Era historians, to contribute academic articles on the Progressive Era to either *Libertarian Forum* or *Journal of Libertarian Studies*, both of which Rothbard edited. See, among others, Arthur A. Ekirch, Jr., "The Reform Mentality, War, Peace, and the National State: From the Progressives to Vietnam," *The Journal of Libertarian Studies* 3, no. 1 (Spring 1979): 55–72; Paul Kleppner, "Religion, Politics, and the American Polity: A Dynamic View of Relationships," *Journal of Libertarian Studies* 6, no. 3 (Summer/Fall 1982): 349–52. During this time, in 1973 Rothbard also gave a lecture series on the Progressive Era at a Cornell University event sponsored by the Institute for Humane Studies. Forrest McDonald was the other speaker. Rothbard's lectures were recorded and titled "20th Century American Economic History." See also Liggio, "A Classical Liberal Life," p. 193; Murray Rothbard, "Selected Bibliographical Essay," (n.d.).

With this work Rothbard planned to continue his project on American history, only now fast forwarding from the change in ideology and government from statism to liberty to the change from liberty to statism. He would chronicle how the battle of Liberty versus Power was lost around the turn of the 20th century. He was not only going to utilize the works of Kolko, but also the works of other notable revisionist historians who wrote on the period in recent years, such as James Weinstein, Paul Kleppner, Richard Jensen, and James Gilbert. Rothbard succinctly described his thesis in a book proposal:

> The purpose of this projected book is to synthesize the remarkable quantity and quality of new and fresh work on the Progressive Era (roughly the late 1890s to the early 1920s) that has been done in the past twenty years. In particular, the object is to trace the causes, the nature, and the consequences of the dramatic shift of the U.S. polity from a relatively *laissez-faire* system to the outlines of the statist era that we are familiar with today.
>
> The older paradigm of historians held the burst of statism in the Progressive Era to be the response of a coalition of workers, farmers, and altruistic intellectuals to the rising tide of big business monopoly, with the coalition bringing in big government to curb and check that monopoly.
>
> Research in the past two decades has overthrown that paradigm in almost every detail.

The burst in statism would be explained by an alliance between big business, big unions, big government, and big intellectuals who were able to take control due to a seismic change in the political system following the election of 1896:

> [T]he essence of Progressivism was that certain elements of big business, having sought monopoly through cartels and mergers on the free market without success, turned to government — federal, state, and local — to achieve that monopoly through government-sponsored and enforced cartelization ...
>
> Allied to these big business elements in imposing Progressivism were what Gilbert calls "collectivist intellectuals," whose goals no longer seem that altruistic. Rather,

they seem like the first great wave of the "New Class" of modern intellectuals out for a share of power and for the fruits of similar governmental cartelization ...

In the last decade, the "new political history" stressing ethno-religious determinants of mass political attitudes, voting, and political parties ... has added another important dimension to this story ... Kleppner explains that the triumph of the Bryan forces in the Democratic Party in 1896 marked the end of the Democrats as a *laissez-faire* party, and the subsequent lack of real electoral choice left a power vacuum for Progressive technocrats, intellectuals, and businessmen to fill.[18]

The original outline of the book was "roughly as follows," and appears to have been the following nine chapters:

Chapter 1: Introduction

Chapter 2: The Failure of Attempts at Monopoly

Chapter 3: Government as Cartelist

Chapter 4: Centralization of the Cities

Chapter 5: Science and Morality: the Intellectual as Corporatist

Chapter 6: The New American Empire

Chapter 7: World War I: the Culmination of the Corporatist System

Chapter 8: The 1920's Corporatism After the War

Chapter 9: Epilogue: to the Present[19]

Chapter 2 would explain the ways in which business attempts at cartelization, mergers, or monopolies failed, whether it was railroads or major industrial firms such as U.S. Steel. Chapter 3 would document the resultant state and federal attempts at cartelization pushed by big businesses, such as the Interstate Commerce Commission (ICC), the Federal Trade Commission (FTC), meatpacking legislation, the Federal Reserve System (FRS), and the importance of the National Civic Federation in spurring the new interventions. Chapter 4 would describe local Progressive politics and the drive by reformers to weaken the ethnic immigrants and push for prohibition and public schools. Chapter 5 would explain the evolution

---

[18]Murray Rothbard, "Roots of the Modern State: The Progressive Era" (n.d.). Reprinted in Preface below, pp. 39–40.

[19]Murray Rothbard, "Roots of the American Corporate State: 1890's–1920's" (n.d.).

of intellectuals into acting as apologists for the new big government, and Chapter 6 would be on the pre-World War I changes in American foreign policy, including interventions in Asia, South America, and the Spanish-American War. Chapter 7 would explain the Wilson administration's push for intervening in the European war, the devolution of the Democratic Party away from its *laissez-faire* heritage, and how the war represented the culmination of the Progressive movement. Chapter 8 would document the Progressivism of Herbert Hoover and the 1920s monetary interventions of Benjamin Strong, and Chapter 9 would briefly extend the analysis up into the present.[20]

When writing the manuscript, Rothbard more or less followed this outline, with one major exception. Instead of postponing the transformation of the Democratic Party to the World War I Chapter 7 (in order to explain the Wilson administration's drive toward war), Rothbard moved it up to right after the failure of the merger movement and monopolies (listed above as Chapter 2). Rothbard decided to move up explaining the Democratic and Republican parties during the third party system up until the election of 1896, when both parties became center-statist and there was no longer a clear *laissez-faire* party in American politics.

Rothbard appears to have worked on the manuscript from 1978 to 1981. Like many of his projects, the book took on a life of its own and grew much bigger than the original plan. By 1981, Rothbard wrote rough drafts of nine chapters, but he was only still on what was planned to be Chapter 3 of the original proposal! Chapter 2 on monopolies grew into three chapters, with two whole chapters devoted to the railroad question, which Rothbard initially planned to only visit "briefly." Explaining the third party system and the election of 1896 took three entire chapters, and Rothbard devoted two entire chapters to the Progressive cartelization during the Roosevelt administration, and a stand-alone chapter on the National Civic Federation, and was still not done with what he wanted to write about in the original chapter 3.

By 1981, Rothbard was no longer working on the remaining chapters of the book. But by no means was Rothbard not finishing the book. Instead, he was writing the remaining chapters as papers that were published in the 1980s, early 1990s, or posthumously after his unexpected

---

[20]Rothbard presented brief summaries for each chapter except for Chapter 1, the Introduction. Rothbard apparently never wrote it since he most likely planned to write it after he finished the book.

death in 1995. On the material planned to be in Chapter 4, such as the feminist movement and women's suffrage, urban reform, prohibition, and other aspects of local Progressivism, Rothbard wrote "The Progressive Era and the Family" and "Origins of the Welfare State in America." In addition to the above topics and on the material in Chapters 5 and 7 on intellectuals and World War I, Rothbard wrote "World War I as Fulfillment: Power and the Intellectuals." On the progression of American foreign policy planned for Chapters 6, 7, and 9, Rothbard wrote "Wall Street, Banks, and American Foreign Policy." Rothbard devoted the most space to the origins of the Federal Reserve (part of Chapter 3) and on 1920s monetary interventions (part of Chapter 8), such as the historical sections in *The Mystery of Banking*, "The Federal Reserve as a Cartelization Device, The Early Years: 1913–1930," the historical sections in *The Case Against the Fed*, "The Gold Exchange Standard in the Interwar Years," "The Origins of the Federal Reserve," and "From Hoover to Roosevelt: The Federal Reserve and the Financial Elites."[21] He was selected to be a reviewer in 1985 for Robert

---

[21]Murray Rothbard, *The Mystery of Banking* (New York: Richardson & Snyder, 1983); "The Federal Reserve as a Cartelization Device, The Early Years: 1913–1930," in *Money in Crisis: The Federal Reserve, the Economy, and Monetary Reform,* Barry N. Siegel, ed. (San Francisco: Pacific Institute for Public Policy Research, 1984), pp. 89–136; "Wall Street, Banks, and American Foreign Policy," *World Market Perspective* (August 1984); "The Progressive Era and the Family," in *The American Family and the State,* Joseph R. Peden and Fred R. Glahe, eds. (San Francisco: Pacific Research Institute, 1986), pp. 109–34; "World War I as Fulfillment: Power and the Intellectuals," *Journal of Libertarian Studies* 9, no. 1 (1989): 81–125; *The Case Against the Fed* (Auburn, AL: Mises Institute, 1994); "Origins of the Welfare State in America," *Journal of Libertarian Studies* 12, no. 2 (1996): 193–232; "The Gold-Exchange Standard in the Interwar Years," in *Money and the Nation State: The Financial Revolution, Government and the World Monetary System,* Kevin Dowd and Richard H. Timberlake, Jr., eds. (New Brunswick, NJ: Transaction Publishers, 1998), pp. 105–63; "The Origins of the Federal Reserve," *Quarterly Journal of Austrian Economics* 2, no. 3 (Fall 1999): 3–51; "From Hoover to Roosevelt: The Federal Reserve and the Financial Elites," in Salerno, ed., pp. 263–347.

In addition, Rothbard also wrote on Progressivism in his contributions to Congressmen Ron Paul and Lewis Lehrman's *Minority Report* for the 1981–1982 Gold Commission. In the section completely written by Rothbard on the 19th century, he included his analysis of electoral politics leading up to the election of 1896, and in the section on the 20th century which he partially wrote (many of the initial paragraphs are extremely similar to what appeared in *The Mystery of Banking*), he wrote on his basic thesis of the Progressive Era and the origins of the Federal Reserve. See "A History of Money and Banking in the United States Before the 20th Century" and "Money and Banking in the United States in the 20th Century," in *The Case For Gold: A Minority Report of the U.S. Gold Commission,* Rep. Ron Paul and Lewis Lehrman, eds. (Washington, D.C: Cato

Higgs's *Crisis and Leviathan: Critical Episodes in the Growth of American Government*, in which he wrote an in-depth review that showed he was still deeply immersed and interested in the Progressive Era.[22] Moreover, while teaching at Brooklyn Polytechnic, Rothbard taught a class in 1986 on the Progressive Era, in which he lectured on segments of the book manuscript as well as other Progressive Era essays he had written or was working on.[23]

It could be said that, in the last decade or so of Rothbard's life, aside from working on his all-encompassing history of economic thought, Progressivism was the next most significant area of research on his mind. That Rothbard was interested in Progressivism right up until his untimely death in 1995 can be seen when reading *The Case Against the Fed,* the last book published in his lifetime, since Rothbard devoted a significant portion of it to providing a brief overview of Progressivism and the history of the Federal Reserve. No doubt, if Rothbard lived to write his third volume on the history of economic thought, which planned to cover topics ranging from the 1871 Marginal Revolution to the 1930s Keynesian Revolution and beyond, he would have written extensively about the Progressivist intellectuals.

Rothbard's book manuscript and the essays contained in *The Progressive Era,* represent a lifetime of deep research in American history. Rothbard was deeply immersed in all areas of American history, especially the Progressive Era, and he was able to collate a massive amount of research and facts and synthesize them to create his own unique narrative of the era. The remainder of this introduction will provide a brief overview of the Rothbardian interpretation as well as a general summary of the chapters and essays contained therein.

Rothbard's central thesis is that big businesses had previously tried to cartelize on the free market around the turn of the 20th century, but had

---

Institute, 1982), pp. 111–22.

[22]Robert Higgs, *Crisis and Leviathan: Critical Episodes in the Growth of American Government* (New York: Oxford University Press, 1987). Higgs notes with astonishment that the review ran 26 single spaced pages at probably over 12,000 words and contained a detailed list of bibliographic information he recommended Higgs to include. In addition, he apparently recalled most of the citation information off the top of his head as he did not have access to his library at the time. Robert Higgs, *Murray N. Rothbard: In Memoriam,* Llewellyn H. Rockwell, Jr., ed. (Auburn, AL: Mises Institute, 1995), pp. 56–60.

[23]The class lectures were recorded and titled "The American Economy and the End of Laissez-Faire: 1870 to World War II."

failed to do so. Try as they might, the cartel agreements and mergers failed because of the internal pressure of collaborators cheating and the external pressure of new competitors entering the market to cut prices and break the cartels. Having failed in this endeavor, they turned to government regulations in order to help them cartelize by preventing various forms of price and product competition and preventing new smaller competitors from successfully entering markets by raising their costs. Big Business allied itself with Big Government, who wanted the regulations in order to increase its own power, and Big Unions, to help stifle the radical opposition of labor. However, this was a resurrection of the *ancien régime* in a different form, and it could not simply be imposed on the public who was all too familiar with this system and instilled with relatively *laissez-faire* principles. In order to sell it to the public they needed a new breed of collectivist intellectuals, many of whom were thoroughly convinced of the ways of Bismarckian socialism after receiving their Ph.D.s in Germany in the post-Civil War era. The Alliance of Throne and Altar was back with a vengeance, between the favored government interests and the intellectual apologists, only that this time the intellectuals were not convincing the public that the King's mandate was the word of God and his depredations were divine, but that Big Government was needed in order to improve the public welfare and cure the social problems brought on by unfettered capitalism. In return, the intellectuals were to benefit by becoming professionalized and given lucrative jobs in planning and administering the whole apparatus. The Alliance saw itself as a middle of the road stabilizer between anarchic and outdated *laissez-faire* capitalism and confiscatory and extremist socialism.

This dramatic change at the beginning of the 20th century was not able to be instituted on the existing political system, but occurred after a seismic change in the orientation of the political parties. This resulted from the ethnoreligious political battles between the Democrats and the Republicans in the 1880s and 1890s which led to the climactic election of 1896.

During the third party system (1854–1896) of American politics, the great mass of the public was ideological and learned their respective economic positions from political activists who translated them into ethnocultural and religious terms. On the one hand, there was the Republican Party, "The Party of Great Moral Ideas," dominated by pietist "Yankee" natives. They were "postmillennial" in that they believed in order for Jesus to return to earth and usher in the end of history, they must first bring about a thousand year Kingdom of God. In order to do so, they not only needed to save themselves, but also save others, even if it required state force. Thus the pietists were hell-bent on stamping out all forms of sin, including instituting prohibition and weakening the "Roman Popery" of the Catholic schools, along with other measures such as immigration restriction and women's suffrage (to boost the pietist vote). This paternalistic intervention on the local ethnoreligious level was translated to a paternalistic intervention on the larger economic realm, such as enacting various government subsidies, tariffs, or greenback inflation. On the other hand, there was the Democratic Party, "The Party of Personal Liberty," dominated by liturgical natives and immigrants, such as Catholics and Lutherans. These religious denominations did not have the evangelical zeal to actively save others and stamp out sin, but only to follow the teachings and practices of their respective churches. As a result, they criticized all Republican local interventions as paternalistic drives to meddle and control their lives, correspondingly saw their economic policies as allied, and consequently favored a more *laissez-faire* agenda, including less government spending, low tariffs, and the gold standard. The *laissez-faire* Democrats were also called the Bourbon Democrats, who were generally centered in the Northeast and Midwest, and whose ancestors belonged to the *laissez-faire* wing of the Jacksonian Democrats. The battle of Liberty versus Power was being fought once again in American history.

The Democrats were slowly but surely winning, and in the late 1880s and early 1890s made a remarkable series of gains, shocking the Republican elite. In order to counter this trend, Republican elites strategically decided to downplay ethno-cultural issues and become more hard money in order to stop alienating liturgicals at the expense of aggravating pietists. This also fortuitously coincided with the Panic of 1893, a severe economic depression that (unjustly) hurt the incumbent Bourbon Democrats at the polls. To make matters worse, at the same time the Southern and Western Democratic pietist populists, who were becoming increasingly "Yankee" and activist, were able to wrest control of the Democratic Party machine while the Bourbon leaders were weakened due to the depression. William Jennings Bryan, not Grover Cleveland, was now the standard bearer for the new Democratic Party. Liturgicals went to the Republicans in droves while pietists flocked to the Democrats. With this remarkable turnaround, in the election of 1896 the moderate statist Republican presidential nominee William McKinley resoundingly defeated the pietist inflationist Democratic presidential nominee William Jennings Bryan and established Republican dominance for the next several decades. This ended the third party system of American electoral politics, when the parties were fiercely ideological and polarized, and brought about the fourth party system (1896–1932), when both parties became less ideologically defined and more center-statist, with increasing control granted to bureaucrats from the resultant de-democratization. The weakening of the Bourbon forces reduced the Democrats to minority status, and ended any *laissez-faire* majority party in America. This lacuna, and the increasing similarity and center statism between the two parties due to the recent metamorphosis, created the power vacuum that allowed for the new quadripartite alliance to take hold of America.

With this rejuvenation of the Alliance, embodied in the newly formed National Civic Federation, came a whole spate of "Progressive" measures, including increased railroad regulation, trustbusting, compulsory publicity laws, conservation laws, meatpacking legislation, the Pure Food and Drug Act, employers' compensation laws, safety legislation, the minimum wage, the Federal Reserve System, and the Federal Trade Commission. The once staunchly pietist Progressive intellectuals arguing on behalf of the entire system slowly but surely became increasingly secularized and more committed to using state coercion to ostensibly improve public welfare than to create the Kingdom of God. Moreover, academia in general and its disciplines, such as economics, began to denigrate theory and embrace statistics and empirical analysis in an attempt to vainly ape the natural sciences. The need for greater data collection and inductive reasoning went hand-in-hand with greater government planning and interventionism.

The transformation of the American government and subsequent interventions were not isolated events unconnected to specific financial and political elites, but were deeply related to the growing clash between the two dominant power elites in the ruling oligarchy, the Morgan ambit, which included the financial groups surrounding J.P. Morgan & Company, and the Rockefeller ambit, which included the financial groups surrounding Standard Oil. In the latter part of the third party system, the Morgans were the dominant interest behind the Democratic Party, and the Rockefellers behind the Republican Party. While the last Cleveland administration (1893–1897) was Morgan dominated, the subsequent McKinley administrations (1897–1901) were Rockefeller dominated, with the Morgans as junior partners since they supported McKinley over Bryan. Matters quickly changed when McKinley was assassinated in 1901 and his vice president, the Morgan affiliated Theodore Roosevelt, took office, and the Morgans were to remain the dominant financial group for the next decade. Ultimately, the Roosevelt administrations (1901–1909) were dominated by the Morgan interests, who were largely able to shield their larger corporations from antitrust and divert Roosevelt's "trustbusting" to non-Morgan companies, in particular Standard Oil in 1906. This led to a Rockefeller counterattack, mainly through the more Rockefeller-affiliated William Howard Taft, whose administration (1909–1913) launched antitrust suits against the Morgan-dominated companies U.S. Steel and International Harvester. Infuriated at Taft, the Morgans deliberately sabotaged his reelection by encouraging Roosevelt to come out of retirement and run on the Progressive Party ticket in 1912, which split the Republican vote and allowed the Democrat Woodrow Wilson, with Morgan and other financial affiliations, to squeak by and capture the presidency — the only Democrat to do so in the fourth party era.

The culmination, the apogee, or the "fulfillment" of not only the new warfare state but also Progressivism, was during World War I, when collectivist fever was at its height and there was an enormous desire among businesses, bureaucrats, and intellectuals to top-down cartelize and plan the economy, and to maintain it in some form after the war. In the 1920s, when the Morgans were still dominant, Progressivist activism, though reduced, continued, especially through the efforts of the Secretary of Commerce Herbert Hoover, and government intervention accelerated during his ill-fated term as president, and then especially during Franklin Roosevelt's New Deal, with its fascist tendencies. The Morgans were to remain dominant throughout the 1920s until they were savagely removed from political power during the New Deal, which was supported by the Rockefellers and other anti-Morgan interests. With the end of World War II the modern American welfare-warfare empire had matured and grown into being, with its roots all from the Progressive Era.

The nine chapters of the original book draft and the six published essays describe this thesis, along with its many other facets, in much greater detail. The essays were chosen by the present editor because they were generally hard to find or had not been published previously in a collection of Rothbard's essays.[24]

---

[24]Many of Rothbard's other works on the Progressive Era and beyond, particularly on the Federal Reserve from its origins to World War II, can be found in Rothbard, *A History of Money and Banking*. The essays contained therein should definitely be read in tandem with the current volume.

Chapters 1 and 2, "Railroads: The First Big Business and the Failure of the Cartels" and "Regulating the Railroads" document the history of the railroad industry from the Civil War onward. Much like the later mergers, the railroads, which were previously granted lavish subsidies, tried hard to cartelize on the free market but failed. Correspondingly, many of them turned to government to push for state enforced cartelization, which led to the Interstate Commerce Act in 1887. Armed with this new legislation, the railroads tried to cartelize but were not entirely successful, which resulted in future legislative attempts to control the railroad industry until the regulations and rival interests suffocated the railroads, leading to government ownership during World War I. Chapter 3 "Attempts at Monopoly in American Industry" documents repeated cases of various businesses' failures to monopolize and consequently saw their market share slipping: Standard Oil, U.S. Steel, and International Harvester, among others. This would later instill the drive for government cartelization.

Chapters 4, 5, and 6, "The Third Party System: Pietists vs. Liturgicals," "The Democratic Triumph of 1892," and "1896: The Collapse of the Third Party System and of Laissez-Faire Politics" describe the ethno-cultural background behind the third party system, and the battles fought between the pietist Republicans and liturgical Democrats. This ultimately led to the election of 1896 where the Republicans were able to decisively defeat the Democrats, change the future of American politics, and allow for an unmitigated increase in government intervention in the new century with the Democrats permanently weakened.

Chapters 7, 8, and 9, "Theodore Roosevelt: The First Progressive, Part I," "Theodore Roosevelt: The First Progressive, Part II," and "The National Civic Federation: Big Business Organized for Progressivism" describe the beginnings of this new Progressive alliance and the repeated attempts at various forms of cartelization. The fascinating struggles between the power elites are documented, and Theodore Roosevelt is exposed as a Morgan affiliate whose actions opened the floodgates of Progressivism. The highly touted Progressive reforms are shown to be driven largely by businesses wishing to hamper their competitors and bureaucrats interested in enhancing their own power, and the National Civic Federation is seen as the major organ for the new Progressive partnership to work through.

The remaining chapters are previously published essays. Chapters 10 and 11, "The Progressive Era and the Family" and "Origins of the Welfare State in America" further describe and elaborate on the recent ethnoreligious history. Local Progressivism and various urban reforms are described, ranging from the fight over public schools to the welfare state, along with many urban reformers, economists, and other crusaders. Chapters 12 and 13, "War Collectivism in World War I" and "World War I as Fulfillment: Power and the Intellectuals" describe Progressivism during the war, when business collectivism was at its peak, along with various other Progressive reforms such as prohibition and women's suffrage. The evolution of intellectuals and their turn towards increased interventionism and empiricism are also chronicled.[25]

Chapter 14, "The Federal Reserve as a Cartelization Device: The Early Years, 1913–1930" describes the origins of the Federal Reserve and its subsequent monetary policy during World War I and the 1920s. The Fed is seen to have originated from a coalition of various bankers, especially the Morgans, who wanted a central bank to help them expand credit and solidify the dominance of New York City finance. Later on, in the 1920s, the Fed played an increasingly international role in helping Great Britain return to the gold standard, largely through the efforts of the governor of the New York Fed Benjamin Strong and his connection with the governor of the Bank of England, Montagu Norman. Chapter 15, "Herbert Hoover and the Myth of Laissez-Faire" describes the 1920s Progressivism driven by Herbert Hoover and refutes the myth that Hoover was a noninterventionist and advocate of *laissez-faire* while president during the Great Depression.

The Progressive Era is one of Rothbard's finest achievements as an academic, and should be read by anyone interested in the Progressive Era or American history in general. Rothbard's analysis is essential for anyone who wishes to understand the evolution of the American state from relatively *laissez-faire* leanings in the 19th century to the modern welfare-warfare state of the 20th and 21st centuries.

The nine chapters of the current volume were rough drafts and in many places lacked references. No doubt, judging from his later essays, if Rothbard finished the book, he would have gone back, revised it, and added a plethora of source material for the reader. As editor, I have, albeit imperfectly, done my best to edit the manuscript and track down and cite all of the material in the nine chapters. In addition, I have provided commen-

---

[25]A previously unpublished section of Chapter 13 is included as an appendix.

tary and sources for the reader on various ideas that Rothbard mentioned and planned to later elaborate on but did not. These are either in [Editor's remarks], my additions to existing footnotes, or [Editor's footnote], my entirely new footnotes.

I would like to thank the Ludwig von Mises Institute, and academic vice president Joseph Salerno in particular, for providing me with the opportunity to work on this book. Archivist Barbara Pickard was indispensable in tracking down the book manuscript. In addition, Joseph Salerno, Jonathan Newman, and Chris Calton were very helpful in proofreading various parts of the book. I would also like to thank editor Judy Thommesen for finalizing the book and correcting typographical mistakes. All errors are entirely my own.

Patrick Newman
Lakeland, Florida
April 2017

Preface

The aim of this proposed book is to trace the origins of the current welfare-warfare state in America, in what is loosely called "The Progressive Period," from approximately the mid-1890s to the mid-1920s. Briefly, the thesis is that the rapid upsurge of statism in this period was propelled by a coalition of two broad groups: (a) certain big business groups, anxious to replace a roughly *laissez-faire* economy by a new form of mercantilism, cartelized and controlled and subsidized by a strong government under their influence and control; and (b) newly burgeoning groups of intellectuals, technocrats, and professionals: economists, writers, engineers, planners, physicians, etc., anxious for power and lucrative employment at the hands of the State. Since America had been born in an antimonopoly tradition, it became important to put over the new system of cartelization as a "progressive" curbing of big business by a humanitarian government; intellectuals were relied on for this selling job. These two groups were inspired by Bismarck's creation of a monopolized welfare-warfare state in Prussia and Germany.

The big government created by this business-intellectual partnership had important repercussions for all aspects of American life, in addition to the cartelized and regulated economy. For one thing, the drive of pietists and compulsory "moralists" could now be foisted on the American public in the name of the newly burgeoning medical "science." The result:

Prohibition, antisex laws, antidrug laws, and Sunday blue laws. Another result, which made heavy and effective use of the "morality" theme, was the business-professional drive to centralize and take over the nation's cities, thereby reaping good government as against the wicked and corrupt old urban machines — which were responsive to poorer and immigrant groups. One of the major aspects of this urban centralization was to centralize the public school system, and force children into them, so that the immigrant Catholic groups would be "Christianized" and be inculcated in the values of the American State and the new system.

In foreign affairs, the new partnership of government and business meant a substitution of a new American imperialism for the older roughly "isolationist" and neutralist foreign policy. The U.S. government was now supposed to open up markets for American exports abroad, use coercion to protect American investors and bondholders overseas, and seize territory on behalf of these aims. It was to be willing to go to war on behalf of these aims. The increasing militarism also meant heavy government contracts and subsidies for favored arms manufacturers.

A third group, virtually created by the new system as a junior partner, was labor unions, which were weak until they were called to share the ruling power of the "collectivist planning" of World War I. Creating favored unions was an instrument of cartelization, as well as insuring worker cooperation in the new order. Partly to mold the immigrants more easily, and partly as a boon to labor unions, immigration was virtually abolished during and after World War I, fueled by the racism sponsored by American social scientists.

Thus, from a roughly free and *laissez-faire* society of the 19th century, when the economy was free, taxes were low, persons were free in their daily lives, and the government was noninterventionist at home and abroad, the new coalition managed in a short time to transform America into a welfare-warfare imperial State, where people's daily lives were controlled and regulated to a massive degree. In this way, the coalition, inspired by Bismarck's example and its success in World War I, was able to reach its apogee in Europe, in Mussolini's "corporate state" and derivative political regimes. In the United States, its apogee was reached in Roosevelt's New Deal and post-World War II America.[1]

---

[1][Editor's footnote] Excerpted from Murray Rothbard, "Roots of the American Corporate State: 1890's–1920's" (n.d.).

The purpose of this projected book is to synthesize the remarkable quantity and quality of new and fresh work on the Progressive Era (roughly the late 1890s to the early 1920s) that has been done in the past 20 years. In particular, the object is to trace the causes, the nature, and the consequences of the dramatic shift of the U.S. polity from a relatively *laissez-faire* system to the outlines of the statist era that we are familiar with today.

The older paradigm of historians held the burst of statism in the Progressive Era to be the response of a coalition of workers, farmers, and altruistic intellectuals to the rising tide of big business monopoly, with the coalition bringing in big government to curb and check that monopoly.

Research in the past two decades has overthrown that paradigm in almost every detail. Gabriel Kolko, James Weinstein, James Gilbert, Samuel P. Hays, Louis Galambos and many others have shown that the essence of Progressivism was that certain elements of big business, having sought monopoly through cartels and mergers on the free market without success, turned to government — federal, state, and local — to achieve that monopoly through government-sponsored and enforced cartelization. Modern scholars of Herbert Hoover, such as Ellis W. Hawley, Joan Hoff Wilson, William A. Williams, and Robert F. Himmelberg, have confirmed the new view of Hoover as Progressive and proto-New Dealer.

Allied to these big business elements in imposing Progressivism were what Gilbert calls "collectivist intellectuals," whose goals no longer seem that altruistic. Rather, they seem like the first great wave of the "New Class" of modern intellectuals out for a share of power and for the fruits of similar governmental cartelization. There has been a proliferation of research in the past two decades on these intellectuals, ranging from illuminating general studies by Gilbert, Christopher Lasch, and Arthur A. Ekirch, Jr., among others, to studies of particular groups of professionals, technocrats, or social workers. Much has been done on the history of medical licensing in this period, the rise of the eugenics movement, guild actions by engineers and social workers, and the imposition of the anti-sex laws — Donald K. Pickens, Allen F. Davis, David W. Noble, and Ronald Hamowy, are just a few of the studies that come to mind.

In the last decade, the "new political history" stressing ethno-religious determinants of mass political attitudes, voting, and political parties — notably the work of Paul Kleppner and others such as Richard J. Jensen, Victor L. Shradar, and Ronald P. Formisano — has added another important dimension to this story. Kleppner stresses the intense drive for statism from the mid-19th century by the pietist Protestant groups, particularly of the New England stock, as opposed to the *laissez-faire* and libertarian attitudes of the liturgical Christians, particularly Catholics and high Lutherans. For the remainder of the century, the pietists tried continually to impose prohibition, Sunday blue laws, and enforced public school education as a means of "Christianizing the Catholics"; the liturgicals resisted bitterly. From these personal, religious matters, the party leaders (Republican for the pietists, Democrat for the liturgicals) expanded the interests of their followers to the economic realm: the pietists tending to favor big government, subsidies and regulations, the liturgicals in favor of free trade and free markets. Kleppner explains that the triumph of the Bryan forces in the Democratic Party in 1896 marked the end of the Democrats as a *laissez-faire* party, and the subsequent lack of real electoral choice left a power vacuum for Progressive technocrats, intellectuals, and businessmen to fill.

Tightening public school control as a means of molding Catholic and immigrant children became important in the Progressive Era, which saw the completion of compulsory education in all the states. The research of Joel Spring, Clarence J. Karier, Colin Greer, and others have revised the older starry-eyed view of the growth of the public school system.

Many of the Progressive intellectuals can best be described as a fusion of supposedly scientific technocracy with a pietist background or pietist allies. As James H. Timberlake points out, the Prohibition movement finally succeeded when wartime was joined to the dictates of medical "science" and long-time pietist crusading.

Finally, Progressivism brought the triumph of institutionalized racism, the disfranchising of blacks in the South, the cutting off of immigration, the building up of trade unions by the federal government into a tripartite big government, big business, big union alliance, the glorifying of military virtues and conscription, and a drive for American expansion abroad.

In short, the Progressive Era ushered the modern American politico-economic system into being. Despite the spate of studies in the past two decades, no one has yet put all the pieces together into a coherent explanatory framework. That will be the aim of this book.[2]

---

[2][Editor's footnote] From ibid.

CHAPTER 1

Railroads:
The First Big Business and the
Failure of the Cartels

1. SUBSIDIZING THE RAILROADS

Railroads were the first Big Business, the first large-scale industry, in America. It is therefore not surprising that railroads were the first industry to receive massive government subsidies, the first to try to form substantial cartels to restrict competition, and the first to be regulated by government.[1]

It was the decade of the 1850s, rather than as once believed, the Civil War, that saw the beginnings of America's epic story of rapid and remarkable growth.[2] The railroads, leading the parade, had spurted ahead of canals as the major form of inland transportation during the 1840s. In the 1850s the railroads established a formidable transportation network as far west as the Mississippi. During the 1860s, the railroads reached westward across the Continent, spurred by massive federal land grants, which eclipsed state government subsidies in this crucial period.

---

[1]Since this book is not meant to be a history of late 19th-century industry or of railroads, we do not discuss here fully the land grants and other subsidies to railroads. What we are interested in is an historical analysis of the development of railroad regulation and other manifestations of statism.

[2]See Ralph Andreano, ed., *The Economic Impact of the American Civil War,* 2nd ed. (Cambridge, MA: Schenkman, 1967).

The Republicans had proved able to use their virtual one-party control of Congress during and immediately after the Civil War, to enact the nationalist and statist economic program they had inherited from the Whigs, a program which included massive subsidies to business in the form of protective tariffs to industry and land grants to railroads. Before the Civil War, the Democratic Party, roughly the *laissez-faire* party since its inception in the late 1820s, had clearly been the permanent majority of the country: the Democrats were only out of the presidential office for two terms in over three decades. But with the Democrats demoralized, seceded from the Union or branded as traitors, the Republicans saw their golden opportunity and drove through their program.[3]

One example of the way in which the railroads fed at the public trough during the 1860s is the case of the 800,000 acre Cherokee tract in southeastern Kansas. The tract was grabbed from the Cherokees by the federal government, and then sold, in one chunk, to James F. Joy, known as "The Railroad King," and head of the Kansas City, Fort Scott, and Gulf Railroad. The sale to Joy, negotiated in secret, was a curious one, since he was not the high bidder for the land. There was a great deal of protest when it was discovered that the sale made no provisions for settlers some 20,000 strong, who had already homesteaded the land. Finally, the government, which had sold the land to Joy at $1.00 an acre on generous credit terms, allowed the settlers to buy their land from Joy for an average sum of $1.92 per acre in cash.

Joy's highly favorable treatment at the hands of the federal government may have been related to the fact that Secretary of the Interior Orville H. Browning, the director of the public lands and the man who had negotiated the sale, was James Joy's brother-in-law. Not only that: Browning had been Joy's attorney, and was soon to be so again. And the man employed by Joy to negotiate with Browning over the Cherokee land was none other than Browning's own law partner. A cozy little group![4]

Of nearly 200 million acres of valuable land in the original federal grants, almost half were handed over to the four large transcontinental railroads: Central Pacific, Southern Pacific, Union Pacific, and Northern

---

[3][Editor's footnote] For more on the political history of the country and the free-market orientation of the Democratic Party in the 19th century, see Chapter 4 below, pp. 109–21.

[4]See Paul W. Gates, "The Homestead Law in an Incongruous Land System," *The American Historical Review* (July 1936): 672–75.

Pacific.[5] The typical *modus operandi* of these railroads was as follows: (1) a small group of inside promoters and managers would form the railroad, putting up virtually no money of their own; (2) they would use their political influence to get land grants and outright loans (for the Union and Central Pacific) from the federal government; (3) they would get aid from various state and local governments; (4) they would issue a huge amount of bonds to sell to the eager public; and (5) they would form a privately-held construction company, issuing themselves bonds and shares, and would then mulct *themselves* as managers of the railroad (or rather, mulct railroad shareholders and bondholders) by charging the road highly inflated construction costs.

The Central Pacific was founded by four Sacramento merchants — "The Big Four": Collis P. Huntington, the dominant partner; Mark Hopkins, the inside man who managed the books; Charles Crocker, who ran the construction work; and Leland Stanford, who took care of the political end by becoming Governor of California. Stanford saw to it that the state and local governments in California along the route kicked in substantial aid to the Central Pacific. One example of his methods occurred when the people of San Francisco voted on a $3 million bond issue to be contributed to the Central Pacific Railroad. To make sure that the people voted correctly, the Governor's brother, Philip Stanford, drove to the polls and distributed gold pieces to the voters, who duly obliged their benefactors.

The four founders had the idea of launching the railroad. But how to do so with only the paltry sum of $200,000 between them? The partners understood where the economics of the business truly lay — in obtaining a lucrative federal charter for the road. Collis Huntington took the $200,000 with him to Washington in his trunk, and when he was through lobbying in Washington, his money was all gone — in a mysteriously unrecorded manner — but the charter for the Central Pacific Railroad was theirs. The charter was the key, for it not only handed nine million acres in land grants to the road, but it also agreed to pay a subsidy in government bonds, amounting to $26 million to serve as a first mortgage on the railroad. Once the charter was received, money would be pouring into the railroad from federal and state governments, and from the sale of stocks and especially bonds to the public.

---

[5]See Alfred D. Chandler, Jr., ed., *The Railroads: The Nation's First Big Business* (New York: Harcourt, Brace & World, 1965), pp. 49–50.

The profits siphoned off by the four founders came largely through their creation of the Credit and Finance Corporation as a separate construction company for the Central Pacific, a company which had the sole right to purchase all material and actually to construct the road. The CFC was wholly owned and directed by the four founders of the Central Pacific, and the founders, as heads of the railroad, made sure to pay munificent and extravagant sums to themselves as the construction company, thereby fleecing the shareholders and bondholders of the railroad. The railroad paid a total of $79 million to the CFC for the construction work, funds acquired from governments and investors, and it has been estimated that over $36 million was in excess of reasonable cost for the construction. Typical of the great waste in construction was the time when the burgeoning Central Pacific encountered the small, already existing Sacramento Valley Railroad along its route. The economic course would have been to simply buy the Sacramento Valley road; instead, the Central Pacific built its own, longer line around it in a twisting and senseless route. The reason: "because it was cheaper to build at the government expense than to buy a railroad already existing ..."[6]

The same device was used for the Union Pacific, which, laying track westward from Omaha, joined the Central Pacific in Utah. In this case, the insiders' construction company was the Crédit Mobilier, the federal land grants to the railroad totaled 12 million acres, and the bond subsidy was $27 million. The inside directors running the Crédit Mobilier charged the Union Pacific $94 million for constructing the road, when $44 million was the estimated true cost.

This time, the distributor of the largesse to Congressmen and other government officials to induce them to vote for chartering the road was Republican Representative Oakes Ames of Massachusetts. Ames distributed the stock of the real profit-maker, the Crédit Mobilier, judiciously to key members of Congress in advance of the vote, either giving them the stock outright or charging them next to nothing. They became known, unsurprisingly, as the "Railway Congressmen." As Ames put it, he distributed the stock "where it will do most good for us." For, "we want more friends in this Congress. There is no difficulty in getting men to look after their own property." The payoff list included the "Christian Statesman"

---

[6]Matthew Josephson, *The Robber Barons: The Great American Capitalists, 1861–1901* (New York: Harcourt, Brace & World, 1962), p. 88. [Editor's remarks] Ibid., pp. 78–89; Chandler, ed., *The Railroads*, p. 50.

Vice President Schuyler Colfax of Indiana, James G. Blaine of Maine, Secretary of the Treasury George S. Boutwell, future president James A. Garfield of Ohio, Senator Henry Wilson of Massachusetts, and a dozen other Congressmen, including James Brooks of New York, House minority leader, as a sop to the Democrats. As for Oakes Ames himself, he not only received some stock for his trouble, but his shovel manufacturing firm surprisingly received the Crédit Mobilier contract for shovels in constructing the railroad.[7]

The railroad financier with closest ties to the Republican administrations was the redoubtable banker, Jay Cooke, head of Jay Cooke & Co. A small Philadelphia financier at the outset of the Civil War, Cooke had the vision to found his banking house and to wangle from the federal government a monopoly on underwriting the massive bond issues floated during the war. To sell them to the gullible public, Cooke launched the first modern propaganda campaign for selling the bonds, employing thousands of subagents and such slogans for the credulous as "A national debt a national blessing."

Cooke obtained the highly lucrative monopoly underwriting concession from Washington through his influence on Secretary of the Treasury Salmon P. Chase. Cooke's journalist brother, Henry, was a long-time aide of Chase, from the latter's tenure of Governor of Ohio. Henry then followed Chase to Washington. After extensive wining and dining of Chase, and after demonstrating his propaganda methods in selling government bonds, Jay Cooke won the coveted concession that was to make him one of the richest men in America and his new Jay Cooke & Co. by far the leading investment bank. Cooke became widely known as "The Tycoon," and the phrase "as rich as Jay Cooke" became a popular saying.

Cooke found many ingenious ways to expand the market for his bonds. He bribed financial reporters and Congressmen extensively, and he demanded kickbacks in bond purchases from every war contractor and military supplier. Particularly adroit was Cooke's success in taking Chase's

---

7[Editor's footnote] Josephson, *The Robber Barons,* pp. 78, 89–93, 164; Chandler, ed., *The Railroads*, p. 50. One of the promoters of the Union Pacific was Grenville M. Dodge. Dodge, who previously was helpful in getting Iowa Republicans to support Abraham Lincoln for president in 1860, later was promoted to an army general in the Civil War and was tasked with removing the Indians from the Union Pacific's land. Part of the railroad's costs were subsidized in this manner. Murray Rothbard, "Bureaucracy and the Civil Service in the United States," *Journal of Libertarian Studies* 11, no. 2 (Summer 1995): 39–41.

plan and persuading Congress to transform the American banking system. The notes of state chartered banks, which constituted all the banks in the country before the onset of the Civil War, were taxed out of existence by the federal government, to be replaced by the notes of a few newly chartered, large-scale national banks. The legal structure of the national banks, in turn, was such that the amount of bank notes they could issue was based on how many federal bonds they held. Hence, by lobbying for a new, centralized banking system dependent upon government bonds, Cooke assured himself a huge increase in the market for the very bonds over which he had acquired a monopoly.[8]

Considering Cooke's credentials, it is no wonder that the biggest land bonanza of all the railroad charters, the Northern Pacific, enjoying its federal gift of 47 million acres, should have fallen into the hands of the Tycoon, in 1869.

Before launching actual construction of the Northern Pacific, Cooke lobbied in Washington in 1870 for a new charter, which provided for Jay Cooke & Co. to be the sole fiscal agent of the railroad, and for Cooke's bank to receive the enormous fee of 12% as well as 20% in Northern Pacific stock, for all bonds it was able to sell.

Thus, Cooke did not need a separate construction company to mulct the other shareholders and bondholders of the railroad, as did his counterparts in the Central and Union Pacific boondoggles; for he already had his private banking house in place. Cooke's handsome charter was aided by the fact that America's leading politicians rushed to help the Northern Pacific in return for shares of its stock. Cooke's old friend, the now Chief Justice of the U.S. Supreme Court, Salmon P. Chase, even offered to become president of the Northern Pacific at a "good salary." Other powerful stockholders brought in by Cooke were: Vice President Schuyler Colfax, future President Rutherford B. Hayes of Ohio, and Secretary of the Treasury Hugh McCulloch. President Ulysses S. Grant's wholehearted favor was assured by the influence of his old friend and advisor Henry

---

[8][Editor's footnote] Josephson, *The Robber Barons*, pp. 53–58. For more on Jay Cooke and the 1863 and 1864 National Banking Acts, see Murray Rothbard, "A History of Money and Banking in the United States Before the Twentieth Century," in *A History of Money and Banking in the United States: The Colonial Era to World War II*, Joseph Salerno, ed. (Auburn, AL: Mises Institute, 2005 [1982]), pp. 132–47; Patrick Newman, "Origins of the National Banking System: The Chase-Cooke Connection and the New York City Banks," *Independent Review* (Winter 2018).

Cooke, and of his private secretary, General Horace Porter, who offered his friendly services to Cooke in return for a handsome bribe.

The payoff to Northern Pacific was opposed by a rival group, who sought similar favors for a new Southern Pacific Railroad. The major backer for the Southern Pacific group was Speaker of the House James G. Blaine, of Maine, one of the powers of the Republican Party. To persuade Blaine of the error of his ways, Jay Cooke & Co. granted the Speaker a sizable personal loan based on collateral that was not investigated with the bank's usual care.

With the charter firmly in tow, Jay Cooke geared up a mammoth propaganda machine such as he had used to successfully sell government bonds in the Civil War. Traveling agents were hired, and newspapermen were systematically bribed to sing the praises of the Northern Pacific and of the climate along its prospective route. The purpose was twofold: to induce the general public to buy Northern Pacific bonds; and to induce settlers to immigrate to the Northwestern territories along the route. The migrants would have to buy the land granted to the railroad and to become customers of the railroad after it was built. Favored stockholder Henry Ward Beecher, the most celebrated minister in the country, wrote blurbs for the railroad in his *Christian Union*; and Cooke's hired pamphleteers had the fertile imagination to claim the climate of the future states of Minnesota and Montana to be "a cross between Paris and Venice."[9]

By the early 1870s, however, the bonanza era for the railroads and their promoters had come to an abrupt end. The reasons were threefold. In the first place, there was a general revulsion at the way in which the railroads had been able to outdo each other in feeding hugely at the public

---

[9][Editor's footnote] Josephson, *The Robber Barons,* pp. 93–99. For a comparison between the inefficient government sponsored transcontinentals created by the 1862 and 1864 Pacific Railway Acts with the more private Great Northern operated by James J. Hill, see Burton Folsom, Jr., *The Myth of the Robber Barons: A New Look at the Rise of Big Business in America* (Herndon, VA: Young America's Foundation, 2007 [1987]), pp. 17–39. The main drawback of the government sponsored transcontinentals was that they were not funded through market savings but instead government loans and land grants, and were thus not disciplined by profit and loss. By granting subsidies, the government diverted resources away from where consumers would have spent their money (and hence valued more highly). See Murray Rothbard, *Man, Economy, and State with Power and Market* (Auburn, AL: Mises Institute 2009 [1962]), pp. 946–53, 1040–41. That transcontinental railroads still would have been created can be seen through Hill's Great Northern, built after buying the previously subsidized and bankrupt St. Paul & Pacific Railroad, which received a land grant far smaller than the other transcontinentals.

trough. 1871 was the year of the last federal land grant to the railroads, for the decade of the 1870s saw a widespread "antimonopoly" movement, which also succeeded in slowing down state and local aid to new railroads. In some states, new constitutions prohibited government loans to corporations (which, in those days, meant mainly railroads).

The revulsion against public partnership with railroads coincided with the second reason, the renaissance of the Democratic Party. For the eager mercantilism of the 1860s reflected the virtual absence in Congress on the political scene of the traditionally *laissez-faire* party. By the early 1870s, the Democratic Party had recouped its fortunes, only to have the presidential election purloined from Samuel Tilden in 1876. From the early 1870s to the mid-1890s, the Democratic Party was to be almost as strong as the Republicans, often controlling at least one house of Congress if not so often the presidency itself. Apart from their ideological affinities, the Democrats could be expected to make political capital out of Republican corruption, so much of which had centered on the railroads.

The third reason for the end of the railroad bonanza was the shocking bankruptcy and collapse of the mighty Jay Cooke in the Panic of 1873.[10] One problem with massive government aid is that it subsidizes inefficiency, and the far from completed Northern Pacific was increasingly in huge financial arrears. Also, the Tycoon's touch in selling bonds was no longer so magical as it had been in peddling government securities. Led by the powerful Rothschilds, European bankers and investors stayed away in droves from Northern Pacific bonds — a striking contrast to the general enthusiasm of European investors in American railroads during the latter half of the 19th century. Meanwhile, at home, the brash new firm of investment bankers, Drexel, Morgan & Co., headed by Cooke's Philadelphia rival, Anthony Drexel, and by young John Pierpont Morgan of New York, acted against Cooke and helped bring about the failure of Cooke's U.S. government bond issue in early 1873. Half a year later, all of these factors combined to cause the failure and bankruptcy of Jay Cooke & Co., precipitating the Panic of 1873. As a result, Cooke was now succeeded by

---

[10][Editor's footnote] For more on Jay Cooke, the inflationist bent of the railroads, and the Panic of 1873, see Rothbard, "A History of Money and Banking," pp. 148–56. For the background behind the Panic of 1873 and evidence that the length and severity of the ensuing depression was exaggerated, see Patrick Newman, "The Depression of 1873–1879: An Austrian Perspective," *Quarterly Journal of Austrian Economics* (Winter 2014): 485–97.

J.P. Morgan as the nation's leading investment banker.[11] Since Morgan was a Democrat, his ascension symbolized the important political shift returning the country to a genuine two-party system.

2. The Rationale of Railroad Pricing

The "anti-monopoly" and later movements that wanted government to do something about the railroads arose partly in response to the outrageous handouts that government had granted to the roads. The healthy demand of the protestors was to stop or rollback the subsidies: the former successfully stopped the land grant process, while the latter focused on a demand for local governments to tax unused land that the railroads had received as a bonus and were holding off the market. Many of the protestors went further, however, and demanded various forms of regulation to hold down railroad rates, especially for freight, which was economically far more significant than passenger service.

The public demand for rate regulation, when not based on self-interest (as will be seen below), reflected a profound ignorance of the basic economics of railroad pricing. The idea that rates were in some sense "too high," or that railroads were monopolies, ran against the hard fact that railroads were tremendously and even fiercely competitive, and that the consuming public was being served, not only by land-based transportation across the Continent,[12] but also by continued, competitive, and substantial lowering of freight rates.

Railroads competed between the same cities and towns, they also competed with each other between regions, and they competed with canals and coastal shipping. Obviously, as in any other commodity pricing, the

---

[11]([Editor's remarks] Josephson, *The Robber Barons*, pp. 165–73.) Since Morgan and August Belmont, the Rothschilds' agent in New York, were generally allied, we may speculate that the Rothschilds' rebuff to the Northern Pacific bonds may have been part of a successful cabal to bring down Jay Cooke and replace him with Morgan in the American banking firmament. On the Morgan-Belmont-Rothschild alliance, see Stephen Birmingham, *"Our Crowd": The Great Jewish Families of New York* (New York: Pocket Books, 1977). ([Editor's remarks] Ibid., pp. 39, 44–45, 73, 94, 131, 152–57). Morgan had other important European connections. His father, Junius, was an American-born banker at the London branch of George Peabody & Co.

[12]It is difficult for the modern reader to comprehend that, before the advent of the railroads, there was literally no way to move over land apart from unsatisfactory local dirt roads. Hence, before the mid-19th century, transportation had to take place over water, and centers of population and production had to be locally nearby.

prices of railway rates were set by the degree of competition in the various areas. Along routes where railroads competed directly with canals or coastal shipping, freight rates were forced lower than where such competition did not exist. There was intra-railroad competition between regions developing between the several transcontinental railroad routes. There was also fierce competition between the five competing "trunk lines" between the Eastern cities and the Midwest — The Erie, Baltimore & Ohio (B&O), Pennsylvania, New York Central, and Grand Trunk. It is interesting that, in their public arguments, the various railroads argued that rates "should" be set in accordance with whatever pricing "theory" benefited the particular road. Thus, the Baltimore & Ohio and Pennsylvania railroads, which were the shortest of the five trunk lines, argued that rates should be set according to *distance*, which of course would allow them to undercut their competitors. The New York Central, which had the lowest costs of operation (easier grades, denser traffic, etc.) argued that rates should be determined solely by operating costs. And the Grand Trunk, weak and perpetually teetering on the edge of bankruptcy, claimed that prices should only be high enough to cover operating costs, ignoring dividends and interest.[13]

There was also vigorous competition between railroads serving the same cities. By the mid-1880s, indeed, there was scarcely a large town in the United States that wasn't served by two or more railroads. For one example, there were in this period no less than 20 competitive railway routes between St. Louis and Atlanta.

Complaints by customers (farmers, merchants, and other shippers) and by the general public about freight rates generally centered around the railroad practice of multiform pricing, of charging one shipper different rates from another. In each case, the shippers paying higher rates denounced the action as "price discrimination" stemming from some sort of conspiracy indulged in by the railroads. But in each case, there were sound economic reasons for the pricing practice. The complaints may be grouped into several categories.

(1) Continuing complaints that railroads were charging lower, proportional, per-mile rates for *long-haul* as compared to *short-haul* traffic. But such pricing was the result, not of some demonic conspiracy against the short-haul areas, but of the economics of the situation. In the first place, railroads had high fixed terminal costs — the costs of loading and

---

[13]See Edward C. Kirkland, *Industry Comes of Age: Business, Labor, and Public Policy, 1860–1897* (New York: Holt, Rinehart, and Winston, 1961), pp. 77–79.

unloading at the two terminals for each shipment — which were incurred regardless of the length of the trip. These would tend to yield lower rates for longer hauls. Secondly, the Western railroads, in particular, were built far ahead of traffic and therefore had to keep freight rates low in order to induce farmers and others to develop the region. This would account for lower "through," long-haul interstate rates from West to East.

The Eastern farmers, hit hard by the competition from the West, were of course more disposed to rail about conspiracy than to consult the economic reasons for the differences in freight rates. They complained about the resulting loss of their "natural" markets in the Eastern cities. Similar bitter complaints about higher rates were indulged in by Eastern merchants and agricultural-based manufacturers, who saw themselves outcompeted by products made further west. Thus, millers in Rochester denounced the lower freight rates enjoyed to their New York City makers by the millers in Minneapolis.

(2) One would think that the Western farmers, at least would be delighted by the lower rates on long-haul through traffic from West to East. But true to both human nature and the political value of pressure and complaints, the Western farmers, too, claimed to be unhappy. *They* protested the higher local rates they had to pay, as well as the discounts that railroads gave to large as compared to small shippers.

The rationale for granting discounts for large shipments should be familiar to the current reader. Larger orders reduce the risk of producing or shipping a desired minimum volume; and larger orders are less costly to process, since there is a certain fixed cost for writing out and processing any given order.

(3) As indicated above, railroad rates will naturally tend to be lower where competition is fiercer, either with other roads in the same town, other regions, or with other forms of transportation. Thus, New York City, with many competing railroads, paid far lower rates per mile on grain shipped from Chicago than did Pittsburgh, which was only served by one railroad, the Pennsylvania. Worchester, Massachusetts merchants paid more for their Western grain than did the merchants from more distant Boston. Naturally, the result was continued grumbling from cities which considered themselves disadvantaged.

(4) The most intense and persistent griping over alleged geographical freight rate "discrimination" has been Southern charges that the South has always been forced to pay substantially higher freight rates than other regions, particularly the East. In a notable article, the eminent historian

David M. Potter has explained these persistently higher Southern rates by demonstrating their economic rationale.[14]

Potter uncovered several reasons for the higher freight rates in the South. In the first place, the density of population is greater in the East, the lower density of traffic in the South imposing higher costs. Secondly, the principal shipment from the South has been cotton. Railroads early realized that they had to "classify" commodities when deciding on freight rates; for heavy, bulky commodities selling at a low cost per unit weight could not afford to pay the high freight rates per ton-mile that lighter-weight, more specialized consumer commodities could afford. Hence, if they were to move these bulky commodities at all, the railroads had to classify the bulky commodities such as coal, wheat, livestock, ore, or cotton into lower rate categories than, say, groceries or clothing. Hence, to make up for the low rates which the Southern railroads had to charge for cotton, they had to set comparatively high rates on other, higher-grade goods, including Northern goods that were shipped southward.

Thirdly, it was the peculiarity of Southern rail traffic that there were for a long time no trunk roads for long-haul traffic from the South to the Eastern markets. Instead, the railroad traffic was local, carrying produce from the interior to the coastal ports, thence to ship by the coastal trade. Local traffic meant higher freight rates. Indeed, the stiff water competition in much of the South — one the coastal route, by river boats on the large and small rivers — meant unusually lower railroad rates on the competing routes, and correspondingly higher local rates where this competition was absent.

Fourthly, even after trunk lines were built, the only through traffic was triangular: shipping foodstuffs from the Midwest to the South, and cotton from South to East. This meant one-way traffic, a costly process which meant little or no return shipments to reduce overhead costs. Again, the result was higher through rates in the Southern trade.

(5) Particularly troubling to critics was the practice of railroads in granting "rebates" off freight rates to their shippers. It was charged that the practice was discriminatory and monopolistic and was used to grant special privileges to favored shippers, such as Standard Oil.

---

[14]David M. Potter, "The Historical Development of Eastern-Southern Freight Relationships," *Law and Contemporary Problems* (Summer 1947): 420–23.

What the critics failed to realize was that, far from being in some way "monopolistic," granting rebates was precisely the major way by which railroads *competed* with each other and with other forms of transportation. The practice of giving discounts off list price to attract or hold customers is a common one in industry now, and there are few accusations that the custom is either monopolistic or discriminatory. The point is that business firms, understandably, do not like to cut prices. If they are forced, by competition, to cut prices, they try at first not to change their lists, but instead, hoping such cuts will be temporary, grant off-list discounts to their customers. The price-cutting process begins with one or two customers, either to gain new customers or to keep them from shifting to a competitor.

If the discounts cannot be sustained, they will disappear and the list will be maintained; but if the general trend turns out to be toward lower prices, the discounts or rebates will spread, especially as other customers tend to find out and demand similar treatment. In short, lower prices will tend to manifest themselves through the spread of discounts off-list.[15]

There is another reason for the prevalence of rebates: that businesses are often willing to charge less in return for a *definite* order. As one railroad man explained in U.S. Senate hearings on the widespread use of rebates: "A man may say, 'I can give you so much business.' If you can depend on that you may make definite arrangements accordingly."[16]

We can see, then, that pricing in the business world, in contrast to the neatly determined quantities and charts of the economics textbooks, is a continuing process of *discovery* — of trying to figure out what the best and most profitable prices may be in any given situation.[17] This is particularly

---

[15][Editor's footnote] Rothbard's reasoning for why firms prefer to engage in secret price discounts rather than publicly stated price cuts is an illuminating explanation for why many prices may appear "stickier" than what they actually are. The historical price data which supposedly look stable over long periods of time may not be the actual prices which transactions are conducted at. Hidden price increases can also occur through reclassifications of goods in pricing categories or charging for previously free services. In his class lectures on this point, Rothbard mentioned the work of George Stigler. See George Stigler and James Kindahl, *The Behavior of Industrial Prices* (New York: NBER, 1970); Murray Rothbard, "The Railroading of the American People" in *The American Economy and the End of Laissez-Faire: 1870 to World War II,* 75:00 onward. Of course, prices are not perfectly flexible, but neither are they as rigid as commonly believed.

[16]Kirkland, *Industry Comes of Age,* p. 84.

[17][Editor's footnote] Rothbard's emphasis on pricing as a discovery process is a major

true of railroads, which have had to price literally thousands of items over a myriad of different routes and conditions.

Perhaps this complexity of the discovery process accounts for the fact that railroad rebates, far from being confined to a few large shippers such as Standard Oil, were widespread during the latter half of the 19th century for petroleum refining as well as in most other industries. Such rebates were one of the major ways in which railroads competed with each other. Thus, the New York Central typically had six thousand cases of "special contracts," or rebates, outstanding; and in California, rebates were granted on virtually every contract. Reductions off list could easily go as far as 50%.

(6) At once the most important and the most absurd charge was that railroad rates were "too high" in the decades after the Civil War. There is, first of all, the lack of any rational and non-arbitrary standard to determine how high or how low the price "should have been." But, apart from that, one of the remarkable phenomena of these decades was the continuing and massive fall in freight rates over the years. It was an era that ushered in a new age of cheap transportation over vast distances.

Generally, the railroad rates fell, as did other prices, during recessions, but did not rise nearly as much during succeeding booms. As a result, the trend was rapidly downward. These were glorious decades in America

---

theme in Austrian economics. The argument is that competition, far from being accurately captured in the staid end state model of perfect competition where buyers and sellers have no influence on prices and possess perfect information, is actually better described as a dynamic interactive process where rivalrous buyers and sellers have to appraise the pertinent market data, make speculative forecasts, and continually adjust their behavior. The market process, or the actions of entrepreneurs engaging in economic calculation to allocate scarce resources, is one of equilibration rather than equilibrium. Markets are efficient and welfare enhancing even if they are not in perfect competition or general equilibrium. See Murray Rothbard, *Man, Economy, and State*, pp. 687–98, 720–39; Dominick T. Armentano, *Antitrust and Monopoly: Anatomy of a Policy Failure*, 2nd ed. (Oakland, CA: Independent Institute, 1990), pp. 13–48, and the sources of other Austrians cited therein. Rothbard later in his life did criticize the discovery procedure paradigm and preferred to characterize entrepreneurs in the market as appraisers and uncertainty bearers instead of discoverers. See Murray Rothbard, "The End of Socialism and the Calculation Debate Revisited," in *Economic Controversies* (Auburn, AL: Mises Institute, 2010 [1991]), pp. 845–48. For an analysis of the railroad industry which uses the perfectly competitive benchmark and therefore ignores the above argument, see Robert Harbeson, "Railroads and Regulation, 1877–1916, Conspiracy or Public Interest?" *Journal of Economic History* (June 1967): 230–42. For an Austrian perspective on the "natural monopoly" concept of which railroads were frequently assumed to be, see Chapter 9 below, p. 288.

when the increased supply of goods and services emanating from our own Industrial Revolution lowered most prices. As in all of the 19th century except for periods of wartime inflation, the general trend of prices was downward. But even in relation to other falling prices, the fall in railroad freight rates was truly remarkable.

The fall in rates took several forms. One was an outright and evident fall in nominal rates. Over the decades, these nominal rates fell by one-half to two-thirds. Thus, the price for shipping wheat from Chicago to New York fell from 65 cents per 100 pounds in 1866 to 20 cents thirty-one years later. Dressed beef shipments between the two cities fell from 90 cents per 100 pounds in 1872 to 40 cents by the end of the century. In westbound traffic from New York to Chicago, the most expensive, or Class 1 goods, fell in price from $2.15 per 100 pounds in the spring of 1865, to $.75 at the end of 1888. Class 4 goods fell, during the same period, from $.96 to $.35.

The most remarkable rate cuts occurred during the great rate wars of 1876–77, between the great trunk lines, soon after the completion of the Baltimore & Ohio route to Chicago in 1874. Class 1 rates fell, in those two years, from $.75 to $.25 per 100 pounds, while class 4 rates fell to $.16. Eastbound freight rates from Chicago to New York dropped phenomenally by 85%, from $1.00 to $.15. Passenger rates were cut in half in this brief period.

Apart from the outright reductions in rates, real freight rates were also lowered by improving the services supplied by the railroads, such as providing storage or carting services without charge. One particular method of lowering freight rates without nominally doing so was by systematically re-classifying commodities from higher to lower-paying categories. Thus, the nominal rates in each class could remain the same, but if goods were transferred from higher to lower rate categories, the real effect was to lower the cost of railroad transportation. For example, before 1887, two-thirds of all the items shipped westward in trunk-line roads were bracketed into high class 1 to class 3 categories; after that year, reclassification in 1887 left only 53% of the items in these highest three classes.

That same year, a huge increase was granted by the trunk lines in the number of types of items that were entitled to lower rates for being shipped in full carload lots. Before that year, only 14% of westbound items on the trunk lines were entitled to discounts in carloads; afterwards, fully 55% of the items were entitled to the same privilege. Hence, real freight rates fell because more items could now obtain quantity discount privileges.[18]

Overall, railroad rates had fallen far below the wildest dreams of the Grangers and the other anti-railroad movements of the 1870s. Albert Fishlow, indeed, estimates that, by 1910, "real freight rates [had fallen by] more than 80 percent from their 1849 level, and real passenger charges 50 percent."[19]

One particularly piquant group of complainers against the railroads were the railroad investors themselves. Often mulcted by unscrupulous promoters and inside managers (as in the case of the major transcontinental roads), induced by eager local, state, and federal governments to over-expand and wastefully manage their operations, the railroad owners found, over the decades, a none too munificent rate of return sinking even lower. Thus, around 1870, railroad bond yields averaged about 6% while stock dividends were approximately 7%; by the end of the century, average bond yields had sunk to 3.3% and dividends to 3.5%. In addition to this virtually 50% drop, only 30–40% of railroad stock paid any dividend at all during the 1890s.[20] Railroad bankruptcies and reorganizations were extensive during the same decade.

3. The Attempts to Form Cartels

Early in the career of large-scale railroads, some railroad men sought a way out from the rigors of competition and competitive price-cutting.

---

[18]Kirkland, *Industry Comes of Age*, pp. 79–80, 83–84, 93–94.

[19]Albert Fishlow, "Productivity and Technological Change in the Railroad Sector, 1840–1910," in National Bureau of Economic Research, *Output, Employment and Productivity in the United States After 1800* (New York, 1966), p. 629.

[Editor's remarks] The Grangers were a farmer protest movement that advocated restrictive railroad regulation, among other interventions. The economic suffering of farmers in the late 19th century was overblown. In general, the real price of freight for western farmers was roughly constant throughout this period, and their terms of trade improved. Nor were they crippled by rising real interest payments, in fact, interest rates were competitive, most farmers did not take out mortgages, and mortgages that were taken out were short term and anticipated future deflation. Farmer anger was mainly due to their income rising less than other groups, and the increased competitiveness and changing environment they operated in. See Charles Morris, *The Tycoons* (New York: Owl Books, 2005), pp. 115–17; Susan Previant Lee and Peter Passell, *A New Economic View of American History* (New York: W.W. Norton & Co, 1979), pp. 292–301.

[20]Kirkland, *Industry Comes of Age*, p. 71.

What they sought was the time-honored device of the *cartel* agreement, in which all the firms in a certain industry agree to raise their selling prices. If the firms could be trusted to abide by the agreement, then all could raise prices and every firm could benefit.

The general public conceives of price-raising and price-fixing agreements to be as easy as a whispered conversation over cocktails at the club. They are, however, extremely difficult to arrange and even harder to maintain. For prices have been driven low by the competition of supply and production; in order to raise prices successfully, the firms will *also* have to agree to cut production. And there is the sticking point: for no business firm, no entrepreneur, and no manager likes to cut production. What they prefer to do is expand. And, if the businessman is to agree, grudgingly, to cut production, he has to make sure that his competitors will do the same. And then there will be interminable quarrels about how much production each firm is supposed to cut. Thus, if several firms are, collectively, producing 1 million tons of Metal X and selling it at $100 a ton, and the firms wish to agree to raise the price to $150 a ton, they will have to agree on how far below the million tons to cut production, and *who* should cut *how much*. And such agreements are at best very difficult to arrive at.

But this is only the beginning of the headaches in store for our cartelists. Generally, they will agree on quota production cuts under the output of a base year, usually the current year of operation. So, if the cartel is being formed in the year 1978, firms A, B, C, etc. may each agree to cut its output in 1979 20% below the previous year. But very quickly in the cartel agreement, and more and more as time goes on, human nature is such that each businessman and manager is thinking as follows: "Darn it, why am I stuck with the maximum production based on 1978 production? This is now 1979 (or 1980, etc.) and now we have installed such-and-such a new process, or we have such-and-such a hotshot product or salesman, that I *know*, if our company were all free to compete and to cut prices, we could sell more, pick up a larger share of the market, and make more profits, than we did that year." As 1978 recedes more and more into the past, and 1978 conditions become more obsolete, each firm chafes increasingly at the bit, longing to be able to cut prices and compete once more. A firm might petition the cartel for an increased quota, but other firms, whose production would have to be cut, would protest bitterly and turn down the request.

Eventually, the internal pressures within the cartel become too great, and the cartel falls apart, prices tumbling once more. A characteristic pattern of cartel breaking is *secret price-cutting*. The restless firm, anxious to cut prices, decides to try to have its cake and eat it too. While its boobish fellow-producers keep sticking to the agreed cartel price of, say, $150 a ton, our hypothetical firm approaches a few customers whom it is anxious to keep, or others whom it is eager to acquire. "Look, because you're such a great person and your firm is such a good one, I'm going to let *you* have our metal for $130 a ton. In return, I want you to keep quiet about it, so that your and our competitors won't find out about the deal." For a few months, this will work, and the firm will be reaping extra profits at its competitors' expense. But, truth will get out, and eventually the word spreads to the firm's other customers and competitors about the secret price-cut. Other customers will demand similar treatment, the competitors will self-righteously denounce our firm as a "rate-buster," a "cheat," and a traitor, and the cartel will dissolve in intensified competition, price-cutting, and intra-industry recriminations.

That is one inexorable way in which a cartel will break up: from internal pressure, pressures arising from the firms within the cartel. But there is another, equally formidable, source of insurmountable pressure to crack the cartel: external pressure, from outside the cartel. For here is the cartel in our hypothetical metal industry. Outside firms, outside investors, clear-sighted entrepreneurs seeking profits, look at this industry and see that a cartel has been formed, its price has gone up by 50%, and consequently, the industry is now enjoying unaccustomed profits. To extend our hypothetical case, suppose that the cartel has raised its profits from 5% to 15%. Outside investors say: "Aha! These fellows have a good thing going. Why shouldn't *I*, who am not bound in any sense by the cartel agreement, nip into this industry, build a new plant and a new firm, and undercut the cartel? I could sell at $130 a ton, and besides, I could build an entirely new plant with the latest equipment and the latest processes, while these fellows would have to compete possessing older and partially obsolete plants." And so, the higher price and the higher profit rates acts as an umbrella and a lure to tempt new and possibly more competitive firms into the industry.

How will the cartel meet the challenge of new and dangerous competitors? If it wishes to keep the high cartel price, it will have to draw the new firm into the cartel, by assigning the firm a production quota of its own. But that would mean that the old firms, each of which detests the idea of cutting production in the first place, would have to cut still more — and all for the benefit of a new and unwelcome interloper. It is unlikely that the new firm could be absorbed into the cartel, and therefore the likely event is a breakup of the cartel, with prices tumbling down again. Except that *this* time the permanent result will be a menacing new competitor which might well out-compete and drive out some of the existing firms. And even if the new firm *is* absorbed into the cartel, the success can only be temporary, since *more* new firms will continue to be attracted to the industry, and the problem will begin all over again. Eventually, the cartel will bust up, from the external pressure of new entrants into the industry.

Thus, every cartel, every voluntary agreement by competing firms to raise prices and cut production, will inexorably break apart from internal and/or external pressures. A cartel cannot long succeed on the free market.[21]

In every industry that has ever attempted the cartel device, the story has been the same repeatedly confirming the above basic economic insight. In the case of the railroads, the plot repeats itself, except that the cartels were called "pools," production was freight shipments, prices were freight rates, and price-cutting took the form of secretly increasing rebates to shippers.

The first important railroad pool was the Iowa Pool, formed in 1870.[22] The twin cities of Omaha, Nebraska — Council Bluffs, Iowa were the eastern terminus of the great new transcontinental Union Pacific-Central Pacific route to California. The rail route from Chicago westward to Omaha therefore took on enormous importance. There were three major

---

[21][Editor's footnote] Rothbard elsewhere argued that even if a cartel was able to successfully restrict output and raise prices, this is not evidence that there is an overall restriction in production, since the cut down in an industry's production releases nonspecific factors and allows them to be absorbed by other industries, who can now increase their production of goods. The sustainable higher price of the cartel is evidence that the industry overproduced, and the resources are more highly valued in other industries. The fact that time and time again, most cartels were not successful is evidence that consumers valued the resources more highly in the cartelized industries than elsewhere. Rothbard, *Man, Economy, and State*, pp. 638, 690. Governments can sustain cartels by forcibly weakening the internal and external mechanisms that break them. For a survey of the various ways in which government intervention cartelizes markets, see ibid., pp. 1089–1147. As will be extensively shown below, virtually all of these were enacted during the Progressive Era.

[22]See Julius Grodinsky, *The Iowa Pool: A Study in Railroad Competition, 1870–1884* (Chicago: University of Chicago Press, 1950). There were fitful attempts to organize railroad pools in the mid and late 1850s, including one by the trunk lines, but they broke up quickly and with little effect. See Alfred D. Chandler, Jr., *The Visible Hand: The Managerial Revolution in American Business* (Cambridge, MA: The Belknap Press of Harvard University Press, 1977), p. 135.

competing routes between Chicago and Omaha: the most northerly, the Chicago and Northwestern; the Chicago, Rock Island, and Pacific ("The Rock Island Line"); and the most southerly "Burlington System" (among other things, interconnecting the Chicago, Burlington, and Quincy with the Burlington and Missouri railroads). As luck would have it, the three competitors were controlled by two businessmen and their associates. The entire Burlington System was controlled by James F. Joy, the "Railroad King," backed by a group of Boston capitalists. Meanwhile, John F. Tracy, backed by numerous capitalists, including Dutch finance, controlled both the Chicago and Northwestern and the Rock Island Line.

With only two businessmen controlling the three competing lines, conditions seemed ripe for a cartel. Both men were eager for the experiment, since both Joy and Tracy had overborrowed in order to acquire their holdings and were in shaky financial shape. And so, in late 1870, Tracy initiated the formation of the Iowa Pool, which tried to prop up freight rates by reducing aggregate traffic and by pooling half the earnings of the three lines and equally dividing the Pool — thereby greatly reducing the incentive to engage in competitive profit-seeking or price-cutting.[23]

Despite the seemingly favorable conditions, and the long official life of the cartel (until 1884), the Iowa Pool was plagued with grave difficulties from the very beginning and broke up after only four years. Competitive rate-cutting, breaking the agreement, occurred early and on many levels. There was, first, severe rate-cutting even *within* the Burlington System and within the Tracy holdings — the sales managers and managerial heads of each railroad understandably wishing to increase the profits of their own organization. There was also vigorous competition and rate-cutting between the Burlington and the Tracy railroads, with charges of "cheating" rife between the various parties. But intra- and inter-organizational rivalry did not complete the competitive picture in the Iowa Pool. For the entire transcontinental railroad system was also in vigorous competition with the Pacific Mail Steamship line, which sailed between the East and West Coasts with overland carriage across Panama. In 1870 there was also an agreement between the Steamship line and Union Pacific to prop up freight rates and allocate an agreed division of traffic between railroad and steamship: in effect, to impose maximum shipping quotas on each mode of transportation in order to raise freight rates. By 1873, however, a rate

---

[23]More specifically, the railroads pooled 50% of their freight receipts and 55% of their earnings from passenger traffic.

war developed between the steamships and the railroads, helping to push the entire Pool into collapse a year later.

Another important factor in the breakup of the Pool was the intervention of the Union Pacific. For one of the first actions of the Iowa Pool was the demand of the Union Pacific a higher share of the transcontinental, Chicago-San Francisco railroad income. Angered, the Union Pacific decided to crush this demand by dealing with the individual members of the Burlington System, and also by shifting more business to the St. Louis rather than the Chicago terminus. All this competition, from within and without the Pool, led to its collapse after only four years of turbulent operation.[24]

The next important pool was an attempt to cartelize trunk line railroads insofar as they were making shipments in the burgeoning new petroleum industry. Ever since the first oil well had been drilled in Titusville, Pennsylvania, in 1859, crude oil had been extracted from western Pennsylvania oil fields and refined largely in Cleveland. At the behest of Thomas A. Scott, head of the Pennsylvania Railroad, in 1871 three great trunk lines, the Pennsylvania, the Erie, and the New York Central formed the South Improvement Company. In order to raise freight rates, the company allocated maximum quotas of oil shipments among themselves. The Pennsylvania was to obtain 45% of oil shipments, while the Erie and the New York Central were each allocated 27.5% of the oil freight. To make sure that the railroads stuck to their agreement, a group of oil refiners was brought into the pact, the refiners being pledged to act as "eveners" to insure that each railroad would not exceed its quota of petroleum freight.

What were the refiners to get in return for providing such essential service to the railroad cartel? They were to obtain freight rebates up to 50%. Furthermore, they were promised a subsidy amounting to a rebate on all oil shipments made by refiners *outside* the South Improvement Company agreement. And since the refiners within the group were acting as eveners for *all* petroleum shipments made by these railroads, they received waybills for these shipments and were therefore able to police the honesty of the railroads in keeping the subsidy agreement.

Oil refining was a highly competitive industry, and so, despite the fact that the South Improvement pool meant higher freight rates, some

---

[24][Editor's footnote] Grodinsky, *The Iowa Pool*, passim; Gabriel Kolko, *Railroads and Regulation: 1877–1916* (Princeton, NJ: Princeton University Press, 1965), p. 8.

refiners were willing to join the pool in order to gain a rebate-and-subsidy advantage over their competitors. Besides, they might succeed in cartelizing oil refining as well. The complying refiners were led by the largest oil refiner in the industry, John D. Rockefeller's Standard Oil Company of Ohio (SOHIO). Originating in 1867 as the partnership of Rockefeller, Flagler & Andrews Co., SOHIO was formed as a $1 million corporation three years later. While Rockefeller was hardly averse to achieving a monopoly, he was skeptical of the success of the cartel and entered it only with reluctance. The South Improvement Pool, indeed, turned out to be still-born; when news of the agreement leaked out, angry pressure by the other refiners and by crude oil producers forced the dissolution of the cartel. As will be seen below in Chapter 3, John D. Rockefeller then turned to the merger route in an attempt to achieve a monopoly in oil refining.[25]

The first important Eastern pool was formed in August 1874. Competition between the great East-Midwest trunk lines had been intense during the Panic of 1873, with a consequent decline in freight rates. The three major trunk lines — New York Central, Erie, and Pennsylvania — were also worried about the imminent completion of a new competition in the Baltimore & Ohio, which would clearly send rates down further. As a result, the presidents of the three trunk lines met at Saratoga, New York, at the home of New York Central's William H. Vanderbilt, and hammered out an agreement to keep up freight rates, and to appoint two regional commissions to enforce the agreement.

But the trunk line agreement soon dissolved from pressures both within and outside the cartel. John W. Garrett, president of the B&O, decided to keep out of the agreement in the hope of outcompeting the other roads and picking up a larger share of the freight business. Externally, the Grand Trunk of Canada took advantage of the pact to open up a new northerly trunk line route from Chicago to Boston via Canada. The result was a speedy collapse of the agreement, and bitter rate wars between the trunk lines followed during 1875 and particularly 1876.[26]

Desperate, the trunk lines called in Albert Fink, German-born engineer and former vice president of the Louisville & Nashville Railroad who

---

[25][Editor's footnote] Allan Nevins, *Study in Power: John D. Rockefeller, Industrialist and Philanthropist* (New York: Charles Scribner's Sons, 1953), vol. 1, pp. 95–131; Kirkland, *Industry Comes of Age*, p. 84. Also see Chapter 3 below, pp. 93–98.

[26]See D.T. Gilchrist, "Albert Fink and the Pooling System," *Business History Review* (Spring 1960): 33–34; Kolko, *Railroads and Regulation*, pp. 8–9.

had become the foremost theoretician, promoter, and manager of railroad pools. By 1873, Fink was urging for the railroads to raise and equalize their rates, and to do it through cartel agreements and divisions of the traffic. Fink was fresh from forming the Southern Railway and Steamship Association in the fall of 1875, in which 32 railway lines formed such an agreement, naming Fink himself as commissioner of the Association with power to supervise the agreement.

In 1877, the trunk lines decided to call in Fink to help them try again. In April, the four largest trunk lines signed the Seaboard Differential Agreement, fixing eastbound freight rates to Philadelphia and Baltimore at 2 and 3 cents per 100 pounds less than to New York or Boston. On westbound traffic, differentials on some freight was the same; on others, it was as much as 6 and 8 cents per 100 pounds. The Seaboard Agreement reflected a shift of power from New York to Baltimore and Philadelphia, with Vanderbilt's New York Central and the Erie forced to agree to maintain freight rates higher than the Pennsylvania Railroad, which had its eastern terminus in Philadelphia, or the B&O, which ended in Baltimore. The agreement was engineered by Philadelphia financier Anthony J. Drexel and J.P. Morgan of Drexel, Morgan, and Co., a major stockholder as well as creditor of the Baltimore & Ohio. Pressure was also put on by allied English bankers, headed by Morgan's father Junius S. Morgan.

In July 1877, a reinforcing agreement between the four trunk lines allocated quotas of all westbound freight from New York: the Erie and the New York Central to receive 33% each, the Pennsylvania 25%, and the remaining 9% to the B&O. Moreover, the railroads established a Trunk Line Association, headed by Albert Fink, to regulate and supervise the pool and rate agreements. August of the following year, the trunk lines and major Western railroads expanded the cartel idea to form a Western Executive Committee to fix and raise rates and pool freight; and in December, at the suggestion of the ubiquitous Fink, the Trunk Line Association and Western Executive Committee formed a Joint Executive Committee to supervise the entire integrated agreement, headed again by Albert Fink. Fink and the Joint Executive also supervised regional subcommittees in all the major cities included in the agreement. By 1881, pooling of freight was extended to eastbound traffic as well.

And yet, this mightiest and continuing attempt to create a voluntary railroad pool proved, like its predecessors, to be a dismal failure. From the beginning, the Grand Trunk line of Canada kept cutting rates, and the completion of the Grand Trunk line to Chicago made matters worse.

Furthermore, rate cutting by railroads within the cartel kept plaguing Fink and the railroads, largely through secret rebates which Fink could not detect until it was too late and much damage had been done to the rate structure and the relative shares of the market. Competitive rebates to shippers were concealed by such deceptive devices as billing freight from more distant points than actually used, under-recording of weight, and spurious classification of freight into cheaper categories of freight rates than had been agreed. Fink tried to counter these practices with a system of freight inspection, but lacking coercive police power, there was little that he could do.

As early as February 1878, Fink attempted to blacklist all railroad executives granting secret rebates; but, a month later, the division of freight between Detroit and Milwaukee was already collapsing in competitive rate and shipping wars. In 1878 and again in 1880 severe rate wars and competition for freight broke out between the trunk lines themselves.

From the beginning of the agreement, the merchants and shippers of New York had been understandably unhappy at the fixed competitive disadvantage that New York was suffering in relation to Philadelphia and Baltimore. Finally, in 1881, under pressure from these merchants and their Boards of Trade, the New York Central broke ranks and initiated a fierce rate war; in three months during 1881, freight rates were cut in half, East and West. Fink tried desperately to stem the tide by gaining an agreement to raise rates to the pre-rate war level and to try to crack down on zealous railroad sales managers (freight agents and freight solicitors) who engaged in secret rebates in order to gain sales. But all this was in vain. In March 1882, Fink and the Joint Executive tried once more, appointing a Joint Agent at every important traffic center, with the power to examine all the railroads' books and bills of lading. But by the end of the year, this attempt had collapsed as well.

One of the major reasons for the failure of Fink and the trunk cartels was the truly heroic activities of one of the most maligned railroad financiers of this era: Jay Gould. In his search for profits, Gould was inadvertently the people's champion by his inveterate activities as "traitor" and "rate-buster," as wrecker of railroad cartels.[27] Ever alert to profits to be

---

[27]Interestingly enough, Gould has been maligned by left-wing historians as well. Thus, the perfervid Matthew Josephson refers to Gould as "Mephistopheles," and speaks of "A Jay Gould [who] flies about preying upon the rich debris ..." Josephson, *The Robber Barons*, pp. 170, 192.

made from undercutting railroad pools and cartels, Gould would either break the agreement from within or build external railroads to compete with the bloated and vulnerable railroad pool.

Thus, it was Gould who initiated much of the Eastern rate wars of 1881–1883 by building the West Shore Railroad in New Jersey as well as the Delaware, Lackawanna and Western in New York to compete directly with the New York Central.[28] In his fascinating re-evaluation of Jay Gould, Julius Grodinsky demonstrates how this "disturber of the peace" benefited the public and shippers by continually building new railroads and breaking railroad pools and rate agreements. Gould performed this function repeatedly in the Middle-West and West, as well as the East. Grodinsky also points out that the extensive rate wars initiated by Gould in the 1870s and 1880s left freight rates permanently far lower than they had been before. And that Gould's rate-cutting benefited even the railroads in the long-run by forcing lower costs and greater efficiency upon the roads, as well as leading to a long-run growth of freight traffic.[29]

All in all, by the mid-1880s the railroads generally were in the position that Gabriel Kolko describes for the Eastern trunk cartelists by 1883:

> By this time the Joint Executive Committee was merely an empty piety without real power or meaning. Fink warned the railroad men that they would lose money by their policies — which they very well realized — but he was unable to obtain their cooperation. There were too many parties,

---

[28]On the trunk lines, Fink, and Gould, see Gilchrist, "Albert Fink and the Pooling System," pp. 34–46; Kolko, *Railroads and Regulation*, pp. 17–20. [Editor's remarks] Lee Benson, *Merchants, Farmers, and Railroads: Railroad Regulation and New York Politics, 1850–1887* (Cambridge, MA: Harvard University Press, 1955), pp. 39–54; Paul W. MacAvoy, *The Economic Effects of Regulation: The Trunk-Line Railroad Cartels and the Interstate Commerce Commission Before 1900* (Cambridge, MA: The MIT Press, 1965), pp. 39–109. For the Joint Executive Committee, significant price wars occurred in 1881, 1884, and 1885. The long run trend of the official grain rate declined from 40 cents per 100 pounds at the beginning of 1880, to 30 cents in early 1883, to 24 cents in mid-1886. See Robert H. Porter, "A Study of Cartel Stability: the Joint Executive Committee, 1880–1886," *Bell Journal of Economics* (Autumn 1983): 311.

[29]Gould filled the image of the self-made man that fitted so many of the entrepreneurs of these decades, including Rockefeller and James J. Hill. Gould was born poor in upstate New York, taught himself surveying, and went on to become a brilliant speculator and corporate financier. See Julius Grodinsky, *Jay Gould: His Business Career, 1867–1892* (Philadelphia: University of Pennsylvania Press, 1957).

too many potential areas of friction, for successful control to come via voluntary agreements.[30]

In 1884, the freight rate structure was in collapse, and the Trunk Line Association "did little more than stand by helplessly." During that year, Charles Francis Adams, Jr., scion of the famous Massachusetts family, and one of the leaders of the Trunk Line Association, wrote that one of its meetings

> struck me as a somewhat funereal gathering. Those comprising it were manifestly at their wit's end. ... Mr. Fink's great and costly organization was all in ruins. ... They reminded me of men in a boat in the swift water above the rapids of Niagara.[31]

The trunk lines struggled to another agreement in late 1885, but it was again to collapse the following year. And the railroad associations in other regions of the country were doing no better. Alfred Chandler's conclusion is apt: "By 1884 nearly all the railroad managers and most investors agreed that even the most carefully devised cartels were unable to control competition."[32]

---

[30]Kolko, *Railroads and Regulation,* p. 20. [Editor's remarks] Ibid., pp. 7–20.

[31]Quoted in Gilchrist, "Albert Fink and the Pooling System," p. 46.

[32]Chandler, *The Visible Hand,* p. 142. [Editor's remarks] Ibid., pp. 137–43.

CHAPTER 2

Regulating the Railroads

1. THE DRIVE FOR REGULATION

Characteristically, it was Albert Fink who saw it first. If the railroads could not form successful cartels by voluntary action, then they would have to get the government to do the job for them. Only government compulsion could sustain a successful cartel. As Fink put it in a letter as early as 1876, "Whether this cooperation can be secured by voluntary action of the transportation companies is doubtful. Governmental supervision and authority may be required to some extent to accomplish the object in view."[1]

The railroad men were scarcely averse to calling in government to help solve their problems. As we have seen, the railroads had been hip deep in government subsidy for many years, and particularly since the Civil War. Of the railroad presidents in the 1870s, 80% held political jobs before, during, or after their tenure. Specifically, of 53 railroad presidents in the 1870s, 28 held down political jobs before or during their presidency, and 14 went into them after they left their railroad posts.[2]

---

[1]Gilchrist, "Albert Fink and the Pooling System," pp. 32–33.

[2]Ruth Crandall, "American Railroad Presidents in the 1870's: Their Backgrounds and Careers," *Explorations in Entrepreneurial History* (July 15, 1950), p. 295. Cited in Kolko, *Railroads and Regulation*, p. 15. [Editor's remarks] For the dominance of railroad interests in the presidential administrations of the post-Civil War years, see Philip H. Burch, Jr.,

Railroad regulation by the states was renewed after the Civil War, beginning with the establishment of the Massachusetts Railroad Commission in 1869. Historians once thought that these state commissions had been put in by farmers to lower railroad rates, but then it was discovered that much of the agitation for regulation came from groups of merchants in specific localities who were disturbed at the pattern of railroad rates, especially the relative height in their own localities. But far from the state commissions being at all anti-railroad, there is strong evidence that the railroads welcomed the commissions and tried to use them to cartelize. Thus, Charles Francis Adams, Jr., of the patrician Adams family, chief architect of the Massachusetts law and Chairman of the Railroad Commission, was scarcely a pariah in the railroad industry. On the contrary, he went on to become a railroad pool administrator and then to be president of the Union Pacific. Moreover, Chauncey M. Depew, attorney for the New York Central, and William H. Vanderbilt, head of the New York Central, were early converts to the regulatory concept. As Depew later wrote, he had become "convinced of their necessity ... for the protection of both the public and the railroads ..."[3]

Much has been made of the fact that the New England and New York commissions of the 1870s and 1880s were merely advisory, and could only hold public hearings and encourage publicity, while Illinois and several other Midwestern states gave their commissions compulsory rate-setting powers. In practice, however, there was little difference, and the "weak" state commissions were scarcely voluntary. As the Senate Committee on Interstate Commerce reported in 1887, concerning the Massachusetts Commission, the railroad men obeyed the commission's edicts because

> self-interest admonishes them of the supreme folly of encouraging or engaging in a losing contest with the forces of public opinion as concentrated and made effective through the commission. It is not because the managers, directors, or stockholders personally shrink from public criticism, but because back of the commission

Elites in American History: The Civil War to the New Deal (New York: Holmes & Meier Publishers, Inc., 1981), pp. 15–67.

[3]Kolko, *Railroads and Regulation*, pp. 16–17.

stands the legislature and back of the legislature stands
the people ...[4]

But state regulation was proving too diverse and inefficient; in particular, it was impossible to regulate the vitally important through rates,
the rates on shipments that extended beyond the boundaries of any one
state. And so, while farmers complained that state commissions were too
friendly to railroads, railroad men began to turn to federal regulation,
to federal cartelization, as the solution. In the summer of 1877, John A.
Wright, a director of the Pennsylvania Railroad, wrote in the *Railway World*
that the federal government must "protect" the railroads from speculators competing ruthlessly toward "cutthroat" competition in railway rates.
The federal government should not only control railroad investments and
charters, but should fix freight and passenger rates, to be enforced "under
penalty of criminal prosecution."[5]

By 1879, there was general agreement among railroad pool executives,
including Albert Fink, that the federal government would have to step in
to cartelize railroad freight, for the pools could not succeed without governmental enforcement. In the same year, Joseph Nimmo, Jr., head of the
first government railroad statistics department, reported that

> At the present time railroad managers appear to be quite
> generally of the opinion that the only practicable rem-
> edy for the evils of unjust and improper discriminations,
> is to be found in a confederation of the railroads under
> governmental sanction and control, the principle of the
> apportionment of competitive traffic being recognized as
> a feature of such a confederation.[6]

The Interstate Commerce Act of 1887, regulating the railroads, was
one of the first federal regulatory acts in American history. The Act began
with a bill introduced in the House by Democratic Representative James
H. Hopkins of Pittsburgh, in 1876 at the behest of a group of independent oil producers of western Pennsylvania. The major provision of the
Hopkins Bill was the outlawing of railroad rebates. Gabriel Kolko is the
first historian to point out that the motives of the Pennsylvania oil men

---

[4]Kirkland, *Industry Comes of Age*, p. 120.

[5]Kolko, *Railroads and Regulation*, p. 14.

[6]Ibid., pp. 26–27.

were not anti-railroad. Quite the contrary, they were pro-railroad and anti-Standard Oil. The oil men were peeved at the superior competition of Standard Oil and its ability to get rebates from the railroads. Bested at competition, they turned to use the federal government to hobble their successful competitor. Formed into the Petroleum Producers' Union the following year, the Union championed the railroads and wailed that Standard Oil was enslaving the giant New York Central, Pennsylvania, and B&O railroads. The railroads were delighted to form an alliance with the weaker oil men, in order to rid themselves of the annoyingly competitive device of rebating; this may be seen in the fact that the Hopkins Bill was apparently written by the attorney for the Philadelphia and Reading Railroad.[7]

The Pennsylvania oil men quickly organized a massive petition campaign for the Hopkins Bill. Over 2,000 signatures of Pennsylvania oil producers and Pittsburgh businessmen poured into the Congress agitating for the Hopkins proposal. The Hopkins Bill died in committee, but a similar bill, drafted by the Petroleum Producers' Union, was introduced in early 1878, by Representative Lewis F. Watson of Pennsylvania. Rapidly, nearly 15,000 signatures on petitions poured into the House from Pennsylvania, attacking rebates and railroad rate "discrimination." The Pennsylvania legislature, followed by Indiana and Nevada, sent similar resolutions to Congress during 1879.

There began almost a decade of jockeying among railroads and other interests on the precise form that federal railroad cartelization would take. The Watson Bill was reported out of the House Commerce Committee headed by Representative John H. Reagan of Texas, and the new Reagan Bill had been amended to outlaw railroad pooling. The Reagan Bill quickly passed the House in December, 1878.[8] While happy to see rebates outlawed,

---

[7]Ibid., pp. 21–22.

[8][Editor's footnote] The motivation behind the Reagan bill has not been sufficiently explored until recently. Railroad tycoon Thomas Scott's fledgling empire, the Texas & Pacific and the Pennsylvania, was involved in heated conflicts with other large railroad giants in the 1870s. The former was wrestling with Collis P. Huntington's Central Pacific for control of transportation from California to the South, and the latter against the Erie and New York Central for Standard Oil's lucrative oil shipments. Scott wanted federal subsidies to strengthen the Texas & Pacific in order to compete with Huntington. John Reagan of Texas was eager to help Scott in order to get a transcontinental railroad in his congressional district, a goal he long desired. This was mixed in with the election of Rutherford B. Hayes and the Compromise of 1877, in which the Republicans were able to offer vague promises to

the railroads wanted the pool agreements to be enforced rather than pro-hibited, and this prohibition was their major objection to the Reagan Bill. As Albert Fink testified before the Senate the following year, the railroads wanted to carry out the objective of the Reagan Bill. Fink approved the outlawing of rebates and the requirement to publicize rates (thus having a chilling effect on *secret* rebates); he also urged a legalized and enforced pooling process, to be governed by a federal railroad commission. Prefig-uring the later provisions of the Interstate Commerce Act, Fink suggested the following clauses:

> Section 3. That all competing railroad companies shall jointly establish a tariff for all competing points.
>
> Section 4. That the tariff so established shall be submit-ted to a commission of experts appointed by the Federal Government, and if they find that the tariff is just and equitable and based upon correct commercial principles ... then such tariff shall be approved, and shall become the law of the land, until changed in the same manner by the same authority.
>
> Section 5. In cases where railroad companies cannot agree upon such tariffs, or upon any other questions such as might lead to a war of rates between railroad companies, the questions of disagreement shall be settled by arbitra-tion, the decision of the arbitrator to be enforced in the United States Courts.[9]

The railroads preferred the Rice Bill of 1879 in the House, and the later Henderson Bill, both written by railroad leader Charles Francis Adams.

Southern Democrats — including John Reagan — in the form of subsidies to the Texas & Pacific in return for their admittance for the electoral commission to count the disputed electoral ballots for Hayes. After the election the Republicans reneged, so Scott received no federal subsidies, and Reagan no transcontinental railroad. The subsequent Reagan Bill, which outlawed pooling and interstate rebates to shippers and discrimination, was designed to strengthen Scott's empire and hamper its rivals connected with Standard's *de facto* railroad cartel. The prohibition of rebates and rate discrimination applied only to interstate trade, shrewdly designed to cripple the Pennsylvania's competitors. Moreover, the Texas & Pacific opposed price discrimination in favor of government involvement with rate setting. See Samuel DeCanio, *Democracy and the Origins of the American Regulatory State* (New Haven, CT: Yale University Press, 2015), pp. 149–79.

[9]Gilchrist, "Albert Fink and the Pooling System," p. 40.

The bill, which called for a federal railroad commission to legalize and enforce railroad pooling, was endorsed by notables of the Pennsylvania and Erie railroads.

The jockeying in Congress for the next several years was largely over the details of regulation, especially over the railroads' desire to legalize pooling and to administer the statue by a regulatory commission. In testimony before the House Commerce Committee in 1884, railroad men were overwhelmingly in favor of regulation, particularly if administered by an appointed commission. John P. Green, vice president of the Pennsylvania Railroad, declared that "a large majority of the railroads in the United States would be delighted if a railroad commission or any other power could make rates upon their traffic which would insure them six per cent dividends, and I have no doubt, with such a guarantee, they would be very glad to come under the direct supervision and operation of the National Government."[10]

Writing to Massachusetts Representative John D. Long on why the railroads were so insistent on a federal commission, the shrewd Charles Francis Adams pointed out:

> If you only get an efficient Board of Commissioners, they could work out of it whatever was necessary. No matter what sort of bill you have, everything depends upon the men who, so to speak, are inside of it, and who are to make it work. In the hands of the right men, any bill would produce the desired results.[11]

What those desired results were, and why federal regulation was needed, were spelled out in an 1884 article in the *Chicago Railway Review* by George R. Blanchard, head of the Erie. Clearly, such great pools as even the Joint Executive Committee could not succeed in imposing joint rates on the railroads. Therefore, what was needed was "a national railway commission to cooperate with and not oppose this recognized committee ... their cooperative traffic federations [of the railroads] which are intended, within just limits, to secure uniformity, stability and impartiality among railways, their patrons and the States, should be reinforced, ratified and legalized by an intelligent public conviction."[12]

---

[10]Kolko, *Railroads and Regulation*, p. 35. See also pp. 26–29.

[11]On March 1, 1884. Ibid., p. 37.

[12]Ibid., p. 38.

In hearings before the Senate Interstate Commerce Committee during 1885, dozens of prominent railroad men testified, and all but one strongly endorsed at least the principle of federal regulation. Almost all the railroad leaders favored a regulatory commission. In more detail, many called for legalizing of pools and for the outlawing of rebates. In reporting out the regulatory bill by Senator Shelby M. Cullom of Illinois, the Committee pointed to its support among the railroad interests.

In the meanwhile, a former vice president of the Erie Railroad wrote to the *Commercial and Financial Chronicle* criticizing traditional American adherence to *laissez-faire*: "It has always been the fashion in this country to argue that the less government we have the better, and that this constitutes the main advantage of this country over Europe. But there are some things that the Government must do if society is to hold together" — in particular, assist the railroads through regulation.[13] In turn, free-market adherents were horrified at the unanimity with which railroads and shippers alike were calling "for the same soothing syrup — legislative enactment."[14]

By late 1886, the Senate had passed over the Cullom Bill and the House the Reagan Bill. Both bills outlawed rebates; neither gave the federal government the power to fix railroad rates directly. The railroads were in favor of the Senate bill because, unlike the Reagan Bill, it did not explicitly outlaw private railroad pools and, more particularly, because it established a federal commission to work its will in interpreting and enforcing a vague law, whereas the Reagan Bill left enforcement solely to the courts. In a conference of the two houses, Reagan conceded all points to the Senate, except to maintain the prohibition on pooling. The country was given a law vague in all matters except outlawry of rebates and of some rate discrimination in favor of long-haul freight. The power of interpretation and enforcement in the courts was given to a five-man commission. The compromise bill, backed by the railroads, passed both houses overwhelmingly in January 1887 by a vote of 36 to 12 in the Senate, and 219 to 41 in the House.[15]

---

[13]In *Commercial and Financial Chronicle* (July 4, 1885), p. 7. Quoted in Kirkland, *Industry Comes of Age*, p. 127.

[14]*Commercial and Financial Chronicle* (June 6, 1885), pp. 666–68. Quoted in ibid., p. 127.

[15][Editor's footnote] Kolko, *Railroads and Regulation*, pp. 43–44; George W. Hilton, "The Consistency of the Interstate Commerce Act," *Journal of Law and Economics* (October, 1966): 103–07. For a survey of the diverse opinions on government regulation by railroad leaders and other businessmen, see Edward A. Purcell, Jr., "Ideas and Interests: Businessmen and the Interstate Commerce Act," *Journal of American History* (December 1967):

The *Chicago Inter-Ocean*, a leading railroad magazine, summed up the railway men's case for the Interstate Commerce Act shortly before its passage:

> Perhaps the strongest argument that can be presented in favor of the passage of this bill is found in the fact that many of the leading railway managers admit the justice of its terms and join in the demand for its passage. ... The irregularities that have gradually crept into [the railroads] ... got beyond their capacity to manage. ...The effort to maintain rates was equally unsuccessful. Then came the last resort — the pool — but that, too, proved impotent. ... And now, acknowledging the inefficiency of their own weak inventions ... the managers are content to leave the settlement of the whole matter to the law-making power of the country ...[16]

With the law passed, "everything depend[ed]," as Adams had said, on who the Interstate Commerce Commissioners would be. The first Commission, in particular, would set the pattern for the future with its interpretations and rulings. Would the railroads, or the shippers, or the farmers, control this commission? Or, more precisely, whom would President Grover Cleveland appoint?

The United States was, politically, in the midst of a new era: in 1884 the Democratic Party had, in the person of Grover Cleveland, captured the presidency for the first time since the Civil War. From now until the late 1890s, the United States would be a genuine two-party country once again, with power shifting easily from one party to the other. We have mentioned above that, in the Panic of 1873, J.P. Morgan had succeeded the fallen Jay Cooke as the nation's premier investment banker. And since the railroads were the only genuine big business in these decades, this meant the successor as the leading railroad financier. But while Jay Cooke

---

561–78; DeCanio, *Democracy and the Origins of the American Regulatory State,* pp. 173–74. That the Erie and New York Central opposed the Reagan bill because it would weaken their position relative to the Pennsylvania, or that the Union Pacific, Central Pacific, and Southern Pacific were opposed to a rival transcontinental railroad, is not surprising. In addition, some railroads opposed the ICC because they were not fully satisfied with the results, and it is not a stretch to assume that since some railroads thrived at breaking rate agreements and cartels, others opposed the measure as well.

[16]January 2, 1887. Quoted in Kolko, *Railroads and Regulation,* p. 41.

had been a Republican, J.P. Morgan was a Democrat. If we consider that August Belmont, U.S. representative of the powerful European banking house of Rothschild, was treasurer of the national Democratic Party for many years, we can see that such financial powers as Morgan and Belmont wielded enormous influence over the personnel and the policies of the Democratic Party.[17]

Before the Civil War, the Democratic Party had been the *laissez-faire*, minimal government party in America. This continued to be the case, although not quite as strongly. But the party was now vulnerable, for if Morgan, Belmont, and financiers or railroad men in their ambit should begin to shift to a statist position in one or more areas, the Democratic Party was likely to follow. And this is in fact what happened.

J.P. Morgan had become the foremost sponsor of railroad pools, and his as well as other railroads had now endorsed the ICC as an instrument of imposed cartelization. The new President, Grover Cleveland, was also generally in favor of *laissez-faire,* but he had long been in the railroad ambit. When he ran for Governor of New York in 1882, he was known, with considerable justice, as a "railroad attorney" in Buffalo. Cleveland had been an attorney for several railroads, including the New York Central. His pro-railroad appointments to the New York Railroad Commission were consistent with this image.[18] Cleveland also had a close long-time relationship with J.P. Morgan. During his administration as President, he frequently consulted with both Morgan and Belmont Jr., and Cleveland's old law partner, Francis Lynde Stetson, later became the attorney for J.P. Morgan and Co. and one of the most important counselors in the Morgan circle.[19]

The railroad men therefore regarded Cleveland as safe, and they turned out to be right. Cleveland did not, of course, veto the Interstate Commerce Act. His appointments to the ICC were even more revealing. At the urging of Senator Cullom, Cleveland chose as chairman the distinguished jurist, Thomas McIntyre Cooley. A proponent of strict construc-

---

[17][Editor's footnote] Burch, *Elites in American History,* pp. 50, 60, 87, 115.

[18]See Benson, *Merchants, Farmers, and Railroads,* pp. 181–82, 187–88, 200. [Editor's remarks] Cleveland's first presidential administration was also dominated by railroad interests, even more so than the preceding Republican regimes. Burch, *Elites in American History,* p. 91.

[19][Editor's footnote] For more on the Cleveland-Morgan connection, see Chapter 7 below, pp. 199–200.

tion and *laissez-faire*, Cooley unfortunately chose the railroad industry to make his most conspicuous exception to this general rule. This choice was perhaps not unconnected with his accepting employment, from 1882 on, as administrator and arbitrator in Albert Fink's Joint Executive Committee railroad pool. In addition, Cooley served since 1885 as a receiver for the Wabash Railroad. As a result of accepting these posts, Cooley had shifted by 1887 to favoring government legalization and control of pooling through a federal commission.

Of the four other commissioners, two were leading railroad men. Augustus Schoonmaker had been associated with Cleveland in New York politics, and then had become a railroad attorney; and Aldace F. Walker was a veteran railroad man who was to resign after two years on the ICC to become head of the major railroad rates association, and eventually to be chairman of the board of the Atchison, Topeka & Santa Fe. The other two members were hack Democratic politicians, one of whom had already been a state railroad commissioner in Alabama. It was no wonder that the *Railway Review* hailed the appointments: "Fortunately, its present membership is not made up of the stuff that is liable to shrink from doing what it conceives to be its duty ..."[20]

The Interstate Commerce Commission quickly moved in the direction desired by the railroads. On the one hand, the ICC allowed the railroads themselves to suspend the provision prohibiting discrimination against short-haul rates when it was advantageous for them to be higher, thereby giving the ICC sanction to their practices. Aldace Walker wrote that this policy was "capable of very general application ... and it is a fact that as a prevention of rate wars and destructive competition it is already recognized by intelligent railroad men as better than the pool."[21] On the other hand, the railroad men were anxious to have the ICC follow strictly the prohibition of rebates to shippers, and the ICC eagerly complied. Railroad leaders kept a vigilant eye on violations of the new law by their competitors and enthusiastically turned them into the authorities. As Charles Francis Adams, Jr., now president of the Union Pacific, declared: "... we would welcome the rigid and literal enforcement of every provision of the interstate commerce act."[22]

---

[20]*Railway Review* (April 16, 1887): 220. Kolko, *Railroads and Regulation*, pp. 47–49.

[21]Aldace F. Walker to Joseph Nimmo, Jr., November 22, 1887. Quoted in ibid., p. 52.

[22]Speech in December 1888. Ibid., p. 57.

At first, the railroads, under the friendly regime of the ICC, were able to raise rates, but soon, by the end of 1887, the dreaded rebates began again as a few railroads decided to compete vigorously once more. The railroads decided to try to bring pools in by the back door. While pools were technically outlawed, voluntary rate associations, which simply fixed rates *without* allocating freights and markets, were still legal. Indeed, Professor George Hilton concurs with pro-railroad opinion at the time that the language of the Interstate Commerce Act, taken from the original Cullom Bill, "almost compels" collusive ratemaking on the part of the railroads.[23]

The ICC was therefore in keeping with the law when, to the delight of the railroads, it decided to give its sanction and imprimatur to the freight rates worked out by the railroad rate associations — in short, to use the federal government to ratify rates decided upon by private railroad cartels. Despite the official outlawry of pools, therefore, the ICC was to serve as a powerful instrument of railroad cartels.

It is no wonder that, very soon after its inception, the Interstate Commerce Act and the ICC were lauded by the railway men, while the merchants' and farmers' groups who had high hopes for the ICC quickly came to call for its repeal. Thus, during 1890, numerous merchants and farmers groups called for repeal of the outlawry of pro-long haul discrimination, while the Detroit and Indianapolis Boards of Trade went so far as to call for outright repeal of the Interstate Commerce Act because it protected railroads and raised railway rates.[24]

But if the ICC looked with favor at cartel rates fixed by rate associations, it had no power to fix or enforce them. As competition resumed and freight rates fell further, the presidents of the leading Western roads were called to New York by the tireless J.P. Morgan to seek ways of maintaining freight rates and enforcing violations of the anti-rebate law. The railroad men met with the ICC commissioners in 1889, and the ICC encouraged the railroads to form what would virtually be a pool agreement. As a result, 22 roads signed an agreement to keep freight rates from falling; and, while no shares of freight were formally allocated between the roads, thus keeping narrowly within the letter of the law, the agreement authorized the railroads to take such steps as may be necessary and legal "to secure to

[23]Hilton, "The Consistency of the Interstate Commerce Act," pp. 108–09.
[24]Kolko, *Railroads and Regulation,* pp. 50–53.

each Company its due share of the competitive traffic."[25] The pool, with its agreement to ration business and thereby allow a raise in rates, was back in all but name. And this time the ICC was there to help enforce it.

The new cartel organization called itself the "Inter-State Commerce Railway Association," and it avowed that its purpose was "to exercise their power and influence in the maintenance of rates and the enforcement of all the provisions of the Inter-State Law." It was, in short, merely altruistically interested in law enforcement! The Association pledged itself to enforce the agreement by notifying the ICC of any violation of law. And, to top matters off, and to underscore the incestuous relationship the new Association had with the ICC, Aldace Walker resigned as a member of the ICC to become chairman of the new organization. Gabriel Kolko aptly calls the Association, "in fact nothing more than a massive railway effort to interpret and enforce, with Commission sanction, the Act of 1887."[26]

The presidents of the Pennsylvania and New York Central railroads, the representative of the Northwest Railroad Board, and Charles Francis Adams, Jr., were all enthusiastic about the agreement. In imitation, ten major Eastern lines signed a similar agreement in February, appointing the ubiquitous cartelist Albert Fink as its commissioner. Again, the sanctimonious purpose was "to aid in the enforcement of the provisions of the Interstate Commerce Law," and to inform on all violations to the Commission.[27]

But even with ICC sanction, the winds of competition proved far too great for the railroad cartels. By the spring of 1889, vehement rate wars in the West had wrecked the Association. Repeated attempts to establish rate associations in the Southwest and to reconstitute the one in the West continued to fail, despite J.P. Morgan's best efforts and the ICC endorsement. Rates continued to fall, sparked by secret competitive rebates, throughout the 1890s. The railroads continued to try to form and reconstitute rate associations, but all to no avail. In late 1895, 31 major Eastern roads set up the Joint Traffic Association, along almost the same lines as the defunct Inter-State Commerce Railway Association. The U.S. Supreme Court killed the association in October 1898 by calling such agreements illegal pools, following a similar decision the previous year. But it should

---

25Ibid., pp. 57–59.

26Ibid., p. 60.

27Ibid., p. 61.

be noted that the Association had foundered on the rock of competition and rate-cutting before the court's decision was announced.[28]

Throughout the 1890s, the railroads agitated for what were called "legalized pools," but were actually pools that would be legally enforceable. In bills sponsored or written by railroads and submitted to Congress, railroad pools would fix rates, and then the ICC would ratify and enforce them. As the attorney for the B&O, who wrote one of the bills, declared: "we say unhesitatingly we are not afraid for one instant of the intervention of the Commission. We do not want an agreement to go into effect without their approval ..." The railroad point of view was put cogently by A.B. Stickney, president of the Minnesota & Northwestern Railroad, in a book written in 1891:

> For a quarter of a century they [the railroads] have been attempting, by agreements between themselves, to make and maintain uniform and stable rates. But as such contracts are not recognized as binding by the law, they have rested entirely on the good faith of each company, and to a great extent upon the capacity as well as good faith of each of the traffic officials and employees. In the past they have not been efficacious, and ... it is too much to hope for any sufficient protection to the rights of owners growing out of such agreements. ... Their alternative protection is the strong arm of the law. Let the law name the rates, and let the law maintain and protect their integrity.[29]

---

[28]Ibid., pp. 72–73, 83. On railroad competition up to the early 1890s, see also Julius Grodinsky, *Transcontinental Railway Strategy, 1869–1893: A Study of Businessmen* (Philadelphia: University of Pennsylvania Press, 1962), pp. 312–429. On the ICC as an attempt to enforce railroad cartelization, see MacAvoy, *The Economic Effects of Regulation*, pp. 110–204.

[29]Quoted in ibid., *Railroads and Regulation*, pp. 74–75, 77. [Editor's remarks] Some critics of Kolko have argued that since many railroads were just trying to get the government to enforce their voluntary cartel agreements and uphold contracts that they mutually agreed upon, they were not nearly as interventionist as Kolko and others have portrayed them. See Robert L. Bradley, Jr. and Roger Donway, "Reconsidering Gabriel Kolko: A Half-Century Perspective," *Independent Review* (Spring 2013): 570–71, 573. It is important to note that, at least from Rothbard's perspective, the free market does not enforce promises unless some goods have already been physically exchanged. This includes cartel agreements, which are explicitly dealt with in Rothbard, *Man, Economy, and State*, p. 181. See also Murray Rothbard, *The Ethics of Liberty* (New York: New York University Press, 2002 [1982]), pp. 133–48. Therefore, the drive for railroads to get the government to enforce their cartel arrangements does constitute as an intervention.

But despite the enthusiastic support of the ICC, Congress stubbornly refused to pass any such legislation. Now, after 1898, even the rate association route was declared illegal by the courts. As a result, railroad and ICC pressure on Congress for legalized pools intensified still further.

2. STRENGTHENING THE INTERSTATE COMMERCE COMMISSION

And so, by the turn of the century, the railroad leaders had realized that the existing Interstate Commerce Act was not sufficiently powerful to act as a successful cartelizer of the railroad industry. For the first decade of the 20th century, as Hilton states, "the history of the statutory authority of the ICC is best interpreted as an effort to convert the Act of 1887 into an effective cartelizing statute."[30]

To aid in this effort, the railroad men were fortunate in the man who succeeded the pro-railroad Shelby M. Cullom in 1899 as chairman of the Senate Interstate Commerce Committee. He was the even more pro-railroad and more vigorous Stephen Benton Elkins of West Virginia, who quickly became the most important Congressional influence on railroad legislation. Elkins had always had his eye on the main chance. During the 1870s he had become the largest landowner in New Mexico by shrewd use of his post as U.S. District Attorney; he then was fortunate enough to marry the daughter of Henry G. Davis, a coal and railroad tycoon in West Virginia. Through this marriage, Elkins became the largest mine owner in the Atlantic area; he and his father-in-law also controlled the West Virginia Central and Pittsburgh Railroad. In short, Elkins' passion for the interests of the railroads was not unconnected with his own status as railroad owner.[31]

The railroad cartelists were also fortunate in the sudden accession to the presidency of the United States of Theodore Roosevelt, the preeminent political symbol of Progressivism whose long political career was always close to the House of Morgan.[32] By the end of the 1890s, Morgan had gained far more predominance in the railroad industry than he had ever had before, and his drive for cartelization — in general industry as well as

---

[30]Hilton, "Consistency of the Interstate Commerce Act," p. 110.

[31]Kolko, *Railroads and Regulation,* pp. 90–91.

[32]For more on the Roosevelt-Morgan connection, see Chapter 7 below, pp. 203–28.

railroads — had intensified. It is no wonder that Morgan's ally Roosevelt would come to be labelled as the railroad men's "best friend."[33]

The first fruit of the new cartelizing drive was the Progressive Elkins Anti-Rebating Act of 1903. Rebates had been outlawed in the Act of 1887, but this mighty instrument of intense competition had continued to flourish, even though hidden, in the form of such devices as false classification and underestimating the weights of freight. Alexander J. Cassatt, president of the Morgan-associated Pennsylvania Railroad since 1899, had long been dedicated to cartels and "stabilization." His attempt to end Pennsylvania rebates to the powerful Carnegie Steel Co. led to a mighty battle in which Andrew Carnegie and George Jay Gould threatened to build parallel railroads, while Morgan countered with a powerful attempt at monopoly in the steel industry known as United States Steel.[34] Cassatt did not hesitate to turn to the secular arm by having his general counsel, James A. Logan, write the Elkins Bill in 1901 to crack down on rebating. Logan told a press conference that if his bill should pass, the railroads would "no longer be subject to the dictation of the great shippers as to rates and facilities."[35] The original Elkins Bill as it passed the Senate also achieved the long-standing railroad objective of legalizing pooling; while the final compromise bill did not officially legalize pools, it did the equivalent by declaring rates jointly arrived at by railroads to be legal, and providing that any joint rate filed with the ICC "shall be conclusively deemed to be the legal rate, and any departure from such rate, or any offer to depart therefrom to be an offense ..."[36] The Elkins Act also made corporations as well as individuals liable for violations and provided that both the giver and receiver of rebates could be prosecuted. Thus, not only did the Elkins Act of 1903 greatly strengthen the prohibition of rebates, but it restored the legalization of associated rates that the Supreme Court had knocked down a half-decade before.

The railroads exulted at the passage of the Elkins Act which passed unanimously in the Senate and with virtually no opposition in the House. The *Railroad Gazette* declared that the law should have been passed five

---

[33]Kolko, *Railroads and Regulation*, p. 155.

[34]([Editor's remarks] Gabriel Kolko, *The Triumph of Conservatism* (Glencoe, IL: The Free Press, 1963), p. 32.) For more, see Chapter 3 below, pp. 98–100.

[35]Kolko, *Railroads and Regulation*, pp. 94–97.

[36]Ibid., p. 100.

years earlier, and gloated that "all that will be asked of the Commissioners by the public will be that they go ahead and catch every law-breaking rate-cutter in the country."[37]

Various merchant and shipper groups were not satisfied with the existing law, and they agitated after 1903 for outright rate-fixing powers to be given to the ICC. They were opposed by other shippers, however, including the National Association of Manufacturers, which reversed itself on the issue. As a result of this split, and of railroad opposition, such bills as the Esch-Townsend Bill were ultimately defeated in Congress.[38]

A different law, the Hepburn Act, written in the councils of the Roosevelt administration, passed Congress almost unanimously in 1906. As Kolko points out, historians have made a great to-do about the Hepburn Act as an allegedly controversial "reform" measure directed against the railroads while overlooking the fact (a) that the controversies were all minor, and (b) that everyone, especially including the railroads, accepted the principles of the bill and quibbled only over details. An examination of the Hepburn Act reveals why the railroads and railroad journals praised the law. Perhaps most importantly, the Hepburn Act strengthened the

---

[37]*Railroad Gazette* (February 20, 1903): 134. Quoted in ibid., p. 101. The importance of the Elkins Act, which has been rather neglected by historians, is underscored by George Hilton as revealing "the overall framework of regulation" of the railroads. George W. Hilton, "Review of Albro Martin, *Enterprise Denied,*" *Bell Journal of Economics and Management Science* (Autumn 1972): 629. ([Editor's remarks] The above article is a trenchant critique of Albro Martin's *Enterprise Denied*, a book on railroads which criticized parts of Kolko's thesis. Rothbard earlier praised the article in "Recommended Reading," *Libertarian Forum* (December, 1972): 6. See Albro Martin, *Enterprise Denied: The Origins of the Decline of the American Railroads, 1897–1917* (New York: Columbia University Press, 1971). However, as shown below, Rothbard does agree with some aspects of Martin's thesis, such as that after 1910 the railroads drowned under the ICC's regulations.) Even Chandler, who is generally unsympathetic to the cartelizing interpretation of railroad legislation, concedes that the railroads overwhelmingly supported the Elkins Act, although he fails to realize that the Act strengthened the ICC and legalized joint railroad rates. Chandler, *The Visible Hand*, p. 174.

[38][Editor's remarks] Kolko, *Railroads and Regulation*, pp. 103–06, 118–20. There has been much discussion over the railroad opposition to regulation in 1904 and 1905. Some have argued, contra Kolko, that the railroads were unanimously opposed to any new regulation. See Martin, *Enterprise Denied*, pp. 111–14; Richard H.K. Vietor, "Businessmen and the Political Economy: The Railroad Rate Controversy of 1905," *Journal of American History* (June, 1977): 50–53. However, Kolko argued that the railroad opposition, especially in the Senate Committee meetings, was mainly directed against the Esch-Townsend Bill, which allowed the ICC to fix definite rates, and in speeches and railroad journals they were more sympathetic to other types of regulation. Kolko, *Railroads and Regulation*, pp. 117–44.

Elkins Act against rebating. For one thing, it extended the law to cover express and sleeping-car railroads, private-car lines, and pipe-lines, thus extending the cartel by bringing competing forms of transportation under the same regulation. Secondly, the Hepburn Act outlawed railroads transporting products which they owned themselves, a measure aimed at competing "industrial roads," such as anthracite railroads, which owned coal mines.[39] Third, it required 30 days' notice for rate changes, which slowed down competitive rate cutting, and rebate penalties were stiffened, with fines equaling three times the value of the rebate, and a possible penalty of two years imprisonment was imposed for violating the law. Fourth, the railroad cartel was expanded by outlawing free passes by railroads to their customers, as well as various other free services to shippers. This, of course, was the equivalent of compulsory raising of rates by outlawing forms of price-cutting. Fifth, if rates arrived at by railroads were challenged by shippers, the ICC had the right to set its own maximum rates, if it found those rates not to be "just, fair, and reasonable." The ICC's rulings would be subject to review by the courts, and even though these were to be *maximum* rates, giving them the force of law made collusion between the railroads much easier, and hence strengthened the cartels.[40]

Particularly enthusiastic about the Hepburn Act was A.J. Cassatt, head of the Pennsylvania Railroad, who proclaimed his agreement with Roosevelt's position. The Pennsylvania pointed out, in its 1906 Annual Report, that its aim of achieving the end of rebating having been achieved with the Hepburn Act, and "the maintenance of tariff rates [having] been practically secured," it could go ahead and sell the stock it had purchased in its competitors.[41] G.J. Grammar of the New York Central exulted in the compulsory elimination of the free passes and services. Key railroad leaders such as John W. Midgley (a veteran pool organizer) and Samuel Spencer were anxious to bring private-car railroad lines under regulation. The

---

[39]The *Railway and Engineering Review* spoke for most railroad opinion in hailing the provision of the new law outlawing industrial railroads: "... the 'Industrial Roads' will go out of business. They ought never to have been allowed to begin it." *Railway and Engineering Review*, Sept. 15, 1906, p. 714. Quoted in Kolko, *Railroads and Regulation*, p. 150. [Editor's remarks] Ibid., pp. 144–51.

[40]See Hilton, "Review of Albro Martin, *Enterprise Denied*," p. 269. [Editor's remarks] Hilton's controversial argument regarding the cartelizing effect of maximum rates seems to have been that the railroads could push for a higher maximum rate, and by making this rate official, downward price cutting from it could be deemed illegal.

[41]Quoted in Kolko, *Railroads and Regulation*, p. 147.

Railway and Engineering Review crowed over the abolition of the industrial railroads. E.H. Harriman, second only to Morgan in controlling railroads, favored the Hepburn Act. And, upon its passage, George W. Perkins, partner of J.P. Morgan & Co., wrote to Morgan that the new law "is going to work out for the ultimate and great good of the railroads. There is no question but that rebating has been dealt a death blow."[42]

The railroads had been so exercised about the rebating problem that the executives of virtually all of the Western roads had met in December 1905, to consider steps to combat the practice. They decided to inform the ICC of all violations of the law.

The Hepburn Act was drawn up by Attorney-General William H. Moody. President Roosevelt had consulted with several railroad leaders, including Cassatt, Midgley, and Spencer. Roosevelt had been converted to the railroad cause, and to the desirability of railroad pools, by his Secretary of the Navy Paul Morton, formerly vice president of the Morgan-controlled Atchison, Topeka & Santa Fe Railroad.[43]

In his December, 1905 message to Congress, Roosevelt explained his call for railroad regulation in terms of restricting railroad competition, of protecting "good" as against "bad" (that is, particularly vigorous) competitors:

> I believe that on the whole our railroads have done well and
> not ill; but the railroad men who wish to do well should not
> be exposed to competition with those who have no such
> desire, and the only way to secure this end is to give some
> Government tribunal the power to see that justice is done
> by the unwilling exactly as it is gladly done by the willing.
> Moreover, if some Government body is given increased
> power the effect will be to furnish authoritative answer on
> behalf of the railroad whenever irrational clamor against

---

[42]Perkins to Morgan, June 25, 1906. Quoted in ibid., p. 148. [Editor's remarks] Harriman favored the act relative to more hostile regulation. By late 1906, his clout with Roosevelt had significantly deteriorated. See Chapter 7 below, pp. 223–28.

[43]Ibid., pp. 111 and 125. We know, too, that Roosevelt's chairman of the Bureau of Corporations James R. Garfield, was consulting during 1905 with two powerful corporate attorneys: Victor Morawetz, of the Atchison, Topeka & Santa Fe, and Francis Lynde Stetson, personal lawyer for J.P. Morgan. Probably, Morawetz and Stetson were most influential in beginning the drive for what later would become the Federal Trade Commission, but railroad matters "might" also have been discussed. Ibid., p. 113.

it is raised, or whenever charges made against it are dis-
proved.[44]

Contemplating the growing drive for what would become the Hepburn Act, the *Wall Street Journal* keenly noted the enthusiasm by the railroad men as well as the growing general business interest in their own
regulation:

> Nothing is more noteworthy than the fact that President
> Roosevelt's recommendation in favor of government
> regulation of railroad rates and Commissioner Garfield's
> recommendation in favor of federal control of interstate
> companies have met with so much favor among managers
> of railroads and industrial companies. It is not meant by
> this that much opposition has not developed, for it has ...
>
> The fact is that many of the railroad men and corporate
> managers are known to be in favor of these measures, and
> this is of vast significance. In the end it is probable that all
> of the corporations will find that a reasonable system of
> federal regulation is to their interest. ... It is known that
> some of the foremost railroad men of the country are at
> this time at work in harmony with the President for the
> enactment of a law providing for federal regulation of
> rates which shall be equitable both to the railroads and
> to the public.[45]

One consequence of the Hepburn Act indicates, contrary to accepted
propaganda, whom the act really injured and whom it benefited. As soon
as the act was passed, the New York Central happily complied by abolishing free storage facilities for New York flour merchants, the Chicago
and Eastern Illinois Railroad inaugurated charges for switching, and free
car service and loading in Philadelphia was abolished. The *Railway World*
happily reported that:

> notwithstanding the fears of many that railroads would
> be hurt by the operation of the law, no complaint has been
> heard from railroad men against its general provisions.
> On the contrary, the complaints are coming from the

---

[44]Ibid., p. 115.

[45]*Wall Street Journal*, December 28, 1904. Quoted in ibid., p. 120.

shippers, who were supposed to be the chief beneficiaries of the law.[46]

In 1910, Congress passed the Mann-Elkins Act completing the trilogy of cartelizing railroad acts passed during the first decade of the 20th century. The original bill of the Taft administration would have legalized railroad agreements to fix freight rates — a measure that the railroads had long yearned for. The roads could not get this provision through Congress, and they had to accept the clause that the ICC might suspend and review railroad rate changes.

In point of fact, the railroads welcomed governmental review and approval of rates provided this power were used primarily to prevent rate *reductions* rather than increases. To insure this, the railroads welcomed the achievement of an old demand in the Mann-Elkins Act: the creation of a new, special Federal Court of Commerce with the power to review all ICC rate decisions on appeal. It was expected by everyone that the new Commerce Court would be solidly pro-railroad, and so it proved to be. The chairman of the Commerce Court was the previous chairman of the ICC, Martin A. Knapp, who had long opposed competition in railroads and favored legalized pooling enforced by the government, and he now reaffirmed this stand, as well as calling for higher railroad rates.[47]

Also a force for cartelization was another provision of Mann-Elkins, reestablishing the original prohibition, in the Interstate Commerce Act, of rate discrimination for long-haul over short-haul traffic — a clause that had been nullified in the Supreme Court's *Alabama Midland Railway* decision in 1897. By restoring this prohibition, Congress strengthened railroad cartels by preventing competitive rate reductions for long-haul traffic.

Professor Hilton trenchantly sums up the effect of the Mann-Elkins and other acts:

> The investigation and suspension procedures established in 1910 and recognized for decades, were a powerful inhibition to promiscuous rate reduction, and the Mann-Elkins Act's revision in Section 4 of the Act of 1887 restored its effectiveness against the practice of charging more for a shorter haul than for a longer haul. Without an effective Section 4, the Commission was unable to

---

[46]*Railway World*, August 29, 1906, p. 729. Quoted in ibid., p. 150.

[47][Editor's footnote] Ibid., p. 199.

put down rate wars in which a railroad cut rates between points which it served in rivalry to parallel railroads below the level of rates to intermediate points.

Basically, what the legislation of 1903, 1906, and 1910 did was rectify the adverse judicial decisions of the 1890s and otherwise patch up the Commission's statutory body of authority so that it could accomplish what Congress had set out to do in 1887: stabilize the railroad cartels without pooling.[48]

But the railroads were getting worried about the performance of their creation, the ICC, as witness their eagerness to place as many rate-setting powers as possible in the Commerce Court. For the organized shippers, with their interest in lower rates, were growing in political strength. They had managed to block important pro-railroad Taft administration provisions in Congress, and they grew in influence after 1910. In consequence, the ICC repeatedly rejected rate increases urged by the railroads after 1910, and, after the Supreme Court emasculated the powers of the Commerce Court in 1912, the shippers persuaded Congress to abolish the latter the following year.[49]

But despite their uneasiness at shipper influence on the ICC, for the nation's railroads there was no turning back. They were strongly committed to federal government regulation, and the stronger the better.[50] For

---

[48]Hilton, "Review of Albro Martin, *Enterprise Denied,*" p. 630. As Kolko points out, the Supreme Court's decisions of the late 1890s, striking down various rate regulations and refusing to sanction cartel agreements, were *not,* as most historians have believed, "pro-railroad" decisions. On the contrary, they were examples of the Court *clashing* with the railroads. Kolko, *Railroads and Regulation,* pp. 80–83.

[49][Editor's footnote] Ibid., pp. 195–202.

[50][Editor's footnote] Therefore, despite repeated efforts, the ICC was a failure for the railroads and was ultimately captured by the rival shipping interests. Robert Higgs has aptly characterized the situation of growing shipper power thwarting the railroads' efforts:

> Not infrequently, however, business support for regulatory harmonization at the federal level gave birth to an unmanageable offspring. Like Dr. Frankenstein's monster, the newly created federal regulatory agencies often stopped heeding their business progenitors' voice. Within twenty years, for example, the ICC had fallen under the sway of shipper interests, and by refusing to approve reasonable rate increases, the commission proceeded to compress the railroad companies in a merciless cost-price squeeze. So severely had the railroad firms suffered in the decade after 1906 that during

one thing, federal regulation was bound to be more uniform, and therefore more effective in imposing a nationwide cartel, than state regulation, and probably it would be more enthusiastically pro-cartel. In the summer of 1914, the newly formed Railroad Executives' Advisory Committee, including most of the nation's railroads and headed by Frank Trumbull of the Chesapeake & Ohio, called for comprehensive federal control of the country's railroads along the lines of federal control of the banks in the new Federal Reserve Act.[51] E.P. Ripley, president of the Santa Fe Railroad, called explicitly for a partnership between the federal government and the railroads. In return for control over rates, the government would guarantee all railroads a fixed minimum rate of profit. This, opined Ripley, "would do away with the enormous wastes of the competitive system ..."[52] Daniel Willard, head of the Baltimore & Ohio, called for speeding up the process of federalizing railroad regulation, and likened this need to the recent federal regulation embodied in the Federal Reserve and Federal Trade Commission acts.

The shippers had managed to block railroad rate increases before the ICC in 1910 by arguing for greater "efficiency" and "scientific management" on the part of the railroads. The railroad leaders, in their subsequent agitation for enlarged and comprehensive federal regulation, turned the tables by linking the typically progressive concept of "efficiency" with imposing uniformity and eliminating "competitive waste." More specifically, this would come through cooperative, i.e., cartel-like, reductions in service and in railroad traffic, as well as quota allocations of freight, all in the name of efficient elimination of waste. The role of the federal government was to be as supervisor and enforcer of this cartelizing process. All

---

World War I they collapsed, financially exhausted, into the loving arms of the U.S. Railroad Administration; afterward, under the terms of the Transportation Act of 1920, they found themselves reduced to little more than regulated public utilities.

Robert Higgs, "Regulatory Harmonization: A Sweet-Sounding, Dangerous Development," in *Against Leviathan: Government Power and a Free Society* (Oakland, CA: Independent Institute 2004 [2000]), p. 76.

[51][Editor's footnote] Kolko, *Railroads and Regulation*, pp. 219–20. For more on the origins of the Federal Reserve, see Chapter 14 below, pp. 463–78.

[52]*Traffic World*, October 31, 1914, p. 798. In Kolko, *Railroads and Regulation*, pp. 215–16.

this was supposed to require, and indeed was meant as the prop for, higher railroad rates.[53]

All in all, Fairfax Harrison, president of the Chicago, Indianapolis & Louisville Railroad, spoke for the railroad leaders when he declared that the ICC was necessary to assure general increases in rates when profits might be low, and thereby to prop up and increase railway earnings. This would be far better than free competition or the vagaries of state regulation. Trumpeted Harrison: "The day of the Manchester school and laissez faire is gone. ... Personally, I do not repine at the change ..."[54]

In response, the Republican platform of 1916 duly called for total federal control of railroad regulation. For their part, the Democrats were blazing the same path through the views and actions of President Woodrow Wilson. On September 10, 1914, Wilson wrote to Trumbull that, in view of declining railroad earnings, the railroads must be "helped in every possible way, whether by private co-operative effort or by the action, wherever feasible, of governmental agencies ..."[55] The *Railway World* reported massive business approval of Wilson's sentiments, and the Railway Business Association passed a resolution hailing the President. J.P. Morgan, Jr. wrote to Wilson expressing his gratitude for the Trumbull letter.

Moreover, in response to a request from Trumbull, President Wilson, in his December 1915 message to Congress, urged an inquiry into a comprehensive grappling with the nation's railroad problem. Trumbull enthusiastically wired Wilson that "I am confident that you will do for the railroads of this country as much as you have already done for the banks."[56] At the subsequent hearings of the Congressional Joint Committee headed by Senator Francis G. Newlands, established in July 1916, the major railroad position was delivered by Alfred P. Thom, chief counsel of the Railroad Executives' Advisory Committee. Thom not only called for exclusive federal regulation of the railroads, but also for their protection. He urged the model of the Federal Reserve System, with regional ICC's, ICC setting of minimum as well as maximum rates, and the compulsory

---

[53]See K. Austin Kerr, *American Railroad Politics, 1914–1920: Rates, Wages, and Efficiency* (Pittsburgh: University of Pittsburgh Press, 1968), pp. 16, 22–24.

[54]Fairfax Harrison, "Speech Before the Transportation Club of Indianapolis," March 31, 1911 (1911), p. 1. In Kolko, *Railroads and Regulation*, pp. 206–07.

[55]*Railway Age Gazette*, September 11, September 18, 1914, pp. 462, 506. In ibid., p. 213.

[56]Frank Trumbull to Woodrow Wilson, December 7, 1915. In ibid., p. 223.

federal incorporation of all railroads as well as exclusive federal regulation of railroad security issues.

President Wilson called for strengthening of the ICC along similar lines in August 1916 — as well as advocating higher rates — and repeated his request in his December message to Congress. As we shall see below, the coming of America's entry into World War I in April 1917 paved the way for the culmination of this, as well as other aspects of the progressives' cartelizing programs for American industry. During the war, the railroad cartelists, viewing the "nationalization" of their industry, couldn't have been happier.[57]

---

[57][Editor's footnote] See Chapter 12 below, pp. 379–82, 394–96.

CHAPTER 3

Attempts at Monopoly
in American Industry

1. AMERICA'S INDUSTRIAL REVOLUTION

I n the decades after the Civil War and until the end of the 19th century, America experienced its veritable Industrial Revolution. In an explosion of industrialization, the United States transformed from a predominantly agricultural into an industrial country. In the process, output and living standards soared for a rapidly increasing population. The enormous expansion of production took place through the factory system which, in these decades, replaced the small artisan and craftsman as the predominant form of industrial production. Formerly, the craftsmen typically worked at home on his own tools, with his raw materials sometimes financed by his wholesale merchant customer ("the putting out" or "domestic" system). Now, a capitalist employer, from his own or from his partner's savings, built or purchased buildings, machines, and raw material, and hired a number of employees to work on these materials at a central location. It proved to be efficient in most industries to help increase the scale and size of the factories and firms as markets for the increased production expanded throughout the nation.

There are many indices that reveal the extent of the explosion of production and industrialization in the three decades after the Civil War. Thus, in "real" terms (in constant 1879 dollars), total commodity output increased by three-and-a-half-fold from 1869 to 1899. Agricultural output, in those years, more than doubled, construction increased 2½ times.

Manufacturing output, in contrast, rose almost six-fold in that period, while mining increased eight-fold. In more specific types of production, increases were even more spectacular, led by the blossoming iron and steel industry. Thus, in 1865, 930 thousand short tons of pig iron were shipped in the United States; in 1899, the figure had risen sixteen-fold to 15.25 million tons. And steel ingots and castings produced, rose five-hundred-fold, from 20 thousand long tons in 1867 to 10.6 million long tons in 1899. Structural iron and steel production increased ten-fold, cotton textiles over five-fold, and rails produced rose nearly six-fold. Bituminous coal output rose seventeen-fold from 1865 to 1900, while crude oil production rose twenty-six-fold.

Output per head, and consequently living standards, also rose sharply in this period, despite the large increase in the nation's population. Commodity output per capita nearly doubled in this period, and Gross National Product per capita in constant 1929 prices rose by 80% in the 20 years from 1871 to 1891. In terms of real wages, the average daily wage in all industry rose by 13% from 1865 to 1891, while the cost of living fell on the average of 31% in the same period. The average daily real wages (corrected for price changes) increased by 64%. Then, when we consider that average hours worked dropped from 11 to 10 hours a day in this period, we should add 10% to the average real wage.

So spectacular was the expansion of products that it outstripped the increase in the money supply during this period, so that, *mirabile dictu*, overall prices fell steadily by 2½% per year from 1870 to 1890.[1]

Manufacturing, however, only caught up to the capital advances of railroads by the 1890s. Before then, industrial firms were still largely individual proprietorships or partnerships, with the corporate form confined to railroads and banks. Despite the fact that savings per capita grew rapidly during the 1870s and 1880s, the size of firms was not large enough for most of this period to require a shift from the proprietorship or partnership to the corporate form. As a result, firms were financed largely by the savings of partners or informal debts from friends or relatives. Until the 1890s, therefore, the New York Stock Exchange and other security markets

---

[1] [Editor's footnote] U.S. Department of Commerce, *Historical Statistics of the United States, Colonial Times to 1957* (Washington, D.C.: Government Printing Office, 1960), pp. 7, 90, 115, 127, 139, 355, 365–66, 414–17. For similar statistics on the overall performance of the American economy during this period, see Rothbard, "A History of Money and Banking," pp. 159–66.

were confined to government bonds, railroad stocks and bonds, and bank stocks.

As a result, the crucial role of investment banks, which underwrote and floated the sale of securities, was largely confined to government bonds and railroad securities until the mid-1890s. Hence, the almost exclusive concern of the Houses of Cooke and Morgan for governments and railroads. By the 1890s, however, J.P. Morgan led the way in organizing large-scale industrial corporations and then underwriting and controlling issues of their securities. Thus, Morgan organized the General Electric Company, in the vital new field of electric machinery and lighting, in 1892. On the other hand, while the passing of ownership from the great inventor Thomas Edison to the enlarged Morgan Company symbolized future trends in American industry, the equally great inventor George Westinghouse stubbornly refused to merge with GE in the mid-1890s. The newly formed Westinghouse Company continued to live on the savings and plowed-back profits of George Westinghouse and his fellow stockholders and to spurn any reliance on "Wall Street" and the investment bankers.

Another successful tactic of the investment banking houses was to acquire control of the rapidly burgeoning life insurance companies. Total assets of life insurance companies had increased ten-fold from 1867 to 1897.[2] Since these companies were "owned" by a self-perpetuating board of trustees who could not earn profits from the companies' assets, life insurance executives were more motivated to maintaining assets than to seek profits with alacrity. Hence, they were ripe for takeover by investment banking houses, who could try to gain control of the boards of trustees and have them purchase securities of industrial companies, controlled by the banks themselves.[3]

2. THE PETROLEUM INDUSTRY

As manufacturing developed in the decades after the Civil War, the temptation to seek monopoly, and thereby to attempt to restrict production and raise prices, infected industry after industry. The attempts took two forms. One was cartels, which had the same function as in railroads, with

---

[2][Editor's footnote] *Historical Statistics,* pp. 675–76.

[3][Editor's footnote] For the general transformation of American business, see Chandler, *The Visible Hand,* passim.

the same disastrous effects under the pressure of internal breakup and new external competition. Another form was mergers, an attempt to merge all firms within an industry into One Big Firm, which would then achieve the monopoly goal. To a certain extent, mergers were beneficial and inevitable, as small firms took advantage of the expanding market to grow and merge into larger firms with larger and eventually corporate capitalization, as the corporate form began to replace the self-owned firm or the partnership. Similar mergers took place in the Eastern railroads after 1850, as small lines consolidated into a more efficient, larger line. But it was very different to merge not from natural market forces but because of "ideology," because of the will o' the wisp of achieving monopoly through this route. The result of such mergers was as disastrous and very similar to the result of cartels.

The first important attempt at achieving industrial monopoly was in petroleum, a new industry which began with the first small oil well at Titusville, in northwestern Pennsylvania, in 1859. Quickly springing up to refine the oil pumped into western Pennsylvania were numerous refiners in Cleveland. Emerging very early out of the pack was a business genius, John D. Rockefeller. Rockefeller, who had begun in business as an impoverished bookkeeper, soon rose to be a wholesale commission grocer. By 1863, Rockefeller and Samuel Andrews were the major partners in the largest kerosene refinery in Cleveland, the Excelsior Works. To form the company, Rockefeller invested his own funds and money borrowed from his father, relatives, friends, and associates. By 1867, Rockefeller had formed Rockefeller, Flagler & Andrews Co., with his brother William, Henry M. Flagler and Stephen V. Harkness as newly joined partners. So great was the efficiency and so low the cost of their refineries that the company further expanded and merged with competing refiners, to incorporate in a few years, in 1870, as the Standard Oil Company of Ohio (SOHIO), a company possessing the world's largest oil refining capacity. SOHIO was capitalized at $1 million.

It should be noted that SOHIO was a business and financial alliance of its major owners, of whom Rockefeller was first among equals. From then on, and on into the 20th century, these founding Standard Oil families tended to act together, to ally with one another, and to make investment decisions in tandem. Some of these founding families were: the Flaglers, the Harknesses, the Paynes, the Bostwicks, the Pratts, the Brewsters, the Rogers, and the Archbolds.

We have seen how Rockefeller participated in the South Improvement Company in 1871, a failed attempt to cartelize both Eastern railroads and the oil industry. After that, Rockefeller tried to achieve the same result more permanently by buying out all of his competitors. In contrast to historical legend, Rockefeller did *not* attempt to achieve his dominance in the oil industry by the costly and dangerous process of driving them out of business by cutting prices sharply. Instead, Rockefeller simply bought out his competitors, and paid handsome prices to boot. For one thing, he was anxious to keep the good will of the former owners and to enlist their administrative capacities in the Standard organization.

Neither did Standard achieve its original dominance solely by obtaining railroad rebates. As we have indicated, all refineries, along with other industries, were receiving rebates, some small competitors even receiving larger rebates than Standard. SOHIO achieved its dominance by also being more efficient, by pioneering in innovative ways to cut costs and to improve product. Its costs were lower than its competitors. While Standard launched several technological innovations and improved lubricating oils, its major innovations were in management techniques. SOHIO pioneered in modern corporate management — in the executive committee system, in careful bookkeeping, in corporate accounting, and in systematic managerial reporting to a central review board.

By 1879, Rockefeller had purchased refineries in Pittsburg, Philadelphia, New York, and Baltimore, and had obtained nearly 90% of American oil refining capacity and 80% of the pipelines. In 1882, Rockefeller and his allies expanded to form an overall Standard Oil Trust, with headquarters in New York City and capitalized at $70 million. Individual firms in the different states had exchanged their stock for pro rata shares in the new, seemingly monopoly, trust.

But Standard Oil was never to retain the dominance it had achieved in 1879 — a dominance, by the way, that never even threatened to extend to marketing or to crude oil production. For one thing, Standard Oil's standing ready to purchase any independent oil refinery at a handsome price functioned something like farm price supports in later years. In brief, various shrewd entrepreneurs began to realize that if Rockefeller were foolish enough to stand ready to purchase any oil refineries offered to him, well they would go heavily into a new, profitable business: the building of oil refineries solely for the purpose of "forcing" Rockefeller to buy them. In their haste, these new refineries were sometimes not even fit for the refining of oil; that they should *seem* to be so as to deceive Standard Oil inspectors was sufficient. As a result, Rockefeller found himself on a treadmill, paying out money for a steady stream of new refineries. Finally, in 1881, Rockefeller declared he would no longer pay "blackmail" to these new refineries, and for the next few years, many overtures for sale by new independent refiners were turned down by Rockefeller. By 1885, then, Rockefeller had given up his attempt to achieve monopoly in oil refining by merger and purchase. From then on, there were to continue to be 10–20% of refining capacity outside the Standard Oil network, and ready to step in to increase competition should the opportunity arise.

Typical of common distortions of the truth about the small competitors of Standard Oil is the case of George Rice, a small Ohio refiner, who was lionized in the press for his alleged martyrdom at the house of Standard Oil. In fact, Rice profited handsomely from his competition, so much so that his asking price to Standard kept increasing. At the historians Hidy and Hidy relate:

> ... Rice invited combat by darting into an area, cutting prices until dangerous to profits, and then diverting his efforts to another spot. In 1881, under the title of *Black Death*, he published a pamphlet of anti-Standard statements. ... Standard Oil officials tried to silence him by attempting to purchase his refinery, but they balked at paying his asking price, which rose from an original $20,000 to a final $500,000. This represented either his reassessment of his nuisance value or a remarkable growth in net assets within less than a decade in the face of competition from a monopoly.[4]

Despite its near monopoly of refining, Standard was clearly never able to use its position to restrict production and raise prices. The price of kerosene, the major oil product during this period, fell drastically throughout these decades as oil production greatly increased. Thus, the wholesale price of kerosene fell from 45 cents per gallon in 1863 to 6 cents per gallon in the mid-1890s. Production was increasing to tap a mass market, and, so long as government did not restrict entry into the field, Standard always had to look to its laurels.

---

[4]Ralph W. and Muriel E. Hidy, *Pioneering in Big Business, 1882–1911* (New York: Harper & Bros., 1955), pp. 203–04.

In fact, Standard Oil's virtual monopoly position began to slip by the early 1880s. We have seen how Rockefeller had to abandon trying to achieve a monopoly. More slippage began to occur in the 1890s. Independent pipelines began to grow to challenge Standard's dominance in this area. Finally, after 1900, and long before the anti-trust dissolution of 1911 and unrelated to it, Standard's dominance of petroleum refining began increasingly to fade. Whereas in 1899 Standard Oil had 90% of the petroleum refining in the country, this share had slipped to 84% during 1904–07, to 80% in 1911, and then to 50% (including together all the separate Standard Oil companies) in 1921. The basic reason was an increasingly conservative, stodgy, and bureaucratic management of the Standard Oil complex, a development accelerated by the retirement of the senior Rockefeller and other top executives by the late 1890s.

Specifically, Standard made two grave mistakes because of its deficient entrepreneurial skills after 1900. It failed to grasp the crude oil revolution, namely that more and more crude was being discovered in the Texas, Gulf, and California areas. Rooted completely in the Pennsylvania-Ohio oil fields, Standard only grasped the significance of the new oil discoveries late in the day. As a result, new firms such as Texas Company and Gulf Oil were able to stead a march on Standard. Secondly, Standard was the last major firm to realize that gasoline was replacing kerosene as the major petroleum product, a mighty shift occasioned by the two great technological industrial revolutions of the first decades of the 20th century: the shift from kerosene to electricity in providing light, and the growth of the automobile as the major means of land transportation. As a result, in 1899, 63% of total oil refined was kerosene; 20 years later, however, the percentage was only 15%.

Moreover, new independent refiners were attracted to the petroleum industry by Standard's high profit margins. Whereas there was a total of 67 refiners in 1899, they had more than doubled to 147 by 1911. The independents, furthermore, led Standard in various innovations in petroleum: in the concept of retail gas stations; in the discovery and production of petrochemicals; in tank cars and tank trucks for conveying oil.[5]

5[Editor's footnote] Ibid., pp. 1–49; Nevins, *Study in Power,* vol. 1, pp. 56–76, vol. 2, pp. 54–79; John S. McGee, "Predatory Price Cutting: The Standard Oil (N.J.) Case," *Journal of Law and Economics* (October, 1958): 137–69; Kolko, *The Triumph of Conservatism,* pp. 39–42; Simon N. Whitney, *Antitrust Policies: The American Experience in Twenty Industries* (New York: The Twentieth Century Fund, 1958), p. 143; Harold F. Williamson and Arnold

3. Iron and Steel

Until very recently, iron and steel has been the glamor industry of the Industrial Revolution. Any undeveloped country that wishes to feel modern makes sure to subsidize and force-feed at least one large steel plant. In the United States, however, the iron and steel industry was chronically inefficient throughout the 19th century. The Pittsburg ironmasters were the source of America's first organized movement for a protective tariff in 1820, and for the rest of the century Pennsylvania iron and steel manufacturers were in the forefront of cries for protection against more efficient British imports.

Despite the high Republican tariffs, there were 719 companies either in the blast furnace, steel work, or rolling mill industry in 1889. Throughout the 1880s and 1890s, there were repeated attempts at pools and cartels to reduce production and raise prices. Pools in pig iron, steel, steel billet, wire, and wire-nails all failed, breaking down from failure of one or more firms to abide by the agreement. Finally, a series of extensive mergers and trusts, incorporating 138 companies consolidated into six trusts, merged in turn to form a new mammoth trust-like holding company, the $1.4 billion United States Steel Corporation, in 1901. U.S. Steel was organized by J.P. Morgan, and represents a shift in industry from plowing-back of profits to finance and underwriting by investment banks. The power in the company soon became George W. Perkins, a partner of the House of

---

R. Daum, *The American Petroleum Industry: The Age of Illumination 1859–1899* (Evanston, IL: Northwestern University Press, 1959), pp. 326, 484, 575, 680. See also Armentano, *Antitrust and Monopoly*, pp. 55–73; Robert L. Bradley, Jr., *Oil, Gas, and Government: The U.S. Experience* (Lanham, MD and Washington D.C.: Rowman and Littlefield Publishers and the Cato Institute, 1995), vol. 1, pp. 1067–1105, the latter a doctoral dissertation written under Rothbard.

More recent research has argued that Standard Oil's success was due to its ability to replicate the South Improvement Company in form by successfully controlling its rebates. Standard was able to ensure low rebates for the oil it shipped relative to its competitors, and if a railroad Standard shipped oil with cut rebates for one of their competitors, they would retaliate by reducing the amount of oil it shipped with the railroad. See Elizabeth Granitz and Benjamin Klein, "Monopolization by 'Raising Rivals' Costs: The Standard Oil Case," *Journal of Law and Economics* (April, 1996): 1–47. However, it should be noted that as expected, railroads still did frequently try to cut rebates to Standard's competitors in order to boost their sales, and new oil was discovered and refineries opened up in areas of the country which Standard did not have control over. For a critique of the Granitz and Klein argument that champions the usual efficiency argument, see Morris, *The Tycoons*, pp. 345, 359.

Morgan. Even so, since there were still 223 firms with blast furnaces and 445 steel work and rolling mill companies by the turn of the century, U.S. Steel only controlled 62% of the market.

Yet, despite its enormous size and its large share of the market, U.S. Steel did badly from the beginning by any criteria. U.S. Steel shares, priced at $55 in 1901, fell precipitately to $9 by 1904. Steel's profits also dropped sharply, yielding 16% in 1902 and falling to less than 8% two years later. Steel prices fell steadily, and U.S. Steel did not dare to raise prices for fear of attracting new and active competitors. Finally, in late 1907, Judge Elbert H. Gary, chairman of the board of U.S. Steel and another Morgan man at the company, inaugurated a series of "Gary dinners" among steel leaders, to form "gentlemen's agreements" to keep up the price of steel. But by as early as mid-1908, smaller independents began cutting their prices secretly, and this broke the agreements and forced U.S. Steel and then other majors to follow suit. By early 1909, even the formal structure of the Gary dinners had completely collapsed. Prices consequently fell sharply in 1908 and until U.S. entry into World War I. As Kolko writes, "The collapse of the Gary agreements is an important turning point in the history of steel, for it represents the final failure of the promised stability and profit that motivated the U.S. Steel merger."[6]

Then, despite further mergers acquired by U.S. Steel, and despite its ownership of three-quarters of the Minnesota iron ore fields, U.S. Steel experienced — until the present day — a steady shrinkage in its share of the market. Thus, its share of wire nails fell from 66% in 1901 to 55% in 1910 and its share of ingots and castings declined from 63% in 1901–05 to 52.5% in 1911–1915. In 1909, furthermore, there were still 208 firms with blast furnaces and 446 firms with steel works and rolling mills.

The basic reason for U.S. Steel's steady decline was the curse of all overly-large corporations: technological and entrepreneurial conservatism. As in the case of Standard Oil, U.S. Steel was consistently the last firm to embrace major technological innovations in the steel industry. From 1900 to 1919, the open-hearth steel process largely replaced the Bessemer process as the dominant way of producing steel; U.S. Steel was mired in the Bessemer method and was late in making the change. Similarly, in later decades, U.S. Steel was the last major company to shift from the open-hearth to the basic oxygen process. Largely invested in the production of

---

[6]Kolko, *The Triumph of Conservatism*, p. 36.

heavy steel, U.S. Steel was very slow to enter the new and growing field of lighter steel products, of alloys or of structural steel. It was slow, also, to shift from ore to the use of scrap for raw material.

Hence, the Morgan attempt to create U.S. Steel as a stabilizing force for dominating and monopolizing the steel industry was as dismal a failure as the previous pools and cartels. As Kolko concludes:

> If nothing else, the steel industry was competitive before the World War, and the efforts of the House of Morgan to establish control and stability over the steel industry by voluntary, private economic means had failed. Having failed in the realm of economics, the efforts of the United States Steel group were to be shifted to politics.[7]

4. Agricultural Machinery

By the turn of the century, the agricultural machinery industry was dominated by two large firms: McCormick Harvester, owned by Cyrus McCormick and the McCormick family, and William Deering and Company. When the competition between McCormick and Deering became so intense that they began to buy iron ore and build rolling mills and thereby compete with iron and steel, Judge Gary, Morgan man and chairman of U.S. Steel, took a hand. At his suggestion, George W. Perkins, Morgan partner, threw his weight around and induced McCormick and Deering to merge into a supposedly profitable farm machinery monopoly. Accordingly, in 1902 International Harvester was formed, combining McCormick, Deering and three smaller firms, with Perkins as chairman of the board. International Harvester began with 85% of the harvester market, 96% of the binders, and 91% of the mowers in the United States.

But International Harvester floundered almost immediately. In the 15 months after the merger the firm earned less than 1% profit; and even after extensive reorganization and jettisoning of deadwood the firm, in 1907 only paid 3 to 4% in dividends; and only began paying dividends on its common stock in 1910. Three small firms left out of the merger, Deere and Co., J.I. Case and Co., and Oliver Farm Equipment Co., quickly expanded

---

[7]Kolko, *Triumph of Conservatism*, p. 39. [Editor's remarks] Ibid., pp. 30–39; Armentano, *Antitrust and Monopoly*, pp. 95–100; Butler Shaffer, *In Restraint of Trade: The Business Campaign Against Competition, 1918–1938* (Cranbury, NJ: Associated University Presses, 1997), pp. 123–27.

and developed a full line of machinery. In 1909, there were still 640 farm manufacturing firms in the United States. More significantly, International Harvester's share of the market fell sharply across-the-board. Its share of binders had fallen to 87% in 1911; of mowers to 75%; and of the harvesters it had declined to 80% in 1911 and then to 64% in 1918. Of particular significance, International fell prey quickly to the curse of "monopoly" firms: sluggishness in developing or exploiting innovations.[8]

5. The Sugar Trust

We may mention one more case study of attempted monopolization of an industry: the "Sugar Trust." The sugar refining industry had attempted a cartel in 1882, but the agreement had fallen apart for the usual reasons. Five years later, the industry attempted the merger route toward monopoly, forming the trust, the American Sugar Refining Company.

Conditions for success seemed propitious. The industry was geographically concentrated; of the 23 refineries, ten were located in New York City, of which six were in Brooklyn. And of the latter, the three largest, constituting 55% of total sugar refining capacity in the country, were owned by the Havemeyer family, headed by the formidable Henry O. Havemeyer.

But even so, the trust would not have been attempted were it not for the very high protective tariff that the sugar refiners had managed to wangle from Congress. As Havemeyer later testified before Congress in 1899, "Without the tariff I doubt if we should have dared to take the risk of forming the trust ... I certainly should not have risked all I had ... in a trust unless the business had been protected as it was by the tariff." And, in his testimony, Havemeyer coined a phrase that was to become famous: "The mother of all trusts is the customs tariff bill."[9] Democrats and free traders

---

[8][Editor's footnote] Kolko, *The Triumph of Conservatism*, pp. 45–47; Chandler, *The Visible Hand*, p. 409.

[9]Quoted in Richard Zerbe, "The American Sugar Refinery Company, 1887–1914: The Story of a Monopoly," *Journal of Law and Economics* 12 (October, 1969): 341–42. [Editor's remarks] The protective tariffs that had been a feature of the United States since the Civil War were hotly contested and criticized as fostering domestic monopolies safe from foreign competition which hurt the American consumer. Prominent legislation included the 1861 Morrill Tariff, the 1890 McKinley Tariff, the 1897 Dingley Tariff, and the 1909 Payne-Aldrich Tariff, all of which helped maintain the average level of duties at roughly 40–50%. For more, see Chapter 7 below, pp. 228–29; Gary M. Walton and Hugh Rockoff,

were from then on to link the protective tariff as the necessary condition of the drive toward trusts and monopolization.

The American Sugar Refining Company, when formed in 1887, possessed 80% of the refining capacity of the country. The importance of the tariff in making the attempt is seen by comparing the British and American prices. Thus, in 1886, the price of British refined sugar, including transportation costs to the United States, was $4.09 per cwt. This compared to the price of American refined sugar, which amounted to $6.01. Thus, it is clear that only the protective tariff allowed the American industry to compete at all.

The American Sugar Refining Co. promptly did what it had been formed to do: cut production and raise prices. Its 20 plants were dismantled and reduced to ten, and it was able to raise its price to $7.01 in 1888 and $7.64 in 1889.

But a grave problem quickly arose, for as the Sugar Trust cut its own production, independents, eager to take advantage of the higher prices, *increased* theirs, so that the Trust's share of the total refined sugar market began to fall precipitously: to 73% in 1888 and 66% the following year. Particularly annoying to the Trust was the entrant into the industry, under the umbrella of its own price increases, of Claus Spreckles, "the sugar king of the Sandwich Islands." Spreckles built modern new plants in Philadelphia and Baltimore that were able to outcompete the older refineries. By 1891, the refining capacity of the independents had almost doubled, and prices had fallen drastically to $4.69, and reached $4.35 in 1892.

The Trust was in deep trouble, but the new McKinley Tariff of 1890, which put imported raw sugar on the free list, emboldened it to try once more. And so the Trust bought out Spreckles, merging into the grand new American Sugar Refining Company in 1892, with no less than 95% of the nation's total sugar production.

But there was still a serpent in Eden. For old sugar hands, seeing their opportunity, moved into refining with new and competitive plants. Adolph Segal, for example, posed a similar problem to the Trust that Rockefeller had faced in petroleum: for he apparently made a business out of building sugar refineries which the Trust felt obliged to purchase. In one case, in 1895, Segal built the U.S. Sugar Refining Company at Camden, New Jer-

---

History of the American Economy, 8th ed. (New York: Harcourt Brace & Company, 1998), pp. 462–64. It is important to note, however, that despite this enormous privilege to forming monopolies, market competition still managed to whittle them away.

sey, which, upon purchase by the Trust, was found to be totally inoperative because of the lack of a proper water supply.

As a result of the new competition by independents, the price of sugar, which had risen to $4.84, fell back to $4.12 in 1894, and the American Sugar Refining Co. only had 85% of the sugar market. During the next two years, the refiners attempted another cartel agreement, the agreement covering 90% of sugar production. But the result was the entry into sugar refining, in the next couple of years, of Claus Dorscher and the Arbuckle Brothers. The Arbuckle refinery, in particular, was able to break the cartel, with its low cost and superior product. The Dingley Tariff of 1897, which levied a high tariff on raw sugar, raising its price in the U.S. by 18%, made times still more difficult for the sugar refinery industry. As early as 1898, the Sugar Trust only produced 75% of total national output.

In 1900–01, the industry tried once again. Arbuckle and Havemeyer formed a cartel which included almost all Eastern refiners, and Dorscher and other independents merged into American to bring the Sugar Trust's share of national output back up to 90% by 1902. Sugar prices rose from $4.50 in 1897 to $5.32 in 1900.

Once again, however, the Trust could not maintain a monopoly position. New sugar plants, including a modern one built by Spreckles, again entered the industry. Furthermore, beet sugar, which had only been 4% or less of total sugar production, now received a notable spur from the high Dingley Tariff on raw cane sugar imports. Seeing this, the Sugar Trust tried to maintain its quasi-monopoly position by buying up beet sugar companies after 1901. But, by 1905, American Sugar Refining was forced to abandon this costly policy as a losing proposition. When it did so, in 1905, the Sugar Trust, including its cartel, only controlled 70% of total sugar production, which included 70% of total beet sugar production. Increased competition had also brought sugar prices down to $4.52 by 1906.

After 1905, furthermore, when the Sugar Trust abandoned its policy of buying up competing beet sugar companies, beet sugar won a greater share of the total market (increasing from 4% in 1905 to 14% in 1911), while the Trust's share of beet sugar production fell to 54% in the same year. In fact, its control of the latter was largely soft; it controlled the majority stock of only 8% of the beet sugar market.

By 1917, the share of the Sugar Trust had fallen to 28% of the total market. Indeed, the subsequent story of the American Sugar Refining Company is strongly reminiscent of the history of U.S. Steel:

There is no evidence to indicate that the sugar refiners were successful in their aim of reestablishing the cartel. Consequently, with wisdom and faith, they turned to one of the more efficient cartel promoters, the government. The government was singularly successful in cartelizing the industry during World War I during the Food Administration Act.[10]

6. OVERALL ASSESSMENT

A typical example of the rapid rise and fall of the trust, peaking during the great merger wave of 1897–1901, was the National Biscuit Company. It was formed in 1898 as a great combination of three previous regional combinations, designed to monopolize the biscuit market, to purchase competitors, and to control competition by restricting production and raising prices. The result was disaster, as the National Biscuit Company admitted in a remarkable confession in its Annual Report for 1901. Announcing a complete change of policy from its previous aim of controlling competition, the Annual Report declared:

> When we look back over the four years [since National Biscuit Company was founded], we find that a radical change has been wrought in our methods of business. ... [W]hen this company started, it was thought that we must control competition, and that to do this we must either fight competition or buy it. The first meant a ruinous war of prices, and a greater loss of profit; the second, a constantly increasing capitalization. Experience soon proved to us that, instead of bringing success, either of these courses, if persevered, must bring disaster. This led us to reflect whether it was necessary to control competition ... we soon satisfied ourselves that within the Company itself we must look for success.
>
> We turned our attention and bent our energies to improving the internal management of our business, to

---

[10]Zerbe, "The American Sugar Refinery Company," p. 367; Chandler, *The Visible Hand,* p. 328. [Editor's remarks] In addition, see Richard Zerbe, "Monopoly, The Emergence of Oligopoly and the Case of Sugar Refining," *Journal of Law and Economics* (October, 1970): 501–15; Armentano, *Antitrust and Monopoly,* pp. 50–51.

getting full benefit from purchasing our raw materials in large quantities, to economizing the expenses of manufacture, to systematizing and rendering more effective our selling department; and above all things and before all things to improve the quality of our goods and the condition in which they should reach the customer.

It became the settled policy of this Company to buy out no competition ...[11]

By the turn of the 20th century, in fact, businessmen had become disillusioned with trust combinations. In trust after trust, higher prices brought about by the combine simply attracted new and powerful competitors — and this after the trust had expended a great deal of resources in buying out previous competition. As the influential *Iron Age* lamented, trouble confronted the trust especially "where the combination is naming confessedly high prices for its goods and is at the same time under heavy expenses on account of buying out competitors or subsidizing them to keep out of the market." Moreover, the *New York Financier* stated:

The most serious problem that confronts trust combinations today is competition from independent sources... When the papers speak of a cessation of operation in certain trust industries, they fail to mention the awakening of new life in independent plants ...[12]

In his study of the success of the trusts at the end of the 19th century, Arthur S. Dewing divided the waves into the first, from the late 1880s to 1893, and the second and by far the larger wave, from 1897–1901 or a little later. He concluded that the trusts came to a sudden halt simply because they turned out badly.[13] They did not succeed in suppressing competition; they did not realize the heady expectations of their founders. Shares of stock in the new trusts steadily declined, and few managed to pay dividends. Many of the trusts even failed outright.

---

[11]Quoted in Alfred D. Chandler, Jr., "The Beginnings of Big Business in American Industry," *Business History Review* (Spring 1959): 11–13.

[12]*The Iron Age* (September 20, 1900): 7; (November 1, 1900): 43; *The New York Financier* (June 11, 1900). Quoted in Marian V. Sears, "The American Businessman at the Turn of the Century," *Business History Review* (December, 1956): 391.

[13]They did not cease because of fear of anti-trust prosecution, which then had barely served as a threat to mergers. For more, see Chapter 7 below, pp. 210–29.

Taking a random sample of 35 trusts formed during both waves, Dewing found as follows: that the average earnings of the separate firms just before the formation of the trust was about 20% *greater* than the trust in its first year, and was also greater than the average earnings of the trust in its first ten years or in its tenth year. Furthermore, the average expected estimates of the promoters and bankers responsible for the trusts exceeded actual first year earnings by 50%, and was also considerably higher than over the first ten years. Of the 35 combinations, only four had earnings equal to expectations.[14]

There are other ways of revealing similar conclusions. Thus, of nearly 100 consolidations formed in 1899–1900, three-quarters were not paying dividends in 1900. Alfred L. Bernheim's study of 109 corporations with a capitalization of $10 million and up in 1903, found that 16 failed before 1914, 24 paid no dividends during 1909–1914, and only 22 paid dividends of over 5% during this period. The average dividend for this period was a puny 4.3% for these companies. Or, put another way, of the 50 largest corporations in 1909, 27 had dropped out of the 100 by 1929, while 61 of the 100 in 1909 had dropped out of the ranks by the latter year.[15]

Dewing concluded from this study that businesses who analogized from economies of scale to a quest for One Big Firm in their industry had committed a grave error. They overlooked that there *were* definite limits to the economic size of a firm. In particular, managerial ability, individual human judgment, and initiative are extremely scarce and cannot be automated and routinized into one giant firm. Mere large size, he pointed out, was often a handicap in competing with smaller, more mobile competitors — competitors who had lower overhead costs, who could leave the industry in bad years and return in good ones, and who could shop around quietly for raw materials without being so big as to significantly raise their own costs. Moreover, he might have added that smaller competitors were very often better innovators, less bureaucratic, and more open to new ideas and new methods; indeed, they were not struck with obsolescing fixed plants.

Dewing concluded with these wise words:

---

[14]Arthur S. Dewing, "A Statistical Test of the Success of Consolidations," *Quarterly Journal of Economics* (1921), pp. 84–101. See also Arthur S. Dewing, *The Financial Policy of Corporations*, 2 vols. 5th ed. (New York: Ronald Press, 1953).

[15]Sears, "The American Businessman," pp. 391–92; Kolko, *Triumph of Conservatism*, pp. 27–29.

I have been impressed throughout by the powerlessness of mere aggregates of capital to hold monopoly; I have been impressed, too, by the tremendous importance of individual, innate ability, or its lack, in determining the success or failure of any enterprise. With these observations in mind, one may hazard the belief that whatever "trust problem" exists will work out its own solution. The doom of the inefficient waits on no legislative regulation. It is rather delayed thereby. Restrictive regulation will perpetuate the inefficient corporation, by furnishing an artificial prop to support natural weakness; it will hamper the efficient by impeding the free play of personal ambition.[16]

We have pointed out earlier in this chapter that industrial corporations and stock shares only appeared in the mid-1890s. It is no coincidence, therefore, that it was the investment bankers, who promoted and underwrote such corporations — led by J.P. Morgan — who took the lead in forming corporate mergers in the same period and attempting to achieve the alleged advantages of monopoly prices. U.S. Steel was but one example of such a failed monopoly.

In manufacturing as well as railroads, then, mergers as well as cartels had systematically failed to achieve the fruits of monopoly on the free market.[17] It was time, then, for those industrial and financial groups who had sought monopoly to emulate the example of the railroads: to turn to government to impose the cartels on their behalf. Except that even more than in the railroads, the regulation would have to be ostensibly in *opposition* to a business "monopoly" on the market, and even more would it have to be put through in conjunction with the opinion-molding groups in the society. The stage was set, at the turn of the 20th century, for the giant leap into statism to become known as the Progressive Period.

---

[16]Arthur S. Dewing, *Corporate Promotions and Reorganizations* (Cambridge, MA: Harvard University Press, 1914), pp. vii–viii.

[17][Editor's footnote] For similar evidence that mergers generally invited new competition and were not successful, see Naomi Lamoreaux, *The Great Merger Movement in American Business, 1895–1904* (New York: Cambridge University Press, 1985).

CHAPTER 4

The Third Party System: Pietists vs. Liturgicals

How could America experience a great leap into statism after 1900, a leap that went virtually unchallenged? What happened to the long-standing American tradition of individual liberty and *laissez-faire*? How could it so meekly roll over and play dead after having been dominant, or at least vibrant, during the last half of the 19th century, and for over half a century before that? To answer this question, we must explore what the "new political historians," in the past decade, have been analyzing as the sudden end of the "third party system" in the United States in the year 1896.[1] It was that sudden collapse that spelled the doom of *laissez-faire* in American party politics and paved the way for the unchallenged statism of the Progressive Period and, indeed, for the remainder of the 20th century.

1. The Third Party System

For the last decade or so, political historians have been analyzing not merely individual elections, but the way in which the political parties and their constituencies have interrelated, persisted, and then changed over time. They have identified a series of "party systems," of such structural

---

[1][Editor's footnote] A condensed version of Chapters 4–6 can be found in Rothbard, "A History of Money and Banking," pp. 169–79.

political relationships, in American history. The first was between the Federalists and the Democratic-Republicans, a conflict which began in the 1790s and continued approximately until the War of 1812. After that, America had a single party, which continued until the late 1820s, when the Democratic Party was developed to challenge the existing party, and this precipitated the formation of the Whig Party in opposition. The Democrats vs. the Whigs, lasting from the 1820s until the 1850s, constituted the second American party system. The formation of the Republican Party in the 1850s over the slavery question and the disappearance of the Whigs precipitated the third party system.

The most important point to note is that all three party systems in the 19th century differed radically from the American party system today. Political scientists, journalists, and the Establishment generally laud the current two party system as gloriously *non*-ideological — as providing very little choice between fuzzy programs which overlap almost completely — so that the only choice in this bipartisan haze of issues is between the personalities of the candidates rather than the programs of the parties. Political *parties*, and more particularly party programs and platforms, mean very little these days in the actual conduct of government, particularly in the dominant executive branch, whether on the federal, state, or local level. Deprived of meaningful choice, the public manifests increasing apathy, voter participation rates steadily drop, and more and more people call themselves "independent" rather than identify with any particular party.

It was not always thus. In the 19th century, during all three party systems, the parties were fiercely ideological. Their constituencies were partisan, and voter participation rates in elections were very high. Platforms meant something and were battled over. So firmly drawn were the lines that it was rare for a Republican to vote Democrat or *vice versa*; disenchantment in one's party was rather reflected in a failure to vote. The drive of each party, therefore, was not to capture the floating independent voter by moving toward the middle, but, on the contrary, to whip up the enthusiasm of its own militant supporters, and thereby to "bring out the new vote."

Throughout the 19th century — with the single and grave exception of slavery — the Democratic Party (and before it, the Democratic-Republicans) was the libertarian, *laissez-faire* party — the "party of personal liberty," of free trade, of hard money, the separation of the economy, religion, and virtually everything else from the State; the opponent of Big Government, high taxes, public works ("internal improvements"), judicial oligarchy, or federal power, the champion of the free press, unrestricted immigration, state and individual rights. The Federalists, on the other hand, and after them the Whigs and then the Republicans, were the party of statism: of Big Government, public works, a large public debt, government subsidies to industry, protective tariffs, opposition to aliens and immigrants, and of cheap money and government control of banking (through a central bank, or later, through the quasi-centralized national banking system). The Whigs, in particular, strove to use the State to compel personal morality: through a drive for Prohibition, Sunday blue laws, or a desire to outlaw the Masons as a secret society. The Republicans, who were essentially the Whigs with the admixture of anti-slavery Democrats, became known quite aptly as "the party of great moral ideas." After the Civil War, when slavery was no longer a blot on America, the Democrats could be a far less sullied champion of personal liberty, while the Republican drive for "moral ideas" became more susceptible to libertarian irony, being fully coercive and now in no sense liberating.[2]

The first party system began in the 1790s when the Democratic-Republican Party was launched in order to combat the Federalist program of economic statism: high tariffs, public works, centralized government, public debt, government control of banking and cheap money, and of repressive federal tyranny against Democratic critics in the press. The Democratic-Republicans also strove to end the ultimate control of the government by a judicial oligarchy and to end militarism by abolishing the navy and standing army. After winning with Thomas Jefferson's assumption to the presidency in 1800 and partially achieving their platform, the Democratic-Republicans faltered and then themselves began to go down the road to federalism by driving toward war with their ancient foe, Great Britain. The pro-British Federalists were effectively destroyed for opposing the War of 1812, but their program was put into effect by their foes in the course of launching and fighting a (necessarily statist) war: high protective tariffs, federal domestic excise taxation, a central bank, inflationary bank credit expansion, public debt, public works, and, to boot, a one party system by the end of the war.

Brooding in retirement at Monticello, Jefferson lamented at what his Virginia successors to the presidency, James Madison and James Monroe, had wrought. They had ended by installing a one party Federalism without the Federalists. Being human, Jefferson was not as keenly alive to his own

---

[2]The Republicans, much less the Whigs, had no interest, however, in freeing the slaves in the South — only preventing an expansion of slave labor into the Western territories.

crucial role in launching the drive toward war and therefore toward the very Federalism that he so bitterly deplored. Inspired and converted by separate weekend pilgrimages to Monticello, two important young politicians: Thomas Hart Benton of Missouri and especially Martin Van Buren of New York, determined to take up the mighty task of creating a new political party, a party designed to take back America from Federalism, and to restore the good old principles of '76 (the American Revolution and the Declaration of Independence) and of '98 (of the Kentucky and Virginia Resolutions which called for a virtual revolution of states against the despotic national Alien and Sedition Laws). Basing themselves in New York, Missouri, and on the old Jeffersonians in Virginia, the new party sought a charismatic leader and found him in Andrew Jackson. The new Democratic Party was born, dedicated to personal liberty, minimal government, free trade, hard money, and the separation of government from banking. The opposition Whigs revived the nationalist-statist Federalist program, except that the Whigs were more interested in compulsory morality and restricting the flood of immigrants, and adopted demagogic democratic techniques and rhetoric in contrast to the frankly elitist and anti-universal suffrage and anti-democratic outlook of the Federalist Party.

It should be noted that in both of the first two party systems, the libertarian, *laissez-faire* party slowly but surely began to establish itself as the dominant majority party in America. The Federalists faded with the triumph of Jefferson, but Jeffersonian principles could not survive the drive that he himself had launched toward war. In the second party system, too, the Democrats began to establish themselves as the majority party, and it seemed once again as if America would move rapidly toward the libertarian, *laissez-faire* ideal. On the federal level, the quite feasible Jacksonian plan was to have eight years of Jackson, eight of Van Buren, and eight of Benton — 24 solid years in which to achieve their goals. Eight years of Jackson from 1828 to 1836 was indeed succeeded by four years of Van Buren. Then, the timetable was briefly interrupted by the victory of the first modern demagogic presidential campaign, replete with all the propaganda techniques we are now familiar with: slogans, parades, buttons, all engineered by the master Whig political technician, Thurlow Weed. But everyone knew that the Democrats, who could easily copy these techniques four years later, would win in 1844, and Van Buren prepared to resume the victorious timetable. But then, the great issue of the expansion of slavery came to split the Democratic Party — in the form of the admission of Texas to the Union as a slave state — and Jackson and Van Buren also split on the issue. While the Democrats remained Jacksonian in most matters, Jacksonianism was pushed to the background as the Democrats became a Southern-based pro-slave party. The Republican Party, including some Northern Democrats, was then founded in the 1850s to become the party opposed to slave expansion and, then, in the Civil War, to uphold the unitary power of the national Union as against the right of state secession. The third American party system had begun.

The Republican Party, which only got 40% of the popular vote in 1860, seized the opportunity presented by the South's walkout and the resulting near one party Congress to ram through the old Whig economic program: inflationary paper money, central control over banking, high tariffs, massive government subsidies to railroads, high federal excise taxation over the "immoral" commodities liquor and cigarettes, plus such centralizing and statist measures as conscription and the income tax. It is no wonder that the Republicans should have been dominant during and immediately after the War in the Reconstruction period.[3]

---

[3][Editor's footnote] For a similar broad overview of the history of America's libertarian tradition up to the Civil War, see Murray Rothbard, *For a New Liberty: The Libertarian Manifesto*, 2nd ed. (Auburn, AL: Mises Institute, 2011 [1978]), pp. 7–10. The narrative is only present in the revised edition. It is described more in depth in Murray Rothbard, "Report on George B. DeHuszar and Thomas Hulbert Stevenson, *A History of the American Republic*, 2 vols." in *Strictly Confidential: The Private Volker Fund Memos of Murray N. Rothbard,* David Gordon, ed. (Auburn, AL: Mises Institute, 2010 [1961]), pp. 96–136. For a Rothbardian analysis of the Jacksonians that stresses the ethno-religious aspects, see Leonard Liggio, "Murray Rothbard and Jacksonian Banking," in *The Contributions of Murray Rothbard to Monetary Economics* (Winchester, VA: The Durell Institute, 1996), pp. 8–17.

For more on the libertarian strengths and weaknesses of the Jeffersonians and Jacksonians and the rifts in the Democratic Party over the slavery and territorial expansion issue, see Arthur Ekirch, Jr., *The Decline of American Liberalism* (Oakland, CA: Independent Institute, 2009 [1955]), pp. 55–115; Jeffrey Hummel, *Emancipating Slaves, Enslaving Free Men: A History of the American Civil War* (Chicago, IL: Open Court, 1996), pp. 76–128. The Locofocos were a Northeastern branch of the Jacksonian Democracy most dedicated to *laissez-faire,* including in the monetary sphere. Their leader was the social theoretician William Leggett. See Lawrence White, "Foreword," in William Leggett, *Democratik Editorials: Essays in Jacksonian Political Economy* (Indianapolis, IN: Liberty Fund, 1984), pp. xi–xix; Lawrence White, "William Leggett: Jacksonian editorialist as classical liberal political economist," *History of Political Economy* 18 (1986): 307–24. For a sweeping history of the Locofoco movement, see Anthony Comegna, "'The Dupes of Hope Forever': The Loco-Foco or Equal Rights Movement, 1820s–1870s" (doctoral dissertation in history, University of Pittsburgh, 2016).

For an overview of America's monetary history during this time, see Rothbard, "A History of Money and Banking," pp. 68–147. For more on the hard money aspects of the Jacksonian Democracy at the federal level, see Murray Rothbard, *An Austrian Perspective on*

Many historians are under the erroneous impression that the Republicans continued to be dominant until 1912, or even until 1932, with only two terms of Grover Cleveland's presidency interrupting the smooth march of Republican victory. This impression, however, is mistaken. As the new political historians have reminded us, the Democratic Party captured the House of Representatives in 1874 — and followed by *really* gaining the presidency in 1876, only to see it purloined in Congress by the Republicans in a bargain that liquidated Reconstruction in the South. From 1874 until 1896, a space of 22 years, the two parties were nip-and-tuck in all races for the Congress and the presidency. From 1875 to 1895, the Republicans controlled the House of Representatives in only two out of the ten sessions, reaching the peak of their control in 1888 with 51.1% of the House membership. But, on the other hand, though the Democrats controlled the House in eight of the ten sessions, their peak membership was 71% in 1890, and only five times did they receive as much as 55.0% of the total vote. In the five presidential contests between 1876 and 1892, the Republicans captured only three races, and two of the victories (1876 and 1888) were achieved with fewer popular votes than the Democratic nominee. The Republican presidential nominee did not receive a majority of the popular vote in *any* election between 1876 and 1892, and had a plurality only in 1880, and then by only a couple thousand votes. On the other hand, the Democrats only controlled the Senate twice in the 20 year period in 1878–80 and 1892–94. Only once did the Republicans control the presidency and both houses of Congress at the same time, and only once did the Democrats accomplish the same feat.

Furthermore, the Democrats were slowly gaining the ascendancy, so that, as happened at the end of the two previous party systems, the Democratic Party was slowly but inexorably moving toward long run dominance. This development was embodied in the Democratic landslide to capture the House in 1890 and in Cleveland's easy return to a second term in the presidency in 1892, which carried the Democrats to control both houses of Congress for the first clean sweep since the Civil War.[4] And then something

---

the History of Economic Thought: Classical Economics (Auburn, AL: Mises Institute, 2006 [1995]), vol. 2, pp. 210–16, 232–35.

[4]The long run decline of the Republicans in this period is seen by the fact that in 1860, the Republican Party captured 59% of the vote in the North Atlantic states and 54% in the Midwest; while in 1892, the percentages had declined seven percentage points, to 52% and 47% respectively. Furthermore, the South had been re-Democratized and far more intensively

happened to clobber the Democratic Party in 1896, and to reduce it to a rather pathetic minority party at least until 1912 (and more accurately until 1928 since Woodrow Wilson's election in 1912 was only made possible by a grave split within Republican ranks). What cataclysmic event occurred in 1896 — so much so as to usher in a new, fourth party system for the next 32 years — will be the subject of the next few chapters.

2. PIETISTS VS. LITURGICALS: THE POLITICAL PARTY CONSTITUENCIES

In 1970, in a brilliant and seminal work titled *The Cross of Culture: A Social Analysis of Midwestern Politics: 1850–1900,* Professor Paul Kleppner provided a cogent and illuminating explanation for the constituencies of the third party systems. It is a thesis since amply confirmed by other historians.[5] The thesis explains not only which groups tended to support which parties, but also the specific *process* by which that support was generated and strengthened.

Briefly, the Kleppner thesis holds that "Pietist" religious groups tended (a) to favor statism, both in the personal and the economic spheres, and (b) therefore consistently supported the Republicans as the statist party, while the Liturgicals, consisting largely of Catholics and conservative Lutherans (a) favored liberty, both in the personal and economic spheres, and (b) therefore supported the Democrats as the Libertarian party. Kleppner, indeed, in examining detailed voting and religious records for the Midwestern states, breaks down Lutherans and other Protestant groups into varying *degrees* of Pietism and Liturgicalism and is able to show a one-to-one correlation between the degree of commitment to the liturgical outlook and the degree of voting support to the Democratic Party. The great exception to this correlation, of course, was the South, overwhelmingly

---

than before the Civil War, after the end of the Reconstruction period. In the presidential election of 1892, the Democrats gained 46% of the popular vote, and the Republicans only 43%, with the rest going to minor parties. It looked as if the Democrats were on the threshold of becoming the dominant party in the United States. [Editor's remarks] For the above statistics, see Paul Kleppner, *The Cross of Culture: A Social Analysis of Midwestern Politics, 1850–1900* (New York: The Free Press, 1970), pp. 5–6.

5[Editor's footnote] Some of the historians and their works Rothbard is referring to are Richard J. Jensen, *The Winning of the Midwest: Social and Political Conflict, 1888–1896* (Chicago: University of Chicago Press, 1971); Samuel T. McSeveney, *The Politics of Depression: Political Behavior in the Northeast, 1893–1896* (Oxford: Oxford University Press, 1972); Paul Kleppner, *The Third Electoral System, 1852–1892: Parties, Voters, and Political Cultures* (Chapel Hill: University of North Carolina Press, 1979).

pietist and yet which voted Democratic because of the special circumstances, memories, and consequences of the Civil War.

The genesis of these differing world outlooks Kleppner analyzes as beginning with basic theology. The pietists were those who held that each individual, rather than the church or the clergy, was responsible for his own salvation. Salvation was a matter, not of following prescribed ritual or even of cleaving to a certain fixed creed, but rather of an intense emotional commitment or conversion experience by the individual, even to the extent of believing himself "born again" in a special "baptism of grace." Moreover, the outward sign — the evidence to the rest of society for the genuineness and the permanence of a given individual's conversion —was his continuing purity of behavior. And since each individual was responsible for his own salvation, the pietists concluded that society was duty-bound to aid each man in pursuing his salvation, in promoting his good behavior, and in seeing as best it could that he does not fall prey to temptation. The emphasis of the pietists was on converting the maximum number of persons, and in helping them to become and to remain sound.

Society, therefore, in the institution of the State, was to take it upon itself to aid the weaker brethren by various crusading actions of compulsory morality, and thus to purge the world of sin. The secular and the religious were to be conjoined. In the second half of the 19th century, the pietists concentrated on agitating for three such compulsory measures on the state and local level, to save liturgical "sinners" despite themselves: Prohibition, to eradicate the sin of alcohol; Sunday blue laws, to prevent people from violating the Sabbath; and, increasingly toward the end of the century, compulsory public schooling to "Americanize" the immigrants and "Christianize the Catholics," and to use the schools to transform Catholics and immigrants (often one and the same) into pietistic Protestant and nativist molds.

The pietists, then, typically concentrated on the purity and propriety of each individual's behavior. They were not particularly interested in creed or formal theology, and since the emphasis was each individual's direct confrontation with Christ, they were not particularly concerned with which specific church the person might join. The typical pietist, therefore, switched denominations with relative ease. The pietists, consequently, went heavily for numerous interdenominational societies for social reform; the prohibition drives being a good case in point.[6]

The liturgicals, on the other hand — largely Catholics and German Lutherans, and also Anglicans — had a very different theological and moral outlook. For the liturgical, the path toward salvation was in the hands of the Church and its priests, and what the individual needed to do was to believe in and practice the prescribed ritual. Given these intellectual rather than emotional beliefs and those rituals, the individual church member need not worry continually over his own salvation; and, as for the salvation of his fellow citizens, that could be accomplished, insofar as was possible, if they joined the Church. The Church rather than the State, then, was in charge of morality and salvation, and hence the State need and should have nothing to do with moral and theological matters. As Professor Jensen, whose studies of the Middle West have confirmed Kleppner's findings, has put it: "[For the liturgical] the Church itself would attend to all matters of morality and salvation ... hence the State had no right to assert a role in delineating public morality."[7]

The liturgical was also rather sensibly puzzled over the intense hostility of the pietists toward alcohol, especially when Jesus himself had drunk wine. "We do not believe in making sin what God made not sin," was a typical liturgical response. To the liturgical, sin was not such "impure" behavior as drinking alcohol, but heresy and refusal to believe the theological creed of the Church or to obey its prescribed ritual. As Jensen summarized the difference: the Methodists expelled members for impure behavior; the liturgicals for heresy. It was quite clear, moreover, that such theological

---

6[Editor's footnote] Rothbard would later expand on this thesis using eschatology (the doctrine of last things) and describe the religious interventionists as "Yankee Postmillennial Pietists," who were evangelized through the frenzied revivals of Reverend Charles Grandison Finney during the Second Great Awakening of the late 1820s. They were a group of pietist English descendants that lived in rural New England, upstate New York, Northern Ohio, Northern Indiana, and Northern Illinois, who were "postmillennialist" in that they believed the world must be improved for a thousand years before Jesus would return to usher in the end of history. In order to bring about this "Kingdom of God," the postmillennial pietists took it as their moral duty to stamp out the sin of others, even if it required the coercive hand of government. Over time, these crusaders lost their religious zeal and became "secularized," but still maintained their enthusiasm for wielding state force. See Chapters 10, 11, and 13 below, pp. 295–99, 327–40, 397–407, 420–36. See also Gary North, "Millennialism and the Progressive Movement," *Journal of Libertarian Studies* 12 (Spring 1996): 121–42.

7Jensen, *The Winning of the Midwest*, p. 64.

matters as heresy and liturgy could hardly be considered matters for State intervention and enforcement.

It should be noted that while liturgicals consisted mainly of such groups as Catholics and Lutherans, they also included some sects, such as orthodox Calvinists, who emphasized creed rather than ritual, and so could not in the strict sense be called "liturgical." Their attitude toward the vital importance of the particular church and of correct belief was similar, however, and this set them apart from the pietistic Protestants. Such groups included "Old School" Presbyterians and a few groups of Baptists.

The liturgical correctly perceived the pietist as the persistent, hectoring busybody and aggressor: hell-bent to deprive him of his Sunday beer and his voluntarily supported parochial schools, so necessary to preserve and transmit his religion and his values. While the pietist was a pestiferous crusader, the liturgical wanted nothing so much as to be left alone. It is no wonder that the Republican Party, the party of the pietists, the party that catered to prohibitionists, blue-law agitators and compulsory public school advocates, was known throughout this period as "the party of great moral ideas." While the Democrats, the party of the liturgicals, the party deeply opposed to compulsory morality, were known as the "party of personal liberty."[8,9]

---

[8]We are not trying to claim any apodictic certainty for these causal connections. That is, it is perfectly *possible* to have pietists who are consistent libertarians, or who are inconsistent between personal and economic liberty, and it is perfectly possible to have liturgicals who are statists or who are inconsistent. All we are claiming is that this is what the contrasting religious groups in America in the late 19th century believed, and that this is how their belief system originated and developed. We are not making any similar claims for any other time or place in world history. ([Editor's remarks] For a prominent example of one such pietist libertarian described by Rothbard, in which he explicitly cites the work of Kleppner and Jensen, see Murray Rothbard, "Introduction" in *Lysander Spooner: Libertarian Pietist, Vices Are Not Crimes* [Cupertino, CA: Tanstaafl, 1977], pp. xiii–xvii).

It should be noted, however, that the leadership on behalf of economic freedom and individual liberty taken by the British pietists in the 18th and 19th centuries, as well as earlier, may be a bit deceiving. For these Dissenters or Nonconformists were reacting against an established Anglican (liturgical) Church, and they would naturally favor religious liberty when confronting a State in opposition hands. It should also be pointed out that British Liberalism in that era was continually being split by the penchant of the Nonconformist masses to be (a) in favor of Prohibition, and (b) in favor of crushing the Irish Catholics. In that way the Liberal party's devotion to individual liberty was repeatedly undercut and comprised.

[9][Editor's footnote] Kleppner, *The Cross of Culture*, pp. 71–91; Jensen, *The Winning of the Midwest*, pp. 58–88.

To a late 20th-century observer, one of the most puzzling things about 19th-century party politics is the enormous amount of interest and passion spent on economic issues. Professors who can scarcely interest their own students in economic matters must marvel at presidential campaigns at which such esoteric matters as protective tariffs, central banking, and gold and silver standards were intense objects of general public attention and partisan debate. How did the mass of the public get interested in such arcane matters?

The Kleppner analysis explains this enigma. The interest and passions of both party constituencies were *first* engaged on the religious-cultural, the gut local level. The constant prods were such issues as liquor, blue laws, and the public schools. Then, with partisan passions engaged on the local and religious level, the leaders and ideologists of both parties were able to widen the consciousness of their respective constituencies to brilliantly link up the local with the national, the personal with the economic. Thus, the Republican leaders would tell their pietist constituents "You believe in strong state and local governments to protect the morals of the public. In the same way, you should favor strong federal government to protect Americans from cheap foreign competition, to expand their purchasing-power through plentiful money and cheap credit (through greenbacks, government control of the banking system, or free silver), government subsidies to business and large-scale public works expenditures."

At the same time, the Democratic leaders would tell their liturgical constituents, "You know that the pietists are determined to deprive you of your wholesome pleasures such as beer and Sunday sports in the name of their own peculiar version of morality. They are trying to take away your parochial schools. Now the same pietists, the same Republicans, who are nagging and oppressing you on the state level are also trying to interfere with your liberty and property on the federal level. They are trying to expand their local moral paternalism to national economic paternalism. They are trying to tax you to subsidize privileged interests, they are trying to keep you from consuming cheap foreign products, and they are trying to deprive you of the fruits of your thrift and savings through cheap money and inflation."

In short, both parties were able to link up statism and Big Government in Washington and at home, to connect the economic and the personal. The Republicans, the party of statism, lined up squarely against the

Democrats, the party of liberty.[10] In those decades, there was continuing drift of both parties from the center, no deliberate fuzzing of the issues and of all differences. On the contrary, the differences were emphasized in order to appeal to the respective constituencies and to keep their interest fired up.

Many historians have concluded that, throughout most of the 19th century, there was an anti-immigrant animus by native-born Americans, and that the Democrats became the immigrant-based party while the Republicans attracted the nativists. But Kleppner shows that the basic division was not *really* between native-born and immigrants, or between English speaking and foreigners. Pietistic Scandinavian immigrants, for example, identified with native WASPs very quickly and readily voted Republican. The real division was Pietist vs. Liturgical, and it so happened that the bulk of immigrants were indeed liturgicals, so as to make these immigrants a made-to-order target for pietist bigotry. Restricting immigration would almost certainly hit far more severely at liturgicals, and hence benefit the Republican Party.

The emergence of different forms of the Christian religion as the key to political conflicts lends an ironic twist to American history. For twice in the history of America, Christianity had virtually died out. The first time was in the early decades of the 18th century, when Calvinism had given way to the new Enlightenment trends of liberalism and rationalism. But orthodox Christianity revived in the 1730s and 1740s with the Great Awakening — a new form of pietist Christianity which swept the colonies through the revivalist and evangelical methods of intensely emotional and frenzied conversions.[11]

But then, late in the 18th century, Christianity began to die once more — to be replaced by the rationalist deism of the Enlightenment. By the

---

[10][Editor's footnote] The post-Civil War *laissez-faire* and hard money Democrats were known as the "Bourbons." They were generally centered in the Northeast, but were also in the Midwest. On the other hand, there were the much more statist and inflationist "Populist" Democrats, based in the South and Far West. The Democratic upheaval in 1896 refers to the Populist faction defeating the Bourbon Democracy and transforming the party from one that championed *laissez-faire* to one that was much more supportive of government interventionism. See Rothbard, "Report on George B. DeHuszar," pp. 137–39, 148.

[11][Editor's footnote] Further analysis of religion in early American history can be found in Murray Rothbard, *Conceived in Liberty*, vol. 2, *"Salutary Neglect": The American Colonies in the First Half of the Eighteenth Century* (Auburn, AL: Mises Institute, 2011 [1975]), pp. 654–71.

time the United States was founded, it was clear that Christianity was giving way across the board — among the upper classes and among the general public.

For the second time, however, Christianity made a remarkable comeback — and once again through a series of frenzied revivals that took place throughout the country in the 1820s and 1830s. These revivals, of course, were necessarily pietist, and pietism's emotional and crusading tone and thrust began with this final upsurge of the early 19th century. Apart from a few Anglicans, there had been very few liturgicals in the America of the 1790s. Essentially, native WASPs were pietist; the ranks of the liturgicals were to be fed, during the 19th century, by Catholic and Lutheran immigrants from Europe.

From the beginning of the revival movement in the 1820s, the resurrected pietists began to form organizations to root out sin among their fellow men. Their two dominant concerns were the sins of slavery and of alcohol. At first, the idea was to ban the saloon, presumably the central iniquity in the dissemination of alcohol. By the late 1830s, the pietists had escalated their demands to include total abstinence and total prohibition, including wine and beer as well as hard liquor. In 1851, the pietists began to succeed, getting liquor totally banned in Maine. This step was followed by numerous other prohibition laws or constitutional amendments in 12 states during the early 1850s.

After 1855, however, the pietists temporarily abandoned the prohibitionist crusade to concentrate on slavery. After the Civil War, the pietists were able to devote all their energies to the evils of alcohol. In 1868, the pietistic prohibitionists founded a secret society, the Good Templars, which soon had 400,000 members. In Michigan, in the following year, the Templars helped form the Prohibitionist Party; the foundation of the Women's Christian Temperance Union followed in 1874. By the 1880s, prohibition had become the leading political issue in the Middle West and in most of the rest of the country.[12]

3. Pietists vs. Liturgicals in the Midwest

The Pietist/Liturgical analysis has been worked out most fully for the vitally important Midwestern states, the area where Kleppner himself did his pioneering research, concentrating particularly on three critical states:

---

[12][Editor's footnote] Jensen, *The Winning of the Midwest,* pp. 68–70.

Michigan, Ohio, and Wisconsin. In the Midwest, the Republicans began in the 1860s with a substantial lead, obtaining approximately 55% in the presidential elections, while the Democrats obtained about 44%. But then, after 1874, the Republicans could no longer obtain a clear majority. The Republican vote ranged from 49% to 52% from 1876 to 1888, and then fell to 47% in 1892. In Michigan, Ohio, and Wisconsin, the Republicans fell below 50% of the vote by 1874, and never really gained a majority after that. The Democratic rise did not match the Republican decline, the Democratic vote in the Midwest ranging narrowly from 45% to 47% in the presidential contests from 1884 to 1892. It should not be thought that there was any significant shift of blocs of voters from Republican to Democratic; on the contrary, two forces were at work: a defection of Republican voters to third parties, especially the Prohibitionists, and a shift of the relative voting population, so that strong Republican areas became a smaller proportion, and strong Democratic areas a larger proportion, of the total vote.[13]

As Kleppner points out, the nip-and-tuck struggle in the Midwest was in no sense urban vs. rural, categories that historians tend to look for in explaining conflict. Elections were extremely close, for example, in all the urban areas of the region. In 1888, in the 14 largest cities of Michigan, the Democrats averaged 48% of the vote while the Republicans averaged the same 48%, in the 22 largest cities in Ohio, the respective averages were 48% and 49%, and in the 9 major cities in Wisconsin, the Democrats averaged 46% and the Republicans 45%. It could not get closer than that. What is more, there had been little change in these relative percentages since the 1876 presidential race.

Neither could any class differentiation in voting be detected within the urban wards. In 1888, the correlation between the Democratic percentage and the percentage of working class in the wards was an extremely low +.035, a figure very close to zero. In Detroit, one wealthy ward gave the Democrats 46% of the vote, while another voted a substantial 56% for the Democracy. One the other hand, one very poor ward voted over 70% Democratic, while another, even poorer ward, voted only 47%. On the other hand, if we examine the religious composition of the wards, the party constituencies become clear. The strongest Democratic ward was the most heavily Catholic, largely Polish, while another poor and heavily

---

[13][Editor's footnote] Kleppner, *The Cross of Culture*, pp. 8–9.

working class ward had a low Democratic vote, and it was very heavily native-born and Protestant.

Similarly, in Milwaukee, while the four wealthiest wards only voted 40% Democratic in 1888, the five poorest only voted 37%. The poorest and most working-class ward, on the other hand, also voted the strongest Democratic in the city (68%), but another poor and working class ward was also the weakest Democratic (13%); the explanation is that the former was almost wholly Polish Catholic, while the latter was strongly Protestant.

In Chicago, in the same year, the correlation between the percentage of Catholics in each ward and the percentage voting Democratic was a very high +.90, and this correlation persisted whether within lower-class or upper-class wards, the former wards correlating at +.88 and the latter at +.90.

Orthodox historians have claimed that the farmers in this period were overwhelmingly Republican. But the difference was not very great, and in Ohio, in 1888, the parties tied (Republicans at 49%, Democrats at 48%). There was no significant correlation, furthermore, between party votes and the degree of rural prosperity; in fact, townships of the same economic level *within* the same rural county often differed widely in their party affiliation. There was no visible correlation, either, by occupation. Neither was there any native-born vs. immigrant bloc; far from being a monolith, immigrants varied widely in their voting patterns. The key, then, for both rural and urban areas, was ethnic-religious factors, which in contrast to the economic, have not been considered "real" by most historians.[14]

Let us, following Paul Kleppner's research, go down the list of ethnic-religious groups and examine their voting records.[15] Historians have been seduced by the prominence of Carl Schurz, German immigrant and leading Liberal Republican, into believing that the Germans were largely Republican.[16] But Schurz was an anti-clerical liberal, who spoke only for

---

[14][Editor's footnote] Ibid., pp. 19–34.

[15][Editor's footnote] Ibid., pp. 36–69.

[16][Editor's footnote] After the Civil War, there were two main factions of the Radical Republicans. The first, headed by Charles Sumner, was in favor of free trade and resuming specie payments. The second, headed by Thaddeus Stevens, was in favor of high tariffs and greenbacks. The Sumner faction lost out and eventually morphed into the Liberal Republicans who, in addition to the above policies, were in favor of ending reconstruction and especially enacting civil service reform, driven by their northern Yankee postmillennial

his own small group of prominent anti-clericals; most Germans were staunchly Catholic or Lutheran, who would tend to reach against, rather than follow, the anticlericals. Most Germans were Democratic and anti-Republican.[17] By the late 1880s, there were approximately one-and-a-half million German Protestants in the Middle West, and another one-and-a-half million Catholics. The German Catholics were overwhelmingly Democratic: in every section, urban or rural, of every state in the Midwest, on every economic level, and in every occupation. Every single German Catholic parish voted Democratic, from 1876 to 1888.

The one million Lutherans were grouped in diverse sects, ranging from conservative and ultra-liturgical down to largely pietist. The proportion voting Democratic correlates one-to-one with the degree by which each sect was liturgical. Thus, the most liturgical group was the Wisconsin Synod, which voted overwhelmingly Democratic. The next most liturgical group was the Missouri Synod, which voted less heavily Democratic, and so down the line.

A second factor determining voting was the province of Germany from which the voters had originally hailed. But here, too, different provinces of Lutherans differed in the degree to which they were liturgical or pietist. Pietism was strongest in Southern and Western Germany, especially in Wurttemberg, while it was weakest in Northern and Eastern Germany, in particular Pomerania. Hence, the Pomeranians were the strongest Democrats, and the Wurttembergers were the least Democratic.[18] The most liturgical provincial group was the "Old Lutherans," who had come early to the United States from Pomerania in the years 1839 to 1845. They had emigrated in reaction to the attempts of the Prussian monarchy to compel the unification of the Lutheran with the Reformed Churches. The Old Lutherans were therefore fiercely anti-evangelical and anti-pietist, and their townships tended to vote far more Democratic than others.

---

background. They would later be known as "Mugwumps," or independent northeastern voters who favored free market policies and civil service reform. See Rothbard, "Bureaucracy and the Civil Service in the United States," pp. 42–43, 55–56, 71–72.

[17]Even the great Schurz, when campaigning for the Republicans in his own hometown, was greeted by his fellow German-Americans with a barrage of rotten eggs and shouts of "ein verdammte Republikaner"; William F. Whyte, "Chronicles of Early Watertown," *Wisconsin Magazine of History* 4 (1920–21): 288–90. Cited in Kleppner, *Cross of Culture*, p. 38.

[18]The rank order of Democratic voting, as well as degree of Liturgicalism, was as follows, beginning with the most Democratic province: Pomeranians, Hanoverians, Mecklenbergers, Oldenburgers, Palatines, and Wurttembergers.

Even the Old Lutherans, as with the other provinces, split in accordance with the degree of their devotion to liturgy. Thus, the ultra-liturgical among the Old Lutherans joined the Wisconsin Synod, while those rather less devoted to liturgy entered into the conservative but less rigorous Missouri Synod. As we might expect, the most heavily Democratic of the German Lutherans were the districts peopled by Old Lutheran members of the Wisconsin Synod. For example, let us consider two townships in Wisconsin of Old Lutheran Germans. Lebanon township, Dodge County, consisting of members of the Wisconsin Synod, averaged no less than 90% Democratic from 1870 to 1888. On the other hand, Mequon township, Ozaukee County, consisting of Old Lutherans, Missouri Synod, averaged 75% Democratic during that period.

On the other hand, if we take Pomeranians who were *not* "Old Lutherans," they were far less Democratic than the latter, but, again, *within* that group, the Wisconsin Synod members were far more Democratic than the Missouri Synod. Thus, within the same county of Wisconsin, Marathon County, Berlin township (made up of non-Old Lutheran Pomeranians of the Wisconsin Synod) voted 76% Democratic in 1880, while Texas township (consisting of Pomeranians of the Missouri Synod), voted only 47% Democratic in that year.

The Missouri Synod, in its turn, was far more liturgical than other German Lutheran groups. A striking contrast may be seen between two groups of (non-Old Lutheran) Pomeranians in the same Presque Isle County, in Michigan. In 1888, the Missouri Synod Pomeranians, who made up the voters of Moltke township in that county, voted 59% Democratic. On the other hand, Bismark township, comprised of Pomeranian members of the pietistic General Council, voted only 8% Democrat in the same year.

The Mecklenbergers were less liturgical and less Democratic than the Pomeranians, but again, the Wisconsin Synod members were more Democratic than the Missouri or other synods. Thus, Greenville township, in Outagamie County, Wisconsin, a Wisconsin Synod Mecklenberger area, voted 59% Democratic, while Plymouth township, Sheboygan County, made up of Missouri Synod Mecklenbergers, voted 36% Democrat. And in the same Marquette County in Wisconsin, made up of a mixed group of Pomeranians and Mecklenbergers, Mecan township, consisting of members of the Wisconsin Synod, voted 72% Democratic while Crystal Lake township, of the Missouri Synod, voted only 46% Democrat.

A third factor influencing voting patterns was the backlash effect; that is, in those townships or wards where opposing religious groups lived side by side, friction and hostility came much more intensely to the fore. In particular, in those townships where German Lutherans, even highly liturgical ones, had to rub elbows with their ancient foes, the ultra-liturgical Catholics, the Lutherans tended to vote more heavily Republican. A striking example is two townships in Manitowoc County, Wisconsin. In Mishicott township, made up of Wisconsin Synod Germans, the vote in 1880 was 87% Democratic; but in Manitowoc township, consisting of a mixed group of Wisconsin Synod and German Catholics, the Lutherans in reaction voted Republican *en masse*, making the total Democratic vote only 33%.

The German Sectarians, evangelical and pietistic to the core, advocates of Prohibition and a holy Sabbath, voted largely Republican. The German Evangelicals voted heavily Republican, as did the United Brethren and the German Methodist Episcopals. On the other hand, the German Reformed Church, though pietistic, hated the more extreme German Evangelicals and voted mildly Democratic, although the vote fluctuated considerably over time. In general, the Sectarian groups — in the backlash effect — voted more strongly Republican if living near other, more liturgical, Germans, while they were willing to vote more evenly for the Democrats if there were no other German religious groups in the vicinity.

The Scandinavians, whether recent immigrants or not, voted very strongly anti-Democratic.[19] This included the Norwegian Lutherans, whose votes for the Democratic Party varied from 0 to 38%, and most places fluctuated only from 0 to 8%. Why was this true even of the Norwegian Synod, which tended to be liturgical? The reasons were rooted in recent Norwegian history. The Norwegian Lutheran Church was a compulsory, State Church — one that was highly formalized and liturgical. By the turn of the 19th century, a pietistic reaction took place in Norway, led by Hans Nielsen Hauge, which was revivalist and evangelical. The Haugeans, however, formed a movement *within* the state Lutheran Church, and never broke off from the official church. And since, the Norwegian Church had a very low ratio of clergy to population, there grew up a great many lay services in the country, headed by Haugean laymen. So influential were the Haugeans that a less pietistic but highly influential movement, the Johnsonian Awakening

---

[19]The percentage of Democratic or anti-Democratic is a better gauge than the percentage of Republican, since such third parties as the Prohibitionists were ultra-pietist, and thereby should be added to the Republicans to constitute the anti-Democratic vote.

headed by Gisle Johnson, developed within the State Church in the 1840s and 1850s. The pietistic Johnsonian pastors were willing to work with the more extremely pietistic Haugean laymen to reform the Church. The result was a thoroughgoing pietizing, or evangelizing, of the Norwegian Synod.

Hence, while in the United States, the Haugeans headed by Elling Eielsen, broke off from the Norwegian Synod to form their own sect, both wings of Norwegian Lutherans were heavily pietistic and hence strongly anti-Democratic. But whereas, the Norwegian Synod Lutherans ranged between 0 and 38% Democratic, the more extreme Haugeans tended to vote about 5% Democratic. Both wings were strongly anti-alcohol and in favor of stern anti-Sabbath-breaking laws.

The Swedish Lutherans, for their part, were even more Republican than the Norwegians, ranging from 0 to 28% Democratic. The Swedes, pastors as well as laymen, had about all been pietistic dissenters within the established liturgical church of Sweden. It is clear from the Norwegian and the Swedish examples that the Democratic vs. Republican breakdown was *not* really "native" vs. "immigrant." For, in contrast to Catholic immigrants, the pietistic Scandinavian immigrants took their place very promptly with the Republican Party. Even though, the Norwegian Synod operated their own parochial schools, more important to them were the pietistic issues of the drinking of liquor and the "desecration" of the Sabbath.

The British-Americans, English, Cornish, or Welsh were pietist and were also heavily Republican and anti-Democratic. Within the Gaelic British community, the ardently pietistic Welsh Methodists were more strongly anti-Democrat than the Cornish Methodists. Thus, in Iowa County, Wisconsin, two townships made up mainly of Cornish Methodists, Dodgeville and Mineral Point, voted 34% and 44% Democratic respectively in 1880, whereas Linden and Mifflin townships, both largely Welsh Methodists, voted 25% and 24% Democratic. And, in Columbia County, Wisconsin, Hazel Green township, which was mainly Cornish Methodist, voted 47% Democratic, while nearby Courtland township, being Welsh Methodist, voted only 18% Democratic. In Michigan, on the other hand, the Cornish voted about 20% less Democratic than they did in Wisconsin, for in the former state there were constant battles between the Cornish and the Irish Catholics, who were heavily Democratic; again the backlash effect was at work.

A fascinating example of a meaningful religious breakdown of even a township vote was Wilkesville township, in Vinton County, Ohio. Wilkesville township, in 1880, voted 51% Democratic. But this moderate figure conceals a dramatic split between two precincts within the township, a split that took place even though both precincts were very poor farming areas. And yet, the eastern precinct voted 21% Democratic, while the western precinct voted 72%. The difference was that the eastern precinct was English and Welsh Methodist, while the western precinct was Irish Catholic.

As for the Irish, the Catholics, both urban and rural, were very strongly Democratic, while the Protestants, being pietist, were equally strongly Republican. Among the Canadians, the Protestant English Canadians were heavily Republican, while the French Catholics were equally strongly Democratic. We can see the ethnic religious factor at work, again, within the same occupational group. Baraga township in Baraga County, Michigan, and Saulte Ste. Marie township, in Chippewa County, both lumbering areas, which were French Canadian, voted heavily Democratic (78% and 67% in 1876, respectively). Also in Chippewa, on the other hand, Pickford, the English Canadian lumbering township, voted strongly Republican in 1888 (only 36% Democratic), and Hiawatha township, in Schoolcraft County, also English Canadian and lumbering, voted only 22% Democratic in 1876.

Among the Dutch, as we would now expect, the Catholics were strongly Democratic, racking up 94% of the vote in some precincts in 1876, while the Reformed were strongly anti-Democratic, voting as low as 19%. The Dutch Reformed Church of Michigan was less Calvinistic than one might expect. For in the 1830s in Holland, a pietistic "New Light" secession occurred in the Reformed Church, led by Gijsbertus Voetius. Voetius stressed pietism and puritanical conduct and opposed a formal orthodox creed. A group of Voetius followers emigrated from Holland to western Michigan in 1846, led by Albertus Christiaan Van Raalte. By the 1850s, however, a group of rather more traditional Calvinists broke off from the Van Raaltean Dutch Reformed Church and formed the "Christian" or "True" Reformed Church. As we might expect, while both groups of Dutch Reformed in Michigan were anti-Democratic, the Van Raalte faction was far more so. Thus, in Ottawa County, a Dutch Protestant stronghold, the Dutch Reformed townships of Georgetown and Zeeland voted 38% and 33% Democratic in 1876. But Blendon and Oliver townships, in the same county, which contained more Dutch Christian Reformed members, voted 46% Democratic in the same year.

The "natives" — defined as the second generation of native born who generally had emigrated from New England or the Middle Atlantic states, tended to vote Republican, but the proportions varied greatly — not by economic status or by state of origin, but by the degree of pietism. The

great exception is migrants from the South, who tended to keep supporting their sectional loyalty and vote Democratic. Here the Southern Presbyterians tended to be less strongly Democratic — and hence less tied to
past struggles — than the Southern Baptists or the Disciples of Christ.
Among these "Old Stock" religious sects, highly pietistic New York Methodists, the Congregationalists, and the Free Will Baptists tended to be
very strongly Republican, while the less pietistic and more rationalistic
Presbyterian was strongly Republican but not nearly as heavily. The lesser
degree of support for Republicans among Presbyterians reflected a split
between the "Old School" and "United" Presbyterians, who were largely
liturgical, and the "New School" pietists. The two wings had formally
reunited in 1869, but the fundamental differences remained. For their
part, the New York Baptists were about evenly split — again reflecting
the fragmentation of Baptist sects between varying degrees of pietist or
liturgical. Thus, the small group of Free Will Baptists were ultra-pietist;
as can be seen in the table below. On the other hand, the Primitive Baptists were ultra-Calvinists, and therefore liturgical. The far larger group of
Regular Baptists were themselves fragmented: most local churches being
pietist and others (such as the Landmarkeans) being liturgical. The pietistic Quakers were strongly Republican but they, too, were divided. The
Quakers from Pennsylvania, in Penn township, Cass County, Michigan,
voted 41% Democratic in 1876 while the Quakers, who had moved from
Pennsylvania to North Carolina, got fiercely involved in the fight against
slavery, and then moved West, voted only 17% Democratic in Calvin
township of the same county.

Within the Catholic groups, all were Democratic, but some were
more overwhelmingly so than others. The Poles and Irish tended to be
most overwhelmingly Democratic, followed slightly behind by the Germans, Dutch, and Bohemians, and then by the French Acadians and "Old
French" Catholics of French extraction. The non-Catholic Bohemians, in
contrast, tended to vote Republican.

Paul Kleppner presents a ranked tabulation of the average Democratic
voting percentages of the religious groups in an illuminating way to summarize the above conclusions. He divides them into "natives," second-
generation and older stock native Americans, and "immigrants," including actual immigrants and first-generation born in the United States. The
table is as follows:

PROPORTION VOTING DEMOCRATIC[20]

"IMMIGRANT" RELIGIOUS GROUPS		"NATIVE" RELIGIOUS GROUPS	
Irish Catholics	95%	Disciples of Christ	60%
Polish Catholics	95%	Southern Baptists	60%
German Catholics	85%	Southern Presbyterians	55%
Dutch Catholics	85%	New York Baptists	45%
Bohemian Catholics	80%	Presbyterians	30%
French Canadians	75%	Quakers	15%
Old French	70%	Congregationalists	10%
German Lutherans	55%	New York Methodists	10%
German Reformed	55%	Free Will Baptists	5%
Danish Lutherans	45%		
Dutch Christian Reformed	45%		
German Sectarians	35%		
Dutch Reformed	30%		
Norwegian Lutherans	30%		
Cornish Methodists	25%		
English Canadians	15%		
Swedish Lutherans	10%		
Irish Protestants	5%		
Welsh Methodists	5%		
Norwegian Haugeans	5%		

With the ethnoreligious demographics of the Midwest broken down, we can now begin to analyze the crucial political issues that consumed the region in the late 1880s and early 1890s, which brings us one step closer towards understanding the election of 1896.

---

[20]Adapted from ibid., p. 70.

4. REFORM AND THE DRIVE FOR PROHIBITION[21]

We have pointed out that, in the early 1850s, the pietists had managed to outlaw alcohol in 12 states. The leading Midwestern states — Illinois, Ohio, Michigan, Iowa, and Indiana — were among those who joined the drive, and the Minnesota Territory also outlawed liquor. In the resurgent drive for prohibition after the Civil War, the prohibitionists attempted to pass constitutional amendments outlawing liquor in all the Midwestern states in the early 1880s. Added to this drive was a move for local option laws for prohibiting the saloon in numerous counties, cities, and townships. As in most of the United States, Prohibition was the most vital issue in the Middle West during the 1880s.

The Catholics, as we have indicated, were overwhelmingly opposed to Prohibition. There emerged within the Catholic Church, however, and among the Irish-American clergy, a quasi-pietistic movement akin to French Jansenism, which pervaded the French Church and had deeply influenced Irish seminarians studying in France since the 18th century. Led by Archbishop John Ireland of St. Paul, this pietistic movement stressed evangelistic missionary fervor as well as strict personal moral standards of behavior. Archbishop Ireland, while not in favor of total prohibition of alcohol, did take a quasi-prohibitionist stance: leading a Catholic temperance movement, condemning saloons, and urging local option prohibition as well as very high license fees to be imposed on saloons. Ireland, in fact, was a founder of the Anti-Saloon League, which was to take the lead in the drive for total prohibition. In his quasi-prohibitionist stance, Ireland was supported by other neo-Jansenist bishops: including James Cardinal Gibbons of Baltimore, Bishop John Spalding of Peoria, and Bishop John Keane of Dubuque. He also found many adherents in the Paulist order. The neo-Jansenists formed the Catholic Total Abstinence Union, held Catholic retreats that were organized to closely resemble pietistic Protestant revival meetings. With his beliefs, it is not surprising that Archbishop Ireland was less than wholly devoted to the Catholic parochial schools, and was himself an ardent member and advocate of the Republican Party.

---

[21][Editor's footnote] For more on prohibition and pietism, including up into World War I, see Chapter 13 below, pp. 400–07. For a general history of the prohibition movement in the United States, see Mark Thornton, "The Fall and Rise of Puritanical Policy in America," *Journal of Libertarian Studies* 12 (Spring 1996): 146–57.

The pietistic softness on prohibition of this small circle of clerics had little influence among the Irish Catholic masses, much less the Catholic voters of other ethnic groups. Indeed, both the Germans and the Poles resented what they considered to be Irish hegemony within the American Church. The Germans were bitter, also, about Archbishop Ireland and about what they considered to be a Jansenistic trend and an underemphasis on liturgy in the American Church. Ireland they denounced as a "Puritan" Republican who was bent on "Protestantizing" the Catholic Church.

The Protestant Episcopal Church was firmly anti-prohibitionist, particularly its Anglican, or high-church, wing which was dominant in the Middle West. The only prohibitionists among them were in the far less liturgical, low-church minority. The views of the Anglicans on Prohibition were well expressed by Bishop Charles C. Grafton of Fond du lac, Wisconsin. Puritanism, he declared, tries to lessen the temptation to intemperance

> by force, law, or prohibition. It is a judicial mode of dealing with a moral problem. The Church looks rather to the aid of moral restraint, and to the aid of grace. ... For great as is the evil of any fleshly sin, it often, by the shame it brings, leads to repentance ... while on the other hand the spiritual sins of pride, self-sufficiency ... are more deadly because unsuspected and more lasting ...[22]

Among the Presbyterians, the more doctrinally oriented Calvinists tended to be "wets," in favor of drinking in moderation. It should not be surprising that the high-church Episcopelians were mainly Democrats, while the low-church members tended to support the Republican Party. An example was the leading wet Presbyterian minister from New York City, the Rev. Howard Crosby. The leading Calvinist theologian in America, Charles Hodge of Princeton University, favored the use of more liturgy in the Presbyterian Church and was also bitterly opposed to Prohibition.

Two leading Presbyterian laymen, who faced each other twice for the presidency of the United States, reflected the differences within the Church in their attitudes toward religion and politics. The outstanding Calvinistic Presbyterian attorney from Buffalo, Grover Cleveland, was the son of a Calvinist clergymen, a leading Democrat, a wet, and a *bon vivant*;

---

[22]Jensen, *The Winning of the Midwest*, p. 78.

the prim pietistic Benjamin Harrison of Indiana was a dry and a leading Republican.

As for the German Lutherans, the conservative and liturgical Missouri Synod, a "wet" group in favor of moderate drinking, spoke for many Liturgicals when it denounced Prohibition as "directly adverse to the spirit, the method and the aim of Christian morals." For the prohibitionist, "instead of relying on God's spirit, ... puts his trust in fallible legislators ... the tricks and treacheries of politicians."[23]

The change in ethnoreligious demographic factors was crucial to the change in the prohibition question, and hence the overall question of the Midwest.

---

[23]From the *Lutheran Witness* (February 7, 1889). Cited in Jensen, *The Winning of the Midwest*, p. 83. [Editor's remarks] See ibid., pp. 69–83.

CHAPTER 5

The Democratic
Triumph of 1892

1. The Road to Democratic Triumph

1892 was the great year of resurgent Democratic triumph. It was the first time since the Civil War that the Democratic Party controlled the presidency as well as both Houses of Congress. The 3% difference in the popular vote (Democrats 46%, Republicans 43%, and minor parties 11%) was by far the largest gap in the totals since the Democratic presidential candidate Samuel Tilden swept the popular vote in 1876. In the Middle West, the Republicans had carried all six states (Ohio, Michigan, Wisconsin, Illinois, Indiana, and Iowa) in 1888; now the Democrats won three (Illinois, Indiana, and Wisconsin), and almost tied in Ohio.

The great shift in Democratic fortunes, however, had come two years earlier, in the Congressional elections of 1890. Before 1890, the House of Representatives was 51.1% Republican; after 1890, it was no less than 71% Democratic. The Democrats controlled nearly every large state. In the Middle West, the Democratic peak in the House came in 1890, with slippage taking place in the 1892 elections. Put another way, the Middle West in 1888 was a Republican stronghold: of the six states (Illinois, Indiana, Ohio, Iowa, Michigan, and Wisconsin), the Republicans had six governors and the majority of five Congressional delegations. Only Indiana was a doubtful state. Yet, by 1889–1890, a spectacular reversal had taken place: nearly all the governors and all the Congressional delegations were Democratic.

One partial explanation was the slight but steady decline in Republican fortunes, and improvement in Democratic status, throughout this period. This relative shift cannot be ascribed to shifts in the urban and rural electorate. It is true that the urban proportion of the electorate in the Middle West rose from 1870 to 1890, but the pattern of slight decline in Republican fortunes occurred similarly in both urban and rural areas. The key to the changing fortunes was, as we have indicated, ethno-religious. The main key, as we shall see below, was the liquor question, and the conflicting views on the issue held by pietists and by liturgicals.[1]

In Michigan, Ohio, and Wisconsin, for example, over the twenty year period there was a marked decline in the Baptist and Methodist proportion of the electorate and a marked rise in Catholics and Lutherans, and among the Lutherans it was the Germans who were growing the most rapidly. By 1890, the Catholics were the largest single religious group in the region. Part of the reason was a higher birth rate among Catholics, both Irish and German; more important was the heavy immigration during the 1870s and 1880s — an immigration in which the largest role was played by the Irish and German Catholics and Lutherans. This and other such Catholic immigration, such as the Poles and Bohemians, far outstripped the immigration of Scandinavian Lutherans.

At its inception in the 1850s, the Republican Party, centering on opposition to the expansion of slavery, was in that sense a moralistic party. It therefore attracted other crusading groups, including Prohibitionists, strict Sabbatarians, German anticlericals, and Know-Nothings who wished to curtail or eliminate foreign immigration.[2] In short, it was pietism in politics, and hence, outside of the South, the Republican Party attracted the Methodists, Presbyterians, Norwegian Lutherans and Dutch Reformers. On the other hand, the Democratic Party, as the traditional party of *laissez-faire*, attracted the immigrant Catholics and German Lutherans.

After the war, it seemed clear to knowledgeable politicians that the German Lutherans were the swing vote, since the other religious groups were firm in one party or the other. By their quixotic choice in 1872 of the New York Republican reformer and prohibitionist Horace Greeley for president — the epitome of the pietistic crusader — the Democrats totally

---

[1][Editor's footnote] Kleppner, *Cross of Culture*, pp. 130–36.

[2][Editor's footnote] The Know-Nothing, or the American Party, was an anti-immigration and anti-Catholic party in the 1850s.

alienated the German Lutherans and went down to a crushing defeat.[3] As a result, the Democratic resurgence was postponed for another four years.

Ohio and Wisconsin were conquered by the Republicans in 1872, but the party promptly threw away its winning momentum. For in both states, the Republicans quickly enacted prohibition statutes under the pressure of the Women's Prayer Crusade against alcohol. The reaction of the German Lutherans to this hated prohibition was intense, as the Republicans lost both states in the elections of the following year (in Wisconsin, the Republican vote fell from 55% to 45% the following year, while in Ohio the Republican poll fell from 53% to 48%).

The Republican politicos then began the process of separating themselves from the bulk of their constituency in order to woo the German Lutheran swing vote. The risk was that their militancy would be angered and fall away from the cause or shift to minor parties. The maneuver was to woo the German Lutherans by playing down Prohibition and Sunday blue laws, while stressing anti-Catholicism and opposition to subsidizing Catholic parochial schools with tax-supported funds. Thus, future president Rutherford B. Hayes won the Ohio gubernatorial race in 1875 by at one and the same time bitterly attacking the Catholic "menace" to the public schools and, although denouncing liquor, *also* coming out against government-mandated prohibition.[4] Similarly, Harrison Luddington, Republican nominee for governor of Wisconsin in 1875, stridently denounced the Catholics and public funds for parochial Catholic schools; at the same time, he scored heavily with the Lutherans for being the Mayor of Milwaukee who refused to enforce that city's prohibition law.

On the other hand, part of the steady Republican decline during these decades may be attributed to the steady alienation of the ultra-pietist Republicans by the leaders' moderation on prohibition and Sabbath laws. We have seen that the Republican decline in the 1870s and 1880s was

---

[3][Editor's footnote] Horace Greeley also was a supporter of the protectionist tariff, anathema to the traditional members of the Democracy, and so a group of the more classical liberal members, later called the Bourbon Democrats, nominated Charles O'Conor on the Straight-Out Democrat ticket for president in 1872, although he did not officially accept the nomination. See Rothbard, "Bureaucracy and the Civil Service in the United States," pp. 58–59.

[4][Editor's footnote] Hayes was from the pro-reformer group of Republicans described earlier and he was also ardently pro-hard money, which further helped him win over the Germans. His Democratic rival, Governor William Allen, supported soft money policies. See ibid., p. 62.

greater than the Democratic increase — the difference consisted of third-party defections from the Republican ranks, to such parties as the Greenbackers in the 1870s and later the Prohibitionists. Apart from the ex-Southerners, the Greenbackers — crusaders for inflationary paper money — in the Midwest were ex-Republicans; in any case, they were almost all pietists: Methodists, Baptists, and Norwegian and Swedish Lutherans. There was hardly a Catholic or a German Lutheran amongst them.[5]

During the 1880s, the Prohibitionist voters were almost all defecting Republicans, including the Scandinavian Lutherans but above all the Methodists, Native, Welsh and Cornish.

Despite these defections, the Republican leaders, seeing the rapid growth of German Lutherans among the electorate, increasingly committed themselves to the policy of moderation on prohibition and Sabbatarian legislation. In Ohio, the Republican Party was torn between the moderate policy of John Sherman and William McKinley, and the strident prohibitionism of Joseph Foraker. It became increasingly clear during the 1880s that Foraker succeeded in his races for governor only when he moderated his prohibitionism and confined his pietist appeals to denouncing the Catholics for undermining the public schools. In Detroit, too, the Republican businessmen formed the Michigan Club in 1884 and came to dominate Republican politics in the city. The Michigan Club turned sharply away from Old Stock pietism and turned toward appealing to the immigrant German Lutherans. As a result, in 1890, the Republicans nominated an urban wet for governor of Michigan after the Democrats, in a remarkable and ominous hint for the future, had nominated an Old Stock pietistic dry.

We come, then, to the question: why the great shift toward the Democrats in 1890? In Ohio and Wisconsin, the reason was a massive shift of German Lutherans from the Republicans to the Democrats so much so as to carry Wisconsin for Grover Cleveland. Michigan, which will be discussed more in depth below, was an unusual case; here the 1890 shift toward the Democrats took place among native Protestants in southern Michigan, while Catholics strengthened their support for the Democrats in the Upper Peninsula. The native Protestants were attracted by the unusual Democratic nomination for governor of a pietistic dry. Two years

---

[5][Editor's footnote] Kleppner argues that the fact that many pietist leaders actually attacked Greenbackism was implicit recognition that the philosophy had large appeal among the rank and file Yankee pietists. See Kleppner, *The Third Electoral System*, p. 293.

later, however, the Democrats returned to their traditional nominating pattern; the native pietists went back to the Republicans, while the former Democrats returned to their old party.[6]

Orthodox historians explain the massive rise in Democratic fortunes in 1890 to reaction against the high McKinley Tariff of that year. But, for one thing, the Ohio shift came the year before, in 1889, and it has not been explained why the German Lutherans should suddenly get so upset about the protective tariff. Neither can the rise of the Populist Party in 1892 be said to have affected this shift between the two major parties. Overall, the Populists attracted about as many Democrats as Republicans, and they attracted far more Prohibitionists than either of the major parties. The inflationary and strongly pro-statist Populists were basically a farmer party of native, British, Norwegian, and Swedish pietists. As a rural pietist party, it is no wonder that the bulk of its voters had been Prohibitionists.

To explain the great Democratic rise in 1890, we must examine the situation in various special states. Ohio, as we have seen, shifted strongly Democratic first, in 1889, largely because of the change in the German Lutheran vote. The explanation for this change is clear: an upsurge in prohibitionism.

Ohio had never gone prohibitionist, thanks to the voting strength of the Cincinnati Germans. The Republican drys had submitted a constitutional amendment to outlaw liquor in 1883, but the voters had defeated the proposal. Failing to get a whole loaf, the prohibitionists decided on half: strict and expensive licensing laws, particularly on saloons. In 1885, the Ohio legislature imposed a stiff tax on liquor, and it followed in 1888 by raising the tax and by prohibiting the sale of alcohol on Sunday. The Ohio officials sagely failed to enforce the law in German areas. As a result, in the following year, the Cincinnati Law and Order Association (known locally as the "Evangelical Stranglers") petitioned Governor Foraker to enforce the law prohibiting the sale of liquor on Sunday.

Foraker now harkened to his old prohibitionist faith. He accepted the petition, and he summarily removed the Cincinnati police board and appointed a new one to enforce the law. This action precipitated the "Saloon-Keepers' Rebellion." Saloon-keepers and liquor dealers organized a League for the Preservation of Citizen's Rights to combat the law. 300 German saloon-keepers resolved to stay open on Sundays in defiance of

---

6[Editor's footnote] Kleppner, *The Cross of Culture*, pp. 95–143.

the law. Not only in Cincinnati, but throughout the state, Law and Order Associations sprang up. They also supported Governor Foraker's request for a constitutional amendment to allow the state to control election boards in cities and thereby to eliminate "corruption" — that is, victories by urban machine Democrats.

In the fall elections in Ohio in 1889, the Democrats were silent on the liquor laws for fear of alienating their Southern Baptist and Disciples of Christ supporters. They did call, however, for Home Rule for the Ohio cities, which would have meant non-enforcement of the law in German areas. The League for the Preservation of Citizen's Rights called for the repudiation of Governor Foraker, who was seeking a third term. All this was enough to induce a massive swing of German Lutherans into the Democratic camp, and Democratic Representative James Campbell won the election for governor.

In the presidential election of 1892, in which the Democrats almost tied the Republicans, the Democrats were able to keep some of the German Lutherans who had defected three years earlier. The remainder of the gain over 1888 came from a defection of many Republican pietists to the Prohibitionist ranks, a defection spurred by the current dominance of the moderate McKinley faction in the Republican Party of Ohio. Seeing the handwriting on the wall, for example, the McKinley group had dropped the idea of enforcing the Sunday closing law.

It is instructive to see how the Democrats, led in the press by the *Cincinnati Enquirer*, were able to argue for the libertarian Democratic positions in the presidential race in 1892 by linking them up to the struggle over prohibition three years earlier. Thus, the major national issues were the Democratic attack on the protective McKinley Tariff, and on the Republican Force Bill, a final attempt to bring back Reconstruction and impose Federal supervision of Congressional elections in the South. On the tariff, the Democrats linked the governmental paternalism of the tariff to the paternalism of prohibition. On the Force Bill, the Democrats could link it with prohibition by denouncing in both cases the Republican assault on home rule and local government, by attempting in both cases to centralize power in the hands of "Republican fanatics," and to suppress individual liberty. In both cases, the issue was liberty against Puritan meddling and paternalism.

For their part, the Republicans, while countering with their habitual stance as the "party of morality," raised a more moderate note by attacking the defectors to the Prohibition Party and other minor parties as "cranks" and "meddling prohibitionists." It was in this unwonted tone of attack upon moral crusading that the Republicans anticipated their momentous shift of policy four years later.

Even the seemingly well entrenched Representative William McKinley had been narrowly beaten in the Democratic landslide by German defectors. Rapidly moderating his stand on prohibition, McKinley was able to buck the Democratic tide by defeating Governor Campbell in 1891, sweeping in a Republican legislature as well. Not only was McKinley the long-time leader of the moderates on pietistic issues, but he was also shrewd enough to reverse his previous pro-inflation and pro-silver stand — in short, to adopt the sort of pro "sound money" and gold standard position previously associated with the Democratic Party. This was particularly effective against Governor Campbell, who had come out for free silver. As a result, Ohio was almost the only major state where the Republicans did well in 1891.

1889 was also an ominous year for the Republicans in Indiana. In Indianapolis, in the fall of that year, a group of wealthy Republicans and pietistic ministers organized the High-License League of Indianapolis, dedicated to raising the annual license fee for saloons. In response, the Republican administration raised the fee from $100 to $250. As a result, the Democrats swept Indianapolis in a triumphant coalition including businessmen opposed high taxes, classical liberals, and anti-prohibitionist Germans.[7]

In Wisconsin too, the Democrats swept the state in 1890, due largely to a massive shift of German Lutherans from the Republican ranks. Two years later, the Democrats retained enough of these defectors to enable them to carry Wisconsin for the presidency.

Wisconsin, with the exception of two years, had been controlled by the Republicans ever since the Civil War. The exception was 1872–73, when a stiff saloon licensing law, put through by the Republicans, shifted enough Germans out of the Republican ranks to carry the state for the Democrats. The Republicans, under the shrewd leadership of "Boss" Elisha Keyes and Philetus Sawyer, then refused to enforce the licensing laws and thereby were swept back into power.

---

[7][Editor's footnote] Ibid., pp. 144–47, 154–55; Jensen, *The Winning of the Midwest*, pp. 115–18, 154–57.

The critical issue in Wisconsin, however, turned out to be not prohibition but another pietist-liturgical conflict: the status of parochial schools. After the Republicans had absorbed the lesson in moderation for many years, the new Republican governor in 1889, William Dempster Hoard, recommended the enforcement of a dead letter compulsory education law requiring the language of all schools, public or private, to be in English.

In response, the Wisconsin legislature, in the spring of 1889, passed the notorious Bennett Law, which (1) imposed compulsory attendance for children in school, and (2) decreed that the language of such a school, whether public or private, could only be in English. This meant, in the concrete, that any German-language schools would henceforth be illegal. The Bennett Law hit hard not only at the German Catholic parochial schools, but also at the German-language parochial schools operated by the Lutheran churches. The Wisconsin Synod, which ran 164 parochial schools in the state, one-third of which used only English, denounced the law as "oppressive and tyrannical" and attacked its encroachment on "parental rights and family life." The Missouri Synod, which ran 136 German-language parochial schools, attacked the law for violating the "natural rights of parents" and their liberty of conscience.

At the end of December, the German Lutherans set up a state committee to combat the Bennett Law. In February, 19 Lutheran congregations in Milwaukee made repeal of the Bennett Law the crucial political issue. The three Catholic bishops of Wisconsin, all Germans, also attacked the law as interfering "with the rights of the Church and of the parent." The German-language press linked the law to nativism and prohibitionism, and the Lutherans and Catholics were angered still further by the fact that some of the hated German anticlerical liberals — along with the German pietist groups — favored the despotic law.

As a consequence, in the Milwaukee municipal election of 1890, an election that took place before the passage of the protectionist McKinley Tariff, the Democrats overthrew the Republican mayor. The cause of this landslide in the first real Democratic victory in Milwaukee in fifteen years was a massive defection to the Democrats in the German Lutheran wards, aided by a further strengthening of Democratic support in German Catholic areas. In consequence, the Republican vote in Milwaukee, which had been 47% in 1888, now fell drastically to 30%. The Democratic nominee, the affable Yankee humorist George Peck, had denounced the Bennett Law in no uncertain terms as unjust, and infringing on the natural liberty of conscience and the natural right of parental control.

In May, a group of leading Wisconsin Lutherans called a state-wide anti-Bennett Law convention for June. The convention was addressed by George Peck, the new Democratic mayor of Milwaukee. Scores of Anti-Bennett Law Clubs burgeoned throughout Wisconsin. The Missouri Synod and allied Lutherans organized systematically in every parish against the law. The German Catholics were equally bitter; Archbishop Katzen of Green Bay declared that "as Bishop of this Diocese [I] should consider anyone who did not vote for repeal of the [Bennett] law a traitor to the Catholic Church."[8]

In August, the Democratic state platform denounced the Bennett Law, and intelligently linked it to other examples of Republican paternalism, state and federal: to the sumptuary laws, high spending, the protective tariff, the Force Bill, and centralization of power. The Democrats were also aided in public opinion by the fact that the Prohibitionist Party, thoroughly hated by all German Catholics and Lutherans, endorsed the Bennett Law in its 1890 platform.

In the Republican Party, two conflicting groups appeared. The dominant faction, headed by Governor William Dempster Hoard, ardently favored the Bennett Law. The Hoard faction, which included Representatives Nils Haugen and Robert M. La Follette, demanded a part declaration in support of the law, in the name of adherence to "principle." The Hoard faction had its way at the state convention and won the re-nomination of Governor Hoard. The Hoard group were responding to local pietist pressures, to anti-Catholicism, and to a drive by the Wisconsin Dairymen's Association, of which Hoard was a member, to teach more English to the state's farmers. Haugen, a Norwegian immigrant, represented a highly pietistic region in the west and northwest of the state, consisting mainly of Norwegians and Swedes. La Follette also came from a heavily pietistic area.

The minority moderates, headed by State Chairman Henry C. Payne and U.S. Senator John C. Spooner, tried in vain to dump Governor Hoard and to call openly for repeal of the Bennett Law. They were responding to the massive defection underway from Republican ranks by the German Lutherans. Governor Hoard, an intensely pietistic newspaper owner and an amateur in politics, did not ease matters by bitterly denouncing German parents and pastors and endorsing the Bennett Law to the hilt.

---

[8]Quoted in Jensen, *The Winning of the Midwest,* p. 132.

In the November, 1890 elections, the German Lutherans reacted by shifting *en masse* to the Democratic camp; the Republicans were crushed by what was called at the time the "Lutheran Landslide." Even the faithfully Republican and slightly liturgical Norwegian Synod Lutherans deserted the Republican camp, not by voting for the hated Democrats but by staying away from the polls. The Norwegian Synod had established Norwegian-language parochial schools, and even the pietistic Norwegians and Swedes — especially the recent immigrants — were embittered by the attack on their home tongues.

As a result, Governor Hoard was smashed by the Democrat George Peck. To the Hoard campaign slogan, "The Little Schoolhouse, STAND BY IT!" the Democrats had countered, "Peck and ALL the Schools!" The Bennett Law was promptly repealed, with half of the Republican legislators joining the Democrats in the vote. By 1892, while many German Lutherans returned to the Republican ranks, enough stayed Democratic to carry the state for Cleveland.[9]

The Bennett Law was modelled after the Edwards Law passed in Illinois in 1889, and pushed through by the State Superintendent of public instruction, Richard Edwards. The reaction in Illinois was very similar. The Germans, even including the anticlerical liberals, rallied to defend the right of instruction in the German language. The Republican Party came out strongly for the public schools, as well as for prohibition, and they re-nominated Edwards for superintendent. The Democrats, in contrast, called for repeal of the Edwards law, as violating the natural rights of parents. With the Edwards law as well as prohibition and Sunday closing laws as the crucial issues in Illinois, the Democrats were able to win the state, to capture Cook County, and to recapture the city of Chicago. The hated Edwards was defeated handily by the Democratic candidate Henry Raab.

In 1892, the Democratic momentum continued. Grover Cleveland was the first Democrat since the Civil War to carry the state of Illinois, sweeping Cook County by 33,000 votes and carrying in the Democratic candidate for governor.[10]

In Michigan, the voting pattern in 1890 was unusual. In the Upper Peninsula, the Democrats gained strength among Catholics and lost votes among Protestants. The reason was that, culturally, the Upper Peninsula

---

[9][Editor's footnote] Ibid., pp. 122–48.

[10][Editor's footnote] Ibid., pp. 118–19, 134–35, 148, 161.

of Michigan was really an extension of northeastern Wisconsin, and so the educational agitation for and against the Bennett Law deeply affected opinion there. In particular, French Canadian Catholics strengthened their devotion to the Democrats, while English Canadian Protestants became even more Republican. The conflict over the Bennett Law in Wisconsin had polarized the Upper Peninsula even more than before.

The political situation in southern Michigan was particularly odd. The Republican moderates, coming to dominate politics in the state, as we have seen, decided to reject a typical pietist farmer for governor and instead nominated an urban wet, James M. Turner, mayor of Lansing. In response, the Michigan Democracy nominated for governor Edwin B. Winans, a prohibitionist Old Stock farmer. The result was that in southern Michigan many Catholics defected to the Republicans, while many more angry Republican pietists failed to vote or supported the Prohibitionist Party. The result was a large defection from Republican ranks and a Democratic victory in the state.

Two years later, however, the parties reverted to type: the Democrats returned to their traditional nominating pattern, the defecting Catholics returned, and the large number of defecting pietists returned to Republican ranks. This meant that Michigan reverted, in 1892, to its pre-1890 status as a solid Republican state.[11]

Iowa was another state in which the Republicans were overturned by the prohibition issue. Iowa had always been totally controlled by the Republican Party. In 1855, the pietistic Whigs had passed a constitutional amendment prohibiting the manufacture and sale of alcohol. The Republicans, concentrating on slavery as the major issue, promptly exempted beer and wine from the ban, permitted local option, and didn't enforce the law in counties opposed to it.

After the Civil War, the Republicans began to succumb to intense pressure by the prohibitionists. The W.C.T.U., the Sons of Temperance, and the Order of Good Templars spread the dry gospel, and the Prohibitionist Party was formed, with the Methodists leading the pietistic sects in the new crusade. In Iowa, the dry political pressure was led by the Iowa State Temperance Alliance.

Throughout the late 1860s and early 1870s, the drys were able to pass ever more stringent licensing and local option laws. At the Republican

---

[11][Editor's footnote] Kleppner, *The Cross of Culture*, pp. 172–77.

convention of 1875, a coalition of dry and inflationist pietists almost gained the gubernatorial nomination for their leader, General James B. Weaver, later to be a Populist presidential candidate. Four years later, the drys finally captured the Republican Party in Iowa, which voted to push for an amendment to the state constitution which would join Maine and Kansas as the only totally prohibitionist states in the Union. The Prohibitionist Party in the state collapsed, for its members hastened to join the Republicans.

The climax came in June 1882, when the Iowa public voted on a prohibition amendment after it was twice recommended by a Republican dominated legislature. The Temperance Alliance mobilized men and women in every part of the state, calling for prohibition in the name of Christian morality and American civilization.

The Democrats denounced the prohibitionists as "puritanical fanatics" trying to impose sumptuary laws and aggressing the liberty of the individual. The Democrats colorfully denounced the Republicans as "the tool of fanatical preachers," and as heading a "Holy Alliance of ... abolitionists, Whigs, Know-Nothings, Sunday and Cold Water Fanatics."[12]

But the opposition was in vain. The prohibition amendment passed by 55% to 45%, by a margin of 30,000 votes. One immediate and lasting result of the vote was the enraging of the German population of Iowa. Before 1882, the fourteen most-heavily German counties of Iowa habitually voted 55% Republican. After voting 39% for the dry referendum, the Republican percentage in these German counties fell permanently to the 36–44% range.

The same defection of German Catholics can be seen in the changed voting patterns of the heavily Catholic city of Dubuque. 50% Republican in 1881, Dubuque dropped to 28% Republican in the fall 1882 reelections (after voting 15% dry in the referendum) and picked up to only 38% in 1885. Particularly striking were two German wards: Ward 3, which fell from 51% Republican in 1881 to 23% the following year (after voting 10% dry), and Ward 5, which dropped from 63% to 22% Republican (after voting 6% dry).

The next winter, however, the Iowa Supreme Court invalidated the amendment on a procedural error. The Republicans, seeing the firestorm of opposition, did not dare to resubmit the amendment. To mollify the

---

12[Editor's footnote] Jensen, *The Winning of the Midwest,* p. 92.

pietists, the Republicans continued to widen the scope of prohibition by statute. In 1884, the Republicans rammed through one of the stiffest prohibition laws in the country. In towns and villages where sentiment was dry, saloons were forced to close. But in the larger towns and cities, the law was openly flouted.

At first, the laws were poorly enforced in wet areas. But in 1887 and 1888, Governor William Larrabee decided to enforce the law to the hilt and more restrictive laws were passed. Informers were given bonuses for revealing the existence of illicit liquor. The officials conducted raids on people suspected of harboring illegal alcohol.

The furor over prohibition reached a peak in Iowa during 1889. A massive flouting of the prohibition laws had polarized sentiment in the state between repeal of prohibition and inflicting ever harsher punishments in order to enforce the law. At the Republican state convention, control was seized from the professionals by the eager ultra-pietist amateurs, who had packed county conventions with radical prohibitionists. Joseph Hutchinson, an amateur politician and wholesale grocer, was nominated for governor; he delivered a paean to prohibition, calling it a "struggle for morality, for the reduction of corruption ... for the true elevation of the human race."[13] Hutchinson made it clear that the fundamental choice before the voter was between modern civilization on the one hand, and that "cursed barracuda," the saloon, on the other.

The prohibitionists and pietists enthusiastically backed Hutchinson, particularly the W.C.T.U., the Good Templars, and the Methodist Church, which demanded the unconditional surrender of liquor, as well as the repudiation of such halfway measures as licensing and local option. The Methodists also called for the outlawing of all desecration of the Sabbath, including ball games, the publishing of newspapers, and railroad service.

For their part, the Democrats shrewdly selected for governor Horace Boies, a former Republican, a personal teetotaler, and even a member of the Good Templars, but who staunchly opposed prohibition, centralized power, and paternalistic government. Boies, however, did favor local option and high license fees for saloons.

Horace Boies became the first Democrat ever to become governor of Iowa since the Civil War, obtaining 50% of the vote to Hutchinson's 48%.

---

[13][Editor's footnote] Ibid., p. 105.

The following year, the Democrats gained the majority of the Iowa Congressional delegation.

Analyzing the composition of the drop in the Republican vote, from 52% in 1888 to 48% the following year, it becomes clear that the major transformation came in the cities. In 1888, out of nine cities in Iowa with 14,000 or more population, the Democrats carried four, with an overall total of 52% of the urban vote. But the following year, Horace Boies swept all nine, with a massive 64% of the vote.

Breaking down the vote by religion, while Old Stock towns and counties, Norwegian, Swedish, and Bohemian townships slightly lowered the proportion of the Republican vote; the biggest Republican losses were in the nine German urban wards, the vote falling from 28% to 15%.

The drys also exercised control over the 1891 Republican convention, calling for total prohibition, and shouting down the possibility of local option. The Democratic slate, however, continuing to attack prohibition, swept to victory in a remarkably high voter turnout; and Governor Boies won reelection, handing the Republicans their worst defeat in the history of Iowa.

The Republicans had learned their lesson. Two years later, in the 1893 convention, the Republican pros were able to take back their party from the enthusiastic amateur drys. The successful comeback was headed by former Senator James Harlan, the founder and Grand Old Man of the Iowa Republican Party, and himself a devout Methodist and temperance man. The professional forces managed to carry repeal of the 12-year Republican commitment to total prohibition and to bury the compulsory education issue as well. Instead, local option and high license fees for liquor were installed in the platform. To win back the German voters, staunch opponents of cheap money and inflation, the Iowa Republicans even abandoned their cheap money plank and adopted an anti-inflation stance. Armed with their new-found moderation, the Republicans were able to recapture the governorship that year on behalf of the moderate Frank Jackson.[14]

---

[14][Editor's footnote] Ibid., pp. 91–115, 200–03, 215–16.

2. The Republicans Regroup

A. *The Retreat from Prohibition*

As the Republicans slipped into becoming the minority party in state after state in the early 1890s, it became increasingly clear to their political leaders that something drastic would have to be done; notably, radically pietist measures would have to be soft-pedalled so as not to aggravate the German Lutherans and other liturgical voters. We have seen how in response to Democratic victories, the Republicans in Ohio and Iowa moved quickly to soften or jettison their prohibitionist platform; in both states, furthermore, the Republicans began to shift from their previous inflationist and pro-silver stance toward the advocacy of the gold standard and sound money. In Wisconsin, they were willing to backtrack on the Bennett Law and its assault on German parochial schooling.

In this move toward jettisoning their pietist doctrines, the lead was taken by the Ohio Republican leadership of Governor William McKinley, and his mentor and party boss, chairman of the Ohio and later the national Republican Party, the industrialist Marcus Alonzo Hanna. In his term as governor, from 1892 to 1896, McKinley succeeded in suppressing the pietists in the Ohio party. And then, when Joseph Foraker returned to control the party that year, the prohibitionists found to their chagrin that their old champion had learned his lesson too, and that Foraker was now a determined wet.

In Wisconsin, former Governor Hoard tried a comeback by promoting such ardent pietists and prohibitionists as Representative Nils Haugen and then Representative Robert La Follette as governor. The Republican professional, however, finally beat out Haugen and La Follette in the 1890s, and eliminated the old Republican lust for moral crusading. In Michigan, the leading Republican pietist was the mayor of Detroit, Hazen Pingree. During the 1890s, the state Republican machinery, led by Senator James McMillan, maneuvered hard to limit or eliminate Pingree's influence, finally succeeding in saving the GOP in Michigan from reacquiring a strongly pietist image. In Illinois and Indiana, in the meantime, the Republican moderates were able to defeat the pietists with comparative ease.

The Republicans were thus retreating *en masse* from prohibitionist and pietist concerns during the early 1890s. No major Republican newspaper endorsed total prohibition; the furthest they would go was regulation, high license fees, and local option. The Republican politicians increasingly avoided the vexed issue altogether, calling it a purely local matter. The veteran Ohio Republican Senator John Sherman went so far as to assert that matters of religion, morality, and temperance should not be political issues. A far cry from the old "party of great moral ideas." Another disillusioning situation for the prohibitionists is that the great bulk of Republican politicians themselves imbibed alcohol. How then could they be trusted?

The tension between the Republicans and their pietist constituents was also growing to the bursting point because, while the Republicans were becoming more moderate, the prohibitionists were becoming increasingly fanatical. Originally, the prohibitionists had habitually referred to themselves as temperate, as men of temperance. By the 1880s and 1890s, however, this was no longer true: the prohibitionists now spoke of themselves as "radicals." It was no longer enough to attack hard liquor; denunciations of beer were now stepped up. The saloon came in for increasing vilification, violent raids were conducted on them, and Law and Order Legions in large cities acted to stamp out illegal sales of liquor. By 1885, there were 500 such local leagues throughout the country, with 60,000 members.

Not only that: the youth were becoming more pietistic and more militant prohibitionists than their elders. The pietist youth exuded a deep hatred for the saloons, expressed through Young People's Christian Societies and interdenominational Sunday school programs. The W.C.T.U., partly through its highly successful mandatory temperance hygiene classes in the public schools, were able to enlist 200,000 youngsters in their youth affiliate, the Loyal Temperance Legion.

The success in radicalizing middle-class pietist youth is shown by the fact that 2/3 of all college students in the Midwest were enrolled in pietist denominations, and that most of them joined the highly moralistic Young Men's Christian Association. The faculty and students at Iowa State University endorsed prohibition. Particularly remarkable was a presidential preference poll of undergraduates at the University of Chicago in 1892. The eventual winner, Democrat Grover Cleveland, obtained 52 votes, while incumbent Republican President Benjamin Harrison received 151 votes, and the Populist James B. Weaver obtained 3. But the astounding fact is that the winner of the poll was the Prohibitionist Party candidate, John Bidwell, who received 164 votes.

But what was an increasingly militant prohibitionist constituency going to do politically in the face of growing Republican reluctance and a declining Prohibitionist Party? The Prohibitionist Party foundered on the question of a single issue on alcohol *versus* a broad-range pietist, genuine third-party organization. A similar split led to the collapse of the anti-Catholic American Protective Association, which could not decide in 1896 whether to endorse McKinley for president or to establish a third political party of its own. The upshot was the gradual disappearance of the Prohibitionist movement as a group of enthusiastic amateurs and its replacement by an extremely effective and professional single-issue lobby, the Anti-Saloon League, founded in 1893. The Anti-Saloon League, willing to concentrate first on local option laws and to build up steadily from there, rewarded or punished politicians purely on the single issue of alcohol. Its tactic was to triumph in a quarter-century.[15]

B. Restricting Immigration[16]

The Republicans were fully aware that the secular demographic trend, fueled by the arrival of Catholic and other liturgical immigrants, was against them. During the 1880s, while British and Scandinavian immigration had reached new highs, they were surpassed by German and Irish immigration, the latter being the highest since the famous influx of the late 1840s and early 1850s. During the same decade, the "new immigration" from southern and eastern Europe, especially Catholics from Italy, began to make its mark.

Their defeat in the presidential election of 1892 intensified the hatred of Catholics and Catholic immigrants in the Republican Party. The predecessors of the Republicans, the Whigs, had been strongly nativist and anti-Catholic, and the short-lived Know-Nothings, from whose ranks many Republicans had emerged in the mid-1850s, flourished on an exclusively anti-immigrant and anti-Catholic program. Now the embittered Republicans turned to a policy of immigration restriction. If the Catholics could not constitutionally be deported, they could at least be prevented from tipping the balance further.

---

[15][Editor's footnote] Ibid., pp. 194–208.

[16][Editor's footnote] For more on pietism and immigration restriction, especially in relation to the public school movement, see Chapter 10 below, pp. 299–308. For a general history of compulsory public education in the United States, see Murray Rothbard, "Compulsory Education in the United States," in *Education, Free & Compulsory* (Auburn, AL: Mises Institute, 1999 [1971]).

The first break in the American tradition of free and unrestricted immigration came in the act of 1882, when the federal government assumed at least formal control over immigration (previously regulated by the states, principally New York).[17] The United States, instead of the several states, was to tax each entrant a modest fifty cents to accumulate an immigrant welfare fund, and ex-convicts or other people likely to become a public charge were to be denied admission.

In the late 1880s, working class activists, concerned with restricting the supply of incoming labor, obtained legislation in several states barring aliens from various types of employment. In particular, aliens were prohibited from employment on public works. The U.S. House of Representatives passed a bill in 1886 banning "nondeclarant" aliens (those who had not yet declared their intentions of becoming U.S. citizens) from employment on public works. When the Senate failed to pass the bill, Illinois, Wyoming, and Idaho proceeded to bar such aliens from state or municipal works projects.

More sweepingly, in 1885, the Knights of Labor and other working class groups persuaded the Congress to outlaw contract labor, the system under which a European immigrant was assured of a specific job in the U.S. before he arrived. The outlawing of contract labor, of course, tended to increase those immigrants likely to become a public charge and thereby added further to the restriction on immigration.[18]

In addition to workers attempting to restrict immigrant competition, the pietists and prohibitionists centered on the Catholic immigrants as their major foe. Thus, the Presbyterian Synod of 1887 declared:

> The ranks of the drinking men are constantly recruited
> by the influx of bibulous and intemperate foreigners. The
> great majority of these alien immigrants, now over a half
> million annually, are addicted to the case of strong drinks,
> as well as steeped in ignorance and vice.

And the Reverend T.W. Cuyler, president of the National Temperance Society, put it even more strongly in the summer of 1891: "How much

---

[17][Editor's footnote] Although the much more well-known Chinese Exclusion Act was also passed in 1882, it bore little relation to the immigration restrictions on Europeans, both ideologically and politically. See John Higham, *Strangers in the Land: Patterns of American Nativism, 1860–1925* (New Brunswick, NJ: Rutgers University Press, 1955), p. 167.

[18][Editor's footnote] Ibid., pp. 44–49.

longer [will] the Republic ... consent to have her soil a dumping ground for all Hungarian ruffians, Bohemian bruisers, and Italian cutthroats of every description?"[19]

Immigration restrictions were sought by the Independent Presbyterians, the National Temperance Convention in 1891, and the Prohibition Party in 1892. The late 1880s saw a blossoming of nativist and anti-Catholic organizations agitating to restrict immigration. The large Civil War veterans' organization, the Grand Army of the Republic, long associated with the Republican Party and now reaching its peak membership of 400,000, began to denounce immigrants who were allying themselves politically with "copperheads and ex-rebels," i.e., with Southerners in the Democratic Party.[20]

Patriotic secret societies, nativist and anti-Catholic, led by the newly burgeoning Junior Order of United American Mechanics, with 60,000 members in 1889 and 160,000 in the 1890s, began to flourish in the late 1880s. Other such fraternal orders, all founded in Pennsylvania, were the Order of United American Mechanics and the Patriotic Order Sons of America.

Also newly active was a group of secret anti-Catholic societies, including the United Order of Deputies, with fifteen thousand working-class members, who demanded that employers discharge all Catholics. By far the leading anti-Catholic organization was the American Protective Association, founded in Clinton, Iowa in 1887 by attorney Henry F. Bowers. A.P.A.

---

[19]Jensen, *The Winning of the Midwest*, pp. 187–89.

[20]Whereas President Cleveland vetoed Republican-passed veterans' pensions and aid to veterans' bills and refused to attend the G.A.R. convention in 1887, Benjamin Harrison favored veteran pensions. In 1882, nearly half of the Republican appointees in Washington were Union veterans, whereas Democratic appointees of the Senate were largely Confederate veterans. In the Iowa Legislature of 1893, 70% of the Republicans eligible to have served were Civil War veterans, whereas only 39% of the eligible Democrats were veterans. In 1888, a poll of disabled veterans at the Ohio Soldiers and Sailors Home voted 3:1 for Harrison over Cleveland. [Editor's remarks] Ibid., pp. 22–25.

In an unpublished manuscript, Rothbard wrote in depth on the origins of Civil War pensions and their relation to the rise of the future welfare state. Pensions to Union soldiers were strongly supported by the Republicans, and they became a favorite way to spend the Treasury's surplus to appeal to a new burgeoning interest group. During the Harrison administration the Dependent and Disability Pension Act was passed in 1890, sharply increasing veterans' payments and contributing to the Republican "Billion Dollar Congress." See Murray Rothbard, "Beginning the Welfare State: Civil War Veterans' Pensions" (n.d.).

members took secret oaths never to vote for a Catholic or to employ one if a Protestant were available.

The A.P.A. grew steadily across the upper Mississippi Valley, especially in large towns and cities where Catholics were prevalent. The A.P.A. helped the Republicans sweep the ordinarily Democratic city of Omaha in 1891, and the following year it elected a Congressman from Saginaw, Michigan. Acquiring 70,000 members by 1893, the A.P.A. suddenly burgeoned to a mammoth half a million members the following year, centering in the Midwest but also stretching eastward through the Great Lakes area.

The A.P.A. was almost exclusively Republican. It aided McKinley's reelection as Ohio governor in 1893, and in Michigan, Kentucky, and Nebraska, the organization was close to the Republican Party leadership.

Thus, the Republican Party had considerable incentive to push for immigration restriction in the late 1880s and early 1890s: both in response to the pietism of its constituents and in reaction to the growing demographic dominance of the immigrant-sustained Democratic Party. But there was also another powerful reason: the Republicans might moderate most of their formerly cherished pietism, but there was one overriding plank to which they were deeply committed: the protective tariff. The pro-tariff manufacturers decided that to gain the support of the working classes against the powerful Democratic assault on the tariff as a special privilege, the Republicans should offer the native workers a *quid pro quo*: protection of *their* foreign competitors, the immigrants. In that way, the manufacturers' privileges and cartels sustained by the tariff would be sweetened by cartelization of the labor force to restrict entry into the work force.[21] The idea of such a bargain in mutual special privilege was particularly pushed by James M. Swank, general manager of the American Iron

---

[21]Another example of joint business-worker restrictionism sponsored by the Republicans was the drive to outlaw the sale of the products of prison labor. Thus, New York State, in its Constitutional Convention of 1894, passed an amendment prohibiting the sale of products of prison labor. The amendment was supported by labor unions as well as by those businesses who were competing against the output of convict labor, in particular the manufacturers of brooms and brushes and other manufacturers whose labor was a large part of production costs. The Republican sponsor of the amendment at the Convention pointed out that it was simply a logical extension of the Republican Party's long-standing commitment to the protection of both the manufacturer and the laborer from "unfair" competition. The opponents correctly but vainly charged that the amendment was "class legislation," and that prisons could no longer be self-sustaining and would become a far greater burden on the taxpayer.

and Steel Association. It is no coincidence that the inefficient iron and steel industry had led the drive for a protective tariff from its earliest days, after the War of 1812, until the end of the century.

By the late 1880s, the Republicans stepped up their agitation for the restriction of immigration. Republican conventions in Pennsylvania and Ohio in 1887, as well as in California the following year, came out for restriction. Senator Justin Morrill, Republican of Vermont, a veteran protectionist and advocate of federal intervention in education, introduced a bill for immigration restriction in 1887. Three years later, Congress moved toward legislative action. Senator William E. Chandler, Republican of New Hampshire, became chairman of the Senate's first standing committee on immigration in 1890 and thereby assumed the lead of the restrictionist movement. The following year, Congress assumed sole jurisdiction over immigration and put teeth in existing restrictions on entry by compelling steamship companies to carry back all immigrants rejected by U.S. inspectors. This law had a chilling effect on the willingness of steamship companies to carry immigrants to the U.S. The act of 1891 also provided, for the first time, for deporting illegal aliens within one year of entry, or for deporting aliens who might become public charges "from causes existing prior to his landing." The act also added to the categories of the excluded polygamists and those with a "loathsome and dangerous" contagious disease. The ban on contract labor was also broadened by adding those immigrants encouraged to arrive by employer advertisements.

The restrictionists in Congress, led by Chandler's committee, attempted to take advantage of a cholera scare in the fall of 1892, to pass a moratorium on all immigration for an entire year. They were not successful in stampeding Congress, however.

Failing the suspension, the restrictionists, led by Chandler and by Representative Henry Cabot Lodge of Massachusetts, drove toward a literacy test for all immigrants. The restrictionists' hand was strengthened by the fall elections in 1894, which installed Republican majorities in both houses of Congress. At the same time, the Immigration Restriction League was founded in Boston by a half-dozen young Brahmins. The League spread a nationwide propaganda and Washington lobbying critical of the new immigration from southern and eastern Europe, which allegedly contained a host of illiterates and criminals.

In the winter of 1895, the Immigration Restriction League's bill was introduced and spearheaded by now-Senator Lodge and by Representative Walker McCall of Massachusetts. The bill provided for the exclusion of all men and women over the age of 14 who could not read and write. Lodge and McCall stressed racial arguments against the Italians and other southern Europeans. The literacy bill passed the House overwhelmingly during 1896, and the Senate in December. But President Cleveland, in one of his last acts in office, vetoed the bill, and the Senate failed to override.

In addition to restricting entry, the nativists could do something about the voting rights of immigrants already in the United States. Restriction-ists urged a lengthening of the waiting period for naturalization. More-over, eighteen southern and western states allowed aliens to vote on a sim-ple declaration of intent to become a citizen. The nativists began a trend back to the original American prohibition of alien suffrage, but by the end of the century 11 states still allowed aliens to vote.[22]

C. Pietism and Women's Suffrage[23]

Voting need not only be restricted; it could also be *expanded*, provided that pietists would hope to benefit more than proportionately. Specifically, women could be granted the vote, in the knowledge that immigrant Cath-olic women would not be likely to vote in as great proportions as native-born WASPs. As Professor Grimes concludes:

> I am ... arguing that the evidence indicates that to a large extent, at least in the West, the constituency granting woman suffrage was composed of those who also sup-ported prohibition and immigration restriction and felt woman suffrage would further their enactment.[24]

Like most reform movements, such as prohibition, the women's suf-frage movement was heavily pietist from the very beginning. The strongly pietist third parties, such as the Prohibition Party and the Greenback Party, supported women's suffrage throughout, and the Populists tended in that direction before their amalgamation into the Democracy in 1896. Later, the Progressive Party of 1912 was the first major national convention to

---

[22][Editor's footnote] Higham, *Strangers in the Land*, pp. 56–105.

[23][Editor's footnote] For more on the relationship between progressivism, pietism, and women's suffrage, see Chapters 10 and 11 below, pp. 309–14, 332–33, 340–41. For their involvement in World War I, see Chapter 13 below, pp. 408–13. For the published version of this section, see Chapter 10 below.

[24]Alan P. Grimes, *The Puritan Ethic and Woman Suffrage* (New York: Oxford University Press, 1967), p. xii.

permit women delegates and to select a woman elector. Of the two major parties, the Democrats paid no attention to the women suffrage question, while the Republicans made vague noises in a favorable direction. The suffragettes saw as their major enemies the party bosses of the Republican and especially the Democratic parties, and in particular the liquor interests, who, in the words of the philippic by Susan B. Anthony and Ida H. Harper, were "positively, unanimously, and unalterably opposed to woman suffrage."[25]

Perhaps one reason for this determined opposition was the great prominence in the suffragette movement of the Women's Christian Temperance Union, founded in 1874, upon the pledge: "I hereby solemnly promise, God helping me, to abstain from all distilled, fermented and malt liquors, including wine, beer and cider, and to employ all proper means to discourage the use of and traffic in the same." The W.C.T.U., led by Frances E. Willard, had, by 1900, established chapters in 10,000 towns and cities across the country and enjoyed a membership of 300,000. Of all women's organizations mentioned in Anthony and Harper's *History of Woman Suffrage*, the W.C.T.U. received the greatest amount of space. That they were also involved in curfew, anti-gambling, anti-smoking, and anti-sex laws — actions lauded by the woman suffrage movements — is clear from the following passage in Anthony and Harper:

> [The W.C.T.U.] has been a chief factor in State campaigns for statutory prohibition, constitutional amendment, reform laws in general and those for the protection of women and children in particular, and in securing anti-gambling and anti-cigarette laws. It has been instrumental in raising the "age of protection" for girls in many States, and in obtaining curfew laws in 400 towns and cities. ... The association protests against the legalization of all crimes, especially those of prostitution and liquor selling.[26]

Not only did Susan B. Anthony begin her career as a professional prohibitionist, but her two successors as president of the leading suffragette

[25]Susan B. Anthony and Ida H. Harper, *The History of Woman Suffrage* (Rochester: Susan B. Anthony, 1902), vol. 4, p. xiii; cited in Grimes, *The Puritan Ethic*, p. 84.

[26]Anthony and Harper, *History of Woman Suffrage*, pp. 1046–47; cited in Grimes, *Puritan Ethic*, p. 85.

organization, the National American Woman Suffrage Association, were also ardent prohibitionists. Her immediate successor, Mrs. Carrie Chapman Catt, also began as a prohibitionist, while the next president, Dr. Anna Howard Shaw, began her career as a lecturer for the W.C.T.U.[27]

The Women's Christian Temperance Union crystallized out of an anti-liquor "Women's Prayer Crusade" that began in Hillsboro, Ohio in 1874, and swept the nation. As Eleanor Flexner put it: "Bands of singing, praying women held meetings, not only in churches but on street corners, penetrating into the saloons themselves and closing them by the thousands."[28] When the effort fizzled, a permanent organization the W.C.T.U. was established in Cleveland to carry on the anti-liquor crusade on a systematic basis.

The W.C.T.U.'s leading spirit, Frances E. Willard, was protypically born of New England stock parents who had moved westward to study at Oberlin College, the nation's center of aggressive, evangelical pietism, and later to settle in Wisconsin. Miss Willard began as corresponding secretary of the W.C.T.U. and, in two years she unseated the previous president and led the organization to the espousal of woman suffrage. Guided by Miss Willard, the W.C.T.U. began its pro-suffrage activities by demanding that women vote in local option referenda on prohibition. As Miss Willard put it: the W.C.T.U. wanted women to vote on this issue because "majorities of women are against the liquor traffic ..."[29]

Opposition to liquor and to the saloon cut against immigrant and liturgical culture, which not only sanctioned drinking, but where the neighborhood saloon was the major social and political institution. The saloon was an all-male institution, and hence was on a collision course with woman suffrage as well as prohibition.

Similarly, whenever there was a voter's referendum on woman suffrage, the foreign-born, responding to immigrant culture and reacting against the feminist support of prohibition, voted consistently against woman suffrage. In Iowa, the Germans voted against such suffrage; in California, the Chinese were opposed; and in South Dakota, where a ref-

---

[27]See Aileen S. Kraditor, *The Ideas of the Woman Suffrage Movement, 1890–1920* (New York: Columbia University Press, 1965), pp. 11–13. Also see ibid., pp. 58–61.

[28]Eleanor Flexner, *Century of Struggle: The Woman's Rights Movement in the United States* (New York, Atheneum, 1970), p. 182.

[29]Ibid., p. 183.

erendum on woman suffrage was defeated in 1890 by the massive margin of 55,000 to 22,000, Susan B. Anthony and Ida Harper wrote bitterly that "there were 30,000 Russians, Poles, Scandinavians and other foreigners in the State, most of whom opposed woman suffrage."

Testifying for woman suffrage before the U.S. Senate Judiciary Committee in 1880, Susan B. Anthony expressed the nativism and racism of much of the feminist movement, in explaining the voter's defeat of woman suffrage in a Colorado referendum in 1877:

> In Colorado, ... 6,666 men voted "Yes." Now, I am going to describe the men who voted "Yes." They were native-born white men, temperance men, cultivated, broad, generous, just men, men who think. On the other hand, 16,007 voted "No." Now, I am going to describe that class of voters. In the southern part of that State there are Mexicans, who speak the Spanish language. ... The vast population of Colorado is made up of that class of people. I was sent out to speak in a voting precinct having 200 voters; 150 of those voters were Mexican greasers, 40 of them foreign-born citizens, and just 10 of them were born in this country ...[30]

The cities, where "sin," alcohol, immigrants, and Catholics abounded, were the centers of opposition to woman suffrage, while the WASP rural areas tended to favor it. The Oregon referendum of 1900, for example, lost largely because of opposition in the "slums" of Portland and Astoria. In 1896, the woman suffrage referendum in California was heavily supported by the bitterly anti-Catholic American Protective Association.[31] The amendment lost by 137,000 to 110,000 votes, and the Anthony and Harper volume expresses great disappointment about the heavy loss in Alameda County, "a most unpleasant surprise, as the voters were principally Republicans and

---

[30]Grimes, *The Puritan Ethic,* pp. 87–88.

[31]In Massachusetts, where women had had the vote in school board elections since 1879, large numbers of Protestant women turned out in 1888 to drive Catholics off the school board. In contrast, Catholic women scarcely voted, "thereby validating the nativist tendencies of suffragists who believed that extension of full suffrage to women would provide a barrier against further Catholic influence." Jane Jerome Camhi, "Women Against Women: American Antisuffragism 1880–1920" (unpublished doctoral dissertation in history, Tufts University, 1973), p. 198. Also see ibid., p. 104, and James J. Kenneally, "Catholicism and Woman Suffrage in Massachusetts," *Catholic Historical Review* (April, 1967): 253.

Populists, both of whom were pledged in the strongest possible manner in their county conventions to support the amendment..." As Grimes writes, "The implication here, and frequently throughout the various volumes of the *History*, was that the Republican Party should provide the natural home for the woman suffrage movement."[32]

The pietist/liturgical split on the woman suffrage question is seen in a report by a Colorado feminist explaining the defeat in the 1877 referendum: the Methodists (most strongly pietistic) were "for us," the less pietistic Presbyterians and Episcopalians "fairly so," and while the Roman Catholics "were not all against us," clearly they were expected to be.[33]

It is evident from their writings that much of the drive for woman suffrage came from middle- and upper-class WASP women who deeply resented the fact that their social inferiors, lower-class immigrants and "foreigners," were allowed to vote while they were not.[34] Thus, as Anthony and Harper put it:

> ... a real democracy has not as yet existed, but ... the dangerous experiment has been made of enfranchising the vast proportion of crime, intemperance, immorality and dishonesty, and barring absolutely from the suffrage the great proportion of temperance, morality, religion and conscientiousness; that, in other words, the worst elements have been put into the ballot box and the best elements kept out. This fatal mistake is even now beginning to dawn upon the minds of those who have cherished an ideal of the grandeur of a republic, and they dimly see that in woman lies the highest promise of its fulfillment. Those who fear the foreign vote will learn eventually that there are more American-born women in the United States than foreign-born men and women; and those who dread the ignorant vote will study the statistics and see

---

[32]Grimes, *The Puritan Ethic*, p. 90.

[33]Ibid., p. 92. Camhi states that, in the last two decades of the 19th century, "the more hierarchical the church organization and the more formal its ritual, the greater was its opposition to woman suffrage, while the democratically organized churches with little dogma tended to be more receptive." Camhi, "Women Against Women," p. 200.

[34]Where women were given the vote in Chicago, before the general adoption of woman suffrage, the highest percentage of women voters appeared in the middle- rather than the working-class wards. Ibid., p. 331.

that the percentage of illiteracy is much smaller among women than among men.[35]

Four western states adopted woman suffrage in the early and mid-1890s. Two, Wyoming and Utah, were simply repeating a practice as new states that they had adopted much earlier as territories: Wyoming in 1869 and Utah in 1870. Utah adopted woman suffrage as a conscious policy by the Mormons to weight political control in favor of their polygamous members, in contrast to the Gentiles, largely miners and settlers who were either single men or who had left their wives in the East. Idaho, which was dominated both by Populists and by Mormons in the southern part of the state, adopted woman suffrage in a referendum in 1896. Wyoming, the first territory to adopt woman suffrage, did so in an effort to increase the political power of its settled householders, in contrast to the transient, mobile, and often lawless single men who peopled that frontier region. The measure was also expected to attract more of the sober kind of migrants into Wyoming.

No sooner had Wyoming Territory adopted woman suffrage than it became evident that the change had benefited the Republicans, particularly since women had mobilized against Democratic attempts to repeal Wyoming's Sunday prohibition law. In 1871, both houses of the Wyoming legislature, led by its Democratic members, voted to repeal woman suffrage, but the bill was vetoed by the Republican territorial governor, John A. Campbell, who had been appointed by President Grant.

Another state adopting woman suffrage in the 1890s was Colorado, which passed it by a referendum in 1893. The reason was the dominance in Colorado politics of the pro-inflation and pietistic Populists, then at the peak of their popularity in that state. In the referendum, the Populist counties gave a majority of 6,800 on behalf of woman suffrage; while the Republican and Democratic counties voted a majority of 500 *against* the measure. Moreover, in the state legislature which submitted the woman suffrage amendment to the voters in 1893, the party breakdown of voting was as follows: Republicans, 19 for woman suffrage and 25 against; Democrats, 1 in favor and 8 against; Populists, 34 in favor and 4 against.

It may be thought paradoxical that a movement born and centered in the East should have had its first victories in the remote frontier states

---

[35]Anthony and Harper, *A History of Woman Suffrage*, vol. 4, p. xxvi; cited in Grimes, *The Puritan Ethic*, p. 94. See also ibid., p. 91.

of the Mountain West. But the paradox clears when we realize the pietist-WASP nature of the frontiersmen, many of them hailing originally from the birthplace of American pietism, New England. As the historian Frederick Jackson Turner, that celebrant of pietist frontier ideals, lyrically observed:

> In the arid West these pioneers [from New England] have halted and have turned to perceive an altered nation and changed social ideals. ... If we follow back the line of march of the Puritan farmer, we shall see how responsive he has always been to *isms*. ... He is the prophet of the "higher law" in Kansas before the Civil War. He is the Prohibitionist of Iowa and Wisconsin, crying out against German customs as an invasion of his traditional ideals. He is the Granger of Wisconsin, passing restrictive railroad legislation. He is the Abolitionist, the Anti-mason, the Millerite, the Woman Suffragist, the Spiritualist, the Mormon, of Western New York.[36]

---

[36]Cited in Grimes, *The Puritan Ethic*, pp. 97–98.

CHAPTER 6

1896:
The Collapse of the
Third Party System and of
Laissez-faire Politics

1. THE FIRST COLLAPSE: 1894

In the cataclysmic year 1896 the face of American politics was changed forever. With the capture of the Democratic Party by the inflationist, statist forces of William Jennings Bryan, the old Democracy of free trade, hard money, personal liberty, and minimal government was gone forever. As Grover Cleveland mournfully pronounced, "... the Democratic party as we knew it is dead."[1]

The orthodox historical view holds that the Bryanite conquest of the Democratic Party resulted from the Depression of 1893. In response to the depression, the masses, led by the farmers of the South and West and clamoring for increased government intervention and the greater purchasing power provided by cheap money, swept Bryan into the presidential nomination in

---

[1]See Allan Nevins, ed., *The Letters of Grover Cleveland* (Boston: Houghton Mifflin, 1933), pp. 440–41, 525. Cited in Paul Kleppner, "From Ethnoreligious Conflict to 'Social Harmony': Coalitional and Party Transformations in the 1890s," in *Emerging Coalitions in American Politics*, S.M. Lipset, ed. (San Francisco: Institute for Contemporary Studies, 1978), p. 42.

the summer of 1896. There are, on its face, several grave problems with this conventional interpretation. In the first place, if the masses were clamoring for Bryan, why was he beaten decisively in the election by McKinley and then crushed in the general election twice again in 1900 and in 1908? These decisive defeats, permanently reversing the upward Democratic trend until 1892, do not look like mass clamor. Furthermore, if the Bryan nomination was a reaction to the depression, why did the Bryan forces continue to dominate the Democracy from then on, long after the depression was over? Merely asserting that the public came to understand that the modern economy requires statism and government intervention explains nothing and only reveals the bias of the liberal historian.

But more importantly, why did Bryan lose the 1896 election so heavily? The Bryanite historians, reflecting the charges of the Bryan forces at the time, fall back on contemporary charges of coercion or corruption in the polling places; the masses *wanted* to vote for Bryan, but were intimidated into voting Republican instead. But this conventional charge is singularly unconvincing. In the first place, corruption — equally on both sides — was a marked feature of all the elections in this era, and there is no evidence whatever that there was any sudden or significant increase in pro-Republican corruption in 1896. Secondly, the Bryan forces did not charge *rural* coercion or corruption; the coercion was supposed to be over laborers by employers in the urban areas. And yet, the Australian secret ballot was by now prevalent and such coercion would have been unfeasible. Moreover, it must be noted that Bryan, though concededly far below the Democratic urban vote in 1892, was yet *stronger* than the Democratic urban vote in the intervening Congressional elections of 1894. Does this mean that the coercion of workers by Republican employers was *less* against the hated Bryan in 1896 than it had been against the conservative Democrats two years earlier? Finally, none of this even begins to explain why Bryan was rejected by the very Midwestern farmers who were supposed to be ardent Bryan supporters and whom no one claims were coerced.[2]

Poor Grover Cleveland had the ill fortune to assume office just after the Depression of 1893 had begun, and just soon enough to be hit with the blame by the voting public. The bankruptcy of the Philadelphia and Reading Railroad had come two weeks before Cleveland's inauguration in March, and then, in early May, the panic and its attendant bankruptcies hit

---

[2]Kleppner, *The Cross of Culture*, p. 297.

the American economy.[3] The result was, indeed, a cataclysmic defeat for the Democrats in the Congressional elections of 1894. In the elections of 1892, 61.2% of the House of Representatives was Democratic; but after the fall 1894 elections, only 29.4% of the House was Democrat, a disastrous loss of no less than 113 seats. The catastrophic declines hit across the board, in every region, occupation, ethnic, religious, and income group, and Democratic strength was in many areas at an all-time low. In the Midwest, the Democratic voting percentage fell an average of 9.9%, from 46.9% in 1892 to 37.0% two years later. In Ohio and Wisconsin, Democratic strength was at an all-time low, as was virtually true of Michigan as well.

Despite all the talk among historians of an "agrarian upheaval" in the 1890s, the urban areas in the Northeast and the Midwest reacted even more sharply against the Democracy in 1894 than did the rural areas. Taking urban as against rural areas, for example, Democratic voting dropped 13 points in urban Michigan (from 50% to 37%) from 1892 to 1894, and 18 points in rural Michigan (from 48% to 30%); dropped 16 points (from 50% to 34%) in urban Wisconsin, and 8 points (from 47% to 39%) in rural Wisconsin; and fell 7 points (from 49% to 42%) in urban Ohio, in contrast to 4 points (from 46% to 42%) in the rural parts of that state. The conclusion is that while Democratic strength fell in all parts of the state, it declined more heavily in urban areas, except for Michigan.

Furthermore, the large losses for the Democracy transcended income levels; wealthy and poor rural counties dropped their support to a similar extent. Moreover, the decline was trans-ethnic, with the various ethnic and religious groups all cutting their votes for the Democrats the degree varying with the intensity of Democratic loyalties.

Another point for the Midwest is that Republican gains did not match Democratic losses. For the region as a whole, the Democratic loss of 9.9 points in 1894 was matched by a gain of only 6.7 points by the Republican Party. The difference represented a gain of support for the Populist Party, which also gained from declines suffered by the Prohibitionists.

Thus, in rural Wisconsin, while all income classes cut their support of the Democrats to the same extent, the decline in Democratic

---

[3][Editor's footnote] For more on the Panic of 1893, see Rothbard, "A History of Money and Banking," pp. 167–69. For the ensuing political crisis, see Robert Higgs, *Crisis and Leviathan: Critical Episodes in the Growth of American Government* (New York: Oxford University Press, 1987), pp. 77–105. The entire book is indispensable for understanding the transformation of ideology and government during the Progressive Era and later years.

strength among religious and ethnic groups depended on the intensity of each group's Democratic commitment. Thus, the highly conservative and liturgical Wisconsin Synod Lutherans reduced their support of the Democracy by a lower amount than the less conservative Missouri Synod. German Catholics cut their support of the Democrats by an even lesser amount, and still lower were the defections of the Irish Catholics. Only the staunchly devoted Polish Catholics, of all the ethnic groups, actually *increased* their support of the Democracy in 1894.

In urban districts, too, the Democrats lost across the board among all income, occupational, and ethnic-religious groups. In some cases, Republican votes increased commensurately; in others, defecting Democrats either failed to vote at all or voted Populist. Defections from the Democrats were even greater among the depressed miners and lumbermen.[4]

The impact of the Depression caused the public to stress economic issues more intensively than before. In 1890, the Sherman Silver Purchase Act had cemented an alliance between the Republicans and the inflationist, pro-silver forces, and tended to ally the latter to the protectionist cause, the Republicans being above all the party of the protective tariff. The Democrats, as well as being free traders, had been historically a solidly hard-money, gold standard party, and the Democratic platform of 1892 condemned the Silver Purchase Act and called for its repeal.[5] True to its commitment, the first act of the new Cleveland administration was to push through repeal, which enabled the Republicans to pull out the demagogic stops and blame the silver purchase repeal for the Depression.[6]

---

[4][Editor's footnote] Kleppner, *The Cross of Culture*, pp. 179–90.

[5][Editor's footnote] Rothbard's evidence that the Democratic Party was more hard money than the Republicans in the post-Civil War era, concentrating on the 1860s and 1870s, can be found in Rothbard, "A History of Money and Banking," pp. 150–53. See also pp. 156–59, 167. By the end of the 1880s, many more Republicans, especially in the East, favored hard money policies. The Republican campaign platform of 1888 supported the use of both gold and silver, and true to its pledge, President Harrison signed the Sherman Silver Purchase Act. See Allan Nevins, *Grover Cleveland: A Study in Courage* (New York: Dodd, Mead, 1932), pp. 465–66.

[6]Unfortunately, Cleveland made the fateful decision to go back on his platform commitment to repeal the 10% tax on state bank notes, in force since the Civil War. This tax had destroyed the decentralized, free banking system of pre-Civil War America, and had replaced it with a quasi-centralized and more inflationary banking system. Repeal would have changed the banking system in the strong direction of decentralized free banking, and while it would not really have been inflationist, the pro-inflationary South and West believed differently. The Cleveland administration, then, could have split the inflationist

In response, and in despair at the increased defections to the pro-silver and inflationist Populists, the Democrats, at least in the South and West, continued to shift their positions and to take up the free silver cause. The two parties continued and intensified their differences, however, on the protective tariff question.

Pledged to tariff reduction, the Democrats drove through the Wilson-Gorman Act in 1893–94; unfortunately, however, the Southern and far Western Democracy, increasingly infected with Populist views, forced the Democrats to pass an income tax measure as part of the total package. Although rather astute businessmen and such New York and New Jersey Democratic leaders as U.S. Senator David B. Hill (N.Y.) and James Smith, Jr. (N.J.) fought against the income tax, the increasingly statist South and West were able to push it through, with the passive support of Cleveland, who was willing to accept the new tax in return for the tariff cut.[7] Some

---

South and West while fostering rather than crippling the long-standing Democratic free banking and hard money principles.

[7] The Democrats, in passing an income tax, were also responding to Republican taunts of where government revenue would be coming from if tariffs were significantly lower. There was, of course, another answer: that pre-Civil War America had gotten along nicely with free trade *and* no income tax, and reduced spending could have restored that kind of a revenue system. [Editor's remarks] Cleveland was ultimately dissatisfied with the minor tariff reductions in the Wilson-Gorman Act and allowed the bill to become law without his signature. The income tax was later struck down by the Supreme Court as unconstitutional in 1895, and the Wilson-Gorman Tariff was replaced by the 1897 Dingley Tariff, which reaffirmed protectionism. The income tax would return in the Taft administration, and alongside the rate reducing Underwood Tariff, the 16th Amendment was passed under the Taft and Wilson administrations in 1913. The passage of the income tax was due to a coalition of groups favoring tariff reduction but eager to find a substitute source of revenue. They were the progressive populists who wanted to reduce income inequality, manufacturing export firms, and those involved in South American and Asian foreign direct investment. The latter also had a vested interest in using the tax to fund the growing pension plans and naval military buildup, which would be used to protect their overseas investments. Although under the initial law the tax only hit the upper class with the top rate at 7%, during World War I the government extended its encroachment, and rates skyrocketed, including on the middle class. See Chapter 7 below, pp. 206–07; Higgs, *Crisis and Leviathan*, pp. 97–103, 112–13, 150–52; Ben Baack and Edward John Ray, "The Political Economy of the Origin and Development of the Federal Income Tax," in *Emergence of Modern Political Economy*, Robert Higgs, ed. (Greenwich, CT: JAI Press, 1985), pp. 121–38.

A high income tax penalizes up-and-coming entrepreneurs who earn high annual incomes relative to their wealth at the expense of existing wealthy entrepreneurs who earn relatively low annual incomes. As a result, it reduces income mobility and ossifies the existing

Democrats were still able to champion their old low-tax and low-budget principles, however. Thus, in Wisconsin, the Democrats pointed out the depression relief their tax-cutting policies caused.

On generally weak economic grounds because of the Depression, the Democrats in 1894 tried to shift grounds to cultural issues, and therefore launched a blistering attack on the newly burgeoning American Protective Association. For the benefit of the German Lutherans, the Democrats stressed the nativist as well as the anti-Catholic policies of the A.P.A. In response, the Republicans intensified the regroupment of issues already underway; it would be folly to lose their current advantage on economic issues by alienating Lutherans and other potential defectors from the Democracy, and where the moderates were in control, the Republicans tried to avoid close identification with the A.P.A. Thus, in Wisconsin, the Republican Establishment managed to defeat the pietist Nils Haugen, an ardent supporter of the nativist and anti-parochial school Bennett Law, for the gubernatorial nomination. The moderates even wanted to nominate a German Lutheran for state treasurer, but were defeated by the furious opposition of the "La Follette gang," the pietist Haugen–La Follette faction in the state party.[8]

2. THE FINAL COLLAPSE: 1896

One of Paul Kleppner's great contributions is to show, for the first time, that the Democratic collapse of 1894 and 1896 were two very different movements with different explanations and occurring in very different segments of the population. Overall, the critical nature of both elections is seen by the unusually high degree of voter turnout in both cases, as well as in the fact that a very close contest was replaced by overwhelming Republican strength. Thus, in the Midwest, a difference between the two parties of plus or minus 3% throughout the region from 1888 to 1892 was replaced by a Republican margin of 16% in 1894, 11% in 1896, and 12.5% in 1900. Suddenly, the Democrats had been reduced to the status of

---

elite. See Ludwig von Mises, *Human Action* (Auburn, AL: Mises Institute, 2008 [1949]), pp. 804–05.

[8][Editor's footnote] McSeveney, *The Politics of Depression*, pp. 35–41, 87–100; Kleppner, *The Cross of Culture*, pp. 255–59; Jensen, *The Winning of the Midwest*, pp. 213–18; Richard Franklin Bensel, *The Political Economy of American Industrialization, 1877–1900* (Cambridge: Cambridge University Press, 2000), pp. 136, 139–40, 417–18; Gretchen Ritter, *Goldbugs and Greenbacks: The Antimonopoly Tradition and the Politics of Finance in America, 1865–1896* (Cambridge: Cambridge University Press, 1997), p. 243.

a permanent minority party. But the overall figures are misleading. For the crucial point about 1896 is the great difference in the type of party support than had been true two years before.

The first difference to be pointed out between 1894 and 1896 is the enormous drop of the minor party vote in the latter year. In fact, the minor party vote in the Midwest (Prohibitionist and Populist) had risen from 1892 to 1894 and then dropped far below the 1892 level in the 1896 election. Thus, the major party vote (combined Democrat and Republican) in Michigan was 91% in 1892, fell to 88% two years later, and then rose to 97% in 1896, a startling 9 point gain in the major party totals. Similarly, in Ohio the progression was 95% in 1892, 89% in 1894, and 99% in 1896; in Wisconsin, it was 94%, 90%, and 98% in 1896. Thus, what had been in a sense a four-party system suddenly became a veritable two party system in 1896 (or, a one-and-a-half party system, with the Republicans in a permanent majority). In short, *both* Republicans and Democrats made overall voting gains in 1896 as compared to 1894.

But particularly important is the *sort* of gains and losses experienced by both parties. For the old ethnic and religious verities in voting patterns were now broken. And the new and startling ethnic and religious pattern continued unbroken in 1900; in short, a new, fourth party system had emerged in the United States.

A key to the difference between 1894 and 1896 is that, while the defectors from the Democrats tended to return to the fold in the latter year, another and permanently significant shift occurred: a massive shift of traditional liturgicals from the Democrats to the Republicans, and of pietists from Republicans to Democrats. Thus, the biggest Democratic gains in Michigan and Ohio took place in traditionally Republican, Old Stock, and British counties.

What happened? The key factor was the conquest of the Democratic Party at the July 1896 national convention by William Jennings Bryan and the forces of inflation and free silver. An upheaval was occurring in the Democratic Party. The South, by now a one-party Democratic region, was having its own pietism transformed by the 1890s. Quiet pietists were now becoming evangelical, and Southern Protestant organizations began to call for prohibition. The new, sparsely settled Mountain states, many of them with silver mines, were also largely pietist. The existing hard money, *laissez-faire* Democracy of President Cleveland was suddenly and tragically repudiated; the traditional Democracy, the party of the fathers, was gone forever. The Bryanite victory had been made possible by the Depression-created heavy Democratic losses in the East and Midwest in 1893 and 1894, losses that swung the balance of national party leadership to the perpetually Democratic South and to the free-silver Mountain states of the West. The Bryan conquest was the result.

Bryan claimed to represent the "toiling masses," the workers and farmers of America, and championed silver and inflation against the Eastern "interests." Conventionally, historians have claimed that Bryan succeeded at least among his beloved rural and agrarian voters. Yet, if we examine the figures, a very different pattern emerges. In the Midwest, for example, Bryan gained only a *minority* of the rural vote, and in Michigan and Wisconsin that vote was *very much lower* than the Democrats had obtained in 1892 (41.0% as against 47.8% in Michigan, 37.2% as against 47.4% in Wisconsin). Similarly, the Bryan urban vote was also far below the 1892 levels. It is true that in each case, both urban and rural, the Democratic vote tended to be better than the 1894 disaster, but this was cold comfort to the Democrats when the enormous distance from 1892 was realized. It is true that if we compare the urban-rural Democratic percentages in the Midwest for the two presidential years, the Democrats had been very slightly better in urban areas before and were now generally better in rural areas. But this hardly constitutes a great rural strength, considering the Democrats being in a hopeless minority even there.

Kleppner has examined Democratic percentages by detailed size of "urban" unit, from 2,500 population to 100,000 and over, in Michigan and in Wisconsin.[9] From his study it is clear that, in 1892, there was no trend by size of place in Wisconsin, and a very slight increase of Democratic support in the larger urban areas in Michigan. Democratic support fell drastically across the board in 1894, even more in small towns in Michigan and in larger cities in Wisconsin. In 1896, Democratic support — with the exception of Detroit — bounced back from two years earlier, but far below the 1892 levels in every area. In general, over the Midwest, he did badly in both, and there was generally no greater difference in urban and rural patterns than had existed since the 1870s.

What of the income class? Is there any support for the view that Bryan was beloved by the urban working poor? If we take the various wards in Chicago, we find an erratic pattern of votes from upper- to lower-class wards in 1892 (ranging from upper through middle and lower class, we

---

[9]Kleppner, *The Cross of Culture*, p. 286. [Editor's remarks] Ibid., pp. 273–86.

get Democratic percentages in that year of 45%, 56%, 45%, 57%, and 63%). The Depression years of 1893 and 1894 saw steady and catastrophic declines of Democratic votes across the board in all income class categories (from 1892 to 1894, we see the following point reductions ranging from upper- to lower-class wards 16%, 24%, 15%, 25%, and 22%). Then all wards bounced back in 1896, but still far below the 1892 levels. It is true that the Democrats fared slightly less badly in the lower wards, but what we see, overwhelmingly, is an across-the-board multi-class repudiation of the Democracy (ranging from upper- to lower-class wards, the Democratic point losses from 1892 to 1896 were 18%, 17%, 12%, 15%, and 14%). The non-class nature of the Bryan vote may be seen even more clearly in Detroit, where, again, the Democrats did badly in all wards, but where they were able to bounce back better was in the rich wards than in the poorer. Thus, in 1892, the Democrats earned 52.2% in the richest wards and 59.0% in the working class wards. In 1894, they fell by 12 points in the rich wards to 40.4% and by 16 points in the working-class wards to 43.3%. In 1896, however, while the Democrats were able to rise a bit in the rich wards of Detroit to 41.2%, in the working-class wards they fell even more sharply, to the same 41.2%.

Similarly, there was no income cohesion in the rural areas. Marginal and prosperous townships behaved very differently among themselves, with no clear differences between the two groups. As Kleppner concludes on the rural areas, "there was no discernible relationship between receptivity to the Bryan candidacy and degree of economic prosperity." In general, "as economic groups, neither urban workers nor farmers reacted favorably to the candidate and his gospel of commodity price inflation."[10] And the Bryan candidacy met a similarly disastrous fate in the Northeast as well.[11]

What happened to the Democracy? Why didn't rural America respond to the agrarian economic appeals of the Bryanites? Simply, because the Bryan Democrats were most aggressively *not* the Democratic party of the fathers; they were neither the party of the liturgicals nor of personal and economic liberty. On the contrary, the Bryanites were both extreme economic statists *and* extreme religious and cultural pietists. All too far from the "party of personal liberty," the Bryanites were statists and pietists across the board, ever more moralistic than the old Republican enemy.

---

[10]Ibid., pp. 291, 294. [Editor's remarks] Ibid., pp. 273–93.

[11]See McSeveney, *The Politics of Depression*.

And when we consider that the Republicans had been moving rapidly, and moved still further during the 1896 McKinley campaign, toward the moderate center and away from statist pietism, we can readily understand the massive defection of the liturgicals from the Bryan Democracy and toward the Republicans or toward dropping completely out of the political process. Democratic loyalists, whom even a depression could not budge, were driven out of their party home by the invasion and triumph of the Bryanite forces.

Conversely, the conquest by Bryan heralded a substantial movement of pietists into the Democratic camp. Some were Old Stock Republicans; others were Prohibitionists and Populists. Indeed, that in effect is what happened to these latter two parties: a dissolution into the newly reconstructed pietistic and statist Democracy. In the Midwest, the Populists were of two breeds. There were the "1892 Populists," who had begun as Republicans and then, disgusted by the Republican "sellout" to German Lutherans and to the saloon, moved to the Prohibitionist Party. Most were native Methodists, British and Welsh Methodists, or Norwegian and Swedish Lutherans — dedicated pietists all. In 1892, many of these shifted into the new Populist Party. Then, in 1894, the many Democrats defecting because of the Depression joined the Populist ranks. The "1892 Populists," then, were originally Republicans whose main motivation was pietism; the "1894 Populists" were ex-Democrats whose main worry was economic.

Unsurprisingly, the two breeds of Populists reacted differently to the critical 1896 election. The pietistic 1892 Populists, ex-Republicans, moved solidly into the Democratic ranks; similarly, the Prohibitionists voted overwhelmingly for their fellow-prohibitionist Bryan in 1896. On the other hand, most of the ex-Democrat 1894 Populists shifted into the Republican ranks. Most of the Republican gains in 1896, indeed, came either directly from Democrats or from the ex-Democrat 1894 Populists.

The explanation was squarely ethnic-religious: pietist vs. liturgical. For a half-century, the Democrats had been the party of the Catholics and other liturgicals; the Republicans (and other minor parties) had been the party of the pietists, the coercive reformers and statists trying to reform the liturgicals by the use of the police. Now, suddenly, in 1896, a new party system arrived: the Catholics, repelled by the ultra-pietistic Bryanites, shifted *en masse* into the Republican Party that was prepared to receive their votes and support.

In the Midwest, the biggest shifts came in Michigan. A large majority of Catholics had voted Democratic in the 1892 and 1894 elections. Now, in 1896, an actual majority of Catholics shifted into the Republican ranks. The German Lutherans shifted to the same degree away from the Democracy. Conversely, Old Stock Protestants shifted toward the Democrats for the first time, although they often continued to give a majority to the Republicans who had not, after all, experienced the convulsive upheaval that had transformed the Democracy. The Republican change had been gradual, in the direction of fuzzy centrism, and its leadership continued to be the same.

In Detroit, Catholic wards shifted *en masse* from Democrat to Republican, regardless of economic class, and German Lutheran wards maintained their 1894 defection into Republican ranks. In Michigan cities where the Democrats had been strong until 1892, the Democrats continued to lose voters in 1896, while in cities with large numbers of Old Stock Protestant voters, the Democrats scored heavy gains. In short, the liturgical areas not only failed to bounce back from 1894, but suffered greater Democratic reverses; whereas Democrats gained votes in pietist areas. This result obtained regardless of the size of the town or city.

The same pattern held for rural areas of Michigan. In Calhoun County, the Democrats gained in every rural township except one, Fredonia, a German Lutheran unit, the only place in the county where the Democrats did less well than in 1892. Fredonia voted 55.5% Democratic in 1892 and a poorer 52.6% in 1896. The Republican gains were even more striking: 35.4% in 1892 and 44.6% in 1896. In contrast, the Methodist township of LeRoy, in the same county, shifted massively from the Republican into the Democratic camp. In 1892, LeRoy had voted only 30.4% Democratic, and the vote had dropped to a meager 11.4% in 1894. Yet, in 1896, LeRoy voted 47.9% for the Democrats, a plurality of the total vote. The Republican vote in LeRoy, a whopping 70.4% in 1894, fell to 47.6% two years later.

Similarly for other rural counties. The average Democratic gain in St. Joseph County was a huge 32.4 points. The German Lutherans in Mottville scored the lowest Democratic gain, 9.2 points, and thereby were the only township in the county to do less well for the Democrats than in 1892. In contrast, the Evangelical Association Germans of Park township scored a 45.3 point Democratic gain over 1894, and 35.5 points above the 1892 level. Neither did it make any difference whether the pietistic or liturgical townships were marginal or prosperous rural units. Thus, Park, a poor rural township, voted 60.5% Democratic in 1896, while Lockport, a prosperous Evangelical Association German township in the same county, voted 63.1% for the Democrats.

A striking change occurred in Branch County. In 1892, the Democrats had carried only one of Branch's 16 rural townships; in 1896, they carried 11. The biggest Democratic gains came among the pietistic Methodists and Presbyterians. Thus, California township, consisting of Presbyterians, Methodists, and Congregationalists, voted a decisive 62.1% Democratic in 1896. But in 1892, it had voted 44.2% Democrat, a percentage which fell catastrophically to 5.0% in 1894 and then rose to new heights two years later. Similarly, Methodist Gilead, fell from 39% in 1892 to 13.0% in 1894, and then bounced up to 60.5% two years later.

Similarly in eastern Michigan's rural Washtenaw County. The Democrats in 1896 were stronger than in 1892 in four townships in the county. The townships differed widely in their economic condition; they ranged from "marginal" to "very prosperous." But in each case the township was native pietist Protestant: Presbyterians, Congregationalists, Methodists, and Baptists. In contrast were the Irish Catholic and German Lutheran townships. The Irish units rose slightly over the nadir of 1894 in their Democratic voting, but they remained on the average 10.1 points below their 1892 average. The German Lutheran units fared even worse for the Democracy, sinking below the 1894 levels and falling to 15.6 points below 1892.

In Houghton County on the Upper Peninsula of Michigan, the votes of the copper miners depended, once again, on their religious orientation. The Catholic miners in Hancock and Portage voted less Democratic than in 1892 *or* 1894, while pietist voters shifted into the Democratic ranks. In fact, there is a virtual 1:1 correlation between the Catholic or Protestant nature of the township and whether the Democrats lost or gained strength from 1894 to 1896. Even the devotedly Republican and anti-Catholic English Canadians in Houghton County now voted a majority for William Jennings Bryan.

The Ohio pattern was much the same, among the farming as well as the mining townships. In Wisconsin, Democratic losses were most striking among those very groups — Catholic and German Lutherans — who had remained steadfast to the Democracy in the 1894 depression. While the Catholics of Wisconsin did not go as far as their co-religionists in Michigan and give an actual majority to the Republicans, the degree of their defection from the Democrats was severe. The defection also varied among ethnic and cultural groups. The Irish Catholics defected the least, with only two Wisconsin units voting less Democratic than in 1894; all of them, however, registered less Democratic than in 1892. So severe was the trauma that even the loyal Polish Catholics fell away; every Polish unit reduced the degree of its Democratic support. The German and Bohemian Catholics defected more severely; 70% of German Catholic units in Wisconsin, for example, registered lower Democratic voting percentages than in 1894, much less 1892. And while no Irish or Polish Catholic unit in 1896 presumed to vote a Republican majority, 27.2% of the German Catholic and 50.0% of the Bohemian Catholic units voted Republican. Not a single one had failed to vote a Democratic majority either in 1892 or 1894.

The pattern was even more striking among the German Lutherans of Wisconsin. In Dodge County, for example, the German Lutherans of Hustisford township had voted a whopping 84.8% Democratic in 1892, and their support scarcely faltered in 1894, falling only to 81.8%. Similarly, German Lutheran Theresa township voted 90.7% Democrat in 1892 and 81.3% in 1894. Yet these two loyal townships, willing to serve through the hardships of the depression, could not countenance the takeover of their beloved party by the Bryanite enemy. In 1896, Hustisford voted only 46.0% Democratic, and Theresa only 42.7%. The pattern held throughout the state. Every German Lutheran unit voted less Democratic in 1896 than in 1892, and only 11.3% of them rose higher than the catastrophic depression lows of 1894. Over the whole state, the Democrats carried 85.2% of the German Lutheran units in 1892, 59.2% in 1894, and only 29.6% in 1896 — the lowest German Lutheran support for the Democracy in half a century.

Conversely, as Catholics and German Lutherans moved from Democrat to Republican, the pietists moved in the opposite direction. Wisconsin townships with Methodists, Swiss Reformed, and Evangelical Association Germans raised their Democratic vote from 10 to 13 points over 1892 levels. Among the Norwegian Lutherans, the more intensely pietistic Haugeans, previously far more Republican than the Norwegian Synod, now shifted more strongly into the Democratic camp. The Norwegians still voted more Republican, but the Democratic minority was higher than it had been in a generation. The highly pietistic Swedish Lutherans reacted in the same way as the Haugeans. Again, while a majority remained Republican, the Democratic minority was now three to four times the percentage in 1892. Thus, in Swedish Burnett County, the Democratic vote was higher than in 1892 in every unit, and the average Democratic vote was 21.4% points higher than in 1892.

A similar pattern held true for the urban areas of Wisconsin. In Milwaukee, the Democratic vote fell below the 1892 level in all but one of the wards, and the Republican percentage, 54.1%, was higher than it had been in a decade. Whereas the Irish and Polish Catholic wards fell only about 4 points below 1892 percentages, the defection was far more serious among German Catholics and Lutherans. A majority of both groups of Milwaukee Germans voted for the Republicans. The Democratic vote by German Catholics fell 12.9 points below the 1892 average. Only among non-Lutheran Protestants in Milwaukee did Bryan run above the 1892 Democratic norm.

Milwaukee, due to a local labor dispute and controversy over the Polish language in the public schools, had a more favorable Democratic climate for Catholics than the rest of the state. In the other urban areas of Wisconsin, the Democrats not only trailed their 1892 vote among Catholics and German Lutherans, they frequently fell even below 1894. The Democrats fell below 1894 in 37 of the state's 51 urban areas; the degree of loss correlated strongly with the proportion of Catholics in the city's voting population. Size of urban area mattered little in the voting shifts.[12]

The massive weakening of the Democratic Party was duplicated in the Northeastern states. The defecting Cleveland Democrats either returned to the fold in 1900 or, more likely, became Republican or dropped out of politics altogether. The German Democrats defected massively in New York, New England, and the Middle-West; one straw in the wind was the German-American Sound Money League, founded in 1896 and supporting the Republicans, which included such notables as Carl Schurz and Jacob H. Schiff, head of the Kuhn-Loeb investment bank.

While the Germans favored free trade and opposed a protective tariff, they were particularly incensed at inflation and free silver and staunchly supported the gold standard. Hence, they were willing to swallow the protective tariff to vote for McKinley and the Republican pro-gold position, however newly won, and against the hated inflationist Bryan. Hence it was the Germans who led the march to McKinley and the Republicans. Many of the Germans, who could not bring themselves to vote Republican directly, voted for the new National (Gold) Democratic Party, which had broken off from the Democrats in disgust.

A leading German Democrat in Illinois, Henry Raab, who had become state superintendent of education in an upsurge against the anti-German parochial school Edwards Law, typified the reaction of German

---

[12][Editor's footnote] See Kleppner, *The Cross of Culture*, pp. 316–38.

Democrats to the political crisis of 1896. Several years earlier, in 1891, Raab had written of the conservatism and anti-emotionalism of the German religion and their desire to maintain their customs and ideals from political aggression. Raab asserted that the American patriotism of the Germans lay in their "courageous struggle against 'bi-metallism' and 'Greenback inflation'; now the determination to pay with honest money, that is patriotism."[13] Now, in 1896, Raab left the party of gold, voted Gold Democrat, and supported William McKinley.

Decisive for the Germans of Milwaukee was the address by the Bryanite Populist-Democratic candidate for Congress, Robert Schilling. Sounding for all the world like modern Friedmanites or Keynesians, Schilling told the assembled Germans of Milwaukee in a campaign speech that it didn't really matter what commodity was chosen as money, and that "gold, silver, copper, paper, sauerkraut or sausages" would do equally well as money. The German masses laughed Schilling off the stage, and the shrewdly opportunistic Republicans promptly adopted as their campaign slogan "Schilling and Sauerkraut" and swept Milwaukee.

So intense was the German-American devotion to gold and hard money that even the German communist-anarchist Johann Most, leader of a movement that sought the eventual abolition of money itself, actually came out for the gold standard during the 1896 campaign!

The *Illinois Staats-Zeitung*, looking back on the 1896 campaign and the decisive shift of the German electorate, summed up its motivations:

> They [the Germans] have had many complaints against the Republican party, which ... annoyed them continually with Prohibition laws, Sunday-closing laws, and school laws. The Germans consequently turned their backs upon the Republicans, with the result that Cleveland was twice elected, and if the Democrats had not inscribed repudiation, bankruptcy, and dishonor upon their colors as a result of their union with the Populists, the Germans would have supported them this time also ...[14]

Since the Irish Catholics bolted less drastically from the Democracy than the other groups, they remained to pick up the pieces and assume control of the Democratic Party, especially in the big cities. In the North-

---

[13]Jensen, *The Winning of the Midwest*, p. 293.
[14]*Illinois Staats-Zeitung*, November 21, 1896. Cited in ibid., p. 295.

east, the wholesale defection of the Cleveland Protestants left control within the party to the Irish Catholics, who proceeded for the first time in ensuing years to nominate and even elect Irish Catholic governors in New York, New Jersey, and New England. In the two years after McKinley's election, the Irish-led Democrats ousted Republican mayors from a host of big cities in the Northeast and Midwest: New York City, Chicago, Cincinnati, Cleveland, Detroit, Akron, Dayton, Springfield, and Milwaukee. Partly, the Irish stuck to the party as a strategy of gaining control; partly, it was a function of the pervasive dependence of the Irish on municipal government jobs and hence on party patronage.

In short, the election of 1896 left the United States with a new party system: a centrist and moderately statist Republican Party with a comfortably permanent majority of the country, and a minority Democratic Party roughly confined to the one party South and to Irish-controlled big cities of the Northeast and Midwest, which were nevertheless a minority in those regions. Gone was the sharp conflict of ideology or even of ethnic-religious values; both parties were now moderately statist in different degrees; both parties contained pietists and liturgicals within their ranks. The McKinley Republicans were happy to be known as the "party of prosperity" rather than the "party of great moral ideas." The familiar lack of clear and genuine ideological choice between two dominant parties so characteristic of modern America was beginning to emerge. Above all, there was no longer a political party, nor a clear-cut constituency, devoted to the traditional American ideology of *laissez-faire*.

3. THE TRANSFORMATION OF THE PARTIES

The key to the drastic change in the American party system in 1896, then, was the ideological change in each of the major parties. The forces of hopped-up pietistic Bryanism had captured the Democratic Party and changed its character forever from its ancient *laissez-faire* principles. At the same time, McKinleyite pragmatism had transformed the Republican Party from the home of statist pietism, from the "party of great moral ideas," to a moderate statist organization cleaving only to the protective tariff, and dumping any emphasis on such emotional and pietistic issues as prohibition or Sunday blue laws. The pull of the newfound Republican pragmatism combined with the push of the Bryanite takeover to drive the liturgicals into the Republican Party and cement Republican hegemony for a generation.

How did the fatal transformations take place? In the first place, in both parties, the metamorphosis was made possible by the short-run but cataclysmic Democratic losses, matched by Republican victories, in the state and Congressional elections of 1894 — losses and victories brought about by the general blame placed upon the Cleveland administration for the Depression. In the Democratic Party, the losses concentrated in the Northeast and Midwest seemed to discredit Cleveland and his hard money and *laissez-faire* policies, and also toppled *laissez-faire* and Clevelandite officeholders, with the power vacuum bringing the pro-inflationist and pietist South and mountain West into national leadership in the Democratic Party. In the Republican Party, too, the cause of pragmatic moderation, which McKinley and others had preached for several years, was advanced by the new Republican officeholders of 1893 and 1894 who did not want to be retired by liturgical constituents after the Depression was over. As a corollary, their increased majorities freed the Republicans from their political dependence on the Prohibition Party and its small but important marginal bloc of voters. Furthermore, the depression made economic issues more important relative to personal issues in the eyes of the voters and gave the Republican moderates leeway to deemphasize the "social" issues for once and for all and to become, in their own claim, the "party of prosperity."

The important transforming role of the new Republican state legislators in previously Democratic districts is shown by the fact that, in the 1894 and 1895 sessions, they voted more nearly like their Democratic predecessors than like traditional Republicans. This was definitely true of Iowa, Illinois, and Wisconsin. In the 1894 session of the Ohio legislators, the new Republicans voted cohesively to weaken a local liquor option bill, and then finally to defeat this prohibitionist measure. In Michigan, the new Republicans consistently voted not to discuss prohibition, as well as to table petitions from evangelical religious groups calling for a prohibition referendum. Furthermore, they united to table a favorite measure of the American Protestant Association to repeal the Michigan law permitting Catholic bishops to hold the property of their churches in trust.[15]

William McKinley came to the 1896 Republican convention as the obvious front-runner. In 1890, as chairman of the House Ways and Means

[15]Paul Kleppner, "The Demise of Ethnoreligious Politics, 1900–1920," in "The Demise of Ethnocultural Politics: Parties and Voters, 1896–1920" (Unpublished paper delivered at the 1980 annual meetings of the Organization of American Historians, San Francisco, April 1980), vol. 3, pp. 22–23.

Committee, McKinley had given his name to the highest protective tariff in American history and thereby became inextricably linked with the hottest Republican issue. It was an issue that endeared McKinley to the protected manufacturers fearful of foreign competition and anxious, furthermore, to organize cartels or mergers under cover of the tariff umbrella protecting them from foreign competition. This was particularly true of the manufacturers of western Pennsylvania and of McKinley's home state of Ohio. Furthermore, McKinley established his front-running status by bucking a Democratic tide, and by raising the banner of pragmatism, winning of governorship of Ohio.

William McKinley, though a Methodist of Ulster Scot ancestry, learned early the value of a moderating and integrative role across the religious and ethnic groups. His career in law and politics was developed in Stark County, Ohio, where he found it necessary to appeal to a large proportion of German Lutheran and German and Irish Catholic voters. Furthermore, his family's connections with iron manufacturing also led McKinley to stress economic issues and the protective tariff. America's inefficient iron and steel industry had led the cry for a protective tariff ever since 1820, and had continued to do so in the protectionist years after the Civil War.

McKinley's long-time friend, political boss, and mentor in the new pragmatic approach was the Cleveland industrialist Marcus Alonzo Hanna. As a coal and iron magnate, Hanna also championed the protective tariff. Hanna was a long-time friend and business associate of John D. Rockefeller and provided the channel by which the Cleveland oil refiner was able to influence the powerful Ohio Republican Party, a party which gave no less than five presidential nominees to the national party between 1876 and 1920.[16] Hanna had been a high-school chum of Rockefeller's at Central High, Cleveland, and his coal and iron business was economically closely allied with Standard Oil. Relatives of Hanna were direct investors in the stock of the closely held Standard Oil Trust.

Hanna repeatedly loaned money to the ever hard-pressed McKinley while in office, and in 1893 Hanna organized a secret consortium of industrialists to salvage the Governor when he went bankrupt. It was Hanna who engineered the McKinley nomination, promptly became national

---

[16][Editor's footnote] During the post-Civil War era, virtually all of the Republican and Democrat candidates came from the Midwest and New York, respectively.

chairman of the party, and was then, at McKinley's instigation, elevated to the U.S. Senate the year after McKinley's election to the presidency.

But while McKinley was the leading candidate for the nomination, he had a problem. The Republican Party had been the home of the inflationists and the free-silver forces, and Congressman McKinley had repeatedly voted for silver purchase acts and for free-silver. He was therefore distrusted by the pro-gold Morgan forces and the rest of Wall Street, which considered McKinley — and with good reason — dangerously soft on silver and inflation. The Morgans, it is true, were traditionally Democrats, but the impending takeover of the Democracy by the wild-eyed Bryanites forced them to focus on their allies within the Republican Party, and look to that party for salvation. Also distrusting McKinley's silverite record was the powerful Speaker of the House Thomas B. Reed of Maine, who presented himself for the nomination.

Furthermore, McKinley would aggravate the Morgans further by refusing to agree to the Morgans' candidate for the presidency, the prominent banker and close friend of Morgan, Levi P. Morton, as a consolation choice for vice president. Morton, currently the governor of New York, was former vice president of the United States under Benjamin Harrison and president of the Morton Trust Company, which was later to form the nucleus for the Morgan-dominated Guaranty Trust Company.

From the summer of 1895 until the Republican convention in June of the following year, the Morgan forces put enormous pressure upon McKinley and Hanna to abandon silver as well as trimming upon the currency issue, to advocate gold openly and squarely. The sources of pressure included William C. Beer, attorney for the Morgan-controlled New York Life Insurance Company; Whitelaw Reid, publisher of the *New York Tribune;* and Senator Henry Cabot Lodge of Massachusetts. They were joined by Thomas C. Platt, Republican boss of New York State, who was fueled by an $85,000 fund provided by the American Bankers Association. McKinley and his associates had prepared a Republican monetary plank calling for the maintenance of the "existing standard." Forwarding this insertion to McKinley, Whitelaw Reid urged, in commenting upon Wall Street opinion:

> The anxiety here, on the whole subject of the money plank to be adopted next week [in late June at St. Louis], can hardly be exaggerated. There seems to be no doubt that the most conservative bankers are extremely apprehensive that any hesitation on our part to take the squarest

sound money ground would bring a great and probably sudden depression in values. On the other hand, there is no doubt that the enclosed plank ... will be followed by an appreciation in values.[17]

Finally, on the eve of the Republican convention, McKinley capitulated and committed himself wholeheartedly to the gold standard. In its platform, the Republican Party declared itself "unreservedly for sound money" and "unalterably opposed to every measure calculated to debase our currency, or impair the credit of the country." It concluded that it was "opposed to the free coinage of silver" except by international agreement, and that "until such agreement can be obtained the existing gold standard must be preserved."[18]

The adoption of the firm gold standard plank by the Republican Party drove the Silver Republicans out of the convention and out of the party. Their leader, Senator Henry Teller of Colorado, one of the founders of the Republican Party, mounted the rostrum at the convention and announced that he and 33 other delegates, largely from the mountain states of Montana, Colorado, Utah, and Idaho, were bolting the convention and the Republican Party. Clearly, they were planning to leave for the reconstituted Democratic Party that was widely expected to emerge the following month at Chicago.[19]

The Silver Republicans were gone, but it was a bargain price for the Republicans to pay for becoming the gold party in the United States. For, in return, the Republicans were able to attract not only the Morgans and

---

[17]Cited in Matthew Josephson, *The Politicos, 1865–1896* (New York: Harcourt, Brace & World, 1964), p. 657.

[18]Ibid., p. 660. [Editor's remarks] Ibid., pp. 639–61; Burch, *Elites in American History,* pp. 136, 185; Kleppner, *The Cross of Culture,* pp. 347–48; Ferdinand Lundberg, *America's 60 Families* (New York: The Vanguard Press, 1938), pp. 57–59.

[19]Senator Teller himself owned $2,000,000 in silver and other mining stock. This points up the role of the silver mining interest in pushing for Bryan and free silver. Silver advocates Senators John P. Jones and William Stewart of Nevada were both wealthy silver mine operators. Marcus Daly, major owner of the great Anaconda mines in Montana, fought for free silver and was the main subsidizer of the American Bimetallic League, which employed Bryan as a lecturer. Daly and his Anaconda associates spent $289,000 to obtain delegates for free silver at the Democratic convention, and Daly gave $50,000 more to the Bryan campaign after the nomination. William Randolph Hearst, young newspaper publisher and son of Daly's late partner at Anaconda was the major press supporter for the Bryan campaign. [Editor's remarks] Josephson, *The Politicos,* pp. 663–64.

Wall Street, but also the Germans and other liturgicals devoted to gold and sound money.[20]

The next month, in July at Chicago, the Bryanites achieved their conquest of the Democratic Party at the national convention. Their triumph had been prefigured for the past two years, as the Bryanites had captured state after state party in the South and West. Even the Midwestern state parties fell, with only staunch Wisconsin remaining in pro-gold hands. After teetering back and forth, the Michigan Democracy finally fell to the Bryan forces, with the result that the Democrats lost the state for a decade.

At Chicago, the Democrats repudiated their own sitting president, Grover Cleveland, adopted a radically new platform, and, for the first time since the Civil War, turned away from the Northeast and chose as their presidential nominee someone from west of the Mississippi.

William Jennings Bryan was born of small-town pietist stock in southern Illinois. As a southern Baptist, Bryan's father was a leading Democrat and one-time State Senator. Bryan was the quintessential pietist and believer in state paternalism and compulsory morality, believing in the Christian duty of the state to create a "safe" social atmosphere for the righteous. So marked were these traits in Bryan that his leading biographer calls him a "political evangelist," while another distinguished historian has dubbed Bryan a "Revivalist."[21] Moving to Lincoln, Nebraska as a young attorney, Bryan quickly rose in Democratic Party politics. As a Democrat, he could not yet commit himself or his party to prohibition, but he soon made his mark as a personal temperance man, and he managed to commit

---

[20][Editor's footnote] With McKinley firmly committed to gold, his subsequent success in 1896, and the affirmative Gold Standard Act of 1900, the Morgans, and other big bankers could gather their forces and now concentrate on monetary reform to correct the defects of the National Banking System and replace it not with free banking, but with a more centralized and cartelized system of monetary expansion — namely, a central bank. This was in contrast to the more blatant congressional inflationism of the Bryanite Democracy. For the early years of the 20th century surrounding this drive, see Murray Rothbard, "The Origins of the Federal Reserve," in *A History of Money and Banking in the United States: From the Colonial Era to World War II*, Joseph Salerno, ed. (Auburn, AL: Mises Institute, 2005 [1999]), pp. 185–208.

[21]Paolo E. Coletta, *William Jennings Bryan, I: Political Evangelist, 1860–1908* (Lincoln: University of Nebraska Press, 1960); Richard Hofstadter, *The American Political Tradition and the Men Who Made It* (New York: Vintage Books, 1961), p. 186. [Editor's remarks] See also Kleppner, *The Cross of Culture*, pp. 338–48.

the state party in 1889 to restricting the flow of liquor through high license fees.

The following year, Bryan ran successfully for Congress. With many liturgicals living in a district which encompassed both Lincoln and Omaha, Bryan managed to pick up votes from both sides of the prohibition issue for his middle-of-the road stance. Instead, he stressed the veteran Democratic issue of opposition to the protective tariff. But two years later, Omaha had been reapportioned out of Bryan's district, which was now significantly more pietist, native Protestant, prohibitionist, and agrarian. In his campaign for reelection, Bryan could adopt free silver as his major cause and thereby win over the votes of the pietistic agrarian Populists in his district.

At the Chicago Democratic convention, the fateful result was prefigured by the first tussle at the meeting, one in which Clevelandite Senator David. B. Hill of New York moved that the convention endorse the Cleveland administration. When the motion was voted down, the pattern of the convention, and of the new Democratic Party, was clear.

The Cleveland Democracy was now squarely confronted with what their course of action should be. Probably the only hope for the old *laissez-faire* Democracy would have been an immediate and massive bolt, a blistering denunciation of the Bryanites, and the creation of a new "third" party to carry the Clevelandite banner. This might have kept the liturgical and *laissez-faire* constituency, and the new party could either have continued permanently, or else dissolved into a recaptured Democratic Party. A bolt and denunciation was the courageous course advocated by a group headed by New York Governor Roswell P. Flower and 25 other New York delegates, including financier Perry Belmont and Wall Street lawyer Frederic R. Coudert. But the New York Clevelandite leaders, Senator Hill and Cleveland's financial and political mentor William C. Whitney, decreed otherwise. The Cleveland forces temporized instead and merely decided to abstain from future ballots or even vote in token fashion for former Governor Robert E. Pattison of Pennsylvania.

Having lost their best chance, the Cleveland Democrats tried to decide what to do. Financier Whitney pleaded with McKinley to soft-pedal the protective tariff and thereby form a broad coalition against Bryanism; McKinley, however, was willing to soft-pedal everything else, but protectionism, after all, was both his own and his party's only distinctive program remaining. The Clevelandites, therefore, decided at last to form a third party, the National Democrats, or "Gold Democrats," who met in September at Indianapolis. The best and most dramatic candidate for the Gold Democrats would have been President Cleveland himself, but he refused any nomination in advance. The new party then nominated Senator John M. Palmer of Illinois for president and Simon B. Buckner of Kentucky for vice president. The fact that Palmer had been a Union general and Buckner a Confederate general in the Civil War symbolized the desire of the Gold Democrats to bury the old North-South hatchet. The platform, prepared by the veteran head of the Wisconsin Democracy, Senator William F. Vilas, not only came out strongly for the gold standard and denounced free silver; it also denounced protectionism, free silver's ally in the governmental creation of special privilege. It went on to attack all forms of governmental paternalism. The National Democratic platform was the last gasp of the old hard money, *laissez-faire* Democracy. The major support for the new party came from the "Honest Money Democrats" of Illinois and of other Midwestern and Border states. They had found their state parties captured by the Bryanites and were therefore desperate enough to form another party. The Eastern Clevelandites, however, still controlled their local parties and were therefore less willing to form a new one. The Southern Democrats, also, were too worried about Populists or about a possible Republican revival to dare to bolt the party.

The Eastern sound money Democrats also failed to support the third party because of their understandable but short-sighted eagerness to defeat Bryan in the election made them virtual or outright champions of McKinley. This was the route taken by Whitney, Flower, Coudert, Representative William Bourke Cockram of New York's Tammany Hall, and the financier Thomas Fortune Ryan. Cleveland himself approved of the National Democrats but vacillated in public support. Leading New York supporter of the Gold Democrats was Calvin Tompkins, head of the state committee of the new party and chairman of the ardently pro-gold Sound Currency Committee of the Reform Club of New York, an organization which was also fervently in favor of free trade. In contrast to the other short-sighted Clevelandites, Tompkins saw the need for a long-run sound money party, which could educate the public permanently and form a continuing structure for the hard-money constituency in the country.

Unfortunately, even Palmer and National Gold Democrat Chairman William D. Bynum of Indiana envisioned the new party as merely a pro-McKinley move rather than the beginnings of a permanent organization on behalf of *laissez-faire* Democracy. Apart from Tompkins, only Ellis B.

Usher, chairman of the Wisconsin Gold Democrats, saw the party as a permanent way of keeping alive the flickering flame of personal and economic liberty — of rebuilding the old Democracy in a new institutional form.

Beset by a lack of spirit and vision, the National Democratic Party unsurprisingly played only a minor role in the 1896 campaign. They polled only roughly 133,000 votes out of 13.7 million and achieved balance-of-power status only in Kentucky and California. The National Democrats quickly faded from view after the election. The last chance to preserve *laissez-faire* Democracy was lost. But, to be fair, even the best will in the world might not have established the National Democrats as a permanent political force. For the liturgicals shifted to the Republicans, rather than the National Democrats, precisely because they correctly perceived the new McKinley Republicanism as having abandoned pietism and changed to a pragmatic and centrist party.[22]

The woes of the Democrats intensified after the election. The Eastern sound-money men were scarcely rewarded for not joining the National Democracy. On the contrary, in the wake of the smashing Democratic defeat, the old-stock Protestants who had run the Democratic Party in the Eastern cities (men such as Grover Cleveland, Calvinist — and hence creedal rather than pietist — Presbyterian from Buffalo) were now removed from leadership positions and deposed by men rising up from the predominantly Irish constituency. But the Irish Democrats soon found that it had been easier to unite Catholic and Lutheran ethnic groups under the benign leadership of old-line WASPS; throughout New England the new Irish domination of the Democratic Party rapidly alienated newly burgeoning Italian and French Catholic voters, who now proved amendable to the lures of the new, open Republican Party. In urban eastern areas, the growing identification of the Democracy as "the Irish party" succeeded in repelling other Catholic and liturgical voters and cemented the Republican Party as the national majority party.[23]

In addition to these troubles, the Democracy became shaken after Bryan's takeover by prohibitionist sentiment. The South became converted

---

[22][Editor's footnote] McSeveney, *The Politics of Depression,* pp. 163–76. For more on the National Democrats, see David T. Beito and Linda Royster Beito, "Gold Democrats and the Decline of Classical Liberalism, 1896–1900," *Independent Review* (Spring 2000): 555–75.

[23]Kleppner, "Demise of Ethnocultural Politics," vol. 3, pp. 23–24. There is particular evidence for this new Irish dominance in New Haven, Providence, and Boston.

to prohibitionism and was now the preeminent sectional stronghold of the Democratic Party. The post-Bryan Democracy outside of the South was not cohesively prohibitionist, but it was racked by powerful struggles over the issue within each state party. In some Eastern states, such as New York and Massachusetts, the internal battle was quickly won by the wets and Catholics. In others, however, the battle was closer and longer-lasting. Thus, in Ohio in 1905, the Democrats gained the endorsement of the powerful Anti-Saloon League by nominating a prohibitionist for governor against a post-McKinley Republican. In New Jersey, Anti-Saloon League endorsement of the rising progressive Democrat Woodrow Wilson ensured his election for governor in 1910 and put him on the road to the presidency. The Anti-Saloon endorsement raised the turnout rate in the rural, native Protestant southern counties of the state by a remarkable 10 to 15 percentage points over the 1906 election, and Wilson's share of the vote increased by 12 to 20 points above the Democratic gubernatorial vote four years earlier.[24]

What of the other minor parties, the Populists and the Prohibitionists? The inflationist and statist Populists, gleeful at the Bryan victory as a triumph for their principles, happily nominated Bryan for president and later dissolved themselves into the Democratic Party. The Farmers' Alliance movement, as much prohibitionist and pro-Sabbath law as they were agrarian statists, also supported Bryan to the hilt. While Bryan did not openly come out for prohibition, the prohibitionists correctly perceived him as one of their own. While the Prohibition Party refused to fuse into the Democracy, much fusion for Bryan occurred at the county level throughout the Midwest. Indeed, when the national convention of the Prohibition Party insisted (as "narrow gaugers") on keeping to one issue and to their separate entity, the "broad gaugers" split from the Prohibition Party and formed the National Party, dedicated to fusing prohibitionists with the new Bryanite Democracy. Their support, added to the whole support of state and local W.C.T.U. organizations, brought most prohibitionists into the Bryan camp. In effect, then, the Prohibition Party also dissolved into the Bryanite Democracy.

Populists for Bryan habitually hailed his candidacy as the new "moral crusade," a crusade against the "saloon power" and the embodiment of a new "party of piety." Bryanite "silver clubs" arose throughout the South

---

[24]Ibid., pp. 24–25, 55–56.

and West, behaving like revival meetings on an all-out moral crusade, and thereby frightening the liturgicals as much with their style and rhetoric as well as the substance of their program.

As Professor Kleppner writes:

> The tripartite cooperation of Democrats, Populists, and Prohibitionists was the type of grand union of "reform-ers" that many of the Midwestern Prohibition leaders especially had sought for several years. ... Bryanites were not concerned with a mere reactivation of old loyalties, but with the creation of a new coalition of voters. They hoped to draw support from the Prohibition, Populist, and Republican ranks by appealing to the concern of such voters for the creation of a moral society. To reinforce the proclivity of these voters to shift to the "new party of morality" ... they employed free silver ideology. It was intended ... to function as a morally toned ideology enlist-ing the support of voter groups that looked to the use of government power as a remedy for society's increasing amorality ...
>
> Because they were relatively more concerned with conversion than with reactivation or reinforcement of old commitments, both Bryan and his Midwestern sup-porters deemphasized their Democratic lineage and their connections with the old Democratic ideology. The image they projected of themselves was not that of "negative government," but of a government dedicated to the use of *positive action* to remedy social inequities. This was not the Democracy whose usual program was a litany of "thou shalt nots," but a Democracy espousing that very type of government which for over half a century had repelled religious ritualists [liturgicals].[25]

How did the old-line Democratic leaders and organs of opinion coun-ter the Bryanites and persuade their readers and supporters to shift to the formerly hated Republicans? They attacked free silver, not primarily on economic grounds, but as part of the Bryanite betrayal of the principles of the old Democratic Party. In short, the Cleveland Democrats correctly

---

[25]Kleppner, *The Cross of Culture*, pp. 354, 361–62.

pointed out to their constituents that Bryan was the reverse of a true Democrat in the previous scheme of things. Specifically, Bryanism was a violation of the old Democratic belief in "personal liberty," for it was yet another attempt to "regulate things ... and to propose laws governing the habits, pursuits, and beliefs of men."[26] And German anti-Bryan papers argued that Bryan was at heart a prohibitionist.

For their part, the new McKinley Republican Party cooperated enthusiastically in welcoming liturgicals into their ranks. They abandoned the old pietist symbolism and presented themselves now not as the party of morality, but as the party of prosperity sheltered by the protective tariff. In Wisconsin, for example, the Republicans followed this strategy by rejecting Robert M. La Follette, pietist, champion of the Bennett Law, and friend of the nativist and anti-Catholic American Protective Association, in deference to the fierce opposition of German Lutheran leaders.

The A.P.A., indeed, was in a quandary in the 1896 election. Previously solidly Republican, the A.P.A. had fought the moderate McKinley bitterly in Ohio politics and had supported the prohibitionist Foraker. The A.P.A. was also embittered at McKinley's willingness to appoint Catholics to public office and at his refusal to appoint leading A.P.A. members. In 1896, the A.P.A. fought McKinley's nomination with great bitterness. During the spring, the National Advisory Board of the A.P.A. accused Governor McKinley of having discriminated in favor of Catholics and against native-born Protestants in his appointments to public office. And in May, both the Executive Committee and the Campaign Committee of the A.P.A. publicly denounced McKinley and announced the support for *any other* Republican candidate.

The upshot was dissension and confusion during the 1896 campaign in A.P.A. ranks. Indeed, the consequence was the rapid disintegration of the A.P.A. and its early disappearance from American life. A.P.A. attacks, however, greatly aided McKinley's ability to attract Catholic support.[27,28]

---

[26]Cited in Ibid., p. 364.

[27][Editor's footnote] Kleppner, *The Cross of Culture*, pp. 349–52.

[28]While Jews were not politically important at this time, it might be pointed out that Bryanite pietism had distinctively anti-Semitic overtones. President Cleveland and the gold standard were attacked as agents of the "European Jew Rothschild," it being noted that the Belmonts, as Rothschild agents, had long been highly influential in the old Democratic Party. Herman Ahlwardt, a leading German born anti-Semite, endorsed Bryan in *The Gentile News*. More importantly, Mrs. Mary Elizabeth Lease, the great woman orator of Kansas

William McKinley gained the presidency in the first decisive Republican victory for the office since 1872 as the first presidential candidate of either party since 1876 to gain a majority of the popular vote. And, as we have pointed out, he began a long era of Republican control of the presidency along with both houses of Congress. McKinley's presidency quickly moved to bury old divisive pietist concerns. Prohibitionism was scuttled by the Republicans, was only revived by the Progressive movement, and was fastened on the country by the temporarily resurgent Democrats, and then only under cover of war.[29] The woman suffrage movement also died out after 1896 and was revived 15 years later by the Progressive movement.[30] And, while President McKinley formally supported the immigration restrictionists' drive for a literacy test, the Republican enthusiasm for the bill was gone. For many Republicans observed that liturgicals and the foreign-born vote had shifted to McKinley, and the newly powerful German groups were organizing strongly to prevent immigration restriction. Officers of 150 German-American societies condemned any such bill as a revival of Know-Nothingism and bigotry, and German and other nationalities formed an Immigration Protective League to combat restrictionism. The House simply failed to act on immigration restriction in 1898, and the agitation died. Once again, it took the Democratic Party and World War I to put an end to America's tradition of free immigration.[31]

Some of the new dimensions of the new American party-system which emerged from the 1896 election may be seen in a study by Paul Kleppner. Kleppner compares the average partisan leads in the various regions in the two decades, 1882–1892, the final and mature years of the third party-

---

Populism, attacked President Cleveland as "the agent of Jewish bankers and British gold," while leading Minnesota populist and prohibitionist Ignatius Donnelly wrote a novel *Caesar's Column,* prophesying a future society ruled and exploited by a Jewish world oligarchy. McSeveney, *The Politics of Depression,* pp. 186–87.

[29]But neither party could be called the prohibitionist or the anti-prohibitionist party. On this as on almost all other issues, neither party stood for anything definite and enduring anymore. Both had become the confused and confusing centrist parties that we know all too well today. [Editor's remarks] For more on the national enactment of prohibition and the 18th Amendment, which passed in 1919 under the guise of World War I, see Chapter 13 below, pp. 400–07.

[30][Editor's remarks] See Chapter 13 below, pp. 408–13. These efforts eventually culminated in the 19th Amendment, which enacted nationwide female suffrage in 1920.

[31][Editor's footnote] Higham, *Strangers in the Land,* pp. 106–07. The Immigration Act of 1917 finally passed the literacy test requirement. From there, quotas emerged in the 1920s. See also Chapters 10 and 13 below, pp. 314–16, 411–13.

system, and 1894–1904, the beginnings of the fourth party-system. The average partisan leads for the two periods are as follows:

Partisan Leads (Percentage points)[32]		
	1882–1892	1894–1904
New England	8.1 R	23.6 R
Mid-Atlantic	0.1 R	16.9 R
East-North-Central	1.1 R	14.8 R
West-North-Central	18.1 R	23.5 R
South	32.6 D	39.1 D
Border	10.9 D	0.6 D
Mountain	11.7 R	3.8 D
Pacific	3.5 R	15.5 R
U.S.: Non-South	2.4 R	14.5 R
U.S.: Total	3.7 D	7.7 R

It is clear that a one-party Democratic South with a slight Republican lead or tie in the rest of the country had been transformed into an even more one-party South with a strong Republican lead everywhere else. More specifically, a comfortably Republican New England was now heavily Republican, the evenly fought Middle Atlantic states were now solidly Republican, and the equally evenly fought East-North-Central (roughly what we have called "the Midwest") was now also decisively in the Republican camp. The same fate had hit the previously narrowly Republican Pacific states, while the previously solidly Democratic Border areas were now nip-and-tuck. The fact that Bryanite free-silver agitation had changed the thinly-populated western Mountain states from firmly Republican to narrowly Democratic was hardly sufficient comfort for the bushwhacked Democratic Party.

The unchallenged hegemony of the Republican Party was reflected in all of America's political institutions. For instance, the previously close presidential races where there was either a tie in the popular vote or a

---

[32]Kleppner, "Party Transformations in the 1890s," p. 44.

Democratic lead was now replaced by significant Republican victories. In 1876, Samuel Tilden notably bested Rutherford B. Hayes in the popular vote (50.9% versus 47.9%), despite not getting the presidency. In 1880, James Garfield narrowly beat Winfield Scott Hancock (48.27% versus 48.25%), while Grover Cleveland accomplished the same against James Blaine in 1884 (48.9% versus 48.3%). In 1888, the Democrats won the popular vote again but did not gain the presidency when Cleveland lost to Benjamin Harrison (48.6% versus 47.8%). In the 1892 rematch, Cleveland defeated Harrison by a sizable lead (46% versus 43%). But starting in 1896, the Republicans dominated the next several elections. In 1896, William McKinley triumphed over William Jennings Bryan (51% versus 46.7%) and won by an even larger lead in the 1900 rematch (51.6% versus 45.5%). Theodore Roosevelt crushed Alton B. Parker in 1904 (56.4% versus 37.6%), and William Howard Taft won by a similarly large margin against Bryan in 1908 (51.6% versus 43%). Not only was there a Republican president from 1896 until the party split temporarily in 1912, but so too were the other political structures. Whereas only once since the mid-1870s until the mid-1890s did any one party control the presidency and *both* houses of Congress, now, from 1897 through 1911, the Republicans continuously and simultaneously controlled all three organs. Between 1894 and 1904, the Republicans elected 70.6% of all the members of non-Southern state legislators, and from 1894 to 1931 the Republicans elected no less than 67.2% of the governors of the Midwestern and Western states, as well as 83.1% of the governors in the New England and mid-Atlantic regions. The South was one-party Democratic, and only the relatively insignificant Mountain states experienced any sort of vibrant two-party contest.

Not only did liturgicals shift heavily to the Republican Party after 1896, but, ironically, the new moderate McKinley Republicanism, the "Party of Prosperity," which had clung only to the protective tariff of the old-time Republican issues, was eventually even able to attract many pietists back from the lures of Bryan Democracy. In consequence, the crushing of Bryan in the presidential elections of 1900 and 1908 was even more decisive than in 1896. Kleppner has examined typically pietist and liturgical areas in the two decades. Six Pennsylvania German counties, +5.5% Democratic in the 1882–1892 decade, shifted to +6.6% Republican in the following ten years. Even more decisively, the liturgical Wisconsin Germans, an average of +24.7% Democratic in ten counties in the first period, shifted to +1.6% Republican in the latter. In contrast, ten counties of pietistic Pennsylvania

Yankees, +10.3% Republican in the first decade, increased their margin to +23.1% Republican in the next; while ten counties of pietistic Wisconsin Scandinavians, +24.8% Republican in the former, shifted to a whopping 45.5% Republican in the latter. Turnout rates fell in all these groups, ranging from a drop of 11% to 20%. Even the largely liturgical big cities, heavily Democratic cities (Boston, Brooklyn), shifted to nip-and-tuck contests; Baltimore fell from heavily Democratic to decisively Republican, while Chicago shifted from solidly Democratic to heavily Republican.

Thus, after 1896, neither major party could any longer be considered the home of consistent ideology or of emphatically pietist or liturgical religious values. Both parties were a mixed bag. The new Republican hegemony, as well as the even stronger Democratic hegemony in the South, combined with the great decline of sharp ideological or ethno-religious conflict between the parties, led to a precipitate drop in voter turnout in state and national elections. The following table of average voter "turnout rates" (percentages of eligible persons voting) for the two-party systems was presented by Professor Kleppner:

TURNOUT PERCENTAGES[33]			
	1874–1892	1900–1918	Changes in Turnout
New England	56.4	47.9	-8.5
Mid-Atlantic	67.9	55.1	-12.8
East-North-Central	74.9	61.3	-13.6
West-North-Central	64.8	61.7	-3.1
South	56.1	24.6	-31.5
Border	66.4	65.8	-0.6
Mountain	54.8	74.1	+19.3
Pacific	52.8	43.6	-9.2
U.S.: Non-South	67.3	57.6	-9.7
U.S.: Total	64.8	51.1	-13.7

[33]Ibid., p. 44.

The 14 and 13 point turnout drops in the Mid-Atlantic and East-North-Central regions reflected the sudden shift from close conflict to Republican hegemony, as did, to a slightly lesser degree, the drops in New England and the Pacific states. The extreme drop in Southern participation rates reflected also the disenfranchisement of blacks that took place in this period.[34] Only in the relatively unimportant Border and Mountain regions, where the intensity of party conflict heightened instead of slackened, did turnout rates stay the same or even increase.[35]

Looking at the turnout rates for the presidential elections, we can see even more starkly from the following table the steady and drastic decline in voter participation:

---

[34]The Southern turnout rate in presidential elections declined from about 75% in 1876 to about 68% from 1880–88, a decline reflecting the end of Reconstruction and the ouster of northern "carpetbagging" whites from the South. Then, a series of sharp declines occurred, to 60% in 1892 and 1896, then to 50% in 1900, and finally to approximately 38% in 1904 and in subsequent elections. These declines, in poor white as well as black turnout, reflected the imposition of the poll tax and of literacy requirements for voting throughout the South during this period. They also reflected the failure of the pietist-Republican Force Bill in 1891, which would have imposed federally supervised elections in Southern state elections to ensure black voting. See Jerrold G. Rusk and John J. Stucker, "The Effect of the Southern System of Election Laws on Voting Participation: A Reply to V.O. Key, Jr.," in *The History of American Electoral Behavior*, J. Sibley, A. Bogue, and W. Flanigan, eds. (Princeton: Princeton University Press, 1978), pp. 198–250. Also see J. Morgan Kousser, *The Shaping of Southern Politics: Suffrage Restrictions and the Establishment of the One-Party South, 1880–1910* (New Haven, CT: Yale University Press, 1974).

[Editor's remarks] The Jim Crow segregation laws enacted during this time were openly championed by Southern Progressives. This support was not a "blind spot" of the well-intentioned reformers, but rather part and parcel of their interventionist agenda to control and cartelize society to benefit special interest groups (such as the Anglo-Saxon white worker). See William L. Anderson and David Kiriazis, "Rents and Race: Legacies of Progressive Policies," *Independent Review* (Summer 2013): 115–33, and Chapter 9 below, pp. 292–93.

[35]The alternative view to that presented here holds that the sharp drop in post-1896 voter turnout stemmed from the adoption of personal registration requirements for voting in nearly every state. But such explanation ignores the fact that (a) voter turnout nevertheless *increased* in the Mountain states where party conflict intensified, and (b) the registration requirements were imposed only in the cities, but turnout declines occurred with equal severity in the rural as in the urban areas. See the following works of Walter Dean Burnham: *Critical Elections and the Mainsprings of American Politics* (New York: W.W. Norton, 1970), "Theory and Voting Research: Some Reflections on Converse's Change in the American Electorate," *American Political Science Review* (September, 1974): 1002–23, and "Rejoinder," ibid., pp. 1050–57; and also see Kleppner, "Party Transformations in the 1890s," p. 465.

TURNOUT RATES IN PRESIDENTIAL ELECTIONS OUTSIDE OF THE SOUTH[36]	
1896	78.3
1900	71.6
1904	64.7
1908	67.9
1912	55.9
1916	59.7

To put these figures in perspective, voter turnout rates in presidential elections had risen from 55–58% from 1828–36, to 80.2% in 1840, after which they ranged from 70% to 84%. The post-1896 declines dropped turnout rates back to pre-1840 levels.

Not only did voter turnout drastically decline, but the character of that turnout changed sharply to reflect the new conditions of American political parties. Before 1896, as we might expect, turnout rates were much higher among church members than among those unaffiliated with churches; now, however, turnout of church members dropped far more precipitously. In the third electoral system, the poor tended to vote more proportionately than the wealthy, but now the relative participation of the poor declined greatly. The same is true of young, and first- and second-generation foreign voters. Old habits die hard, and we would expect the new trend toward non-voting to hit first and deepest among the young, newly-eligible age groups. Thus, between 1876 and 1892, 62.1% of newly eligible non-southern voters turned out to the polls, but from 1900 to 1916, only 41.2% of the newly eligible bothered to vote.[37]

As Kleppner states:

... the electoral demobilization that occurred was neither uniform nor random in its social effects, but clearly and

---

[36]From Howard W. Allen and Jerome Clubb, "Progressive Reform and the Political System," *Pacific Northwest Quarterly* (July, 1974): 140. [Editor's remarks] Turnout rates as a percentage of the voting age population remained subdued throughout the 20th and 21st centuries and has hovered around 50–60%.

[37]Kleppner, "Demise of Ethnocultural Politics," vol. 3, pp. 27–32, 67.

strongly class skewed. The participation gap was most noticeable among voters towards the bottom end of the economic scale, and — even net of these economic effects — among younger-aged cohorts. Around the turn of the century, in other words, electoral politics seemed to lose much of its earlier capacity to arouse the enthusiasm of most citizens and to enlist their active participation.[38]

But how could voter interest decline drastically, especially among the poor and the young, in the very Progressive Era (approximately 1900–1917), which has been trumpeted by the Progressives themselves and laudatory historians as the voice of "the people" and the "march of expanding democracy"? Obviously, historians have, at least until the last decade or so, unfortunately taken the progressives at face value. The march of triumphal democracy was, in stark reality, a mere camouflage for an assault on democracy and on freedom on behalf of the burgeoning coalition of technocratic and Big Business elites.

For the new non-ideological party system and demobilized electorate meant also that the political party *itself* became far less important in deciding government policy. And, along with the parties, their constituencies — the voting public — became less important in influencing government actions. This decline of the political party as well as its voting constituency left a power vacuum which, as will be detailed below, the new order of experts, technocrats, and organized economic pressure groups rushed to fill. The dominance of the new elites alienated still more citizens and swelled the ranks of non-voters. The way was paved for the Progressive period.

As Paul Kleppner sums up the new trend:

> ... the cumulative effect of noncompetitiveness and mass demobilization, combined with legal changes downgrading the role of the party as organization, was to lower party effectiveness as a mobilizing agency and thus to reduce its capacity to shape policy outputs. Freeing elected decisions-makers from the constraints of the party was a requisite condition to increase the policy-shaping role of other political institutions capable of articulating group interests. As the party's role as a

---

[38]Ibid., p. 33.

determinant of legislative voting behavior declined, for example, the influence of functionally organized economic interest groups increased. That was accompanied by an accelerated tendency to remove large clusters of policy from even the potential influence of party behavior by shifting decision-making from elected to appointed bodies. Done in the name of "efficiency" and "expertise," the consequence of that removal was further to insulate decision-making from organized mass opinion. That insulation was an indispensable stage in the efforts of cosmopolitan elites to eliminate the party as a critical source of localist resistance to the centralizing impulses of corporate capitalism.[39]

---

[39]Kleppner, "Party Transformations in the 1890s," p. 59. Also see Kleppner, "Demise of Ethnocultural Politics," vol. 3, pp. 33ff.

[Editor's remarks] Many alleged instances of a democratization of politics during the Progressive Era, such as the 17th Amendment in 1913, which allowed for the direct election of senators instead of being chosen by the state legislatures, or the push for the political primaries, still fit in this schema. Their main effect was to reduce the ideological and institutional role of the political parties, allowing anyone to run based off of their public relations and contributed toward the transformation of politics into a bland popularity contest. This was highly related to the increased centralization and similarity of the parties, and the creation of the vacuum for technocrats and policymakers to control everything behind the scenes. Moreover, the 17th Amendment weakened state legislatures, and hence state governments, and transferred this power into the hands of the federal government. The diminished ability of the states to check the power of the federal government allowed for a greater expansion and consolidation of government activities.

CHAPTER 7

Theodore Roosevelt: The First Progressive, Part I

1. FINANCIAL INFLUENCE ON POLITICAL PARTIES

Before 1896, the Democratic Party was roughly a party devoted to free trade and the gold standard, while the Republican Party stood squarely for a protective tariff and was more amenable to inflationist experimentation. Put very simply, the Democrats were particularly congenial to and influenced by Wall Street investment bankers, notably the Morgan interests and by the European Rothschilds, acting through their New York agent, August Belmont, who was for many years national treasurer of the Democratic Party. The Republicans, on the other hand, were more susceptible to the influence of manufacturers seeking a protective tariff, in particular Pennsylvania iron and steel men, who had been in the forefront of the struggle for high tariffs ever since 1820. One of the main leaders of the Republican Party during the Civil War and the immediate post-war years was Representative Thaddeus Stevens, Pennsylvania iron manufacturer, and a leading proponent of the protective tariff as well as irredeemable Greenback money.[1]

---

[1][Editor's footnote] On the relationship between protectionist iron manufacturers and greenbackism, see Rothbard, "A History of Money and Banking," pp. 147–48. The protectionists shrewdly realized that when off a gold standard, currency inflation, in addition to

The two Democratic administrations of Grover Cleveland were heavily influenced by the Morgans and allied Wall Street interests. Cleveland himself got his start as a railroad lawyer in Buffalo, including for Morgan-affiliated railroads such as the New York Central. In between terms Cleveland became associated with the powerful New York City law firm Bangs, Stetson, Tracy, and MacVeagh. The original senior partner of the firm was Charles E. Tracy, J.P. Morgan's brother in law. After Tracy died in 1887, Francis Lynde Stetson became the main partner. Stetson was Cleveland's close friend, political advisor, and Wall Street law associate at the firm, and was also the counsel to J.P. Morgan & Co. Cleveland's major political organizer and Secretary of the Navy in his first cabinet was the brilliant Wall Street financier William C. Whitney, who was affiliated with various railroad interests and later served as the director of several Morgan companies. Whitney's daughter was later to marry Morgan partner Willard D. Straight. But Whitney was doubly blessed by being also closely associated with Standard Oil and the Rockefellers, a mainly Republican family, as his brother in law Oliver H. Payne was a close associate with Rockefeller in the ownership of Standard Oil. His first Secretary of War was the Boston Brahmin William C. Endicott, who had married into the wealthy Peabody family. George Peabody had established a banking firm which included J.P. Morgan's father as a senior partner; and a Peabody had been best man at J.P.'s wedding.

Another leading Cleveland associate was the prominent Boston attorney Richard Olney, Attorney-General and then Secretary of State in the second Cleveland administration. His first Secretary of State was Thomas F. Bayard, who had strong ties to August Belmont, allied to the Morgans and Rothschilds, and August's son Perry worked for Bayard in Congress. Before assuming office, Olney was the counsel to the Morgan affiliated Boston & Maine Railroad, as well as to the Burlington Railroad. Other Cleveland advisers included Morgan himself, Stetson, and August Belmont Jr., himself a Rothschild agent.

After he left the presidency, Grover Cleveland was, at the suggestion of J.P. Morgan, made a trustee of the Equitable Life Assurance Society, and participated in stock speculation with Whitney and Oliver Payne.[2]

---

providing cheap credit, also acts as a surrogate tariff since the foreign exchange market quickly anticipates the future rise in prices, which means that the exchange rate depreciates more than the current rise in prices and so net exports increase.

[2][Editor's footnote] Burch, *Elites in American History*, pp. 72, 88–89, 97–98, 118–19, 123, 150; Lundberg, *America's 60 Families*, pp. 56–57; Ron Chernow, *The House of Morgan: An*

If the Cleveland administration was heavily Morgan-tinged, the Republican Party and the McKinley administration was even more under the domination of John D. Rockefeller and Standard Oil. In the House, the powerful Speaker Thomas B. Reed of Maine was an old and close friend of Henry H. Rogers, an early associate of Rockefeller and one of the major owners of Standard Oil. The unquestioned boss of the New York Republican Party was Thomas C. Platt, an old friend and schoolmate of John D. Rockefeller's at Owego High School in upstate New York. Dominating the Senate from his post as head of the Finance Committee was Nelson W. Aldrich of Rhode Island, arch-protectionist and father-in-law of John D. Rockefeller, Jr. Aldrich entered the Senate in 1881 as a moderately prosperous wholesale grocer, and then, after 30 years of devotion to the public service, he died a multimillionaire.

Throughout his career in Congress, William McKinley of Ohio was associated with the cause of protectionism. Devoted in particular to Ohio iron manufacturing, McKinley was born into an iron-mongering and therefore protectionist family. McKinley's political and financial mentor, who engineered his political career and his presidential nomination and saved him from bankruptcy while Governor of Ohio, was Marcus Alonzo Hanna, coal operator and iron manufacturer. A business associate as well as an old friend and classmate of Rockefeller at Central High in Cleveland, Hanna was John D.'s conduit to influence over the Ohio and the national Republican Parties. As soon as McKinley became president, he had the Ohio legislature make Mark Hanna Senator from Ohio; other Senators from that state were once Henry B. Payne, father of the Standard Oil partner, and the newly elected Joseph B. Foraker, who as a Senator was a recipient of Standard Oil stipends.

McKinley's cabinet reflected a strong Rockefeller Standard Oil influence. His Secretary of State was the veteran Ohio Republican John Sherman, whom Hanna had backed for the presidential nomination a decade earlier and who currently took his Senate position. Sherman's son-in-law was a former financial advisor to Rockefeller. Secretary of Treasury was Lyman J. Gage, close to the Rockefeller-controlled National City Bank and previous president of the First National Bank of Chicago, who, after leaving the Cabinet, became president of the Rockefeller-controlled United States Trust Co. Gage's hand-picked assistant at the Treasury, Frank A.

American Banking Dynasty and the Rise of Modern Finance (New York: Touchstone, 1990), pp. 74–75.

Vanderlip, later moved to the Rockefeller-controlled National City Bank, eventually becoming its president. His second Ambassador to the Court of St. James was Joseph H. Choate, distinguished attorney for Standard Oil. Secretary of the Navy was John Davis Long, who was later appointed to be a director of the United States Trust Co. while still in office.

Driven from their Democratic home by the victory of the Bryanites, the Morgan interests backed the prominent Wall St. banker Levi P. Morton, governor of New York and former vice president, for the Republican presidential nomination in 1896. Defeating Morton and refusing him another turn at the vice presidency, McKinley made amends to the Morgans by picking as his running-mate Garret A. Hobart. Hobart had the bad taste to continue in his posts as director of a Morgan dominated bank, an insurance company, and a railroad even while vice president. In addition, William McKinley eventually granted the War Department cabinet post to Elihu Root, a brilliant attorney for Ryan and then for J.P. Morgan. Moreover, McKinley's Secretary of the Interior was Cornelius N. Bliss, close associate of Morgan and Ryan, and a director of the Equitable Life Assurance Society. In McKinley's second term, the Attorney-Generalship was granted to Philander C. Knox of Pittsburgh, who served as counsel for the nation's leading steel manufacturer Carnegie Steel which was to help form U.S. Steel, which was in turn also dominated by Morgan. Knox was a close friend and associate of Andrew Carnegie's partner and right-hand man, Henry Clay Frick, and a director of the great Pittsburgh banks of the House of Mellon. It was Frick who personally urged McKinley to name Knox to the Attorney-General post.

In September, 1901, early in President McKinley's second term, a fateful event occurred which changed the face of American politics. One of the several "lone nuts" who have suddenly appeared in American history to assassinate an American president gunned down William McKinley, and the brilliantly crafted McKinley-Hanna-Rockefeller regime crumbled into dust. For, as fate would have it, his successor was the colorful young New Yorker Vice President Theodore Roosevelt, beholden to a very different and clashing set of financial interests. The first — and the quintessential — "progressive" American president had been catapulted into power.[3]

---

[3][Editor's footnote] Burch, *Elites in American History*, pp. 134–44, 183–85; Lundberg, *America's 60 Families*, pp. 57–65; John Flynn, *God's Gold: The Story of Rockefeller and His Times* (New York: Harcourt, Brace and Company, 1932), p. 353. See also Chapter 14 below, pp. 469–70.

2. T.R.: THE MAKING OF A PROGRESSIVE

Teddy Roosevelt was America's first progressive president and it was during his administration that progressivism began to take shape as a political force, on the urban and state, as well as federal, levels.

An aristocratic New Yorker, Roosevelt went to Harvard, and there married into the top Brahmin families of the Boston financial oligarchy. His first wife, Alice Lee, was the daughter of George Cabot Lee, and was related to the Cabots, Lees, and Higginsons (the latter of the Boston investment banking firm of Lee, Higginson & Co.). The Boston financial group was generally allied to the Morgan interests. In Boston, he gained a life-long friend and close political mentor, the rising young politician Henry Cabot Lodge, also a member of the Cabot family.

After a stint as New York Assemblyman, the death of his first wife and a bitter break with his reform friends on his supporting the Republican ticket in 1884, Roosevelt moved west to his South Dakota ranch. Returning to New York, he was badly beaten for the mayoralty of New York City in 1886, and he retired to writing historical works. It seemed that, at the age of 28, Teddy Roosevelt's political career was already at an end.

But in 1889, the new President Benjamin Harrison was induced by the powerful Congressman Henry Cabot Lodge to appoint Teddy Roosevelt head of the Civil Service Commission. So ardent was Roosevelt in this post that he was reappointed by the Democratic president Grover Cleveland.[4]

In addition to a strong nationalist policy, devotion to militarism and a large navy, and to a Republican protective tariff, Roosevelt had long called for an ever-greater strengthening of the civil service system. Here, he joined the principal "reform" cause in the decades after the Civil War, a cause that prefigured the later progressive call for taking "politics" out of government. Civil service reform was the first proto-progressive cause to blend moralistic attacks on "corruption" with a supposedly scientific plea for "efficiency" and non-partisanship in government. The idea was to end or limit the "spoils system" by taking ever more government jobs out of politics, freeing bureaucrats in their posts, and making hiring and

---

[4][Editor's footnote] William Henry Harbaugh, *Power and Responsibility: The Life and Times of Theodore Roosevelt* (New York: Farrar, Straus and Cudahy, 1961), passim; Lundberg, *America's 60 Families*, p. 238. See also Burch, *Elites in American History*, pp. 146–47 for evidence of the familial ties of the Oyster Bay Roosevelts to Morgan and Vanderbilt interests.

promotion subject to "objective" written tests of "merit" rather than political party or ideology.

The civil service system, however, which began in force with the Pendleton Act of 1883, had vitally important but unacknowledged effects. For the consequence was to build and preserve a continuing ruling oligarchy that was not subject to the democratic check of the voting public. "Nonpartisanship" and civil service "protection" meant the fastening of a permanent bureaucratic elite upon the hapless public. It paved the way for rule by the expert rather than by political representatives. And there was another built-in consequence of civil service. If Party A appoints its members and then freezes them in place via civil service, this meant that, when Party B came into power, it could no longer find jobs for the party faithful in the good old way of ousting the members of Party A. Instead, Party B could only reward its followers by creating new jobs which it, in turn, could freeze into civil service. In short, the advent of civil service brought a powerful incentive for either party to multiply the number of government officials and bureaucrats.[5]

In 1895, Roosevelt was made president of the Police Board of New York City. The blustering Roosevelt immediately began to make his mark in a way that was becoming standard for "reform" politicians: a pietistic crackdown on liquor and Sunday business. Specifically, T.R. began a ferocious enforcement of the Republican-sponsored Raines Law, which mandated Sunday closing for liquor stores and saloons. The crackdown was particularly effective against neighborhood saloons and beer gardens, the latter the habitual Sunday entertainment of German-Americans. As a not unintended consequence, the result was a crippling of the political power of the saloonkeepers, the major political influence in liturgical-ethnic neighborhoods, and also habitually the bulwark of the urban Democratic Party.

Soon Germans protested against the Raines Law in New York City, and the Liquor Dealers' Association claimed that 90% of the saloonkeepers had been driven into bankruptcy by Roosevelt's rigorous prosecution of the law. Even the reform-fusion Mayor, William L. Strong, who had appointed the unpopular police commissioner, stated at a public dinner: "I found that the Dutchman [Roosevelt] whom I had appointed meant to

---

[5][Editor's Footnote] For a history of civil service reform leading up to the Pendleton Act, see Rothbard, "Bureaucracy and the Civil Service in the United States."

turn all New Yorkers into Puritans."[6] The Mayor urged T.R. — in vain — to relax his enforcement of the law, while Roosevelt was denounced and threatened, and a bomb was sent to him in the mail. The Chairman of the Republican County Committee in Manhattan went so far as to read T.R. out of the party in a desperate attempt to hold the German-American vote. But, with Roosevelt holding fast, the Republican Party went down to a crushing defeat in the ensuing election, with 30,000 German-Americans bolting to the Democratic Party. The state legislature then managed to revive saloons by authorizing the sale of liquor in hotels serving meals, an act which spawned a host of new pseudo-hotels and saloons, institutions which Roosevelt found he could not effectively stamp out.[7]

In 1896, Roosevelt and his friend Senator Lodge backed the pro-gold standard Speaker of the House Thomas B. Reed of Maine for president, and we have seen the role that Lodge played in forcing the Morgan-Wall Street pro-gold standard plank upon William McKinley. After McKinley's election, Roosevelt returned to the federal arena. At the insistence of Lodge and of T.R.'s good friends, Cincinnati millionaires Mr. and Mrs. Bellamy Storer, who had helped to bail McKinley out of bankruptcy four years earlier, Roosevelt was made Assistant Secretary of the Navy.

All his life Theodore Roosevelt had thirsted for war — any war — and military glory. In 1886, hearing of possible conflict with Mexico, Roosevelt offered to organize his South Dakota ranch hands into a cavalry battalion to lead against that country. In 1892, Roosevelt hailed U.S. demands for Chilean indemnity for injuries to U.S. sailors at Valparaiso, and he dreamt of leading a cavalry charge. Two years later, he demanded annexation of the Hawaiian Islands and the construction of a Nicaraguan canal. In 1895, T.R. lauded President Cleveland's hawkish anti-British position in the Venezuela boundary dispute, and he looked forward to war with Britain as a means of conquering Canada. That year, he wrote to Lodge that "... This country needs a war," which incited reformer and President Charles W. Eliot of Harvard to denounce Roosevelt's "doctrine of jingoism, this chip-on-the-shoulder attitude ... of a ruffian and a bully," and claimed that Roosevelt and Lodge were "degenerated sons of Harvard." Roosevelt in turn grouped together Eliot and reformer Carl Schurz with "the futile sen-

[6]Harbaugh, *Power and Responsibility,* p. 85.

[7][Editor's footnote] Harbaugh, *Power and Responsibility*, pp. 81–86; Matthew Josephson, *The President Makers: The Culture of Politics and Leadership in an Age of Enlightenment, 1896–1919* (New York: Harcourt, Brace and Company, 1940), pp. 50–64.

timentalists of the international arbitration type," who would lead to "a flabby, timid type of character, which eats away at the great fighting qualities of our race."

Now, as Assistant Secretary, Roosevelt called for the building of more battleships and dreamt of war with Japan and the annexation of Hawaii. Representative Thomas S. Butler of Pennsylvania, a member of the House Naval Affairs Committee in 1897, wrote that "Roosevelt came down here [to Washington] looking for war. He did not care whom we fought as long as there was a scrap."[8] Also yearning for war *per se* were the scholars, theoreticians, and politicos of T.R.'s circle: Senator Lodge, the Brahmin historian Brooks Adams, Ambassador to Great Britain John Hay, and T.R.'s naval mentor, Captain Alfred T. Mahan. Roosevelt's friend Justice Oliver Wendell Holmes, Jr. held war to be "divine" and held that the United States needed war to substitute danger for comfort.

After the U.S. battleship *Maine* exploded in the Havana harbor on February 15, 1898, Secretary of the Navy John D. Long, leaving the office for the day on February 25, warned the impetuous jingo Roosevelt not to take "any step affecting the policy of the administration without consulting the President or me." Instead, T.R. seized the opportunity to violate these instructions and to change American policy by sending a fateful telegram to Commodore George Dewey, ordering Dewey's squadron out of Hong Kong and, in the event of war with Spain, to blockade the Spanish fleet on the Asian coast and then to proceed to offensive operations in the Philippines. While Secretary Long was furious, he failed to countermand T.R.'s telegram, so when the U.S. went to war in April, Dewey sailed to Manila Bay and eventually the U.S. conquered the Philippines.[9]

---

[8]Henry F. Pringle, *Theodore Roosevelt, A Biography* (New York: Harcourt, Brace and Co., 1931), p. 171. [Editor's remarks] Ibid., pp. 165–71.

[9]For more on Roosevelt's foreign policy, see below. [Editor's remarks] Rothbard planned on devoting significantly more space to the evolution of foreign policy during the Progressive Era before World War I, but unfortunately did not write it. In general, during this time there was a transformation from the *laissez-faire* "isolationist" foreign policy of the United States to a bellicose, interventionist, and paternalistic approach that created an imperial empire in parts of South America and Asia to subjugate the "inferior" races. It is essential to understand that these ideas were not *antithetical*, but *complementary* to the entire progressive ideology. The president's powers were correspondingly strengthened, and the new empire was supported by progressive economists and planners who were eager to get new jobs in planning and administering the new system. This included the "Dollar Diplomacy" system, which was a gold exchange standard where dollars were the reserve currency used by the other subjugated countries.

When war came, Teddy Roosevelt at last found the military action he had lusted for all his life. With his equally pro-war friend Colonel Leonard Wood, T.R. formed the First Volunteer Cavalry, the "Rough Riders." T.R.'s and the Rough Riders' military prowess in Cuba was less than overwhelming; indeed, Roosevelt displayed a penchant for charging his men into ambush and absorbing extremely heavy losses. But although getting ambushed or surrounded twice and losing over a quarter of his men, Teddy Roosevelt managed to emerge elated and to parlay his military exploits into public legend.[10]

Back from the war, Roosevelt was urged upon the Republican Party as a gubernatorial candidate by the powerful Chauncey M. Depew, president of the Morgan-controlled New York Central Railroad. T.R.'s campaign was heavily financed by the Morgan-controlled Mutual Life Insurance company, along with other insurance companies, while J.P. Morgan apparently gave the campaign $10,000.[11] T.R. ran his successful campaign strictly

---

The transformation of foreign policy began in the second Cleveland administration in South America, at the behest of bankers eager to subsidize export growth, prod open foreign markets, and diminish Great Britain's influence. McKinley enormously accelerated this trend through the 1898 Spanish American War, in which the United States took control of the Philippines, Hawaii, Cuba, and Puerto Rico. Roosevelt continued the expansion of militarism by cracking down on Philippine guerillas, instituting the Roosevelt Corollary, which expanded the more defensive Monroe Doctrine and declared that the U.S. had the right to directly intervene in Latin American countries, creating the machismo Great White Fleet, and the Morgan backed seizure of Panama from Columbia by inciting a revolution. Taft, although less expansionist, maintained the new foreign policy by intervening in Cuba, Nicaragua, and the Dominican Republic. Wilson embodied the fulfillment of the new imperialist executive state by invading Mexico and other South American countries and enlarged U.S. imperialism to a world-wide level by getting involved in World War I.

See Murray Rothbard, *Wall Street, Banks, and American Foreign Policy* (Auburn, AL: Mises Institute, 2011 [1984]), pp. 3–23 and "The Origins of the Federal Reserve," pp. 208–34. See also, among others, Joseph Stromberg, "William McKinley: Architect of the American Empire," in *Reassessing the Presidency: The Rise of the Executive State and the Decline of Freedom*, John Denson, ed. (Auburn, AL: Mises Institute, 1999), pp. 319–39; Thomas Woods, Jr., "Theodore Roosevelt and the Modern Presidency," in idem, pp. 352–61; William Marina, "From Opponent of Empire to Career Opportunist: William Howard Taft as Conservative Bureaucrat in the Evolution of the American Imperial System," in idem, pp. 385–411; Joseph Stromberg, "The Spanish-American War as Trial Run, or Empire as its Own Justification" in *The Costs of War: America's Pyrrhic Victories*, John Denson, ed. (Auburn, AL: Mises Institute, 1999), pp. 169–201.

[10][Editor's footnote] Harbaugh, *Power and Responsibility*, pp. 96–98, 101–07; Josephson, *The President Makers*, pp. 66–89.

[11][Editor's footnote] Pringle, *Theodore Roosevelt*, p. 208; Burch, *Elites in American History*,

upon the issue of the war and his Rough Riders, denouncing the Democrats as being unpatriotic for giving reluctant support to the war and demanding that the United States must help its new conquests because "our flag has gone" to these lands.[12]

Teddy Roosevelt's term as governor has, until recent years, been neglected by historians, but now it is realized that his policies as governor prefigured his immediately succeeding years in the presidency.[13] Roosevelt moved quickly on his long-time favorite front, the extension of civil service. Working closely with George McAneny, secretary of the Civil Service Reform Association, Roosevelt drove through a civil service expansion greater than any other previously obtained in the United States.

In collaboration with labor union leaders, social workers, and wealthy Midwest Baptists, Roosevelt urged putting more teeth in labor laws, centralizing and expanding the enforcement. In addition, the maximum 10-hour-per-day labor law was expanded to all women workers. Industrial establishments in residential homes were cracked down on by imposing licensing laws and by permitting factory inspectors to enter all shops without restriction. Such laws were designed to restrict labor competition, and — in the name of repressing "sweatshops" — suppress efficient competition to the larger and more politically powerful enterprises.

Roosevelt also urged a larger governmental role in tenement housing. The drive for repressing and regulating tenement housing was largely an upper- and middle-class, as well as pietist, concern for the morals — for the "vice" and the "corruption" amidst the ethnic poor of the tenements. The upper-class guardian of the morals of the poor, Mrs. Josephine Shaw Lowell, successfully urged Governor Roosevelt to expand the vagrancy law, a meat-axe available to coerce people without visible means of support, and to round up and punish pimps. Then, at the behest of Methodist Bishop Henry Codman Potter and reform Republican F. Norton Goddard, Roosevelt put through further legal restrictions on the numbers "racket" and on any prize fighting for a fee. The new anti-numbers law went so far as to make it a misdemeanor even to possess a policy slip, while the ban on prize fighting was bitterly opposed by Tammany Hall, the leader of the New York City Democracy. Both repressive

---

pp. 131–33; Lundberg, *America's 60 Families*, p. 67.

[12][Editor's footnote] Pringle, *Theodore Roosevelt*, pp. 205–07; Harbaugh, *Power and Responsibility*, pp. 111–12; G. Wallace Chessman, *Governor Theodore Roosevelt: The Albany Apprenticeship, 1898–1900* (Cambridge, MA: Harvard University Press, 1965), p. 84.

[13]Thus, see Chessman, *Governor Theodore Roosevelt*.

measures passed the legislature. Furthermore, Roosevelt put through a bill for a state tenement house regulatory commission, which in turn put through a new housing code in 1901 that soon became a model for all the states in the nation. The code, which restricted the supply of new housing, and thereby raised costs in the name of higher quality, was put through by a commission of such wealthy reformers and social workers as I.N. Phelps Stokes, James B. Reynolds, Robert W. DeForest, and corporate lawyer Paul D. Cravath.[14]

Theodore Roosevelt was to be the first president dedicated to government conservation of public land, timber, and other natural resources. The conservation movement has always enjoyed an uncritical "press," it being almost always assumed that conservationists can only be motivated by disinterested love of nature. In fact, the conservation movement, as we shall see further below, has been an alliance of elitist groups, one part of that coalition upper-class people who wish to repress further growth and thereby preserving both their own enclaves of wealth and the natural scene around them, while others have been private real estate, timber, and other interests, such as railroads, who wish to keep potentially competing public land and natural resources off the market, thereby maintaining and raising the value of their own assets and income. A final and crucial part of the coalition are the experts and technocrats, the professional bureaucrats and managers of the natural resources.[15]

The aristocratic hunter and sportsman Teddy Roosevelt had organized the Boone and Crockett Club, the premier advocates of forest conservation, at his home in 1887. The Boone-and-Crocketters were devotees of the "scientific forestry" schemes of wealthy young New York forester Gifford Pinchot, a member of the Club and, after 1898, Chief of the U.S. Division of Forestry.[16] Governor Roosevelt's two leading advisers on conservation

---

[14][Editor's footnote] The New York State Tenement Act of 1901 raised building costs and limited construction of low income housing, thereby reducing availability. Through nighttime inspections, urban city reformers also tried to clamp down on the "lodger evil," where poor ethnic immigrants would sublet their apartments in order to accumulate enough savings to later purchase a home. Zoning laws later came about with a similar purpose to limit apartments to only families. Due to the regulations, by the 1920s real estate developers shied away from low income housing, which then led to calls for subsidies to construction companies or outright public provision. See David T. Beito and Linda Royster Beito, "The 'Lodger Evil' and the Transformation of Progressive Housing Reform, 1890–1930," *Independent Review* 20, no. 4 (Spring 2016): 485–508.

[15][Editor's footnote] For more on the conservation movement, see Chapter 8 below, pp. 252–72.

[16]For Pinochet's influence on Roosevelt, see Muriel Olivi Fisher, "The Evolution of the

were disciples of Pinchot: C. Grant La Farge, who persuaded Roosevelt to turn to Pinchot for advice on the forestry section of his message to the legislature, and James MacNaughton, representative of the McIntyre Iron Association, owner of 90,000 acres of Adirondack forest land. Pinchot's cozy relations with private timber interests were typified by his offer to use the services of his Forestry Bureau to aid private timber owners in managing their forests.

At the behest of Pinchot and of the Boone and Crockett Club, Governor Roosevelt urged the legislature to centralize the five–man state forest, fish, and game commission into a one-man agency. The plan was to succeed after Roosevelt left office; in the meanwhile, he appointed as head of the board the president of the Boone and Crockett Club, W. Austin Wadsworth, wealthy landowner and sportsman.[17]

A particularly important pre-figuring of progressivism on a federal level was Governor Roosevelt's attitude toward the "trust problem." A major part of T.R's annual message of 1900 was devoted to this question. As we have seen, 1898 and 1899 saw a tidal wave of mergers and consolidations, generally known as "trusts" — in an attempt to achieve monopolies in each of the various industries. The Sherman Antitrust Act of 1890 was considered a dead letter, and certainly none of the merger promoters considered it a problem.

The McKinley administration pursued a *laissez-faire* attitude toward the trusts, with Mark Hanna affirming that antitrust laws were a "war on corporations pure and simple" and a "war on business success." In the fall of 1899, Hanna lauded the writings of ex-labor leader and economist George Gunton, who had denounced antitrust proposals as a "Crusade Against Prosperity." Hanna's reflection of Rockefeller's *laissez-faire* views on trusts at the time is not surprising, and neither is the fact that Gunton was receiving subsidies from Standard Oil.[18]

Conservation Cartel and its Effect on Forest Resource Policy" (unpublished M.A. essay in history, University of San Diego, 1979), pp. 86–87.

[17][Editor's footnote] Chessman, *Governor Theodore Roosevelt*, pp. 77–91, 200–33, 242–52.

[18]For the regular subsidization of Gunton by Standard Oil, see Hidy and Hidy, *Pioneering in Big Business*, pp. 600, 660. That these subsidies were fairly widely known at the time can be seen in Joseph Dorfman, *The Economic Mind in American Civilization, 1865–1918* (New York: Viking Press, 1949), vol. 3, p. xxx. Gunton's article was in *Gunton's Magazine* (September 1899).

But Teddy Roosevelt and his financial allies were in the process of taking a very different line on the trusts. Roosevelt turned for advice to three distinguished economists, each of whom were taking in various ways a pro-government cartelist, rather than a *laissez-faire* position. One was the Columbia University professor, Edwin R.A. Seligman, of the distinguished investment banking family of J. & W. Seligman; another was President Arthur Twining Hadley of Yale. A third was Jeremiah W. Jenks, Cornell University professor and chief advisor to the U.S. Industrial Commission, a federal blue ribbon panel investigating the trusts. A key adviser was Secretary of War Elihu Root, once and future Ryan and Morgan lawyer.

Roosevelt emerged from these consultations determined to move toward government regulation and cartelization of the trusts and of corporations generally. In a speech in late September, 1899, Roosevelt urged the regulation of trusts first through compulsory publicity, then, if necessary, through taxation, and finally through licensing. Trusts and the accumulation of wealth were perfectly legitimate, Roosevelt was soon to hold, but regulation was needed when fortunes were acquired in a predatory manner.[19]

Jenks and Seligman had long been members of the "new school" of economics which, over a decade earlier, had frankly repudiated the idea of *laissez-faire* in favor of increasing state control of the economy. In the course of favoring the establishment of the Interstate Commerce Commission in 1887, Seligman had written:

> We must recognize the monopolies as existing facts, but hold them under control. ... Competition has had its day and has proved ineffective. Let us be bold enough to look the facts straight in the face and not shrink from the logical conclusions of our premises. Recognize the combinations but regulate them.[20]

---

[19]By this time, even McKinley was moving toward the idea of compulsory publicity for corporations. This can be seen in his establishment of the U.S. Industrial Commission, for which see pp. 214–17.

[20]Edwin R.A. Seligman, "Railway Tariffs and the Interstate Commerce Law, II," *Political Science Quarterly* (September, 1887): 374; quoted in Sidney Fine, *Laissez Faire and the General-Welfare State: A Study of Conflict in American Thought, 1865–1901* (Ann Arbor: University of Michigan Press, 1956), p. 338. Also see Jeremiah W. Jenks, "Capitalistic Monopolies and Their Relation to the State," *Political Science Quarterly* (September 1894): 486–505.

Arthur Hadley has been wrongly classified by historians as an advocate of *laissez-faire*. But while not as eager to regulate railroads and industrial combinations as some of his statist conferees, Hadley pioneered in the Rooseveltian idea of compulsory publicity. In the mid-1880s, Hadley advocated a federal regulatory commission for the railroads, but one whose powers would be essentially confined to forced publicity. Similarly, coerced publicity was his proposed remedy for industrial combinations.[21]

Compulsory publicity has a twofold cartelizing effect not generally understood by the public. In the first place, as we have seen with the vigorous competitive effect of secret rebates by the railroads, secrecy is a great spur to competitive rivalry. If business firms can somehow engineer the coercing of publicity about their rivals, they will be able to know much more about their competitors' affairs, their pricing and production policies, and hence cartel agreements, formal or informal, become far more enforceable and active competition may be crippled. Secondly, the cost of making reports and obeying government regulations puts an extra burden on small, new, and innovative competitors and hampers their chances of competing with existing and more staid large firms.

After Governor Roosevelt's speech in the fall of 1899, Jeremiah Jenks drew up a bill for Roosevelt to submit to the legislature. Newly incorporated firms were to be offered a lower tax in exchange for provisions for compulsory publicity.[22] Roosevelt then got Jenks to write a magazine article defending the bill, and induced leading state legislators to confer privately on the bill with Jenks, with Francis Lynde Stetson, attorney for J.P. Morgan and Co., and with Victor Morawetz, an attorney for Morgan railroads.

Due to the opposition of the Republican machine in New York State, the Roosevelt-Jenks bill failed to passage, but the stage was set for Roosevelt's trust policies as president of the United States.[23]

---

[21]See Arthur Twining Hadley, *Railroad Transportation* (New York, 1885); Hadley, "American Railroad Legislation," *Harper's Monthly Magazine* (June, 1887): 141–50; Hadley, "Private Monopolies and Public Rights," *Quarterly Journal of Economics* (October, 1886): 28–44; Hadley, "The Formation and Control of Trusts," *Scribner's* (November, 1889): 604–10; Hadley, *Economics* (New York, 1896); Hadley, "The Good and Evil of Industrial Combination," *Atlantic Monthly* (March, 1897): 377–385; cited in Fine, *Laissez Faire*, pp. 71–73.

[22]The full text of the proposed law is to be found in Jeremiah W. Jenks and Walter E. Clark, *The Trust Problem*, 5th ed. (Garden City, N.Y.: Doubleday, Doran and Co., 1929), Appendix C, pp. 323–43.

[23][Editor's footnote] Chessman, *Governor Theodore Roosevelt*, pp. 158–76.

The death of relatively unimportant Vice President Garrett Hobart in November, 1899 left a vacancy in this No. 2 and previously Morgan post. Teddy Roosevelt had deliberately cultivated good relations with the press, and this blustering and colorful figure was now boosted around the country for the vice presidential spot. McKinley was opposed, however, and Mark Hanna was vehemently hostile to T.R., referring to him as "erratic," "unsafe," and "a madman." After the veteran Iowa Senator William Allison turned down a McKinley offer for the nomination, McKinley and Hanna offered the vice presidential spot to Secretary of the Interior Cornelius Bliss, a New York banker and Morgan-Ryan associate. This offer was in the venerable tradition of the dominant faction in the party offering the second spot as a consolation prize to the subordinate faction. Bliss, too, refused, however, and then the president offered the post to his Secretary of War Elihu Root, another powerful figure in the Morgan ambit. But when Root too refused, McKinley was subject to the powerful pressures for Roosevelt from New York boss Tom Platt, close to the Mellon interests, and Senator Henry Cabot Lodge. Particularly powerful was the lobbying for Roosevelt by Morgan partner George W. Perkins, a close friend of both Hobart and Roosevelt. At last, McKinley and Hanna succumbed, and Teddy Roosevelt was nominated as vice president.[24]

It is not surprising that as soon as the election of 1900 was over, Teddy Roosevelt gave a lavish dinner in honor of J.P. Morgan.[25] No such gift was ever more deserved. It was clear to everyone that the battle between Roosevelt and Hanna for the presidential prize in 1904 had already begun. But all bets were off when a "lone nut" gunman assassinated William McKinley and Teddy Roosevelt fortuitously became president of the United States.

3. T.R. AS PRESIDENT: THE "GOOD" TRUSTS

Theodore Roosevelt's first — and one of his most important — moves toward regulation in the presidency was presaged in his first message to Congress upon assuming the presidency in December 1901. Reviving an old proposal for a new Cabinet Department of Commerce and Labor, to

---

[24][Editor's footnote] John A. Garraty, *Right-Hand Man: The Life of George W. Perkins* (New York: Harper & Bros., 1960), pp. 221–22; Josephson, *The President Makers*, pp. 106–10; Pringle, *Theodore Roosevelt*, pp. 216–223; Herbert D. Croly, *Marcus Alonzo Hanna* (New York: MacMillan Company, 1912), pp. 310–18.

[25]Lundberg, *America's 60 Families*, p. 68.

serve as a means of subsidizing commerce and industry, Roosevelt spoke of the department having the power to investigate corporations and to publicize their findings. Roosevelt also eyed a federal board, like the ICC, to supervise industrial combination. His address was cleared with two good friends who were also Morgan partners, George W. Perkins and Robert Bacon.

Throughout the summer of 1902, Roosevelt peppered his speeches with calls for compulsory publicity in order to curb business "evils." He found a strong ally in Attorney-General Philander Knox, an attorney close to the Mellon interests and Henry C. Frick, now a major shareholder in Morgan's U.S. Steel. Knox urged T.R. to establish a commission with compulsory powers to obtain information from interstate corporations, and to report to the president, who, in turn could or could not publicize the information as he saw fit. This provision appealed to Roosevelt's strong *penchant* for personal power, as well as to his commitment to compulsory publicity.

In early 1903, Roosevelt submitted a proposal to Congress to add to a previously proposed new Department of Commerce and Labor a Bureau of Corporations, the Bureau to have full compulsory powers to "investigate the operations and conduct of interstate corporations" and to convey that information to the president.[26]

Prefiguring the Bureau of Corporations proposal was the U.S. Industrial Commission, an investigatory body created by act of Congress in June 1898 to inquire into the economy, collect information, and recommend legislation to Congress. The Commission consisted of five Senators appointed by the vice president (the president of the Senate), five Congressmen appointed by the Speaker of the House, and nine men appointed by the president with the consent of the Senate. The Commission issued 19 volumes of reports from 1900 until its demise in February 1902.

The first chairman of the Industrial Commission, Senator James H. Kyle of North Dakota, was a Populist Senator from North Dakota and one of the most left-wing members of the Senate. But more significant than the official members of the Commission was the expert staff that did the actual investigating and guided its deliberations. All of them were of

---

[26][Editor's footnote] Kolko, *The Triumph of Conservatism*, pp. 66–67, 69–71; Lundberg, *America's 60 Families*, p. 69; John A. Garraty, *Right-Hand Man*, p. 223; Pringle, *Theodore Roosevelt*, pp. 340–42; Arthur M. Johnson, "Theodore Roosevelt and the Bureau of Corporations," *Mississippi Valley Historical Review* 45 (March, 1959): 573–74.

the new school of interventionist economists. Professor William Z. Ripley of Harvard, the Commission's expert on transportation, was to exult a decade later that the "foremost railroad presidents of the United States [were] approving a policy of federal government regulation, which, when I approved it on paper ten years ago, was characterized [by] ... a leading railroad man ... as 'pernicious.'"[27]

Roswell C. McCrea, highly paced in the academic world as Dean of the Wharton School of Finance, was the Industrial Commission's expert on taxes and transportation. McCrea looked forward eagerly to a welfare state. The Commission's expert on labor and immigration was Dr. John R. Commons, perhaps America's leading progressive economist and hence its outstanding champion of the emerging corporate state. His role in the progressive movement will be detailed more extensively below.[28] Above all, the Commission's authority on trusts and combinations was none other than Jeremiah W. Jenks, who therefore shaped the Commission's recommendations in this vital area.

The Preliminary Report of the Industrial Commission, submitted in 1900, was a thoroughly Jenksian document. The object of its recommendations was to prevent corporations or industrial combinations from deceiving investors or the public. Therefore, the Commission recommended compulsory reporting and data of all sorts to the stockholders, and to the government, and making the corporations subject to government inspection. The Preliminary Report had the effrontery to claim that "the purpose of such publicity is to encourage competition" when, as we have seen, the point was precisely the opposite. Indeed, the Commission went on to cite what it considered the horrors of secret railroad rebates to shippers before the advent of the ICC as an example of monopolization. Hence, its determination to do for general industry what the outlawry of secret rebates was supposed to be doing for the railroads.[29]

The Final Report of the Industrial Commission in 1902, continued the previous recommendations, and added a good deal more. It was recommended that federal and state anti-trust laws be strengthened and

---

[27]William Z. Ripley, "Are Our Railroads Fairly Treated?" In *Year Book of the Economic Club of New York* (1916), vol. 3, p. 209; quoted in Joseph Dorfman, *The Economic Mind in American Civilization*, vol. 3, p. 319.

[28][Editor's footnote] See Chapters 9, 11, and 13 below, pp. 291–94, 333–40, 359–60, 430–32.

[29]The full text of the Preliminary Report is in Jeremiah W. Jenks, *The Trust Problem,* 3rd ed. (New York: McClure, Phillips & Co., 1903), pp. 261–66.

enforced, with a particular crackdown on the "vicious practice of discrimination between customers" — that is, secret or open price-cutting to one or more customers at a time. State legislation was advocated, such as Massachusetts' new law regulating the floating of new stock issues, and a federal franchise tax, progressive in relation to earnings, was recommended on all interstate corporations. And, finally, as the kickoff to the official proposal for the Bureau of Corporations, the Commission recommended such a Bureau for investigation, reports, and publicity, perhaps as a preparation for a compulsory federal incorporation law.[30]

Angry that so many of the industrial mergers of the late 1890s had failed, the Final Report of the Industrial Commission also demanded that the accounting profession develop methods to "protect" investors from the alleged "watering" of stock capital in the formation of the "trusts." In reality, the watering was not a swindle, but a legitimate aspect of entrepreneurial activity. If the promoters of a particular trust or corporation are overoptimistic about its profits and estimate its future earning power — and therefore the current value of its stock — too highly, well then, each investor is free to disagree with these estimates. No one held a gun to the head of the investors in the failed trust combinations of the 1890s. The paternalistic idea that government exists to protect everyone from their own folly also meant, in this case, regulation to keep out some usually new marginal promoters for the benefit of older and stronger competitors. The cause of regulation and cartelization was thereby furthered.[31]

---

[30]Jenks and Clark, *The Trust Problem*, pp. 317–22. The Commission also urged federal subsidies to agriculture, including cartelizing agriculture through federal inspection of export products, especially meat, and the fixing of standard grades for cereals. It also recommended the establishment of a Pure Food and Drug section of the Department of Agriculture, with the power to outlaw the interstate shipment of "impure" food and drugs. It urged continuing the setting aside of the public domain for forest reserves, the conservationist taking of land out of use. The ICC was to be strengthened and given the power to regulate railroad rates. The states were urged to enact uniform laws prohibiting child labor, thereby raising wages for competing adult workers, and to pass anti-"sweatshop" laws and anti-truck laws crippling small business competition. An eight-hour day for miners was urged, thereby helping to restrict entry of workers into the field and raising wage rates for the miners remaining. As a further subsidy to labor unions and aid to restrictionism of labor, Congress was urged to regulate the interstate movement of private detectives for strike-breaking, to repress the movement of convict-made products between states, and to draft codes for railway labor. U.S. Industrial Commission, vol. 19, *Final Report* (Washington, D.C.: General Printing Office, 1902). Also see Fine, *Laissez Faire*, pp. 367–69.

[31][Editor's footnote] A common criticism of the free market is that it provides products or

The nascent accounting profession leaped to the support of the Industrial Commission's strictures, as well as to its call for compulsory publicity and periodic accounting audits, of all the trusts and corporations, for two reasons: the Industrial Commission proposals meant a great deal more work for the accounting profession, and accountants were annoyed because "going concern" capitalization, such as what the trust promoters had engaged in, was necessarily a subjective procedure. The accountants' penchant for "objective," "scientific" measurement was offended by the fact that all estimates of future earning power are necessarily subjective estimates. As Previts and Merino state, the accountants "objected to 'going concern' capitalization procedures because earning power could not be objectively measured."[32] Perhaps so, but the capital values of any business firm happen to be the discounted sum of expected future earnings of that firm, and those expected earnings, in the nature of reality and of the market, are necessarily speculative and subjective. This might be unfortunate for the "scientific" pretensions of some members of the accounting profession, but that is the way things are.[33]

---

working standards that are "poor quality" and is rife with "imperfect" and "asymmetric" information, so even if regulation has a cartelizing effect, it can still be beneficial. Against this, it is important to note that only the market can provide the optimal — ascertainable only by demonstrated consumer preferences — level of regulation, and it has institutional features to ensure that bad products are driven from the market. Entrepreneurs are incentivized to provide reliable goods in order to maximize long term profits, and consumers and investors learn the particular attributes they care about through competitive advertising among firms. Product quality and working standards rise over time as entrepreneurs increase their savings and embark upon more roundabout processes of production and engage in technological innovation. Regulation that raises quality artificially stymies this crucial progressing process of the market, slows down the rate of growth, and defies the preferences of consumers. See Rothbard, *Man, Economy, and State with Power and Market*, pp. 1069–74, 1096–1101; Mises, *Human Action*, pp. 613–19.

[32]Gary John Previts and Barbara Dubis Merino, *A History of Accounting in America* (New York: Ronald Press, 1979), p. 170. The Final Report of the Industrial Commission urged compulsory annual audited reports by large corporations, the audit to be subject to government regulation. The minority of the Industrial Commission went further to advocate a bureau in the Treasury Department, which would register all corporations and obtain a financial report, make examinations, and publish information. Ibid., pp. 133–35.

[33]George Stigler points out that the advent of new issue regulations by the Securities and Exchange Commission does not seem to have appreciably protected the investor. As Stigler states, for security as well as for all other protective regulation, "Public regulation weakens the defenses the consumer has in the market and often imposes new burdens upon him, without conferring corresponding protections. The doctrine of *caveat emptor* has not lost its force: the only change is that now the consumer must beware of different threats, and

President Roosevelt's chief business ally in driving the Bureau of Corporations bill through Congress was George W. Perkins, a Morgan partner and in the process of being Morgan's right-hand man in forming the two giant "trusts," United States Steel and International Harvester. Perkins agreed totally with Roosevelt's conception of federal regulation of trusts. Like Roosevelt, Perkins believed that there were "good trusts" and "bad trusts," and, like T.R., he believed that his own U.S. Steel and International Harvester were conspicuous examples of the good. So influential was Perkins in establishing the Bureau that when the president signed the bill into law, he gave one of the two pens he used to George Perkins.[34]

Only one important financial group stood opposed to the Bureau of Corporations bill. In a way, it was strange, since three leading representatives of the Standard Oil trust, John D. Archbold, Henry H. Rogers, and John D. Rockefeller himself, had all testified strongly in favor of a federal incorporation law and federal regulation of corporate publicity before the U.S. Industrial Commission. John D. Rockefeller advocated that there be

> First, Federal legislation under which corporations may be created and regulated, if that be possible. Second, in lieu thereof, State legislation *as nearly uniform as possible* encouraging combinations of persons and capital for the purpose of carrying on industries, but permitting State supervision ...[35]

But now, with Morgan ally Theodore Roosevelt at the helm, Standard Oil took a very different tack. Archbold lobbied heavily against the Bureau of Corporations bill, and John D. Rockefeller, Jr. sent telegrams to several

---

threats which he is less well equipped to defend against." George J. Stigler, "Can Government Protect the Consumer?" in *The Citizen and the State* (Chicago: University of Chicago Press, 1975 [1971]), p. 181. [Editor's remarks] For a similar analysis behind the origins of the Securities Act of 1933 and the Securities Exchange Act of 1934 that stresses government enforced cartelization, see Murray Rothbard, "From Hoover to Roosevelt: The Federal Reserve and the Financial Elites," in *A History of Money and Banking in the United States: The Colonial Era to World War II*, Joseph T. Salerno ed. (Auburn, AL: Mises Institute, 2005), pp. 320–30.

[34]John A. Garraty, *Right-Hand Man,* p. 223. [Editor's remarks] George Perkins was heavily affiliated with J.P. Morgan and has been called one of Roosevelt's "most important informal advisors" and "J.P. Morgan's chief governmental emissary." Burch, *Elites in American History,* pp. 158–59. See also Chernow, *House of Morgan,* pp. 105–12.

[35]Quoted in Kolko, *The Triumph of Conservatism,* p. 64.

key Senators against the bill. President Roosevelt demagogically seized the opportunity to hold a press conference deceitfully charging that the widely hated John D. *Senior* sent the telegram. It was to be the first shot in a savage war against Standard Oil. Given T.R.'s ability to manipulate the press for his ends, Congress rushed to pass the bill in February 1903. T.R. promptly made his private secretary, George B. Cortelyou, Secretary of the new Department of Commerce and Labor and appointed as first Commissioner of Corporations young James R. Garfield, son of the late president and former staff attorney for the Civil Service Commission when Roosevelt served as its head. Before Garfield was selected, his appointment was cleared with and approved by Francis Lynde Stetson, attorney for the House of Morgan, and fellow alumnus with Garfield from Williams College.

After a year or more of operation, business was quite content with Garfield's administration of the Bureau. In his annual December 1904 message to Congress, T.R. declared that the Bureau had "been able to gain not only the confidence, but, better still, the co-operation of men engaged in legitimate business." Garfield himself, in the Bureau's first report in the same month, declared that "In brief, the policy of the Bureau in the accomplishment of the purposes of its creation is to cooperate with, not antagonize the business world; the immediate object of its inquiries is the suggestion of constructive legislation, not the institution of criminal prosecutions." Garfield also pleased most big businessmen by coming out in favor of federal licensing of corporations, a recommendation that caused George W. Perkins to call up Garfield and congratulate him warmly. Even John D. Rockefeller, Sr., so soon to feel the wrath of T.R., praised Garfield's proposal, because "the Federal government would scarcely issue its license to a corporation without at the same time guaranteeing to its beneficiaries an adequate degree of protection." But Rockefeller was soon to find out that, as far as Roosevelt was concerned, Standard Oil would not be a firm that he would be interested in "protecting."[36]

In the same month, February 1903, as it passed the Bureau of Corporations bill, Congress also passed the Elkins Anti-Rebating Act of 1903 at the behest of the Morgan railroads trying to outlaw railroad rebates to shippers.[37] The satisfaction with which big business greeted Roosevelt's

---

[36]Ibid., pp. 77–78. [Editor's remarks] Ibid., pp. 71–72; Josephson, *The President Makers*, p. 147.

[37]See Chapter 2 above, pp. 80–81.

policies on federal control of corporations and railroad rates was embodied in an editorial of late December 1904 by the influential *Wall Street Journal*:

> Nothing is more noteworthy than the fact that President Roosevelt's recommendation in favor of government regulation of railroad rates and Commissioner Garfield's recommendation in favor of federal control of interstate companies have met with so much favor among managers of railroad and industrial companies. It is not meant by this that much opposition has not developed, for it has ...
>
> The fact is that many of the railroad men and corporation managers are known to be in favor of these measures, and this is of vast significance. In the end it is probable that all of the corporations will find that a reasonable system of federal regulation is to their interest.[38]

In 1904 and 1905, the Roosevelt administration entered into a cozy arrangement with the two major Morgan-controlled trusts, International Harvester and United States Steel, both of them organized and supervised by T.R.'s close friend George W. Perkins. In 1904, Garfield and Attorney-General William H. Moody agreed to Harvester's proposal that they would not prosecute any violations of the law provided that the company would conform in the future. In return, Harvester cooperated by giving any desired information to the Bureau; after all, as Harvester financier Cyrus H. McCormick told Garfield, "International Harvester was in entire sympathy with some program of this sort."[39]

There matters lay until, in December 1906, Congress passed a resolution ordering the Bureau of Corporations to investigate International Harvester. Harvester was delighted to comply. Meeting with Garfield and his deputy and eventual successor Herbert Knox Smith in January were Perkins, McCormick, and Harvester's chief spokesmen, Judge Elbert H. Gary, chairman of the board of U.S. Steel. Gary and Roosevelt had formed a close working relationship since 1902. Gary, seconded by Perkins and McCormick, told Garfield and Smith that "he believed in the work of the Bureau and the necessity of Governmental supervision of large corporations, and that he felt that the president and the Bureau, representing his

---

[38] *Wall Street Journal*, December 28 1904. Quoted in Kolko, *Triumph of Conservatism*, p. 78.
[39] Ibid., p. 74.

policy, was a strong safeguard both to the removal of abuses and to the prevention of violent attacks on private rights in general that might otherwise come." Furthermore, they informed Garfield that a Bureau report would show that they were operating in America at a loss, and "then they would have just ground for raising American prices."[40]

Lo and behold, however, a threat appeared to this friendly arrangement. Attorney-General Charles Joseph Bonaparte, a patrician Baltimorean who had met Roosevelt as a young civil service reformer, insisted on bringing suit against Harvester for some of its overseas activities. When Bonaparte failed to take even the hint of President Roosevelt to deter action until the Bureau investigation was complete, Herbert Knox Smith, former assistant head and now the head of the Bureau, wrote an impassioned letter to Roosevelt. The letter detailed all the arrangements and understandings the Bureau had worked out with the Morgan interests. Smith pointed out that "The attitude of the Morgan interests generally, which control this company, has been one of active cooperation," and any prosecution would abandon the crucial policy of distinguishing sharply between "good" and "bad" trusts. Attacking the "economic absurdity" and unenforceability of the Sherman Act, Smith pointed out the beneficent alternative of federal regulation through compulsory publicity. Smith then warned that "it is a very practical question whether it is well to throw away now the great influence of the so-called Morgan interests, which up to this time have supported the advanced policy of the administration, both in the general principles and in the application thereof to their specific interests, and to place them generally in opposition."[41] A few days later, Roosevelt ordered Bonaparte to drop the suit.

U.S. Steel's arrangement with the Roosevelt administration occurred a bit later than Harvester's, but it was activated considerably earlier. In late 1904, in one of his frequent meetings with T.R., Judge Gary proposed

---

[40]Ibid., pp. 119–20.

[41]Smith to Roosevelt, September 21, 1907. Quoted in Johnson, "Theodore Roosevelt and the Bureau of Corporations," pp. 588–89. Also see Kolko, *The Triumph of Conservatism*, pp. 121–22. Bonaparte was something of an anomaly; in 1899, he had unequivocally denounced any attempt at governmental regulation or restraint of industrial combinations. He was also, as H.L. Mencken later pointed out, "that strangest of hybrids, a Catholic Puritan," being one of the leading backers of the Baltimore Anti-Vice Society. One of Bonaparte's great attractions for T.R. was that he was of royal blood, being the grand-nephew of Napoleon I. H.L. Mencken, "An American Bonaparte," *A Mencken Chrestomathy* (New York: Knopf, 1949), p. 287.

to the president, that "If at any time you feel that the Steel Corporation should be investigated, you shall have an opportunity to examine
the books and records of all our companies, and if you find anything in
them that you think is wrong, we will convince you that we are right or
we will correct the wrong." To which the president replied, "Well, that
seems to me to be about the fair thing." Shortly thereafter, in January
1905, the House of Representatives ordered the Bureau of Corporations
to investigate U.S. Steel. In November, Gary, Henry Clay Frick, Garfield,
and Roosevelt met at the White House and formalized the arrangement.
U.S. Steel would cooperate with the government and supply information,
while, if the president found a violation of law, publicity would be the only
punishment wielded against the company. Explaining to Garfield why he
was willing to be so cooperative, Judge Gary wrote that "the public utterances of the president, and your statements to me from time to time, have
been such as to show conclusively to my mind that there was no intention
of doing or saying anything that would injure our Corporation or disturb
business conditions." Garfield was delighted; here was "a long step ahead
in fixing the work of the Bureau on the lines I wish."[42]

T.R.'s closeness to the Morgan interests may also be seen in several of
his key appointments. As Secretary of War, T.R. reappointed Elihu Root,
an old and valued friend and adviser, who had been a lawyer for the New
York financier and Morgan ally Thomas Fortune Ryan and later for the
House of Morgan itself, and also served at various times as director of the
Morgan-controlled National Bank of Commerce and Mutual Life Insurance Co. In 1904, Root left the Cabinet to aid J.P. Morgan in reorganiz-
ing Equitable Life Assurance Company to direct Morgan's investments in
China and defend Morgan against T.R. in the Northern Securities case
described below. The following year, Root was rewarded for his efforts by
being appointed T.R.'s Secretary of State, the most powerful post in the
Cabinet. Root, indeed, was T.R.'s original choice as his successor, an offer
which Root, perhaps because of the burden of his "Wall Street" image,
refused.

Root promptly appointed Robert Bacon, Morgan partner and old
Harvard friend of Roosevelt, as Assistant Secretary of State. When Root
left office toward the end of T.R.'s term to become a New York Senator, the
president made Bacon his Secretary of State. In the last two years of his

---

[42]Kolko, *The Triumph of Conservatism*, pp. 79–81.

administration T.R. appointed George von L. Meyer of Boston as his Post-master-General. Meyer was an agent of the House of Morgan and a direc-tor of the Old Colony Trust Company of Boston. Secretary of the Navy during 1904 was Paul Morton, president of Equitable (Ryan-Morgan), and former vice president of the Morgan-dominated Atchison, Topeka, and Santa Fe Railroad, from which post he had advocated federal regula-tion and cartelization of railroads five years earlier. Serving for a while as T.R.'s Assistant Secretary of the Navy was none other than Herbert L. Sat-terlee, J.P. Morgan's son-in-law. Furthermore, Roosevelt made Elihu Root's law partner, Henry L. Stimson, Federal District Attorney of New York, and later obtained for Stimson the Republican nomination for the governor-ship. Shortly after assuming office, Roosevelt appointed Henry C. Payne of Wisconsin to be Postmaster General. Payne was president of the Wisconsin Telephone Company and a director of the North American Company, both Morgan concerns. Roosevelt appointed Payne to Postmaster General as an apparent way of weakening Hanna's grip on the national Republican Party. [43]

The one case that some historians raise as a counter-example to the close affinity between Roosevelt and Morgan was the Northern Securities case. After battling fiercely for control of the Northern Pacific and other competing Western railroads, the Morgan and the Edward H. Harriman-Kuhn-Loeb interests effected a détente, forming the Northern Securities Company in 1901 as a holding company for the merged railroads with an agreed-upon allocation of the stock. Without consulting Root or other advisers, and consulting only Attorney-General Philander Knox, in one of the first acts of his administration Roosevelt decided to revive the virtually moribund Sherman Act and to launch an anti-trust suit against Northern Securities in February 1902.

There is no question about the fact that Morgan was upset at the suit, especially about not being consulted or advised in advance. But this in itself is no indication of a fundamental break between Morgan and the president. Morgan's personal visit to Roosevelt over the suit has become famous, but its significance has been misconstrued. Morgan is supposed to have told T.R.: "If we have done anything wrong, send your man [i.e., the Attorney-General] to my man [Morgan's lawyer] and they can fix it up." T.R. is supposed to have rejected this offer of détente, but to have

---

[43][Editor's footnote] Burch, *Elites in American History*, pp. 150, 155, 189, 191; Lundberg, *America's 60 Families*, pp. 64, 70, 72; Kolko, *The Triumph of Conservatism*, p. 84; Josephson, *The President Makers*, pp. 118, 407; Pringle, *Theodore Roosevelt*, pp. 501, 538.

gone on to assure Morgan that he was planning no further foray against U.S. Steel or any of the other Morgan trusts. After Morgan left, T.R. was supposed to have turned to Knox to observe that Morgan "could not help regarding me as a big rival operator, who either intended to ruin all his interests or else could be induced to come to an agreement to ruin none."[44]

The main point, however, is that Roosevelt clearly agreed to Morgan's deal. Or, at least, all of his subsequent actions, in and out of the presidency, supports this conclusion. For although the U.S. government won a technical victory against Northern Securities in the Supreme Court's decision of March, 1904, the upshot of the suit was not to injure either Northern Securities or the Morgan interests. Suffice it to say that only the formal device of the holding company in this situation was banned. Overall,

> The Northern Securities Case was a politically popular act, and it has strongly colored subsequent historical interpretations of Roosevelt as a trustbuster. It did not change the railroad situation in the Northwest, the ownership of the railroads in that region, nor did it end cooperation among the Hill-Morgan and Harriman lines. Roosevelt never asked for a dissolution of the company, or a restoration of competition.[45]

Indeed, according to one historian, "by the terms of the [court's] decree the Morgan-Hill ownership in the railroads was increased at the expense of Harriman."[46] Perhaps that was, after all, the ultimate point of the whole affair. The House of Morgan, in fact, was enough satisfied with Teddy Roosevelt's performance in office to donate $150,000 to T.R.'s reelection in 1904.[47]

4. T.R. AS PRESIDENT: THE "BAD" TRUSTS

Considering later events, the Northern Securities case may have been, not a break with Morgan at all, but the opening shot in Theodore Roosevelt's

---

[44]In Joseph B. Bishop, *Theodore Roosevelt and His Time* (New York, 1920), vol. 1, p. 184–85.

[45]Kolko, *The Triumph of Conservatism*, p. 67.

[46]Lundberg, *America's 60 Families*, p. 71. Also see Josephson, *The President Makers*, p. 130. [Editor's remarks] For evidence that the Northern Securities Company did not restrain competition between the railroads, see Armentano, *Antitrust and Monopoly*, pp. 51–55.

[47][Editor's footnote] Josephson, *The President Makers*, p. 167; Lundberg, *America's 60 Families*, p. 83.

war with Morgan's great financial rival, E.H. Harriman. After the Roosevelt administration leaked dark hints during the fall of 1906 about breaking up the Harriman railroad lines of Union Pacific and Southern Pacific, Harriman understandably linked this threatened persecution to his refusal to donate a large sum of money to the Republican campaign that year. When one of Harriman's attorneys, Maxwell Evarts, tried to intercede with the president, Roosevelt burst out: "Well, you don't know what Morgan and some of these other people say about Harriman."[48] The following spring, one of Harriman's employees stole a letter sent by Harriman to his chief counsel in late 1905, expressing his disillusion with Roosevelt, with the sums of money that Harriman had contributed to Roosevelt and the broken promises that T.R. had made to him in return. The letter was published in the press, to which Roosevelt retorted by vilifying Harriman at a press conference, attacking him as a dangerous "wealthy corruptionist."

An important clash of the Morgan and Harriman interests involving the Roosevelt administration occurred in 1907. Morgan was intent on consolidating his control of the entire New England railroad system under the aegis of his New Haven Railroad. In the spring of 1907, he accomplished the most important step in this process: purchase by New Haven of the Boston & Maine Railroad. Before assuming final control, Morgan, Charles S. Mellen, president of the New Haven, and other Morgan executives had an audience with Roosevelt where they won his approval of the merger, thus fending off any anti-trust suit. In addition to his general affinities with Morgan, one of Morgan's key allies in this merger, was Lee, Higginson & Co., whose partner, George Cabot Lee, Jr., was a former brother-in-law of T.R.'s. The major opponent of the merger on the other hand, was E.H. Harriman, who himself was trying to acquire the Boston & Maine.

But keeping up a hysterical drumfire of public criticism of the merger was the wealthy progressive Boston corporate lawyer, Louis D. Brandeis, who somehow managed to gain for himself, both in the press at the time and among historians afterward, the reputation of being a "people's advocate" removed from the sordid economic interests of the day. In reality, as was fully known to his enemies at the time, Brandeis was an attorney for Morgan's great investment banking rival, Kuhn-Loeb, which in turn was

---

[48]George Kennan, *E.H. Harriman* (Boston: Houghton and Mifflin, 1922), vol. 2, p. 224. Also see Josephson, *The President Makers*, pp. 240–42. J.P. Morgan's hatred of Harriman was legendary. "Punk" was just one of the habitual epithets that Morgan would use to refer to Harriman. See Birmingham, *"Our Crowd,"* pp. 189, 222.

the investment bank for the Harriman interests. When T.R., under public pressure, finally filed an anti-trust suit against the New Haven-Boston
& Maine merger in May 1908, Roosevelt's old friend and major political
mentor, Henry Cabot Lodge, long allied to the Morgan interests, wrote to
T.R. informing him of the facts of life: namely, that Louis Brandeis was
really a tool of Harriman and Kuhn-Loeb. In response, Roosevelt in effect
dropped the suit.[49]

But the outstanding example of a "bad" trust, from T.R.'s point of view,
was Standard Oil. Roosevelt had never forgiven McKinley and Hanna — of
the Rockefeller wing of the Republican Party — for stubbornly resisting his
nomination for vice president in 1900. Then, the Rockefellers angered T.R.,
as we have seen, by lobbying against his Bureau of Corporations Bill. The
Standard Oil people tried to induce Mark Hanna to run for the Republican
nomination in 1904 against the upstart Roosevelt; but the Hanna boom,
which much worried the president, was cut short by Hanna's death in the
early part of the year. There is evidence that the Rockefeller forces then
swung their support to Judge Alton B. Parker, the colorless Democratic
nominee, who got roundly clobbered by Roosevelt in the 1904 election.[50]

In Roosevelt's second term, his first full term elected on his own,
he concentrated an assault on Standard Oil. From 1905 on, Roosevelt
directed the Bureau of Corporations to focus its attentions upon, i.e., to
persecute, Standard Oil. In explanation, Roosevelt vindictively admitted
many years later: "It [Standard Oil] antagonized me before my election,
when I was getting through the Bureau of Corporations bill, and I then
promptly threw down the gauntlet to it."[51] Another important consider-
ation is that Morgan's hated foe, Harriman, was financially allied with the
Rockefellers.[52]

---

[49][Editor's footnote] Kolko, *Railroads and Regulation*, pp. 156–61. For more on Brandeis,
see Rothbard, "From Hoover to Roosevelt," pp. 322–23.

[50]Thomas W. Lawson, Boston financier and former associate of John D. Archbold and Henry H. Rogers of Standard Oil, testified before a U.S. Senate subcommittee on campaign contributions that Rogers "practically gave their agents at the [Democratic] convention *carte
blanche* to nominate Mr. Parker." See Lundberg, *America's 60 Families*, pp. 85–86. Also see
Clarence W. Barron, *More They Told Barron* (New York: Harper & Bros., 1931), p. 51.

[51]Johnson, "Theodore Roosevelt," p. 584.

[52][Editor's footnote] For this and the Rockefeller ambit's foray into banking and other investments, see Josephson, *The Robber Barons*, pp. 394–403.

In 1906, President Roosevelt launched what can only be considered a savage prosecution of Standard Oil. It was the first really serious and major use of the Sherman Anti-trust Act as a weapon against industrial corporations. First, the Bureau of Corporations reported, in the spring of 1906, that Standard Oil, by accepting railroad rebates, had violated the cartelizing Elkins Anti-Rebating Act. In September 1907, the Roosevelt administration filed a far more important — and ultimately successful — suit to dissolve Standard Oil under the Sherman Act. When Standard Oil, alarmed, offered a détente, Roosevelt turned the idea down, for to T.R., both Standard Oil and Harriman were "setting the pace in the race for wealth under illegal and improper conditions," and were the embodiments of the "bad," as contrasted to the "good" Morgan trusts.[53]

Teddy Roosevelt's motive for launching his brutal assault on Standard Oil have not been fully explained by historians. His alleged hostility to trusts is belied by his sharp distinction between "good" and "bad" ones, and the aligning of the Morgan trusts as good and Morgan's opponents as bad.[54] Personal slights can hardly account for the persistence of the hostility. Nor does the alignment of Roosevelt with Morgan and the

---

[53]Kolko, *The Triumph of Conservatism*, pp. 123–25.

[54][Editor's footnote] Roosevelt's characterization as a trustbuster has been greatly exaggerated. In the entire seven-and-a-half years of his presidency, only 44 antitrust cases were initiated, with at most 10 against actually large companies. Although he initiated more than his predecessor McKinley, under the four-year presidency of his successor Taft 80 suits were initiated. In addition,

> Roosevelt's "bad trusts" were basically "non-Morgan trusts," such as the Rockefeller-controlled Standard Oil Co. [or] the Harriman-dominated Union Pacific Railroad. ... Conversely, Roosevelt's "good trusts" usually turned out to be big Morgan-controlled companies, such as U.S. Steel Corp. and International Harvester Co., ... no action was taken against either of these giant concerns (although some federal officials were so inclined), partly because of Roosevelt's implicit trust in Morgan-backed firms and the quiet, though highly effective pressure applied by such influential Morgan men as George W. Perkins and Elbert H. Gary, board chairman of the U.S. Steel Corp. [Burch, *Elites in American History*, pp. 164–165. Also see Josephson, *The President Makers*, p. 242.]

It should be noted that Roosevelt was not a complete tool to the Morgan interests; his erratic personality and certain actions during his political career did cause some headaches and annoyances, such as the Northern Securities Case. However, he allowed himself to be surrounded and influenced by Morgan and his affiliates, and overall his actions were beneficial to the ambit.

Morgan-Rockefeller division provide a satisfactory explanation *per se*. For these divisions had persisted for decades. The point is that previously, the Rockefeller-Morgan contests were far more gentlemanly, and centered on such issues as higher or lower tariffs. The sudden bringing of the anti-trust weapon out of a disused closet, and the use of it to go for the Rockefeller jugular, can only be explained by some new conditions — something new that might have entered the Morgan vs. Rockefeller conflict and intensified it greatly.

The origins of the Sherman Antitrust Act of 1890 has, unfortunately, not been subjected to the kind of withering revisionist analysis that Gabriel Kolko and others have employed on the later regulatory measures of the Progressive Era.[55] One thing is clear: conservative old Republican Senator John Sherman of Ohio can in no way be considered an opponent of big business. We do know that the Republican Party was increasingly under attack by the Democrats for their protectionist policies and that one of the cogent Democratic charges is that it was a high protective shield behind which trusts and cartels could form, free of at least external competition. Committed as they were to the protective tariff, the Republicans demagogically countered the argument by passing a measure supposedly designed to combat trusts. The fact that it was illogical to create a governmental shield for trusts and then use government force to try to dissolve them, is not something that would long stop any politician who felt he could get away with the illogic.

Furthermore, we know that the Sherman Act was rarely used by any of the administrations, and that it sunk into innocuous desuetude by the time of the McKinley administration. That it was designed as a sop to public opinion and to take the heat off the tariff therefore seems likely.

But there was another motivation prompting Senator Sherman personally. Sherman had been a candidate for the presidential nomination since 1880, and with the backing of Mark Hanna, seemed to be winning his lifelong desire at the convention in 1888. The frontrunner in the bal-

---

[55]The only major work on the origins of the Sherman Act is an old one, hopelessly mired in the outmoded world-view of the masses rising up to curb big business. See Hans B. Thorelli, *The Federal Antitrust Policy: The Origination of an American Tradition* (Baltimore: Johns Hopkins Press, 1955). For an excellent critique of Thorelli's anti-business bias from an economic historian who supports antitrust and is outside the revisionist tradition, see William L. Letwin, "The Origins of Antitrust Policy," *Journal of Political Economy* (April, 1956): 156–59. Also see Letwin, *Law and Economic Policy in America: The Evolution of the Sherman Antitrust Act* (New York: Random House, 1965).

loting until unexpectedly beaten by Benjamin Harrison of Indiana, the embittered Sherman blamed his defeat on Michigan Governor Russell Alger, one of his rivals for the presidential nomination. Sherman publicly accused the wealthy Alger of bribing pledged Southern delegates away from Sherman at $50 a head, and there is considerable evidence that Sherman's charge was not unfounded.

It was only after his defeat that Sherman evinced a sudden interest in antitrust legislation, particularly with regard to the hated Russell Alger's monopoly Diamond Match Company, of which Alger "the Diamond Match King" was a principal financier. We know that Sherman read with great glee to the Senate, as an example of a harmful monopoly, the full text of the Michigan Supreme Court decision in the case of *Richardson v. Buhl and Alger* (1889), in which the court declared a specific contract between the organizers of the Diamond Match Company to be unenforceable because it aimed at a monopoly in the match industry. And, significantly, it has been reported that when President Harrison signed the Sherman Antitrust Act, he remarked to his aide, "John Sherman has fixed General Alger."[56]

To return to our central problem: was there any change in objective economic conditions that might account for a desire by the Morgan interests

---

[56]The reported statement is in Matilda Gresham, *Life of Walter Quintin Gresham* (1919), vol. 2, p. 632. The Michigan law case is *David M. Richardson v. Christian H. Buhl and Russell A. Alger*, 77, Mich. 632 (1889). See Letwin, *Law and Economic Policy*, pp. 87–92, especially p. 92n. Thorelli dismisses the problem in a prissy and naïve note: "The present writer is unable to believe that such a personal matter would play a part of significance as a factor motivating Sherman with regard to the antitrust bill or, in fact, any other major legislative measure." Thorelli, *The Federal Antitrust Policy*, p. 168n. [Editor's remarks] Ibid., pp. 49–50, 402. See Robert L. Bradley, Jr., "On the Origins of the Sherman Antitrust Act," *Cato Journal* 9, no. 3 (Winter 1990): 737–42, which presents an account of Sherman's motives very similar to Rothbard's. Alger actually only had a limited relationship with the company, and Sherman intentionally exaggerated it in order to hurt Alger's future political career. In addition, for other similar studies that Rothbard's analysis foreshadowed, which argue that Sherman Antitrust was not passed to protect the consumer but instead for other motives (such as to protect inefficient businesses at the expense of more efficient competitors or to divert attention away from the 1890 McKinley Tariff), see Thomas J. DiLorenzo, "The Origins of Antitrust: An Interest-Group Perspective," *International Review of Law and Economics* 5 (1985): 73–90; Thomas W. Hazlett, "The Legislative History of the Sherman Act Re-examined," *Economic Inquiry* 30 (April, 1992): 263–76. For a study behind the motivations of antitrust at the state level, see Donald J. Boudreaux and Thomas J. DiLorenzo, "The Protectionist Roots of Antitrust," *Review of Austrian Economics* 6, no. 2 (1993): 81–96.

to trot out the formerly innocuous Sherman antitrust weapon and launch a savage assault upon Standard Oil? The answer is yes: the eruption of the International Oil War.

5. The International Oil War

For decades, American petroleum was the oil used by other countries in Europe and Asia, and by the early 1880s, Standard Oil had a virtual monopoly of refined petroleum exports, with kerosene for oil lamps as the major product. Then, in the mid-1890s, the refinery financed by the Nobel brothers Robert and Ludvig, in Baku, Russia, began to challenge the exclusive Standard dominance of foreign oil markets. The Swedish Nobel brothers had by then built pipelines and steam-run oil tankers in Russia, and its Baku refinery in the Caucuses pioneered the continuous distillation process two decades before it would be adopted in Standard Oil refineries. By the mid-1880s, the powerful Rothschild Bank in Paris began to collaborate with the Nobels in production and refining, and also in delivering oil by railroad tank car from the Black Sea to the lucrative markets in Western Europe.

By the late 1880s, it was clear that Standard Oil was in for a fight; the Nobel-Rothschild alliance was matching Standard markets in Western Europe with the help of kerosene that was cheaper and of higher quality than the American product. Due to the growth of Russian and other foreign crude, the American proportion of the world's crude oil output had fallen rapidly from 85% in 1882 to 53% in 1888. Of the kerosene sold for export, about 90% of the American product was marketed by Standard Oil. Meanwhile, Russian crude production at Baku rose from 13% of the world's output in 1882 to 38% nine years later.

J.C. Chambers, American Consul in Batum, in the Caucuses, waxed livid in assessing the growth of Russian oil. Perhaps his anger was connected to his doubling as the eyes and ears of Standard Oil in the region. In his consular reports, in the late 1880s, Chambers charged the Russians with having a "quixotic ambition to drive the American oil from the markets of the world." And William Herbert Libby, Standard Oil's roving ambassador to the world, pinpointed the "support of the Russian government" and of key European bankers in accounting the meteoric rise of Baku oil.[57]

---

[57]Hidy and Hidy, *Pioneering in Big Business*, p. 135. By the early 1880s, the U.S. State Department acted as a foreign arm of Standard Oil by instructing its representatives abroad to

To counter the Nobel-Rothschild alliance, Standard set up its own aggressive marketing affiliates and subsidiaries abroad. As a result, Standard's Anglo-American Oil had captured 71% of the British oil import market by 1891. By the 1890s, the Nobel-Rothschild Russian interests had gained only a third of the British kerosene market and a fifth of Western Europe's. Asia and Latin America, as well as the rest of the European market, were Standard Oil's. Standard seemed secure in its world dominance.

In the early 1890s, Baron Alphonse de Rothschild offered a cartel arrangement to John D. Archbold of Standard Oil, with Rothschild being willing to guarantee Standard 80% of the world oil market. What happened then is unclear. The offer was surely tempting, especially since Standard's proportion had by then fallen to 70%. But nothing was achieved beyond a series of limited agreements from time to time. The U.S. Consul General in St. Petersburg reported that the negotiations broke down because the Russian Finance Minister, supporting the Nobel-Rothschilds, refused to give his backing to such concessions to Standard Oil. Or perhaps Harvey O'Connor is right that

> The world was still Standard's oyster; and while it was obliged reluctantly to witness cheaper Russian markets, it was by no means willing to formalize any such seizure through written agreement.[58]

But then there came into this idyll for the Rockefellers a cloud no bigger than a man's hand. Aeilko Jans Zijlker, a Dutch tobacco planter, had discovered a remarkably productive oil well in northern Sumatra in 1885. In 1890, Zijlker, aided by Dutch financial interests, formed the Royal Dutch Company in Amsterdam to exploit the Sumatran oil. During the 1890s, Royal Dutch, managed by J.B. August Kessler, grew rapidly and began to compete sturdily with Standard in East Asian markets. At the same time, Russian Baku oil began to compete in Asian markets. The problem had been transportation. In 1892, the Rothschild interests granted to the transport firm of Marcus Samuel & Company a commitment of ten years supply of Russian kerosene to be shipped to the Far East. The Samuel brothers and the London Rothschilds jointly managed to per-

---

study and oppose any foreign laws or ordinances that would hamper Standard's operations. Ibid., p. 137. [Editor's remarks] Ibid., pp. 130–31.

[58]Harvey O'Connor, *World Crisis in Oil* (New York: Monthly Review Press, 1962), p. 34. [Editor's remarks] Ibid., pp. 29–34; Hidy and Hidy, *Pioneering in Big Business*, pp. 236–37.

suade the British-run Suez Canal board to allow oil tankers (previously considered too dangerously explosive) to pass through the Canal.

Samuel & Co. prospered, and in early 1898, it expanded to include a large number of oil merchants in the great Shell Transport & Trading Company. Shell grew apace, snapping up highly productive Indonesian oil wells that had been unwisely scorned by both Standard and Royal Dutch. Shell also invaded American crude oil markets, being considerably more farsighted than Standard in seeing the importance of newly-discovered Texas crude, and contracted with Gulf Oil for its products. Shell was aggressive, detested Standard Oil, and was ready for bear. As one out-raged Standard exporter agent in Java reported back in 1899 about Shell: "They advertise everywhere, loudly, broadly, and boldly about how they are going to run the Standard Oil Co. out of Netherlands India, and have been doing that steadily for the last four years until my ears are tired and sick of such trashy rubbish."[59]

But the growth of Royal Dutch was even more striking. Two Standard Oil experts, sent to survey the East Indies situation in 1897, were deeply impressed, writing back that "In the whole history of the oil business, there has never been anything more phenomenal than the success and rapid growth of the R.D. Co."[60] Accordingly, William H. Libby, during the years 1895 to 1897, offered to buy out Royal Dutch and make it a marketing subsidiary of Standard Oil. Unfortunately for Standard, it shortsightedly offered the Royal Dutch stockholders less than 94% of the current market value of their shares; and so Standard's chance to recoup its dominance of the Asian market was lost.[61]

By 1901, the three world giants were eyeing each other hungrily but warily. In that year, Standard offered to buy out a majority of Shell stock, after which it proposed to take over Royal Dutch. The Rothschilds, however, were aiming at a Shell merger with Royal Dutch in order to challenge Standard

[59]Hidy and Hidy, *Pioneering in Big Business*, p. 260. [Editor's remarks] O'Connor, *World Crisis in Oil*, pp. 38–43.

[60]Hidy and Hidy, *Pioneering in Big Business*, p. 264.

[61]In 1898, Royal Dutch shrewdly managed to insulate itself against any possible Standard takeover of its stock. A special class of stockholders was newly created, which had the sole right to choose directors and to change the capitalization of the company. Instead of the stock shares being made out to the bearer, as before, the new stock could only be sold if so authorized by a general meeting of the special shareholders. One could become such a stockholder only by invitation, and the only ones eligible for such invitation were those eligible to gain a mining concession in the Dutch East Indies. Ibid., pp. 266–67.

Oil throughout the world. After the Dutch, too, rejected Standard's offers, Royal Dutch's new manager, the young Hendrik August Wilhelm Deterding predicted that "before long it would have to defend its independence in a life-and-death struggle." The dynamic Deterding, who was eventually to become known as "the Napoleon of petroleum" was intensely hostile toward Standard, which he referred to in florid terms as "the abhorred ogre of the industry, pitilessly devouring all that is newly-born."[62]

A full merger between Shell and Royal Dutch was still not possible because of personality conflicts between Deterding and Shell's dominant owner Sir Marcus Samuel, the Lord Mayor of London. In 1902, the Asian sales of the two companies were merged by setting up the new Asian Petroleum Company, with one-third ownership each by Shell, Royal Dutch, and Baron de Rothschild. Deterding was to be the manager, with Sir Marcus holding veto power over him as chairman of the board. The result was a great upsurge in the fortunes of Royal Dutch in the Far East. Finally, in 1907, Royal Dutch and Shell merged outright to form the powerful Royal Dutch Shell group, run by Deterding, who now moved to London and was dubbed Sir Henri by the British.

It should be noted that a fierce international oil war between the two giants began in 1902 and continued for many years thereafter, and that Shell had early formed an alliance with Mellon-run Gulf Oil in supplying it with Texas crude. Indeed, since the early 1890s, Mellon oil companies had competed with Standard Oil for petroleum markets in Europe.[63] And since the Morgans were long-time allies of the Rothschilds, could we not interpret T.R.'s ferocious assault on Standard Oil as an integral part of the world-wide oil war — a war assisted by former Morgan-and-Mellon lawyer, Attorney General Philander Knox?[64]

---

[62]O'Connor, *World Crisis in Oil*, p. 43.

[63][Editor's remarks] O'Connor, *World Crisis in Oil*, pp. 43–46.

[64]On Morgan-Rothschild ties, see Birmingham, *"Our" Crowd*, pp. 152, 156. [Editor's remarks] See also G. Edward Griffin, *The Creature from Jekyll Island: A Second Look at the Federal Reserve* (Westlake Village, CA: American Media, 1994), pp. 413–19.

Knox left the attorney general position to become a senator in mid-1904, so he couldn't have been that crucial in the government's antitrust suit against Standard Oil. Regardless, Rothbard's international motivation for explaining Roosevelt's harsh attack on Rockefeller, which he at another time described as one which "there are no hard facts to prove it," provides an intriguing global dimension to the clash between the Morgan and Rockefeller financial groups during the Progressive Era and beyond. In a later unwritten chapter, Rothbard planned to describe how Roosevelt's successor in 1908, William Howard

The Progressive Era

Taft, although put in by the Morgan ambit, was actually closer to the Rockefeller forces. As a result, in the middle of his presidency the Taft administration started to initiate antitrust suits against Morgan companies, in particular U.S. Steel and International Harvester, as retaliation for the Roosevelt assault on Rockefeller interests. Therefore, in order to deny Taft reelection in 1912 the Morgan interests formed the Progressive Party and put Roosevelt on the ticket. This heavily pietist, intellectual, and Morgan-laden party was able to deny Taft reelection and allow for the Democratic candidate, Woodrow Wilson, to win the White House. See Chapters 10, 11, and 13 below, pp. 316–18, 350–51, 402–43; Rothbard, *Wall Street, Banks, and American Foreign Policy*, pp. 13–23; Lundberg, *America's 60 Families*, pp. 98–11; Josephson, *The President Makers*, pp. 405, 426–48; Kolko, *The Triumph of Conservatism*, pp. 164–72, 190–216; Burch, *Elites in American History*, pp. 173–74.

Wilson was linked to the Morgan ambit, and the Morgans' strong political power continued during World War I, including the drive for war and, aside from a brief Rockefeller-Harding regime cut short, was maintained throughout the 1920s in the Coolidge and Hoover administrations. Then, during the Great Depression, the banking reform and other measures under Franklin Roosevelt's New Deal were a savage attack on the Morgan Empire by opposing Rockefeller affiliated financial groups. By the time of World War II, the Morgans were now the subsidiary financial elite. See Chapters 11 and 14 below pp. 356, 478–90; Rothbard, "From Hoover to Roosevelt," pp. 297–347; Alexander Tabarrok, "The Separation of Commercial and Investment Banking: The Morgans vs. The Rockefellers," *Quarterly Journal of Austrian Economics* 1, no. 1 (1998): 1–18.

CHAPTER 8

Theodore Roosevelt: The First Progressive, Part II

1. THE MEAT PACKING MYTH

One of the earliest acts of Progressive regulation of the economy was the Meat Inspection Act, which passed in June 1906. The orthodox myth holds that the action was directed against the "beef trust" of the large meat packers, and that the federal government was driven to this anti-business measure by popular outcry generated by the muckraking novel, *The Jungle,* by Upton Sinclair, which exposed unsanitary conditions in the Chicago meat-packing plants.[1]

Unfortunately for the myth, the drive for federal meat inspection actually began more than two decades earlier and was launched mainly by the big meat packers themselves. The spur was the urge to penetrate

---

[1]Even as perceptive an analyst as Simon Whitney was taken in by the myth. See Whitney, *Antitrust Policies,* p. 35. [Editor's remarks] Consumer protection, such as food regulation, was one of the main planks of Roosevelt's famous "Square Deal," the others being corporate regulation and conservation of natural resources. In his two terms as president, Roosevelt made great advances toward these cartelizing goals and later championed a "New Nationalism" that advocated similar progressive measures. Although there were differences in emphasis, Woodrow Wilson's "New Freedom" was a similar program that stressed tax reform, federal regulation of business, and monetary reform. Like Roosevelt, Wilson carried out all of these during his presidency.

the European market for meat, something which the large meat packers thought could be done if the government would certify the quality of meat and thereby make American meat more highly rated abroad. Not coincidentally, as in all Colbertist mercantilist legislation over the centuries, a governmentally-coerced upgrading of quality would serve to cartelize — to lower production, restrict competition, and raise prices to the consumers. It, furthermore, socializes the cost of inspection to satisfy consumers, by placing the burden upon the taxpayers instead of on the producers themselves.[2]

More specifically, the meat packers were concerned to with combating the restrictionist legislation of European countries, which, in the late 1870s and early 1880s, began to prohibit the import of American meat. The excuse was to safeguard the European consumer against purportedly diseased meat; the probable major reason was to act as a protectionist device for European meat production.

Partly at the behest of the major meat packers, Chicago and other cities imposed and then strengthened a system of meat inspection, and the Secretary of the Treasury, on his own and without Congressional authorization, set up an inspection organization to certify exported cattle as free of pleuropneumonia in 1881. Finally, after Germany prohibited the importation of American pork, ostensibly because of the problem of disease, Congress, responding to the pressure of the large meatpackers, reacted in May 1884 by establishing a Bureau of Animal Industry within the Department of Agriculture "to prevent the exportation of diseased cattle" and to try to eliminate contagious diseases among domesticated animals.

But this was not enough, and the Department of Agriculture kept agitating for additional federal regulation to improve meat exports. Then, in response to the hog cholera epidemic in the United States in 1889, Congress, again pressured by the big meat packers, passed a law in the summer of 1890 compelling the inspection of all meat intended for export. But the European governments, claiming to be unsatisfied because live animals at the time of slaughter remained uninspected, continued their prohibitions of American meat. As a result, Congress, in March 1891, passed the first

---

[2][Editor's footnote] Rothbard is referring to Jean-Baptiste Colbert, economic czar of France under the reign of Louis XIV. He supported extremely mercantilist policies that created a system of cartels through artificially high "standards of quality." See Murray Rothbard, *An Austrian Perspective on the History of Economic Thought: Economic Thought Before Adam Smith* (Auburn, AL: Mises Institute, 2006 [1995]), vol. 1, pp. 216–20, 246–49.

important compulsory federal meat inspection law in American history. The Act provided that all live animals must be inspected, and it managed to cover most animals passing through interstate commerce. Every meat packer involved in any way whatever in export had to be inspected in detail by the Department of Agriculture, and violations were punishable by imprisonment as well as fine.

This rigid inspection law satisfied European medicine, and European countries swiftly removed their prohibition on American pork. But the European meat packers were upset in proportion as their physicians were satisfied. Quickly, the European packers began discovering ever higher "standards" of health — at least as applied to imported meat — and European governments responded by reimposing import restrictions. The American meat industry felt it had no other choice but escalating its own compulsory inspection — as the minuet of ever higher and hypocritical standards continued. The Department of Agriculture inspected more and more meat and maintained dozens of inspection stations. In 1895, the department was able to get Congress to strengthen meat inspection enforcement. By 1904, the Bureau of Animal Industry was inspecting 73% of the entire U.S. beef kill.[3]

The big problem for the large packers was their smaller competitors, who were able to avoid government inspection. This meant that their smaller rivals were outside the attempted cartelization and benefited by the advantage of being able to ship uninspected meat. To succeed, the cartel had to be extended to, and imposed upon, the small packers.

The much publicized "beef trust," or cartel among the major packers to agree on prices and restrict production and competition, had indeed been in existence since the mid-1880s. But in an industry with free entry and numerous small producers, and with meat growing in the hands of thousands of stock raisers, the beef trust had no impact on meat prices. Moreover, the competition from small meat packers was increasing. During the 1880s, the number of meat packing establishments in the United States had increased sharply from 872 in 1879 to 1,367 ten years later. Under the impact of federal cartelization, the number of firms declined to

---

[3] [Editor's footnote] Smaller local butchers, resentful of the competitive power of the Chicago packers, also falsely charged that they were selling diseased meat in order to underprice them. This gave credibility to the European governments who said that American meat was diseased. Gary D. Libecap, "The Rise of the Chicago Packers and the Origins of Meat Inspection and Antitrust," *Economic Inquiry* 30 (April, 1992): 242–62.

1,080 in 1899, but then competitive pressure increased, with the number of firms rising to 1,641 in 1909, an increase of 52% in the first decade of the 20th century. Another gauge is that the meat packers other than the three largest firms accounted for 65% of meat production in 1905, and the percentage rose to 78% in 1909.

In March 1904, responding to pressure from organized livestock growers, the House of Representatives passed a resolution calling for the Bureau of Corporations to investigate the alleged impact of the beef trust on prices and meatpacking profits. The Bureau's report, issued one year later, angered the muckrakers, populists, and livestock interests by pointing out, quite accurately, that the meatpacking industry was substantially competitive, and that the packer cartel had no particular impact on meat prices.

Until early 1906, all the popular agitation against the meat industry was focused on the alleged monopoly, and scarcely at all on sanitary conditions. Articles in English and American magazines in the previous two years attacking sanitary conditions in meatpacking houses had no impact on the public. In February 1906, Upton Sinclair's *The Jungle* was published and revealed many alleged horrors of the meat packing industry. Shortly thereafter, Roosevelt sent two Washington bureaucrats, Commissioner of Labor Charles P. Neill and civil service lawyer James B. Reynolds, to investigate the Chicago industry. The famous "Neill-Reynolds" report that apparently confirmed Sinclair's findings, in fact, only revealed the ignorance of the officials, as later congressional hearings indicated that they poorly understood how slaughterhouses worked and confused their inherently foul nature with unsanitary conditions.

Shortly after *The Jungle* came out, J. Ogden Armour, owner of one of the biggest packing firms, wrote an article in the *Saturday Evening Post* defending government inspection of meat and insisting that the large packers had always favored and pushed for inspection. Armour wrote:

> Attempt to evade it [government inspection] would be, from the purely commercial viewpoint, suicidal. *No packer can do an interstate or export business without Government inspection.* Self-interest forces him to make use of it. Self-interest likewise demands that he shall not receive meats or by-products from any small packer, either for export or other use, unless that small packer's plant is also "official" — that is, under United States Government inspection.

> This government inspection thus becomes an impor-
> tant adjunct of the packer's business from two viewpoints.
> It puts the stamp of legitimacy and honesty upon the
> packer's product and so is to him a necessity. To the public
> it is *insurance* against the sale of diseased meats.[4]

Government meat inspection which also lures the public into always thinking the food is safe and reduces competitive pressures to improve meat quality.

In May, Senator Albert J. Beveridge of Indiana, a leading Progressive Republican and old friend of Morgan partner George W. Perkins, introduced a bill for strengthening the compulsory inspection of all meat, including meat products and preservatives, passing through interstate commerce, as well as fixing standards for sanitation within the meatpacking plants. The bill was vigorously supported by Secretary of Agriculture James Wilson. The funds appropriated for federal inspection were quadrupled compared to the existing law, from $800,000 to $3 million. The Beveridge bill passed both houses of Congress nearly unanimously at the end of June.

The large meat packers were enthusiastically in favor of the bill, designed as it was to bring the small packers under federal inspection. The American Meat Producers' Association endorsed the bill. At the hearings of the House Committee of Agriculture on the Beveridge bill, Thomas E. Wilson, representing the large Chicago packers, put their support succinctly:

> We are now and have always been in favor of the exten-
> sion of the inspection, also to the adoption of the sanitary
> regulations that will insure the very best possible condi-
> tions. ... We have always felt that Government inspection,
> under proper regulations, was an advantage to the live
> stock and agricultural interests and to the consumer ...[5]

One advantage to imposing uniform sanitary conditions on all meat-packers is that the burden of the increased costs would fall more heavily

---

[4]J. Ogden Armour, "The Packers and the People," *Saturday Evening Post* 178 (March 10, 1906): 6, italics in original. Quoted in Kolko, *Triumph of Conservatism*, p. 102. This entire section is based on Kolko's account in ibid., pp. 98–108; also see ibid., pp. 51–53, 75, 81–82.

[5]Quoted in ibid., p. 105.

on the smaller than on the bigger plants, thereby crippling the smaller competitors even further.

The major battle over the Beveridge bill was who was to pay for the increased government inspection. The big packers, naturally enough, wanted the taxpayers to keep paying the costs as they had in the past. They also objected to the bill's provision to compel canning dates placed on meat products, for fear of discouraging consumer purchases of cans stamped at more remote dates. The packers' objections were embodied in amendments by James W. Wadsworth, chairman of the House Committee on Agriculture, amendments which were drafted by Samuel H. Cowan, attorney of the National Live Stock Association. When President Roosevelt attacked the Wadsworth amendments after approving them privately earlier, Wadsworth answered him with "I told you ... that the packers insisted before our committee on having a rigid inspection law passed. Their life depends on it, and the committee will bear me out in the statement that they placed no obstacle whatever in our way ..."[6]

The House passed the Wadsworth bill and the Senate the Beveridge original, but the House stood firm, and the big packers got all that they had wanted, the bill being signed by the president at the end of June. The cans would not be dated, and the taxpayers would pay the entire cost of inspection. George W. Perkins was delighted, and he wrote to J.P. Morgan that the new law "will certainly be of very great advantage when the thing once gets into operation and they are able to use it all over the world, as it will practically give them a government certificate for their goods ..."

The opposition to the Wadsworth amendment was scarcely based on anti-business views. Beveridge himself declared, quite sensibly, that "an industry which is infinitely benefited by the Government inspection ought to pay for that inspection instead of the people paying for it." The same position was advanced by the *New York Journal of Commerce*.

The leftish opponents of business were not fooled by the Beveridge-Wadsworth law. Senator Knute Nelson realized that the law was a meat packer's bonanza: "Three objects have been sought to be accomplished — first, to placate the packers; next, to placate the men who raise the range cattle, and, third, to get a good market for the packers abroad." Even Upton Sinclair himself was not fooled; he realized that the new law was designed to benefit the packers; the intention of his expose, in any case,

---

[6] *Washington Post,* June 15, 1906. In ibid., p. 106.

was not to impose higher standards for meat as it was to improve the living conditions of the packinghouse workers, which he himself admitted was scarcely accomplished by the new law. Hence his famous quote: "I aimed at the public's heart, and by accident I hit it in the stomach." Sinclair looked back on the event:

> I am supposed to have helped clean up the yards and improve the country's meat supply — though this is mostly delusion. ... But nobody even pretends to believe that I improved the conditions of the stockyard workers.

Neither was Secretary of Agriculture Wilson under any delusions who favored or opposed the new law. Meeting with the large packers shortly after the bill passed, Wilson told them: "... the great asset that you gentlemen are going to have when we get this thing to going will be the most rigid and severe inspection on the face of the earth." To which the packers responded with "loud applause." Swift & Co. and the other large meat packers took out giant ads trumpeting the new law asserting that its purpose "is to assure the public that only sound and wholesome meat and meat food products may be offered for sale. ... It is a wise law. Its enforcement must be universal and uniform."

During the next few years, Senator Beveridge tried to restore the idea of the packers paying for their inspection, but he got no support from Roosevelt and opposition from his Secretary of Agriculture. Meanwhile, the packers continued to defend the Bureau of Animal Industry and its inspections, and they even sought unsuccessfully to strengthen inspection further.[7]

2. HARVEY W. WILEY AND THE PURE FOOD AND DRUG ACT

Neither was the Pure Food and Drug Act, passed on the same day as the Meat Inspection Act, a triumph of the "people" over the "interests." The

---

[7]Ibid., 107–08. [Editor's remarks] See also Jim Powell, *Bully Boy: The Truth about Theodore Roosevelt's Legacy* (New York: Crown Forum, 2006), pp. 158–69. For a different account from Kolko similar to the traditional narrative, see James Harvey Young, *Pure Food: Securing the Federal Food and Drugs Act of 1906* (Princeton, NJ: Princeton University Press, 1989), pp. 221–52. The packers were naturally disturbed at the flagrant lies Sinclair wrote slandering their industry, and also at the original Beveridge bill. Against this, and Roosevelt's threat to release the similarly untruthful Neill-Reynolds report, they even offered to enact their own voluntary regulations. However, they supported new regulation if the taxpayers were forced to pay and if smaller firms were also included. As documented above, they were successfully able to steer the new legislation according to their desires.

pure food agitation had been carried on for years by business interests in general, and specifically by large food companies anxious to use the government in a mercantilist way to cartelize, restrict competition, and impose higher relative costs on small business competitors.

In the early 1880s, the leadership of the drive for pure food legislation was taken by Dr. Harvey W. Wiley, the leading food chemist for the federal Department of Agriculture. Wiley combined in his person the leading forces making for Progressivism and statism in the late 19th and early 20th centuries: an amalgam of pietism, of a technocratic drive by new corps of "experts," and of powerful business interests.

Harvey W. Wiley was born an Indiana farm boy to a father of Ulster Scot background who was a lay preacher in the pietistic Campbellite sect.[8] But more important than the specific sect to the Wiley home was a non-sectarian and pietistic devotion to strict adherence to the Sabbath. At Hanover College in Indiana, young Wiley began his lifelong obsession with "purity," and began discoursing on the importance of purity of body, mind, and soul. He was early convinced that tobacco and pork were foul "impurities" that marred the perfection of one's body.

In his commencement address at Hanover in 1867, the 23-year old Wiley combined the themes of purity, pietism, and supposedly value-free medicine in ways that would foreshadow his later career. He declared that man must preserve his God-like "purity" of body and mind, and he exalted the nobility of the physicians, men who "guard the holy covenant God made with man." The physician, Wiley conceded, may not be able to make man immortal, but "he may help to make the probation state [man's life on earth] a proper place of preparation for the precious life that beckons from beyond the misty hills ..."[9]

Wiley then went to tutor in languages at Northwestern Christian University, a Campbellite university in Indianapolis, after which Wiley went to Indiana Medical College, acquiring an M.D. in 1871. Wiley then shifted to chemistry, becoming a professor of chemistry at Indiana Medical School the following year, then obtaining a B.S. in chemistry at Harvard, after which he became professor of chemistry at Northwestern Christian

---

[8]See the definitive, though overly laudatory, biography of Wiley and his crusade, in Oscar E. Anderson, Jr., *The Health of a Nation: Harvey W. Wiley and the Fight for Pure Food* (Chicago: University of Chicago Press, 1958).

[9][Editor's footnote] Ibid., pp. 2–9.

in 1873, followed by a professorship of chemistry at the newly founded Purdue University in the following year.

Five years later, Dr. Wiley studied medicine, chemistry, and physics at the University of Berlin, where he was inspired by Dr. Sell's government laboratory for the detecting of impurities in food and drink. It was at Berlin that Wiley picked up his lifelong interest in sugar chemistry and began his permanent alliance with the sugar industry and government in the U.S.

In 1881, Wiley began to agitate for the government's protection of the consumer from adulterated sugar products in the state of Indiana. Specifically, he called for a state requirement that sugar and syrup products be required to carry labels detailing their composition. The compulsory labelling law would have had several significant effects. By requiring compulsory publicity, it would cripple trade and brand-name secrets, thereby helping to restrict competition and cartelize the sugar industry. The law would also have the Colbertist or mercantilist effect of cartelizing through allegedly higher "quality" imposed on the consumer by coercion.

In addition, Wiley cemented his alliance with the sugar industry by agitating for the notion that the United States should be self-sufficient in sugar, and therefore that imported sugar should be kept out of the United States by a prohibitively high tariff. His alliance with government began in 1881 when Indiana passed a law regulating the manufacturer and sale of commercial fertilizers and named Dr. Wiley as the "state chemist" in charge of testing these products.

During the early 1880s, Wiley launched several abortive attempts to go into the sugar manufacturing business himself. He tried to buy a defunct beet-sugar plant in Boston to make glucose, a new product which he had lauded, and to organize a glucose plant in Indiana. Both of these failed. He also hoped to make sugar from sorghum cane, and organized a small Indiana company to make preliminary investigations on the subject, and he was happy enough with his results to believe it would be successful in the future.

In an address before the Indiana State Board of Agriculture in January 1883, Dr. Wiley, by now one of America's leading sugar chemists, made clear the extent to which he was wedded to sugar. "Let me make the sweets of the nation and I don't care who makes the laws. ... The consumption of sugar is a measure of progress in civilization," Wiley thundered, "Childhood without candy would be Heaven without harps."[10] Wiley added, with

---

[10]Ibid., p. 28. [Editor's remarks] Ibid., pp. 9–16, 20–23, 26–28.

no trace of irony, that "nothing is ever gained for a cause by an overstatement of its claims." He also commended the possibilities for profit in the manufacture of sugar from sorghum.

At this point, the federal Commissioner of Agriculture fired as the department chemist the obstreperous and notoriously pro-sorghum Dr. Peter Collier. To appease the politically powerful sorghum growers, the Commissioner was forced to appoint the notoriously pro-sorghum Harvey Wiley in 1883 as chief chemist.

Wiley leaped to his new role, agitating at length for a protective tariff to keep out efficient foreign sugar and to subsidize a domestic sugar industry into being. As a lifelong Republican in a Republican administration, Wiley was simply singling out his own favorite tariff in a party wedded to the concept of keeping out imports in competition with American industry. Free trade, Wiley opined, was but "the tender tropical nursling of the college hot-houses and professional dilettantism." When asked what would happen to foreign sugar growers put out of work by an American protective tariff, Wiley displayed the arrogant attitude toward Third World people typical of the Progressive. The native, Wiley opined, "sullenly lolling in the sun ... can look up and see cocoanuts and bananas; he will not starve nor freeze."[11]

In his scientific work for the Department of Agriculture, Wiley also devoted much time and energy to subsidizing the sugar industry, specifically a search for economic methods of producing sugar from sorghum, cane, and beet — especially sorghum. Despite his eminence in the field, Wiley's sorghum experiments during the 1880s were consistent flops. Congressional appropriations for these schemes, however, were repeatedly salvaged by the Republican Senator Preston B. Plumb of Kansas, who was subject to pressure by Kansas agriculturalists looking for salvation by sorghum. Even Wiley's seemingly successful diffusion process for Louisiana sugarcane turned out to be a failure. Wiley, however, continued to be enthusiastic about government subsidizing of sugar manufacture, and he also advocated a governmental school to teach people the ways of sugar production.

Neither consistent failure nor the changes in government, however, seemed to deter the federal government from continuing to finance and even expand Dr. Wiley's activities. For one thing, Wiley proved early to be an expert maneuverer in the corridors of power. Although a Republican,

---

[11]Ibid., pp. 35–36, 39.

Wiley was not ousted by the Cleveland administration in 1885 because he managed to persuade Cleveland to appoint his old friend, farm editor Norman J. Colman, as the Commissioner of Agriculture. Then, when Jeremiah Rusk, former governor of Wisconsin, became Secretary of Agriculture under the Harrison administration, Wiley was able to work very closely with the new Secretary.

The following year, 1890, Wiley and Rusk worked closely together with wealthy Philadelphia financier Hamilton Disston. Disston had bought a million acres of swamp and wetlands in Florida for the production of sugar cane, organizing the Florida Sugar Cane Co. for that purpose. Disston then successfully lobbied through Congress a grant to the Department of Agriculture of funds for research in improving sugar cane production. The grateful Rusk and Wiley promptly constructed their experimental station on a site on Disston's soil, only four miles from his sugar factory. Disston, of course, was only too happy to lease the land for free to the Department of Agriculture, since the station could only boost the market for Disston's sugar and his entire acreage.

By the mid-1890s, it was clear to everyone that the idea of any sort of economic production of sugar from sorghum was a total failure, and that furthermore there was no real domestic sugar industry of any consequence. Wiley, of course, blamed the misfires neither on his grandiloquent attempts at subsidy nor on his consistent string of research failures; no, he charged, the problem was that the sugar tariff was not yet high enough.[12]

If one of Dr. Wiley's lifelong passions was the promotion of American sugar, the other was the outlawry of food or farm products that he considered "impure." In the decades after the Civil War, municipal boards of health had issued ordinances on pure milk and meat. More to the point, dairy interests forced through protective laws in some states against competing milk or butter products, e.g. against such "adulterated" competitors as oleo-margarine. Farmers in many states tried to stop "adulterated fertilizers," and we have seen that Dr. Wiley was enlisted in Indiana's crusade as early as 1881. There were a few state food and drug laws, but they were enforced only in Massachusetts.

On the federal level, there was only a pre-Civil War law banning the importation of adulterated drugs. In the mid-1880s, Dr. Wiley took the

---

[12][Editor's footnote] Ibid., pp. 36–39, 56, 59–60, 65.

lead in agitating for a food and drug law on the federal level. In 1884, Wiley and several state chemists had organized the Association of Official Agricultural Chemists, which issued its reports in the Department of Agriculture's Bulletins. Two years later, when Wiley was president of the Association, he induced it to expand its scope from commercial fertilizers to the entire area of agricultural chemistry, including the adulteration of food.

It should be noted that Wiley's primary interest in this field was *not* in safeguarding the public health; it was in outlawing all changes in the definition of a product, since he considered all such changes in name as fraud. In short, Wiley sough to freeze the composition of all products in their original mold. It should be clear that such a law would not only cartelize industry and impose Colbertian mercantilism, but it would also cripple competition from new and imaginative innovators and freeze the status quo in industry. That the motivation for this drive was economic was admitted by Agricultural Commissioner Colman, who wanted to eradicate food adulteration by means of tough state and federal laws. His "chief concern," Anderson stated, "was the plight of the honest producer faced with the competition of adulterated" products.[13]

The Department of Agriculture, Division of Chemistry, kicked off its campaign against impure food in its Bulletin #13, issued in 1887. To popularize its findings among the public, Wiley hired Alexander J. Wedderburn, farm editor, pure food enthusiast, and secretary of the legislative committee of the farm lobby group the Virginia Grange, to write Bulletin #25 in 1890. The Bulletin saw fraud everywhere, and particularly worried about the export markets which were being injured by the poor reputation of American food. Wedderburn's Bulletin called for national legislation to remedy the evil.

Public agitation for a national pure food law, however, was not launched first by Wiley and the Department of Agriculture. It was begun by Francis B. Thurber, a leading wholesale grocer in New York City. In the summer of 1880, Thurber got his brother-in-law, Major Henry C. Meyer, editor of the *Plumber and Sanitary Engineer*, to persuade the National Board of Trade, the leading organization of merchants, to sponsor a $1000 contest in the *PSE* for the best essay drafting legislation against food adulteration.

---

[13]Ibid., p. 71. [Editor's remarks] Ibid., pp. 68–71.

The winner of the contest was Professor G.W. Wigner, president of the Engineering Society of Public Analysts; the judges of the contest then drafted a model bill along Wigner's lines, a bill then endorsed by the National Board of Trade and many local boards. While the bill failed to pass, it served as the model for numerous state laws during the 1880s.

In late 1886, the American Society for the Prevention of the Adulteration of Food, a Philadelphia-based outfit, called a national convention in Washington for January 1887 to draft pure food legislation. The convention, representing commercial organizations, trade journal and boards of health, endorsed the 1880 Board of Trade bill. A larger convention the following year included food manufacturers and distributors and also endorsed legislation against harmful adulteration and compelling the labelling of the composition of products. The 1888 convention was led by the organized grocers, frankly, in order "to protect the honest businessmen from the competition of the adulterator and to build public confidence," but it was also, as Anderson notes, "an attempt to capture the initiative to the end that any legislation enacted would in objectives and details conform to the business point of view."[14] Also heavily involved in the convention were numerous agricultural interests. There were the dairy producers, who wanted protection from such "fraud" as oleomargarine, corn and hog growers, who wanted protection against adulterated lard and inspection of slaughtered animals for export in order to prevent Europe from discriminating against them. As stated earlier, they succeeded with the 1891 law. And there were, of course, the public health professionals who wanted an expansion of their jobs and prestige.

Specific agricultural interests managed to obtain governmental crippling of their competitors. In 1886, the dairy interests won a federal tax against the manufacture and sale of oleomargarine. A bill crippling the production of "adulterated" lard passed the House in 1890 but failed in the Senate because of the opposition of the cottonseed oil interests, who were successfully making composed lard, lard mixed with cottonseed oil.

More generally, Congress passed a bill in 1888 prohibiting the manufacture and sale of adulterated food and drugs in the District of Columbia, which of course has always been conceded to be constitutionally under federal control. But the first important general federal bill mandating pure

[14]Ibid., p. 76. [Editor's remarks] pp. 71–76.

food and drugs was submitted in 1890 by Senator Algernon S. Paddock of Nebraska, chairman of the Senate Committee on Agriculture and Forestry. The Committee reported out of the bill to protect consumers and producers against adulteration and, most significantly, to raise the reputation of American food products in export markets abroad. The bill mandated labelling of components and outlawed adulteration, as well as prohibiting allegedly injurious ingredients. The following year, Wiley induced Paddock to amend the bill to tighten up enforcement and place responsibility for enforcement in a food section within his own division of chemistry. In early 1892, Senator Paddock delivered a speech hailing his bill as protecting the pocketbook as well as the health of consumers, and as helping the farmer by strengthening our export markets.

Lobbying for the Paddock bill were many farm organizations, including the Alliance and the Grange, state legislatures, boards of trade, and wholesale grocery and drug associations. Opposed to it were the cottonseed oil producers, as well as the manufacturers of other new and mixed products, which would be first in line to be attacked as an "adulteration" from the "purity" of the original definition of any particular product. The bill passed the Senate but died in the House, facing as it did a public which was either apathetic or positively opposed to a pure food and drug act as an illegitimate and paternalistic intervention of government into their lives.

Speaking for the Paddock bill before the Franklin Institute, Dr. Wiley conceded that only a small part of food adulteration injured the consumers. He was more worried about them spending their money in ways that he considered unwise; the poor were purchasing food that was "ostensibly pure and nutritious, but in reality valueless."[15] His concern for the consumer's pocketbook, however, was conveniently forgotten when he pointed out to his colleagues in the Department of Agriculture that if adulteration were outlawed, the farmers' markets would broaden, and food prices would rise. Or, to put it in starker terms, competition in food products would be crippled, supply would therefore be reduced, and food and farm prices would rise. Which was perhaps the point of the whole enterprise.

The second Cleveland administration was a difficult time for Wiley, for Secretary of Agriculture J. Sterling Morton insisted on spending cuts and bureaucratic dismissals in the department. However, the food and

---

[15]Ibid., p. 80. [Editor's remarks] Ibid., pp. 76–80.

drug crusade pressed on. Most states enacted pure food and drug laws during the 1890s; the initiative came from industrial and merchant groups anxious to protect themselves against competition. In the late 1890s, the Association of Official Agricultural Chemists launched reports, studies, and addresses against adulteration. Heading the Associations' committee on food standards, and therefore spearheading this drive, was Dr. Harvey Wiley. By 1897, Wiley urged the Paddock bill as a model law for all states and got his proposed bill introduced in the House by Republican Representative Marriott Brosius of Pennsylvania. The Brosius bill outlawed adulteration, compelled the labelling of food contents, and barred poisonous ingredients. Wiley's Division of Chemistry in the Department of Agriculture was to examine samples of food and to regulate products in interstate commerce.

Favoring the bill were the National Grange and Farmers' National Congress, interested in cartelizing the food industry. Particularly advocating the bill was a new overall organization designed to lobby for a pure food and drug law, the National Pure Food and Drug Congress, which was set up at a convention in March 1898. The Congress, consisting of 150 delegates from 24 states, was called by a group including health officers and wholesale grocers of the District of Columbia. The Congress was the idea of Alexander J. Wedderburn, former propagandist in the service of Dr. Wiley and now master of the State Grange of Virginia. Wiley was the chairman of the Congress's advisory committee, and later chairman of its legislative committee, which got Brosius to revise his bill.[16]

Wiley's concern for "purity" was designed to put competitive innovation into a straitjacket. Thus, Wiley vigorously opposed adding blends to straight whiskey and harshly criticized rectified whiskey because he though it "fraudulent" to call it "whiskey," and he felt that such an "impure" product had to be injurious to the health.

Subsequent pure food and drug bills, shepherded by Dr. Wiley, were strongly backed by farmers' groups, such as the National Grange, by commercial organizations such as the National Board of Trade, the National Retail Grocers' Association, the National Wholesale Druggists' Association, the National Retail Liquor Dealers' Association, the Proprietary Association of America, and, last but not least, the American Pharmaceutical and American Medical Association. Soon, the National Association

---

16[Editor's footnote] Ibid., pp. 121–23.

of Manufacturers, the American Baking Powder Association, and many individual companies contributed heavy support for a pure food and drug bill, drawn up by Dr. Wiley and submitted to the House by Representative William P. Hepburn. Finally, under the impact of the meat packing excitement, Wiley's bill passed the Congress almost unanimously in 1906, with Theodore Roosevelt giving the measure at least passive support. Wiley acknowledged that the "great majority" of food manufacturers supported the bill.[17]

The Pure Food and Drug Act was a continuation of previous congressional bills and legislations on the state level. It prohibited "adulteration" (to be decided by bureaucrats and the special interests they represented), which cracked down on certain forms of competition, and required "honest labeling," which added additional costs on firms that did not previously do so. At the helm was Dr. Wiley and his Bureau of Chemistry in the Department of Agriculture.[18]

Wiley's passion for pure food and drugs dovetailed neatly, after the passage of the law, with his equally dominant lifelong passion for sugar. After the frustrations of the Democratic Cleveland administration, the Republican McKinley administration gladdened Wiley's heart by restoring and expanding Wiley's sugar beet experiments. For a domestic sugar beet industry had now been made viable by the Dingley Tariff Act of 1897, which doubled the duty on imported sugar. Wiley's studies and subsidized

---

[17][Editor's footnote] Ibid., p. 133; Kolko, *The Triumph of Conservatism*, pp. 109–10.

[18][Editor's footnote] The Bureau of Chemistry would eventually morph into the Food and Drug Administration in the 1920s and 1930s. Rothbard planned to elaborate on the cartelization of the drug industry and the medical profession further, but unfortunately did not do so. The drug industry and medical profession were believed to be vastly unsafe until government regulation, with unsuspecting consumers buying addicting and dangerous medicines and medical treatments from quack salesmen and heterodox doctors. While sensational for the media, addiction and death were overblown and, in fact, partially caused by prior regulations. In addition, the mainstream medical profession also practiced treatments that would be considered dangerous and ineffective by today's standards. In 1910, the Flexner Report, written by Abraham Flexner, brother of Simon Flexner, head of the Rockefeller Institute for Medical Research, proposed a licensing system for medical schools and hospitals that artificially raised quality and blocked out many black, female, and Jewish doctors as well as proprietary hospitals and alternative forms of medicine. See, among others, Murray Rothbard, "Government Medical Insurance," in *Making Economic Sense* (Auburn, AL: Mises Institute, 1995), pp. 76–77; Mark Thornton, *The Economics of Prohibition* (Salt Lake City: University of Utah Press, 1991), pp. 52–65; Dale Steinreich, "100 Years of Medical Fascism," *Mises Daily* (April, 2010).

experiments now greatly aided the beet sugar industry. At the first annual convention of the American Beet Sugar Association in 1904, Dr. Wiley was introduced with the encomium that "We have had no more loyal and staunch friend."

Harvey W. Wiley, as befitting a Progressive, was an ardent imperialist, and he vigorously supported the American annexations of Hawaii, Puerto Rico, and the Philippines. But his devotion to American sugar took precedence over imperial concerns, and he opposed President Roosevelt, whom he had generally supported, over T.R.'s desire to import Cuban sugar for free or at reduced duties after it had become our virtual protectorate.

If Harvey Wiley was ruthless with foreign sugar, he was even more bitterly opposed to any competitive substitute for sugar, especially if he could also stigmatize it as "artificial" and "impure," in contrast to his favorite commodity. Teddy Roosevelt soon broke with the spiritual mentor of the Pure Food and Drug law, and the issue was the problem of saccharin. Wiley did his best to outlaw saccharin, thereby gladdening the hearts of his friends and associates in the sugar industry. Wiley denounced saccharin as a "deception" because it provided a cheap substitute for sugar; since it was devoid of food value, according to Wiley, it must therefore be harmful. The solicitor and associate chemist of the Department of Agriculture, appointed by the president as a check upon the obstreperous Wiley, pronounced saccharin harmless and should therefore be permitted in food if labelled as such. Finally, in January 1908, T.R. appointed a higher board in the Department to pass on differences of opinion over adulterated food and thereby to overrule Wiley; as a special dig at Wiley, the board was headed by Ira Remsen, the distinguished discoverer of saccharin.

It is no accident that the emotional T.R. should have broken with Wiley over the saccharin question, for Roosevelt was accustomed to take saccharin in his daily coffee and was therefore convinced that Wiley was hopelessly addled in his attempt to deprive the president of his favorite sweetener.[19]

Wiley's biographer perceptively summed up the man whose crusading passion had shifted from pietist Christianity to the new salvation of mankind by science or, more particularly, by scientists, professionals, and technocrats in the name of value-free science. As Anderson puts it: "Science filled the void left by the loss of faith. ... Perhaps [Wiley's] views ...

---

[19][Editor's footnote] Kolko, *The Triumph of Conservatism*, p. 110; Anderson, *Health of a Nation*, pp. 99–103, 209–11.

stemmed from his heritage of evangelical Christianity, a heritage whose theological superstructure had lost its meaning for him but whose burning zeal for social justice remained."[20]

3. THEODORE ROOSEVELT AND THE CONSERVATION CRUSADE

The conservation movement, past and present, has generally been painted in sweetness and light, as disinterested nature lovers leading the "people" in war against corporate interests who wished to exploit and plunder natural resources. The actual facts were quite different. As Professor Samuel P.

---

[20]Ibid., p. 85. [Editor's remarks] See also Powell, *Bully Boy*, pp. 152–57, 168–82. Powell notes that food quality was going up through improvements such as canned and frozen food, better preservatives, and improved railroad transportation (including refrigeration of dressed meats). See also Clayton A. Coppin and Jack High, *The Politics of Purity: Harvey Washington Wiley and the Origins of Federal Food Policy* (Ann Arbor: University of Michigan Press, 1999). It is worth quoting several passages (pp. 31, 167–68) from the authors on the entire matter:

> A striking fact about the Pure Food and Drugs Act of 1906, a fact with which every interpretation of the act must come to terms, is that urban workers and families did not agitate for its passage or enforcement. No general outbreak of disease or death from food in the cities was recorded. No epidemic of malnutrition swept through the urban populace. No public outcry over food was ever heard from the working classes. The movement for a national food law came from food commissioners, agricultural chemists, manufacturers of expensive foods, representatives from rural agricultural states, and a small number of middle-class women. The rhetoric of regulation was "pure food for the mass consumer," but its impetus came from the professional classes ...
>
> When the patina of public-spirited reform is removed, we find that the cumulative interaction of commercial and bureaucratic competition led to the passage of the Pure Food and Drugs Act in 1906. These two competitive forces, rather than consumer health or business fraud, also account for Wiley's actions as a regulator of food and drugs. ... His enforcement of the act did not improve the health of the consumer, the plane of competition among producers, or the honesty and integrity of government officials. If anything, Wiley's enforcement worsened the ability of consumers to make informed judgements about food and drugs. His claims about the healthfulness of various foods and preservatives were not well-founded. ... The firms that Wiley opposed were not shady operations designed to bilk the consumer. They were reputable firms that were as forthright in their commercial and political dealings as the firms that Wiley supported.

Hays, the pioneering revisionist historian of the conservation movement, has declared:

> The crusading quality of the conservation movement has given it an enviable reputation as a defender of spiritual values and national character. ... [But] conservation neither arose from a broad popular outcry, nor centered its fire primarily upon the private corporation. Moreover, the corporations often supported conservation policies, while the "people" just as frequently opposed them. In fact, it becomes clear that one must discard completely the struggle against corporations as the setting in which to understand conservation history ...[21]

As in so many other aspects of the progressive movement, conservation constituted a shift of control or ownership of natural resources from private to governmental hands in order to subsidize and cartelize private interests in that area. In the name of "scientific" management, government intervention took two forms: either subsidize research and development in natural sources or withhold resources indefinitely from use, thereby cartelizing the resource, and raising prices for private producers and increasing the capital value of resources already in private hands. Thus, as in so much of the Progressive Era, professionals and technocrats formed a congenial alliance with private interests.

We have already noted Theodore Roosevelt's early interest in forest conservation and his close friendship with the man who was to become the unquestioned leader of the forest conservation movement, Gifford Pinchot. After training in forestry in France and Germany, the wealthy young Pinchot became a consultant for private forest owners, advocating European techniques of "scientific forestry." In 1895, President Cleveland's Secretary of the Interior Hoke Smith, responding to growing pressure by Eastern nature lovers, appointed Harvard Professor Charles S. Sargent to a National Forestry Committee, of which Pinchot was a member. The committee's report deplored the pro-use attitude of the cities of the West and urged a systematic permanent withdrawal and reserving of forest land by the federal government. Responding to the committee, President Cleveland created 21.3 million acres of forest reserves in early 1897, making 39.0

---

[21]Samuel P. Hays, *Conservation and the Gospel of Efficiency: The Progressive Conservation Movement, 1890–1920* (Cambridge, MA: Harvard University Press, 1959), pp. 1–2.

million acres of total reserves. In 1898, Gifford Pinchot became Chief of the Division of Forestry and, in 1900, head of the new Bureau of Forestry — by 1905 called the Forest Service— in the Department of Agriculture. The previous head of the Division, the German-American and German-trained Bernhard Fernow, had been relatively harmless, confining himself to the study of individual trees and to dispensing technical information. Fernow had not been a crusader.

Pinchot, however, set out the convert the nation to scientific forestry. He rapidly formed an alliance with private timber companies, proselytizing and aiding them in forestry techniques. Some of the largest timber owners in the country had sought his assistance, including the Kirby Lumber Company of Texas, the Northern Pacific Railroad, and the Weyerhaeuser Lumber Company in the Pacific Northwest. By 1905, Pinchot had aided the owners of three million acres of timber and had helped manage almost 200,000 acres. In 1901, Pinchot and his colleagues in scientific forestry formed the Society of American Foresters, and in a few years they were able to convert the older group, the American Forestry Association, from an aesthetic admiration of forests and arbors into an organization on behalf of the new scientific forestry. As a result of Pinchot's efforts, private lumbermen joined the AFA, and by 1909, the Association had an advisory board including representatives of nine lumbermen's organizations.

When Congress failed to appropriate money for a clerk in the Bureau of Forestry, the private lumbermen raised the funds for three years in a row; furthermore, they endowed a chair in forestry at Yale, assisted forestry students in field training, and formed lobbying groups in behalf of Pinchot and his Forest Bureau in Congress.

As soon as Roosevelt became president, he began reserving more and more parts of the public domain from private homesteading and into the permanently governmental national forests. In his first year as president, Roosevelt created 13 new forests totaling 15.5 million acres. When in 1907, Congress, in alarm at Roosevelt's grabbing new forest reserves, revoked his authority to create new reserves in six Western states, T.R. spitefully rushed to set aside 75 million additional acres of forests before the bill became law, bringing the grand total up to 151 million acres. In late 1905, Roosevelt transferred control of the national forests from the Department of the Interior to his friend Pinchot and the Forest Service. Furthermore, Roosevelt and Pinchot gave the impetus to a bill finally passed in 1911 as the Weeks Act, which purchased large areas of private land in the East to be set aside by the Forest Service as national forest.

How did the private timber interests stand on this policy of sequestering forests under permanent government ownership? Roosevelt himself answered this question by announcing that "The great users of timber are themselves forwarding the movement for forest preservation." J.H. Cox has pointed to the great support of this Progressive forest reservation policy by the timber interests and lumber manufacturers of the Northwest:

> lumber manufacturers and timber owners ... had arrived at a harmonious understanding with Gifford Pinchot as early as 1903. ... In other words the government by withdrawing timber lands from entry and keeping them off the market would aid in appreciating the value of privately owned timber.[22]

The *American Lumberman*, official journal of the lumbering industry, as well as the National Lumber Manufacturers' Association, expressed similar approval during this period.

In addition to the timber owners, the lumber *users* also weighed in for compulsory conservation in the interests of preserving their future supplies. Hardwood users were particularly eager to set aside the Appalachian mountain range as a hardwood area, and they became active in the AFA as well as backing Pinchot in the Forest Service. Hardwood users who joined the advisory board of the AFA by 1909 included the Tight Barrel Stave Manufacturers' Association, the National Association of Box Manufacturers, the Carriage Builders' National Association, and the National Slack Cooperage Manufacturers' Association.

The timber interests were, of course, all too aware that compulsory sequestering of forest lands by the federal government would raise the prices and value of their timber. The alliance between industry and bureaucrats for higher prices was nowhere more stark than in the drive for higher tariffs on foreign lumber. If conservation of domestic resources had truly been their primary aim, then the "scientific" foresters in the federal bureaucracy should have been fervently eager to import foreign timber in

---

[22]J.H. Cox, "Organization of the Lumber Industry in the Pacific Northwest, 1889–1914," (unpublished doctoral dissertation, department of history, University of California, 1937), pp. 174–77; quoted in E. Louise Peffer, *The Closing of the Public Domain: Disposal and Reservation Policies, 1900–50* (Stanford, CA: Stanford University Press, 1951), p. 57. On Roosevelt's statement, see ibid., p. 56. [Editor's remarks] See ibid., pp. 16–17; Hays, *Conservation and the Gospel of Efficiency*, pp. 29–30, 47–48.

order to slow down domestic production. Instead, the foresters joined the timber industry in advocating higher tariffs.

Until the 1890s, American policy had been to allow public lands, including timber, to pass into private ownership as soon as they were homesteaded by private users. The beginning of the end of homesteading came with the General Land Law Revision Act of 1891, which granted the president power to create national forest reserves by mere proclamation. This power was installed by the political pressure of the American Forestry Association and the American Association for the Advancement of Science, aided by President Harrison.

The impetus for the 1891 measure had been upper-class "preservationist," a romantic desire to use government to preserve pristine forests and game animals intact. But Pinchot and Roosevelt were "scientific" cartelists and were soon able to elbow the preservationists aside. In the inter-bureaucratic maneuvering that won control for his Forest Service as against the Department of the Interior, Pinchot was able to use his powerful political allies, the Western stockmen, who were anxious to lease the forests to graze their animals. So fond were the stockmen of Pinchot's policies that the American National Livestock Association, from 1901 onward, passed resolutions endorsing Pinchot and the transfer of the national forests to his control. Thus Pinchot was able to keep Eastern game preservationist organizations from converting the national forests from all commercial use into game preserves. Roosevelt and Pinchot even turned against their old colleagues in the Boone and Crockett Club and managed to squash the Club's proposal to reserve game areas in the national forests.

Grazing under lease, indeed, soon became a far more important commercial use of the national forests than lumbering, thus cementing still further the alliance between the Roosevelt administration and the Western stockmen. This happy partnership between government as the owner and private firms as users or leasers of the land demonstrates that private firms do not necessarily oppose government ownership.

The Western grazing range had long been a mess, the direct result of the antiquated homesteading law which had governed U.S. land policy since the Civil War. The maximum homesteading acreage of 160 was well suited to the wet agriculture of the lands east of the Mississippi; but on the dry land of the Western prairie, 160 acres was an absurdly small technological unit for a farm. But since the 160-acre maximum still remained in force, the result, for decades, was a vast "open range," owned by the federal government, but used in common on a first-come, first-served basis by private users. The result of this "land communism" in the West was that the private users had a strong incentive to use up the soil or land as rapidly as possible, before their competitors could use it, and then to move onto the rest of the range. On the other hand, there was a *negative* incentive for maintaining or improving the soil, since any person or firm who invested in the soil could not keep other users from looting these improvements. The result was destruction of the soil and grassland, as well as a failure to maintain or restore, let alone improve, these resources.[23]

Many private firms favored this system, since they could operate with little capital and without the burden of maintaining the land. But the result was not only destruction of the soil, but also chaos, conflict, and the "range wars" between competing users of the land familiar to fans of Western films. All this from the failure of the federal government to allow private property in the Western range.

Samuel Hays writes:

> Moving their livestock from the higher alpine ranges during the summer to the lower grazing lands in the winter, cattle and sheepmen could operate profitability with little capital and no privately owned land. Chaos and anarchy, however, predominated on the open range. Congress had never provided legislation regulating grazing or permitting stockmen to acquire range lands. Cattle and sheepmen roamed the public domain, grabbing choice grazing areas before others could reach them first. Cattlemen fenced range for their exclusive use, but competitors cut the wire. Resorting to force and violence, sheepherders and cowboys "solved" their disputes over grazing lands by slaughtering rival livestock and murdering rival stockmen. Armed bands raided competing herds and flocks and patrolled choice areas to oust interlopers. Absence of

---

[23] [Editor's footnote] In contrast to overconsumption from public ownership, under a system of private ownership firms have an incentive to maximize profits by only harvesting a fraction of the resource (such as timber, soil, animals, or fish) at a time to allow the resource to replenish for future use. In addition, over time firms innovate in technologies that allow for more efficient utilization of resources. Entrepreneurs use the price system to estimate whether or not a resource is more highly demanded in the present or the future. For more on the economics of conservation, see Rothbard, *Man, Economy, and State*, pp. 1122–33.

the most elementary institutions of property law created confusion, bitterness, and destruction.

Amid this turmoil the public range rapidly deteriorated. Originally plentiful and lush, the forage supply was subjected to intense pressure by increasing use. The number of Western cattle grew rapidly after the Civil War; a rising sheep industry claimed its right to share in the public range; and settlers transformed grazing lands into more valuable cropland. The public domain became stocked with more animals than the range could support. Since each stockman feared that others would beat him to the available forage, he grazed early in the year and did not permit the young grass to mature and reseed. Under such conditions the quality and quantity of available forage rapidly decreased; vigorous perennials gave way to annuals and annuals to weeds.[24]

By the end of the 19th century, the Department of Agriculture estimated that overgrazing had reduced the capacity of public grazing lands by 50% in the previous ten years.[25]

Cattlemen, sheepmen, and farmer-settlers formed three groups that used both governmental and private violence to try to keep their competitors off the public range. State and community boosters, favoring a growing population, sided with the farmers. These farm groups established state immigration commissions to encourage migrants from the East and strongly opposed any private homesteading or fencing by cattlemen or leasing by grazers. Cattlemen tried to do the reverse and, to discourage settlement. Often, cattlemen would buy up all the water rights in an area to deny farmers the use of water. Sheepmen were hated by the cattlemen, because sheep, guided by herders, were more mobile and could forage more quickly. Furthermore, cattle would often refuse to graze where sheep had previously been. Cattlemen managed to obtain state laws to prohibit sheep grazing near villages or to tax sheep entering from another state.

---

[24]Hays, *Conservation*, pp. 50–51. [Editor's remarks] See ibid., pp. 31, 33–34, 36, 40–41; Peffer, *Public Domain*, pp. 12–14.

[25]Peffer, *Public Domain*, p. 27. By 1944, the U.S. Forest Service estimated that the range lands in the public domain had been depleted by two-thirds from their original virgin condition. Hays, *Conservation*, p. 50n. On the dust storms of the 1930s as the result of previous overgrazing and public land policies, see Peffer, *Public Domain*, p. 220.

Cattlemen originally tried to amend the homestead laws to enable them to homestead cattle ranches, but Congress refused. Then, cattlemen simply fenced portions of the open range, but Congress banned that practice in 1885. On railroad or state-owned lands, cattlemen were permitted to lease. And so, in default of the private ownership option, cattlemen from the 1880s on agitated for Congress to lease the public range to the stockmen. For, in that, at least land communism would be eliminated, and cattle would be assured, at least for certain periods, of lands that they could graze exclusively.

The scientific foresters and agriculturalists also favored leasing for grazing, for then, they felt, the soil and grass of the public domain could be at least partially restored. And in contrast to private ownership, the government and its forest and agricultural technologists could regulate the cattle and sheep and the use of the land. Both interests, then — that of the stockmen and of the scientific bureaucracy — would be fostered by a leasing program.

Gifford Pinchot and his fellow scientific foresters waged a successful battle, from the turn of the century on, against the preservationist policy of the Department of the Interior during the 1890s. In 1894, the Secretary of the Interior prohibited all grazing in the national forests. But in 1897, Congress passed the Forest Management Act, which paved the way for the Interior Department to allow grazing. From then on, Pinchot was able eventually to gain the upper hand, and grazing won out, aided by the head of Pinchot's Division of Grazing, a prominent Arizona sheepman and founder of the Arizona Wool Growers' Association, Albert F. Potter.

Apart from the national forests, what of the rest of the public domain? Why not apply livestock grazing leasing there as well? Roosevelt and Pinchot formed an alliance with the Western cattlemen who had long agitated for leasing, but they realized they were stirring up a political hornets' nest. The first leasing bill, introduced into the House in 1901, was defeated by the Western settlers, whose only concession was to expand the allowed homesteading acreage to 640 in western Nebraska, still an absurdly small acreage for cattle ranches.

T.R. set up a Public Lands Commission in 1903–04, that, predictably, reported in favor of grazing leases on the public domain. But T.R. moved slowly, waiting until after his re-election in 1904, and finally introduced a leasing bill in 1907, aided by James R. Garfield, who had become Secretary of the Interior in March. The House defeated the bill, however, and

Congress continued to defeat Pinchot's efforts for the next decade, until he finally abandoned hope.

The accession of James Garfield to the Secretary of the Interior's office was a bureaucratic triumph for Gifford Pinchot. The previous Secretary, Ethan A. Hitchcock, was a preservationist; now this son of former president Garfield, a cartelizing ally of T.R.'s in the new Bureau of Corporations, was to be a firm Pinchot ally in the new concept of "scientific" conservation.

Theodore Roosevelt's setting aside of 75 million acres for forest reserves in early 1907, in defiance of Congressional will, particularly angered the bulk of the West anxious to use the sequestered land. There was particularly bitter hatred against Gifford Pinchot, the originator and inspirer of T.R.'s forest policy and, since 1905, in total control of the national forests. In response, the governor of Colorado called a Public Lands Convention of Westerners to protest against "Pinchotism."

In reaction against this growth of opposition, T.R., once again at the suggestion of Pinchot, whipped up a nationwide "Conservation Movement" as a supposedly grassroots crusade. The movement was proposed at the convention of the Deep Waterways Association in the fall of 1907 and officially launched at the Conference of Governors held at the White House in May 1908. Roosevelt managed to line up in support of the conservation crusade not only many members of his Cabinet and of the Supreme Court, but also 38 state governors, William Jennings Bryan, soon to be the Democratic presidential standard-bearer for the third time. intellectuals and magazine editors, and such industrialists as Andrew Carnegie and railroad magnate James J. Hill.

Such was the propaganda barrage of this Roosevelt-created movement that not only the Republican platform, but also the Democrats, in 1908 endorsed the new fad. Most of the enthusiasts for forest conservation in the West were, of course, urban Easterners, many of them dilettantes and statist reformers in other areas. Such prominent and wealthy Chicago urban reformers as Alfred N. Baker and Walter L. Fisher now joined enthusiastically in the conservation movement.[26] Such women's groups as

---

[26]Pinchot induced Fisher in 1908 to become president of the Conservation League of America, which Pinchot had newly formed to be an umbrella group for 20 national conservation associations. The CLA proved ineffectual, and after that Pinchot dedicated his organizing efforts among the public to the National Conservation Association, which he formed a year later.

the General Federation of Women's Clubs and especially the Daughters of the American Revolution now became particularly enthusiastic about conservation, the DAR maintaining a special Committee on Conservation, headed by Pinchot's mother, Mrs. James Pinchot. Pinchot himself fawned on the DAR as spelling "only another name for the highest form of conservation, that of vital force and intellectual energy."[27]

These reformers disliked the big cities growing up around them, seemingly replacing the values of pietist religion, sobriety, and thrift with secularism, immorality, and profligacy. Conservation, on the other hand, seemed to promise preservation of the beauties of nature and the maintenance of rural values. Many of the wealthy conservation crusaders prided themselves on having abandoned "materialism" on behalf of such higher, nonmaterial ideals as parks and forests. A women's representative declared at a meeting of the National Conservation Congress that "We feel that it is for us, who are not wholly absorbed in business, to preserve ideals that are higher than business ..." And one enthusiast exulted that "National Parks represent opportunities for worship through which one comes to understand more fully certain of the attributes of nature and its Creator."[28]

We have seen, however, that many groups concerned with business also supported the conservation crusade, notably the private timber interests and the Western cattlemen. Thus, Leonard Bronson, manager of the National Lumber Manufacturers Association, was quite frank about the reason that the lumber industry favored forest reserves. As he wrote to the progressive Republican Senator Albert J. Beveridge of Indiana: "from a selfish standpoint alone the heavy timber owners of the West are heartily in favor of the reserves; for the mere establishment of these reserves has increased the value of their holdings very heavily by withdrawing from the market timber which otherwise would be competitive."[29] And then there

---

[27]At the convention of the National Conservation Congress, 1911. Quoted in Hays, *Conservation*, p. 142. [Editor's remarks] Ibid., pp. 36–38, 51–58, 60–63, 99–102.

[28]Quoted in ibid., p. 145.

[29]See Fisher, "The Evolution of the Conservation Cartel," pp. 89–90, 117–18; James Penick, Jr., *Progressive Politics and Conservation: The Ballinger-Pinchot Affair* (Chicago: University of Chicago Press, 1968), p. 36. Leading supporters of the forest conservation movement included N.W. McLeod, president of the National Lumber Manufacturers Association; George K. Smith, secretary of the Association; R.A. Long, president of the Southern Lumber Manufacturers Association; and F.J. Hagenbarth, president of the National Livestock Association. Also backing the national forest movement were the National Board of Trade, the National Business League, and the National Association of Manufacturers.

were the railroads. Recall that the land-grant railroads had received vast subsidies of land from the government: not only rights-of-way for their roads, but 15-mile tracts on either side of the line. Government reservation of public lands greatly raised the price received by the railroads when they later sold this land to new inhabitants of the area. The railroads were not ignorant of the monopolistic advantages that would be conferred upon them by conservation laws; in fact, the railroads were the financial "angel" of the entire conservation movement. James J. Hill, as we have seen, was an ardent conservationist. The Western railroads, it turns out, paid $45,000 annually in secret subsidy to a leading conservationist magazine, *Maxwell's Talisman*, and financed the Washington conservation lobby. Clearly, one reason was that subsidized irrigation, Maxwell's major concern, would stimulate farm settlement and transportation. But another was, as shown above, that if the federal government reserved its public domain or forests from use, settlers would be forced instead on railroad grant land, and the value of their lands, as well as the traffic on their railroads, would increase. Thus, the National Irrigation Congress, the most vigorous advocate of the Roosevelt conservation program — particularly federal irrigation subsidies — was financed by the transcontinental and the Burlington and Rock Island railroads, to the tune of $39,000 out of their annual budget of $50,000. The railroads were led, in this subsidy, by James J. Hill.[30]

Subsidized irrigation was a frankly developmental part of the new "conservation" program. The program had begun in 1888, when Congress authorized the first water resources investigation by the U.S. Geological Survey. Young engineer Frederick Haynes Newell organized this work and continued it as chief hydrographer; Newell also served as secretary of the National Geographic Society during the 1890s. From the beginning, private corporations, interested in developing water and irrigation, enthusiastically encouraged the socialization of their research costs through the

---

[30]The effectiveness of the National Irrigation Congress was destroyed when a congressional investigation revealed this hidden railroad financing. See below; also see Hays, *Conservation*, pp. 10, 178; Peffer, *Closing of the Public Domain*, p. 54; H.C. Hansbrough, *The Wreck: An Historical and Critical Study of the Administrations of Theodore Roosevelt and William Howard Taft* (1913), p. 52. [Editor's remarks] The U.S. land grant system can be seen as a case of "land-engrossment." The U.S. government "owned" a vast amount of land that was either unappropriated land not homesteaded or previously appropriated land acquired through conquest. To the extent that the government sold unappropriated land directly to settlers or gave that land to the railroads, which they sold, settlers were forced to pay a price, or a tax, for free land. See Rothbard, *Ethics of Liberty*, pp. 63–75.

Geological Survey and lobbied for ever-larger congressional appropriations.

Private irrigation in the West proved to be a bust in the Depression of 1893, after which the private irrigators turned to the federal government to finance these uneconomic ventures for them. The Carey Act of 1894, sponsored by Senator Robert Carey (R., Wyo.), granted a million acres of federal land to each Western state to allow the states to finance irrigation. But this, too, was not enough, so in the late 1890s, Newell and other federal officials joined with private Western interests to demand outright federal financing.

The propaganda campaign for federal financing was led by a young northern California lawyer, George H. Maxwell, who was inspired by a quixotic vision of depopulating urban centers and settling urban types on the land. The crusader Maxwell first converted the National Irrigation Congress, in 1896, to the idea of federal financing, a conversion which must not have been very difficult. He then converted private business groups by arguing that federal irrigation would increase Western farm population and broaden Western markets for Eastern business. Probably even more influential was the opportunity of subsidy to all forms of agri-business. In their annual conventions in 1898, the National Board of Trade, the National Business Men's League, and the National Association of Manufacturers all endorsed federal aid to irrigation and continued to do so thereafter. The following year, the indefatigable Maxwell organized his own National Irrigation Association to lobby for the cause; the NIA published his own monthly *Maxwell's Talisman*. By 1900, the propaganda coalition had done its work so well that both major parties adopted federal irrigation plans in their platforms.

The major booster of federal irrigation in Congress was a Representative Francis G. Newlands (D., Nev.), a wealthy silver mine owner. After the bimetallic cause lost out, Newlands shifted to emphasize irrigation, pushing a Reclamation Act through Congress in 1902. The Reclamation Act provided a new device to finance federal irrigation projects in the West: all receipts from the sale of public land in the West go to a special fund for irrigation works in those states. The Reclamation Act also delighted conservationists by giving maximal power to finance projects to the Secretary of the Interior so that he would not have to be restricted by the necessity of getting annual appropriations from the people's representatives in Congress. In this way, scientific expertise would replace taxpayer and democratic control.

Eastern Republicans were understandably critical of the reclamation bill for subsidizing Western farmers at the expense of Eastern competition; but the West was able to spring a *tu quoque* by attacking the Rivers and Harbors bills that had long subsidized Eastern lands. But the main force behind the passage of the Reclamation Act was Theodore Roosevelt, who had enthusiastically backed federal irrigation in the 1900 campaign, and had long been personally influenced by both Pinchot and Newell. In his first message to Congress, the new president asked for the advice of these two men, and he then drove through the Reclamation Act. It was not surprising that T.R. appointed Frederick Newell to be head of the new Reclamation Service, which later became a Bureau directly under the Secretary of the Interior in 1907.

Federal irrigation of course boosted the prices of the subsidized land. Much of the land was owned by speculators, who had either homesteaded the land originally or purchased it from homesteaders, and these speculators were mainly men of moderate means. The higher land prices, which both government irrigators and large corporate developers were now obliged to pay, irritated these powerful groups. The private ditch and reservoir companies found, too, that the speculator-settlers were not interested in immediate development and therefore had no interest in the purchase of their water. For their poor forecasting of demand, the private irrigation companies often went bankrupt. To try to shore up the companies, the Carey Act of 1894 provided that any settlers who bought land in the new irrigation projects would be forced to purchase water rights from the private company that had constructed the irrigation works. Carey himself had experienced financial difficulties in previous irrigation schemes, which he had promoted, and tried to eliminate them in the future by this tie-in plan. The Reclamation Act of 1902 extended this compulsory tie-in of land and water rights from state to federal projects. Not only that: in the same act, the federal government took up the entire burden by retaining title to all irrigation reservoirs and large ditches and agreeing to maintain and operate them forever. Bankruptcy of uneconomic private irrigation projects would no longer be a stumbling-block to excessive and hasty development through subsidized irrigation; for now, the federal government and the taxpayer would take on the task.

But the comforting umbrella of the Reclamation Service applied only to ditch, reservoir, and farming sites after it had approved a certain project. The compulsory tie-in provisions did not apply if settlers already owned the sites. And speculator-settlers had usually been alerted by many years of boosterism and agitation for the particular project. The next step, then, was accomplished in the Reclamation Act: for both government and corporate developers to pressure the Congress to authorize the Secretary of the Interior to withdraw all land from homesteading that might be capable of being irrigated. Under the pressure of Frederick H. Newell, Chief of the Bureau of Reclamation, the Secretary agreed to withdraw any lands from possible private use as long as the Bureau felt it might irrigate them at some time in the future. Here was an important example of large private land developers joining enthusiastically with bureaucrats and technocrats in urging the federal government to keep land off the market and out of the hands of homesteaders and settlers. Moreover, they agitated for the repeal of the Desert Land Act of 1877, under which a private settler could homestead 320 acres of federal desert land if he irrigated the land himself. This sort of private competition was scarcely welcome to the large corporate irrigators who yearned for a federal-state irrigation partnership.

The West generally favored rapid private settlement and development through the broadest possible homesteading of the public lands. They strongly opposed any such reservation of the public domain as was pushed by Roosevelt's forest conservation or Reclamation Bureau irrigation policy. And yet so greedy was the West for public subsidy that they were willing to swallow the reservation clauses in order to pass the Reclamation Act of 1902. In pushing through the bill, Teddy Roosevelt spoke grandly of helping the noble homesteader, whose interests he was quick to suppress in his forest and irrigation reservation programs. The West was so lured by subsidy and the rhetoric of homesteading that it supported the bill.

So the Reclamation Act was passed by a coalition of subsidized Westerners, technocrats, and Eastern businessmen and manufacturers sensing increased Western markets for their products. Understandably bitterly opposed were the Midwestern farmers, who saw the competition of Western farmers subsidized by themselves along with other taxpayers. The Midwestern Democracy took the lead in the opposition. One of the most trenchant attacks was levelled by Representative John S. Snook (D., Oh.), who pointed out that the pioneer-farmer in the Midwest had accomplished his survival and prosperity by his own efforts:

> He accomplished all this by his own efforts. ... He over-
> came all these difficulties unaided and alone. He never
> received, yea, more than that, he never asked, for a cent of

government aid. And now you propose to tax him and the
fruits of his unaided toil to build up a great farming section where products will be raised to compete with those
he raises ..."[31]

As is typical of men who wish to force others to sacrifice in their own
behalf, the Western leaders accused the Midwesterners of following their
"narrow and selfish local and personal interest." The *advocates* of irrigation
subsidies, in contrast, were men of "Americanism" and of "broad-minded
statesmanship."[32] To which Representative William P. Hepburn (R., Iowa)
made the proper reply:

If I were not one of the most amiable and polite men in
this House, I would take the liberty of saying that the
proposition involved in this bill is the most insolent and
impudent attempt at larceny that I have ever seen embodied in a legislative proposition. These gentlemen simply
do what? They ask us ... to give away an empire in order
that their private property may be made valuable.

With the Reclamation Act safely passed, the technocrat-large developer-
transcontinental railroad coalition lobbied vigorously during the Roosevelt
administration for the repeal of the Desert Land Act, repeal of the Timber
and Stone Act of 1878, which permitted homesteading of public land valuable for timber and stone, and generally to constrict private homesteading in
the West to the technologically absurd maximum of 160 acres. Accordingly,
on October 22, 1903, President Roosevelt appointed a three-man Public
Lands Commission, consisting of Pinchot, Newell, and chairman William A.
Richards, former governor of Wyoming and now Commissioner of the General Land Office in the Department of Interior. The following year, the Commission's report duly pushed for the conservationist program, including:
greater reservation of public land from private use, the repeal of the Timber
and Stone Act, and the reduction of the Desert Land Act entries to 160 acres.

The Public Lands Commission report quickly met with the hearty
approval of the president of the National Board of Trade, the National

[31]Quoted in Peffer, *Public Domain*, p. 36. Another leader against the Reclamation Act was
Representative James M. Robinson (D., Ind.). [Editor's remarks] Ibid., pp. 33–35; Hays,
Conservation, pp. 6–7, 10–12, 14–15, 18, 21.

[32]See the outpouring by Senator Clarence D. Clark (R., Wyo.), in Peffer, *Public Domain*,
pp. 36–37.

Association of Manufacturers, the National Business League of America, and the National Irrigation Association.[33] George Maxwell mobilized his entire propaganda machine, including the transcontinental railroads and manufacturing organizations, behind the commission report.

Despite this formidable pressure and the repeated pleas of the president, Congress, led by the citizens of the West themselves, blocked passage of the commission's measures. In particular, they saw that repression of homesteading, especially through the reservation of lands and forests, would cripple development of the West. As E. Louise Peffer writes about the Roosevelt period:

> It appears ironical that, in a period of such heart-felt sympathy for the homesteader and concern over preserving for his benefit all the remaining good land, every effort seemed to be aimed at cutting down his opportunities. Back in the 1880s, when there was still desirable land left, he could legitimately acquire under the various land laws enough land to make up quite sizable holdings. By 1905, when by general admission there remained very little of the type upon which a man could make a living on the area permitted, the administration was doing everything to cut down the amount that one man could legally acquire to the 160 acres allowed by the Homestead Law. The West argued that it was humanly impossible to succeed under those circumstances. ... To succeed on such undesirable land, the entryman had to have double or more the acreage allowed by the Homestead Law.[34]

Superficially, it may seem inconsistent for Roosevelt and his conservation program to stress reservation and withdrawal on some occasions, and subsidized development on others. But there is a deeper consistency to all parts of the program. In every case, land and natural resources are taken out of free, private settlement and development and converted to State regulation and control, in partnership with a relatively few privileged private interests. Where government takes resources off the market, the aim is to restrict and cartelize lands or resource industries. Where government subsidizes development, it is carefully limited to a partnership with

---

[33]See ibid., pp. 46, 47n.

[34]Ibid., pp. 54–55.

selected private interests instead of left open to the competition of the free market. Statism — corporate statism — was the key. Thus, the members and colleagues of the Public Lands Commission continued to meet informally after its formal existence was over, and, as Hays writes, a common theme underlay their efforts: "The old practice of disposing of nonagricultural lands to private owners, Pinchot and others argued, must give way to public ownership and public management."[35]

The consistency of the conservation program was greatly aided by the fact that the various wings of conservationists generally worked in tandem. As we have indicated, forest reservationists and irrigationists assiduously promoted each other's cause. This collaboration was greatly aided by the forest cover-flood control mythology that had been adopted by the conservationists. The familiar argument ran that forests were essential in absorbing rainfall, retarding stream runoff, checking soil erosion, and therefore preventing floods and preserving uniformity of the water supply. Irrigationists, private power and water supply corporations, municipal water departments, and forest and worker scientists joined in this seemingly powerful and "scientific" argument for forest reservation. The alliance began as early as the Harrison administration in the early 1890s, when the president was prevailed upon by southern California groups, panicky over forest cover flood and soil erosion, to create the San Bernardino National Forest. The major lobbyist for this National Forest was General Adolph Wood, president of the Arrowhead Reservoir Company, a private corporation engaged in storing water for power, irrigation, and general domestic use. Wood was understandably interested in turning to state and federal government to subsidize the long-run supply of his water.[36]

By the latter years of the Roosevelt administration, the T.R. conservationists had expanded the irrigation program and the irrigation-forestry alliance into a comprehensive statist program for federal "multiple-purpose river development." The multiple-purpose concept grew also out of a dozen years of enthusiasm for governmental subsidies to river navigation. The river development movement arose throughout the country in the late 1890s, led invariably by urban merchants and manufacturers, anxious to force the general taxpayer to subsidize river transport. One problem is that shippers, after 1898, faced a continuing rise in railroad freight rates,

---

[35]Hays, *Conservation*, p. 69.

[36]Ibid., pp. 22–26.

reversing the trend of previous decades. Part of a counter-drive was to lobby government to promote inland navigation for a cheaper form of transportation — cheaper for themselves, of course, not for the taxpayers. Local merchants and manufacturers easily persuaded local and regional booster groups that federal funds in *their* area would promote that area as against competing towns and regions.

For many years, the enthusiasts for the expensive "new waterway" boondoggles were thwarted by Congress, led by the shrewd representative Theodore E. Burton (R., Ohio), chairman of the House Rivers and Harbors Committee. Burton, a lawyer, banker, and water transportation expert, argued that the proposed river improvements and inland canals were far too expensive and would have little effect on railway rates. In frustration, the waterway agitators formed the National Rivers and Harbors Congress in 1901, regrouping five years later to become the most powerful lobby for the waterway movement. It urged a $50 million annual federal river development program and, at its December 1908 meeting, endorsed a vast $500 million federal bond issue for waterway development, as well as a permanent commission whose task would be to propose new projects.

In 1907, Roosevelt's conservationist leaders gathered all these conservationist threads together to formulate the concept of multiple-purpose river basin development. Forests would be reserved for their own sake and also to regulate stream flow of water, reservoirs would be built to control floods, promote irrigation, and generate hydroelectric power, and rivers would be developed for navigation and all these other functions. The vast expense involved meant federal funds and federal control; not only had local and private funding proved inadequate for the irrigation desired by the new planners, but rivers, after all, run interstate, and therefore, if they are to be planned by government, require federal operation and control. Newell, Pinchot, and Garfield were crucial to formulating and pushing for the new concept. So too was W.J. McGee, the chief theoretician and organizer of the new multiple-purpose river basin movement. A self-taught geologist and anthropologist from Iowa, and at this point assistant head of the Bureau of Ethnology in the Roosevelt administration, McGee worked tirelessly to persuade all branches of the conservation movement of the new dispensation. Daily he peppered Roosevelt, Pinchot, and Garfield with ideas and suggestions; he drew up presidential messages and organized conferences. McGee pushed Newell into expanding irrigation projects to their effects on river flows, and he urged Newell on the new National Rivers and Harbors Congress.

In February 1907, McGee urged upon T.R. the creation of a federal Inland Waterways Commission. Roosevelt accepted the idea the following month, including on the Commission, appointing Pinchot and Newell to it and giving McGee the critical post of Commission Secretary. From that point on, multiple-purpose river development became a leading conservation policy of President Roosevelt. A crucial figure aiding the commission was Marshall O. Leighton, Chief Hydrographer for the U.S. Geological Survey, who had worked on flood control problems. As advisory hydrographer to the Inland Waterways Commission, Leighton drew up the practical engineering plans for a mammoth development scheme for the Ohio River System, consisting of no less than one hundred reservoirs for flood control, from which the federal government would produce and sell the power for the alleged self-financing of the project.

In December 1907 Senator Francis Newlands presented a bill incorporating the findings of the Commission, establishing the Inland Waterways Commission as a permanent body with the power not only to investigate, but also to decide upon water projects, with Congress providing a permanently available fund of $50 million for their financing. That is, the president could replenish the fund when it fell sharply below the $50 million level.

Despite the enthusiastic support of Roosevelt, this leap into statism was successfully blocked by the opposition of Representative Burton and the Army Corps of Engineers, who wished to confine water projects to navigation aid only, and who stoutly denied the theory that forest cover retarded the runoff of water. While the comprehensive multiple-purpose concept failed, it proved a harbinger of the future. As Hays puts it: "Although Congress approved few of its proposals, the Roosevelt administration for the first time worked out the general principles and specific elements of the multiple-purpose approach to river development which the New Deal put into practice over two decades later."[37]

As we have pointed out, the forest stream-flow theory was critical to the allegedly scientific basis for the technocratic enthusiasm for integrated multi-purpose development. Unfortunately, the scientific basis of this well-known theory was shaky at best. Oddly enough, for alleged scientists,

---

[37]Ibid., p. 91. [Editor's remarks] Ibid., pp. 93–94, 102–03.

their enthusiasm for the theory waxed not in proportion to the evidence behind it, but to the political popularity of forest conservation and multiple-purpose development. Though tentative at first, confidence of the conservationists in the theory swelled after the conservationist victories from 1902 on, reaching a peak in the struggles over the Inland Waterways Commission proposals six years later.

From the counterattack by the Army Corps of Engineers came scientific arguments which punctured the new forest cover myth. Lieutenant Colonel Hiram Martin Chittenden, a veteran of river control, delivered an influential paper before the American Society of Civil Engineers in September 1908 which set up a devastating barrage against the myth. Chittenden pointed out that there was no quantitative evidence of any impact of deforestation on river flow. Furthermore, the existence of forests can cut both ways, for forest litter accumulates water and thereby adds to floods. As for soil erosion, wrote Chittenden, it is caused by poor agricultural practices rather than deforestation. Other Corps engineers did quantitative studies that showed no correlation between forested or deforested conditions on particular rivers with the incidence of floods. Willis Moore, head of the U.S. Weather Bureau, argued also that floods are caused by excessive precipitation period, and that water runoff is not materially affected by any other factor; "high waters are not higher and the low waters are not lower than formerly," i.e., than before deforestation.

The devastating attacks of Chittenden and Moore began the inexorable decline, at least in scientific circles, of the forest cover stream-flow theory.

Professor Gordon Dodds sums up his illuminating discussion of the stream-flow controversy as follows:

> The stream-flow controversy not only illustrates the emotionalism of the conservation movement and its misrepresentations of science but also reveals much about the contemporary concepts of science itself. ... Pressed by their critics who were proposing the new quantitative methodology [in contrast to casual observation], the forestry advocates, some of whom were privately aware of their own methodological weaknesses, fell back upon enthusiasm, and, on occasion, duplicity. Their commitment was to a cause, not to scientific evidence if the evidence contravened the cause. ... Although their evidence for the forest-stream-flow theory was dubious, the conservationists, as

progressives were wont to do, framed their arguments in
moralistic terms by stigmatizing their enemies as milita-
rists, monopolists, traditionalists, and other opprobrious
creatures ...

Men like Chittenden, who fought the conservationists, were as dedicated to the public interest ... as Pinchot
and his followers. They were, in addition, more successful as scientists in pointing the way to rewarding studies of forest influences. Yet their services to science and
their assistance in saving the taxpayers vast expenditures
of public money for reforestation for flood control have
gone unrecognized in historical studies, whereas the
conservationists appear as farsighted guardians of the
national estate.[38]

Despite the setbacks to the multiple-purpose river concept, Theodore
Roosevelt had launched a modern movement that was already on the way
to long-run triumph. In the fair-sounding name of "conservation," he set
the pace for the accelerating future withdrawal of vast parts of the federal
domain from ownership, production, or use, and for federal control of the
natural resources of the nation.[39]

[38]Gordon B. Dodds, "The Stream-Flow Controversy: A Conservation Turning Point," *Journal of American History* (June, 1969): 67–69.

[39][Editor's footnote] For more on the conservation policies of Theodore Roosevelt, see Powell, *Bully Boy*, pp. 13–16, 183–210, 256–62. Powell chronicles the various ways in which subsidized irrigation systems and dams, eagerly supported by Western politicians, led to inefficiency and a misallocation of resources.

CHAPTER 9

The National Civic Federation: Big Business Organized for Progressivism

At about the same time the nation acquired its first progressive President Theodore Roosevelt, various big business leaders decided to organize on behalf of the new concept, one which has in recent years been termed "corporate liberalism." The nation was to be guided into the new path of a strong State, expanding, regulating, and governing all in behalf of a tripartite coalition led by Big Business, by means of Big Government, and creating Big Unionism as junior partner. Or rather, a quadripartite coalition, since economists and other intellectuals were needed to argue for and help plan the new system. How fitting, then, that the major big business-led organization for the new dispensation should itself include all four of these groups![1]

---

[1][Editor's footnote] Rothbard here is alluding to the famous rebirth of the "Alliance of Throne and Altar," which occurred between progressive economists and government in the early 20th century. During the Progressive Era, big business turned to big government in order to cartelize, and both in turn needed planners to sell their interventions to the public and convince them that government sponsored monopolies were not being created. Instead of saying that the king was divine, the new court apologists said big government was necessary to improve welfare. In return, the collectivist intellectuals would benefit from the power and prestige of planning the new system, which was more lucrative than what existed in a *laissez-faire* regime. The secularization of the Alliance and the transformation

1. The Origins: The Chicago Civic Federation

The National Civic Federation (NCF), the major organization for the new statism, was organized in 1900 by Ralph M. Easley, a former school-teacher and journalist, and a self-styled conservative Republican. The NCF emerged out of the Chicago Civic Federation (CCF), which itself was launched in a blend of pietist reform, corporate statism, and high-level foreign influence.

The CCF began as the result of frenetic denunciations of vice, gambling, and prostitution in Chicago by the pietistic Englishman William T. Stead, editor of the distinguished London magazine *Review of Reviews*. The culmination of Stead's agitation over sin in Chicago came at a mass meeting in the city's Civic Center Club in November 1893, at which Stead hoped to establish a Chicago form of his "Civic Church," a London group Stead had helped to organize. The November meeting selected an organizing committee, which in turn incorporated the Civic Federation of Chicago in early 1894. President of the new CCF was Lyman J. Gage, head of the First National Bank of Chicago, a man strongly in the Rockefeller ambit who was later to become Secretary of the Treasury in the McKinley administration. Secretary of the CCF and operating head was Ralph Easley. A majority of posts in the new CCF was held by a group of wealthy Chicago businessmen.[2]

Stead, the spiritual founder of the CCF, was a powerful figure in England as a religious reformer and editor, and even more so behind-the-scenes. A social reformer and ardent English imperialist, Stead was a disciple of the English art critic and social philosopher John Ruskin and

---

of economists during this time from *laissez-faire* philosophers to activist government planners was heavily related to the fact that many Yankee postmillennial pietist reformers went to Bismarck's Germany to get their Ph.D.s and became instilled with German socialism and centralization. See Chapters 11 and 13 below, pp. 333–30, 420–61; Murray Rothbard, "The Anatomy of the State" in *Egalitarianism as a Revolt Against Nature and Other Essays* (Auburn, AL: Mises Institute, 2000 [1965]), pp. 61–64; *For a New Liberty*, pp. 67–77; James Gilbert, *Designing the Industrial State: The Intellectual Pursuit of Collectivism in America, 1880–1940* (Chicago: Quadrangle Books, 1972); Frank Tariello, Jr., *The Reconstruction of American Political Ideology, 1865–1917* (Charlottesville: University Press of Virginia, 1981).

[2] On the Chicago Civic Federation, see David W. Eakins, "The Development of Corporate Liberal Policy Research in the United States, 1885–1965," (doctoral dissertation in history, University of Wisconsin, 1966), pp. 60–66.

was instrumental in bringing Ruskin's young Oxford as well as Cambridge disciples together with an older Ruskinian, Cecil Rhodes. In early 1891, Rhodes and Stead had formed a secret society to spread the cause of social imperialism, the "Society of the Elect." Rhodes was the leader, and Stead was on the executive committee, along with Alfred (later Lord) Milner. Other devotees of the circle included future Prime Minister Arthur (Lord) Balfour and the powerful investment banker, Lord Rothschild.[3]

The new CCF lost little time in plunging into political activity in Chicago. It pioneered in upper-class municipal "reform" efforts, which would later become so prominent during the Progressive Era. It drafted and pushed through expansion of civil service in Illinois. Various academics worked with the wealthy businessmen in the CCF, including Albion W. Small, University of Chicago sociology professor, and particularly Chicago political economy professor Edward W. Bemis, member of the five-man nominating committee of the Federation. Both Small and Bemis had been students of the formidable progressive economist Richard T. Ely, and both followed Ely enthusiastically into statism.

Very quickly, the well-organized CCF branched out into national affairs, holding four national conferences, one on American foreign policy in 1898. The most publicized and important conference held by the CCF — which led directly to the formation of the National Civic Federation — was the Chicago Conference on Trusts, held in 1899. Ralph Easley traveled across the nation mobilizing delegates and support for the conference. Indeed, the Conference took on semi-official status, since some governors, including Theodore Roosevelt in New York, were induced to send delegations to the Chicago Conference.

Most speeches at the Conference, spearheaded by progressive economists Jeremiah W. Jenks, Edward Bemis, and John R. Commons, asserted that the trust was here to stay and trusts needed to be regulated by government. Even the supposedly radical Democratic leader William Jennings Bryan, while more aggressively anti-business in rhetoric, ended by

---

[3]See Carroll Quigley, *The Anglo-American Establishment: From Rhodes to Cliveden* (New York: Books in Focus, 1981), pp. 33–40. [Editor's remarks] In the early 1910s, this organization would establish Round Table groups in Britain, the U.S., and other countries. The U.S. branch would later be involved in setting up the highly influential and Morgan-dominated Council on Foreign Relations. See Chapter 13 below, pp. 447–48, Rothbard, *Wall Street, Banks, and American Foreign Policy*, pp. 39–32; Griffin, *The Creature from Jekyll Island*, pp. 270–74.

advocating a very similar program. The Conference also touched off the compulsory publicity agitation which marked the early days of the corporate reform movement.

So successful was the Chicago Conference on Trusts that the leadership of the CCF determined, by unanimous vote of the executive committee in September, 1899, to organize a national civic federation with Easley at the head, a task accomplished the following year. The more progressive and corporatist leaders then joined the new NCF while the more conservative, local-minded members continued to run the CCF.

2. ORGANIZING THE NCF

Helping Easley organize the ambitious new NCF was Jeremiah W. Jenks, Oscar S. Straus of the New York department store family and later to become Secretary of Commerce and Labor under Theodore Roosevelt, and Samuel Gompers and John Mitchell of the AFL (the American Federation of Labor). Also on the Advisory Council of the new federation were Richard T. Ely, Bemis, Commons, the Columbia University economist E.R.A. Seligman of the powerful international banking family, and the intriguing Albert Shaw.

Shaw, a political scientist and a disciple of Ely, was later to be a leading advisor of Theodore Roosevelt, and he had spoken before the Chicago Conference on Trusts. As a leading magazine editor of *The American Review of Reviews*, Shaw lent the power of the press to the corporatist cause. When John D. Rockefeller came to launch his General Education Board, Albert Shaw became one of the trustees of the powerful new foundation. An interesting point about Shaw is that he became the long-time editor of the journal in 1891 when it was set up by William T. Stead, editor of the London *Review of Reviews*.

Easley's success was marked and rapid, and very quickly official leadership of the new NCF was assumed by top Rockefeller ally Marcus A. Hanna as first president of the NCF, by Chicago utilities tycoon Samuel Insull, Chicago banker Franklin MacVeagh (later Secretary of the Treasury), Andrew Carnegie, and — inevitably — several partners of J.P. Morgan and Company. By 1903, the National Civic Federation included representatives of nearly one-third of all the 367 corporations worth more than $10 million, and it also included one-fourth of the largest railroads. George W. Perkins, Morgan's main man in the political sphere, was prominent in the organization. August Belmont Jr., prominent Democrat and

Rothschild agent in the U.S., was elected president of the NCF on Hanna's death. At various times, the executive committee of the NCF also included such prominent politicians as ex-President Grover Cleveland, Roosevelt's Attorney-General Charles J. Bonaparte, T.R.'s close friend Nicholas Murray Butler of Columbia University, T.R.'s Secretary of State Elihu Root, George B. Cortelyou, Roosevelt's private secretary, later his Secretary of the Treasury, and finally president of Consolidated Gas, and Secretary of War under T.R. and then President William Howard Taft. It is clear, in short, that the NCF represented a coalition of top big business interests with the Morgans the most prominent, but with Rothschilds and Rockefellers also included.[4]

3. The Clash over Unions

The union problem was a particularly sticky one for the NCF, for two major reasons: many businessmen were stubbornly *laissez-faire* and particularly were opposed to unionism, and unions scarcely existed, except in such non-competitive (between localities) industries as the building trades, the cartelized railroads, and in certain skilled crafts where unions could exclude competing labor. Overall, unions did not rise above a meagre 6% of the labor force until America's entry into World War I, and they were usually well below that figure. But those unions that did exist were perfectly suited for the corporatist ideal: monopolistic craft unions grouped in the AFL unions which had abandoned the early radical socialism of the Knights of Labor, and were prepared to take their place in a corporatist order — a role that would be far greater than any they could possibly achieve in a free market.

And so, labor leaders played a prominent role in the National Civic Federation from the very beginning. Samuel Gompers, longtime head of the AFL, was first vice president of the NCF from its inception until his death in 1924. John Mitchell, head of the United Mine Workers, was chairman or co-chairman of the Trade Agreements Department of the NCF from 1904 to 1911. The heads of the railroad Brotherhoods, powerful craft unions in the railroad industry, were on the NCF executive committee.

The Trade Agreements Department was organized in 1904 to promote unionism among employer groups. It was jointly chaired for four

---

[4][Editor's footnote] James Weinstein, *The Corporate Ideal in the Liberal State, 1900–1918* (Boston: Beacon Press, 1968), pp. 8–11; Burch, *Elites in American History*, pp. 135, 156, 166, 170, 184.

years by Mitchell and a prominent employer, Francis L. Robbins of the Pittsburg Coal Company. The Department engineered union agreements with the New York clothing trades, the iron molders, the newspaper publishers and the Typographical Union, between Theatrical Managers and the Musicians Protective Association, the New York Metal Trades Association and the Boilermakers Union, bituminous coal operators and the struggling United Mine Workers, and U.S. Steel and the Metal Workers Union.

Many of the progressive big businessmen, however, while eager to foist corporatist unionism on the rest of the country, balked at dealing with unions in their own plants. Leading the parade favoring unions for everyone but themselves were men prominent in the Morgan ambit: George W. Perkins, Cyrus McCormick of International Harvester, and Judge Elbert Gary of U.S. Steel.

Typical was the fact that August Belmont Jr. was boosted vigorously as successor to Hanna as president of the NCF by the union leaders in the organization. Despite these cordial relations, Belmont refused to have anything to do with unions in his own Interborough Rapid Transit Company on the New York City subways.

Opposing the big-business-dominated NCF was the newly organized National Association of Manufacturers. Formed in 1895 as a small, low-profile group to promote foreign trade, the NAM was taken over in 1902 by an aggressive group of small businessmen in the Middle West, dedicated to free markets and hostility to labor unions. Revealingly, Easley condemned the NAM and like-minded capitalists as "anarchists"; he saw the NCF as a third way between radical socialism on the one hand and "anarchist," free-market capitalism on the other. As Easley wrote to a supporter, "our enemies are the Socialists among the labor people and the anarchists among the capitalists."[5]

For their part, the NAM leaders angrily saw the National Civic Federation as "part and parcel" of the AFL and as a proponent of "the most virulent form of socialism, closed shop unionism." They also attacked the threat they saw in "socialized industry," and they perceptively saw the NCF, as a later historian would sum it up, "as a conspiracy between the magnates and the unionists aimed directly at them." As Professor Wiebe puts it, the threat

---

[5]Easley to Joseph L. Bristow, July 17, 1909. In Weinstein, *The Corporate Ideal in the Liberal State*, p. 11. [Editor's footnote] Ibid., pp. 5–15.

of "big labor and big business combined horrified members of the NAM, who believed their future depended upon an economic fluidity which the recently formed trusts and the AFL would destroy."[6] Meanwhile, Ralph Easley was sneering at the NAM anti-union employers as small fry; they included "none of the great employers of labor representing basic industries, such as coal, iron and steel, building trades and railroads."[7]

The conflict between the two groups was dramatized by the anti-union action taken by one of the leaders of the newly-constituted National Association of Manufacturers, James W. Van Cleave, head of the Buck's Stove and Range Company of St. Louis. The Metal Polishers Union had struck the Buck's Company for union recognition, and the AFL, in 1908, had organized a secondary boycott of the Buck's Company in support of the strike. Van Cleve responded by filing suit to try and obtain an injunction against the boycott. At that point, Wall Street lawyer Alton B. Parker, Democratic presidential candidate in 1904 and later president of the NCF, became the defense counsel for Gompers, while much of the AFL defense was secretly financed by Andrew Carnegie, steel magnate in the Morgan ambit, who was also the NCF's biggest contributor.[8]

4. The Drive for Workmen's Compensation Laws

If the pro-union attitude of the NCF offended anti-union employers, the Civic Federation's increasing attention to promoting welfare and the welfare state after 1905 avoided such alienation. The Welfare Department of the NCF was founded in 1904 and took on an accelerating role by the following year. By 1911 it had 500 employer-members. Its task was to promote a voluntary paternalistic welfare program by the corporations toward their workers, promoting a sense of team spirit and a kind of feudalistic loyalty by the workers to the corporation. As Weinstein puts it, the approach of the Welfare Department "was to promote sympathy and a sense of identification

---

[6]Robert H. Wiebe, *Businessmen and Reform: A Study of the Progressive Movement* (Cambridge, MA: Harvard University Press, 1962), p. 31.

[7]Weinstein, *The Corporate Ideal in the Liberal State*, p. 16.

[8]Van Cleave won a temporary injunction against the AFL secondary boycott in the federal courts, but two years later the Supreme Court reversed. Bucks was one of the few cases where the courts enjoined peaceful persuasion rather than the use of union violence. See Sylvester Petro, "Injunctions and Labor Disputes, 1880–1932, Part I," *Wake Forest Law Review* 14 (June, 1978): 485, 488, 550.

between the employer and his employees by integrating the lives and the leisure time of the workers with the functioning of the corporation."[9]

More important was the National Civic Federation's push for welfare state measures. Particularly important was its leadership driving for workmen's compensation laws. Under the sensible and cogent doctrine of the common law, employers were not liable for accidents to workers if: (a) other workers were responsible for the accident (the fellow-servant defense), (b) if the worker knew the risk and therefore could be held to have voluntarily assumed it (the assumption-of-risk defense), or (c) if the worker himself contributed to the accident by his negligence (the contributory negligence defense). In this period, labor unions did not favor workmen's compensation laws; rather, they called for changing liability laws to make the employer liable when the worker himself did not contribute to the accident. By 1907, agitation had managed to pass such "employer liability" laws in 26 states. Most of these laws applied only to railroads, however, where unions were strongest, and limited only the fellow-servant, the weakest of the three employer defenses.

Progressive employers, in contrast, began moving in this period toward workmen's compensation laws. From their point of view, these laws would confer several important benefits. First, they would forestall the threat of employer liability laws; the payments would be far less, and the costs would be spread among all the employers, not only those with the highest rates of accidents. Second, and more important, the taxpayers would be forced to pay a large proportion of the costs of compensation. In contrast, say, to voluntary insurance, the taxpaying public would be forced to pay for the bureaucracy of the regulatory commissions and to socialize the costs of accident insurance under state insurance plans. Third, the laws would impose high fixed costs for compliance and for accident prevention, which would fall with particular severity on smaller competitors. Hence, workmen's compensation laws, in the name of humanitarianism and progress, would advance the cartelization of industry. Specifically in line with cartelization, such large firms, which had already instituted voluntary workmen's compensation plans such as International Harvester and U.S. Steel, could now impose higher costs on their competitors by agitating for the government legislation. And fourth, for anti-union employers,

[9]Weinstein, *The Corporate Ideal in the Liberal State*, p. 19.

workmen's compensation would reduce benefits workers might expect from unions and lead them to look elsewhere.

Thus, at the annual 1911 meeting of the National Civic Federation, August Belmont Jr. announced that he had induced half a dozen major corporations, from Edison Electric and Otis Elevator to Ingersoll-Rand to come out for workmen's compensation laws. Andrew Carnegie also endorsed the idea. The NCF frankly saw a major reason as the forestalling of any application of employer liability laws to manufacturing. In the meanwhile, the always far-sighted George W. Perkins stressed workmen's compensation as part of a broad reach toward industrial cartelization. As Perkins explained at the 1909 annual meeting of the NCF, "Cooperation in business is taking and should take the place of ruthless competition." To succeed, this "new order" must demonstrate that it is better for the laborer as well as for capital and the consumer.[10]

The NCF began its drive for workmen's compensation in 1908, establishing an Industrial Insurance Commission with George W. Perkins as chairman. This commission was rather quiescent, however; the major drive was launched the following year when new president Seth Low appointed past-president August Belmont Jr. as head of a new Department on Compensation for Industrial Accidents and Their Prevention. From then on, the NCF was at the center of the movement for workmen's compensation legislation. Among those involved in the NCF agitation were the prominent progressive reformer Louis D. Brandeis, active in the Massachusetts branch of the NCF, the vice president of Metropolitan Life Insurance Company, and a representative of the Sage Foundation Fund. At the 1909 annual meeting, workmen's compensation was strongly defended by George M. Gillette, head of Minneapolis Steel and Machinery Company and president of the Minnesota Employers' Association; Louis B. Schram, head of the labor Committee of the U.S. Brewers Association, and Major J.G. Pangborn of the Baltimore and Ohio Railroad. By 1909, too, the NCF had managed to convert Samuel Gompers and the AFL to the idea of compensation laws.

In the meanwhile, by 1910 the small manufacturers of the NAM had also been converted to workmen's compensation. By the spring of 1911, journalist Will Irwin noted that the entire business community was now in favor of workmen's compensation laws. The only remaining holdouts

---

[10]Ibid., pp 41–47.

against this "scientific system," he opined, were "a few old-time manufacturers who can see nothing but next year's dollar."[11]

The NCF proceeded to draw up model workmen's compensation bills and to agitate for them on the state and federal levels. There were no state laws before 1909; but, as in so many other areas of statism in 20th-century America, President Roosevelt led the way by pushing a federal compensation act through Congress in 1908.

The actual drive for workmen's compensation legislation was sparked by August Belmont Jr. Shortly after becoming head of the NCF Compensation Department in 1909, Belmont appointed a legal committee headed by P. Tecumseh Sherman, a conservative lawyer and former Commissioner of Labor in New York, to draw up a model bill. Sherman was particularly inspired by the German system of compulsory medical, old age, and accident insurance. Realizing that this comprehensive welfare state model could not be established in the United States all at once, he frankly called his proposed model state workmen's compensation bill "a halfway measure — a mere entering wedge."[12] Completed by the spring of 1910, the model bill was sent to all state governors and legislators interested in the problem.

In contrast to the stereotype of older historians, the major opposition to the Sherman Bill within the NCF was from big businessmen urging Sherman to have the courage to be far more radical. One leading critic within the Federation was Raynal C. Bolling of U.S. Steel, who declared that workmen's compensation should be nothing less than universal and compulsory (Sherman had extended it only to hazardous industries), and applied to agriculture and domestic work as well as manufacturing. Also leading an unsuccessful call for more radical legislation were George M. Gillette, head of the Minnesota Employers' Association, and Hugh V. Mercer, a Minnesotan appointed to study workmen's compensation in that state.

In 1909, New York became the first state to pass a compulsory workmen's compensation law. After the NCF flooded the states with the model Sherman bill the following year, former-president Theodore Roosevelt addressed the annual meeting of the NCF and called for workmen's compensation laws. During the year 1911, the number of state workmen's compensation laws jumped from one to thirteen.

---

[11]Ibid., pp. 47–51.

[12]Ibid., p. 52.

But a temporary hitch suddenly developed in the rapid march to Paradise. In the spring of 1911, the New York Court of Appeals in *Ives v. South Buffalo Railway Co.* unanimously held the compensation law to be unconstitutional, an assault on the common law and deprivation of property without due process. In many ways, the courts proved to be the last stronghold of the old *laissez-faire* order.

While the courts had outlawed compensation acts before without provoking much comment, times were now changing rapidly. Teddy Roosevelt led the howls of outrage, writing that the path of necessary "social reform" was being blocked. The progressive magazine *Survey* significantly and trenchantly noted that the court would not have struck down workmen's compensation "if a board of broad gauge business men [with]... responsibility for vast property interests on their shoulders" had constituted the judges' bench. *Survey* particularly pointed to the wise statesmanship in this matter of J.P. Morgan, E.H. Gary, Andrew Carnegie, and Jacob H. Schiff — all but the last solidly in the Morgan ambit, and the latter the head of Kuhn-Loeb. Sure enough, the *Ives* decision was promptly denounced by Sherman, the National Civic Federation, and by the redoubtable Francis Lynde Stetson, long-time Morgan lawyer and now attorney for Morgan's International Harvester Company. The NCF called for Congress to pass federal compensation legislation.

Moving quickly and obediently to bury *Ives*, the New York State legislature in 1913 proposed a constitutional amendment to remove the protection of due process in the case of workmen's compensation. In the former times, this drastic assault on private property would have caused a great furor; now it passed overwhelmingly both in the legislature and among the public. In December 1913, the Conference of New York State Republicans, led by the formidable Elihu Root, unanimously passed a resolution hailing the new amendment and trumpeting the new spirit of government intervention. "Changed and changing social and industrial conditions impose new duties on government," the Republicans opined. The party must therefore "meet industrial and social demands of modern civilization."[13]

Seeing the handwriting on the wall, other state courts began to ratify compensation legislation. By 1920, all but six states had workmen's com-

---

[13]Weinstein, *The Corporate Ideal in the Liberal State*, pp. 55–56, 58, 61.

pensation laws in force, and the federal government had widened its coverage to all of its own employees.[14]

5. Monopolizing Public Utilities

Another aspect of progressive reform pushed by the NCF was the transformation of public utilities in the United States. The thrust here was to change from a roughly free market in utilities toward outright grants of monopoly privilege. The public utility — the gas, electric, or trolley franchises — was to be protected from competition and regulated by the state or municipality so as to provide a guaranteed, fixed rate of profit. For those lucky enough to obtain utility franchises, this seemed like paradise.

The NCF established a Commission on Public Ownership of Public Utilities in late 1905, ostensibly to engage in a scientific, impartial study of the public utility question and of the results of public ownership, which had become the prevalent system in Europe. The Commission was chaired by Melville E. Ingalls, chairman of the board of the Big Four Railroad, and its first vice-chairman was John Mitchell of the United Mine Workers. Other members of the executive committee of the Commission included Frank A. Vanderlip of the Rockefeller-oriented National City Bank, prominent investment banker Isaac N. Seligman, wealthy reformer Jacob Riis, Louis D. Brandeis, and utilities magnate Samuel Insull, who was previously affiliated with Thomas Edison and General Electric. It also included the leading progressive economist John R. Commons of the University of Wisconsin. Ingalls and Commons were featured in a tour of Britain and the U.S., studying public utilities. Finally, in 1907, the Commission issued a three-volume report, whose tone was set by Samuel Insull and whose views were close to that of the National Electric Light Association, the trade association of the electric utility industry. Public utilities were to be legal grants of monopoly, to be regulated by public utility commissions established by government. In contrast to the NELA, however, the NCF commission took no stand on municipal ownership.[15]

14[Editor's footnote] For more on workmen's compensation laws, see Price Fishback and Shawn Kantor, *A Prelude to the Welfare State: The Origins of Workers' Compensation* (Chicago: University of Chicago Press, 2000). For a similar analysis of the motivations behind the Social Security System, in which larger businesses tried to saddle their smaller competitors with a costly pension system, see Chapter 11 below, pp. 356–60.

15[Editor's footnote] Weinstein, *The Corporate Ideal in the Liberal State*, pp. 24–25.

Insull had formed these views nearly a decade earlier, learning them from Chicago traction magnate Charles Tyson Yerkes. Yerkes, in the late 1890s, had a problem, his system of public utilities could, under state law, only receive monopoly franchises for 20 years' duration, and hence one part or another of his utility empire had to have its franchise renewed every few years. Yerkes was willing and able to bribe city councilmen to keep renewing the franchises, but he found that he could not float long-term bonds for companies that might lose their monopoly status in a few years' time.

Taking advantage of the election of a purchasable Republican governor, Yerkes managed to have introduced a series of bills in the 1897 Illinois legislature, which presaged Wisconsin progressivism by a decade. They would have extended all traction franchises by 50 years and removed control of transportation from city councils and transferred it to an expert, allegedly non-partisan state regulatory commission. This not only would have placed the mantle of science on monopoly privilege; it would, of course, have considerably reduced Charles Tyson Yerkes' bribery costs.

While Yerkes' bills presaged progressive reform, he came a cropper because of another aspect of the burgeoning progressive ethos that he had violated. A vital part of urban progressivism, as shall be seen further below, was a frenetic attack on the "corruption" of politicians, and it was the bribery issue that laid Yerkes low.[16] Even such progressive business organizations as the powerful Chicago Civic Federation turned on Yerkes, and his measures went down to defeat.[17]

---

[16][Editor's footnote] Rothbard planned to elaborate on the de-democratization described earlier in Chapter 6 (pp. 196–97) and tie it in with the urban municipal reform movement. This movement was driven largely by upper-class pietist businessmen and professionals to take various elected "party machine" positions out of politics and replace them with centralized bureaucratic commissions of experts shielded from voters. Far from being championed by the poor and middle classes, this drive was seen as weakening ethnic-liturgical power in politics by removing local ward influence on the political structure. See Chapters 10, 11, and 13 below, pp. 302–08, 318–20, 323, 440–41; Weinstein, *The Corporate Ideal in the Liberal State,* pp. 92–116; Samuel P. Hays, "The Politics of Reform in Municipal Government in the Progressive Era," *The Pacific Northwest Quarterly* 55, no. 4 (1964): 157–69; Murray Rothbard, "H.L. Mencken: The Joyous Libertarian," *The New Individualist Review* (Summer 1962): 24; Murray Rothbard, "Historical Origins," in *The Twelve Year Sentence,* William F. Rickenbacker, ed. (San Francisco, CA: Fox & Wilkes, 1999 [1974]), pp. 20–25.

[17]Forrest McDonald, *Insull* (Chicago: University of Chicago Press, 1962), pp. 84–88.

Learning from Yerkes' abortive program and applying it to electric utilities, Samuel Insull launched progressivism in public utilities in his presidential address before the National Electric Light Association in June 1898. He urged his fellow electric utility magnates to get the industry regulated by state commissions with the full power to fix rates and the quality of service. In contrast to Yerkes' bold grab for monopoly, Insull, more sensitive to public relations, stressed the government's rate-making power rather than the attendant long-run monopoly franchise. Most of the utilities executives were shocked at this assault on *laissez-faire*, but Insull garnered a few supporters and appointed them to the association's new Committee on Legislative Policy.

While the Committee languished for lack of support in the industry, Insull instructed the employees of his Chicago Edison and Commonwealth Electric companies in advertising and public relations, and established one of the first public relations departments in industry in 1901.

The threat of the municipal rate regulation and municipal ownership of public utilities, which had given rise to the NCF's Commission study in 1905, provided an impetus for the eventual success of the regulated monopoly movement. The idea of municipal ownership of electric utilities had been launched in the 1880s and 1890s by electric equipment salesmen, who wanted electric power subsidized by the taxpayers, and gas companies, which wanted to stifle the growing competition of electricity by having it supplied by local governments. Municipal ownership grew after the mid-1890s and reached a peak in 1905–06 when interest yields were low and the municipal bond market was strong. Transportation companies were the principal area of government ownership, but public electric companies grew as well. From 1902 to 1907, the number of publicly-owned plants were growing at twice the rate of private electric plants. This was particularly true in the small cities; more than 80% of municipally-owned electric plants were in cities of less than 5,000 population.

In response to this trend, the National Electric Light Association was moved to establish a Committee on Municipal Ownership, which grew two years later into the Committee on Public Policy. The new Committee included Insull and most of the people on his earlier Legislative Policy Committee. The new Public Policy Committee lobbied energetically for state regulatory commissions, basing its propaganda on its own report of 1907, which paralleled the recommendations of the NCF Commission report of the same year. The NELA Public Policy Committee report stressed that the NELA should favor state commission regulation, with

the power to control franchise, establish rates, and enforce a uniform system of accounting as well as making all pertinent information public —
thus adding to the cartelization and decreasing competition in the utility
industries. The Committee particularly stressed the threat of municipal
ownership as the alternative, deliberately ignoring the third alternative of
free competition and free markets.[18]

The municipal ownership threat died shortly thereafter, living long
enough to act as a goal toward monopoly privilege. The Panic of 1907
drove up interest rates and shattered the municipal bond markets, especially for the weak smaller cities.[19]

The National Civic Federation was never content to stop at theory;
theory, in the pragmatic progressive tradition, was to be the groundwork
for political action. The NCF Commission report was used by Professor
Commons, one of its authors, to draw up the Wisconsin public utilities
law as part of Commons' promotion of the "Wisconsin Idea" while working for Charles McCarthy's Legislative Reference Bureau in that state. The
progressives in Wisconsin pushed the law through in the spring of 1907,
establishing the Wisconsin Railroad Commission and setting the model
for the other states. Similar laws quickly followed in New York and Massachusetts. The result was the monopolization of the public utilities industry,
the end of competitive "discriminatory" pricing, and the raising of rates.
As Weinstein sums it up:

> By 1909 many industry people had begun to look favor-
> ably on regulation by state commissions and to understand
> the advantages of taking utilities regulation out of politics.
> The underlying principles of the regulatory legislation
> supported responsible private ownership, and the experts
> appointed to the new commission were almost invariably
> conservative in that they did not question the framework
> of the utilities industry. The result, therefore, was to intro-

---

[18][Editor's footnote] For evidence on the relative effectiveness of competition in providing gas, a public utility, to Chicago before government restrictions in the late 1890s, see
Werner Troesken, *Why Regulate Utilities? The New Institutional Economics and the Chicago
Gas Industry, 1849–1924* (Ann Arbor: University of Michigan Press, 1996), pp. 25–53. For
more on Samuel Insull and public utilities regulation, see Robert L. Bradley, Jr., *Edison to
Enron: Energy Markets and Political Strategies* (Salem, MA: M&M Scrivener Press, 2011),
pp. 19–221, 493–522.

[19]See McDonald, *Insull*, pp. 113–21.

duce stability in the industry and to "raise public morality" through the removal of discriminatory rates.[20]

Spearheading the NCF drive for state public utilities regulation was Emerson McMillin, banker and president and director of several gas, electric, and traction companies; collaborating with him was Teddy Roosevelt's ex-secretary George B. Cortelyou, now head of Consolidated Gas of New York. When some utilities magnates balked at the possible effect of regulatory commissions on the floating of utilities bonds, McMillin shrewdly pointed out that state utilities commissions performed the valuable function of supervising utilities' finances and their bond issues, both calculated to assist in the financing of public utilities.

By the fall of 1913, Ralph Easley was able to write to President Seth Low of the success of the drive for public utilities regulation. "Twenty five years ago," he exulted "we would have regarded this as a species of socialism," but now utilities are submitting, with many railways even embracing regulation, "joyfully in some cases."[21]

6. REGULATING INDUSTRY

On the national level, the NCF, as might be expected, was close to President Roosevelt and his Bureau of Corporations. In its first annual report in 1904 the Bureau attacked the Sherman Antitrust Act and proposed that it be replaced by another kind of legislation, one that regulates trusts by

---

[20]Weinstein, *The Corporate Ideal in the Liberal State*, pp. 25–26. See also the similar estimate of Balthasar H. Meyer, president of the Wisconsin Railroad Commission, in 1909. The industry pushing for utilities regulation in this period was invariably the electric utility industry; other utilities tended to oppose regulation. See McDonald, *Insull*, p. 121.

[21]Weinstein, *The Corporate Ideal in the Liberal State*, pp. 34–35. [Editor's remarks] For more on the origins of public utilities, see Thomas J. DiLorenzo, "The Myth of Natural Monopoly," *Review of Austrian Economics* 9, no. 2 (1996): 43–58. As DiLorenzo, borrowing from Rothbard, points out, one of the main problems with "public utilities" is that they occur on public, and not private, streets, which interferes with the ability of entrepreneurs to effectively engage in economic calculation.

Of course, in so called "natural monopolies" earning profits, as with all goods, there is always competitive pressure from other potential innovative producers of substitute products. Cost-price and franchise regulation leads to inefficient and cumbersome firms unable to quickly change when their costs change, reduces rivalrous innovation, incentivizes firms to "transfer" some of their profits into costs, and invites regulatory capture. Moreover, it neglects the fact that a firm's costs and therefore prices are not objectively available to the regulator, but must be appraised and discovered by the entrepreneur.

eliminating "improper rebates, discrimination, and unfair combinations." Each one of these proposed crackdowns was well calculated to cripple the most effective forms of competition and the market's ability to break up cartels and monopoly.

The NCF leadership then moved to draw up proposed legislation along the Rooseveltian lines. Spurred by Melville E. Ingalls, chairman of the Big Four Railroad, and more especially by August Belmont Jr., the NCF first established a commission to rewrite the antitrust laws. But soon it concluded that more powerful and dramatic action was needed. Drawing on the CCF experience of the Conference on Trusts, the NCF called in Professor Jenks, steeped in the experience of organizing the previous conference. Before going ahead with the new conference, Easley won the unofficial but powerful blessing of President Roosevelt and his Secretary of Commerce and Labor Oscar Straus.

The NCF's National Conference on Trusts and Combinations was held in Chicago in October, 1907. It drew 492 delegates from 147 delegations appointed by state governors, business and labor associations, and civic groups. Businessmen were in the overwhelmingly majority, seconded by a sprinkling of academics, politicians, and reformers. The revered president Nicholas Murray Butler of Columbia served as chairman and convenient front man. The Conference urged that railroads be permitted to enter into rate agreements, as recommended by the ICC and Roosevelt, that Congress establish a commission to amend the Sherman Act to regulate competition, establish federal licensing of corporations, and endorse trusts "in the public interest" (in short, Teddy Roosevelt's "good trusts"), and that the Bureau of Corporations be empowered to require compulsory publicity from large corporations. It was a program designed to quicken the hearts of big corporations and the Roosevelt administration.

So delighted were Roosevelt and the Congressional leaders with the Conference proposals that they easily induced the NCF to draw up the required bill and not wait for any commission. Seth Low, new president of the NCF, established an informal committee of leading corporatists to draw up the desired bill for industrial regulation. It was truly a gathering of the eagles. Businessmen on the committee included among others Judge Gary, chairman of the board of U.S. Steel, Isaac N. Seligman and James Speyer, top New York investment bankers, the ubiquitous Morgan man, George W. Perkins, and August Belmont Jr. Labor leaders included Samuel Gompers and John Mitchell, while progressive academia was well represented by President Butler and Jeremiah W. Jenks; from the media there came the inevitable Albert Shaw. Also on the committee were Judge Alton B. Parker, who had made the disastrous Democratic run for the presidency in 1904, and Herbert Knox Smith, Roosevelt's Commissioner of Corporations, representing the administration. Actually drawing up the bill were two formidable and also ubiquitous lawyers in the Morgan ambit: Morgan's own attorney Francis Lynde Stetson and Victor Morawetz, counsel to the Atchison, Topeka and Santa Fe Railroad.

Working eagerly and at top speed, this formidable committee came up with a bill in February 1908, and it was approved by the NCF shortly afterwards. Working closely and approvingly with Stetson and Morawetz was Commissioner Smith. The NCF bill, obediently introduced into Congress by Representative William P. Hepburn, gave the Bureau of Corporations power to approve any corporate contract or merger in advance, thus lending a selective imprimatur of the federal executive to combinations, and to supervise and veto a host of daily operations of business firms. Unions were also to be exempt from the antitrust laws.

A firestorm of opposition descended upon Congress, however, from small- and medium-size businesses across the country. Organizations of such businesses, including the National Association of Manufacturers, the Merchants Association of New York, and the Board of Trade of New York, opposed the legislation. They objected not only to the pro-union provision but also to allowing the executive branch to pick and choose between good and bad corporate actions. The Roosevelt administration was forced to withdraw its support for the bill, and Perkins wrote to Smith that "if the opponents to Governmental supervision could only know how intelligently and how fairly you have worked for the very highest and best interests of American corporations, I am sure they would abandon their present attitude." As Seth Low correctly wrote to the President, "the large interests, such as Judge Gary represents, are still loyally behind our bill. The objection comes from the mercantile element ..."[22]

It was time to regroup, and the NCF then turned to an alternative approach suggested by Ingalls and Andrew Carnegie to accomplish the same purpose by setting up a new interstate trade commission, to do for general

[22]See Weinstein, *The Corporate Ideal in the Liberal State*, pp. 77–82. For the preceding Conference on trusts in 1907, see ibid., pp. 73–76. Also see Kolko's account in *The Triumph of Conservatism*, pp. 129–38. Kolko lays exclusive emphasis for Roosevelt's withdrawal of support on personal opposition to the pro-union clause of the NCF-Hepburn bill. He thereby downplays the effects of the pressure from small and medium businesses.

business, as it was often put, what the ICC had already done for the railroads. The embryo of the Federal Trade Commission had come into being.[23]

7. ALLIED GROUP: THE AMERICAN ASSOCIATION FOR LABOR LEGISLATION

If the National Civic Federation was an organization of corporatist big businessmen with a sprinkling of intellectual and academic allies, the American Association for Labor Legislation (AALL) was an organization of corporatist intellectuals financed by Big Business.

The AALL was a spinoff of the American Economic Association, which had originally been organized to foster the new spirit of statism among economists. The AALL was organized by a committee established at the 1905 annual meeting of the AEA, and its first annual meeting two years later was held in conjunction with the meeting of the economists' association. First president of the AALL was the inevitable Richard T. Ely, and its long-time executive secretary was John B. Andrews, a research associate of Ely and John R. Commons, and a collaborator with Commons in various tomes on industry and labor.

---

[23][Editor's footnote] Rothbard planned on devoting additional space later to the Clayton Antitrust Act and the Federal Trade Commission, the Bureau of Corporation's successor, both of which were created under the Wilson administration in the fall of 1914. The five-man commission was dominated by pro-business sentiment from the outset, and in the words of prominent commission member Edward N. Hurley, it was intended "to do for general business" what the ICC, the Federal Reserve, and the Department of Agriculture did for railroads, bankers, and farmers. Influential advisors to the Commission included familiar names such as Louis D. Brandeis and Victor Morawetz, railroad executive Walker D. Hines, and Arthur Eddy. The latter was an important corporate lawyer who proclaimed in his influential book that "Competition is War, and 'War is Hell.'"

The acts helped eliminate competitive price discrimination and various market forms, such as holding companies and tying agreements. This benefited larger existing firms and smaller firms engaged in intrastate commerce. With regards to larger businesses, which vertically or horizontally integrated due to cost advantages, they would benefit at the expense of their medium-size competitors, who could only afford to partially integrate through various market agreements now deemed "restrictions" on competition. The FTC would later hold "trade practice conferences" in the 1920s in order to meet with industry members to figure out "unfair" practices, such as price discrimination and secret price cutting. For the origins of the acts see Murray Rothbard, "Left and Right: The Prospects for Liberty," in *Egalitarianism as a Revolt Against Nature and other Essays,* (Auburn, AL: Mises Institute, 2000 [1965]), pp. 40–41; Kolko, *The Triumph of Conservatism,* pp. 255–78; Weinstein, *The Corporate Ideal,* 82–89. See also Chapters 12, 13, 14, and 15 below, pp. 383–86, 389–94, 448–49, 464–65, 473–74, 519–24; Shaffer, *In Restraint of Trade,* pp. 51–90.

The AALL worked the labor and "social welfare" end of the corporatist street. It was organized as a branch of the International Association for Labor Legislation and received a government subsidy from the Bureau of Labor Statistics to publish an English edition of the Bulletin of the International Labor Bureau.

As self-proclaimed "scientists," AALL claimed not to take a partisan stand in economic or industrial conflicts, but it pretentiously asserted that its "only allegiance is to the general welfare." As such, it supported uniform labor legislation among the states. In addition, a 1914 AALL national conference, including businessmen, state, and labor officials, agreed on the idea of stabilizing employment, on calling for state and federal unemployment agencies to provide tax-supported free employment service to workers and employers, and on the desirability of some form of compulsory unemployment insurance. The conference quickly inspired Governor Martin Glynn, Democrat of New York, to push through a bill establishing a state employment agency. In the following year, AALL called for a planned program of public works to relieve unemployment — a program well calculated, of course, to subsidize the construction industry.

In subsequent years, AALL drafted model bills pushing for employment agencies, workmen's compensation, compulsory health insurance, increased safety legislation, a minimum wage unemploying marginal workers, and child labor laws, a "humanitarian" program outlawing the employment of minors and thereby freeing adult workers from their unwelcome and often successful competition. In 1916, Congress passed the Kern-McGillicuddy Bill, which had been drafted by AALL and which applied workmen's compensation to federal employees.[24]

---

[24][Editor's footnote] The minimum wage and other proposals by progressive economists had strong racist and sexist underpinnings. Many economists and other social theorists were strong believers in eugenics, which stated that society could effectively plan and control the racial quality of the labor force in order to improve and thereby enhance social welfare. As a result, they were intensely worried about the flood of "inferior" immigrants from Asia and parts of Europe diluting the labor pool and undercutting the wages of the superior Anglo-Saxon white man. They were also concerned about female workers, who were undercutting the male breadwinners and not being properly allocated to the household to raise children. A minimum wage and other labor regulations, such as immigration restriction and maximum hour legislation, would unemploy the less skilled immigrants and females and protect the jobs of the superior white males. See Chapters 10 and 13 below, pp. 314–16, 412–13; Thomas C. Leonard, *Illiberal Reformers: Race, Eugenics & American Economics in the Progressive Era* (Princeton, NJ: Princeton University Press, 2016), pp. 141–85. The entire book is crucial for understanding the transformation of the economics profession

The idea behind the seemingly innocuous and merely "efficient" drive for uniform labor legislation, and also behind much of the push for workmen's compensation and other social welfare measures, was to enable paternalistic employers, who had already established private welfare programs, to impose higher costs on their "non-socially conscious" competitors. As Eakins puts it:

> A number of pieces of Progressive legislation were not only supported but also were, in a number of important instances, drafted by [enlightened] businessmen. These men, many of them "corporate liberals," could support some regulation on the grounds that a uniform application of the laws by the states or the federal government would permit the socially conscious employer to compete on an even footing with the individualistic cost-cutting employer. There would be no room for "unscrupulous" [i.e., successfully competitive] employers.

He goes on with a candid quote from the New York Branch of AALL in 1910: "To set limits to this competition, to establish standards in law which it cannot overcome, and thus to put an end to the process of exploitation are the meaning and purpose" of the AALL.[25]

AALL included the standard business-politician mix, but with a broader spectrum of statist intellectuals than the NCF. A particularly important politician was Woodrow Wilson, while Governor of New Jersey

---

from *laissez-faire* to one of interventionist technocrats and planners, and the inherent paternalism and elitism motivating it.

Of course, modern progressivism has replaced eugenics with egalitarianism, or equality for all. However, it is not really egalitarianism but elitism in a different form, since everyone must be made equal except the intellectuals and opinion molders, who are still chosen to plan society and run people's lives. See Murray Rothbard, "Egalitarianism and the Elites," *Review of Austrian Economics* 8, no. 2 (1995): 39–57.

[25]Eakins, *The Development of Corporate Liberal Policy Research*, pp. 84–85. [Editor's remarks] This "exploitative competition" was already declining regardless of recent progressive legislative efforts. Since 1900, workers' living standards rose through higher real wages, a decline in hours of work per week, reduced child labor, earlier retirement, and better working standards. This occurred primarily due to the normal progression of an unfettered capitalist economy and not legislation that only codified existing trends. See Claudia Goldin, "Labor Markets in the Twentieth Century," in *The Cambridge Economic History of the United States,* Stanley Engerman and Robert Gallman, eds. (Cambridge: Cambridge University Press, 2000), vol. 3, pp. 549–624; Price Fishback, "The Progressive Era," in *Government and the American Economy* (Chicago: University of Chicago Press, 2007), pp. 307–08.

and later while president; Wilson was an officer of AALL for five years. Wilson's Secretary of Commerce, businessman William Redfield, was also active in the AALL. Unionists Gompers and Mitchell were also in AALL. Corporatist intellectuals included such NCF stalwarts as Ely, Commons, and Jenks, and AALL published a book by Jenks (1910) on *Governmental Action for Social Welfare*. NCF consultant Henry R. Seager, professor of political economy at Columbia, was a three-term president of AALL, and in his AALL-published work, *Social Insurance, A Program of Social Reform* (1910) Seager set forth much of the basic AALL doctrine. He called for "an aggressive program of governmental control and regulation" on behalf of the "common welfare." The idea of freedom from government interference is obsolete, Professor Seager thundered, and must be replaced by active government promotion of the common welfare. His ideal was the compulsory state insurance plans for accident, disease, and unemployment modelled after Europe. Three years earlier, Seager had pioneered in proposing a uniform minimum wage law.[26]

A major difference from NCF is that AALL included a raft of frankly leftist and socialist intellectuals; its spectrum of statist and collectivist intellectuals was considerably broader than NCF. This included socialists such as Florence Kelley, Victor Berger, W.D.P. Bliss, and Robert Hunter.

Corporatist big business control remained secure, however. Officers of AALL included corporate liberal financiers and industrialists like the Bostonian Edward A. Filene, and Charles M. Cabot, Gerard Swope of General Electric and investment banker Isaac Seligman. Financers of AALL included such financial notables as Judge Elbert Gary of United States Steel, Mrs. Madeline Astor, John D. Rockefeller, Anne Morgan, daughter of J.P., and the Kuhn-Loeb-connected banker Felix Warburg.

Big business support and control of AALL demonstrates the fallacy of the traditional sharp separation by historians of progressives into "business moderates" and "radical intellectuals." In actuality, there was no genuine separation, but rather an interpenetration, a happy collaboration between big business supporters and intellectuals, whether moderate or radical corporatist, marching hand-in-hand into the New Order.[27]

---

[26]Eakins, *Development of Corporate Policy Research*, pp. 91–93.

[27]See the incisive discussion by Eakins of this question in ibid., pp. 85–86.

CHAPTER 10

The Progressive Era and the Family

While the "Progressive Era" used to be narrowly designated as the period 1900–1914, historians now realize that the period is really much broader, stretching from the latter decades of the nineteenth century into the early 1920s. The broader period marks an era in which the entire American polity — from economics to urban planning to medicine to social work to the licensing of professions to the ideology of intellectuals — was transformed from a roughly *laissez-faire* system based on individual rights to one of state planning and control. In the sphere of public policy issues closely related to the life of the family, most of the change took place, or at least began, in the latter decades of the nineteenth century. In this paper we shall use the analytic insights of the "new political history" to examine the ways in which the so-called progressives sought to shape and control select aspects of American family life.

1. Ethnoreligious Conflict and the Public Schools

In the last two decades, the advent of the "new political history" has transformed our understanding of the political party system and the basis of political conflict in nineteenth century America. In contrast to the party

Originally published in *The American Family and the State*, Joseph R. Peden and Fred R. Glahe, eds. (San Francisco: Pacific Research Institute, 1986), pp. 109–34.

systems of the twentieth century (the "fourth" party system, 1896–1932, of Republican supremacy; the "fifth" party system, 1932–? of Democratic supremacy), the nineteenth century political parties were not bland coalitions of interests with virtually the same amorphous ideology, with each party blurring what is left of its image during campaigns to appeal to the large independent center. In the nineteenth century, each party offered a fiercely contrasting ideology, and political parties performed the function of imposing a common ideology on diverse sectional and economic interests. During campaigns, the ideology and the partisanship became fiercer and even more clearly demarcated, since the object was not to appeal to independent moderates — there were virtually none — but to bring out the vote of one's own partisans. Such partisanship and sharp alternatives marked the "second" American party system (Whig versus Democrat, approximately 1830 to the mid-1850s) and the "third" party system (closely fought Republican versus Democrat, mid-1850s to 1896).

Another important insight of the new political history is that the partisan passion devoted by rank-and-file Democrats and Republicans to national economic issues, stemmed from a similar passion devoted at the local and state level to what would now be called "social" issues. Furthermore, that political conflict, from the 1830s on, stemmed from a radical transformation that took place in American Protestantism as a result of the revival movement of the 1830s.

The new revival movement swept the Protestant churches, particularly in the North, like wildfire. In contrast to the old creedal Calvinist churches that stressed the importance of obeying God's law as expressed in the church creed, the new "pietism" was very different. The pietist doctrine was essentially as follows: Specific creeds of various churches or sects do not matter. Neither does obedience to the rituals or liturgies of the particular church. What counts for salvation is only each individual being "born again" — a direct confrontation between the individual and God, a mystical and emotional conversion in which the individual achieves salvation. The rite of baptism, to the pietist, therefore becomes secondary; of primary importance is his or her personal moment of conversion.

But if the specific church or creed becomes submerged in a vague Christian interdenominationalism, then the individual Christian is left on his own to grapple with the problems of salvation. Pietism, as it swept American Protestantism in the 1830s, took two very different forms in North and South, with very different political implications. The Southerners, at least until the 1890s, became "salvationist pietists," that is, they believed that the emotional experience of individual regeneration, of being born again, was enough to ensure salvation. Religion was a separate compartment of life, a vertical individual-God relation carrying no imperative to transform man-made culture and interhuman relations.

In contrast, the Northerners, particularly in the areas inhabited by "Yankees," adopted a far different form of pietism, "evangelical pietism." The evangelical pietists believed that man could achieve salvation by an act of free will. More particularly, they also believed that it was *necessary* to a person's *own salvation* — and not just a good idea — to try his best to ensure the salvation of everyone else in society:

> "To spread holiness," to create that Christian commonwealth by bringing all men to Christ, was the divinely ordered duty of the "saved." Their mandate was "to transform the world into the image of Christ."[1]

Since each individual is alone to wrestle with problems of sin and salvation, without creed or ritual of the church to sustain him, the evangelical duty must therefore be to use the state, the social arm of the integrated Christian community, to stamp out temptation and occasions for sin. Only in this way could one perform one's divinely mandated duty to maximize the salvation of others.[2] And to the evangelical pietist, sin took on an extremely broad definition, placing the requirements for holiness far beyond that of other Christian groups. As one antipietist Christian put it, "They saw sin where God did not." In particular, sin was any and all forms of contact with liquor, and doing anything except praying and going

---

[1] The quotations are, respectively, from the *Minutes of the Ohio Annual Conference of the Methodist Episcopal Church, 1875*, p. 228; and the *Minutes of the Annual Meeting of the Maine Baptist Missionary Convention, 1890*, p. 13. Both are cited in Kleppner, *The Third Electoral System, 1853–1892*, p. 190. Professor Kleppner is the doyen of the "new political," also known as the "ethnocultural," historians. See also his *The Cross of Culture*.

[2] In contrast to previous Christian groups, which were either amillennial (the return of Jesus will bring an end to human history) or premillennial (the return of Jesus will usher in a thousand-year reign of the Kingdom of God on earth), most evangelical pietists were postmillennialists. In short, whereas Catholics, Lutherans, and most Calvinists believed that the return of Jesus is independent of human actions, the postmillennialists held that Christians must establish a thousand-year reign of the Kingdom of God on earth as a necessary precondition of Jesus's return. In short, the evangelicals will have to take over the state and stamp out sin, so that Jesus can then return.

to church on Sunday. Any forms of gambling, dancing, theater, reading of novels — in short, secular enjoyment of any kind — were considered sinful.

The forms of sin that particularly agitated the evangelicals were those they held to interfere with the theological free will of individuals, making them unable to achieve salvation. Liquor was sinful because, they alleged, it crippled the free will of the imbibers. Another particular source of sin was Roman Catholicism, in which priests and bishops, arms of the Pope (whom they identified as the Antichrist), ruled the minds and therefore crippled the theological freedom of will of members of the church.

Evangelical pietism particularly appealed to, and therefore took root among, the "Yankees," i.e., that cultural group that originated in (especially rural) New England and emigrated widely to populate northern and western New York, northern Ohio, northern Indiana, and northern Illinois. The Yankees were natural "cultural imperialists," people who were wont to impose their values and morality on other groups; as such, they took quite naturally to imposing their form of pietism through whatever means were available, including the use of the coercive power of the state.

In contrast to evangelical pietists were, in addition to small groups of old-fashioned Calvinists, two great Christian groups, the Catholics and the Lutherans (or at least, the high-church variety of Lutheran), who were "liturgicals" (or "ritualists") rather than pietists. The liturgicals saw the road to salvation in joining the particular church, obeying its rituals, and making use of its sacraments; the individual was not alone with only his emotions and the state to protect him. There was no particular need, then, for the state to take on the functions of the church. Furthermore, the liturgicals had a much more relaxed and rational view of what sin really was; for instance, *excessive* drinking might be sinful, but liquor per se surely was not.

The evangelical pietists, from the 1830s on, were the northern Protestants of British descent, as well as the Lutherans from Scandinavia and a minority of pietist German synods; the liturgicals were the Roman Catholics and the high-church Lutherans, largely German.

Very rapidly, the political parties reflected a virtually one-to-one correlation of this ethnoreligious division: the Whig, and later the Republican Party consisting chiefly of the pietists, and the Democratic Party encompassing almost all the liturgicals. And for almost a century, on a state and local level, the Whig/Republican pietists tried desperately and determinedly to stamp out liquor and all Sunday activities except church (of course, drinking liquor on Sunday was a heinous double sin). As to the Catholic Church, the pietists tried to restrict or abolish immigration, since people coming from Germany and Ireland, liturgicals, were outnumbering people from Britain and Scandinavia. Failing that and despairing of doing anything about adult Catholics poisoned by agents of the Vatican, the evangelical pietists decided to concentrate on saving Catholic and Lutheran youth by trying to eliminate the parochial schools, through which both religious groups transmitted their precious religious and social values to the young. The object, as many pietists put it, was to "Christianize the Catholics," to force Catholic and Lutheran children into public schools, which could then be used as an instrument of pietist Protestantization. Since the Yankees had early taken to the idea of imposing communal civic virtue and obedience through the public schools, they were particularly receptive to this new reason for aggrandizing public education.

To all of these continuing aggressions by what they termed "those fanatics," the liturgicals fought back with equal fervor. Particularly bewildered were the Germans who, Lutheran and Catholic alike, were accustomed to the entire family happily attending beer gardens together on Sundays after church and who now found the "fanatic" pietists trying desperately to outlaw this pleasurable and seemingly innocent activity. The pietist Protestant attacks on private and parochial schools fatally threatened the preservation and maintenance of the liturgicals' cultural and religious values; and since large numbers of the Catholics and Lutherans were immigrants, parochial schools also served to maintain group affinities in a new and often hostile world — especially the world of Anglo-Saxon pietism. In the case of the Germans, it also meant, for several decades, preserving parochial teaching in the beloved German language, as against fierce pressures for Anglicization.

In the last three decades of the nineteenth century, as Catholic immigration grew and the Democratic Party moved slowly but surely toward a majority status, the Republican, and — more broadly — pietist pressures became more intense. The purpose of the public school, to the pietists, was "to unify and make homogeneous the society." There was no twentieth century concern for separating religion and the public school system. To the contrary, in most northern jurisdictions only pietist-Protestant church members were allowed to be teachers in the public schools. Daily reading of the Protestant Bible, daily Protestant prayers and Protestant hymns were common in the public schools, and school textbooks were rife with anti-Catholic propaganda. Thus, New York City school textbooks spoke broadly of "the deceitful Catholics," and pounded into their children, Catholic and Protestant alike, the message that "Catholics are necessarily, morally, intellectually, infallibly, a stupid race."[3]

Teachers delivered homilies on the evils of Popery, and also on deeply felt pietist theological values: the wickedness of alcohol (the "demon rum") and the importance of keeping the Sabbath. In the 1880s and 1890s, zealous pietists began working ardently for antialcohol instruction as a required part of the public-school curriculum; by 1901, every state in the Union required instruction in temperance.

Since most Catholic children went to public rather than parochial schools, the Catholic authorities were understandably anxious to purge the schools of Protestant requirements and ceremonies, and of anti-Catholic textbooks. To the pietists, these attempts to de-Protestantize the public schools were intolerable "Romish aggression." The whole point of the public schools was moral and religious homogenization, and here the Catholics were disrupting the attempt to make American society holy — to produce, through the public school and the Protestant gospel, "a morally and politically homogeneous people." As Kleppner writes:

> When they [the pietists] spoke of "moral education," they had in mind principles of morality shared in common by the adherents of gospel religion, for in the public school *all* children, even those whose parents were enslaved by "Lutheran formalism or Romish superstition," would be exposed to the Bible. That alone was cause for righteous optimism, for they believed the Bible to be *"the* agent in *converting* the soul," "the volume that makes human beings *men."*[4]

In this way, "America [would] be Saved Through the Children."[5]

The pietists were therefore incensed that the Catholics were attempting to block the salvation of America's children — and eventually of America itself — all at the orders of a "foreign potentate." Thus, the New

---

[3]Cited in David B. Tyack, *The One Best System: A History of American Urban Education* (Cambridge, MA: Harvard University Press, 1974), pp. 84–85.

[4]Kleppner, *Third Electoral System*, p. 222 n.1.

[5]*Our Church Work* (Madison, WI), July 17, 1890. Cited in ibid., p. 224.

Jersey Methodist Conference of 1870 lashed out with their deepest feelings against this Romish obstructionism:

> *Resolved,* That we greatly deprecate the effort which is being made by "Haters of Light," and especially by an arrogant priesthood, to exclude the Bible from the Public Schools of our land; and that we will do all in our power to defeat the well-defined and wicked design of this "Mother of Harlots."[6]

Throughout the nineteenth century, "nativist" attacks on "foreigners" and the foreign-born were really attacks on liturgical immigrants. Immigrants from Britain or Scandinavia, pietists all, were "good Americans" as soon as they got off the boat. It was the diverse culture of the *other* immigrants that had to be homogenized and molded into that of pietist America. Thus, the New England Methodist Conference of 1889 declared:

> We are a nation of remnants, ravellings from the Old World. ... The public school is one of the remedial agencies which work in our society to diminish this ... and to hasten the compacting of these heterogeneous materials into a solid nature.[7]

Or, as a leading citizen of Boston declared, "the only way to elevate the foreign population was to make Protestants of their children."[8]

Since the cities of the North, in the late nineteenth century, were becoming increasingly filled with Catholic immigrants, pietist attacks on sinful cities and on immigrants both became aspects of the anti-liturgical struggle for a homogeneous Anglo-Saxon pietist culture. The Irish were particular butts of pietist scorn; a New York City textbook bitterly warned that continued immigration could make America "the common sewer of Ireland," filled with drunken and depraved Irishmen.[9]

---

[6]*Minutes of the New Jersey Annual Conference of the Methodist Episcopal Church, 1870,* p. 24. Cited in ibid., p. 230. Similar reactions can be found in the minutes of the Central Pennsylvania Methodists in 1875, the Maine Methodists in 1887, the New York Methodists of 1880, and the Wisconsin Congregationalists of 1890.

[7]*Minutes of the Session of the New England Annual Conference of the Methodist Episcopal Church, 1889,* p. 85. Cited in ibid., p. 223.

[8]Tyack, p. 84, n.3.

[9]Ibid., p. 85, n.3.

The growing influx of immigrants from southern and eastern Europe toward the end of the nineteenth century seemed to pose even greater problems for the pietist progressives, but they did not shrink from the task. As Ellwood P. Cubberley of Stanford University, the nation's outstanding progressive historian of education, declared, southern and eastern Europeans have

> served to dilute tremendously our national stock, and to corrupt our civil life. ... Everywhere these people tend to settle in groups or settlements, and to set up here their national manners, customs, and observances. Our task is to break up these groups or settlements, to assimilate and amalgamate these people as a part of our American race and to implant in their children ... the Anglo-Saxon conception of righteousness, law and order, and popular government ...[10]

2. PROGRESSIVES, PUBLIC EDUCATION, AND THE FAMILY: THE CASE OF SAN FRANCISCO

The molding of children was of course the key to homogenization and the key in general to the progressive vision of tight social control over the individual via the instrument of the state. The eminent University of Wisconsin sociologist Edward Alsworth Ross, a favorite of Theodore Roosevelt and the veritable epitome of a progressive social scientist, summed it up thus: The role of the public official, and in particular of the public school teacher, is "to collect little plastic lumps of human dough from private households and shape them on the social kneadingboard."[11]

The view of Ross and the other progressives was that the state must take up the task of control and inculcation of moral values once performed by parents and church. The conflict between middle- and upper-class urban progressive Anglo-Saxon Protestants and largely working-class Catholics was sharply delineated in the battle over control of the San Francisco

---

[10]Ellwood P. Cubberley, *Changing Conceptions of Education in America* (Boston: Houghton Mifflin, 1909), pp. 15–16.

[11]Edward Alsworth Ross, *Social Control* (New York, 1912). Cited in Paul C. Violas, "Progressive Social Philosophy: Charles Horton Cooley and Edward Alsworth Ross," in *Roots of Crisis: American Education in the 20th Century,* C.J. Karier, P.C. Violas, and J. Spring, eds. (Chicago: Rand McNally, 1973), pp. 40–65.

public school system during the second decade of the twentieth century. The highly popular Alfred Roncovieri, a French-Italian Catholic, was the elected school superintendent from 1906 on. Roncovieri was a traditionalist who believed that the function of schools was to teach the basics, and that teaching children about sex and morality should be the function of home and church. Hence, when the drive for sex hygiene courses in the public schools got under way, Roncovieri consulted with mothers' clubs and, in consequence, kept the program out of the schools.

By 1908, upper-class progressives launched a decade-long movement to oust Roncovieri and transform the nature of the San Francisco public school system. Instead of an elected superintendent responding to a school board elected by districts, the progressives wanted an all-powerful school superintendent, appointed by a rubber-stamp board that in turn would be appointed by the mayor. In other words, in the name of "taking the schools out of politics," they hoped to aggrandize the educational bureaucracy and maintain its power virtually unchecked by any popular or democratic control. The purpose was threefold: to push through the progressive program of social control, to impose upper-class control over a working-class population, and to impose pietist Protestant control over Catholic ethnics.[12]

The ethnoreligious struggle over the public schools in San Francisco was nothing new; it had been going on tumultuously since the middle of the nineteenth century.[13] In the last half of the nineteenth century, San Francisco was split into two parts. Ruling the city was a power elite of native-born old Americans, hailing from New England, including lawyers, businessmen, and pietist Protestant ministers. These comprised successively the Whig, Know-Nothing, Populist, and Republican parties in the city. On the other hand were the foreign-born, largely Catholic immigrants from Europe — Irish, Germans, French, and Italians — who comprised the Democratic Party.

---

[12]The cities were already beginning to reach the point where class and ethnic divisions almost coincided, where, in other words, few working-class Anglo-Saxon Protestants resided in the cities.

[13]For an excellent study and analysis of the ethnoreligious struggle over the San Francisco public schools from the mid-nineteenth through the first three decades of the twentieth century, see the neglected work of Victor L. Shradar, "Ethnic Politics, Religion, and the Public Schools of San Francisco, 1849–1933" (Ph.D. dissertation, School of Education, Stanford University, 1974).

The Protestants early tried to use the public schools as a homogenizing and controlling force. The great theoretician and founder of the public school system in San Francisco, John Swett, "the Horace Mann of California," was a lifelong Republican and a Yankee who had taught school in New Hampshire before moving West. Moreover, the Board of Education was originally an all-New England show, consisting of emigrants from Vermont, New Hampshire, and Rhode Island. The mayor of San Francisco was a former mayor of Salem, Massachusetts, and every administrator and teacher in the public schools was a transplanted New Englander. The first superintendent of schools was not exactly a New Englander, but close: Thomas J. Nevins, a Yankee Whig lawyer from New York and an agent of the American Bible Society. And the first free public school in San Francisco was instituted in the basement of a small Baptist chapel.

Nevins, installed as superintendent of schools in 1851, promptly adopted the rule of the New York City schools: Every teacher was compelled to begin each day with a Protestant Bible reading and to conduct daily Protestant prayer sessions. And John Swett, elected as Republican state superintendent of public instruction during the 1860s, declared that California needed public schools because of its heterogeneous population: "Nothing can Americanize these chaotic elements, and breathe into them the spirit of our institutions," he warned, "except the public schools."[14]

Swett was keen enough to recognize that the pietist educational formula meant that the state takes over jurisdiction of the child from his parents, since "children arrived at the age of maturity belong, not to the parents, but to the State, to society, to the country."[15]

A seesaw struggle between the Protestant Yankees and Catholic ethnics ensued in San Francisco during the 1850s. The state charter of San Francisco in 1855 made the schools far more responsive to the people, with school boards being elected from each of a dozen wards instead of at large, and the superintendent elected by the people instead of appointed by the board. The Democrats swept the Know-Nothings out of office in the city in 1856 and brought to power David Broderick, an Irish Catholic who controlled the San Francisco as well as the California Democratic Party. But this gain was wiped out by the San Francisco Vigilance Movement, a

---

[14]Ibid., p. 14 n.13.

[15]Rousas John Rushdoony, "John Swett: The Self-Preservation of the State," in *The Messianic Character of American Education: Studies in the History of the Philosophy of Education* (Nutley, N.J.: Craig Press, 1963), pp. 79–80.

private organization of merchants and New England-born Yankees, who, attacking the "Tammany" tactics of Broderick, installed themselves in power and illegally deported most of the Broderick organization, replacing it with a newly formed People's Party.

The People's Party ran San Francisco with an iron hand for ten years, from 1857 to 1867, making secret nominations for appointments and driving through huge slates of at-large nominees chosen by a single vote at a public meeting. No open nomination procedures, primaries, or ward divisions were allowed, in order to ensure election victories by "reputable" men. The People's Party promptly reinstalled an all-Yankee school board, and the administrators and teachers in schools were again firmly Protestant and militantly anti-Catholic. The People's Party itself continually attacked the Irish, denouncing them as "micks" and "rank Pats." George Tait, the People's Party-installed superintendent of schools in the 1860s, lamented, however, that some teachers were failing to read the Protestant Bible in the schools, and were thus casting "a slur on the religion and character of the community."

By the 1870s, however, the foreign-born residents outnumbered the native-born, and the Democratic Party rose to power in San Francisco, the People's Party declining and joining the Republicans. The Board of Education ended the practice of Protestant devotions in the schools, and Irish and Germans began to pour into administrative and teaching posts in the public school system.

Another rollback began, however, in 1874, when the Republican state legislature abolished ward elections for the San Francisco school board, and insisted that all board members be elected at large. This meant that only the wealthy, which usually meant well-to-do Protestants, were likely to be able to run successfully for election. Accordingly, whereas in 1873, 58% of the San Francisco school board was foreign-born, the percentage was down to 8% in the following year. And while the Irish were approximately 25% of the electorate and the Germans about 13%, the Irish were not able to fill more than one or two of the 12 at-large seats, and the Germans virtually none.

The seesaw continued, however, as the Democrats came back in 1883, under the aegis of the master politician, the Irish Catholic Christopher "Blind Boss" Buckley. In the Buckley regime, the post-1874 school board dominated totally by wealthy native-born, Yankee businessmen and professionals, was replaced by an ethnically balanced ticket with a high proportion of working-class and foreign-born. Furthermore, a high proportion of Irish Catholic teachers, most of them single women, entered the San Francisco schools during the Buckley era, reaching 50% by the turn of the century.

In the late 1880s, however, the stridently anti-Catholic and anti-Irish American Party became strong in San Francisco and the rest of the state, and Republican leaders were happy to join them in denouncing the "immigrant peril." The American Party managed to oust the Irish Catholic Joseph O'Connor, principal and deputy superintendent, from his high post as "religiously unacceptable." This victory heralded a progressive Republican "reform" comeback in 1891, when none other than John Swett was installed as superintendent of schools in San Francisco. Swett battled for the full reform program: to make everything, even the mayoralty, an appointive rather than an elective office. Part of the goal was achieved by the state's new San Francisco charter in 1900, which replaced the 12-man elected Board of Education by a four-member board appointed by the mayor.

The full goal of total appointment was still blocked, however, by the existence of an elective superintendent of schools who, since 1906, was the popular Catholic Alfred Roncovieri. The pietist progressives were also thwarted for two decades by the fact that San Francisco was ruled, for most of the years between 1901 and 1911, by a new Union Labor Party, which won on an ethnically and occupationally balanced ticket, and which elected the German-Irish Catholic Eugene Schmitz, a member of the musician's union, as mayor. And for eighteen years after 1911, San Francisco was governed by its most popular mayor before or since, "Sunny Jim" Rolph, an Episcopalian friendly to Catholics and ethnics, who was pro-Roncovieri and who presided over an ethnically pluralistic regime.

It is instructive to examine the makeup of the progressive reform movement that eventually got its way and overthrew Roncovieri. It consisted of the standard progressive coalition of business and professional elites, and nativist and anti-Catholic organizations, who called for the purging of Catholics from the schools. Particular inspiration came from Stanford educationist Ellwood P. Cubberley, who energized the California branch of the Association of Collegiate Alumnae (later the American Association of University Women), led by the wealthy Mrs. Jesse H. Steinhart, whose husband was later to be a leader in the Progressive Party. Mrs. Steinhart got Mrs. Agnes De Lima, a New York City progressive educator, to make a survey of the San Francisco schools for the association. The report, presented in 1914, made the expected case for an "efficient," business-like, school system run solely by appointed educators. Mrs. Steinhart also organized the Public Education Society of San Francisco to agitate for progressive school reform; in this she was aided by the San Francisco Chamber of Commerce.

Also backing progressive reform, and anxious to oust Roncovieri, were other elite groups in the city, including the League of Women Voters, and the prestigious Commonwealth Club of California.

At the behest of Mrs. Steinhart and the San Francisco Chamber of Commerce, which contributed the funds, Philander Claxton of the U.S. Office of Education weighed in with *his* report in December 1917. The report, which endorsed the Association of Collegiate Alumnae study and was extremely critical of the San Francisco school system, called for all power over the system to go to an appointed superintendent of schools. Claxton also attacked the teaching of foreign languages in the schools, which San Francisco had been doing, and insisted on a comprehensive "Americanization" to break down ethnic settlements.

The Claxton Report was the signal for the Chamber of Commerce to swing into action, and it proceeded to draft a comprehensive progressive referendum for the November 1918 ballot, calling for an appointed superintendent and an appointed school board. This initiative, Amendment 37, was backed by most of the prominent business and professional groups in the city. In addition to the ones named above, there were the Real Estate Board, elite women's organizations such as the Federation of Women's Clubs, wealthy neighborhood improvement clubs, and the San Francisco *Examiner*. Amendment 37 lost, however, by two to one, since it had little support in working-class neighborhoods or among the teachers.

Two years later, however, Amendment 37 passed, aided by a resurgence of pietism and virulent anti-Catholicism in postwar America. Prohibition was now triumphant, and the Ku Klux Klan experienced a nationwide revival as a pietist, anti-Catholic organization. The KKK had as many as 3,500 members in the San Francisco Bay Area in the early 1920s. The anti-Catholic American Protective Association also enjoyed a revival, led in California by a British small businessman, the anti-Irish Grand Master Colonel J. Arthur Petersen.

In opposing Amendment 37 in the 1920 elections, Father Peter C. Yorke, a prominent priest and Irish immigrant, perceptively summed up the fundamental cleavage: "The modern school system," he declared, "is not satisfied with teaching children the 3 Rs…it reaches out and takes possession of their whole lives."

Amendment 37 passed in 1920 by the narrow margin of 69,200 to 66,700. It passed in every middle- and upper-class Assembly District, and lost in every working-class district. The higher the concentration of foreign-born voters in any district, the greater the vote against. In the Italian precincts 1 to 17 of the 33rd A.D., the Amendment was beaten by 3 to 1; in the Irish precincts, it was defeated by 3 to 1 as well. The more Protestant a working-class district, the more it supported the Amendment.

The bulk of the lobbying for the Amendment was performed by the ad hoc Educational Conference. After the victory, the conference happily presented a list of nominees to the school board, which now consisted of seven members appointed by the mayor, and which in turn appointed the superintendent. The proposed board consisted entirely of businessmen, of whom only one was a conservative Irish Catholic. The mayor surrendered to the pressure, and hence, after 1921, cultural pluralism in the San Francisco school system gave way to unitary progressive rule. The board began by threatening to dock any teacher who dared to be absent from school on St. Patrick's Day (a San Francisco tradition since the 1870s), and proceeded to override the wishes of particular neighborhoods in the interest of a centralized city.

The superintendent of schools in the new regime, Dr. Joseph Marr Gwinn, fit the new dispensation to a tee. A professional "scientist" of public administration, his avowed aim was unitary control. The entire package of typical progressive educational nostrums was installed, including a department of education and various experimental programs. Traditional basic education was scorned, and the edict came down that children should not be "forced" to learn the 3 Rs if they didn't feel the need. Traditional teachers, who were continually attacked for being old-fashioned and "unprofessional," were not promoted.

Despite continued opposition by teachers, parents, neighborhoods, ethnic groups, and the ousted Roncovieri, all attempts to repeal Amendment 37 were unsuccessful. The modern dispensation of progressivism had conquered San Francisco. The removal of the Board of Education and school superintendent from direct and periodic control by the electorate had effectively deprived parents of any significant control over the educational policies of public schools. At last, as John Swett had asserted nearly 60 years earlier, schoolchildren belonged "not to the parents, but to the State, to society, to the country."

3. ETHNORELIGIOUS CONFLICT AND THE RISE OF FEMINISM

A. Women's Suffrage

By the 1890s, the liturgically oriented Democracy was slowly but surely winning the national battle of the political parties. Culminating the battle was the Democratic congressional victory in 1890 and the Grover Cleveland landslide in the presidential election of 1892, in which Cleveland carried both Houses of Congress along with him (an unusual feat for that era). The Democrats were in way of becoming the majority party of the country, and the root was demographic: the fact that most of the immigrants were Catholic and the Catholic birthrate was higher than that of the pietist Protestants. Even though British and Scandinavian immigration had reached new highs during the 1880s, their numbers were far exceeded by German and Irish immigration, the latter being the highest since the famous post-potato-famine influx that started in the late 1840s. Furthermore, the "new immigration" from southern and eastern Europe, almost all Catholic — and especially Italian — began to make its mark during the same decade.

The pietists became increasingly embittered, stepping up their attacks on foreigners in general and Catholics in particular. Thus, the Reverend T.W. Cuyler, president of the National Temperance Society, intemperately exclaimed in the summer of 1891: "How much longer [will] the Republic ... consent to have her soil a dumping ground for all Hungarian ruffians, Bohemian bruisers, and Italian cutthroats of every description?"

The first concrete political response by the pietists to the rising Catholic tide was to try to restrict immigration. Republicans successfully managed to pass laws partially cutting immigration, but President Cleveland vetoed a bill to impose a literacy test on all immigrants. The Republicans also managed to curtail voting by immigrants, by getting most states to disallow voting by aliens, thereby reversing the traditional custom of allowing alien voting. They also urged the lengthening of the statutory waiting period for naturalization.

The successful restricting of immigration and of immigrant voting was still not enough to matter, and immigration would not really be foreclosed until the 1920s. But if voting could not be restricted sharply enough, perhaps it could be *expanded* — in the proper pietist direction.

Specifically, it was clear to the pietists that the role of women in the liturgical "ethnic" family was very different from what it was in the pietist Protestant family. One of the reasons impelling pietists and Republicans toward prohibition was the fact that, culturally, the lives of urban male Catholics — and the cities of the Northeast were becoming increasingly Catholic — evolved around the neighborhood saloon. The men would repair at night to the saloon for chitchat, discussions, and argument — and they would generally take their political views from the saloonkeeper, who thus became the political powerhouse in his particular ward. Therefore, prohibition meant breaking the political power of the urban liturgical machines in the Democratic Party.

But while the social lives of liturgical males revolved around the saloon, their wives stayed at home. While pietist women were increasingly independent and politically active, the lives of liturgical women revolved solely about home and hearth. Politics was strictly an avocation for husbands and sons. Perceiving this, the pietists began to push for women's suffrage, realizing that far more pietist than liturgical women would take advantage of the power to vote.

As a result, the women's suffrage movement was heavily pietist from the very beginning. Ultrapietist third parties like the Greenback and the Prohibition parties, which scorned the Republicans for being untrustworthy moderates on social issues, supported women's suffrage throughout, and the Populists tended in that direction. The Progressive Party of 1912 was strongly in favor of women's suffrage; theirs was the first major national convention to permit women delegates. The first woman elector, Helen J. Scott of Wisconsin, was chosen by the Progressive Party.

Perhaps the major single organization in the women's suffrage movement was the Women's Christian Temperance Union, founded in 1874 and reaching an enormous membership of 300,000 by 1900. That the W.C.T.U. was also involved in agitating for curfew, antigambling, antismoking, and antisex laws — all actions lauded by the women's suffrage movement — is clear from the official history of women's suffrage in the 19th century:

> [The W.C.T.U.] has been a chief factor in State campaigns for statutory prohibition, constitutional amendment, reform laws in general and those for the protection of women and children in particular, and in securing antigambling and anti-cigarette laws. It has been instrumental in raising the "age of protection" for girls in many States, and in obtaining curfew laws in 400 towns and cities. ... The association [W.C.T.U.] protests against the

legalization of all crimes, especially those of prostitution and liquor selling.[16]

Not only did Susan B. Anthony begin her career as a professional prohibitionist, but her two successors as president of the leading women's suffrage organization, the National American Woman Suffrage Association — Mrs. Carrie Chapman Catt and Dr. Anna Howard Shaw — also began their professional careers as prohibitionists. The leading spirit of the W.C.T.U., Frances E. Willard, was prototypically born of New England-stock parents who had moved westward to study at Oberlin College, then the nation's center of aggressive, evangelical pietism, and had later settled in Wisconsin. Guided by Miss Willard, the W.C.T.U. began its prosuffrage activities by demanding that women vote in local option referendums on prohibition. As Miss Willard put it, the W.C.T.U. wanted women to vote on this issue because "majorities of women are against the liquor traffic ..."[17]

Conversely, whenever there was a voters' referendum on women's suffrage, the liturgicals and the foreign-born, responding to immigrant culture and reacting against the pietist-feminist support of prohibition, consistently opposed women's suffrage. In Iowa, the Germans voted against women's suffrage, as did the Chinese in California. The women's suffrage amendment in 1896 in California was heavily supported by the bitterly anti-Catholic American Protective Association. The cities, where Catholics abounded, tended to be opposed to women's suffrage, while pietist rural areas tended to favor it. Thus, the Oregon referendum of 1900 lost largely because of opposition in the Catholic "slums" of Portland and Astoria.

A revealing religious breakdown of votes on an 1877 women's suffrage referendum was presented in a report by a Colorado feminist. She explained that the Methodists (the most strongly pietistic) were "for us," the (less pietistic) Presbyterians and Episcopalians "fairly so," while the Roman Catholics "were not all against us" — clearly they were expected to be.[18] And, testifying before the U.S. Senate Judiciary Committee in favor of women's suffrage in 1880, Susan B. Anthony presented her own explanation of the Colorado vote:

---

[16]Anthony and Harper, *The History of Woman Suffrage*, vol. 4, pp. 1046–47.

[17]Cited in Flexner, *Century of Struggle: The Woman's Rights Movement in the United States*, p. 183.

[18]Anthony and Harper, *The History of Woman Suffrage*, vol. 3, p. 724 n.15.

> In Colorado ... 6,666 men voted "Yes." Now, I am going to
> describe the men who voted "Yes." They were native-born
> men, temperance men, cultivated, broad, generous, just
> men, men who think. On the other hand, 16,007 voted
> "No." Now, I am going to describe that class of voters. In
> the southern part of that State are Mexicans, who speak
> the Spanish language. ... The vast population of Colorado
> is made up of that class of people. I was sent out to speak
> in a voting precinct having 200 voters; 150 of those voters
> were Mexican greasers, 40 of them foreign-born citizens,
> and just 10 of them were born in this country; and I was
> supposed to be competent to convert those men to let me
> have so much right in this Government as they had ... [19]

A laboratory test of which women would turn out to vote occurred in Massachusetts, where women were given the power to vote in school board elections from 1879 on. In 1888, large numbers of Protestant women in Boston turned out to drive Catholics off the school board. In contrast, Catholic women scarcely voted, "thereby validating the nativist tendencies of suffragists who believed that extension of full suffrage to women would provide a barrier against further Catholic influence."[20] During the last two decades of the 19th century "the more hierarchical the church organization and the more formal the ritual, the greater was its opposition to women suffrage, while the democratically organized churches with little dogma tended to be more receptive."[21]

Four mountain states adopted women's suffrage in the early and mid-1890s. Two, Wyoming and Utah, were simply ratifying, as new states, a practice they had long adopted as territories: Wyoming in 1869 and Utah in 1870. Utah had adopted women's suffrage as a conscious policy by the

---

[19]Quoted in Grimes, *The Puritan Ethic and Woman Suffrage*, p. 87.

[20]Camhi "Women Against Women: American Antisuffragism, 1880–1920," p. 198. See also Kenneally, "Catholicism and Woman Suffrage in Massachusetts," p. 253. Joining in the demand that only Protestants be elected to the Boston school board were, in addition to British-American clubs and numbers of Protestant ministers, the W.C.T.U., the Loyal Women of American Liberty, the National Women's League, and the League of Independent Women Voters. See Kleppner, *Third Electoral System,* p. 350 n.1. See also Tyack, pp. 105–06, n.1; and Lois Bannister Merk, "Boston's Historic Public School Crisis," *New England Quarterly* 31 (June, 1958): 172–99.

[21]Camhi, p. 200 n.20. Hierarchically organized pietist churches, like the Methodist or the Scandinavian Lutheran, were no less receptive to women's suffrage than the others.

pietistic Mormons to weight political control in favor of their polygamous members, who contrasted to the Gentiles, largely miners and settlers who were either single men or who had left their wives back East. Wyoming had adopted women's suffrage in an effort to increase the political power of its settled householders, in contrast to the transient, mobile, and often lawless single men who peopled that frontier region.

No sooner had Wyoming Territory adopted women's suffrage than it became evident that the change had benefited the Republicans, particularly since women had mobilized against Democratic attempts to repeal Wyoming's Sunday prohibition law. In 1871, both houses of the Wyoming legislature, led by its Democratic members, voted to repeal women's suffrage, but the bill was vetoed by the Republican territorial governor.

Two additional states adopting women's suffrage in the 1890s were Idaho and Colorado. In Idaho the drive, adopted by referendum in 1896, was led by the ultrapietistic Populists and by the Mormons, who were dominant in the southern part of the state. The Populist counties of Colorado gave a majority of 6,800 for women's suffrage, while the Republican and Democratic counties voted a majority of 500 against.[22]

It may be thought paradoxical that a movement — women's suffrage — born and centered in the East should have had its earliest victories in the remote frontier states of the Mountain West. But the paradox begins to clear when we realize the pietist-Anglo-Saxon-Protestant nature of the frontiersmen, many of them Yankees hailing originally from that birthplace of American pietism, New England. As the historian Frederick Jackson Turner, that great celebrant of frontier ideals, lyrically observed:

> In the arid West these pioneers [from New England] have halted and have turned to perceive an altered nation and changed social ideals. ... If we follow back the line of march of the Puritan farmer, we shall see how responsive he has always been to *isms*. ... He is the Prohibitionist of Iowa and Wisconsin, crying out against German customs as an invasion of his traditional ideals. He is the Granger of Wisconsin, passing restrictive railroad legislation. He is the Abolitionist, the Anti-mason, the Millerite, the

[22]Furthermore, in the Colorado legislature that submitted the women's suffrage amendment to the voters in 1893, the party breakdown of voting was as follows: Republicans, 19 for women's suffrage and 25 against; Democrats, 1 in favor and 8 against; Populists, 34 in favor and 4 against. See Grimes, p. 96 n.16 and passim.

Woman Suffragist, the Spiritualist, the Mormon, of Western New York.[23]

B. Eugenics and Birth Control

Thus the women's suffrage movement, dominated by pietist progressives, was not directed solely to achieving some abstract principle of electoral equality between males and females. This was more a means to another end: the creation of electoral majorities for pietist measures of direct social control over the lives of American families. They wished to determine by state intervention what those families drank and when and where they drank, how they spent their Sabbath day, and how their children should be educated.

One way of correcting the increasingly pro-Catholic demographics was to restrict immigration; another to promote women's suffrage. A third way, often promoted in the name of "science," was eugenics, an increasingly popular doctrine of the progressive movement. Broadly, eugenics may be defined as encouraging the breeding of the "fit" and discouraging the breeding of the "unfit," the criteria of "fitness" often coinciding with the cleavage between native, white Protestants and the foreign born or Catholics — or the white-black cleavage. In extreme cases, the unfit were to be coercively sterilized.

To the founder of the American eugenics movement, the distinguished biologist Charles Benedict Davenport, a New Yorker of eminent New England background, the rising feminist movement was beneficent provided that the number of biologically superior persons was sustained and the number of the unfit diminished. The biologist Harry H. Laughlin, aide to Davenport, associate editor of the *Eugenical News,* and highly influential in the immigration restriction policy of the 1920s as eugenics expert for the House Committee on Immigration and Naturalization, stressed the great importance of cutting the immigration of the biologically "inferior" southern Europeans. For in that way, the biological superiority of Anglo-Saxon women would be protected.

Harry Laughlin's report to the House Committee, printed in 1923, helped formulate the 1924 immigration law, which, in addition to drasti-

---

[23]Frederick Jackson Turner, "Dominant Forces in Western Life," in *The Frontier in American History* (New York: Holt, Rinehart & Winston, 1962), pp. 239–40. Quoted in Grimes, pp. 97–98, n.19.

cally limiting total immigration to the United States, imposed national origin quotas based on the 1910 census, so as to weight the sources of immigration as much as possible in favor of northern Europeans. Laughlin later emphasized that American women must keep the nation's blood pure by not marrying what he called the "colored races," in which he included southern Europeans as well as blacks: for if "men with a small fraction of colored blood could readily find mates among the white women, the gates would be thrown open to a final radical race mixture of the whole population." To Laughlin the moral was clear: "The perpetuity of the American race and consequently of American institutions depends upon the virtue and fecundity of American women."[24]

But the problem was that the fecund women were not the pietist progressives but the Catholics. For, in addition to immigration, another source of demographic alarm to the pietists was the far higher birthrate among Catholic women. If only they could be induced to adopt birth control! Hence, the birth control movement became part of the pietist armamentarium in their systemic struggle with the Catholics and other liturgicals.

Thus, the distinguished University of California eugenicist, Samuel J. Holmes, lamented that "the trouble with birth control is that it is practiced least where it should be practiced most." In the *Birth Control Review,* leading organ of the birth control movement, Annie G. Porritt was more specific, attacking "the folly of closing our gates to aliens from abroad, while having them wide open to the overwhelming progeny of the least desirable elements of our city and slum population."[25] In short, the birth controllers were saying that if one's goal is to restrict sharply the total number of Catholics, "colored" southern European or no, then there is no point in only limiting immigration while the domestic population continues to increase.

The birth control and the eugenics movement therefore went hand in hand, not the least in the views of the well-known leader of the birth control movement in the United States: Mrs. Margaret Higgins Sanger, prolific author, founder, and long-time editor of the *Birth Control Review.* Echoing many of the various strains of progressivism, Mrs. Sanger hailed the emancipation of women through birth control as the latest in applied science and "efficiency." As she put it in her *Autobiography:*

---

[24]Cited in Donald K. Pickens, *Eugenics and the Progressives* (Nashville, Tenn.: Vanderbilt University Press, 1968), p. 67.

[25]Annie G. Porritt, "Immigration and Birth Control, an Editorial," *The Birth Control Review* 7 (September, 1923): 219. Cited in Pickens, p. 73 n.24.

> In an age which has developed science and industry
> and economic efficiency to their highest points, so little
> thought has been given to the development of a science of
> parenthood, a science of maternity which could prevent
> this appalling and unestimated waste of womankind and
> maternal effort.[26]

To Mrs. Sanger, "science" also meant stopping the breeding of the
unfit. A devoted eugenicist and follower of C.B. Davenport, she in fact
chided the eugenics movement for not sufficiently emphasizing this crucial point:

> The eugenists wanted to shift the birth control empha-
> sis from less children for the poor to more children for
> the rich. We went back of that and sought first to stop
> the multiplication of the unfit. This appeared the most
> important and greatest step toward race betterment.[27]

4. Gathered Together: Progressivism as a Political Party

Progressivism was, to a great extent, the culmination of the pietist Protestant political impulse, the urge to regulate every aspect of American life,
economic and moral — even the most intimate and crucial aspects of family life. But it was also a curious alliance of a technocratic drive for government regulation, the supposed expression of "value-free science," and
the pietist religious impulse to save America — and the world — by state
coercion. Often both pietistic and scientific arguments would be used,
sometimes by the same people, to achieve the old pietist goals. Thus, prohibition would be argued for on religious as well as on alleged scientific
or medicinal grounds. In many cases, leading progressive intellectuals at
the turn of the 20th century were former pietists who went to college and
then transferred to the political arena, their zeal for making over mankind, as a "salvation by science." And then the Social Gospel movement
managed to combine political collectivism and pietist Christianity in the
same package. All of these were strongly interwoven elements in the progressive movement.

---

[26]Quoted in Pickens, p. 80 n.24.

[27]Ibid., p. 83.

All these trends reached their apogee in the Progressive Party and its national convention of 1912. The assemblage was a gathering of businessmen, intellectuals, academics, technocrats, efficiency experts and social engineers, writers, economists, social scientists, and leading representatives of the new profession of social work. The Progressive leaders were middle and upper class, almost all urban, highly educated, and almost all white Anglo-Saxon Protestants of either past or present pietist concerns.

From the social work leaders came upper-class ladies bringing the blessings of statism to the masses: Lillian D. Wald, Mary Kingsbury Simkhovitch, and above all, Jane Addams. Miss Addams, one of the great leaders of progressivism, was born in rural Illinois to a father, John, who was a state legislator and a devout nondenominational evangelical Protestant. Miss Addams was distressed at the southern and eastern European immigration, people who were "primitive" and "credulous," and who posed the danger of unrestrained individualism. Their different ethnic background disrupted the unity of American culture. However, the problem, according to Miss Addams, could be easily remedied. The public school could reshape the immigrant, strip him of his cultural foundations, and transform him into a building block of a new and greater American community.[28]

In addition to writers and professional technocrats at the Progressive Party convention, there were professional pietists galore. Social Gospel leaders Lyman Abbott, the Reverend R. Heber Newton, and the Reverend Washington Gladden were Progressive Party notables, and the Progressive candidate for governor of Vermont was the Reverend Fraser Metzger, leader of the Inter-Church Federation of Vermont. In fact, the Progressive Party proclaimed itself as the "recrudescence of the religious spirit in American political life."

Many observers, indeed, reported in wonder at the strongly religious tone of the Progressive Party convention. Theodore Roosevelt's acceptance address was significantly entitled, "A Confession of Faith," and his words were punctuated by "amens" and by a continual singing of Christian hymns by the assembled delegates. They sang "Onward, Christian Soldiers," "The Battle Hymn of the Republic," and finally the revivalist hymn, "Follow, Follow, We Will Follow Jesus," except that "Roosevelt" replaced the word "Jesus" at every turn.

---

[28]See Violas, "Jane Addams and the New Liberalism," in Karier et al., eds. *Roots of Crisis*, pp. 66–83 n.11.

The *New York Times* of August 6, 1912, summed up the unusual experience by calling the Progressive assemblage "a convention of fanatics." And, "It was not a convention at all. It was an assemblage of religious enthusiasts. It was such a convention as Peter the Hermit held. It was a Methodist camp following done over into political terms."[29]

Thus the foundations of today's massive state intervention in the internal life of the American family were laid in the so-called "progressive era" from the 1870s to the 1920s. Pietists and "progressives" united to control the material and sexual choices of the rest of the American people, their drinking habits, and their recreational preferences. Their values, the very nurture and education of their children, were to be determined by their betters. The spiritual, biological, political, intellectual, and moral elite would govern, through state power, the character and quality of American family life.

5. SIGNIFICANCE

It has been known for decades that the Progressive Era was marked by a radical growth in the extension and dominance of government in America's economic, social, and cultural life. For decades, this great leap into statism was naively interpreted by historians as a simple response to the greater need for planning and regulation of an increasingly complex economy. In recent years, however, historians have come to see that increasing statism on a federal and state level can be better interpreted as a profitable alliance between certain business and industrial interests, looking for government to cartelize their industry after private efforts for cartels and monopoly had failed, and intellectuals, academics, and technocrats seeking jobs to help regulate and plan the economy as well as restriction of entry into their professions. In short, the Progressive Era re-created the age-old alliance between Big Government, large business firms, and opinion-molding intellectuals — an alliance that had most recently been embodied in the mercantilist system of the sixteenth through eighteenth centuries.

Other historians uncovered a similar process at the local level, especially that of urban government beginning with the Progressive Era. Using the influence of media and opinion leaders, upper-income and business groups in the cities systematically took political power away from the masses and centralized this power in the hands of urban government responsive to

---

[29]Cited in John Allen Gable, *The Bull Moose Years: Theodore Roosevelt and the Progressive Party* (Port Washington, NY: Kennikat Press, 1978), p. 75.

progressive demands. Elected officials, and decentralized ward representation, were systematically replaced either by appointed bureaucrats and civil servants, or by centralized at-large districts where large-scale funding was needed to finance election races. In this way, power was shifted out of the hands of the masses and into the hands of a minority elite of technocrats and upper-income businessmen. One result was an increase of government contracts to business, a shift from "Tammany" type charity by the political parties to a taxpayer-financed welfare state, and the imposition of higher taxes on suburban residents to finance bond issues and redevelopment schemes accruing to downtown financial interests.

During the last two decades, educational historians have described a similar process at work in public, especially urban, school systems. The scope of the public school was greatly expanded, compulsory attendance spread outside of New England and other "Yankee" areas during the Progressive Era, and a powerful movement developed to try to ban private schools and to force everyone into the public school system.

From the work of educational historians, it was clear that the leap into comprehensive state control over the individual and over social life was not confined, during the Progressive and indeed post-Progressive eras, to government and the economy. A far more comprehensive process was at work. The expansion of compulsory public schooling stemmed from the growth of collectivist and anti-individualist ideology among intellectuals and educationists. The individual, these "progressives" believed, must be molded by the educational process to conform to the group, which in practice meant the dictates of the power elite speaking in the group's name. Historians have long been aware of this process.[30] But the accruing insight into progressivism as a business cartelizing device led historians who had abandoned the easy equation of "businessmen" with "*laissez-faire*" to see that all the facets of progressivism — the economic and the ideological and educational — were part of an integrated whole. The new ideology among business groups was cartelist and collectivist rather than individualist and *laissez-faire*, and the social control over the individual exerted by progressivism was neatly paralleled in the ideology and practice of progressive education. Another parallel to the economic realm, of course, was the increased power and

---

[30]For further discussion of education, see Robert B. Everhart, ed., *The Public School Monopoly: A Critical Analysis of Education and the State in American Society* (San Francisco: Pacific Institute for Public Policy Research, 1982).

income accruing to the technocratic intellectuals controlling the school system and the economy.

If the action of business and intellectual elites in turning toward progressivism was now explained, there was still a large gap in the historical explanation and understanding of progressivism and therefore of the leap into statism beginning in the early 20th century. There was still a need to explain mass voting behavior and the ideology and programs of the political parties in the American electoral system. This chapter applies the illuminating findings of recent "ethnoreligious historians" to significant changes that took place during the Progressive Era in the power of government over the family. In particular, we discuss the movement to expand the power of the public school and the educationist elite over the family, as well as the women's suffrage and eugenics movement, all important features of the Progressive movement. In every case, we see the vital link between these intrusions into the family and the aggressive drive by Anglo-Saxon Protestant "pietists" to use the state to "make America holy," to stamp out sin and thereby assure their own salvation by maximizing the salvation of others. In particular, all of these measures were part and parcel of the long-standing crusade by these pietists to reduce if not eliminate the role of "liturgicals," largely Roman Catholics and high-church Lutherans, from American political life. The drive to stamp out liquor and secular activities on Sundays had long run into successful Catholic and high-church Lutheran resistance. Compulsory public schooling was soon seen as an indispensable weapon in the task of "Christianizing the Catholics," of saving the souls of Catholic children by using the public schools as a Protestantizing weapon. The neglected example of San Francisco politics was urged as a case study of this ethnoreligious political battle over the schools and hence over the right of Catholic parents to transmit their own values to their children without suffering Anglo-Saxon Protestant obstruction. Women's suffrage was seized upon as a means of increasing Anglo-Saxon Protestant voting power, and immigration restriction as well as eugenics was a method of reducing the growing demographic challenge of Catholic voters.

In sum, recent insights into the cartelizing drive of various business interests have provided an important explanation of the rapid growth of statism in the 20th century. Ethnoreligious history provides an explanation of mass voting behavior and political party programs that neatly complement the cartelizing explanation of the actions of business elites.

CHAPTER 11

Origins of the Welfare State in America

S tandard theory views government as functional: a social need arises, and government, semi-automatically, springs up to fill that need. The analogy rests on the market economy: demand gives rise to supply (e.g., a demand for cream cheese will result in a supply of cream cheese on the market). But surely it is strained to say that, in the same way, a demand for postal services will spontaneously give rise to a government monopoly Post Office, outlawing its competition and giving us ever-poorer service for ever-higher prices.

Indeed, if the analogy fails when even a genuine service (e.g., mail delivery or road construction) is being provided, imagine how much worse the analogy is when government is not supplying a good or service at all, but is coercively redistributing income and wealth.

When the government, in short, takes money at gun point from A and gives it to B, *who* is demanding *what*? The cream cheese producer on the market is using his resources to supply a genuine demand for cream cheese; he is not engaged in coercive redistribution. But what about the government's taking from A and giving the money to B? Who are the demanders, and who are the suppliers? One can say that the subsidized, the "donees,"

Originally published in *Journal of Libertarian Studies* 12, no. 2 (1996): 193–232.

are "demanding" this redistribution; surely, however, it would be straining credulity to claim that A, the fleeced, is also "demanding" this activity. A, in fact, is the reluctant supplier, the coerced donor; B is gaining at A's expense. But the really interesting role here is played by G, the government. For apart from the unlikely case where G is an unpaid altruist, performing this action as an uncompensated Robin Hood, G gets a rake-off, a handling charge, a finder's fee, so to speak, for this little transaction. G, the government, in other words, performs his act of "redistribution" by fleecing A for the benefit of B and of himself.

Once we focus on this aspect of the transaction, we begin to realize that G, the government, might not just be a passive recipient of B's felt need and economic demand, as standard theory would have it; instead, G himself might be an active demander and, as a full-time, paid Robin Hood, might even have stimulated B's demand in the first place, so as to be in on the deal. The felt need, then, might be on the part of the governmental Robin Hood himself.

1. Why the Welfare State?

Why has government increased greatly over this century? Specifically, why has the welfare state appeared, grown, and become ever-larger and more powerful? What was the functional need felt here? One answer is that the development of poverty over the past century gave rise to welfare and redistribution. But this makes little sense, since it is evident that the average person's standard of living has grown considerably over the past century-and-a-half, and poverty has greatly diminished.

But perhaps inequality has been aggravated, and the masses, even though better off, are upset by the increased income gap between themselves and the wealthy? English translation: the masses may be smitten with envy and rankle furiously at a growing income disparity. But it should also be evident from one glance at the Third World that the disparity of income and wealth between the rich and the masses is far greater there than in Western capitalist countries. So what's the problem?

Another standard answer more plausibly asserts that industrialization and urbanization, by the late 19th century, deprived the masses, uprooted from the soil or the small town, of their sense of community, belonging, and mutual aid.[1] Alienated and deracinated in the city and in the factory,

---

[1]Harold Wilensky put it baldly and succinctly: "Economic growth is the ultimate cause of

the masses reached out for the welfare state to take the place of their old community.

Certainly it is true that the welfare state emerged during the same period as industrialization and urbanization, but coincidence does not establish causation.

One grave flaw in this urbanization theory is that it ignores the actual nature of the city, at least as it had been before it was effectively destroyed in the decades after World War II. The city was not a monolithic agglomeration but a series of local neighborhoods, each with its own distinctive character, network of clubs, fraternal associations, and street corner hangouts. Jane Jacobs's memorable depiction of the urban neighborhood in her *Death and Life of Great American Cities* was a charming and accurate portrayal of the unity in diversity of each neighborhood, of the benign role of the "street watcher" and the local storekeeper. Large city life in the United States by 1900 was almost exclusively Catholic and ethnic, and both the political and social life of Catholic males in each neighborhood revolved, and still, to an extent, revolves, around the neighborhood saloon. There the men of the neighborhood would repair each evening to the saloon, where they would drink a few beers, socialize, and discuss politics. Typically, they would receive political instruction from the local saloonkeeper, who was generally also the local Democratic ward heeler. Wives socialized separately, and at home. The beloved community was still alive and well in urban America.

On deeper historical inquiry, moreover, this seemingly plausible industrialism explanation falls apart, and not only on the familiar problem of American exceptionalism, the fact that the United States, despite industrializing more rapidly, lagged behind European countries in developing the welfare state. Detailed investigations of a number of industrialized countries, for example, find no correlation whatsoever between the degree of industrialization and the adoption of social insurance programs between the 1880s and the 1920s or the 1960s.[2]

---

welfare state development." Harold Wilensky, *The Welfare State and Equality* (Berkeley: University of California Press, 1975), p. 24.

[2]Thus, Flora and Alber find no correlation between levels of industrialization and social insurance programs of 12 European nations between the 1880s and the 1920s. Peter Flora and Jens Alber, "Modernization, Democratization, and the Development of Welfare States in Western Europe," in *The Development of Welfare States in Europe and America*, Peter Flora and Arnold Heidenheimer, eds. (New Brunswick, NJ: Transaction Press, 1981), pp.

More strikingly, the same findings hold true *within* the United States, where American exceptionalism can play no role. The earliest massive social welfare program in the United States was the dispensing of post-Civil War pensions to aging veterans of the Union Army and their dependents. Yet, these post-Civil War pensions were more likely to aid farmers and small townsmen than residents of large industrial cities. County level post-Civil War pension studies in Ohio in the late 1880s, the peak years for these pension payments, demonstrate a negative correlation between the degree of urbanism, or percentage of people living in homes rather than on farms, and the rates of receipt of pensions. The author of the study concluded that "generally, pensions were distributed to predominantly rural, Anglo-Saxon areas," while the major city of Cleveland had the lowest per capita rate of receipt of pensions.[3] Furthermore, pioneers in unemployment insurance and other social legislation were often the less-industrialized and more rural states, such as Wisconsin, Minnesota, Oklahoma, and Washington state.[4]

Another standard view, the left-liberal or "social democratic model," as its practitioners call it, holds that the welfare state came about not through the semi-automatic functioning of industrialization, but rather through conscious mass movements from below, movements generated by the demands of the presumptive beneficiaries of the welfare state themselves: the poor, the masses, or the oppressed working class. This thesis has been summed up boldly by one of its adherents. Everywhere, he says, the welfare state has been the product of

---

37–80. Likewise, Collier and Messick find no relation between industrialization and the adoption of social insurance programs in 59 nations between the 1880s and the 1960s. David Collier and Richard Messick, "Prerequisites versus Diffusion: Testing Alternative Explanations of Social Security Adoption," *American Political Science Review* 69 (1975): 1299–315. Cited in Theda Skocpol, *Protecting Soldiers and Mothers: The Political Origins of Social Policy in the United States* (Cambridge, MA: Belknap Press of Harvard University Press, 1992), pp. 559–60.

[3]Heywood Sanders, "Paying for the 'Bloody Shirt': The Politics of Civil War Pensions," in *Political Benefits*, Barry Rundquist, ed. (Lexington, MA: D.C. Heath, 1980), pp. 150–54.

[4]Edwin Amenta, Elisabeth Clemens, Jefren Olsen, Sunita Parikh, and Theda Skocpol, "The Political Origins of Unemployment Insurance in Five American States," *Studies in American Political Development* 2 (1987): 137–82; Richard M. Valelly, *Radicalism in the States: the Minnesota Farmer-Labor Party and the American Political Economy* (Chicago: University of Chicago Press, 1989); and Skocpol, *Protecting Soldiers*, pp. 560–61.

> a highly centralized trade union movement with a class-
> wide membership base, operating in close coordination
> with a unified reformist-socialist party which, primarily
> on the basis of massive working class support, is able to
> achieve hegemonic status in the party system.[5]

Certainly, much of this thesis is overdrawn even for Europe, where much of the welfare state was brought about by conservative and liberal bureaucrats and political parties, rather than by unions or socialist parties. But setting that aside and concentrating on the United States, there has been, for one thing, no massively supported socialist party, let along one which has managed to achieve "hegemonic status."

We are left, then, with labor unions as the only possible support for the social-democratic model for the United States. But here, historians, almost uniformly starry-eyed supporters of labor unions, have wildly exaggerated the importance of unions in American history. When we get past romantic stories of strikes and industrial conflicts (in which the union role is inevitably whitewashed if not glorified), even the best economic historians don't bother informing the reader of the meager quantitative role or importance of unions in the American economy. Indeed, until the New Deal, and with the exception of brief periods when unionization was coercively imposed by the federal government (during World War I, and in the railroads during the 1920s), the percentage of union members in the labor force typically ranged from a minuscule 1% to 2% during recessions, up to 5% or 6% during inflationary booms, and then down to the negligible figure in the next recession.[6]

---

[5]Michael Shalev, "The Social Democratic Model and Beyond: Two Generations of Comparative Research on the Welfare State," *Comparative Social Research* 6 (1983): 321. A similar sentiment is: "the welfare state is a product of the growing strength of labour in civil society." John Stephens, *The Transition from Capitalism to Socialism* (London: Macmillan, 1979), p. 89.

[6]The percentage of union membership to the American population, aged 15–64, amounted to only 1.35% in 1871, 0.7% in 1880, and, after the development of the AFL and the modern labor movement in 1886, totaled 1.0% in 1890 and 1.9% in 1900. Lloyd Ulman, *The Rise of the National Trade Union* (Cambridge, MA: Harvard University Press, 1955). The best works on trade union memberships in this period are still Leo Wolman, *The Growth of American Trade Unions, 1880–1923* (New York: National Bureau of Economic Research, 1924), and Leo Wolman, *Ebb and Flow in Trade Unionism* (New York: National Bureau of Economic Research, 1936).

Furthermore, in boom or bust, labor unions, in the free-market environment, were only able to take hold in specific occupations and areas of the economy. Specifically, unions could only flourish as skilled-craft unions (a) which could control the supply of labor in the occupation because of the small number of workers involved, (b) where this limited number constituted a small fraction of the employer's payroll, and (c) where, because of technological factors, the industry in question was not very actively competitive across geographical regions. One way to sum up these factors is to say, in economists' jargon, that the employers' demand schedule for this type of labor is inelastic — that is, that a small restriction in the supply of such labor could give rise to a large wage increase for the remaining workers. Labor unions could flourish, moreover, in such geographically uncompetitive industries as anthracite coal, which is found in only a small area of northeastern Pennsylvania; and the various building trades (carpenters, masons, electricians, joiners, etc.), since building construction in, say, New York City, is only remotely competitive with similar construction in Chicago or Duluth. In contrast, despite determined efforts, it was impossible for unions to prosper in such industries as bituminous coal, which is found in large areas of the United States, or clothing manufacture, where factories can move readily to another, non-unionized area.

It was a shrewd understanding of these principles that enabled Samuel Gompers and the craft unions in his American Federation of Labor to flourish, while other, more radical and socialistic unions, such as The Noble Order of the Knights of Labor, collapsed quickly and faded from the scene.[7]

It should be obvious, then, that the advent and growth of the welfare state in the United States had little or nothing to do with the growth of the labor movement. On the contrary, the growth of labor unionism in America — during World War I and during the 1930s, its two great spurts of activity — were brought about by governmental coercion from above. Labor unions, then, were an effect rather than a cause of the welfare state, at least in the United States.

---

[7]For the classic exposition of Gompersian unionism by an economist and student of John R. Commons, the Wisconsin institutional economist who was virtually Gompers's theoretician, see Selig Perlman, *A Theory of the Labor Movement* (New York: Augustus M. Kelley, 1949); also see the companion volume by Perlman, *A History of Trade Unionism in the United States* (New York: Macmillan, 1922).

2. Yankee Postmillennial Pietism

If it wasn't industrialism or mass movements of the working class that brought the welfare state to America, what was it? Where are we to look for the causal forces? In the first place, we must realize that the two most powerful motivations in human history have always been ideology (including religious doctrine), and economic interest, and that a joining of these two motivations can be downright irresistible. It was these two forces that joined powerfully together to bring about the welfare state.

Ideology was propelled by an intensely held religious doctrine that swept over and controlled virtually all Protestant churches, especially in "Yankee" areas of the North, from 1830 on. Likewise, a growing corollary ideology of statism and corporate socialism spread among intellectuals and ministers by the end of the 19th century. Among the economic interests promoted by the burgeoning welfare state were two in particular. One was a growing legion of educated (and often overeducated) intellectuals, technocrats, and the "helping professions" who sought power, prestige, subsidies, contracts, cushy jobs from the welfare state, and restrictions of entry into their field via forms of licensing. The second was groups of big businessmen who, after failing to achieve monopoly power on the free market, turned to government — local, state, and federal — to gain it for them. The government would provide subsidies, contracts, and, particularly, enforced cartelization. After 1900, these two groups coalesced, combining two crucial elements: wealth and opinion-molding power, the latter no longer hampered by the resistance of a Democratic Party committed to *laissez-faire* ideology. The new coalition joined together to create and accelerate a welfare state in America. Not only was this true in 1900, it remains true today.

Perhaps the most fateful of the events giving rise to and shaping the welfare state was the transformation of American Protestantism that took place in a remarkably brief period during the late 1820s. Riding in on a wave from Europe, fueled by an intense emotionalism often generated by revival meetings, this Second Great Awakening conquered and remolded the Protestant churches, leaving such older forms as Calvinism far behind. The new Protestantism was spearheaded by the emotionalism of revival meetings held throughout the country by the Rev. Charles Grandison Finney. This new Protestantism was pietist, scorning liturgy as papist or formalistic, and equally scornful of the formalisms of Calvinist creed or church organization. Hence, denominationalism, God's Law, and church

328   The Progressive Era

organization were no longer important. What counted was each person's achieving salvation by his own free will, by being "born again," or being "baptized in the Holy Spirit." An emotional, vaguely defined pietist, non-creeded, and ecumenical Protestantism was to replace strict creedal or liturgical categories.

The new pietism took different forms in various regions of the country. In the South, it became personalist, or salvational; the emphasis was on each person achieving this rebirth of salvation on his own, rather than via social or political action. In the North, especially in Yankee areas, the form of the new Protestantism was very different. It was aggressively evangelical and postmillennialist, that is, it became each believer's sacred duty to devote his energies to trying to establish a Kingdom of God on Earth, to establishing the perfect society in America and eventually the world, to stamp out sin and "make America holy," as essential preparation for the eventual Second Advent of Jesus Christ. Each believer's duty went far beyond mere support of missionary activity, for a crucial part of the new doctrine held that he who did not try his very best to maximize the salvation of others would not himself be saved. After only a few years of agitation, it was clear to these new Protestants that the Kingdom of God on Earth could only be established by government, which was required to bolster the salvation of individuals by stamping out occasions for sin. While the list of sins was unusually extensive, the PMPs (postmillennial pietists) stressed in particular the suppression of Demon Rum, which clouds men's minds to prevent them from achieving salvation, slavery which prevented the enslaved from achieving such salvation, any activities on the Sabbath except praying or reading the Bible and any activities of the Anti-Christ in the Vatican, the Pope of Rome and his conscious and dedicated agents who constituted the Catholic Church.

The Yankees who particularly embraced this view were an ethno-cultural group descending from the original Puritans of Massachusetts, and who, beginning in rural New England, moved westward and settled upstate New York ("the Burned-Over District"), northern Ohio, northern Indiana, northern Illinois, and neighboring areas. As early as the Puritan days, the Yankees were eager to coerce themselves and their neighbors; the first American public schools were set up in New England to inculcate obedience and civic virtue in their charges.[8]

---

[8]Those two great ideological and political opponents of the late 1880s and early 1890s, Grover Cleveland and Benjamin Harrison, embodied this battle within the Presbyterian

The concentration of the new statists in Yankee areas was nothing short of remarkable. From the Rev. Finney on down to virtually all the Progressive intellectuals who would set the course of America in the years after 1900, they were, almost to a man, born in Yankee areas: rural New England and their migrant descendants in upstate and western New York, northeastern Ohio (the "Western Reserve," originally owned by Connecticut and settled early by Connecticut Yankees), and the northern reaches of Indiana and Illinois. Almost to a man, they were raised in very strict Sabbatarian homes, and often their father was a lay preacher and their mother the daughter of a preacher.[9] It is very likely that the propensity of the Yankees, in particular, to take so quickly to the coercive, crusading aspect of the new Protestant pietism was a heritage of the values, mores, and world outlook of their Puritan ancestors, and of the community they had established in New England. Indeed, we have in recent years been strikingly reminded of the three very different and clashing groups, all Protestants, who came from very different regions of Great Britain, and who settled in different regions of North America: the coercive, community-oriented Puritans from East Anglia who settled in New England, the manor-and-plantation-oriented Anglian Cavaliers who came from Wessex and settled in the Tidewater South, and the feisty, individualistic Presbyterian Borderers who came from the border country in northern England and southern Scotland and who settled in the Southern and Western back country.[10]

Church. Cleveland, an old-fashioned Calvinist Presbyterian from Buffalo, was the son of a Calvinist clergyman, a Democrat, a "wet" on liquor, and a personal *bon vivant*; the prim, dour Harrison was a pietist Presbyterian from Indiana, and a Republican. See Jensen, *The Winning of the Midwest: Social and Political Conflict, 1888–1896*, pp. 79–80.

[9]Rural, because urban New England centers such as Boston had gone Unitarian during the 18th century. The Unitarians, on the other hand, were allied to the PMPs in advocating a more secular version of the coercive Utopian Kingdom to be achieved by government. On Unitarianism, Calvinism, and the Kingdom of God on Earth, especially as it dominated the public school movement in the 19th century, see the important but neglected work by Rousas John Rushdoony, *The Messianic Character of American Education*, pp. 18–32, 40–48.

[10]See the massive and fascinating work by David Hackett Fischer, *Albion's Seed: Four British Folkways in America* (New York: Oxford University Press, 1989).Whether or not these Borderers, or Scotch-Irish, are Celtic is controversial, with Fischer denying it, and most other authorities, notably Grady McWhiney and Forrest McDonald, maintaining this thesis.

The Rev. Charles Grandison Finney, who essentially launched the pietist sweep, was virtually a paradigmatic Yankee. He was born in Connecticut; at an early age, his father joined the emigration by taking his family to a western New York farm, on the Ontario frontier. In 1812, fully 2/3 of the 200,000 people living in western New York had been born in New England. While a nominal Presbyterian, in 1821 at the age of 29, Finney converted to the new pietism, experiencing his second baptism, his "baptism of the Holy Spirit," his conversion being greatly aided by the fact that he was self-educated in religion and lacked any religious training. Tossing aside the Calvinist tradition of scholarship in the Bible, Finney was able to carve out his new religion and ordain himself in his new version of the faith. Launching his remarkably successful revival movement in 1826 when he was an attorney in northeastern Ohio, his new pietism swept the Yankee areas in the East and Midwest. Finney wound up at Oberlin College, in the Western Reserve area of Ohio, where he became president, and transformed Oberlin into the preeminent national center for the education and dissemination of postmillennial pietism.[11]

The pietists quickly took to statist paternalism at the local and state level: to try to stamp out Demon Rum, Sabbath activity, dancing, gambling, and other forms of enjoyment, as well as trying to outlaw or cripple Catholic parochial schools and expand public schools as a device to Protestantize Catholic children, or, in the common phrase of the later 19th century, to "Christianize the Catholics." But use of the national government came early as well: to try to restrict Catholic immigration, in response to the Irish Catholic influx of the late 1840s, to restrict or abolish slavery; or to eliminate the sin of mail delivery on Sunday. It was therefore easy for the new pietists to expand their consciousness to favor paternalism in national economic affairs. Using big government to create a perfect economy seemed to parallel employing such government to stamp out sin and create a perfect society. Early on, the PMPs advocated government intervention to aid business interests and to protect American industry from the competition of foreign imports. In addition, they tended to advocate public works and government creation of mass

---

[11]On Finney and the revival movement, see Bernard A. Weisberger, *They Gathered at the River: The Story of the Great Revivalists and their Impact Upon Religion in America* (Boston: Little, Brown, 1958). Also see the classic work by Whitney R. Cross, *The Burned-Over District: The Social and Intellectual History of Enthusiastic Religion in Western New York, 1800–1850* (New York: Harper Torchbooks, 1950).

purchasing power through paper money and central banking. The PMPs therefore quickly gravitated toward the statist Whig Party, and then to the vehemently anti-Catholic American (or "Know-Nothing") Party, finally culminating in all-out support for the Republican Party, the "party of great moral ideas."[12]

On the other hand, all religious groups that did not want to be subjected to the PMP theocracy — Catholics, High Church (or liturgical) German Lutherans, old-fashioned Calvinists, secularists, and Southern personal salvationists — naturally gravitated toward the *laissez-faire* political party, the Democrats. Becoming known as the "party of personal liberty," the Democrats championed small government and *laissez-faire* on the national economic level as well, including separation of government and business, free trade, and hard money, which included the separation of government from the banking system.

The Democrat Party was the champion of *laissez-faire*, minimal government, and decentralization from its inception until its takeover by the ultra-pietist Bryanite forces in 1896. After 1830, the *laissez-faire* Democratic constituency was greatly strengthened by an influx of religious groups opposed to Yankee theocracy.

If postmillennial Protestantism provided a crucial impetus toward State dictation over society and the economy, another vital force on behalf of the partnership of government and industry was the zeal of businessmen and industrialists eager to jump on the bandwagon of state privilege. Vital to the Republican coalition, then, were the big railroads, dependent on government subvention and heavily in debt, and the Pennsylvania iron and steel industry, almost chronically inefficient and in perpetual need of high tariffs to protect them from import competition. When industrialists, as was often the case, were at one and the same time Yankee postmillennial pietists seeking to impose a perfect society, and also inefficient industrialists seeking government aid, the fusion of religious doctrine and economic interest became a powerful force in guiding their actions.

---

[12]On the enormous, but neglected, importance of anti-Catholicism and the co-opting of Know-Nothings in the Republican rise to major party status, see William E. Gienapp, "Nativism and the Creation of a Republican Majority in the North before the Civil War," *Journal of American History* 72 (December, 1985): 529–59.

3. Yankee Women: The Driving Force

Of all the Yankee activists in behalf of statist "reform," perhaps the most formidable force was the legion of Yankee women, in particular those of middle- or upper-class background, and especially spinsters whose busy-body inclinations were not fettered by the responsibilities of home and hearth. One of the PMPs' favorite reforms was to bring about women's suffrage, which was accomplished in various states and localities long before a constitutional amendment imposed it on the entire country. One major reason: it was obvious to everyone that, given the chance to vote, most Yankee women would be quick to troop to the ballot-box, whereas Catholic women believed their place to be at home and with the family, and would not bother about political considerations. Hence, women's suffrage was a way of weighting the total vote toward the postmillennialists and away from the Catholics and High Church Lutherans.

The impact of the revivalist transformation of Protestantism in the 1820s and 1830s upon female activism is well described by the feminist historian Carroll Smith-Rosenberg:

> Women's religious movements multiplied. Female revival converts formed Holy Bands to assist the evangelist in his revival efforts. They gathered with him at dawn to help plan the day's revival strategies. They posted bills in public places urging attendance at revival meetings, pressured merchants to close their shops and hold prayer services, and buttonholed sinful men and prayed with them. Although "merely women," they led prayer vigils in their homes that extended far into the night. These women for the most part were married, respected members of respectable communities. Yet, transformed by millennial zeal, they disregarded virtually every restraint upon women's behavior. They self-righteously commanded sacred space as their own. They boldly carried Christ's message to the streets, even into the new urban slums.[13]

The early suffragette leaders began as ardent prohibitionists, the major political concern of the postmillennial Protestants. They were all

---

[13]Carroll Smith-Rosenberg, *Disorderly Conduct* (New York: Alfred A. Knopf, 1985), pp. 85–86.

Yankees, centering their early activities in the Yankee heartland of upstate New York. Thus, Susan Brownell Anthony, born in Massachusetts, was the founder of the first women's temperance (prohibitionist) society, in upstate New York in 1852. Susan B. Anthony's co-leader in generating suffragette and prohibitionist women's activities, Elizabeth Cady Stanton, came from Johnston, New York, in the heart of the Yankee Burned-Over District. Organized prohibitionism began to flourish in the winter of 1873–74, when spontaneous "Women's Crusades" surged into the streets, dedicated to direct action to closing down the saloons. Beginning in Ohio, thousands of women took part in such actions during that winter. After the spontaneous violence died down, the women organized the Women's Christian Temperance Union (W.C.T.U.) in Fredonia (near Buffalo), New York, in the summer of 1874. Spreading like wildfire, the W.C.T.U. became the outstanding force for decades on behalf of the outlawry of liquor.

What is less well known is that the W.C.T.U. was not a one-issue organization. By the 1880s, the W.C.T.U. was pushing, throughout states and localities, for a comprehensive statist program for government intervention and social welfare. These measures included the outlawing of licensed brothels and red light districts, imposition of a maximum 8-hour working day, the establishment of government facilities for neglected and dependent children, government shelters for children of working mothers, government recreation facilities for the urban poor, federal aid to education, mothers' education by government, and government vocational training for women. In addition, the W.C.T.U. pushed for the new "kindergarten movement," which sought to lower the age when children began to come under the purview of teachers and other educational professionals.[14]

4. PROGRESSIVES AND THE GRADUAL SECULARIZATION OF POSTMILLENNIAL PIETISM: ELY, DEWEY, AND COMMONS

A critical but largely untold story in American political history is the gradual but inexorable secularization of Protestant postmillennial pietism over the decades of the middle and late 19th century.[15] The emphasis, almost

---

[14]See Ruth Bordin, *Woman and Temperance: the Quest for Power and Liberty, 1873–1900* (Philadelphia: Temple University Press, 1981). On the postmillenialists and women suffrage, see the excellent work by Grimes, *The Puritan Ethic and Woman Suffrage*.

[15]But see the illuminating article by Jean B. Quandt, "Religion and Social Thought: The Secularizing of Postmillenialism," *American Quarterly* 25 (October, 1973): 390–409.

from the beginning, was to use government to stamp out sin and to create a perfect society in order to usher in the Kingdom of God on Earth. Over the decades, the emphasis slowly but surely shifted: more and more away from Christ and religion, which became ever-vaguer and woollier, and more and more toward a Social Gospel, with government correcting, organizing, and eventually planning the perfect society. From paternalistic mender of social problems, government became more and more divinized, more and more seen as the leader and molder of the organic social whole. In short, Whigs, Know-Nothings, and Republicans were increasingly becoming Progressives, who were to dominate the polity and the culture after 1900; a few of the more radical thinkers were openly socialist, with the rest content to be organic statists and collectivists. And as Marxism became increasingly popular in Europe after the 1880s, the progressives prided themselves on being organic statist middle-of-the-roaders between old fashioned dog-eat-dog *laissez-faire* individualism on the one hand, and proletarian socialism on the other. Instead, the progressive would provide to society a Third Way in which Big Government, in the service of the joint truths of science and religion, would harmonize all classes into one organic whole.

By the 1880s, the focus of postmillennial Christian endeavor began to shift from Oberlin College to the liberal "New Theology" at Andover Theological Seminary in Massachusetts. The Andover liberals, as Jean Quandt points out, stressed "the immanence of God in nature and society, a concept derived in part from the doctrine of evolution." Furthermore, "Christian conversion ... came more and more to mean the gradual moral improvement of the individual." Thus, says Quandt, "Andover's identification of God with all the regenerating and civilizing forces in society, together with its Arminian emphasis on man's moral achievements, pointed toward an increasingly secular version of America's transfiguration."[16] Professor Quandt sums up the gradual but fateful change as a change that amounted to "a secularization of the eschatological vision." As Quandt writes:

> The outpourings of the Holy Spirit which were to usher
> in the kingdom of the 1850s were replaced, in the Gilded
> Age and the Progressive Era, by advances in knowledge,

Also see James H. Moorhead, "The Erosion of Postmillennialism in American Religious Thought, 1865–1925," *Church History* 53 (March, 1984): 61–77.

[16]Quandt, "Secularization," p. 394.

culture, and ethical Christianity. Whereas evangelical Protestantism had insisted that the kingdom would come by the grace of God acting in history and not by any natural process, the later version often substituted the providential gift of science for redeeming grace. These changes toward a more naturalistic view of the world's progress were paralleled by a changing attitude toward the agencies of redemption. The churches and the benevolent societies connected with them were still considered important instruments of the coming kingdom, but great significance was now attached to such impersonal messianic agencies as the natural and social sciences. The spirit of love and brotherhood ... was (now) often regarded as an achievement of human evolution with only tenuous ties to a transcendent deity.[17]

Progressive intellectuals and social and political leaders reached their apogee in a glittering cohort which, remarkably, were almost all born in precisely the year 1860, or right around it.[18]

Richard T. Ely was born on a farm in western New York, near Fredonia, in the Buffalo area.[19] His father, Ezra, a descendant of Puritan refugees from Restoration England, came from a long line of Congregationalist and Presbyterian clergy. Ezra, who had come from rural Connecticut, was a farmer whose poor soil was suited only to grow barley; yet, as an ardent prohibitionist, he refused to give his sanction to barley, since its main consumer product was beer. Highly intense about religion, Ezra was an extreme Sabbatarian who prohibited games or books (except the Bible) upon the Sabbath, and hated tobacco as well as liquor.

Richard was highly religious but not as focused as his father; he grew up mortified at not having had a conversion experience. He learned early to get along with wealthy benefactors, borrowing a substantial amount of money from his wealthy Columbia classmate, Edwin R.A. Seligman, of the New York investment-banking family. Graduating from Columbia in

---

[17]Ibid., p. 396.

[18]See the impressive list of the 1860 and environs cohort of Progressives in Robert M. Crunden, *Ministers of Reform: The Progressives Achievement in American Civilization, 1889–1920* (New York: Basic Books, 1982), pp. 275–76.

[19]For a biography of Ely, see Benjamin G. Rader, *The Academic Mind and Reform: the Influence of Richard T. Ely on American Life* (Lexington: University of Kentucky Press, 1966).

1876, in a country where there was not yet a Ph.D. program, Ely joined most of the economists, historians, philosophers, and social scientists of his generation in traveling to Germany, the land of the Ph.D., for his doctorate. As in the case of his fellows, Ely was enchanted with the third way or organic statism that he and the others thought they found in Hegel and in German social doctrine. As luck would have it, Ely, on his return from Germany with a Ph.D. at the young age of 28, became the first instructor in political economy at America's first graduate university, Johns Hopkins. There, Ely taught and found disciples in a glittering array of budding statist economists, social scientists, and historians, some of whom were barely older than he was, including Chicago sociologist and economist Albion W. Small (b. 1854), Chicago economist Edward W. Bemis, economist and sociologist Edward Alsworth Ross, City College of New York president John H. Finlay, Wisconsin historian Frederick Jackson Turner, and future president Woodrow Wilson.

During the 1880s, Ely, like so many postmillennial pietists remarkably energetic, founded the American Economic Association and ran it with an iron hand for several years; he also founded, and became the first president of, the Institute for Christian Sociology, which pledged "to present ... (God's) kingdom as the complete ideal of human society to be realized on earth." Ely also virtually took over the summer evangelical Chautauqua movement, and his textbook, *Introduction to Political Economy*, became a best-seller, largely by being distributed through, and becoming required reading for, the Chautauqua Literary and Scientific Circle for literally a half-century. In 1891, Ely founded the Christian Social Union of the Protestant Episcopal Church, along with the avowedly socialist Rev. William Dwight Porter Bliss, who was the founder of the Society of Christian Socialists. Ely was also enamored by the socialist "One Big Union" Knights of Labor, which he hailed as "truly scientific" and lauded in his book *The Labor Movement* (1886); the Knights, however, collapsed abruptly after 1887.

Discouraged about not getting a full professorship at Hopkins, Ely, moving through his old student Frederick Jackson Turner, who was teaching at Wisconsin, managed to land not only a professorship at that university in 1892, but also became director, with the highest salary on campus, of a new institute, a School of Economics, Political Science, and History. A gifted academic empire-builder, he managed to acquire funding for an assistant professor, a graduate fellow, and a large library at his institute.

Ely brought his favorite former students to Wisconsin, and Ely and his former and later students became the key advisors to the administration of Robert M. La Follette (b. 1855), who became the Progressive governor of Wisconsin in 1900. Through La Follette, Ely and the others pioneered welfare-state programs on a state level. Significantly, La Follette had gotten his start in Wisconsin politics as an ardent prohibitionist.

The key to Ely's thought was that he virtually divinized the State. "God," he declared, "works through the State in carrying out His purposes more universally than through any other institution."[20] Once again, Professor Quandt sums up Ely best:

> In Ely's eyes, government was the God-given instrument through which we had to work. Its preeminence as a divine instrument was based on the post-Reformation abolition of the division between the sacred and the secular and on the State's power to implement ethical solutions to public problems. The same identification of sacred and secular ... enabled Ely to both divinize the state and socialize Christianity: he thought of government as God's main instrument of redemption.[21]

It must not be thought that Ely's vision was totally secular. On the contrary, the Kingdom was never far from his thoughts. It was the task of the social sciences to "teach the complexities of the Christian duty of brotherhood." Through such instruments as the industrial revolution, the universities, and the churches, through the fusion of religion and social science, there will arrive, Ely believed, "the New Jerusalem" "which we are all eagerly awaiting." And then, "the earth [will become] a new earth, and all its cities, cities of God." And that Kingdom, according to Ely, was approaching rapidly.

A striking example of the secularization of a postmillennial progressive leader is the famed founder of pragmatist philosophy and progressive education, the prophet of atheistic higher Democracy, philosopher John Dewey (b. 1859). It is little known that in an early stage of his seemingly endless career, Dewey was an ardent preacher of postmillennialism and the coming of the Kingdom. Addressing the Students' Christian Association at

[20]Fine, *Laissez Faire Thought and the General-Welfare State*, p. 180.

[21]Quandt, "Secularization," p. 403.

Michigan, Dewey argued that the Biblical notion of the Kingdom of God come to earth was a valuable truth which had been lost to the world, but now, the growth of modern science and the communication of knowledge has made the world ripe for the temporal realization of "the Kingdom of God…the common incarnate Life, the purpose … animating all men and binding them together into one harmonious whole of sympathy." Science and democracy, exhorted Dewey, marching together, reconstruct religious truth, and with this new truth, religion could help bring about "the spiritual unification of humanity, the realization of the brotherhood of man, all that Christ called the Kingdom of God … on earth."

For Dewey, democracy was "a spiritual fact." Indeed, it is the "means by which the revelation of truth is carried on." It was only in democracy, asserted Dewey, that "the community of ideas and interest through community of action, that the incarnation of God in man (man, that is to say, as an organ of universal truth) becomes a living, present thing."

Dewey concluded with a call to action: "Can anyone ask for better or more inspiring work? Surely to fuse into one the social and religious motive, to break down the barriers of Pharisaism and self-assertion which isolate religious thought and conduct from the common life of man, to realize the state as one Commonwealth of truth — surely, this is a cause worth battling for."[22] Thus, with Dewey the final secularization is at hand: the truth of Jesus Christ *was* the unfolding truth brought to man by modern science and modern democracy. Clearly, it was but one small step for John Dewey, as well as for other, similarly situated progressives, to abandon Christ and to keep his ardent faith in government, science, and democracy to bring about an atheized Kingdom of God on earth.[23]

If Richard T. Ely was the leading PMP and progressive in economics and the social sciences, the leading progressive activist was his indefatigable and beloved No. 2 man, Professor John Rogers Commons (b. 1862). Commons was a student of Ely at Johns Hopkins graduate school, but even though he flunked out of graduate school, he continued ever afterward as Ely's right-hand man and perpetual activist, becoming professor of economics at the University of Wisconsin. Commons was a major force in the

---

[22]Crunden, *Ministers of Reform*, pp. 57–58. Also see Quandt, "Secularization," pp. 404–05.

[23]Dewey, as H.L. Mencken put it, was "born of indestructible Vermont stock and a man of the highest bearable sobriety." Dewey was the son of a small town Vermont grocer; his mother was an ardent evangelical Congregationalist. H.L. Mencken, "Professor Veblen," in *A Mencken Chrestomathy* (New York: Alfred A. Knopf, 1949), p. 267.

National Civic Federation, which was the leading Progressive organization pushing for statism in the economy. The National Civic Federation
was a big-business-financed outfit that wrote and lobbied for model legislation on a state and federal level favoring state unemployment insurance,
federal regulation of trade, and regulation of public utilities. Further, it
was the dominant force for progressive policies from 1900 until U.S. entry
into World War I. Not only that, Commons was a founder and the leading
force in the even more explicitly leftist American Association for Labor
Legislation (AALL), powerful from 1907 on in pushing for public works,
minimum wages, maximum hours, and pro-union legislation. The AALL,
financed by Rockefeller and Morgan industrialists, was highly influential
in the 1920s and 1930s. The executive secretary of the AALL was for many
decades John B. Andrews, who began as a graduate assistant of Commons
at the University of Wisconsin.

John R. Commons was a descendant of the famed English Puritan
martyr John Rogers. His parents moved from rural Vermont to the heavily
Yankee, rabidly PMP Western Reserve section of northeastern Ohio. His
father was a farmer, his extremely energetic mother a schoolteacher and
graduate of the virtual PMP headquarters, Oberlin College. The family
moved to northeastern Indiana. Commons' mother, the financial main-
stay of the family, was a highly religious pietist Presbyterian and an ardent
lifelong Republican and prohibitionist. Ma Commons was anxious for
her son to become a minister, and when Commons enrolled in Oberlin
in 1882, his mother went with him, mother and son founding and edit-
ing a prohibitionist magazine at Oberlin. Although a Republican, Commons voted Prohibitionist in the national election of 1884. Commons felt
himself lucky to be at Oberlin, and to be in at the beginnings there of the
Anti-Saloon League, the single-issue pressure group that was to become
the greatest single force in bringing Prohibition to America. The national
organizer of the league was Howard H. Russell, then a theological student
at Oberlin.

At Oberlin, Commons found a beloved mentor, James Monroe, professor of political science and history, who managed to get two Oberlin
trustees to finance Commons' graduate studies at Johns Hopkins. Monroe himself was a deeply religious PMP, a protectionist and prohibitionist,
and for 30 years had been a Republican Congressman from the Western
Reserve. Commons was graduated from Oberlin in 1888 and proceeded to

Johns Hopkins.[24] Before going to Wisconsin, Commons taught at several colleges, including Oberlin, Indiana University, and Syracuse, and helped found the American Institute for Christian Sociology on behalf of Christian Socialism.

Not only did Commons go on to Wisconsin to become the major inspirer and activist of the "Wisconsin Idea," helping to set up the welfare and regulatory state in that region, several of his doctoral students at Wisconsin were to become highly influential in the Roosevelt New Deal. Selig Perlman, who was appointed to the Commons Chair at Wisconsin was, following his mentor, the major theoretician for the policies and practices of Commons' beloved American Federation of Labor. And two of Commons' other Wisconsin students, Arthur J. Altemeyer and Edwin E. Witte, were both high officials in the Industrial Commission of Wisconsin, founded by Commons to administer that state's pro-union legislation. Both Altemeyer and Witte went on from there to be major founders of Franklin Roosevelt's Social Security legislation.[25]

5. Yankee Women Progressives

The Elys, Commonses, and Deweys might have might have been more notable, but the Yankee women progressives provided the shock troops of the progressive movement and hence the burgeoning welfare state. As in the case of the males, gradual but irresistible secularization set in over the decades. The abolitionist and slightly later cohort were fanatically postmillennial Christian, but the later progressive cohort, born, as we have seen, around 1860, were no less fanatical but more secular and less Christian-Kingdom oriented. The progression was virtually inevitable; after all, if your activism as a Christian evangelist had virtually nothing to do with Christian creed or liturgy or even personal reform, but was focused exclusively in using the force of government to shape up everyone, stamp out sin, and usher in a perfect society, if government is really God's major instrument of salvation, then the role of Christianity in one's practical activity began to fade into the background. Christianity became taken for granted, a background buzz; one's practical activity was designed to use

---

[24]See John R. Commons, *Myself* (Madison: University of Wisconsin Press, [1934] 1964).

[25]See Dorfman, *The Economic Mind in American Civilization, 1918–1933*, vol. 4, pp. 395–98.

the government to stamp out liquor, poverty, or whatever is defined as sin, and to impose one's own values and principles on the society.

Not only that, but by the late 19th century, as the 1860 cohort came of age, there arose greater and more specialized opportunities for female activism on behalf of statism and government intervention. The older groups, the Women's Crusades, were short-run activities, and hence could rely on short bursts of energy by married women. However, as female activism became professionalized, and became specialized into social work and settlement houses, there was little room left for any women except upper-class and upper-middle-class spinsters, who answered the call in droves. The settlement houses, it must be emphasized, were not simply centers for private help to the poor; they were, quite consciously, spearheads for social change and government intervention and reform.

The most prominent of the Yankee progressive social workers, and emblematic of the entire movement, was Jane Addams (b. 1860). Her father, John H. Addams, was a pietist Quaker who settled in northern Illinois, constructed a sawmill, invested in railroads and banks, and became one of the wealthiest men in northern Illinois. John H. Addams was a lifelong Republican, who attended the founding meeting of the Republican Party at Ripon, Wisconsin in 1854 and served as a Republican State Senator for 16 years.

Graduating from one of the first all-women colleges, the Rockford Female Seminary, in 1881, Jane Addams was confronted by the death of her beloved father. Intelligent, upper class, and energetic, she was faced with the dilemma of what to do with her life. She had no interest in men, so marriage was not in the cards; indeed, in her lifetime, she seems to have had several intense lesbian affairs.[26]

After eight years of indecision, Jane Addams decided to devote herself to social work and founded the famed settlement house, Hull House, in the Chicago slums in 1889. Jane was inspired by reading the highly influential English art critic John Ruskin, who was an Oxford professor, Christian Socialist, and bitter critic of *laissez-faire* capitalism. Ruskin was the

---

[26]Recent feminist historians have been happy to overcome the reluctance of older historians, and have proudly "outed" the lesbianism of Addams and many other spinster Yankee progressive activists of that epoch. Probably these feminists are right, and the pervasive lesbianism of the movement is crucial to a historical understanding of why this movement got under way. At the very least, they could not simply follow other women and make a career of marriage and homemaking.

charismatic leader of Christian Socialism in England, which was influential in the ranks of the Anglican clergy. One of his disciples was the historian Arnold Toynbee, in whose honor Canon Samuel A. Barnett, another Ruskinian, founded the settlement house of Toynbee Hall in London in 1884. In 1888, Jane Addams went to London to observe Toynbee Hall, and there she met Canon W.H. Freemantle, close friend and mentor of Canon Barnett, and this visit settled the matter, inspiring Jane Addams to go back to Chicago to found Hull House, along with her former classmate and intimate lesbian friend Ellen Gates Starr. The major difference between Toynbee Hall and its American counterparts is that the former was staffed by male social workers who stayed for a few years and then moved on to build their careers, whereas the American settlement houses almost all constituted lifelong careers for spinster ladies.

Jane Addams was able to use her upper-class connections to acquire fervent supporters, many of them women who became intimate and probably lesbian friends of Miss Addams. One staunch financial supporter was Mrs. Louise de Koven Bowen (b. 1859), whose father, John de Koven, a Chicago banker, had amassed a great fortune. Mrs. Bowen became an intimate friend of Jane Addams; she also became the treasurer and even built a house for the settlement. Other society women supporters of Hull House included Mary Rozet Smith, who had a lesbian affair with Jane Addams, and Mrs. Russell Wright, the mother of the future-renowned architect Frank Lloyd Wright. Mary Rozet Smith, indeed, was able to replace Ellen Starr in Jane Addams's lesbian affection. She did so in two ways: by being totally submissive and self-deprecating to the militant Miss Addams, and by supplying copious financial support to Hull House. Mary and Jane proclaimed themselves "married" to each other.

One of Jane Addams's close colleagues, and probable lesbian lover, at Hull House was the tough, truculent Julia Clifford Lathrop (b. 1858), whose father, William, had migrated from upstate New York to Rockford in northern Illinois.[27] William Lathrop, an attorney, was a descendant of the eminent English Nonconformist and Yankee minister, the Reverend

---

[27]On Jane Addams and her friends and colleagues, see Allen F. Davis, *American Heroine: The Life and Legend of Jane Addams* (New York: Oxford University Press, 1973). For a critical assessment of Addams, see Christopher Lasch, *The New Radicalism in America, 1889–1963: The Intellectual as a Social Type* (New York: Random House, 1965), pp. 3–37. It is all too clear that, in her 1910 autobiography, Jane Addams lied by ennobling her motivation for founding Hull House, claiming that it was the sheer horror of watching a bullfight in Spain. None of that alleged horror shines through her letters at the time.

John Lathrop. William became a trustee of the Rockford Female Seminary, and was elected Republican U.S. Senator from Illinois. His daughter Julia was graduated from the Seminary earlier than Addams, and then went on to Vassar College. Julia Lathrop moved to Hull House in 1890, and from there developed a lifelong career in social work and government service. Julia founded the first Juvenile Court in the country, in Chicago in 1899, and then moved on to become the first female member of the Illinois State Board of Charities, and president of the National Conference of Social Work. In 1912, Lathrop was appointed by President Taft as head of the first U.S. Children's Bureau.

Ensconced in the federal government, the Children's Bureau became an outpost of the welfare state and social work engaging in activities that eerily and unpleasantly remind one of the modern era. Thus, the Children's Bureau was an unremitting center of propaganda and advocacy of federal subsidies, programs, and propaganda on behalf of the nation's mothers and children — a kind of grisly foreshadowing of "family values" and Hillary Rodham Clinton's concerns for "the children" and the Children's Defense Fund. Thus, the Children's Bureau proclaimed "Baby Week" in March 1916, and again in 1917, and designated the entire year 1918 as "The Year of the Child."

After World War I, Lathrop and the Children's Bureau lobbied for, and pushed through Congress in late 1921, the Sheppard-Towner Maternity and Infancy Protection Act, providing federal funds to states that set up child hygiene or child welfare bureaus, as well as providing public instruction in maternal and infant care by nurses and physicians. Here we had the beginnings of socialized medicine as well as the socialized family. This public instruction was provided in home conferences and health centers, and to health care professionals in each area. It was also chillingly provided that these states, under the carrot of federal subsidy, would remove children from the homes of parents providing "inadequate home care," the standard of adequacy to be determined, of course, by the government and its alleged professionals. There was also to be compulsory birth registration for every baby and federal aid for maternity and infancy.

Julia Lathrop was instrumental in persuading Sheppard-Towner to change the original bill from a welfare measure to those unable to pay into a bill designed to encompass everyone. At Lathrop put it, "The bill is designed to emphasize public responsibility for the protection of life just as already through our public schools we recognize public responsibility in the education of children." The logic of cumulative government intervention was irresistible; it's unfortunate that no one turned the logic the other way and instituted a drive for the abolition of public schooling.

If none of the opponents of Sheppard-Towner went so far as to call for the abolition of public schooling, James A. Reed (D-Mo.), the staunch *laissez-faire* Senator, did well enough. Caustically, Senator Reed declared that "It is now proposed to turn the control of the mothers of the land over to a few single ladies holding government jobs in Washington. ... We would better reverse the proposal and provide for a committee of mothers to take charge of the old maids and teach them how to acquire a husband and have babies of their own."[28] Perhaps Senator Reed thereby cut to the heart of the motivation of these Yankee progressives.

At about the same time that Jane Addams and friends were founding Hull House, settlement houses were being founded in New York and Boston, also by spinster Yankee females, and also under the inspiration of Toynbee Hall. Actually, the founder of the first ephemeral settlement in New York was the male Stanton Coit (b. 1857), born in northern Ohio to a prosperous merchant, and a descendant of the Puritan Massachusetts Yankee, John Coit. Coit obtained a Ph.D. from the University of Berlin, worked at Toynbee Hall, and then established the short-lived Neighborhood Guild settlement in New York in 1886; it failed the following year. Inspired by this example, however, three Yankee lesbians followed by founding the College Settlement Association in 1887, which established College Settlements in New York in 1889, and in Boston and Philadelphia several years later. The leading female founder was Vida Dutton Scudder (b. 1861), a wealthy Bostonian and daughter of a Congregational missionary to India. After graduating from Smith College in 1884, Vida studied literature at Oxford, and became a disciple of Ruskin and a Christian Socialist, ending up teaching at Wellesley College for over 40 years. Vida Scudder became an Episcopalian, a frank socialist, and a member of the Women's Trade Union League. The two other founders of the College Settlements were Katharine Coman (b. 1857), and her long-time lesbian lover Katharine Lee Bates. Katharine Coman was born in northern Ohio to a father who had been an ardent abolitionist and teacher in upstate New York and who moved to a farm in Ohio as a result of wounds suffered in the Civil War. Graduating from the University of Michigan, Coman taught history and political economy at Wellesley, and later became chairman of the Wellesley

---

[28]Skocpol, *Protecting Soldiers and Mothers*, pp. 500–01.

department of economics. Coman and Bates traveled to Europe to study and promote social insurance in the United States. Katharine Bates was a professor of English at Wellesley. Coman became a leader of the National Consumers League and of the Women's Trade Union League.

The founder of the concept of the Children's Bureau, Florence Kelley, who lobbied for both the Children's Bureau and Sheppard-Towner, was one of the few women activists who was in some way unique and not paradigmatic. In many ways, she did share the traits of the other progressive ladies. She was born in 1859, her father was a wealthy, lifelong Republican Congressman from Philadelphia, William D. Kelley, whose devotion to protective tariffs, especially for the Pennsylvania iron industry, was so intense as to earn him the sobriquet "Pig Iron" Kelley. A Protestant Irishman, he was an abolitionist and Radical Republican.

Florence Kelley differed from her colleagues on two counts: (1) she was the only one who was an outright Marxist, and (2) she was married and not a lesbian. However, in the long run, these differences did not matter very much. For Kelley's open Marxism was not, in practice, very different, in policy conclusions, from the less-systematic Fabian socialism or progressivism of her sisterhood. As such, she was able to take her place at the end of a spectrum that was not really very far from the mainstream of non-Marxian ladies. On the second count, Florence Kelley managed to dispose of her husband in fairly short order, and to palm off the raising of her three children onto doting friends. Thus, home and hearth proved no obstacle to Florence Kelley's militancy.

Graduating from Cornell, Florence went to study at the University of Zurich. There she promptly became a Marxist and translated Engels's *Condition of the Working Class in England* into English. In Zurich, Florence met and married a Russian — Jewish Marxist medical student, Lazare Wischnewetsky, in 1884, moving with her husband to New York, and having three children by 1887. In New York, Florence promptly formed the New York Consumers League and got a law passed for inspecting women in factories. In 1891, Florence fled her husband with her kids and went to Chicago for reasons that remain unknown to her biographers. In Chicago, she gravitated inevitably to Hull House, where she stayed for a decade. During this time, the large, volcanic, and blustery Florence Kelley helped to radicalize Jane Addams. Kelley lobbied successfully in Illinois for a law creating a legal-maximum eight-hour work day for women. She then became the first chief factory inspector in the state of Illinois, gathering about her an all-socialist staff.

Florence Kelley's husband, Dr. Wischnewetsky, had been pushed off the pages of history. But what about her children? While Florence went about the task of socializing Illinois, she was able to pass off the raising of her children onto her friends Henry Demarest Lloyd, prominent leftist *Chicago Tribune* journalist, and his wife, the daughter of one of the owners of the *Tribune*.

In 1899, Florence Kelley returned to New York, where she resided for the next quarter-century at what was by then the most prominent settlement house in New York City, the Henry Street Settlement on the Lower East Side. There, Kelley founded the National Consumers League, and was the chief lobbyist for the federal Children's Bureau and for Sheppard-Towner. She battled for minimum wage laws and maximum-hours laws for women, fought for an Equal Rights Amendment to the Constitution, and was a founding member of the NAACP. When accused of being a Bolshevik in the 1920s, Florence Kelley disingenuously pointed to her Philadelphia blue blood heritage — how could someone of such a family possibly be a Marxist?[29]

Another prominent and very wealthy Yankee woman in New York City was Mary Melinda Kingsbury Simkhovitch (b. 1867). Born in Chestnut Hill, Massachusetts, Mary Melinda was the daughter of Isaac Kingsbury, a prominent Congregationalist and Republican merchant. She was the niece of an executive of the Pennsylvania Railroad and a cousin of the head of Standard Oil of California. Graduating from Boston University, Mary Melinda toured Europe with her mother, studied in Germany, and was deeply moved by socialism and Marxism. Becoming engaged to Vladimir Simkhovitch, a Russian scholar, she joined him in New York when he acquired a post at Columbia. Before marrying Simkhovitch, Mary Melinda became head resident of the College Settlement in New York, studied socialism further, and learned Yiddish so as to be able to communicate better with her Lower East Side neighbors. Even after marrying Simkhovitch and acquiring two children, Mary Melinda founded her own settlement at Greenwich House, joined the New York Consumers League and Women's Trade Union League, and fought for government old-age pensions and public housing.

---

[29]On Kelley, see Dorothy Rose Blumberg, *Florence Kelley: The Making of A Social Pioneer* (New York: Augustus M. Kelley, 1966). Also, see Kathryn Kish Sklar, "Hull House — the 1890s: A Community of Women Reformers," *Signs* 10, no. 4 (Summer 1985): 685–777.

Particularly important for New York statism and social reform were the wealthy and socially prominent Dreier family, which gave rise to several active daughters. The Dreiers were German-Americans, but they could just as well have been Yankees, since they were fervent — if not fanatical — German evangelical pietists. Their father, Theodore Dreier, was an emigrant from Bremen who had risen to become a successful merchant; during the Civil War, he returned to Bremen and married his younger cousin, Dorothy Dreier, the daughter of an evangelical minister. Every morning, the four Dreier daughters and their brother, Edward (b. 1872), were swathed in Bible readings and the singing of hymns.

In 1898, father Dreier died, leaving several million dollars to his family. Eldest daughter Margaret (b.1868) was able to dominate her siblings into engaging in radical and philanthropic activities at her beck and call.[30] To dramatize her altruism and alleged "sacrifice," Margaret Dreier habitually wore shoddy clothes. Active in the Consumers League, Margaret joined, and heavily financed, the new Women's Trade Union League in late 1904, joined by her sister Mary. Soon, Margaret was president of the New York WTUL and treasurer of the national WTUL. Indeed, Margaret Dreier presided over the WTUL from 1907 until 1922.

In the spring of 1905, Margaret Dreier met and married the Chicago-based progressive adventurer Raymond Robins (b. 1873). They had met, appropriately enough, when Robins delivered a lecture on the Social Gospel at an evangelical church in New York. The Robinses became the country's premier progressive couple; Margaret's activities scarcely slowed down, since Chicago was at least as active a center for the welfare reformers as New York.

Raymond Robins had a checkered career as a wanderer and nomad. Born in Florida, deserted by his father and absent a mother, Robins wandered around the country and managed to earn a law degree in California, where he became a pro-union progressive. Prospecting gold in Alaska, he saw a vision of a flaming cross in the Alaska wilds and became a social-gospel-oriented minister. Moving to Chicago in 1901, Robins became a leading settlement house worker, associating, of course, with Hull House and "Saint Jane" Addams.

---

[30]The one sister who slightly broke the Dreier mold was Katherine (b. 1877), an artist and patroness of modern art who, interested in organic philosophy, became pro-Nazi during the 1930s.

Two years after the Robins-Dreier marriage, sister Mary Dreier came to Robins and confessed her overwhelming love. Robins persuaded Mary to transmute her shameful secret passion on the altar of leftist social reform, and the two of them engaged in a lifelong secret correspondence based on their two-person "Order of the Flaming Cross."

Perhaps the most important function of Margaret Dreier for the cause was her success in bringing top female wealth into financial and political support of the leftist and welfare-state programs of the Women's Trade Union League. Included among WTUL supporters were Anne Morgan, daughter of J. Pierpont Morgan; Abby Aldrich Rockefeller, daughter of John D. Rockefeller, Jr.; Dorothy Whitney Straight, heiress to the Rockefeller-oriented Whitney family; Mary Eliza McDowell (b. 1854), a Hull House alumnus whose father owned a steel mill in Chicago; and the very wealthy Anita McCormick Blaine, daughter of Cyrus McCormick, inventor of the mechanical reaper, who had already been inducted into the movement by Jane Addams.[31]

We should not leave the Chicago scene without noting a crucial activist and academic transition to the next generation. An important academic wealthy spinster was Sophonisba Breckinridge (b. 1866), who came from a prominent Kentucky family and was the great-granddaughter of a U.S. Senator. She, too, was not a Yankee, but she was pretty clearly a lesbian. Unhappy as a lawyer in Kentucky, Sophonisba went to the University of Chicago graduate school and became the first woman Ph.D. in political science in 1901. She continued to teach social science and social work at the University of Chicago for the rest of her career, becoming the mentor and probable long-time lesbian companion of Edith Abbott (b. 1876). Edith Abbott, born in Nebraska, had been secretary of the Boston Trade Union League and had studied at the London School of Economics, where she was strongly influence by the Webbs, leaders of Fabian Socialism. She lived and worked, predictably, at a London Settlement House. Then Edith studied for a Ph.D. in economics at the University of Chicago, which she earned in 1905. Becoming an instructor at Wellesley, Edith soon joined her slightly younger sister Grace at Hull House in 1908, where the two sisters lived for the next dozen years, Edith as social research director of Hull House. In the early 1920s, Edith Abbott became Dean of the University of Chicago School of Social Service Administration and co-edited

---

[31]See Elizabeth Ann Payne, *Reform, Labor, and Feminism: Margaret Dreier Robins and the Women's Trade Union League* (Urbana: University of Illinois Press, 1988).

the school's *Social Service Review* with her friend and mentor, Sophonisba Breckinridge.

Grace Abbott, two years younger than Edith, took more of an activist route. The Abbott sisters' mother had come from upstate New York and graduated from Rockford Female Seminary; their father was an Illinois lawyer who became Lieutenant Governor of Nebraska. Grace Abbott, also living at Hull House and a close friend of Jane Addams, became Julia Clifford Lathrop's assistant at the federal Children's Bureau in 1917, and, in 1921, succeeded her mentor Lathrop as head of the Children's Bureau.

If the female social reform activists were almost all Yankee, by the late 19th century, Jewish women were beginning to add their leaven to the lump. Of the crucial 1860s cohort, the most important Jewess was Lillian D. Wald (b. 1867). Born to an upper-middle-class German and Polish-Jewish family in Cincinnati, Lillian and her family soon moved to Rochester, where she became a nurse. She then organized, in the Lower East Side of New York, the Nurses' Settlement, which was soon to become the famed Henry Street Settlement. It was Lillian Wald who first suggested a federal Children's Bureau to President Theodore Roosevelt in 1905, and who led the agitation for a federal constitutional amendment outlawing child labor. While she was not a Yankee, Lillian Wald continued in the dominant tradition by being a lesbian, forming a long-term lesbian relationship with her associate Lavinia Dock. Wald, while not wealthy herself, had an uncanny ability to gain financing for Henry Street, including top Jewish financiers such as Jacob Schiff and Mrs. Solomon Loeb of the Wall Street investment-banking firm of Kuhn-Loeb, and Julius Rosenwald, then head of Sears Roebuck. Also prominent in financing Henry Street was the Milbank Fund, of the Rockefeller-affiliated family who owned the Borden Milk Company.

Rounding out the important contingent of socialist-activist Jews were the four Goldmark sisters, Helen, Pauline, Josephine, and Alice. Their father had been born in Poland, became a physician in Vienna, and was a member of the Austrian Parliament. Fleeing to the United States after the failed Revolution of 1848, Dr. Goldmark became a physician and chemist, became wealthy by inventing percussion caps, and helped organized the Republican Party in the 1850s. The Goldmarks settled in Indiana.

Dr. Goldmark died in 1881, leaving eldest daughter Helen as the head of the family. Helen married the eminent Felix Adler, philosopher and founder of the Society for Ethical Culture in New York, a kind of Jewish Unitarianism. Alice married the eminent Boston Jewish lawyer Louis

Dembitz Brandeis, helping to radicalize Brandeis from moderate classical liberal to socialistic progressive. Pauline (b. 1874), after graduating from Bryn Mawr in 1896, remained single, did graduate work at Columbia and Barnard in botany, zoology, and sociology, and then became assistant secretary of the New York Consumers League. Even more successful an activist was Josephine Clara Goldmark (b. 1877), who graduated from Bryn Mawr in 1898, did graduate work in education at Barnard, and then became publicity secretary of the National Consumers League and author of the NCL's annual handbooks. In 1908, Josephine became chairman of the new NCL Committee on Legislation, and she, her sister Pauline, and Florence Kelley (along with Alice) persuaded Brandeis to write his famed Brandeis brief in the case of *Muller* v. *Oregon* (1908), claiming that the Oregon maximum-hours law for women was constitutional. In 1919, Josephine Goldmark continued her rise by becoming secretary of the Rockefeller Foundation's Committee for the Study of Nursing Education. Josephine Goldmark culminated her career by writing the first hagiographical biography of her close friend and mentor in socialistic activism, Florence Kelley.[32]

6. THE NEW DEAL

It was not long before these progressives and social reformers exerted an impact on American national politics. The Progressive Party was launched in 1912 by the Morgans — the party was headed by Morgan partner George W. Perkins — in a successful attempt to nominate Theodore Roosevelt, and thereby destroy President William Howard Taft, who had broken with his predecessor Roosevelt's Pro-Morgan policies. The Progressive Party included all the spearheads of this statist coalition: academic progressives, Morgan businessmen, social-gospel Protestant ministers, and, of course, our subjects, the leading progressive social workers.

Thus, delegates to the national Progressive convention of 1912 in New York City included Jane Addams, Raymond Robins, and Lillian D. Wald, as well as Henry Moskowitz of the New York Society of Ethical Culture, and Mary Kingsbury Simkhovitch of New York's Greenwich House. True to its feminist stance, the Progressive Party was also the first, except for the Prohibition Party, to include women delegates to the convention, and the

[32]Josephine Goldmark, *Impatient Crusader: Florence Kelley* (Champaign: University of Illinois Press, 1953).

first to name a woman elector, Helen J. Scott of Wisconsin. After the success of the Progressive Party in the 1912 elections, the social workers and social scientists who had flooded into the party were convinced that they were bringing the pristine values (or rather, non-values) of "science" to political affairs. *Their* statist proposals were "scientific," and any resistance to such measures was, therefore, narrow and opposed to the spirit of science and social welfare.

In its permanent organization of 1913, the Progressive Party adopted "A Plan of Work" proposed by Jane Addams just after the election. Its major division was Progressive Science, headed by New York social worker, attorney, and sociologist Frances A. Kellor. Assisting Frances Kellor as director of the Legislative Reference Bureau, a department of the Progressive Science division, was Chicago pro-union labor lawyer Donald Richberg, later to be prominent in the Railway Labor Act of the 1920s and in the New Deal. Prominent in the Party's Bureau of Education was none other than John Dewey. But particularly important was the Party's Department of Social and Industrial Justice, headed by Jane Addams. Under her, Henry Moskowitz headed the Men's Labor committee, and upper-class philanthropist Mary E. McDowell headed Women's Labor. The Social Security Insurance committee was headed by Paul Kellogg, editor of the leading social work magazine, *Survey,* while Lillian Wald played a prominent role in the Child Welfare committee.[33]

More important than the heady few years of the Progressive Party, however, was the accelerating accumulation of influence and power in state and federal government. In particular, the ladies' settlement-house movement exerted enormous influence in shaping the New Deal, an influence that has been generally underrated.

Take, for example, Mary H. Wilmarth, daughter of a gas fixture manufacturer and one of the upper-class Chicago socialites who had been brought into the group of wealthy supporters of Hull House. Soon, Mary Wilmarth was to become one of the major financial supporters of the radical Women's Trade Union League. Mary's sister, Anne Wilmarth, married a Progressive Chicago attorney, the curmudgeon Harold L. Ickes, who soon became legal counsel for the W.T.U.L. During the New Deal, Ickes was to become Franklin Roosevelt's high-profile Secretary of the Interior.

---

[33]On the Progressive Party, see Gable, *The Bull Moose Years.*

At the other end of the social and ethnic spectrum from the Wilmarth sisters was the short, fiery, aggressively single Polish-American Jewess, Rose Schneiderman (b. 1882). One of the most frankly left-wing figures among the female agitators, Miss Schneiderman emigrated to New York in 1890 with her family, and at the age of 21 became the organizer of the first women's local of the Jewish Socialist United Cloth Hat and Cap Makers Union. Rose was prominent in the W.T.U.L and played a key role in organizing the International Ladies Garment Workers Union, landing on that union's Executive Board. Rose Schneiderman was appointed to the Labor Advisory Board during the New Deal.

From Florence Kelley's National Consumers League, there came into the New Deal Molly Dewson, who became a member of Franklin Roosevelt's Social Security Board, and Josephine Roche, who became Assistant Secretary of the Treasury in the New Deal.

But there were significantly bigger fish to fry than these few lesser figures. Perhaps the leading force emerging from the women's statist, social-welfare movement was none other than Eleanor Roosevelt (b. 1884), perhaps our first bisexual First Lady. Eleanor fell under the influence of the passionately radical London prep school headmistress, Madame Marie Souvestre, who apparently set Eleanor on her lifelong course. Back in New York, Eleanor joined Florence Kelley's National Consumers League and became a lifelong reformer. During the early 1920s, Eleanor was also active in working for, and financially supporting, Lillian Wald's Henry Street Settlement and Mary Simkhovitch's Greenwich House. In the early 1920s, Eleanor joined the W.T.U.L. and helped to finance that radical organization, agitating for maximum-hour and minimum wage laws for women. Eleanor became a close friend of Molly Dewson, who later joined the Social Security Board, and of Rose Schneiderman. Eleanor also brought her friend, Mrs. Thomas W. Lamont, wife of the then-most-powerful Morgan partner, into her circle of social-reform agitators.

The woman who rose highest in rank during the New Deal, and who was highly influential in its social legislation, was Madame Frances Perkins (b. 1880), Secretary of Labor and first female Cabinet member in U.S. history. Frances Perkins was born in Boston; both parents, who came from Maine, were active Congregationalists, and her father, Fred, was a wealthy businessman. Frances went to Mt. Holyoke in 1898, where she was elected class president. At Mt. Holyoke, Frances was swept up in the intense religious-pietist wave sweeping that college; every Saturday night, each class would conduct a prayer meeting.

The leader of what we might call the "religious Left" on the campus was American history professor Annabelle May Soule, who organized the Mt. Holyoke chapter of the National Consumers League, urging the abolition of child labor, and of low-wage sweatshops, another prominent statist cause. It was a talk at the Mt. Holyoke by the charismatic Marxist and national leader of the NLC, Florence Kelley, that changed Frances Perkins's life and brought her on the road to lifelong welfare-state reform.

In 1913, Frances Perkins was married, in a secret ceremony, to economist Paul C. Wilson. Wilson was a wealthy, cheerful, but sickly social reformer, providing Frances a good entry into municipal reform circles. While the marriage was supposed to be a love match, it is doubtful how much the marriage meant to the tough-minded Perkins. Her friend, the unmarried welfare activist Pauline Goldmark, lamented that Frances had married, but added that she "did it to get it off her mind." In a gesture of early feminism, Frances refused to take her husband's name. When she was named Secretary of Labor by Franklin Roosevelt, she rented a house with a close friend, the powerful and prodigiously wealthy Mary Harriman Rumsey, daughter of the great tycoon E.H. Harriman. The Harriman family was extremely powerful in the New Deal, an influence that has been largely neglected by historians. Mary Harriman Rumsey, who had been widowed in 1922, was head of the Maternity Center Administration in New York, and under the New Deal, she was chairman of the Consumer Advisory Committee of the National Recovery Administration.[34]

The close interrelation between social work, female activism, and extremely wealthy financiers is seen in the career of Frances Perkins's close friend Henry Bruere (b. 1882), who had been Wilson's best friend. Bruere was born to a physician in St. Charles, Missouri, went to the University of Chicago, attended a couple of law schools, and then did graduate work in political science at Columbia. After graduate school, Bruere resided at College Settlement and then University Settlement, and then went on from there to become Personnel Director at Morgan's International Harvester Corporation.

From then on, Bruere's life was a revolving door, going from social agencies to private corporations and back again. Thus, after Harvester, Bruere founded the Bureau of Municipal Research in New York and became president of the New York City Board of Social Welfare. From

---

[34]On Mrs. Perkins, see George Whitney Martin, *Madame Secretary: Frances Perkins* (Boston: Houghton Mifflin, 1976).

there, it was on to vice president of Metropolitan Life and the CEO of the Bowery Savings Bank, which became his operating base from the late 1920s until the early 1950s.

But Henry Bruere still had plenty of time for good works. In the late 1920s and early 1930s, Bruere was a member of the Executive Committee and Board of the Welfare Council of New York City, leading the drive for government unemployment relief. Bruere was appointed by Perkins as chairman of the New York State Committee on the Stabilization of Industry in 1930, which presaged the National Recovery Administration idea of coerced government cartelization of industry. During the New Deal, Bruere also became an advisor to the federal Home Owners Loan Corporation, Federal Credit Association, to unemployment and old-age insurance, and was an advisor to the Reconstruction Finance Corporation. Bruere also became executive assistant to William Woodin, Roosevelt's first Secretary of the Treasury.

In the meanwhile, however, and this should be underscored, in addition to the high federal posts and social-welfare jobs, Bruere also hobnobbed with the financial greats, becoming a director of Harriman's Union Pacific Railroad and a treasurer of Edward A. Filene's left-liberal Twentieth-Century Fund. Filene was the millionaire retailer who was the major sponsor of the legal activities of his friend and oft-time counselor, Louis D. Brandeis.

As we can see from the case of Henry Bruere, after Yankee women pioneered in welfare and social-work organizations, men began to follow suit. Thus, heavily influenced by their stays at Hull House were the prominent journalist Francis Hackett; the distinguished historian and political scientist Charles A. Beard, who had also stayed at Toynbee House in London; the man who would become one of the most preeminent state-cartelists in American industry, Gerard Swope, head of the Morgans' General Electric Company; and the man who would become one of the major social and labor activists for John D. Rockefeller, Jr., and eventually the Rockefellers' man as Liberal Premier of Canada for many years, William Lyon Mackenzie King.

But perhaps the most important of the male social workers who became prominent in the New Deal was the man who became Roosevelt's Brain Truster, Secretary of Commerce, and eventually the shadowy virtual (if unofficial) Secretary of State, Harry Lloyd Hopkins (b. 1890). Hopkins, along with Eleanor Roosevelt, might be considered the leading statist social worker and activist of the 1880s cohort, the generation after the 1860s founders.

Hopkins was born in Iowa, the son of a harness maker who later operated a general store. Following in the Yankee pietist social gospel mold, Hopkins's Canadian mother, Anna Pickett Hopkins, was a gospel teacher and had become president of the Methodist Home Mission Society of Iowa. Hopkins graduated from Grinnell College in Iowa in 1912 in the social sciences. Moving to New York, Hopkins promptly married the first of three wives, the Jewish heiress Ethel Gross. Hopkins plunged into the settlement-house movement, becoming a resident of the Christodora House in New York before his marriage. He then went to work for the Association for Improving the Condition of the Poor (AICP) and became a protégé of the general director of the AICP, John Adams Kingsbury (b. 1876). Kingsbury, no relation to the wealthy Mary Kingsbury Simkhovitch, had been born in rural Kansas to a father who became a socialist high school principal in Seattle. Kingsbury, on graduation from Teachers College, Columbia, in 1909, went into professional social work.

During the Reform Administration of New York Mayor John Purroy Mitchell, Kingsbury became Commissioner of Public Charities in New York, and Hopkins was executive secretary of the Board of Child Welfare, serving on the Board together with such rising social-reform luminaries as Henry Bruere, Molly Dewson, and Frances Perkins.

From 1917 to 1922, Hopkins administered the Red Cross in the South, returning to New York to become assistant director of the AICP, while Kingsbury became CEO of the highly influential Milbank Fund, which financed many medical and health projects, and was in the Rockefeller orbit. Kingsbury funded a major project for the New York Tuberculosis Association after Hopkins became its director in 1924. Kingsbury became more and more openly radical, praising to the skies the alleged medical achievements of the Soviet Union and agitating for compulsory health insurance in the United States. Kingsbury became such an outspoken agitator against the American Medical Association that the AMA threatened a boycott of Borden's milk (the major business of the Milbank family), and succeeded in getting Kingsbury fired in 1935. But not to worry; Harry Hopkins promptly made his old friend Kingsbury a consultant to Hopkins's make-work Works Progress Administration.

How did Harry Hopkins rise from being a settlement-house worker to one of the most-powerful people in the New Deal? Part of the answer was his close friendship with W. Averill Harriman, scion of the Harriman family, his friendship with John Hertz, partner of the powerful investment-banking firm of Lehman Brothers; and his association with the rising polit-ical leader of the powerful Rockefeller family, Nelson Aldrich Rockefeller. Indeed, when Hopkins was made Secretary of Commerce in the New Deal, he offered the Assistant Secretary post to Nelson Rockefeller, who turned it down.

7. The Rockefellers and Social Security

The Rockefellers and their intellectual and technocratic entourage were, indeed, central to the New Deal. In a deep sense, in fact, the New Deal itself constituted a radical displacement of the Morgans, who had domi-nated the financial and economic politics of the 1920s, by a coalition led by the Rockefellers, the Harrimans, Kuhn-Loeb, and the Lehman Broth-ers investment banking firms.[35] The Business Advisory Committee of the Department of Commerce, for example, which proved highly influential in drawing up New Deal measures, was dominated by the scion of the Harriman family, W. Averill Harriman, and by such Rockefeller satraps as Walter Teagle, head of Standard Oil of New Jersey. Here we have space to trace only the influence of the Rockefellers, allied with the Wisconsin progressives and the graduates of the settlement houses, in creating and imposing on America the Social Security System. Here, too, was the end product of a gradual but sure process of secularization of the messianic ideal of the postmillennial pietists. Perhaps it is only fitting that a move-ment that began with postmillennial Yankee harridans going out into the streets and trying to destroy saloons would conclude with Wisconsin social scientists, technocrats, and Rockefeller-driven experts manipulat-ing the levers of political power to bring about a top-down revolution in the form of the welfare state.[36]

---

[35]See Thomas Ferguson, "Industrial Conflict and the Coming of the New Deal: The Tri-umph of Multinational Liberalism in America," in *The Rise and Fall of the New Deal Order, 1930–1980*, S. Fraser and G. Gerstle, eds. (Princeton, NJ: Princeton University Press, 1989), pp. 3–31.

[36]The Rockefellers were originally ardent postmillennialist Baptists, John D. Sr., hailing originally from upstate New York. John D. Jr., headed the moral as well as philanthropic wing of the Rockefeller Empire, heading a grand jury in New York City in 1920 dedicated to stamping out vice in that city. After World War I, however, the Rockefeller family's hand-picked personal minister, the Reverend Harry Emerson Fosdick, spearheaded the drive of "liberal Protestantism," a secularized version of postmillennialism, in order to repel a ris-ing tide of premillennialist "fundamentalism" in the church. Harry Fosdick became head

Social Security began in 1934 when President Franklin Roosevelt commissioned a triad of his top officials to select the membership of a Committee on Economic Security (CES), which would draw up the legislation for the Social Security system. The three officials were Secretary of Labor Frances Perkins, Director of the Federal Emergency Relief Administration Harry Hopkins, and Secretary of Agriculture Henry A. Wallace. The most important of this triad was Perkins, whose department came closest to jurisdiction over social security, and who presented the administration's viewpoints at Congressional hearings. Perkins and the others decided to entrust the all-important task to Arthur Altmeyer, a Commons disciple at Wisconsin who had been secretary of the Wisconsin Industrial Commission and had administered Wisconsin's system of unemployment relief. When Roosevelt imposed the corporatist collectivist National Recovery Administration (NRA) in 1933, Altmeyer was made director of the NRA Labor Compliance Division. Corporatist businessmen heartily approved of Altmeyer's performance on the task, notably Marion Folsom, head of Eastman Kodak, and one of the leading members of the Business Advisory Council.

Altmeyer's first choice to become chairman of the CES was none other than Dr. Bryce Stewart, director of research for the Industrial Relations Councilors (IRC). The IRC had been set up in the early 1920s by the Rockefellers, specifically John D., Jr., in charge of ideology and philanthropy for the Rockefeller empire. The IRC was the flagship scholarly and activist outfit to promote a new form of corporatist labor-management cooperation, as well as promoting pro-union and pro-welfare-state policies in industry and government. The IRC also set up influential Industrial Relations departments in Ivy League universities, notably Princeton.

Bryce Stewart, however, was hesitant about so openly taking charge of the Social Security effort on behalf of the IRC and the Rockefellers. He preferred to remain behind the scenes, do advisory consulting to the CES, and co-direct a study of unemployment insurance for the Council.

---

of the Federal Council of Churches of Christ, the mainstream liberal Protestant organization. In the meanwhile, John D., Jr. made Fosdick's brother, Raymond Blaine Fosdick, head of the Rockefeller Foundation and eventually John D., Jr's official biographer. Fosdick had been a settlement house worker. The Fosdicks were born in Buffalo to a New England Yankee family. On the Fosdicks, see Murray N. Rothbard, "World War I as Fulfillment: Power and the Intellectuals," *Journal of Libertarian Studies* 9, no. 1 (Winter 1989): 92–93, 120. [Editor's remarks] See Chapter 13 below, pp. 414–19.

Turned down by Stewart, Altmeyer turned to his successor as secretary of the Wisconsin Industrial Commission, Commons disciple Edwin E. Witte. Witte became Executive Secretary of the CES, with the task of appointing the other members. At the suggestion of FDR, Altmeyer consulted with powerful members of the BAC, namely Swope, Teagle, and John Raskob of DuPont and General Motors, about the makeup and policies of the CES.

Altmeyer and Witte also prepared names for FDR to select an Advisory Council to the CES, consisting of employer, union, and "citizen" members. In addition to Swope, Folsom, and Teagle, the Advisory Council included two other powerful corporatist businessmen. The first, Morris Leeds, was president of Leeds & Northrup, and a member of the corporate, pro-union, pro-welfare-state American Association for Labor Legislation. The second, Sam Lewisohn, was vice president of Miami Copper Company, and former president of the AALL. Selected to head the Advisory Council was an academic front man, the much beloved Southern liberal, Frank Graham, president of the University of North Carolina.

Altmeyer and Witte appointed as the members of the key Technical Board of the CES three distinguished experts, Murray Webb Latimer, J. Douglas Brown, and Barbara Nachtried Armstrong, who was the first female law professor at the University of California at Berkeley. All three were IRC affiliates, and Latimer and Brown were, indeed, eminent members of the Rockefeller-IRC network. Latimer, chairman of the Railroad Retirement Board, was a long-time employee of the IRC, and had compiled the IRC's study of industrial pensions, as well as having hammered out the details of the Railroad Retirement Act. Latimer was a member of the AALL and helped administer insurance and pension plans for Standard Oil of New Jersey, Standard Oil of Ohio, and Standard Oil of California.

J. Douglas Brown was head of Princeton's IRC-created Industrial Relations Department and was the point man for the CES in designing the old-age pension plan for Social Security. Brown, along with the big-business members of the Advisory Council, was particularly adamant that no employers escape the taxes for the old-age pension scheme. Brown was frankly concerned that small business not escape the cost-raising consequences of these social security tax obligations. In this way, big businesses, who were already voluntarily providing costly old-age pensions to their employees, could use the federal government to force their small-business competitors into paying for similar, costly, programs. Thus, Brown explained, in his testimony before the Senate Finance Committee in 1935, that the great boon of the employer "contribution" to old-age pensions is that

> it makes uniform throughout industry a minimum cost of providing old-age security and protects the more liberal employer now providing pensions from the competition of the employer who otherwise fires the old person without a pension when superannuated. It levels up cost of old-age protection on both the progressive employer and the unprogressive employer.[37]

In other words, the legislation deliberately penalizes the lower cost, "unprogressive," employer and cripples him by artificially raising his costs compared to the larger employer. Also injured, of course, are the consumers and the taxpayers who are forced to pay for this largess.

It is no wonder, then, that the bigger businesses almost all backed the Social Security scheme to the hilt, while it was attacked by such associations of small business as the National Metal Trades Association, the Illinois Manufacturing Association, and the National Association of Manufacturers. By 1939, only 17% of American businesses favored repeal of the Social Security Act, while not one big business firm supported repeal.

Big business, indeed, collaborated enthusiastically with social security. When the Social Security Board faced the formidable task of establishing 26 million accounts for individuals, it consulted with the BAC, and Marion Folsom helped plan the creation of regional SSB centers. The BAC got the Board to hire the director of the Industrial Bureau of the Philadelphia Chamber of Commerce to serve as head registrar, and J. Douglas Brown was rewarded for his services by becoming chairman of the new, expanded Advisory Council for the Social Security Administration.

The American Association for Labor Legislation was particularly important in developing the Social Security system. This leftist social-welfare outfit, founded by Commons and headed for decades by his student John B. Andrews, was financed by Rockefeller, Morgan, and other wealthy

---

[37]Jill Quadagno, *The Transformation of Old Age Security: Class and Politics in the American Welfare State* (Chicago: University of Chicago Press, 1988), p. 112; Jill Quadagno, "Welfare Capitalism and the Social Security Act of 1935," *American Sociological Review* 49 (October, 1984): 641. Also see G. William Domhoff, *The Power Elite and the State: How Policy is Made in America* (New York: Aldine de Gruyter, 1990).

corporate liberal financial and industrial interests. The AALL was the major developer of disability and health insurance proposals during the 1920s, and then in 1930 turned to work on model state bills for unemployment insurance. In 1932, Wisconsin adopted the AALL's plan and, under the force of AALL lobbying, the Democratic Party incorporated it into its platform. In developing Social Security, key CES Technical Board and Advisory Council posts were staffed with AALL members. Not only that, but in early 1934, Secretary Perkins asked none other than Paul Rauschenbush, the AALL's Washington lobbyist, to draft a bill for Social Security which became the basis for further discussions in the CES. The AALL was also closely associated with Florence Kelley's National Consumers League.

Paul Rauschenbusch had a fascinating pedigree in his own right. Paul was the son of the leading Social-Gospel Baptist minister Walter Rauschenbusch. Paul studied under John R. Commons and was the principle author of the Wisconsin unemployment insurance law. There was even more of a progressive cast to Rauschenbusch, for he married none other than Elizabeth Brandeis, daughter of the famed progressive jurist. Elizabeth also studied under Commons and received a Ph.D. from Wisconsin. What's more, she was also a close friend of the Marxist Florence Kelley and helped edit her aunt Josephine Goldmark's loving biography of Kelley. Elizabeth also helped write the Wisconsin unemployment compensation law. She taught economics at Wisconsin, rising to the post of full professor.

We can conclude by noting, with historian Irwin Yellowitz, that all these reform organizations were dominated and funded by "a small group of wealthy patricians, professional men, and social workers. Wealthy women, including some from New York society, were indispensable to the financing and staffing."[38]

---

[38]Irwin Yellowitz, *Labor and the Progressive Movement in New York State, 1897–1916* (Ithaca, NY: Cornell University Press, 1965), p. 71. See in particular J. Craig Jenkins and Barbara G. Brents, "Social Protest, Hegemonic Competition, and Social Reform: A Political Struggle Interpretation of the American Welfare State," *American Sociological Review* 54 (December, 1989): 891–909; and J. Craig Jenkins and Barbara Brents, "Capitalists and Social Security: What Did They Really Want?" *American Sociological Review* 56 (February, 1991): 129–32.

CHAPTER 12

War Collectivism
in World War I

More than any other single period, World War I was the critical watershed for the American business system. It was a "war collectivism," a totally planned economy run largely by big-business interests through the instrumentality of the central government, which served as the model, the precedent, and the inspiration for state-corporate capitalism for the remainder of the 20th century. That inspiration and precedent emerged not only in the United States but also in the war economies of the major combatants of World War I. War collectivism showed the big-business interests of the Western world that it was possible to shift radically from the previous, largely free-market, capitalism to a new order marked by strong government, and extensive and pervasive government intervention and planning, for the purpose of providing a network of subsidies and monopolistic privileges to business, and especially to large business, interests. In particular, the economy could be cartelized under the aegis of government, with prices raised and production fixed and restricted, in the classic pattern of monopoly, and military and other government contracts could be channeled into the hands of favored corporate

Originally published in *A New History of Leviathan*, Ronald Radosh and Murray N. Rothbard, eds. (New York: E.P. Dutton & Co., 1972), pp. 66–110. Rothbard numbered but did not name the subsections of this essay; to keep all the chapters of the book uniform titles to the subsections have been added by the editor.

producers. Labor, which had been becoming increasingly rambunctious, could be tamed and bridled into the service of this new, state-monopoly-capitalist order, through the device of promoting a suitably cooperative trade unionism, and by bringing the willing union leaders into the planning system as junior partners.

In many ways, the new order was a striking reversion to old-fashioned mercantilism, with its aggressive imperialism and nationalism, its pervasive militarism, and its giant network of subsidies and monopolistic privileges to large business interests. In its 20th-century form, of course, the New Mercantilism was industrial rather than mercantile, since the industrial revolution had intervened to make manufacturing and industry the dominant economic form. But there was a more significant difference in the New Mercantilism. The original mercantilism had been brutally frank in its class rule, and in its scorn for the average worker and consumer.[1] Instead, the new dispensation cloaked the new form of rule in the guise of promotion of the overall national interest of the welfare of the workers through the new representation for labor, and of the common good of all citizens. Hence the importance, for providing a much-needed popular legitimacy and support, of the new ideology of 20th-century liberalism, which sanctioned and glorified the new order. In contrast to the older *laissez-faire* liberalism of the previous century, the new liberalism gained popular sanction for the new system by proclaiming that it differed radically from the old, exploitative mercantilism in its advancement of the welfare of the whole society. And in return for this ideological buttressing by the new "corporate" liberals, the new system furnished the liberals the prestige, the income, and the power that came with posts for the concrete, detailed planning of the system as well as for ideological propaganda on its behalf.

For their part, the liberal intellectuals acquired not only prestige and a modicum of power in the new order, they also achieved the satisfaction of believing that this new system of government intervention was able to

---

[1]On the attitudes of the mercantilists toward labor, see Edgar S. Furniss, *The Position of the Laborer in a System of Nationalism* (New York: Kelley & Millman, 1957). Thus, Furniss cites the English mercantilist William Petyt, who spoke of labor as a "capital material ... raw and undigested ... committed into the hands of supreme authority, in whose prudence and disposition it is to improve, manage, and fashion it to more or less advantage." Furniss adds that "it is characteristic of these writers that they should be so readily disposed to trust in the wisdom of the civil power to 'improve, manage and fashion' the economic raw material of the nation." p. 41.

transcend the weaknesses and the social conflicts that they saw in the two major alternatives: *laissez-faire* capitalism or proletarian, Marxian socialism. The intellectuals saw the new order as bringing harmony and cooperation to all classes on behalf of the general welfare, under the aegis of big government. In the liberal view, the new order provided a middle way, a "vital center" for the nation, as contrasted to the divisive "extremes" of left and right.

1. BIG BUSINESS AND WAR COLLECTIVISM

We have no space here to dwell on the extensive role of big business and business interests in getting the United States into World War I. The extensive economic ties of the large business community with England and France, through export orders and through loans to the Allies — especially those underwritten by the politically powerful J.P. Morgan & Co. (which also served as agent to the British and French governments) — allied to the boom brought about by domestic and Allied military orders, all played a leading role in bringing the United States into the war. Furthermore, virtually the entire eastern business community supported the drive toward war.[2]

Apart from the role of big business in pushing America down the road to war, business was equally enthusiastic about the extensive planning and economic mobilization that the war would clearly entail. Thus, an early enthusiast for war mobilization was the United States Chamber of Commerce, which had been a leading champion of industrial cartelization under the aegis of the federal government since its formation in 1912. The chamber's monthly, *The Nation's Business*, foresaw in mid-1916 that a mobilized economy would bring about a sharing of power and responsibility between government and business. And the chairman of the U.S. chamber's executive committee on national defense wrote to the du Ponts, at the end of 1916, of his expectation that "this munitions question would seem to be the greatest opportunity to foster the new spirit" of cooperation between government and industry.[3]

---

[2]On the role of the House of Morgan, and other economic ties with the Allies in leading to the American entry into the war, see Charles Callan Tansill, *America Goes to War* (Boston: Little, Brown & Co., 1938), pp. 32–134. [Editor's remarks] See also Chapter 14, below, pp. 487–89.

[3]Quoted in Paul A.C. Koistinen, "The 'Industrial-Military Complex' in Historical Perspective: World War I," *Business History Review* (Winter 1967): 381.

The first organization to move toward economic mobilization for war was the Committee on Industrial Preparedness, which in 1916 grew out of the Industrial Preparedness Committee of the Naval Consulting Board, a committee of industrial consultants to the navy dedicated to considering the ramifications of an expanding American navy. Characteristically, the new CIP was a closely blended public-private organization, officially an arm of the federal government but financed solely by private contributions. Moreover, the industrialist members of the committee, working patriotically without fee, were thereby able to retain their private positions and incomes. Chairman of the CIP, and a dedicated enthusiast for industrial mobilization, was Howard E. Coffin, vice president of the important Hudson Motor Co. of Detroit. Under Coffin's direction, the CIP organized a national inventory of thousands of industrial facilities for munitions making. To propagandize for this effort, christened "industrial preparedness," Coffin was able to mobilize the American Press Association, the Associated Advertising Clubs of the World, the august *New York Times,* and the great bulk of American industry.[4]

The CIP was succeeded, in late 1916, by the fully governmental Council of National Defense, whose advisory commission — largely consisting of private industrialists — was to become its actual operating agency. (The council proper consisted of several members of the cabinet.) President Wilson announced the purpose of the CND as organizing "the whole industrial mechanism ... in the most effective way." Wilson found the council particularly valuable because it "opens up a new and direct channel of communication and cooperation between business and scientific men and all departments of the Government ..."[5] He also hailed the personnel of the council's advisory commission as marking "the entrance of

---

[4]The leading historian of World War I mobilization of industry, himself a leading participant and director of the Council of National Defense, writes with scorn that the scattered exceptions to the chorus of business approval "revealed a considerable lack ... of that unity of will to serve the Nation that was essential to the fusing of the fagots of individualism into the unbreakable bundle of national unity." Grosvenor B. Clarkson, *Industrial America in the World War* (Boston: Houghton Mifflin Co., 1923), p. 13. Clarkson's book, incidentally, was subsidized by Bernard Baruch, the head of industrial war collectivism; the manuscript was checked carefully by one of Baruch's top aides. Clarkson, a public relations man and advertising executive, had begun his effort by directing publicity for Coffin's industrial preparedness campaign in 1916. See Robert D. Cuff, "Bernard Baruch: Symbol and Myth in Industrial Mobilization," *Business History Review* (Summer 1969): 116.

[5]Clarkson, *Industrial America in the World War*, p. 21.

the nonpartisan engineer and professional man into American governmental affairs" on an unprecedented scale. These members, declared the
president grandiloquently, were to serve without pay, "efficiency being
their sole object and Americanism their only motive."[6]

Exulting over the new CND, Howard Coffin wrote to the du Ponts
in December, 1916 that "it is our hope that we may lay the foundation
for that closely knit structure, industrial, civil and military, which every
thinking American has come to realize is vital to the future life of this
country, in peace and in commerce, no less than in possible war."[7]

Particularly influential in establishing the CND was Secretary of the
Treasury William Gibbs McAdoo, son-in-law of the president and formerly promoter of the Hudson and Manhattan Railroad and associate of
the Ryan interests in Wall Street.[8] Head of the advisory commission was
Walter S. Gifford, who had been one of the leaders of the Coffin Committee and had come to government from his post as chief statistician of the
American Telephone and Telegraph Co., a giant monopoly enterprise in
the Morgan ambit. The other "nonpartisan" members were Daniel Willard, president of the Baltimore and Ohio Railroad, Wall Street financier
Bernard M. Baruch, Howard E. Coffin, Julius Rosenwald, president of
Sears, Roebuck and Co., Samuel Gompers, president of the AF of L, and
one scientist and one leading surgeon.

Months before American entry into the war, the advisory commission
of the CND designed what was to become the entire system of purchasing war supplies, the system of food control, and censorship of the press.
It was the advisory commission that met with the delighted representatives of the various branches of industry, and told the businessmen to form
themselves into committees for sale of their products to the government,
and for the fixing of the prices of these products. Daniel Willard was,
unsurprisingly, put in charge of dealing with the railroads, Howard Coffin

---

[6]Ibid., p. 22.

[7]Koistinen, "The 'Industrial-Military Complex' in Historical Perspective," p. 385.

[8]Originating the idea of the CND was Dr. Hollis Godfrey, president of the Drexel Institute,
an industrial training and management education organization. Also influential in establishing the CND was the joint military-civilian Kernan Board, headed by Colonel Francis
J. Kernan, and including as its civilian members: Benedict Crowell, chairman of Crowell &
Little Construction Co. of Cleveland and later Assistant Secretary of War; and R. Goodwyn
Rhett, president of the People's Bank of Charleston, and president as well of the Chamber
of Commerce of the United States. Ibid., pp. 382, 384.

with munitions and manufacturing, Bernard Baruch with raw materials and minerals, Julius Rosenwald with supplies, and Samuel Gompers with labor. The idea of establishing committees of the various industries, "to get their resources together," began with Bernard Baruch. CND commodity committees, in their turn, invariably consisted of the leading industrialists in each field; these committees would then negotiate with the committees appointed by industry.[9]

At the recommendation of the advisory commission, Herbert Clark Hoover was named head of the new Food Administration. By the end of March, 1917, the CND appointed a Purchasing Board, to coordinate government's purchases from industry. Chairman of this board, the name of which was soon changed to the General Munitions Board, was Frank A. Scott, a well-known Cleveland manufacturer and president of Warner & Swasey Co.

Yet centralized mobilization was proceeding but slowly through the tangle of bureaucracy, and the United States Chamber of Commerce urged Congress that the director of the CND "should be given power and authority in the economic field analogous to that of the chief of state in the military field."[10] Finally, in early July, the raw materials, munitions, and supplies departments were brought together under the new War Industries Board, with Scott as chairman, the board that was to become the central agency for collectivism in World War I. The functions of the WIB soon became the coordinating of purchases, the allocation of commodities, and the fixing of prices and priorities in production.

Administrative problems beset the WIB, however, and a satisfactory "autocrat" was sought to rule the entire economy as chairman of the new organization. The willing autocrat was finally discovered in the person of Bernard Baruch in early March, 1918. With the selection of Baruch, urged strongly on President Wilson by Secretary McAdoo, war collectivism had

---

[9]As one of many examples, the CND's "Cooperative Committee on Copper" consisted of the president of Anaconda Copper, the president of Calumet and Hecla Mining, the vice president of Phelps Dodge, the vice president of Kennecott Mines, the president of Utah Copper, the president of United Verde Copper, and Murray M. Guggenheim of the powerful Guggenheim family interests. And the American Iron and Steel Institute furnished the representatives of that industry. Clarkson, *Industrial America in the World War*, pp. 496–97; Koistinen, "The 'Industrial-Military Complex' in Historical Perspective," p. 386.

[10]Clarkson, *Industrial America in the World War*, p. 28.

achieved its final form.[11] Baruch's credentials for the task were unimpeachable; an early supporter of the drive toward war, Baruch had presented a scheme for industrial war mobilization to President Wilson as early as 1915.

The WIB developed a vast apparatus that connected to the specific industries through commodity divisions largely staffed by the industries themselves. The historian of the WIB, himself one of its leaders, exulted that the WIB had established

> a system of concentration of commerce, industry, and all the powers of government that was without compare among all the other nations. ... It was so interwoven with the supply departments of the army and navy, of the Allies, and with other departments of the Government that, while it was an entity of its own ... its decisions and its acts ... were always based on a conspectus of the whole situation. At the same time, through the commodity divisions and sections in contact with responsible committees of the commodities dealt with, the War Industries Board extended its antennae into the innermost recesses of industry. Never before was there such a focusing of knowledge of the vast field of American industry, commerce, and transportation. Never was there such an approach to omniscience in the business affairs of a continent.[12]

Big-business leaders permeated the WIB structure from the board itself down to the commodity sections. Thus, Vice Chairman Alexander Legge came from International Harvester Co.; businessman Robert S. Brookings was the major force in insisting on price fixing; George N. Peek, in charge of finished products, had been vice president of Deere & Co., a leading farm-equipment manufacturer. Robert S. Lovett, in charge of priorities, was chairman of the board of Union Pacific Railroad, and J. Leonard Replogle, Steel Administrator, had been president of the American Vanadium Co. Outside of the direct WIB structure, Daniel Willard of the Baltimore & Ohio was in charge of the nation's railroads, and big businessman Herbert C. Hoover was the "Food Czar."

---

[11]Scott and Willard had successively been Chairman, which post was then offered to Homer Ferguson, president of the Newport News Shipbuilding Co. and later head of the United States Chamber of Commerce.

[12]Clarkson, *Industrial America in the World War*, p. 63.

In the granting of war contracts, there was no nonsense about competitive bidding. Competition in efficiency and cost was brushed aside, and the industry-dominated WIB handed out contracts as it saw fit.

Any maverick individualistic firm that disliked the mandates and orders of the WIB was soon crushed between the coercion wielded by government and the collaborating opprobrium of his organized business colleagues. Thus, Grosvenor Clarkson writes,

> Individualistic American industrialists were aghast when they realized that industry had been drafted, much as manpower had been. ... Business willed its own domination, forged its bonds, and policed its own subjection. There were bitter and stormy protests here and there, especially from those industries that were curtailed or suspended. ... [But] the rents in the garment of authority were amply filled by the docile and cooperative spirit of industry. The occasional obstructor fled from the mandates of the Board only to find himself ostracized by his fellows in industry.[13]

One of the most important instrumentalities of wartime collectivism was the Conservation Division of the WIB, an agency again consisting largely of leaders in manufacturing. The Conservation Division had begun as the Commercial Economy Board of the CND, the brainchild of its first chairman, Chicago businessman A.W. Shaw. The Board, or Division, would suggest industrial economies and encourage the industry concerned to establish cooperative regulations. The board's regulations were supposedly "voluntary," a voluntarism enforced by "the compulsion of trade opinion — which automatically policed the observance of the recommendations." For "a practice adopted by the overwhelming consent and even insistence of ... [a man's] fellows, especially when it bears the label of patriotic service in a time of emergency, is not lightly to be disregarded."[14]

In this way, in the name of wartime "conservation," the Conservation Division set out to rationalize, standardize, and cartelize industry in a way that would, hopefully, continue permanently after the end of the war. Arch W. Shaw summed up the division's task as follows: to drastically reduce the number of styles, sizes, etc., of the products of industry, to

---

[13]Ibid., pp. 154, 159.
[14]Ibid., p. 215.

eliminate various styles and varieties, and to standardize sizes and measures. That this ruthless and thoroughgoing suppression of competition in industry was not thought of as a purely wartime measure is made clear in this passage by Grosvenor Clarkson:

> The World War was a wonderful school. ... It showed us how so many things may be bettered that we are at a loss where to begin with permanent utilization of what we know. The Conservation Division alone showed that merely to strip from trade and industry the lumber of futile custom and the encrustation of useless variety would return a good dividend on the world's capital. ... It is, perhaps, too much to hope that there will be any general gain in time of peace from the triumphant experiment of the Conservation Division. Yet now the world needs to economize as much as in war.[15]

Looking forward to future cartelization, Clarkson declared that such peacetime "economizing ... implies such a close and sympathetic affiliation of competitive industries as is hardly possible under the decentralization of business that is compelled by our antitrust statutes."

Bernard Baruch's biographer summarized the lasting results of the compulsory "conservation" and standardization as follows:

> Wartime conservation had reduced styles, varieties, and colors of clothing. It had standardized sizes. ... It had outlawed 250 different types of plow models in the U.S., to say nothing of 755 types of drills ... mass production and mass distribution had become the law of the land. ... This, then, would be the goal of the next quarter of the twentieth century: "To Standardize American Industry"; to make of wartime necessity a matter of peacetime advantage.[16]

Not only the Conservation Division, but the entire structure of wartime collectivism and cartelization constituted a vision to business and government of a future peacetime economy. As Clarkson frankly put it,

---

[15]Ibid., p. 230.

[16]Margaret L. Coit, *Mr. Baruch* (Boston: Houghton Mifflin Co., 1957), p. 219.

> It is little wonder that the men who dealt with the indus-
> tries of a nation ... meditated with a sort of intellectual
> contempt on the huge hit-and-miss confusion of peace-
> time industry, with its perpetual cycle of surfeit and
> dearth and its internal attempt at adjustment after the
> event. From their meditations arose dreams of an ordered
> economic world. ...
>
> They conceived of America as "commodity sectioned"
> for the control of world trade. They beheld the whole
> trade of the world carefully computed and registered in
> Washington, requirements noted, American resources
> on call, the faucets opened or closed according to the
> circumstances. In a word, a national mind and will con-
> fronting international trade and keeping its own house in
> business order.[17]

Heart and soul of the mechanism of control of industry by the WIB
were its 60-odd commodity sections, committees supervising the various
groups of commodities, which were staffed almost exclusively by businessmen from the respective industries. Furthermore, these committees dealt
with over three hundred "war service committees" of industry appointed
by the respective industrial groupings under the aegis of the Chamber of
Commerce of the United States. It is no wonder that in this cozy atmosphere, there was a great deal of harmony between business and government. As Clarkson admiringly described it,

> Businessmen wholly consecrated to government service,
> but full of understanding of the problems of industry,
> now faced businessmen wholly representative of industry
> ... but sympathetic with the purpose of government.[18]

And:

> The commodity sections were business operating Gov-
> ernment business for the common good. ... The war com-
> mittees of industry knew, understood, and believed in the
> commodity chiefs. They were of the same piece.[19]

---

[17]Clarkson, *Industrial America in the World War*, p. 312.

[18]Ibid., p. 303.

[19]Ibid., pp. 300–01.

All in all, Clarkson exulted that the commodity sections were "industry mobilized and drilled, responsive, keen, and fully staffed. They were militant and in serried ranks."[20]

The Chamber of Commerce was particularly enthusiastic over the war service committee system, a system that was to spur the trade association movement in peacetime as well. Chamber president Harry A. Wheeler, vice president of the Union Trust Co. of Chicago, declared that

> Creation of the War Service Committees promises to furnish the basis for a truly national organization of industry whose preparations and opportunities are unlimited. ... The integration of business, the expressed aim of the National Chamber, is in sight. War is the stern teacher that is driving home the lesson of cooperative effort.[21]

The result of all this newfound harmony within each industry, and between industry and government, was to "substitute cooperation for competition." Competition for government orders was virtually nonexistent, and "competition in price was practically done away with by Government action. Industry was for the time in ... a golden age of harmony," and freed from the menace of business losses.[22]

One of the crucial functions of wartime planning was price fixing, set in the field of industrial commodities by the Price Fixing Committee of the War Industries Board. Beginning with such critical areas as steel and copper early in the war and then inexorably expanding to many other fields, the price fixing was sold to the public as the fixing of maximum prices in order to protect the public against wartime inflation. In fact, however, the government set the price in each industry at such a rate as to guarantee a "fair profit" to the high-cost producers, thereby conferring a large degree of privilege and high profits on the lower-cost firms.[23] Clarkson admitted that this system

---

[20]Ibid., p. 309. On the War Industries Board, the commodity sections, and on big-business sentiment paving the path for the coordinated industry-government system, see Weinstein, *The Corporate Ideal in the Liberal State, 1900–1918*, p. 223 and passim.

[21]In *The Nation's Business* (August, 1918): 9–10. Quoted in Koistinen, "The 'Industrial-Military Complex' in Historical Perspective," pp. 392–93.

[22]Clarkson, *Industrial America in the World War*, p. 313.

[23]See George P. Adams, Jr., *Wartime Price Control* (Washington, D.C.: American Council on Public Affairs, 1942), pp. 57, 63–64. As an example, the government fixed the price of

was a tremendous invigoration of big business and hard
on small business. The large and efficient producers made
larger profits than normally and many of the smaller concerns fell below their customary returns.[24]

But the higher-cost firms were largely content with their "fair profit"
guarantee.

The attitude of the Price-Fixing Committee was reflected in the statement of its Chairman, Robert S. Brookings, a retired lumber magnate,
addressed to the nickel industry: "We are not in an attitude of envying you
your profits; we are more in the attitude of justifying them if we can. That
is the way we approach these things."[25]

Typical of the price-fixing operation was the situation in the cotton
textile industry. Chairman Brookings reported in April, 1918, that the
Cotton Goods Committee had decided to "get together in a friendly way"
to try to "stabilize the market." Brookings appended the feeling of the
larger cotton manufacturers that it was better to fix a high long-run minimum price than to take full short-run advantage of the very high prices
then in existence.[26]

The general enthusiasm of the business world, and especially big business, for the system of war collectivism can now be explained. The enthusiasm was a product of the resulting stabilization of prices, the ironing out
of market fluctuations, and the fact that prices were almost always set by
mutual consent of government and the representatives of each industry. It
is no wonder that Harry A. Wheeler, president of the United States Chamber of Commerce, wrote in the summer of 1917 that war "is giving business the foundation for the kind of cooperative effort that alone can make
the U.S. economically efficient." Or that the head of American Telephone
and Telegraph hailed the perfecting of a "coordination to ensure complete
cooperation not only between the Government and the companies, but
between the companies themselves." The wartime cooperative planning
was working so well, in fact, opined the chairman of the board of Republic

---

copper f.o.b. New York at 23 ½ cents per pound. The Utah Copper Co., which produced
over 8% of the total copper output, had estimated costs of 11.8 cents per pound. In this way,
Utah Copper was guaranteed nearly 100% profit on costs. Ibid., p. 64n.

[24]Clarkson, *Industrial America in the World War.*

[25]Adams, *Wartime Price Control,* pp. 57–58.

[26]Weinstein, *The Corporate Ideal in the Liberal State, 1900–1918,* pp. 224–25.

Iron and Steel in early 1918, that it should be continued in peacetime as well.[27]

The vitally important steel industry is an excellent example of the workings of war collectivism. The hallmark of the closely knit control of the steel industry was the close "cooperation" between government and industry, a cooperation in which Washington decided on broad policy, and then left it up to Judge Elbert Gary, head of the leading steel producer, United States Steel, to implement the policy within the industry. Gary selected a committee representing the largest steel producers to help him run the industry. A willing ally was present in J. Leonard Replogle, head of American Vanadium Co. and chief of the Steel Division of the WIB. Replogle shared the long-standing desire of Gary and the steel industry for industrial cartelization and market stability under the aegis of a friendly federal government. Unsurprisingly, Gary was delighted with his new powers in directing the steel industry and urged that he be given total power "to thoroughly mobilize and if necessary to commandeer." And *Iron Age,* the magazine of the iron and steel industry, exulted that

> it has apparently taken the most gigantic war in all history to give the idea of cooperation any such place in the general economic program as the country's steel manufacturers sought to give it in their own industry nearly ten years ago

with the short-lived *entente cordiale* between Judge Gary and President Roosevelt.[28]

It is true that wartime relations between government and steel companies were sometimes strained, but the strain and the tough threat of government commandeering of resources was generally directed at smaller

---

[27]Melvin I. Urofsky, *Big Steel and the Wilson Administration* (Columbus: Ohio State University Press, 1969), pp. 152–53.

[28]Ibid., pp. 153–57. In his important study of business-government relations in the War Industries Board, Professor Robert Cuff has concluded that federal regulation of industry was shaped by big-business leaders, and that relations between government and big business were smoothest in those industries, such as steel, whose industrial leaders had already committed themselves to seeking government-sponsored cartelization. Robert D. Cuff, "Business, Government, and the War Industries Board" (Doctoral dissertation in history, Princeton University, 1966).

firms, such as Crucible Steel, which had stubbornly refused to accept government contracts.[29]

In the steel industry, in fact, it was the big steelmakers — U.S. Steel, Bethlehem, Republic, etc. — who, early in the war, had first urged government price fixing, and they had to prod a sometimes confused government to adopt what eventually became the government's program. The main reason was that the big steel producers, happy at the enormous increase of steel prices in the market as a result of wartime demand, were anxious to stabilize the market at a high price and thus ensure a long-run profit position for the duration of the war. The government-steel industry price-fixing agreement of September, 1917, was therefore hailed by John A. Topping, president of Republic Steel, as follows:

> The steel settlement will have a wholesome effect on the steel business because the principle of cooperative-regulation has been established with Government approval. Of course, present abnormal profits will be substantially reduced but a runaway market condition has been prevented and prosperity extended. ... Furthermore, stability in future values should be conserved.[30]

Furthermore, the large steel firms were happy to use the fixed prices as a rationale for imposing controls and stability on wages, which were also beginning to rise. The smaller steel manufacturers, on the other hand, often with higher costs, and who had not been as prosperous before the war, opposed price fixing because they wished to take full advantage of the short-run profit bonanza brought about by the war.[31]

Under this regime, the steel industry achieved the highest level of profits in its history, averaging 25% per year for the two years of war. Some of the smaller steel companies, benefiting from their lower total capitalization, did almost twice as well.[32]

The most thoroughgoing system of price controls during the war was enforced not by the WIB but by the separate Food Administration, over

---

[29]Urofsky, *Big Steel and the Wilson Administration*, p. 154.

[30]In *Iron Age* (September 27, 1917). Quoted in Urofsky, *Big Steel and the Wilson Administration*, pp. 216–17.

[31]Urofsky, pp. 203–06. Also see Robert D. Cuff and Melvin I. Urofsky, "The Steel Industry and Price-Fixing During World War I," *Business History Review* (Autumn 1970): 291–306.

[32]Urofsky, *Big Steel and the Wilson Administration*, pp. 228–33.

which Herbert Clark Hoover presided as "Food Czar." The official historian of wartime price control justly wrote that the food control program "was the most important measure for controlling prices which the United States ... had ever taken."[33]

Herbert Hoover accepted his post shortly after American entry into the war, but only on the condition that he alone have full authority over food, unhampered by boards or commissions. The Food Administration was established without legal authorization, and then a bill backed by Hoover was put through Congress to give the system the full force of law. Hoover was also given the power to requisition "necessaries," to seize plants for government operation, and to regulate or prohibit exchanges.

The key to the Food Administration's system of control was a vast network of *licensing.* Instead of direct control over food, the FA was given the absolute power to issue licenses for any and all divisions of the food industry, and to set the conditions for keeping the license. Every dealer, manufacturer, distributor, and warehouser of food commodities was required by Hoover to maintain its federal license.

A notable feature introduced by Hoover in his reign as Food Czar was the mobilization of a vast network of citizen volunteers as a mass of eager participants in enforcing his decrees. Thus, Herbert Hoover was perhaps the first American politician to realize the potential — in gaining mass acceptance and in enforcing government decrees — in the mobilizing of masses through a torrent of propaganda to serve as volunteer aides to the government bureaucracy. Mobilization proceeded to the point of inducing the public to brand as a virtual moral leper anyone dissenting from Mr. Hoover's edicts. Thus

> The basis of all ... control exercised by the Food Administration was the educational work which preceded and accompanied its measures of conservation and regulation. Mr. Hoover was committed thoroughly to the idea that the most effective method to control foods was to set every man, woman, and child in the country at the business of saving food. ... The country was literally strewn with millions of pamphlets and leaflets designed to educate the people to the food situation. No war board at

---

[33]Paul Willard Garrett, *Government Control Over Prices* (Washington, D.C.: Government Printing Office, 1920), p. 42.

Washington was advertised as widely as the U.S. Food Administration. There were Food Administration insignia for the coat lapel, store window, the restaurant, the train, and the home. A real stigma was placed upon the person who was not loyal to Food Administration edicts through pressure by the schools, churches, women's clubs, public libraries, merchants' associations, fraternal organizations, and other social groups.[34]

The method by which the Food Administration imposed price control was its requirement that its licensees should receive "a reasonable margin of profit." This "reasonable margin" was interpreted as a margin over and above each producer's costs, and this cost plus "reasonable profit" for each dealer became the rule of price control. The program was touted to the public as a means of keeping profits and food prices *down*. Although the administration certainly wished to stabilize prices, the goal was also and more importantly to *cartelize*. Industry and government worked together to make sure that individual maverick competitors did not get out of line; prices in general were to be set at a level to guarantee a "reasonable" profit to everyone. The goal was not *lower* prices, but uniform, stabilized, non-competitive prices for all. The goal was far more to keep prices *up* than to keep them down. Indeed, any overly greedy competitor who tried to increase his profits above prewar levels by *cutting* his prices was dealt with most severely by the Food Administration.

Let us consider two of the most important food-control programs during World War I: wheat and sugar. Wheat price control, the most important program, came in the wake of wartime demand, which had pushed wheat prices up very rapidly to their highest level in the history of the United States. Thus, wheat increased by one dollar a bushel in the course of two months at the start of the war, reaching the unheard of price of three dollars a bushel. Control came in the wake of agitation that government must step in to thwart "speculators" by fixing maximum prices on wheat. Yet, under pressure by the agriculturists, the government program fixed *by statute*, not maximum prices for wheat but *minima*; the Food Control Act of 1917 fixed a minimum price of two dollars a bushel for the next year's wheat crop. Not content with this special subsidy, the president proceeded to raise the minimum to $2.26 a bushel in mid-1918, a figure that was then

---

[34]Ibid., p. 56.

the precise market price for wheat. This increased minimum effectively fixed the price of wheat for the duration of the war. Thus, the government made sure that the consumers could not possibly benefit from any fall in wheat prices.

To enforce the artificially high price of wheat, Herbert Hoover established the Grain Corporation, "headed by practical grain men," which purchased the bulk of the wheat crop in the United States at the "fair price" and then resold the crop to the nation's flour mills at the same price. To keep the millers happy, the Grain Corporation guaranteed them against any possible losses from unsold stocks of wheat or flour. Moreover, each mill was guaranteed that its relative position in the flour industry would be maintained throughout the war. In this way, the flour industry was successfully cartelized through the instrument of government. Those few mills who balked at the cartel arrangement were dealt with handily by the Food Administration; as Garrett put it: "their operations ... were reasonably well controlled ... by the license requirements."[35]

The excessively high prices of wheat and flour also meant artificially high costs to the bakers. They, in turn, were taken under the cozy cartel umbrella by being required, in the name of "conservation," to mix inferior products with wheat flour at a fixed ratio. Each baker was of course delighted to comply with a requirement that he make inferior products, which he knew was also being enforced upon his competitors. Competition was also curtailed by the Food Administration's compulsory standardization of the sizes of bread loaves, and by prohibiting price cutting through discounts or rebates to particular customers — the classic path toward the internal breakup of any cartel.[36]

In the particular case of sugar, there was a much more sincere effort to keep down prices — due to the fact that the United States was largely an importer rather than a producer of sugar. Herbert Hoover and the Allied governments duly formed an International Sugar Committee, which undertook to buy all of their countries' sugar, largely from Cuba, at an artificially low price, and then to allocate the raw sugar to the various refiners. Thus, the Allied governments functioned as a giant buying cartel to lower the price of their refiners' raw material.

---

[35]Ibid., p. 66.
[36]Ibid., p. 73.

Herbert Hoover instigated the plan for the International Sugar Committee, and the U.S. government appointed the majority of the five-man committee. As Chairman of the committee, Hoover selected Earl Babst, president of the powerful American Sugar Refining Co., and the other American members also represented refiner interests. The ISC promptly fixed a sharp reduction of the price of sugar: lowering the New York price of Cuban raw sugar from its high market price of six and three-quarter cents per pound in the summer of 1917 to six cents per pound. When the Cubans understandably balked at this artificially forced price reduction of their cash crop, the United States State Department and the Food Administration collaborated to coerce the Cuban government into agreement. Somehow, the Cubans were unable to obtain import licenses for needed wheat and coal from the United States Food Administration, and the result was a severe shortage of bread, flour, and coal in Cuba. Finally, the Cubans capitulated in mid-January, 1918, and the import licenses from the United States were rapidly forthcoming.[37] Cuba also induced to prohibit all sugar exports except to the International Sugar Committee.

Apparently, Mr. Babst ensured an extra bonus to his American Sugar Refining Company, for, shortly, officials of competing American refineries were to testify before Congress that this company had particularly profited from the activities of the International Sugar Committee and from the price that it fixed on Cuban sugar.[38]

Although the American government pursued with great diligence the goal of pushing down raw material prices for U.S. refiners, it also realized that it could not force down the price of raw sugar *too* low, since the government had to consider the marginal U.S. cane and beet-sugar producers, who had to receive their duly appointed "fair return." Jointly to harmonize and subsidize both the sugar refiners *and* the sugar growers in the United States, Mr. Hoover established a Sugar Equalization Board that would simultaneously keep the price of sugar *low* to Cuba while keeping it high enough for the American producers. The Board accomplished this feat by buying the Cuban sugar at the fixed low price and then reselling the crop to the refiners at a higher price to cover the American producers.[39]

---

[37]See Robert F. Smith, *The United States and Cuba* (New York: Bookman Associates, 1960), pp. 20–21.

[38]Ibid., p. 191.

[39]Garrett, *Wartime Price Control*, pp. 78–85.

The result of the artificially low prices for sugar was, inevitably, to create a severe sugar shortage, by reducing supplies and by stimulating an excessive public consumption. The result was that sugar consumption was then severely restricted by federal rationing of sugar.

It is not surprising that the food industries were delighted with the wartime control program. Expressing the spirit of the entire war-collectivist regime, Herbert Hoover, in the words of Paul Garrett

> maintained, as a cardinal policy from the beginning, a very close and intimate contact with the trade. The men, whom he chose to head his various commodity sections and responsible positions, were in a large measure tradesmen. ... The determination of the policies of control within each branch of the food industry was made in conference with the tradesmen of that branch. ... It might be said ... that the framework of food control, as of raw material control, was built upon agreements with the trade. The enforcement of the agreements once made, moreover, was intrusted in part to the cooperation of constituted trade organizations. The industry itself was made to feel responsible for the enforcement of all rules and regulations.[40]

Also separate from the War Industries Board were the nation's railroads, which received the greatest single ministration of government dictation as compared to any other industry. The railroads, in fact, were seized and operated directly by the federal government.

As soon as the United States entered the war, the administration urged the railroads to unite as one in behalf of the war effort. The railroads were delighted to comply and quickly formed what became known as the Railroads' War Board, promising faithfully to pursue a goal that they had long sought in peacetime: to cease competitive activities and to coordinate railroad operations.[41] Daniel Willard, president of the Baltimore & Ohio Railroad and Bernard Baruch's predecessor as head of the WIB, happily reported that the railroads had agreed to vest their War Board with complete authority to override individual railroad interests. Under its Chairman, Fairfax Harrison of the Southern Railroad, the War Board estab-

[40]Ibid., pp. 55–56.
[41]See Kerr, *American Railroad Politics, 1914–1920*, pp. 44ff.

lished a Committee on Car Service to coordinate national car supplies. Aiding the coordination effort was the Interstate Commerce Commission, the longtime federal regulatory body for the railroads. Once again, the government-promoted monopoly was an inspiration to many who were looking ahead to the peacetime economy. For several years the railroads had been agitating for "scientific management" as a means of achieving higher rates from the ICC and a governmentally imposed cartelization, but they had been thwarted by the pressure of the organized shippers, the industrial users of the railroads.

But now even the shippers were impressed. Max Thelen, chairman of the California Railroad Commission, president of the National Association of Railway and Utilities Commissions, and the leading spokesman for the organized shippers, agreed that the critical railroad problem was "duplication" and the "irrational" lack of complete inter-railroad coordination. And Senator Francis G. Newlands (D., Nev.), the most powerful congressman on railroad affairs as the chairman of a joint committee on transportation regulation, opined that the wartime experience was "somewhat shattering our old views regarding antitrust laws."[42]

Soon, however, it became clear that the system of voluntary private coordination was not really working well. Traffic departments of individual roads persisted in competitive practices, the railroad brotherhood unions were persistently demanding substantial wage increases, and the railroads and organized shippers locked horns over railroad demands for an across-the-board rate increase. All groups felt that regional coordination and overall efficiency would best be achieved by outright federal operation of the railroads. The shippers first proposed the scheme as a method of achieving coordination and to forestall higher freight rates; the unions seconded the plan in order to obtain wage increases from the government, and the railroads cheerfully agreed when President Wilson assured them that each road would be guaranteed its 1916/17 profits — two years of unusually high profits for the railroad industry. With the federal government offering to take on the headaches of wartime dislocation and management, while granting the roads a very high guaranteed profit for doing nothing, why shouldn't the railroads leap to agreement?

The most enthusiastic administration proponent of federal operation of the railroads was Secretary of the Treasury McAdoo, a former New York

---

[42]Ibid., p. 48.

railroad executive and close associate of the Morgan interests, who in turn were the leading underwriters and owners of railroad bonds. McAdoo was rewarded by being named head of the United States Railroad Administration after Wilson seized the railroads on December 28, 1917.

Federal rule by the Morgan-oriented McAdoo proved to be a bonanza for the nation's railroads. Not only were the railroads now fully monopolized by direct government operation, but also the particular railroad executives now found themselves armed with the coercive power of the federal government. For McAdoo chose as his immediate assistants a group of top railroad executives, and all rate-setting powers of the ICC were shifted to the railroad-dominated Railroad Administration for the duration.[43] The significance of the shift is that the railroads, although largely responsible for the inception and growth of the ICC as a cartelizing agency for the railroad industry, had seen control of the ICC slip into the hands of the organized shippers in the decade before the war. This meant that the railroads had found it very difficult to win freight rate increases from the ICC. But now the wartime federal control of the railroads was shunting the shippers aside.[44]

McAdoo's brazen appointment of railroad men to virtually all the leading positions in the Railroad Administration, to the virtual exclusion of shippers and academic economists, greatly angered the shippers, who had launched an intense barrage of criticism of the system by midsummer of 1918. This barrage came to a head when McAdoo increasingly turned the direction of the RA, including the appointment of regional directors, over to his principal assistant, railroad executive Walker D. Hines. Shippers and ICC commissioners complained that

> railroad lawyers from the entire country descended on Washington, told their troubles to other railroad lawyers

---

[43]McAdoo's "cabinet," which assisted him in running the railroads, included Walker D. Hines and Edward Chambers, respectively chairman of the board and vice president of the Santa Fe R.R.; Henry Walters, chairman of the board of the Atlantic Coast R.R., Hale Holden, of the Burlington R.R., A.H. Smith, president of the New York Central R.R., John Barton Payne, formerly chief counsel of the Chicago Great Western R.R., and Comptroller of the Currency John Skelton Williams, formerly chairman of the board of the Seaboard R.R. Hines was to be McAdoo's principal assistant; Payne became head of traffic. The Division of Operation was headed by Carl R. Gray, president of the Western Maryland R.R. One Unionist, W.S. Carter, head of the Brotherhood of Firemen and Engineers, was brought in to head the Division of Labor.

[44]Kerr, *American Railroad Politics, 1914–1920*, pp. 14–22.

serving on McAdoo's staff, and were "told to go into an adjoining room and dictate what orders they want."[45]

As in the case of the War Industries Board, the railroad executives used their coercive governmental powers to deal a crippling blow to diversity and competition, on behalf of monopoly, in the name of "efficiency" and standardization. Again, over the opposition of shippers, the RA ordered the compulsory standardization of locomotive and equipment design, eliminated "duplicate" (i.e., competitive) passenger service and coal transportation, shut down off-line traffic offices, and ordered the cessation of competitive solicitation of freight by the railroads.

All of these edicts reduced railroad services to the hapless shippers. There were still other coerced reductions of service. One ended the shippers' privileges of specifying freight routes — and thereby of specifying the *cheapest* routes for shipping their goods. Another upset the peacetime practice of making the railroads liable for losses and damages to shipments; instead, the entire burden of proof was placed on the shippers. Another RA ruling — the "sailing day plan" — ordered freight cars to remain in their terminals until filled, thus sharply curtailing service to small-town shippers.

The granting of absolute power to the railroad-dominated RA was cemented by the Federal Control Act of March, 1918, which *ex post facto* legalized the illegal federal takeover. Working closely with railroad lobbyists, the RA, backed by the full support of President Wilson, was able to drive through Congress the transfer of rate-making powers to itself from the ICC. Furthermore, all power was taken away from the invariably shipper-dominated state railroad commissions.

The RA hastened to exercise its rate-setting powers, announcing freight rate increases of 25% across the board in the spring of 1918 — an act that permanently cemented shipper hostility to the system of federal operation. To add insult to injury, the new higher rates were set without any public hearings or consultation with other agencies or interests involved.

---

[45]Ibid., p. 80.

2. Intellectuals and the Legacy of War Collectivism

Historians have generally treated the economic planning of World War I as an isolated episode dictated by the requirements of the day and having little further significance. But, on the contrary, the war collectivism served as an inspiration and as a model for a mighty army of forces destined to forge the history of 20th-century America. For big business, the wartime economy was a model of what could be achieved in national coordination and cartelization, in stabilizing production, prices, and profits, in replacing old-fashioned competitive *laissez-faire* by a system that they could broadly control and that would harmonize the claims of various powerful economic groups. It was a system that had already abolished much competitive diversity in the name of standardization. The wartime economy especially galvanized such business leaders as Bernard Baruch and Herbert Hoover, who would promote the cooperative "association" of business trade groups as secretary of commerce during the 1920s, an associationism that paved the way for the cooperative statism of Franklin Roosevelt's AAA and NRA.

The wartime collectivism also held forth a model to the nation's liberal intellectuals, for here was seemingly a system that replaced *laissez-faire* not by the rigors and class hatreds of proletarian Marxism, but by a new strong State, planning and organizing the economy in harmony with all leading economic groups. It was, not coincidentally, to be a neomercantilism, a "mixed economy," heavily staffed by these selfsame liberal intellectuals. And finally, both big business and the liberals saw in the wartime model a way to organize and integrate the often unruly labor force as a junior partner in the corporatist system — a force to be disciplined by their own "responsible" leadership of the labor unions.

For the rest of his life, Bernard Mannes Baruch sought to restore the lineaments of the wartime model. Thus, in summing up the experience of the WIB, Baruch extolled the fact that:

> many businessmen have experienced during the war, for the first time in their careers, the tremendous advantages, both to themselves and to the general public, of combination, of cooperation and common action ...

Baruch called for the continuance of such corporate associations, in "inaugurating rules" to eliminate "waste" (i.e., competition), to exchange trade information, to agree on the channeling of supply and demand among themselves, to avoid "extravagant" forms of competition and to allocate the location of production. Completing the outlines of a corporate state, Baruch urged that such associations be governed by a federal agency, either the Department of Commerce or the Federal Trade Commission,

> an agency whose duty it should be to encourage, under strict Government supervision, such cooperation and coordination ...[46]

Baruch also envisioned a federal board for the retraining and channeling of labor after the war. At the very least, he urged standby legislation for price control and for industrial coordination and mobilization in the event of another war.[47]

During the 1920s and 1930s, Bernard Baruch served as a major inspiration of the drive toward a corporate state; moreover, many of the leaders of this drive were men who had served under him during the heady days of the WIB and who continued to function frankly as "Baruch's men" in national affairs. Thus, aided by Baruch, George N. Peek, of the Moline Plow Company, launched in the early 1920s the drive for farm price supports through federally organized farm cartels that was to culminate in President Hoover's Federal Farm Board in 1929 and then in Roosevelt's AAA. Peek's farm-equipment business, of course, stood to benefit greatly from farm subsidies. Hoover appointed as first Chairman of the FFB none other than Baruch's old top aide from World War I, Alexander Legge of International Harvester, the leading farm machinery manufacturer. When Franklin Roosevelt created the AAA, he first offered the job of director to Baruch and then gave the post to Baruch's man, George Peek.

Neither was Baruch laggard in promoting a corporatist system for industry as a whole. In the spring of 1930, Baruch proposed a peacetime reincarnation of the WIB as a "Supreme Court of Industry." In September of the following year, Gerard Swope, head of General Electric and brother of Baruch's closest confidant Herbert Bayard Swope, presented an elaborated plan for a corporate state that essentially revived the system of wartime planning. At the same time, one of Baruch's oldest friends, former secretary William Gibbs McAdoo, was proposing a similar plan for a "Peace Industries Board." After Hoover dismayed his old associates by rejecting

---

[46]Bernard M. Baruch, *American Industry in the War* (New York: Prentice-Hall, 1941), pp. 105–06.

[47]Coit, *Mr. Baruch*, pp. 202–03, 218.

the plan, Franklin Roosevelt embodied it in the NRA, selecting Gerard Swope to help write the final draft, and picking another Baruch disciple and World War aide General Hugh S. Johnson — also of the Moline Plow Company — to direct this major instrument of state corporatism. When Johnson was fired, Baruch himself was offered the post.[48]

Other leading NRA officials were veterans of war mobilization. Johnson's chief of staff was another old friend of Baruch's, John Hancock, who had been Paymaster General of the Navy during the war and had headed the naval industrial program for the War Industries Board; other high officials of the NRA were Dr. Leo Wolman, who had been head of the production-statistics division of the WIB; Charles F. Homer, leader of the wartime Liberty Loan drive; and General Clarence C. Williams, who had been Chief of Ordnance in charge of Army war purchasing. Other WIB veterans highly placed in the New Deal were Isador Lubin, United States Commissioner of Labor Statistics in the New Deal; Captain Leon Henderson of the Ordnance Division of the WIB; and Senator Joseph Guffey (D., Pa.), who had worked in the WIB on conservation of oil, and who helped pattern the oil and coal controls of the New Deal on the wartime Fuel Administration.[49]

Another leading promoter of the new cooperation subsequent to his experience as wartime planner was Herbert Clark Hoover. As soon as the war was over, Hoover set out to "reconstruct America" along the lines of peacetime cooperation. He urged national planning through "voluntary" cooperation among businessmen and other economic groups under the "central direction" of the government. The Federal Reserve System was to allocate capital to essential industries and thereby to eliminate the competitive "wastes" of the free market. And in his term as Secretary of Commerce during the 1920s, Hoover assiduously encouraged the cartelization of industry through trade associations. In addition to inaugurating the modern program of farm price supports in the Federal Farm Board, Hoover urged the coffee buyers to form a cartel to lower buying prices, established a buying cartel in the rubber industry, led the oil industry in working toward restrictions on oil production in the name of "conservation", tried repeatedly to raise prices, restrict production, and encourage marketing co-ops in the coal industry, and tried to force the cotton textile

[48]Ibid., pp. 440–43.

[49]See William E. Leuchtenburg, "The New Deal and the Analogue of War," in *Change and Continuity in Twentieth-Century America,* John Braeman et al., eds. (New York: Harper & Row, 1967), pp. 122–23.

industry into a nationwide cartel to restrict production. Specifically in furtherance of the wartime abolition of thousands of diverse and competitive products, Hoover continued to impose standardization and "simplification" of materials and products during the 1920s. In this way, Hoover managed to abolish or "simplify" about a thousand industrial products. The "simplification" was worked out by the Department of Commerce in collaboration with committees from each industry.[50] Grosvenor Clarkson hailed the fact that

> it is probable that there will never again be such a multiplicity of styles and models in machinery and other heavy and costly articles as there was before the restrictions necessitated by the war. ... The ideas conceived and applied by the War Industries Board in war are being applied in peace by the Department of Commerce ...[51]

Not the least of the influential groups dazzled and marked by the experience of war collectivism were the liberal intellectuals. Never before had so many intellectuals and academicians swarmed into government to help plan, regulate, and mobilize the economic system. The intellectuals served as advisers, technicians, framers of legislation, and administrators of bureaus. Furthermore, apart from the rewards of newly acquired prestige and power, the war economy held out to such intellectuals the promise of transforming the society into a "third way" completely different from the *laissez-faire* past that they scorned or the looming proletarian Marxism that they reviled and feared. Here was a planned corporate economy that seemed to harmonize all groups and classes under a strong and guiding nation-state with the liberals themselves at or near the helm. In a notable article, Professor Leuchtenburg saw the war collectivism as "a logical outgrowth of the Progressive movement."[52] He demonstrated the enthusiasm of the Progressive intellectuals for the social transformation effected by

---

[50]See Herbert Hoover, *Memoirs* (New York: Macmillan, 1952), vol. 2, pp. 27, 66–70; on Hoover and the export industries, Joseph Brandes, *Herbert Hoover and Economic Diplomacy* (Pittsburgh: University of Pittsburgh Press, 1962); on the oil industry, Gerald D. Nash, *United States Oil Policy, 1890–1964* (Pittsburgh: University of Pittsburgh Press, 1968); on coal, Ellis W. Hawley, "Secretary Hoover and the Bituminous Coal Problem, 1921–1928," *Business History Review* (Autumn 1968): 247–70; on cotton textiles, Louis Galambos, *Competition and Cooperation* (Baltimore: Johns Hopkins Press, 1966).

[51]Clarkson, *Industrial America in the World War*, pp. 484–85.

[52]Leuchtenburg, "The New Deal," p. 84n.

the war. Thus, the *New Republic* hailed the "revolutionizing" of society by means of the war; John Dewey hailed the replacement of production for profit and "the absoluteness of private property" by production for use. Economists were particularly enchanted by the "notable demonstration of the power of war to force concert of effort and collective planning" and looked for "the same sort of centralized directing now employed to kill their enemies abroad for the new purpose of reconstructing their own life at home."[53]

Rexford Guy Tugwell, ever alert to the advance of social engineering, was soon to look back wistfully on "America's wartime socialism"; lamenting the end of the war, he declared that "only the Armistice prevented a great experiment in control of production, control of price, and control of consumption." For, during the war, the old system of industrial competition had "melted away in the fierce new heat of nationalistic vision."[54]

Not merely the NRA and AAA, but virtually the entire New Deal apparatus — including the bringing to Washington of a host of liberal intellectuals and planners — owed its inspiration to the war collectivism of World War I. The Reconstruction Finance Corporation, founded by Hoover in 1932 and expanded by Roosevelt's New Deal, was a revival and expansion of the old War Finance Corporation, which had loaned government funds to munitions firms. Furthermore, Hoover, after offering the post to Bernard Baruch, named as first Chairman of the RFC, Eugene Meyer, Jr., an old protégé of Baruch's, who had been managing director of the WFC. Much of the old WFC staff and method of operations were taken over bodily by the new agency. The Tennessee Valley Authority grew out of a wartime government nitrate and electric-power project at Muscle Shoals, and in fact included the old nitrate plant as one of its first assets. Moreover, many of the public power advocates in the New Deal had been trained in such wartime agencies as the Power Section of the Emergency Fleet Corporation. And even the innovative government corporate form of the TVA was based on wartime precedent.[55]

---

[53]Ibid., p. 89.

[54]Ibid., pp. 90–92. It was very similar considerations that also brought many liberal intellectuals, especially including those of the *New Republic*, into at least a temporary admiration for Italian Fascism. Thus, see John P. Diggins, "Flirtation with Fascism: American Pragmatic Liberals and Mussolini's Italy," *American Historical Review* (January, 1966): 487–506.

[55]Leuchtenburg, "The New Deal," pp. 109–10.

Wartime experience also provided the inspiration for the public housing movement of the New Deal. During the war, the Emergency Fleet Corp. and the United States Housing Corp. were established to provide housing for war workers. The war established the precedent of federal housing and also trained architects like Robert Kohn, who functioned as chief of production for the housing division of the United States Shipping Board. After the war, Kohn exulted that "the war has put housing 'on the map' in this country," and in 1933, Kohn was duly named by President Roosevelt to be the director of the New Deal's first venture into public housing. Furthermore, the Emergency Fleet Corp. and the United States Housing Corp. established large-scale public housing communities on planned "garden city" principles (Yorkship Village, N.J.; Union Park Gardens, Del.; Black Rock and Crane Tracts, Conn.) — principles finally remembered and put into effect in the New Deal and afterward.[56]

The oil and coal controls established in the New Deal also rested on the precedent of the wartime Fuel Administration. Indeed, Senator Joseph Guffey (D., Pa.), leader in the coal and oil controls, had been head of the petroleum section of the War Industries Board.

Deeply impressed with the "national unity" and mobilization achieved during the war, the New Deal established the Civilian Conservation Corps to instill the martial spirit in America's youth. The idea was to take the "wandering boys" off the road and "mobilize" them into a new form of American Expeditionary Force. The Army, in fact, ran the CCC camps; CCC recruits were gathered at Army recruiting stations, equipped with World War I clothing, and assembled in army tents. The CCC, the New Dealers exulted, had given a new sense of meaning to the nation's youth, in this new "forestry army." Speaker Henry T. Rainey (D., Ill.) of the House of Representatives put it this way:

> They [the CCC recruits] are also under military training and as they come out of it ... improved in health and developed mentally and physically and are more useful citizens ... they would furnish a very valuable nucleus for an army.[57]

---

[56]Ibid., pp. 111–12.

[57]Ibid., p. 117. Roosevelt named union leader Robert Fechner, formerly engaged in war labor work, as director of the CCC to provide a civilian camouflage for the program, p. 115n.

3. The Drive to Prolong War Collectivism

Particularly good evidence of the deep imprint of war collectivism was the reluctance of many of its leaders to abandon it when the war was finally over. Business leaders pressed for two postwar goals: continuance of government price fixing to protect them against an expected postwar deflation, and a longer-range attempt to promote industrial cartelization in peacetime. In particular, businessmen wanted the price *maxima* (which had often served as *minima* instead) to be converted simply into outright minima for the postwar period. Wartime quotas to restrict production, furthermore, needed only to remain in being to function as a frank cartelizing for raising prices in time of peace.

Accordingly, many of the industrial War Service Committees, and their WIB Section counterparts, urged the continuance of the WIB and its price-fixing system. In particular, section chiefs invariably urged continued price control in those industries that feared postwar deflation, while advocating a return to a free market wherever the specific industry expected a continuing boom. Thus, Professor Himmelberg concluded,

> Section chiefs in their recommendations to the Board consistently followed the wishes of their industries in urging protection if the industry expected price declines and release of all controls when the industry expected a favorable postwar market.[58]

Robert S. Brookings, Chairman of the Price-Fixing Committee of the WIB, declared that the WIB would be "as helpful ... during the reconstruction period as we have during the war period in stabilizing values."[59]

From the big-business world, meanwhile, Harry A. Wheeler, president of the United States Chamber of Commerce, presented to Woodrow Wilson in early October 1918, an ambitious scheme for a "Reconstruction Commission," to be composed of all the economic interests of the nation.

The WIB itself concurred and urged the president to allow it to continue after the war. Baruch himself urged on Wilson the continuation of at least the minimum price-fixing policies of the WIB. However, Baruch was gulling the public when he foresaw a postwar WIB as guarding against

---

[58]Robert F. Himmelburg, "The War Industries Board and the Antitrust Question in November 1918," *Journal of American History* (June, 1965): 65.

[59]Ibid.

both inflation and deflation; there was no inclination to impose maximum prices against inflation.

The great problem with these ambitious plans of both industry and government was President Wilson himself. Perhaps a lingering attachment to the ideals, or at least to the rhetoric, of free competition prevented the president from giving any favorable attention to these postwar schemes.[60] The attachment was particularly nourished by Secretary of War Newton D. Baker, of all Wilson's advisers the closest to a believer in *laissez-faire*. Throughout October 1918, Wilson rejected all of these proposals. The response of Baruch and the WIB was to put further pressure on Wilson during early November, by publicly predicting and urging that the WIB would definitely be needed during demobilization. Thus *The New York Times* reported, the day after the Armistice, that

> War Industries Board officials declared there would be
> much work for that organization to do. They foresee no
> serious industrial dislocation with the Government's grip
> on all war industries and material held tight.[61]

The president remained adamant, however, and on November 23 he ordered the complete disbanding of the WIB by the end of the year. The disappointed WIB officials accepted the decision without protest, partly because of expected congressional opposition to any attempt to continue, partly from the hostility to continued controls by those industries anticipating a boom. Thus, the shoe industry particularly chafed at any continuing controls.[62] The industries favoring controls, however, urged the WIB at least to ratify their own price *minima* and agreements for restricting production for the coming winter, and to do so just before the disbandment of the agency. The Board was sorely tempted to engage in this final exploit, and indeed was informed by its legal staff that it could successfully continue such controls beyond the life of the agency even against the will of the president. The WIB, however, reluctantly turned down requests to this effect by the acid, zinc, and steel manufacturers on December 11.[63]

---

[60]Ibid., pp. 63–64; Urofsky, *Big Steel and the Wilson Administration*, pp. 298–99.

[61]Quoted in Himmelburg, "The War Industries Board," p. 64.

[62]Favoring continuing price controls were such industries as the chemical, iron and steel, lumber, and finished products generally. Opposing industries included abrasives, automotive products, and newspapers. Ibid., pp. 62, 65, 67.

[63]Urofsky, *Big Steel and the Wilson Administration*, pp. 306–07.

It only rejected the price-fixing plans, however, because it feared being overturned by the courts should the Attorney General challenge such a decision.

One of the most ardent advocates of continued WIB price control was the great steel industry. Two days after the Armistice, Judge Gary of U.S. Steel urged the WIB to continue its regulations and declared that "The members of the steel industry desire to cooperate with each other in every proper way." Gary urged a three-month extension of price fixing, with further gradual reductions that would prevent a return to "destructive" competition. Baruch replied that he was personally "willing to go to the very limit," but he was blocked by Wilson's attitude.[64]

If the WIB itself could not continue, perhaps the wartime cartelization could persist in other forms. During November, Arch W. Shaw, Chicago industrialist and head of the Conservation Division of the WIB (whose wartime work in fostering standardization was being transferred to the Department of Commerce) and Secretary of Commerce William Redfield agreed on a bill to allow manufacturers to collaborate in "the adoption of plans for the elimination of needless waste in the public interest," under the supervision of the Federal Trade Commission. When this proposal fizzled, Edwin B. Parker, Priorities Commissioner of the WIB, proposed in late November a frankly cartelizing bill that would allow the majority of the firms in any given industry to set production quotas that would have to be obeyed by all the firms in that industry. The Parker plan won the approval of Baruch, Peek, and numerous other government officials and businessmen, but WIB's legal counsel warned that Congress would never give its consent.[65] Another proposal that interested Baruch was advanced by Mark Requa, Assistant Food Administrator, who proposed a United States Board of Trade to encourage and regulate industrial agreements that "promoted the national welfare."[66]

Whatever the reason, Bernard Baruch failed to press hard for these proposals, and so they died on the vine. If Baruch failed to press matters, however, his associate George Peek, head of the Finished Products Division of the WIB, was not so reticent. By mid-December 1918, Peek wrote

[64]Ibid., pp. 294–302.

[65]Himmelberg, "The War Industries Board," pp. 70–71.

[66]Ibid., p. 72; Weinstein, *The Corporate Ideal in the Liberal State*, pp. 231–32.

Baruch that the postwar era must retain the "benefits of proper cooperation." In particular,

> proper legislation should be enacted to permit coopera-
> tion in industry, in order that the lessons we have learned
> during the war may be capitalized ... in peacetime ... Con-
> servation; ... standardization of products and processes,
> price fixing under certain conditions, etc., should con-
> tinue with Government cooperation.[67]

By late December, Peek was proposing legislation for

> some kind of an Emergency Peace Bureau ... in order that
> businessmen may, in conjunction with such a Bureau,
> have an opportunity to meet and cooperate with Govern-
> mental cooperation.[68]

The leading business groups endorsed similar plans. In early December, the Chamber of Commerce of the United States called a meeting of
the various industrial War Service Committees to convene as a "Reconstruction Congress of American Industry." The Reconstruction Congress
called for revision of the Sherman Act to permit "reasonable" trade agreements under a supervisory body. Furthermore, a nationwide Chamber
referendum, in early 1919, approved such a proposal by an overwhelming
majority, and President Harry Wheeler urged the "cordial acceptance by
organized business" of regulation that would ratify business agreements.
The National Association of Manufacturers, before the war devoted to
competition, warmly endorsed the same goals.

The last gasp of wartime cartelization came in February 1919, with the
establishment by the Department of Commerce of the Industrial Board.[69]
Secretary of Commerce William C. Redfield, formerly president of the
American Manufacturers Export Association, had long championed the
view that government should promote and coordinate industrial cooperation. Redfield saw an entering wedge with the transfer of the WIB's
Conservation Division to his department shortly after the Armistice. Red-

---

[67]Himmelberg, "The War Industries Board," p. 72.

[68]Robert D. Cuff, "A 'Dollar-a-Year Man' in Government: George N. Peek and the War
Industries Board," *Business History Review* (Winter 1967): 417.

[69]On the Industrial Board, see Robert F. Himmelberg, "Business, Antitrust Policy, and the
Industrial Board of the Department of Commerce, 1919," *Business History Review* (Spring
1968), pp. 1–23.

field continued the wartime stimulation of trade associations, and to that end established an advisory board of former WIB officials. One of these advisers was George Peek; another was Peek's assistant on the WIB, Ohio lumber executive William M. Ritter. It was Ritter, in fact, who originated the idea of the Industrial Board.

The Industrial Board, conceived by Ritter in January, 1919, and enthusiastically adopted and pushed by Secretary Redfield, was a cunning scheme. On its face, and as promoted to President Wilson and to others in the administration and Congress, the Board was merely a device to secure large price *reductions,* and thereby to lower the inflated level of general prices and to stimulate consumer demand. It was therefore seemingly unrelated to the previous cartelizing drive and hence won the approval of the president, who established the new Board in mid-February. At Ritter's urging, George Peek was named chairman of the IB; other members included Ritter himself, George R. James, head of a major Memphis dry-goods concern and former chief of the Cotton and Cotton Linters section of the WIB; Lewis B. Reed, vice president of the U.S. Silica Co. and another former assistant to Peek; steel castings manufacturer Samuel P. Bush, former head of the WIB's Facilities Division; Atlanta steel-fabricating manufacturer Thomas Glenn, also a veteran of the WIB; and two "outsiders," one representing the Labor Department and the other the Railroad Administration.

No sooner did the IB get under way than it pursued its real, but previously camouflaged, purpose: not to reduce, but rather to stabilize prices at existing high levels. Moreover, the method of stabilization would be the longed-for but previously rejected path of ratifying industrial price agreements arrived at in collaboration with the Board. Deciding on this cartelizing policy in early March, the IB moved toward the first application in a conference with, unsurprisingly, the steel industry on March 19–20, 1919. Opening the conference, Chairman George Peek grandly declared that the event might prove "epoch-making," especially in establishing "real genuine cooperation between Government, industry, and labor, so that we may eliminate ... the possibility of the destructive forces ..."[70] The steel men were of course delighted, hailing the "great chance ... to come into close contact with the Government itself ..."[71] The IB told the steel industry

---

[70]Himmelburg, "The War Industries Board," p. 13.

[71]Professor Urofsky surmised from the orderly and very moderate price reductions in steel during the first months of 1919 that Robert S. Brookings had quietly given the steel

that any agreement to sustain prices agreed upon by the conference would be immune from the antitrust laws. Not only was the price list offered by the IB to the steel men still very high even if moderately lower than existing prices; but Peek agreed to announce to the public that steel prices would not be lowered further for the remainder of the year. Peek advised the steel men that his statement would be their biggest asset, for "I don't know what I wouldn't have given in times past if in my own business I could say that the government of the United States says this is as low a price as you could get."[72]

The IB-steel agreement lowered steel prices by a modest 10% to 14%. The small, high-cost steel producers were disgruntled, but the big steel firms welcomed the agreement as a coordinated, orderly reduction of inflated prices, and especially welcomed the Board's guarantee of the fixed price for the remainder of the year.

The elated IB proceeded with similar conferences for the coal and building materials industries, but two dark clouds promptly appeared: the refusal of the government's own Railroad Administration to pay the fixed, agreed-upon, price for steel rails and for coal; and the concern of the Justice Department for the evident violation of the antitrust laws. The railroad men running the RA particularly balked at the reduced but still high price that they were going to be forced to pay for steel rails — at a rate that they declared was at least two dollars per ton above the free-market price. Walker D. Hines, head of the RA, denounced the IB as a price-fixing agency, dominated by steel and other industries, and he called for the abolition of the Industrial Board. This call was seconded by the powerful Secretary of the Treasury Carter Glass. The Attorney General concurred that the IB's policy was illegal price fixing and in violation of the antitrust laws. Finally, President Wilson dissolved the Industrial Board in early May, 1919; wartime industrial planning had at last been dissolved, its formal cartelization to reappear a decade and a half later.

Yet remnants of wartime collectivism still remained. The high wartime minimum wheat price of $2.26 a bushel was carried over to the 1919 crop, continuing until June, 1920. But the most important carry-over of war collectivism was the Railroad Administration: the government's operation of the nation's railroads. When William Gibbs McAdoo resigned as head

industry the green light to proceed with its own price fixing. Urofsky, *Big Steel and the Wilson Administration*, pp. 307–08.

[72]Himmelburg, "The War Industries Board," p. 14n.

of the RA at the end of the war, he was succeeded by the previous *de facto* operating head, railroad executive Walker D. Hines. There was no call for immediate return to private operation because the railroad industry generally agreed on drastic regulation to curb or eliminate "wasteful" railroad competition and coordinate the industry, to fix prices to ensure a "fair profit," and to outlaw strikes through compulsory arbitration. This was the overall thrust of railroad sentiment. Furthermore, being in effective control of the RA, the roads were in no hurry to return to private operation and jurisdiction by the less reliable ICC. Although McAdoo's plan to postpone by five years the given 1920 date for return to private operation gained little support, Congress proceeded to use its time during 1919 to tighten the monopolization of the railroads.

In the name of "scientific management," Senator Albert Cummins (R., Iowa) proceeded to grant the railroads' fondest dreams. Cummins' bill, warmly approved by Hines and railroad executive Daniel Willard, ordered the consolidation of numerous railroads, and would set the railroad rates according to a "fair," fixed return on capital investment. Strikes would be outlawed, and all labor disputes settled by compulsory arbitration. For their part, the Association of Railroad Executives submitted a legislative plan similar to the Cummins Bill. Also similar to the Cummins Bill was the proposal of the National Association of Owners of Railroad Securities, a group composed largely of savings banks and insurance companies. In contrast to these plans, the Citizens National Railroad League, consisting of individual railroad investors, proposed coerced consolidation into one national railroad corporation and the guaranteeing of minimum earnings to this new road.

All of these plans were designed to tip the prewar balance sharply in favor of the railroads and against the shippers, and, as a result, the Cummins Bill, in passing the Senate, ran into trouble in the House. The trouble was fomented by the shippers, who demanded a return to the status quo ante when the shipper-dominated ICC was in charge. Furthermore, for their part, the wartime experience had embittered the shippers, who, along with the ICC itself, demanded a return to the higher quality service provided by railroad competition rather than the increased monopolization provided by the various railroad bills. Unsurprisingly, however, one of the leading nonrailroad business groups favoring the Cummins Bill was the Railway Business Association, a group of manufacturers and distributors of railroad supplies and equipment. The House of Representatives, in its turn, passed the Esch Bill, which essentially reestablished the prewar rule of the ICC.

President Wilson had put pressure on Congress to make a decision by threatening the return of the railroads to private operation by the given date of January 1, 1920, but, under pressure of the railroads who were anxious to push the Cummins Bill, Wilson extended the deadline to March 1. Finally, the joint conference committee of Congress reported out the Transportation Act of 1920, a compromise that was essentially the Esch Bill returning the railroads to the prewar ICC, but adding the Cummins provisions for a two-year guarantee to the railroads to set rates providing a "fair return" of 5.5% on investment. Furthermore, on the agreement of both shippers and the roads, the power to set *minimum* railroad rates was now granted to the ICC. This agreement was the product of railroads eager to set a floor under freight rates, and shippers anxious to protect budding canal transportation against railroad competition. Furthermore, although railway union objections blocked the provision for the outlawing of strikes, a Railroad Labor Board was established to try to settle labor disputes.[73]

With the return of the railroads to private operation in March, 1920, war collectivism finally and at long last seemed to pass from the American scene. But pass it never really did; for the inspiration and the model that it furnished for a corporate state in America continued to guide Herbert Hoover and other leaders in the 1920s, and was to return full-blown in the New Deal and in the World War II economy. In fact, it supplied the broad outlines for the corporate monopoly state that the New Deal was to establish, seemingly permanently, in the United States of America.

---

[73]On the maneuvering leading to the Transportation Act of 1920, see Kerr, *American Railroad Politics*, pp. 128–227.

CHAPTER 13

World War I as Fulfillment: Power and the Intellectuals

1. INTRODUCTION

In contrast to older historians who regarded World War I as the destruction of progressive reform, I am convinced that the war came to the United States as the "fulfillment," the culmination, the veritable apotheosis of progressivism in American life.[1] I regard progressivism as basically a movement on behalf of Big Government in all walks of the economy and society, in a fusion or coalition between various groups of big businessmen, led by the House of Morgan, and rising groups of technocratic and statist intellectuals. In this fusion, the values and interests of both groups would be pursued through government. Big business would be able to use the government to cartelize the economy, restrict competition, and regulate production and prices, and also to be able to wield a militaristic and imperialist foreign policy to force open markets abroad and apply the sword of the State to protect foreign investments. Intellectuals would be able to use the government to restrict entry into their professions and to

---

Originally published in the *Journal of Libertarian Studies* 9, no. 1 (1989): 81–125.

[1] The title of this paper is borrowed from the pioneering last chapter of Weinstein's excellent work, *The Corporate Ideal in the Liberal State, 1900–1918*. The last chapter is entitled, "War as Fulfillment."

assume jobs in Big Government to apologize for, and to help plan and staff, government operations. Both groups also believed that, in this fusion, the Big State could be used to harmonize and interpret the "national interest" and thereby provide a "middle way" between the extremes of "dog-eat-dog" *laissez-faire* and the bitter conflicts of proletarian Marxism. Also animating both groups of progressives was a postmillennial pietist Protestantism that had conquered "Yankee" areas of northern Protestantism by the 1830s and had impelled the pietists to use local, state, and finally federal governments to stamp out "sin," to make America and eventually the world holy, and thereby to bring about the Kingdom of God on earth. The victory of the Bryanite forces at the Democratic national convention of 1896 destroyed the Democratic Party as the vehicle of "liturgical" Roman Catholics and German Lutherans devoted to personal liberty and *laissez-faire* and created the roughly homogenized and relatively non-ideological party system we have today. After the turn of the century, this development created an ideological and power vacuum for the expanding number of progressive technocrats and administrators to fill. In that way, the locus of government shifted from the legislature, at least partially subject to democratic check, to the oligarchic and technocratic executive branch.

World War I brought the fulfillment of all these progressive trends. Militarism, conscription, massive intervention at home and abroad, a collectivized war economy, all came about during the war and created a mighty cartelized system that most of its leaders spent the rest of their lives trying to recreate, in peace as well as war. In the World War I chapter of his outstanding work, *Crisis and Leviathan*, Professor Robert Higgs concentrates on the war economy and illuminates the interconnections with conscription. In this paper, I would like to concentrate on an area that Professor Higgs relatively neglects: the coming to power during the war of the various groups of progressive intellectuals.[2] I use the term "intellectual" in the broad sense penetratingly described by F.A. Hayek: that is, not merely theorists and academicians, but also all manner of opinion-molders in society — writers, journalists, preachers, scientists, activists of all sort — what Hayek calls "secondhand dealers in ideas."[3]

---

[2]Higgs, *Crisis and Leviathan*, pp. 123–58. For my own account of the collectivized war economy of World War I, see Rothbard, "War Collectivism in World War I," pp. 66–110. [Editor's remarks] See Chapter 12 above.

[3]F.A. Hayek, "The Intellectuals and Socialism," in *Studies in Philosophy, Politics and Economics*

Most of these intellectuals, of whatever strand or occupation, were either dedicated, messianic postmillennial pietists or else former pietists, born in a deeply pietist home, who, though now secularized, still possessed an intense messianic belief in national and world salvation through Big Government. But, in addition, oddly but characteristically, most combined in their thought and agitation messianic moral or religious fervor with an empirical, allegedly "value-free," and strictly "scientific" devotion to social science. Whether it be the medical profession's combined scientific and moralistic devotion to stamping out sin or a similar position among economists or philosophers, this blend is typical of progressive intellectuals.

In this paper, I will be dealing with various examples of individual or groups of progressive intellectuals, exulting in the triumph of their creed and their own place in it, as a result of America's entry into World War I. Unfortunately, limitations of space and time preclude dealing with all facets of the wartime activity of progressive intellectuals; in particular, I regret having to omit treatment of the conscription movement, a fascinating example of the creed of the "therapy" of "discipline" led by upper-class intellectuals and businessmen in the J.P. Morgan ambit.[4] I shall also have to omit both the highly significant trooping to the war colors of the nation's preachers, and the wartime impetus toward the permanent centralization of scientific research.[5]

There is no better epigraph for the remainder of this paper than a congratulatory note sent to President Wilson after the delivery of his war message on April 2, 1917. The note was sent by Wilson's son-in-law and

---

(Chicago: University of Chicago Press, 1967), pp. 178ff.

[4]On the conscription movement, see in particular Michael Pearlman, *To Make Democracy Safe for America: Patricians and Preparedness in the Progressive Era* (Urbana: University of Illinois Press, 1984). See also John W. Chambers II, "Conscripting for Colossus: The Adoption of the Draft in the United States in World War I" (Ph.D. diss., Columbia University, 1973); John Patrick Finnegan, *Against the Specter of a Dragon: the Campaign for American Military Preparedness, 1914–1917* (Westport, CT: Greenwood Press, 1974); and John Gany Clifford, *The Citizen Soldiers: The Plattsburg Training Camp Movement* (Lexington: University Press of Kentucky, 1972).

[5]On ministers and the war, see Ray H. Abrams, *Preachers Present Arms* (New York: Round Table Press, 1933). On the mobilization of science, see David F. Noble, *America By Design: Science, Technology and the Rise of Corporate Capitalism* (New York: Oxford University Press, 1977), and Ronald C. Tobey, *The American Ideology of National Science, 1919–1930* (Pittsburgh: University of Pittsburgh Press, 1971). [Editor's footnote] See below, pp. 453–61.

fellow Southern pietist and progressive, Secretary of the Treasury William Gibbs McAdoo, a man who had spent his entire life as an industrialist in New York City, solidly in the J.P. Morgan ambit. McAdoo wrote to Wilson: "You have done a great thing nobly! I firmly believe that it is God's will that America should do this transcendent service for humanity throughout the world and that you are His chosen instrument."[6] It was not a sentiment with which the president could disagree.

2. PIETISM AND PROHIBITION

One of the few important omissions in Professor Higgs's book is the crucial role of postmillennial pietist Protestantism in the drive toward statism in the United States. Dominant in the "Yankee" areas of the North from the 1830s on, the aggressive "evangelical" form of pietism conquered Southern Protestantism by the 1890s and played a crucial role in progressivism after the turn of the century and through World War I. Evangelical pietism held that requisite to any man's salvation is that he do his best to see to it that everyone else is saved, and doing one's best inevitably meant that the State must become a crucial instrument in maximizing people's chances for salvation. In particular, the State plays a pivotal role in stamping out sin, and in "making America holy." To the pietists, sin was very broadly defined as any force that might cloud men's minds so that they could not exercise their theological free will to achieve salvation. Of particular importance were slavery (until the Civil War), Demon Rum, and the Roman Catholic Church, headed by the Antichrist in Rome. For decades after the Civil War, "rebellion" took the place of slavery in the pietist charges against their great political enemy, the Democratic Party.[7] Then in 1896, with the evangelical conversion of Southern Protestantism and the admission to the Union of the sparsely populated and pietist Mountain states, William Jennings Bryan was able to put together a coalition that transformed the Democrats into a pietist party and ended forever that party's once proud

---

[6]Cited in Gerald Edward Markowitz, "Progressive Imperialism: Consensus and Conflict in the Progressive Movement on Foreign Policy, 1898–1917" (Ph.D. diss., University of Wisconsin, 1971), p. 375, an unfortunately neglected work on a highly important topic.

[7]Hence the famous imprecation hurled at the end of the 1884 campaign that brought the Democrats into the presidency for the first time since the Civil War, that the Democratic Party was the party of "Rum, Romanism, and Rebellion." In that one phrase, the New York Protestant minister was able to sum up the political concerns of the pietist movement.

role as the champion of "liturgical" (Catholic and High German Lutheran) Christianity and of personal liberty and *laissez-faire*.[8,9]

The pietists of the 19th and early 20th centuries were all postmillennialist: They believed that the Second Advent of Christ will occur only *after* the millennium — a thousand years of the establishment of the Kingdom of God on earth — has been brought about by human effort. Postmillennialists have therefore tended to be statists, with the State becoming an important instrument of stamping out sin and Christianizing the social order so as to speed Jesus' return.[10]

Professor Timberlake neatly sums up this politico-religious conflict:

> Unlike those extremist and apocalyptic sects that rejected and withdrew from the world as hopelessly corrupt, and unlike the more conservative churches, such as the Roman Catholic, Protestant Episcopal, and Lutheran, that tended to assume a more relaxed attitude toward the influence of religion in culture, evangelical Protestantism sought to overcome the corruption of the world in a dynamic manner, not only by converting men to belief in Christ but also by Christianizing the social order through the power

---

[8]For an introduction to the growing literature of "ethnoreligious" political history in the United States, see Kleppner, *The Cross of Culture*; and idem, *The Third Electoral System*. For the latest research on the formation of the Republican Party as a pietist party, reflecting the interconnected triad of pietist concerns — antislavery, prohibition, and anti-Catholicism — see Gienapp, "Nativism and the Creation of a Republican Majority in the North before the Civil War," pp. 529–59.

[9]German Lutherans were largely "high" or liturgical and confessional Lutherans who placed emphasis on the Church and its creed or sacraments rather than on a pietist, "born-again" emotional conversion experience. Scandinavian-Americans, on the other hand, were mainly pietist Lutherans.

[10]Orthodox Augustinian Christianity, as followed by the liturgicals, is "a-millennialist," i.e., it believes that the "millennium" is simply a metaphor for the emergence of the Christian Church and that Jesus will return without human aid and at his own unspecified time. Modern "fundamentalists," as they have been called since the early years of the 20th century, are "premillennialists," i.e., they believe that Jesus will return to usher in a thousand years of the Kingdom of God on Earth, a time marked by various "tribulations" and by Armageddon, until history is finally ended. Premillennialists, or "millennarians," do not have the statist drive of the postmillennialists; instead, they tend to focus on predictions and signs of Armageddon and of Jesus' advent.

and force of law. According to this view, the Christian's duty was to use the secular power of the state to transform culture so that the community of the faithful might be kept pure and the work of saving the unregenerate might be made easier. Thus the function of law was not simply to restrain evil but to educate and uplift.[11]

Both prohibition and progressive reform were pietistic, and as both movements expanded after 1900 they became increasingly intertwined. The Prohibition Party, once confined — at least in its platform — to a single issue, became increasingly and frankly progressive after 1904. The Anti-Saloon League, the major vehicle for prohibitionist agitation after 1900, was also markedly devoted to progressive reform. Thus at the League's annual convention in 1905, Rev. Howard H. Russell rejoiced in the growing movement for progressive reform and particularly hailed Theodore Roosevelt as that "leader of heroic mould, of absolute honesty of character and purity of life, that foremost man of this world ..."[12] At the Anti-Saloon League's convention of 1909, Rev. Purley A. Baker lauded the labor union movement as a holy crusade for justice and a square deal. The League's 1915 convention, which attracted 10,000 people, was noted for the same blend of statism, social service, and combative Christianity that had marked the national convention of the Progressive Party in 1912.[13]

---

[11]James H. Timberlake, *Prohibition and the Progressive Movement, 1900–1920* (New York: Atheneum, 1970), pp. 7–8.

[12]Quoted in ibid., p. 33.

[13]The Progressive Party convention was a mighty fusion of all the major trends in the progressive movement: statist economists, technocrats, social engineers, social workers, professional pietists, and partners of J.P. Morgan & Co. Social Gospel leaders Lyman Abbott, the Rev. R. Heber Newton and the Rev. Washington Gladden, were leading Progressive Party delegates. The Progressive Party proclaimed itself as the "recrudescence of the religious spirit in American political life." Theodore Roosevelt's acceptance speech was significantly entitled "A Confession of Faith," and his words were punctuated by "amens" and by a continual singing of pietist Christian hymns by the assembled delegates. They sang "Onward Christian Soldiers," "The Battle Hymn of the Republic," and especially the revivalist hymn, "Follow, Follow, We Will Follow Jesus," with the word "Roosevelt" replacing "Jesus" at every turn. The horrified *New York Times* summed up the unusual experience by calling the Progressive grouping "a convention of fanatics." And it added, "It was not a convention at all. It was an assemblage of religious enthusiasts. It was such a convention as Peter the Hermit held. It was a Methodist camp following done over into political terms." Cited in Gable, *The Bull Moose Years*, p. 75.

And at the League's June 1916 convention, Bishop Luther B. Wilson stated, without contradiction, that everyone present would undoubtedly hail the progressive reforms then being proposed.

During the Progressive years, the Social Gospel became part of the mainstream of pietist Protestantism. Most of the evangelical churches created commissions on social service to promulgate the Social Gospel, and virtually all of the denominations adopted the Social Creed drawn up in 1912 by the Commission of the Church and Social Service of the Federal Council of Churches. The creed called for the abolition of child labor, the regulation of female labor, the right of labor to organize (i.e., compulsory collective bargaining), the elimination of poverty, and an "equitable" division of the national product. And right up there as a matter of social concern was the liquor problem. The creed maintained that liquor was a grave hindrance toward the establishment of the Kingdom of God on earth, and it advocated the "protection of the individual and society from the social, economic, and moral waste of the liquor traffic."[14]

The Social Gospel leaders were fervent advocates of statism and of prohibition. These included Rev. Walter Rauschenbusch and Rev. Charles Stelzle, whose tract *Why Prohibition!* (1918) was distributed, after the United States' entry into World War I, by the Commission on Temperance of the Federal Council of Churches to labor leaders, members of Congress, and important government officials. A particularly important Social Gospel leader was Rev. Josiah Strong, whose monthly journal, *The Gospel of the Kingdom*, was published by Strong's American Institute of Social Service. In an article supporting prohibition in the July 1914 issue, The Gospel of the Kingdom hailed the progressive spirit that was at last putting an end to "personal liberty":

> "Personal Liberty" is at last an uncrowned, dethroned king, with no one to do him reverence. The social consciousness is so far developed, and is becoming so autocratic, that institutions and governments must give heed to its mandate and share their life accordingly. We are no longer frightened by that ancient bogy — "paternalism in government." We affirm boldly, it is the business of government to

---

[14]Timberlake, *Prohibition and the Progressive Movement*, p. 24.

> be just that — Paternal. ... *Nothing human can be foreign
> to a true government.*[15]

As true crusaders, the pietists were not content to stop with the stamping out of sin in the United States alone. If American pietism was convinced that Americans were God's chosen people, destined to establish a Kingdom of God within the United States, surely the pietists' religious and moral duty could not stop there. In a sense, the world was America's oyster. As Professor Timberlake put it, once the Kingdom of God was in the course of being established in the United States, "it was therefore America's mission to spread these ideals and institutions abroad so that the Kingdom could be established throughout the world. American Protestants were accordingly not content merely to work for the kingdom of God in America, but felt compelled to assist in the reformation of the rest of the world also."[16]

American entry into World War I provided the fulfillment of prohibitionist dreams. In the first place, all food production was placed under the control of Herbert Hoover, Food Administration Czar. But if the U.S. government was to control and allocate food resources, shall it permit the precious scarce supply of grain to be siphoned off into the "waste," if not the sin, of the manufacture of liquor? Even though less than 2% of American cereal production went into the manufacture of alcohol, think of the starving children of the world who might otherwise be fed. As the progressive weekly *The Independent* demagogically phrased it, "Shall the many have food, or the few have drink?"

For the ostensible purpose of "conserving" grain, Congress wrote an amendment into the Lever Food and Fuel Control Act of August 10, 1917, that absolutely prohibited the use of foodstuffs, hence grain, in the production of alcohol. Congress would have added a prohibition on the manufacture of wine or beer, but President Wilson persuaded the Anti-Saloon League that he could accomplish the same goal more slowly and thereby avoid a delaying filibuster by the wets in Congress. However, Her-

---

[15]Quoted in Timberlake, *Prohibition and the Progressive Movement*, p. 27. Italics in the article. Or, as the Rev. Stelzle put it, in *Why Prohibition!*, "There is no such thing as an absolute individual right to do any particular thing, or to eat or drink any particular thing, or to enjoy the association of one's own family, or even to live, if that thing is in conflict with the law of public necessity." Quoted in David E. Kyvig, *Repealing National Prohibition* (Chicago: University of Chicago Press, 1979), p. 9.

[16]Timberlake, *Prohibition and the Progressive Movement*, pp. 37–38.

bert Hoover, a progressive and a prohibitionist, persuaded Wilson to issue an order, on December 8, both greatly reducing the alcoholic content of beer and limiting the amount of foodstuffs that could be used in its manufacture.[17]

The prohibitionists were able to use the Lever Act and war patriotism to good effect. Thus, Mrs. W.E. Lindsey, wife of the governor of New Mexico, delivered a speech in November 1917 that noted the Lever Act, and declared:

> Aside from the long list of awful tragedies following in the wake of the liquor traffic, the economic waste is too great to be tolerated at this time. With so many people of the allied nations near to the door of starvation, it would be criminal ingratitude for us to continue the manufacture of whiskey.[18]

Another rationale for prohibition during the war was the alleged necessity to protect American soldiers from the dangers of alcohol to their health, their morals, and their immortal souls. As a result, in the Selective Service Act of May 18, 1917, Congress provided that dry zones must be established around every army base, and it was made illegal to sell or even to give liquor to any member of the military establishment within those zones, even in one's private home. Any inebriated servicemen were subject to courts-martial.

But the most severe thrust toward national prohibition was the Anti-Saloon League's proposed 18th constitutional amendment, outlawing the manufacture, sale, transportation, import, or export of all intoxicating liquors. It was passed by Congress and submitted to the states at the end of December 1917. Wet arguments that prohibition would prove unenforceable were met with the usual dry appeal to high principle: Should laws against murder and robbery be repealed simply because they cannot be completely enforced? And arguments that private property would

---

[17]See David Burner, *Herbert Hoover: A Public Life* (New York: Alfred A. Knopf, 1979), p. 107.

[18]James A. Burran, "Prohibition in New Mexico, 1917," *New Mexico Historical Quarterly* 48 (April, 1973): 140–41. Mrs. Lindsey of course showed no concern whatever for the German, allied, and neutral countries of Europe being subjected to starvation by the British naval blockade.

The only areas of New Mexico that resisted the prohibition crusade in the referendum in the November 1917 elections were the heavily Hispanic-Catholic districts.

be unjustly confiscated were also brushed aside with the contention that property injurious to the health, morals, and safety of the people had always been subject to confiscation without compensation.

When the Lever Act made a distinction between hard liquor (forbidden) and beer and wine (limited), the brewing industry tried to save their skins by cutting themselves loose from the taint of distilled spirits. "The true relationship with beer," insisted the United States Brewers Association, "is with light wines and soft drinks — not with hard liquors ..." The brewers affirmed their desire to "sever, once for all, the shackles that bound our wholesome productions ... to ardent spirits ..." But this craven attitude would do the brewers no good. After all, one of the major objectives of the drys was to smash the brewers, once and for all, they whose product was the very embodiment of the drinking habits of the hated German-American masses, both Catholic and Lutheran, liturgicals and beer drinkers all. German-Americans were now fair game. Were they not all agents of the satanic Kaiser, bent on conquering the world? Were they not conscious agents of the dreaded Hun *Kultur*, out to destroy American civilization? And were not most brewers German?

And so the Anti-Saloon League thundered that "German brewers in this country have rendered thousands of men inefficient and are thus crippling the Republic in its war on Prussian militarism." Apparently, the Anti-Saloon League took no heed of the work of German brewers *in Germany*, who were presumably performing the estimable service of rendering "Prussian militarism" helpless. The brewers were accused of being pro-German, and of subsidizing the press (apparently it was all right to be pro-English or to subsidize the press if one were not a brewer). The acme of the accusations came from one prohibitionist: "We have German enemies," he warned, "in this country too. And the worst of all our German enemies, the most treacherous, the most menacing are Pabst, Schlitz, Blatz, and Miller."[19]

In this sort of atmosphere, the brewers didn't have a chance, and the 18th Amendment went to the states, outlawing all forms of liquor. Since 27 states had already outlawed liquor, this meant that only nine more were needed to ratify this remarkable amendment, which directly involved the federal constitution in what had always been, at most, a matter of police power of the states. The 36th state ratified the 18th Amendment on Janu-

---

[19]Timberlake, *Prohibition and the Progressive Movement*, p. 179.

ary 16, 1919, and by the end of February, all but three states (New Jersey, Rhode Island, and Connecticut) had made liquor unconstitutional as well as illegal. Technically, the amendment went into force the following January, but Congress speeded matters up by passing the War Prohibition Act of November 21, 1918, which banned the manufacture of beer and wine after the following May and outlawed the sale of all intoxicating beverages after June 30, 1919, a ban to continue in effect until the end of demobilization. Thus total national prohibition really began on July 1, 1919, with the 18th Amendment taking over six months later. The constitutional amendment needed a congressional enforcing act, which Congress supplied with the Volstead (or National Prohibition) Act, passed over Wilson's veto at the end of October 1919.

With the battle against Demon Rum won at home, the restless advocates of pietist prohibitionism looked for new lands to conquer. Today America, tomorrow the world. In June 1919, the triumphant Anti-Saloon League called an international prohibition conference in Washington and created a World League Against Alcoholism. World prohibition, after all, was needed to finish the job of making the world safe for democracy. The prohibitionists' goals were fervently expressed by Rev. A.C. Bane at the Anti-Saloon League's 1917 convention, when victory in America was already in sight. To a wildly cheering throng, Bane thundered:

> America will "go over the top" in humanity's greatest battle [against liquor] and plant the victorious white standard of Prohibition upon the nation's loftiest eminence. Then catching sight of the beckoning hand of our sister nations across the sea, struggling with the same age-long foe, we will go forth with the spirit of the missionary and the crusader to help drive the demon of drink from all civilization. With America leading the way, with faith in Omnipotent God, and bearing with patriotic hands our stainless flag, the emblem of civic purity, we will soon ... bestow upon mankind the priceless gift of World Prohibition.[20]

Fortunately, the prohibitionists found the reluctant world a tougher nut to crack.

---

[20]Quoted in ibid., pp. 180–81.

3. Women at War and at the Polls

Another direct outgrowth of World War I, coming in tandem with prohibition but lasting more permanently, was the 19th Amendment, submitted by Congress in 1919 and ratified by the following year, which allowed women to vote. Women's suffrage had long been a movement directly allied with prohibition. Desperate to combat a demographic trend that seemed to be going against them, the evangelical pietists called for women's suffrage (and enacted it in many western states). They did so because they knew that while pietist women were socially and politically active, ethnic or liturgical women tended to be culturally bound to hearth and home and therefore far less likely to vote. Hence, women's suffrage would greatly increase pietist voting power. In 1869 the Prohibitionist Party became the first party to endorse women's suffrage, which it continued to do. The Progressive Party was equally enthusiastic about female suffrage; it was the first major national party to permit women delegates at its conventions. A leading women's suffrage organization was the Women's Christian Temperance Union, which reached an enormous membership of 300,000 by 1900. And three successive presidents of the major women's suffrage group, the National American Woman Suffrage Association — Susan B. Anthony, Mrs. Carrie Chapman Catt, and Dr. Anna Howard Shaw — all began their activist careers as prohibitionists. Susan B. Anthony put the issue clearly:

> There is an enemy of the homes of this nation and that enemy is drunkenness. Everyone connected with the gambling house, the brothel and the saloon works and votes solidly against the enfranchisement of women, and, I say, if you believe in chastity, if you believe in honesty and integrity, then ... take the necessary steps to put the ballot in the hands of women.[21]

For its part, the German-American Alliance of Nebraska sent out an appeal during the unsuccessful referendum in November 1914 on woman suffrage. Written in German, the appeal declared, "Our German women do not want the right to vote, and since our opponents desire the right of

---

[21]Quoted in Grimes, *The Puritan Ethic and Woman Suffrage*, p. 78.

suffrage mainly for the purpose of saddling the yoke of prohibition on our necks, we should oppose it with all our might ..."[22]

America's entry into World War I provided the impetus for overcoming the substantial opposition to woman suffrage, as a corollary to the success of prohibition and as a reward for the vigorous activity by organized women in behalf of the war effort. To close the loop, much of that activity consisted in stamping out vice and alcohol as well as instilling "patriotic" education into the minds of often suspect immigrant groups.

Shortly after the U.S. declaration of war, the Council of National Defense created an Advisory Committee on Women's Defense Work, known as the Woman's Committee. The purpose of the committee, writes a celebratory contemporary account, was "to coordinate the activities and the resources of the organized and unorganized women of the country, that their power may be immediately utilized in time of need, and to supply a new and direct channel of cooperation between women and governmental department."[23] Chairman of the Woman's Committee, working energetically and full time, was the former president of the National American Woman Suffrage Association, Dr. Anna Howard Shaw, and another leading member was the suffrage group's current chairman and an equally prominent suffragette, Mrs. Carrie Chapman Catt.

The Woman's Committee promptly set up organizations in cities and states across the country and on June 19, 1917, convened a conference of over 50 national women's organizations to coordinate their efforts. It was at this conference that "the first definite task was imposed upon American women" by the indefatigable Food Czar, Herbert Hoover.[24] Hoover enlisted the cooperation of the nation's women in his ambitious campaign for controlling, restricting, and cartelizing the food industry in the name of "conservation" and elimination of "waste." Celebrating this coming together of women was one of the Woman's Committee members, the Progressive writer and muckraker Mrs. Ida M. Tarbell. Mrs. Tarbell lauded the "growing consciousness everywhere that this great enterprise for democracy which we are launching [the U.S. entry into the war] is a national affair, and if an individual or a society is going to do its bit it must act with

---

[22]Ibid., p. 116.

[23]Ida Clyde Clarke, *American Women and the World War* (New York: D. Appleton and Co., 1918), p. 19.

[24]Ibid., p. 27.

and under the government at Washington." "Nothing else," Mrs. Tarbell gushed, "can explain the action of the women of the country in coming together as they are doing today under one centralized direction."[25]

Mrs. Tarbell's enthusiasm might have been heightened by the fact that she was one of the *directing* rather than the *directed*. Herbert Hoover came to the women's conference with the proposal that each of the women sign and distribute a "food pledge card" on behalf of food conservation. While support for the food pledge among the public was narrower than anticipated, educational efforts to promote the pledge became the basis of the remainder of the women's conservation campaign. The Woman's Committee appointed Mrs. Tarbell as chairman of its committee on Food Administration, and she not only tirelessly organized the campaign but also wrote many letters and newspaper and magazine articles on its behalf.

In addition to food control, another important and immediate function of the Woman's Committee was to attempt to register every woman in the country for possible volunteer or paid work in support of the war effort. Every woman aged 16 or over was asked to sign and submit a registration card with all pertinent information, including training, experience, and the sort of work desired. In that way the government would know the whereabouts and training of every woman, and government and women could then serve each other best. In many states, especially Ohio and Illinois, state governments set up schools to train the registrars. And even though the Woman's Committee kept insisting that the registration was completely voluntary, the state of Louisiana, as Ida Clarke puts it, developed a "novel and clever" idea to facilitate the program: women's registration was made compulsory.

Louisiana's Governor Ruffin G. Pleasant decreed October 17, 1917 compulsory registration day, and a host of state officials collaborated in its operation. The State Food Commission made sure that food pledges were also signed by all, and the State School Board granted a holiday on October 17 so that teachers could assist in the compulsory registration, especially in the rural districts. Six thousand women were officially commissioned by the state of Louisiana to conduct the registration, and they worked in tandem with state Food Conservation officials and parish Demonstration

---

[25]Ibid., p. 31. Actually Mrs. Tarbell's muckraking activities were pretty much confined to Rockefeller and Standard Oil. She was highly favorable to business leaders in the Morgan ambit, as witness her laudatory biographies of Judge Elbert H. Gary, of U.S. Steel (1925) and Owen D. Young of General Electric (1932).

Agents. In the French areas of the state, the Catholic priests rendered valuable aid in personally appealing to all their female parishioners to perform their registration duties. Handbills were circulated in French, house-to-house canvasses were made, and speeches urging registration were made by women activists in movie theaters, schools, churches, and courthouses. We are informed that all responses were eager and cordial; there is no mention of any resistance. We are also advised that "even the negroes were quite alive to the situation, meeting sometimes with the white people and sometimes at the call of their own pastors."[26]

Also helping out in women's registration and food control was another, smaller, but slightly more sinister women's organization that had been launched by Congress as a sort of prewar wartime group at a large Congress for Constructive Patriotism, held in Washington, D.C. in late January 1917. This was the National League for Woman's Service (NLWS), which established a nationwide organization later overshadowed and overlapped by the larger Woman's Committee. The difference was that the NLWS was set up on quite frankly military lines. Each local working unit was called a "detachment" under a "detachment commander," district-wide and state-wide detachments met in annual "encampments," and every woman member was to wear a uniform with an organization badge and insignia. In particular, "the basis of training for all detachments is standardized, physical drill."[27]

A vital part of the Woman's Committee work was engaging in "patriotic education." The government and the Woman's Committee recognized that immigrant ethnic women were most in need of such vital instruction, and so it set up a committee on education, headed by the energetic Mrs. Carrie Chapman Catt. Mrs. Catt stated the problem well to the Woman's Committee: Millions of people in the United States were unclear on why we were at war, and why, as Ida Clarke paraphrases Mrs. Catt, there is "the imperative necessity of winning the war if future generations were to be protected from the menace of an unscrupulous militarism."[28] Presumably U.S. militarism, being "scrupulous," posed no problem.

Apathy and ignorance abounded, Mrs. Catt went on, and she proposed to mobilize 20 million American women, the "greatest sentiment

---

[26]Ibid., pp. 277, 275–79, 58.

[27]Ibid., p. 183.

[28]Ibid., p. 103.

makers of any community," to begin a "vast educational movement" to get the women "fervently enlisted to push the war to victory as rapidly as possible." As Mrs. Catt continued, however, the clarity of war aims she called for really amounted to pointing out that we were in the war "whether the nation likes it or does not like it," and that therefore the "sacrifices" needed to win the war "willingly or unwillingly must be made." These statements are reminiscent of arguments supporting recent military actions by Ronald Reagan ("He had to do what he had to do"). In the end, Mrs. Catt could come up with only one reasoned argument for the war, apart from this alleged necessity: that it must be won to make it "the war to end wars."[29]

The "patriotic education" campaign of the organized women was largely to "Americanize" immigrant women by energetically persuading them (a) to become naturalized American citizens and (b) to learn "Mother English." In the campaign, dubbed "America First," national unity was promoted through getting immigrants to learn English and trying to get female immigrants into afternoon or evening English classes. The organized patriot women were also worried about preserving the family structure of the immigrants. If the children learn English and their parents remain ignorant, children will scorn their elders, "parental discipline and control are dissipated, and the whole family fabric becomes weakened. Thus one of the great conservative forces in the community becomes inoperative." To preserve "maternal control of the young," then, "Americanization of the foreign women through language becomes imperative." In Erie, Pennsylvania, women's clubs appointed "Block Matrons," whose job it was to get to know the foreign families of the neighborhood and to back up school authorities in urging the immigrants to learn English, and who, in the rather naive words of Ida Clarke, "become neighbors, friends, and veritable mother confessors to the foreign women of the block." One would like to have heard some comments from recipients of the attentions of the Block Matrons.

All in all, as a result of the Americanization campaign, Ida Clarke concludes, "the organized women of this country can play an important part in making ours a country with a common language, a common purpose, a common set of ideals — a unified America."[30]

Neither did the government and its organized women neglect progressive economic reforms. At the organizing June 1917 conference of

---

[29]Ibid., pp. 104–05.

[30]Ibid., p. 101.

the Woman's Committee, Mrs. Carrie Catt emphasized that the greatest problem of the war was to assure that women receive "equal pay for equal work." The conference suggested that vigilance committees be established to guard against the violation of "ethical laws" governing labor and also that all laws restricting ("protecting") the labor of women and children be rigorously enforced. Apparently, there were some values to which maximizing production for the war effort had to take second place. Mrs. Margaret Dreier Robins, president of the National Women's Trade Union's League, hailed the fact that the Woman's Committee was organizing committees in every state to protect minimum standards for women and children's labor in industry and demanded minimum wages and shorter hours for women. Mrs. Robins particularly warned that "not only are unorganized women workers in vast numbers used as underbidders in the labor market for lowering industrial standards, but they are related to those groups in industrial centers of our country that are least Americanized and most alien to our institutions and ideals." And so "Americanization" and cartelization of female labor went hand in hand.[31,32]

---

[31]Ibid., p. 129. Margaret Dreier Robins and her husband Raymond were virtually a paradigmatic progressive couple. Raymond was a Florida-born wanderer and successful gold prospector who underwent a mystical conversion experience in the Alaska wilds and became a pietist preacher. He moved to Chicago, where he became a leader in Chicago settlement house work and municipal reform. Margaret Dreier and her sister Mary were daughters of a wealthy and socially prominent New York family who worked for and financed the emergent National Women's Trade Union League. Margaret married Raymond Robins in 1905 and moved to Chicago, soon becoming longtime president of the league. In Chicago, the Robinses led and organized progressive political causes for over two decades, becoming top leaders of the Progressive Party from 1912 to 1916. During the war, Raymond Robins engaged in considerable diplomatic activity as head of a Red Cross mission to Russia. On the Robinses, see Allen F. Davis, *Spearhead for Reform: the Social Settlements and the Progressive Movement, 1890–1914* (New York: Oxford University Press, 1967).

[32]For more on women's war work and woman suffrage, see the standard history of the suffrage movement, Flexner, *Century of Struggle*, pp. 288–89. Interestingly, The National War Labor Board (NWLB) frankly adopted the concept of "equal pay for equal work" in order to limit the employment of women workers by imposing higher costs on the employer. The "only check," affirmed the NWLB, on excessive employment of women "is to make it no more profitable to employ women than men." Quoted in Valerie I. Conner, "'The Mothers of the Race' in World War I: The National War Labor Board and Women in Industry," *Labor History* 21 (Winter 1979–80): 34.

414   The Progressive Era

4. SAVING OUR BOYS FROM ALCOHOL AND VICE

One of organized womanhood's major contributions to the war effort was to collaborate in an attempt to save American soldiers from vice and Demon Rum. In addition to establishing rigorous dry zones around every military camp in the United States, the Selective Service Act of May 1917 also outlawed prostitution in wide zones around the military camps. To enforce these provisions, the War Department had ready at hand a Commission on Training Camp Activities, an agency soon imitated by the Department of the Navy. Both commissions were headed by a man tailor-made for the job, the progressive New York settlement-house worker, municipal political reformer, and former student and disciple of Woodrow Wilson, Raymond Blaine Fosdick.

Fosdick's background, life, and career were paradigmatic for progressive intellectuals and activists of that era. Fosdick's ancestors were Yankees from Massachusetts and Connecticut, and his great-grandfather pioneered westward in a covered wagon to become a frontier farmer in the heart of the Burned-Over District of transplanted Yankees, Buffalo, New York. Fosdick's grandfather, a pietist lay preacher born again in a Baptist revival, was a prohibitionist who married a preacher's daughter and became a lifelong public school teacher in Buffalo. Grandfather Fosdick rose to become Superintendent of Education in Buffalo and a battler for an expanded and strengthened public school system.

Fosdick's immediate ancestry continued in the same vein. His father was a public school teacher in Buffalo who rose to become principal of a high school. His mother was deeply pietist and a staunch advocate of prohibition and women's suffrage. Fosdick's father was a devout pietist Protestant and a "fanatical" Republican who gave his son Raymond the middle name of his hero, the veteran Maine Republican James G. Blaine. The three Fosdick children, elder brother Harry Emerson, Raymond, and Raymond's twin sister, Edith, on emerging from this atmosphere, all forged lifetime careers of pietism and social service.

While active in New York reform administration, Fosdick made a fateful friendship. In 1910, John D. Rockefeller, Jr., like his father a pietist Baptist, was chairman of a special grand jury to investigate and to try to stamp out prostitution in New York City. For Rockefeller, the elimination of prostitution was to become an ardent and lifelong crusade. He believed that sin, such as prostitution, must be criminated, quarantined, and driven underground through rigorous suppression. In 1911, Rockefeller began his crusade by setting up the Bureau of Social Hygiene, into which he poured $5 million in the next quarter century. Two years later he enlisted Fosdick, already a speaker at the annual dinner of Rockefeller's Baptist Bible class, to study police systems in Europe in conjunction with activities to end the great "social vice." Surveying American police after his stint in Europe at Rockefeller's behest, Fosdick was appalled that police work in the United States was not considered a "science" and that it was subject to "sordid" political influences.[33]

At that point, the new Secretary of War, the progressive former mayor of Cleveland Newton D. Baker, became disturbed at reports that areas near the army camps in Texas on the Mexican border, where troops were mobilized to combat the Mexican revolutionary Pancho Villa, were honeycombed with saloons and prostitution. Sent by Baker on a fact-finding tour in the summer of 1916, scoffed at by tough army officers as the "Reverend," Fosdick was horrified to find saloons and brothels seemingly everywhere in the vicinity of the military camps. He reported his consternation to Baker, and, at Fosdick's suggestion, Baker cracked down on the army commanders and their lax attitude toward alcohol and vice. But Fosdick was beginning to get the glimmer of another idea. Couldn't the suppression of the bad be accompanied by a positive encouragement of the good, of wholesome recreational alternatives to sin and liquor that our boys could enjoy? When war was declared, Baker quickly appointed Fosdick to be chairman of the Commission on Training Camp Activities.

Armed with the coercive resources of the federal government and rapidly building his bureaucratic empire from merely one secretary to a staff of thousands, Raymond Fosdick set out with determination on his twofold task: stamping out alcohol and sin in and around every military camp, and filling the void for American soldiers and sailors by providing them with wholesome recreation. As head of the Law Enforcement Division of the Training Camp Commission, Fosdick selected Bascom Johnson, attorney for the American Social Hygiene Association.[34] Johnson was commissioned a major, and his staff of 40 aggressive attorneys became second lieutenants.

---

[33]See Raymond B. Fosdick, *Chronicle of a Generation: An Autobiography* (New York: Harper & Bros., 1958), p. 133. Also see Peter Collier and David Horowitz, *The Rockefellers: An American Dynasty* (New York: New American Library, 1976), pp. 103–05. Fosdick was particularly appalled that American patrolmen on street duty actually smoked cigars! Fosdick, *Chronicle of a Generation*, p. 135.

[34]The American Social Hygiene Association, with its influential journal *Social Hygiene*,

Employing the argument of health and military necessity, Fosdick set up a Social Hygiene Division of his commission, which promulgated the slogan "Fit to Fight." Using a mixture of force and threats to remove federal troops from the bases if recalcitrant cities did not comply, Fosdick managed to bludgeon his way into suppressing, if not prostitution in general, then at least every major red light district in the country. In doing so, Fosdick and Baker, employing local police and the federal Military Police, far exceeded their legal authority. The law authorized the president to shut down every red light district in a five-mile zone around each military camp or base. Of the 110 red light districts shut down by military force, however, only 35 were included in the prohibited zone. Suppression of the other 75 was an illegal extension of the law. Nevertheless, Fosdick was triumphant: "Through the efforts of this Commission [on Training Camp Activities] the red light district has practically ceased to be a feature of American city

was the major organization in what was known as the "purity crusade." The association was launched when the New York physician Dr. Prince A. Morrow, inspired by the agitation against venereal disease and in favor of the continence urged by the French syphilographer, Jean-Alfred Fournier, formed in 1905 the American Society for Sanitary and Moral Prophylaxis (ASSMP). Soon, the terms proposed by the Chicago branch of ASSMP, "social hygiene" and "sex hygiene," became widely used for their medical and scientific patina, and in 1910 ASSMP changed its name to the American Federation for Sex Hygiene (AFSH). Finally, in late 1913, AFSH, an organization of physicians, combined with the National Vigilance Association (formerly the American Purity Alliance), a group of clergymen and social workers, to form the all-embracing American Social Hygiene Association (ASHA).

In this social hygiene movement, the moral and medical went hand in hand. Thus Dr. Morrow welcomed the new knowledge about venereal disease because it demonstrated that "punishment for sexual sin" no longer had to be "reserved for the hereafter."

The first president of ASHA was the president of Harvard University, Charles W. Eliot. In his address to the first meeting, Eliot made clear that total abstinence from alcohol, tobacco, and even spices was part and parcel of the anti-prostitution and purity crusade.

On physicians, the purity crusade, and the formation of ASHA, see Ronald Hamowy, "Medicine and the Crimination of Sin: 'Self-Abuse' in 19th Century America," *Journal of Libertarian Studies* 1 (Summer 1972): 247–59; James Wunsch, "Prostitution and Public Policy: From Regulation to Suppression, 1858–1920" (Ph.D. diss., University of Chicago, 1976); and Roland R. Wagner, "Virtue Against Vice: A Study of Moral Reformers and Prostitution in the Progressive Era" (Ph.D. diss., University of Wisconsin, 1971). On Morrow, also see John C. Burnham. "The Progressive Era Revolution in American Attitudes Toward Sex," *Journal of American History* 59 (March, 1973): 899, and Paul Boyer, *Urban Masses and Moral Order in America, 1820–1920* (Cambridge, MA: Harvard University Press, 1978), p. 201. Also see Burnham, "Medical Specialists and Movements Toward Social Control in the Progressive Era: Three Examples," in *Building the Organizational Society: Essays in Associational Activities in Modern America,* J. Israel, ed. (New York: Free Press, 1972), pp. 24–26.

life."[35] The result of this permanent destruction of the red light district, of course, was to drive prostitution onto the streets, where consumers would be deprived of the protection of either an open market or of regulation.

In some cases, the federal anti-vice crusade met considerable resistance. Secretary of Navy Josephus Daniels, a progressive from North Carolina, had to call out the marines to patrol the streets of resistant Philadelphia, and naval troops, over the strenuous objections of the mayor, were used to crush the fabled red light district of Storyville, in New Orleans, in November 1917.[36]

In its hubris, the U.S. Army decided to extend its anti-vice crusade to foreign shores. General John J. Pershing issued an official bulletin to members of the American Expeditionary Force in France urging that "sexual continence is the plain duty of members of the A.E.F., both for the vigorous conduct of the war, and for the clean health of the American people after the war." Pershing and the American military tried to close all the French brothels in areas where American troops were located, but the move was unsuccessful because the French objected bitterly. Premier Georges Clemenceau pointed out that the result of the "total prohibition of regulated prostitution in the vicinity of American troops" was only to increase "venereal diseases among the civilian population of the neighborhood." Finally, the United States had to rest content with declaring French civilian areas off limits to the troops.[37]

The more positive part of Raymond Fosdick's task during the war was supplying the soldiers and sailors with a constructive substitute for

---

[35]In Daniel R. Beaver, *Newton D. Baker and the American War Effort, 1917–1919* (Lincoln: University of Nebraska Press, 1966), p. 222. Also see ibid., pp. 221–24; and C.H. Cramer, *Newton D. Baker: A Biography* (Cleveland: World Publishing Co., 1961), pp. 99–102.

[36]Fosdick, *Chronicle of a Generation*, pp. 145–47. While prostitution was indeed banned in Storyville after 1917, Storyville, contrary to legend, never "closed" — the saloons and dance halls remained open, and contrary to orthodox accounts, jazz was never really shut down in Storyville or New Orleans, and it was therefore never forced up river. For a revisionist view of the impact of the closure of Storyville on the history of jazz, see Tom Bethell, *George Lewis: A Jazzman from New Orleans* (Berkeley: University of California Press, 1977), pp. 6–7; and Al Rose, *Storyville, New Orleans* (Montgomery: University of Alabama Press, 1974). Also, on later Storyville, see Boyer, *Urban Masses and Moral Order*, p. 218.

[37]See Hamowy, "Crimination of Sin," p. 262 n. The quote from Clemenceau is in Fosdick, *Chronicle*, p. 171. Newton Baker's loyal biographer declared that Clemenceau, in this response, showed "his animal proclivities as the 'Tiger of France.'" Cramer, *Newton Baker*, p. 101.

sin and alcohol, "healthful amusements and wholesome company." As might be expected, the Woman's Committee and organized womanhood collaborated enthusiastically. They followed the injunction of Secretary of War Baker that the government "cannot allow these ... young men to be surrounded by a vicious and demoralizing environment, nor can we leave anything undone which will protect them from unhealthy influences and crude forms of temptation." The Woman's Committee found, however, that in the great undertaking of safeguarding the health and morals of our boys, their most challenging problem proved to be guarding the morals of their mobilized young girls. For unfortunately, "where soldiers are stationed ... the problem of preventing girls from being misled by the glamour and romance of war and beguiling uniforms looms large." Fortunately, perhaps, the Maryland Committee proposed the establishment of a "Patriotic League of Honor which will inspire girls to adopt the highest standards of womanliness and loyalty to their country."[38]

No group was more delighted with the achievements of Fosdick and his Military Training Camp Commission than the burgeoning profession of social work. Surrounded by handpicked aides from the Playground and Recreation Association and the Russell Sage Foundation, Fosdick and the others "in effect tried to create a massive settlement house around each camp. No army had ever seen anything like it before, but it was an outgrowth of the recreation and community organization movement, and a victory for those who had been arguing for the creative use of leisure time."[39] The social work profession pronounced the program an enormous success. The influential *Survey* magazine summed up the result as "the most stupendous piece of social work in modern times."[40]

---

[38]Clarke, *American Women*, pp. 90, 87, 93. In some cases, organized women took the offensive to help stamp out vice and liquor in their community. Thus in Texas in 1917 the Texas Women's Anti-Vice Committee led in the creation of a "White Zone" around all the military bases. By autumn the Committee expanded into the Texas Social Hygiene Association to coordinate the work of eradicating prostitution and saloons. San Antonio proved to be its biggest problem. Lewis L. Gould, *Progressives and Prohibitionists: Texas Democrats in the Wilson Era* (Austin: University of Texas Press, 1973), p. 227.

[39]Davis, *Spearheads for Reform*, p. 225.

[40]Fosdick, *Chronicle of a Generation*, p. 144. After the war, Raymond Fosdick went on to fame and fortune, first as Under Secretary General of the League of Nations, and then for the rest of his life as a member of the small inner circle close to John D. Rockefeller, Jr. In that capacity, Fosdick rose to become head of the Rockefeller Foundation and Rockefeller's official biographer. Meanwhile, Fosdick's brother, Rev. Harry Emerson, be-

Social workers were also exultant about prohibition. In 1917, the National Conference of Charities and Corrections (which changed its name around the same time to the National Conference of Social Work) was emboldened to drop whatever value-free pose it might have had and come out squarely for prohibition. On returning from Russia in 1917, Edward T. Devine of the Charity Organization Society of New York exclaimed that "the social revolution which followed the prohibition of vodka was more profoundly important ... than the political revolution which abolished autocracy." And Robert A. Woods of Boston, the Grand Old Man of the settlement house movement and a veteran advocate of prohibition, predicted in 1919 that the 18th Amendment, "one of the greatest and best events in history," would reduce poverty, wipe out prostitution and crime, and liberate "vast suppressed human potentialities."[41]

Woods, president of the National Conference of Social Work during 1917–18, had long denounced alcohol as "an abominable evil." A postmillennial pietist, he believed in "Christian statesmanship" that would, in a "propaganda of the deed," Christianize the social order in a corporate, communal route to the glorification of God. Like many pietists, Woods cared not for creeds or dogmas but only for advancing Christianity in a communal way; though an active Episcopalian, his "parish" was the community at large. In his settlement work, Woods had long favored the isolation or segregation of the "unfit," in particular "the tramp, the drunkard, the pauper, the imbecile," with the settlement house as the nucleus of this reform. Woods was particularly eager to isolate and punish the drunkard and the tramp. "Inveterate drunkards" were to receive increasing levels of "punishment," with ever-lengthier jail terms. The "tramp evil" was to be gotten rid of by rounding up and jailing vagrants, who would be placed in tramp workhouses and put to forced labor.

For Woods the world war was a momentous event. It had advanced the process of "Americanization," a "great humanizing process through

came Rockefeller's hand-picked parish minister, first at Park Avenue Presbyterian Church and then at the new interdenominational Riverside Church, built with Rockefeller funds. Harry Emerson Fosdick was Rockefeller's principal aide in battling, within the Protestant Church, in favor of postmillennial, statist, "liberal" Protestantism and against the rising tide of premillennial Christianity, known as "fundamentalist" since the years before World War I. See Collier and Horowitz, *The Rockefellers*, pp. 140–42, 151–53.

[41]Davis, *Spearheads for Reform*, p. 226; Timberlake, *Prohibition and the Progressive Movement*, p. 66; Boyer, *Urban Masses and Moral Order*, p. 156.

which all loyalties, all beliefs must be wrought together in a better order."[42] The war had wonderfully released the energies of the American people. Now, however, it was important to carry the wartime momentum into the postwar world. Lauding the war collectivist society during the spring of 1918, Robert Woods asked the crucial question, "Why should it not always be so? Why not continue in the years of peace this close, vast, wholesome organism of service, of fellowship, of constructive creative power?"[43]

5. THE NEW REPUBLIC COLLECTIVISTS

The *New Republic* magazine, founded in 1914 as the leading intellectual organ of progressivism, was a living embodiment of the burgeoning alliance between big-business interests, in particular the House of Morgan, and the growing legion of collectivist intellectuals. Founder and publisher of the *New Republic* was Willard D. Straight, partner of J.P. Morgan & Co., and its financier was Straight's wife, the heiress Dorothy Whitney. Major editor of the influential new weekly was the veteran collectivist and theoretician of Teddy Roosevelt's New Nationalism, Herbert David Croly. Croly's two coeditors were Walter Edward Weyl, another theoretician of the New Nationalism, and the young, ambitious former official of the Intercollegiate Socialist Society, the future pundit Walter Lippmann. As Woodrow Wilson began to take America into World War I, the *New Republic*, though originally Rooseveltian, became an enthusiastic supporter of the war, and a virtual spokesman for the Wilson war effort, the wartime collectivist economy, and the new society molded by the war.

On the higher levels of ratiocination, unquestionably the leading progressive intellectual, before, during, and after World War I, was the champion of pragmatism, Professor John Dewey of Columbia University. Dewey wrote frequently for the *New Republic* in this period and was clearly its leading theoretician. A Yankee born in 1859, Dewey was, as Mencken put it, "of indestructible Vermont stock and a man of the highest bearable sobriety." John Dewey was the son of a small town Vermont grocer.[44] Although he was a pragmatist and a secular humanist most of his life, it

---

[42]Eleanor H. Woods, *Robert A. Woods: Champion of Democracy* (Boston: Houghton Mifflin, 1929), p. 316. Also see ibid., pp. 201–02, 250ff., 268ff.

[43]Davis, *Spearheads for Reform*, p. 227.

[44]Mencken, "Professor Veblen," p. 267.

is not as well known that Dewey, in the years before 1900, was a postmillennial pietist, seeking the gradual development of a Christianized social order and Kingdom of God on earth via the expansion of science, community, and the State. During the 1890s, Dewey, as professor of philosophy at the University of Michigan, expounded his vision of postmillennial pietism in a series of lectures before the Students' Christian Association. Dewey argued that the growth of modern science now makes it possible for man to establish the biblical idea of the Kingdom of God on earth. Once humans had broken free of the restraints of orthodox Christianity, a truly religious Kingdom of God could be realized in "the common incarnate Life, the purpose ... animating all men and binding them together into one harmonious whole of sympathy."[45] Religion would thus work in tandem with science and democracy, all of which would break down the barriers between men and establish the Kingdom. After 1900 it was easy for John Dewey, along with most other postmillennial intellectuals of the period, to shift gradually but decisively from postmillennial progressive Christian statism to progressive secular statism. The path, the expansion of statism and "social control" and planning, remained the same. And even though the Christian creed dropped out of the picture, the intellectuals and activists continued to possess the same evangelical zeal for the salvation of the world that their parents and they themselves had once possessed. The world would and must still be saved through progress and statism.[46]

A pacifist while in the midst of peace, John Dewey prepared himself to lead the parade for war as America drew nearer to armed intervention in the European struggle. First, in January 1916 in the *New Republic*, Dewey attacked the "professional pacifist's" outright condemnation of war as a "sentimental phantasy," a confusion of means and ends. Force, he declared, was simply "a means of getting results," and therefore would neither be lauded nor condemned per se. Next, in April Dewey signed a pro-Allied-

---

[45]Quoted in the important article by Quandt, "Religion and Social Thought," p. 404. Also see John Blewett, S.J., "Democracy as Religion: Unity in Human Relations," in *John Dewey: His Thought and Influence*, Blewett, ed. (New York: Fordham University Press, 1960), pp. 33–58; and *John Dewey: The Early Works, 1882–1889*, J. Boydstan *et al.*, eds. (Carbondale: Southern Illinois University Press, 1969–71), vols. 2 and 3.

[46]On the general secularization of postmillennial pietism after 1900, see Quandt, "Religion and Social Thought," pp. 390–409; and Moorhead, "The Erosion of Postmillennialism in American Religious Thought," pp. 61–77.

manifesto, not only cheering for an Allied victory but also proclaiming that the Allies were "struggling to preserve the liberties of the world and the highest ideals of civilization." And though Dewey supported U.S. entry into the war so that Germany could be defeated, "a hard job, but one which had to be done," he was far more interested in the wonderful changes that the war would surely bring about in the domestic American polity. In particular, war offered a golden opportunity to bring about collectivist social control in the interest of social justice. As one historian put it,

> because war demanded paramount commitment to the national interest and necessitated an unprecedented degree of government planning and economic regulation in that interest, Dewey saw the prospect of permanent socialization, permanent replacement of private and possessive interest by public and social interest, both within and among nations.[47]

In an interview with the *New York World* a few months after U.S. entry into the war, Dewey exulted that "this war may easily be the beginning of the end of business." For out of the needs of the war, "we are beginning to produce for use, not for sale, and the capitalist is not a capitalist ... [in the face of] the war." Capitalist conditions of production and sale are now under government control, and "there is no reason to believe that the old principle will ever be resumed. ... Private property had already lost its sanctity ... industrial democracy is on the way."[48] In short, intelligence is at last being used to tackle social problems, and this practice is destroying the old order and creating a new social order of "democratic integrated control." Labor is acquiring more power, science is at last being socially mobilized,

---

[47]Carol S. Gruber, *Mars and Minerva: World War I and the Uses of the Higher Learning in America* (Baton Rouge: Louisiana State University Press, 1975), p. 92.

[48]Quoted in ibid., pp. 92–93. Also see Leuchtenburg, "The New Deal and the Analogue of War," p. 89. For similar reasons, Thorstein Veblen, prophet of the alleged dichotomy of production for profit vs. production for use, championed the war and began to come out openly for socialism in an article in the *New Republic* in 1918, later reprinted in his *The Vested Interests and the State of the Industrial Arts* (1919). See Charles Hirschfeld, "Nationalist Progressivism and World War I," *Mid-America* 45 (July, 1963): 150. Also see David Riesman, *Thorstein Veblen: A Critical Interpretation* (New York: Charles Scribner's Sons, 1960), pp. 30–31.

and massive government controls are socializing industry. These developments, Dewey proclaimed, were precisely what we are fighting for.[49]

Furthermore, John Dewey saw great possibilities opened by the war
for the advent of worldwide collectivism. To Dewey, America's entrance
into the war created a "plastic juncture" in the world, a world marked by a
"world organization and the beginnings of a public control which crosses
nationalistic boundaries and interests," and which would also "outlaw
war."[50]

The editors of the *New Republic* took a position similar to Dewey's,
except that they arrived at it even earlier. In his editorial in the magazine's
first issue in November 1914, Herbert Croly cheerily prophesied that the
war would stimulate America's spirit of nationalism and therefore bring it
closer to democracy. At first hesitant about the collectivist war economies
in Europe, the *New Republic* soon began to cheer and urged the United
States to follow the lead of the warring European nations and socialize
its economy and expand the powers of the State. As America prepared to
enter the war, the *New Republic*, examining war collectivism in Europe,
rejoiced that "on its administrative side socialism [had] won a victory that
[was] superb and compelling." True, European war collectivism was a bit
grim and autocratic, but never fear, America could use the selfsame means
for "democratic" goals.

The *New Republic* intellectuals also delighted in the "war spirit" in
America, for that spirit meant "the substitution of national and social and
organic forces for the more or less mechanical private forces operative in
peace. ..." The purposes of war and social reform might be a bit different,
but, after all, "they are both purposes, and luckily for mankind a social
organization which is efficient is as useful for the one as for the other."[51]
Lucky indeed.

As America prepared to enter the war, the *New Republic* eagerly looked
forward to imminent collectivization, sure that it would bring "immense
gains in national efficiency and happiness." After war was declared, the
magazine urged that the war be used as "an aggressive tool of democracy."

---

[49]Hirschfeld, "Nationalist Progressivism and World War I," p. 150.

[50]Gruber, *Mars and Minerva*, p. 92.

[51]Hirschfeld, "Nationalist Progressivism in World War I," p. 142. It is intriguing that for the
New Republic intellectuals, actually existent private individuals are dismissed as "mechanical," whereas nonexistent entities such as "national and social" forces are hailed as being
"organic."

"Why should not the war serve," the magazine asked, "as a pretext to be used to foist innovations upon the country?" In that way, progressive intellectuals could lead the way in abolishing "the typical evils of the sprawling half-educated competitive capitalism."

Convinced that the United States would attain socialism through war, Walter Lippmann, in a public address shortly after American entry, trumpeted his apocalyptic vision of the future:

> We who have gone to war to insure democracy in the world will have raised an aspiration here that will not end with the overthrow of the Prussian autocracy. We shall turn with fresh interests to our own tyrannies — to our Colorado mines, our autocratic steel industries, sweatshops, and our slums. A force is loose in America. ... Our own reactionaries will not assuage it. ... We shall know how to deal with them.[52]

Walter Lippmann, indeed, had been the foremost hawk among the *New Republic* intellectuals. He had pushed Croly into backing Wilson and into supporting intervention, and then had collaborated with Colonel House in pushing Wilson into entering the war. Soon Lippmann, an enthusiast for conscription, had to confront the fact that he himself, only 27 years old and in fine health, was eminently eligible for the draft. Somehow, however, Lippmann failed to unite theory and praxis. Young Felix Frankfurter, progressive Harvard Law Professor and a close associate of the *New Republic* editorial staff, had just been selected as a special assistant

---

[52]Quoted in Hirschfeld, "Nationalist Progressivism, and World War I," p. 147. A minority of pro-war socialists broke off from the antiwar Socialist Party to form the Social Democratic League, and to join a pro-war front organized and financed by the Wilson administration, the American Alliance for Labor and Democracy. The pro-war socialists welcomed the war as providing "startling progress in collectivism," and opined that after the war, the existent state socialism would be advanced toward "democratic collectivism." The pro-war socialists included John Spargo, Algie Simons, W.J. Ghent, Robert R. LaMonte, Charles Edward Russell, J.G. Phelps Stokes, Upton Sinclair, and William English Walling. Walling so succumbed to war fever that he denounced the Socialist Party as a conscious tool of the Kaiser and advocated the suppression of freedom of speech for pacifists and for antiwar socialists. See ibid., p. 143. On Walling, see Gilbert, *Designing the Industrial State*, pp. 232–33. On the American Alliance for Labor and Democracy and its role in the war effort, see Ronald Radosh, *American Labor and United States Foreign Policy* (New York: Random House, 1969), pp. 58–71.

to Secretary of War Baker. Lippmann somehow felt that his own inestimable services could be better used planning the postwar world than battling in the trenches. And so he wrote to Frankfurter asking for a job in Baker's office. "What I want to do," he pleaded, "is to devote all my time to studying and speculating on the approaches to peace and the reaction from the peace. Do you think you can get me an exemption on such highfalutin grounds?" He then rushed to reassure Frankfurter that there was nothing "personal" in this request. After all, he explained, "the things that need to be thought out, are so big that there must be no personal element mixed up with this." Frankfurter having paved the way, Lippmann wrote to Secretary Baker. He assured Baker that he was only applying for a job and draft exemption on the pleading of others and in stern submission to the national interest. As Lippmann put it in a remarkable demonstration of cant:

> I have consulted all the people whose advice I value and they urge me to apply for exemption. You can well understand that this is not a pleasant thing to do, and yet, after searching my soul as candidly as I know how, I am convinced that I can serve my bit much more effectively than as a private in the new armies.

No doubt.

As icing on the cake, Lippmann added an important bit of "disinformation." For, he piteously wrote to Baker, the fact is "that my father is dying and my mother is absolutely alone in the world. She does not know what his condition is, and I cannot tell anyone for fear it would become known." Apparently, no one else "knew" his father's condition either, including his father and the medical profession, for the elder Lippmann managed to peg along successfully for the next ten years.[53]

Secure in his draft exemption, Walter Lippmann hied off in high excitement to Washington, there to help run the war and, a few months later, to help direct Colonel House's secret conclave of historians and social scientists setting out to plan the shape of the future peace treaty and the postwar world. Let others fight and die in the trenches; Walter Lippmann

---

[53]In fact, Jacob Lippmann was to contract cancer in 1925 and die two years later. Moreover, Lippmann, before and after Jacob's death, was supremely indifferent to his father. Ronald Steel, *Walter Lippmann and the American Century* (New York: Random House, 1981), p. 5, pp. 116–17. On Walter Lippmann's enthusiasm for conscription, at least for others, see Beaver, *Newton Baker*, pp. 26–27.

had the satisfaction of knowing that his talents, at least, would be put to their best use by the newly emerging collectivist State.

As the war went on, Croly and the other editors, having lost Lippmann to the great world beyond, cheered every new development of the massively controlled war economy. The nationalization of railroads and shipping, the priorities and allocation system, the total domination of all parts of the food industry achieved by Herbert Hoover and the Food Administration, the pro-union policy, the high taxes, and the draft were all hailed by the *New Republic* as an expansion of democracy's power to plan for the general good. As the Armistice ushered in the postwar world, the *New Republic* looked back on the handiwork of the war and found it good: "We revolutionized our society." All that remained was to organize a new constitutional convention to complete the job of reconstructing America.[54]

But the revolution had not been fully completed. Despite the objections of Bernard Baruch and other wartime planners, the government decided not to make most of the war collectivist machinery permanent. From then on, the fondest ambition of Baruch and the others was to make the World War I system a permanent institution of American life. The most trenchant epitaph on the World War I polity was delivered by Rexford Guy Tugwell, the most frankly collectivist of the Brain Trusters of Franklin Roosevelt's New Deal. Looking back on "America's wartime socialism" in 1927, Tugwell lamented that if only the war had lasted longer, that great "experiment" could have been completed: "We were on the verge of having an international industrial machine when peace broke," Tugwell mourned. "Only the Armistice prevented a great experiment in control of production, control of prices, and control of consumption."[55]

---

[54]Hirschfeld, "Nationalist Progressivism and World War I," pp. 148–50. On the *New Republic* and the war, and particularly on John Dewey, also see Lasch, *The New Radicalism in America*, pp. 181–224, especially pp. 202–04. On the three *New Republic* editors, see Charles Forcey, *The Crossroads of Liberalism: Croly, Weyl, Lippmann and the Progressive Era, 1900–1925* (New York: Oxford University Press, 1961). Also see David W. Noble, "The *New Republic* and the Idea of Progress, 1914–1920," *Mississippi Valley Historical Review* 38 (December, 1951): 387–402. In a book titled *The End of the War* (1918), *New Republic* editor Walter Weyl assured his readers that "the new economic solidarity once gained, can never again be surrendered." Cited in Leuchtenburg, "New Deal, and the Analogue of War," p. 90.

[55]Rexford Guy Tugwell, "America's War-Time Socialism" *The Nation* (1927): 364–65. Quoted in Leuchtenburg, "The New Deal and the Analogue of War," pp. 90–91.

Tugwell need not have been troubled; there would soon be other emergencies, other wars.

At the end of the war, Lippmann was to go on to become America's foremost journalistic pundit. Croly, having broken with the Wilson administration on the harshness of the Versailles Treaty, was bereft to find the *New Republic* no longer the spokesman for some great political leader. During the late 1920s he was to discover an exemplary national collectivist leader abroad — in Benito Mussolini.[56] That Croly ended his years as an admirer of Mussolini comes as no surprise when we realize that from early childhood he had been steeped by a doting father in the authoritarian socialist doctrines of Auguste Comte's Positivism. These views were to mark Croly throughout his life. Thus, Herbert's father, David, the founder of Positivism in the United States, advocated the establishment of vast powers of government over everyone's life. David Croly favored the growth of trusts and monopolies as a means both to that end and also to eliminate the evils of individual competition and "selfishness." Like his son, David Croly railed at the Jeffersonian "fear of government" in America and looked to Hamilton as an example to counter that trend.[57]

---

[56]In January 1927, Croly wrote a *New Republic* editorial, "An Apology for Fascism," endorsing an accompanying article, "Fascism for the Italians," written by the distinguished philosopher Horace M. Kallen, a disciple of John Dewey and an exponent of progressive pragmatism. Kallen praised Mussolini for his pragmatic approach, and in particular for the *élan vital* that Mussolini had infused into Italian life. True, Professor Kallen conceded, fascism is coercive, but surely this is only a temporary expedient. Noting fascism's excellent achievement in economics, education, and administrative reform, Kallen added that "in this respect the Fascist revolution is not unlike the Communist revolution. Each is the application by force ... of an ideology to a condition. Each should have the freest opportunity once it has made a start. ..." The accompanying *New Republic* editorial endorsed Kallen's thesis and added that "alien critics should beware of outlawing a political experiment which aroused in a whole nation an increased moral energy and dignified its activities by subordinating them to a deeply felt common purpose." *New Republic* 49 (January 12, 1927): 207–13. Cited in John Patrick Diggins, "Mussolini's Italy: The View from America," (Ph.D. diss., University of Southern California, 1964), pp. 214–17.

[57]Born in Ireland, David Croly became a distinguished journalist in New York City and rose to the editorship of the *New York World*. Croly organized the first Positivist Circle in the United States and financed an American speaking tour for the Comtian Henry Edgar. The Positivist Circle met at Croly's home, and in 1871 David Croly published *A Positivist Primer*. When Herbert was born in 1869, he was consecrated by his father to the Goddess Humanity, the symbol of Comte's Religion of Humanity. See the illuminating recent biography of Herbert by David W. Levy, *Herbert Croly of the New Republic* (Princeton, NJ: Princeton University Press, 1985).

And what of Professor Dewey, the doyen of the pacifist intellectuals-turned-drumbeaters for war? In a little known period of his life, John Dewey spent the immediate postwar years, 1919–21, teaching at Peking University and traveling in the Far East. China was then in a period of turmoil over the clauses of the Versailles Treaty that transferred the rights of dominance in Shantung from Germany to Japan. Japan had been promised this reward by the British and French in secret treaties in return for entering the war against Germany. The Wilson administration was torn between the two camps. On the one hand were those who wished to stand by the Allies' decision and who envisioned using Japan as a club against Bolshevik Russia in Asia. On the other were those who had already begun to sound the alarm about a Japanese menace and who were committed to China, often because of connections with the American Protestant missionaries who wished to defend and expand their extraterritorial powers of governance in China. The Wilson administration, which had originally taken a pro-Chinese stand, reversed itself in the spring of 1919 and endorsed the Versailles provisions.

Into this complex situation John Dewey plunged, seeing no complexity and of course considering it unthinkable for either him or the United States to stay out of the entire fray. Dewey leaped into total support of the Chinese nationalist position, hailing the aggressive Young China movement and even endorsing the pro-missionary YMCA in China as "social workers." Dewey thundered that while "I didn't expect to be a jingo," Japan must be called to account, and Japan is the great menace in Asia. Thus, scarcely had Dewey ceased being a champion of one terrible world war than he began to pave the way for an even greater one.[58]

6. Economics in Service of the State: The Empiricism of Richard T. Ely

World War I was the apotheosis of the growing notion of intellectuals as servants of the State and junior partners in State rule. In the new fusion of intellectuals and State, each was of powerful aid to the other. Intellectuals could serve the State by apologizing for and supplying rationales for its deeds. Intellectuals were also needed to staff important positions as planners and controllers of the society and economy. The State could

---

[58]See Jerry Israel, *Progressivism and the Open Door: America and China, 1905–1921* (Pittsburgh: University of Pittsburgh Press, 1971).

also serve intellectuals by restricting entry into, and thereby raising the income and the prestige of, the various occupations and professions. During World War I, historians were of particular importance in supplying the government with war propaganda, convincing the public of the unique evil of Germans throughout history and of the satanic designs of the Kaiser. Economists, particularly empirical economists and statisticians, were of great importance in the planning and control of the nation's wartime economy. Historians playing preeminent roles in the war propaganda machine have been studied fairly extensively; economists and statisticians, playing a less blatant and allegedly "value-free" role, have received far less attention.[59]

Although it is an outworn generalization to say that 19th century economists were stalwart champions of *laissez-faire*, it is still true that deductive economic theory proved to be a mighty bulwark against government intervention. For, basically, economic theory showed the harmony and order inherent in the free market, as well as the counterproductive distortions and economic shackles imposed by state intervention. In order for statism to dominate the economics profession, then, it was important to discredit deductive theory. One of the most important ways of doing so was to advance the notion that, to be "genuinely scientific," economics had to eschew generalization and deductive laws and simply engage in empirical inquiry into the facts of history and historical institutions, hoping that somehow laws would eventually arise from these detailed investigations. Thus the German Historical School, which managed to seize control of the economics discipline in Germany, fiercely proclaimed not only its devotion to statism and government control, but also its opposition to the "abstract" deductive laws of political economy. This was the first major group within the economics profession to champion what Ludwig von Mises was later to call "anti-economics." Gustav Schmoller, the leader of

---

[59]For a refreshingly acidulous portrayal of the actions of the historians in World War I, see C. Hartley Grattan, "The Historians Cut Loose," *American Mercury*, August 1927, reprinted in Harry Elmer Barnes, *In Quest of Truth and Justice*, 2nd ed. (Colorado Springs: Ralph Myles Publisher, 1972), pp. 142–64. A more extended account is George T. Blakey, *Historians on the Homefront: American Propagandists for the Great War* (Lexington: University Press of Kentucky, 1970). Gruber, *Mars and Minerva*, deals with academia and social scientism, but concentrates on historians. James R. Mock and Cedric Larson, *Words that Won the War* (Princeton, NJ: Princeton University Press, 1939), presents the story of the "Creel Committee," the Committee on Public Information, the official propaganda ministry during the war.

the Historical School, proudly declared that his and his colleagues' major task at the University of Berlin was to form "the intellectual bodyguard of the House of Hohenzollern."

During the 1880s and 1890s bright young graduate students in history and the social sciences went to Germany, the home of the Ph.D. degree, to obtain their doctorates. Almost to a man, they returned to the United States to teach in colleges and in the newly created graduate schools, imbued with the excitement of the "new" economics and political science. It was a "new" social science that lauded the German and Bismarckian development of a powerful welfare-warfare State — a State seemingly above all social classes — that fused the nation into an integrated and allegedly harmonious whole. The new society and polity was to be run by a powerful central government — cartelizing, dictating, arbitrating, and controlling — thereby eliminating competitive *laissez-faire* capitalism on the one hand and the threat of proletarian socialism on the other. And at or near the head of the new dispensation was to be the new breed of intellectuals, technocrats, and planners, directing, staffing, propagandizing, and "selflessly" promoting the common good while ruling and lording over the rest of society. In short, doing well by doing good. To the new breed of progressive and statist intellectuals in America, this was a heady vision indeed.

Richard T. Ely, virtually the founder of this new breed, was the leading progressive economist and also the teacher of most of the others. As an ardent postmillennialist pietist, Ely was convinced that he was serving God and Christ as well. Like so many pietists, Ely was born (in 1854) of solid Yankee and old Puritan stock, again in the midst of the fanatical Burned-Over District of western New York. Ely's father, Ezra, was an extreme Sabbatarian, preventing his family from playing games or reading books on Sunday, and so ardent a prohibitionist that, even though an impoverished, marginal farmer, he refused to grow barley, a crop uniquely suitable to his soil, because it would have been used to make that monstrously sinful product, beer.[60] Having been graduated from Columbia College in 1876, Ely went to Germany and received his Ph.D. from Heidelberg in 1879. In several decades of teaching at Johns Hopkins and then at Wisconsin, the energetic and empire-building Ely became enormously influential in American thought and politics. At Johns Hopkins he turned

---

[60]See the useful biography of Ely, Rader, *The Academic Mind and Reform*.

out a gallery of influential students and statist disciples in all fields of the social sciences as well as economics. These disciples were headed by the pro-union institutionalist economist John R. Commons and included the social-control sociologists Edward Alsworth Ross and Albion W. Small, John H. Finlay, president of City College of New York, Dr. Albert Shaw, editor of the *Review of Reviews* and influential adviser and theoretician to Theodore Roosevelt, the municipal reformer Frederick C. Howe, and the historians Frederick Jackson Turner and J. Franklin Jameson. Newton D. Baker was trained by Ely at Hopkins, and Woodrow Wilson was also his student there, although there is no direct evidence of intellectual influence.

In the mid-1880s Richard Ely founded the American Economic Association in a conscious attempt to commit the economics profession to statism as against the older *laissez-faire* economists grouped in the Political Economy Club. Ely continued as secretary-treasurer of the AEA for seven years, until his reformer allies decided to weaken the association's commitment to statism in order to induce the *laissez-faire* economists to join the organization. At that point, Ely, in high dudgeon, left the AEA.

At Wisconsin in 1892, Ely formed a new School of Economics, Political Science, and History, surrounded himself with former students, and gave birth to the Wisconsin Idea which, with the help of John Commons, succeeded in passing a host of progressive measures for government regulation in Wisconsin. Ely and the others formed an unofficial but powerful brain trust for the progressive regime of Wisconsin Governor Robert M. La Follette, who got his start in Wisconsin politics as an advocate of prohibition. Though never a classroom student of Ely's, La Follette always referred to Ely as his teacher and as the molder of the Wisconsin Idea. And Theodore Roosevelt once declared that Ely "first introduced me to radicalism in economics and then made me sane in my radicalism."[61]

Ely was also one of the most prominent postmillennialist intellectuals of the era. He fervently believed that the State is God's chosen instrument for reforming and Christianizing the social order so that eventually Jesus would arrive and put an end to history. The State, declared Ely, "is religious in its essence," and, furthermore, "God works through the State in carrying out His purposes more universally than through any other institution."

---

[61]Fine, *Laissez Faire and the General-Welfare State*, pp. 239–40.

The task of the church is to guide the State and utilize it in these needed reforms.[62]

An inveterate activist and organizer, Ely was prominent in the evangelical Chautauqua movement, and he founded there the "Christian Sociology" summer school, which infused the influential Chautauqua operation with the concepts and the personnel of the Social Gospel movement. Ely was a friend and close associate of Social Gospel leaders Revs. Washington Gladden, Walter Rauschenbusch, and Josiah Strong. With Strong and Commons, Ely organized the Institute of Christian Sociology.[63] Ely also founded and became the secretary of the Christian Social Union of the Episcopal Church, along with Christian Socialist W.D.P. Bliss. All of these activities were infused with postmillennial statism. Thus, the Institute of Christian Sociology was pledged to present God's "kingdom as the complete ideal of human society to be realized on earth." Moreover,

> Ely viewed the state as the greatest redemptive force in society. ... In Ely's eyes, government was the God-given instrument through which we had to work. Its preeminence as a divine instrument was based on the post-Reformation abolition of the division between the sacred and the secular and on the State's power to implement ethical solutions to public problems. The same identification of sacred and secular which took place among liberal clergy enabled Ely to both divinize the state and socialize Christianity: he thought of government as God's main instrument of redemption.[64]

---

[62]Fine, *Laissez Faire and the General-Welfare State*, pp. 180–81.

[63]John Rogers Commons was of old Yankee stock, descendant of John Rogers, Puritan martyr in England, and born in the Yankee area of the Western Reserve in Ohio and reared in Indiana. His Vermont mother was a graduate of the hotbed of pietism, Oberlin College, and she sent John to Oberlin in the hopes that he would become a minister. While in college, Commons and his mother launched a prohibitionist publication at the request of the Anti-Saloon League. After graduation, Commons went to Johns Hopkins to study under Ely, but flunked out of graduate school. See Commons, *Myself*. Also see Dorfman, *Economic Mind in American Civilization*, vol. 3, pp. 276–77; Mary O. Furner, *Advocacy and Objectivity: A Crisis in the Professionalization of American Social Science, 1865–1905* (Lexington: University Press of Kentucky, 1975), pp. 198–204.

[64]Quandt, "Religion and Social Thought," pp. 402–03. Ely did not expect the millennial Kingdom to be far off. He believed that it was the task of the universities and of the social sciences "to teach the complexities of the Christian duty of brotherhood" in order

When war came, Richard Ely was for some reason (perhaps because he was in his sixties) left out of the excitement of war work and economic planning in Washington. He bitterly regretted that "I have not had a more active part than I have had in this greatest war in the world's history."[65] But Ely made up for his lack as best he could; virtually from the start of the European war, he whooped it up for militarism, war, the "discipline" of conscription, and the suppression of dissent and "disloyalty" at home. A lifelong militarist, Ely had tried to volunteer for war service in the Spanish-American War, had called for the suppression of the Philippine insurrection, and was particularly eager for conscription and for forced labor for "loafers" during World War I. By 1915 Ely was agitating for immediate compulsory military service, and the following year he joined the ardently pro-war and heavily big-business–influenced National Security League, where he called for the liberation of the German people from "autocracy."[66] In advocating conscription, Ely was neatly able to combine moral, economic, and prohibitionist arguments for the draft: "The moral effect of taking boys off street corners and out of saloons and drilling them is excellent, and the economic effects are likewise beneficial."[67] Indeed, conscription for Ely served almost as a panacea for all ills. So enthusiastic was he about the World War I experience that Ely again prescribed his favorite cure-all to alleviate the 1929 depression. He proposed a permanent peacetime "industrial army" engaged in public works and manned by conscripting youth for strenuous physical labor. This conscription would

---

to arrive at the New Jerusalem "which we are all eagerly awaiting." The church's mission was to attack every evil institution, "until the earth becomes a new earth, and all its cities, cities of God."

[65]Gruber, *Mars and Minerva*, p. 114.

[66]See Rader, *Academic Mind and Reform*, pp. 181–91. On top big business affiliations of National Security League leaders, especially J.P. Morgan and others in the Morgan ambit, see C. Hartley Grattan, *Why We Fought* (New York Vanguard Press, 1929), pp. 117–18, and Robert D. Ward, "The Origin and Activities of the National Security League, 1914–1919," *Mississippi Valley Historical Review* 47 (June, 1960): 51–65.

[67]The Chamber of Commerce of the United States spelled out the long-run economic benefit of conscription, that for America's youth it would "substitute a period of helpful discipline for a period of demoralizing freedom from restraint." Finnegan, *Against the Specter of a Dragon*, p. 110. On the broad and enthusiastic support given to the draft by the Chamber of Commerce, see Chase C. Mooney and Martha E. Layman, "Some Phases of the Compulsory Military Training Movement, 1914–1920," *Mississippi Historical Review* 38 (March, 1952): 640.

instill into America's youth the essential "military ideals of hardihood and discipline," a discipline once provided by life on the farm but unavailable to the bulk of the populace now growing up in the effete cities. This small, standing conscript army could then speedily absorb the unemployed during depressions. Under the command of "an economic general staff," the industrial army would "go to work to relieve distress with all the vigor and resources of brain and brawn that we employed in the World War."[68]

Deprived of a position in Washington, Ely made the stamping out of "disloyalty" at home his major contribution to the war effort. He called for the total suspension of academic freedom for the duration. Any professor, he declared, who stated "opinions which hinder us in this awful struggle" should be "fired" if not indeed "shot." The particular focus of Ely's formidable energy was a zealous campaign to try to get his old ally in Wisconsin politics, Robert M. La Follette, expelled from the U.S. Senate for continuing to oppose America's participation in the war. Ely declared that his "blood boils" at La Follette's "treason" and attacks on war profiteering. Throwing himself into the battle, Ely founded and became president of the Madison chapter of the Wisconsin Loyalty Legion and mounted a campaign to expel La Follette.[69] The campaign was meant to mobilize the Wisconsin faculty and to support the ultrapatriotic and ultrahawkish activities of Theodore Roosevelt. Ely wrote to T.R. that "we must crush La Follettism." In his unremitting campaign against the Wisconsin Senator, Ely thundered that La Follette "has been of more help to the Kaiser than a quarter of a million troops."[70] "Empiricism" rampant.

The faculty of the University of Wisconsin was stung by charges throughout the state and the country that its failure to denounce La Follette was proof that the university — long affiliated with La Follette in state politics — supported his disloyal antiwar policies. Prodded by Ely, Commons, and others, the university's War Committee drew up and circulated a petition, signed by the university president, all the deans, and over 90%

---

[68]Richard T. Ely, *Hard Times: The Way in and the Way Out* (1931), cited in Joseph Dorfman, *The Economic Mind in American Civilization* (New York: Viking, 1949), vol. 5, p. 671; and in Leuchtenburg, "The New Deal and the Analogue of War," p. 94.

[69]Ely drew up a super-patriotic pledge for the Madison chapter of the Loyalty Legion, pledging its members to "stamp out disloyalty." The pledge also expressed unqualified support for the Espionage Act and vowed to "work against La Follettism in all its anti-war forms." Rader, *Academic Mind and Reform*, pp. 183ff.

[70]Gruber, *Mars and Minerva*, p. 207.

of the faculty, that provided one of the more striking examples in United States history of academic truckling to the State apparatus. None too subtly using the constitutional verbiage for treason, the petition protested "against those utterances and actions of Senator La Follette which have given aid and comfort to Germany and her allies in the present war; we deplore his failure loyally to support the government in the prosecution of the war."[71]

Behind the scenes, Ely tried his best to mobilize America's historians against La Follette, to demonstrate that he had given aid and comfort to the enemy. Ely was able to enlist the services of the National Board of Historical Service, the propaganda agency established by professional historians for the duration of the war, and of the government's own propaganda arm, the Committee on Public Information. Warning that the effort must remain secret, Ely mobilized historians under the aegis of these organizations to research German and Austrian newspapers and journals to try to build a record of La Follette's alleged influence, "indicating the encouragement he has given Germany." The historian E. Merton Coulter revealed the objective spirit animating these researches: "I understand it is to be an unbiased and candid account of the Senator's [La Follette's] course and its effect — but we all know it can lead but to one conclusion — something little short of treason."[72]

Professor Gruber well notes that this campaign to get La Follette was "a remarkable example of the uses of scholarship for espionage. It was a far cry from the disinterested search for truth for a group of professors to mobilize a secret research campaign to find ammunition to destroy the political career of a United States senator who did not share their view of the war."[73] In any event, no evidence was turned up, the movement failed, and the Wisconsin professoriat began to move away in distrust from the Loyalty Legion.[74]

---

[71]Ibid., p. 207.

[72]Ibid., pp. 208 n.

[73]Ibid., pp. 209–10. In his autobiography, written in 1938, Richard Ely rewrote history to cover up his ignominious role in the get–La Follette campaign. He acknowledged signing the faculty petition, but then had the temerity to claim that he "was not one of the ringleaders, as La Follette thought, in circulating this petition ..." There is no mention of his secret research campaign against La Follette.

[74]For more on the anti-La Follette campaign, see H.C. Peterson and Gilbert C. Fite, *Opponents of War: 1917–1918* (Madison: University of Wisconsin Press, 1957), pp. 68–72;

After the menace of the Kaiser had been extirpated, the Armistice found Professor Ely, along with his compatriots in the National Security League, ready to segue into the next round of patriotic repression. During Ely's anti–La Follette research campaign he had urged investigation of "the kind of influence which he [La Follette] has exerted against our country in Russia." Ely pointed out that modern "democracy" requires a "high degree of conformity" and that therefore the "most serious menace" of Bolshevism, which Ely depicted as "social disease germs," must be fought "with repressive measures."

By 1924, however, Richard T. Ely's career of repression was over, and what is more, in a rare instance of the workings of poetic justice, he was hoisted with his own petard. In 1922 the much-traduced Robert La Follette was reelected to the Senate and also swept the Progressives back into power in the state of Wisconsin. By 1924 the Progressives had gained control of the Board of Regents, and they moved to cut off the water of their former academic ally and empire-builder. Ely then felt it prudent to move out of Wisconsin together with his Institute, and while he lingered for some years at Northwestern, the heyday of Ely's fame and fortune was over.

7. ECONOMICS IN SERVICE OF THE STATE: GOVERNMENT AND STATISTICS

Statistics is a vital, though much underplayed, requisite of modern government. Government could not even presume to control, regulate, or plan any portion of the economy without the service of its statistical bureaus and agencies. Deprive government of its statistics and it would be a blind and helpless giant, with no idea whatever of what to do or where to do it. It might be replied that business firms, too, need statistics in order to function. But business needs for statistics are far less in quantity and also different in quality. Business may need statistics in its own micro area of the economy, but only on its prices and costs; it has little need for broad collections of data or for sweeping, holistic aggregates. Business could perhaps rely on its own privately collected and unshared data. Furthermore, much entrepreneurial knowledge is qualitative, not enshrined in quantitative data, and of a particular time, area, and location. But government bureaucracy could

Paul L. Murphy, *World War I and the Origin of Civil Liberties in the United States* (New York: W.W. Norton, 1979), p. 120; and Belle Case La Follette and Fola La Follette, *Robert M. LaFollette* (New York: Macmillan, 1953), vol. 2.

do nothing if forced to be confined to qualitative data. Deprived of profit and loss tests for efficiency, or of the need to serve consumers efficiently, conscripting both capital and operating costs from taxpayers, and forced to abide by fixed, bureaucratic rules, modern government shorn of masses of statistics could do virtually nothing.[75]

Hence the enormous importance of World War I, not only in providing the power and the precedent for a collectivized economy, but also in greatly accelerating the advent of statisticians and statistical agencies of government, many of which (and who) remained in government, ready for the next leap forward of power.

Richard T. Ely, of course, championed the new empirical "look and see" approach, with the aim of fact-gathering to "mold the forces at work in society and to improve existing conditions."[76] More importantly, one of the leading authorities on the growth of government expenditure has linked it with statistics and empirical data: "Advance in economic science and statistics ... strengthened belief in the possibilities of dealing with social problems by collective action. It made for increase in the statistical and other fact-finding activities of government."[77] As early as 1863, Samuel B. Ruggles, American delegate to the International Statistical Congress in Berlin, proclaimed that "statistics are the very eyes of the statesman,

---

[75]Thus, T.W. Hutchison, from a very different perspective, notes the contrast between Carl Menger's stress on the beneficent, unplanned phenomena of society, such as the free market, and the growth of "social self-consciousness" and government planning. Hutchison recognizes that a crucial component of that social self-consciousness is government statistics. T.W. Hutchison, *A Review of Economic Doctrines, 1870–1929* (Oxford: Clarendon Press, 1953), pp. 150–51, 427.

[76]Fine, *Laissez Faire and the General-Welfare State*, p. 207.

[77]Solomon Fabricant, *The Trend of Government Activity in the United States since 1900* (New York: National Bureau of Economic Research, 1952), p. 143. Similarly, an authoritative work on the growth of government in England puts it this way: "The accumulation of factual information about social conditions and the development of economics and the social sciences increased the pressure for government intervention. ... As statistics improved and students of social conditions multiplied, the continued existence of such conditions was kept before the public. Increasing knowledge of them aroused influential circles and furnished working class movements with factual weapons." Moses Abramovitz and Vera F. Eliasberg, *The Growth of Public Employment in Great Britain* (Princeton, NJ: National Bureau of Economic Research, 1957), pp. 22–23, 30. Also see M.I. Cullen, *The Statistical Movement in Early Victorian Britain: The Foundations of Empirical Social Research* (New York: Barnes & Noble, 1975).

enabling him to survey and scan with clear and comprehensive vision the whole structure and economy of the body politic."[78]

Conversely, this means that stripped of these means of vision, the statesman would no longer be able to meddle, control, and plan.

Moreover, government statistics are clearly needed for specific types of intervention. Government could not intervene to alleviate unemployment unless statistics of unemployment were collected — and so the impetus for such collection. Carroll D. Wright, one of the first Commissioners of Labor in the United States, was greatly influenced by the famous statistician and German Historical School member, Ernst Engel, head of the Royal Statistical Bureau of Prussia. Wright sought the collection of unemployment statistics for that reason and, in general, for "the amelioration of unfortunate industrial and social relations." Henry Carter Adams, a former student of Engel, and, like Ely, a statist and progressive "new economist," established the Statistical Bureau of the Interstate Commerce Commission, believing that "ever increasing statistical activity by the government was essential — for the sake of controlling naturally monopolistic industries. ..." And Professor Irving Fisher of Yale, eager for government to stabilize the price level, conceded that he wrote *The Making of Index Numbers* to solve the problem of the unreliability of index numbers. "Until this difficulty could be met, stabilization could scarcely be expected to become a reality."

Carroll Wright was a Bostonian and a progressive reformer. Henry Carter Adams, the son of a New England pietist Congregationalist preacher on missionary duty in Iowa, studied for the ministry at his father's alma mater, Andover Theological Seminary, but soon abandoned this path. Adams devised the accounting system of the Statistical Bureau of the ICC. This system "served as a model for the regulation of public utilities here and throughout the world."[79]

---

[78]See Joseph Dorfman, "The Role of the German Historical School in American Economic Thought," *American Economic Review, Papers and Proceedings* 45 (May, 1955): 18. George Hildebrand remarked on the inductive emphasis of the German Historical School that "perhaps there is, then, some connection between this kind of teaching and the popularity of crude ideas of physical planning in more recent times." George H. Hildebrand, "International Flow of Economic Ideas-Discussion," ibid., p. 37.

[79]Dorfman, "Role of the German Historical School in American Economic Thought," p. 23. On Wright and Adams, see Dorfman, *Economic Mind in American Civilization*, vol. 3, 164–74, 123; and Boyer, *Urban Masses and Moral Order*, p. 163. Furthermore, the first professor of statistics in the United States, Roland P. Falkner, was a devoted student of Engel's

Irving Fisher was the son of a Rhode Island Congregationalist pietist preacher, and his parents were both of old Yankee stock, his mother a strict Sabbatarian. As befitted what his son and biographer called his "crusading spirit," Fisher was an inveterate reformer, urging the imposition of numerous progressive measures including Esperanto, simplified spelling, and calendar reform. He was particularly enthusiastic about purging the world of "such iniquities of civilization as alcohol, tea, coffee, tobacco, refined sugar, and bleached white flour. ..."[80] During the 1920s Fisher was the leading prophet of that so-called New Era in economics and in society. He wrote three books during the 1920s praising the noble experiment of prohibition, and he lauded Governor Benjamin Strong and the Federal Reserve System for following his advice and expanding money and credit so as to keep the wholesale price level virtually constant. Because of the Fed's success in imposing Fisherine price stabilization, Fisher was so sure that there could be no depression that as late as 1930 he wrote a book claiming that there was and could be no stock crash and that stock prices would quickly rebound. Throughout the 1920s Fisher insisted that since wholesale prices remained constant, there was nothing amiss about the wild boom in stocks. Meanwhile he put his theories into practice by heavily investing his heiress wife's considerable fortune in the stock market. After the crash he frittered away his sister-in-law's money when his wife's fortune was depleted, at the same time calling frantically on the federal government to inflate money and credit and to re-inflate stock prices to their 1929 levels. Despite his dissipation of two family fortunes, Fisher managed to blame almost everyone except himself for the debacle.[81]

As we shall see, in view of the importance of Wesley Clair Mitchell in the burgeoning of government statistics in World War I, Mitchell's view on statistics are of particular importance.[82] Mitchell, an institutionalist

---

and a translator of the works of Engel's assistant, August Meitzen.

[80]Irving Norton Fisher, *My Father Irving Fisher* (New York: Comet Press, 1956), pp. 146–47. Also Fisher, see *Irving Fisher, Stabilised Money* (London: Allen & Unwin, 1935), p. 383.

[81]Fisher, *My Father*, pp. 264–67. On Fisher's role and influence during this period, see Murray N. Rothbard, *America's Great Depression*, 4th ed. (New York: Richardson & Snyder, 1983). Also see Joseph S. Davis, *The World Between the Wars, 1919–39, An Economist's View* (Baltimore: Johns Hopkins University Press, 1975), p. 194; and Melchior Palyi, *The Twilight of Gold, 1914–1936: Myth and Realities* (Chicago: Henry Regnery, 1972), pp. 240, 249.

[82]Wesley C. Mitchell was of old Yankee pietist stock. His grandparents were farmers in Maine and then in Western New York. His father followed the path of many Yankees in migrating to a farm in northern Illinois. Mitchell attended the University of Chicago, where he

and student of Thorstein Veblen, was one of the prime founders of modern statistical inquiry in economics and clearly aspired to lay the basis for "scientific" government planning. As Professor Dorfman, friend and student of Mitchell's, put it:

> "clearly the type of social invention most needed today is one that offers definite techniques through which the social system can be controlled and operated to the optimum advantage of its members." (Quote from Mitchell.) To this end he constantly sought to extend, improve and refine the gathering and compilation of data. ... Mitchell believed that business-cycle analysis ... might indicate the means to the achievement of orderly social control of business activity.[83]

Or, as Mitchell's wife and collaborator stated in her memoirs:

> ... he [Mitchell] envisioned the great contribution that government could make to the understanding of economic and social problems if the statistical data gathered independently by various Federal agencies were systematized and planned so that the interrelationships among them could be studied. The idea of developing social statistics, *not merely as a record but as a basis for planning*, emerged early in his own work.[84]

Particularly important in the expansion of statistics in World War I was the growing insistence, by progressive intellectuals and corporate liberal businessmen alike, that democratic decision-making must be increasingly replaced by the administrative and technocratic. Democratic or legislative decisions were messy, "inefficient," and might lead to a significant curbing of statism, as had happened in the heyday of the Democratic Party during the 19th century. But if decisions were largely administrative and technocratic, the burgeoning of state power could continue unchecked. The collapse of the *laissez-faire* creed of the Democrats in 1896 left a power vacuum in government that administrative and corporatist types were eager

---

was strongly influenced by Veblen and John Dewey. Dorfman, *Economic Mind in American Civilization*, vol. 3, p. 456.

[83]Dorfman, *Economic Mind in American Civilization*, vol. 4, pp. 376, 361.

[84]Emphasis added. Lucy Sprague Mitchell, *Two Lives* (New York: Simon and Schuster, 1953), p. 363. For more on this entire topic, see Murray N. Rothbard, "The Politics of Political Economists: Comment," *Quarterly Journal of Economics* 74 (November, 1960): 659–65.

to fill. Increasingly, then, such powerful corporatist big business groups as the National Civic Federation disseminated the idea that governmental decisions should be in the hands of the efficient technician, the allegedly value-free expert. In short, government, in virtually all of its aspects, should be "taken out of politics." And statistical research with its aura of empiricism, quantitative precision, and nonpolitical value-freedom, was in the forefront of such emphasis. In the municipalities, an increasingly powerful progressive reform movement shifted decisions from elections in neighborhood wards to citywide professional managers and school superintendents. As a corollary, political power was increasingly shifted from working class and ethnic German Lutheran and Catholic wards to upper-class pietist business groups.[85]

By the time World War I arrived in Europe, a coalition of progressive intellectuals and corporatist businessmen was ready to go national in sponsoring allegedly objective statistical research institutes and think tanks. Their views have been aptly summed up by David Eakins:

> The conclusion being drawn by these people by 1915 was that fact-finding and policymaking had to be isolated from class struggle and freed from political pressure groups. The reforms that would lead to industrial peace and social order, these experts were coming to believe, could only be derived from data determined by objective fact-finders (such as themselves) and under the auspices of sober and respectable organizations (such as only they could construct). The capitalist system could be improved only by a single-minded reliance upon experts detached from the hurly-burly of democratic policy-making. The emphasis was upon efficiency — and democratic policymaking was inefficient. An approach to the making of national economic and social policy outside traditional democratic political processes was thus emerging before the United States formally entered World War I.[86]

---

[85]See in particular Weinstein, *The Corporate Ideal in the Liberal State*; and Hays, "The Politics of Reform in Municipal Government in the Progressive Era," pp. 157–69.

[86]David Eakins, "The Origins of Corporate Liberal Policy Research, 1916–1922: The Political-Economic Expert and the Decline of Public Debate," in *Building the Organizational Society*, Israel, ed., p. 161.

Several corporatist businessmen and intellectuals moved at about the same time toward founding such statistical research institutes. In 1906–07, Jerome D. Greene, secretary of the Harvard University Corporation, helped found an elite Tuesday Evening Club at Harvard to explore important issues in economics and the social sciences. In 1910 Greene rose to an even more powerful post as general manager of the new Rockefeller Institute for Medical Research, and three years later Greene became secretary and CEO of the powerful philanthropic organization, the Rockefeller Foundation. Greene immediately began to move toward establishing a Rockefeller-funded institute for economic research, and in March 1914 he called an exploratory group together in New York, chaired by his friend and mentor in economics, the first Dean of the Harvard Graduate School of Business, Edwin F. Gay. The developing idea was that Gay would become head of a new "scientific" and "impartial" organization, The Institute of Economic Research, which would gather statistical facts, and that Wesley Mitchell would be its director.[87]

Opposing advisers to John D. Rockefeller, Jr., won out over Greene, however, and the institute plan was scuttled.[88] Mitchell and Gay pressed on, with the lead now taken by Mitchell's longtime friend, chief statistician and vice president of AT&T, Malcolm C. Rorty. Rorty lined up support for the idea from a number of progressive statisticians and businessmen, including Chicago publisher of business books and magazines, Arch W.

---

[87]Herbert Heaton, *Edwin F. Gay, A Scholar in Action* (Cambridge: Harvard University Press, 1952). Edwin Gay was born in Detroit of old New England stock. His father had been born in Boston and went into his father-in-law's lumber business in Michigan. Gay's mother was the daughter of a wealthy preacher and lumberman. Gay entered the University of Michigan, was heavily influenced by the teaching of John Dewey, and then stayed in graduate school in Germany for over a dozen years, finally obtaining his Ph.D. in economic history at the University of Berlin. The major German influences on Gay were Gustav Schmoller, head of the Historical School, who emphasized that economics must be an "inductive science," and Adolf Wagner, also at the University of Berlin, who favored large-scale government intervention in the economy in behalf of Christian ethics. Back at Harvard, Gay was the major single force, in collaboration with the Boston Chamber of Commerce, in pushing through a factory inspection act in Massachusetts, and in early 1911 Gay became president of the Massachusetts branch of the American Association for Labor Legislation, an organization founded by Richard T. Ely and dedicated to agitating for government intervention in the area of labor unions, minimum wage rates, unemployment, public works, and welfare.

[88]On the pulling and hauling among Rockefeller advisers on The Institute of Economic Research, see David M. Grossman, "American Foundations and the Support of Economic Research, 1913–29," *Minerva* 22 (Spring–Summer 1982): 62–72.

Shaw, E.H. Goodwin of the U.S. Chamber of Commerce, Magnus Alexander, statistician and assistant to the president of General Electric, like AT&T, a Morgan-oriented concern, John R. Commons, economist and aide-de-camp to Richard T. Ely at Wisconsin, and Nahum I. Stone, statistician, former Marxist, a leader in the "scientific management" movement, and labor manager for the Hickey Freeman clothing company. This group was in the process of forming a "Committee on National Income" when the United States entered the war, and they were forced to shelve their plans temporarily.[89] After the war, however, the group set up the National Bureau of Economic Research, in 1920.[90]

While the National Bureau was not to take final shape until after the war, another organization, created on similar lines, successfully won Greene and Rockefeller's support. In 1916 they were persuaded by Raymond B. Fosdick to found the Institute for Government Research (IGR).[91] The IGR was slightly different in focus from the National Bureau group, as it grew directly out of municipal progressive reform and the political science profession. One of the important devices used by the municipal reformers was the private bureau of municipal research, which tried to seize decision-making from allegedly "corrupt" democratic bodies on behalf of efficient, nonpartisan organizations headed by progressive technocrats and social scientists. In 1910 President William Howard Taft, intrigued with the potential for centralizing power in a chief executive inherent in the idea of the executive budget, appointed the "father of the budget idea," the political scientist Frederick D. Cleveland, as head of a Commission on Economy and Efficiency. Cleveland was the director of the New York Bureau of Municipal Research. The Cleveland Commission also included political scientist and municipal reformer Frank Goodnow, professor of public law at Columbia University, first president of the American Political Science Association and president of Johns Hopkins, and William Franklin Willoughby, former student of Ely, Assistant Director of

---

[89]See Eakins, "Origins of Corporate Liberal Policy Research," pp. 166–67; Grossman, "American Foundations and the Support of Economic Research," pp. 76–78; Heaton, *Edwin F. Gay.* On Stone, see Dorfman, *Economic Mind in American Civilization,* vol. 4, pp. 42, 60–61; and Samuel Haber, *Efficiency and Uplift: Scientific Management in the Progressive Era, 1890–1920* (Chicago: University of Chicago Press, 1964), pp. 152, 165. During his Marxist period, Stone had translated Marx's *Poverty of Philosophy.*

[90]See Guy Alchon, *The Invisible Hand of Planning: Capitalism, Social Science, and the State in the 1920's* (Princeton, NJ: Princeton University Press, 1985), pp. 54ff.

[91]Collier and Horowitz, *The Rockefellers,* p. 140.

the Bureau of Census, and later president of the American Association for Labor Legislation.[92] The Cleveland Commission was delighted to tell President Taft precisely what he wanted to hear. The Commission recommended sweeping administrative changes that would provide a Bureau of Central Administrative Control to form a "consolidated information and statistical arm of the entire national government." And at the heart of the new Bureau would be the Budget Division, which was to develop, at the behest of the president, and then present "an annual program of business for the Federal Government to be financed by Congress."[93]

When Congress balked at the Cleveland Commission's recommendations, the disgruntled technocrats decided to establish an Institute for Government Research in Washington to battle for these and similar reforms. With funding secured from the Rockefeller Foundation, the IGR was chaired by Goodnow, with Willoughby as its director.[94] Soon Robert S. Brookings assumed responsibility for the financing.

When America entered the war, present and future NBER and IGR leaders were all over Washington, key figures and statisticians in the collectivized war economy.

By far the most powerful of the growing number of economists and statisticians involved in World War I was Edwin F. Gay. Arch W. Shaw, an enthusiast for rigid wartime planning of economic resources, was made head of the new Commercial Economy Board by the Council of National Defense as soon as America entered the war.[95] Shaw, who had taught at and

---

[92]Eakins, "Origins of Corporate Liberal Policy Research," p. 168. Also see Furner, *Advocacy and Objectivity*, pp. 282–86.

[93]Stephen Skowronek, *Building a New American State: The Expansion of the National Administrative Capacities, 1877–1920* (Cambridge: Cambridge University Press, 1982), pp. 187–88.

[94]Vice chairman of the IGR was retired St. Louis merchant and lumberman and former president of Washington University of St. Louis, Robert S. Brookings. Secretary of the IGR was James F. Curtis, formerly Assistant Secretary of the Treasury under Taft and now secretary and deputy governor of the New York Federal Reserve Bank. Others on the board of the IGR were ex-President Taft, railroad executive Frederic A. Delano, uncle of Franklin D. Roosevelt and member of the Federal Reserve Board, Arthur T. Hadley, economist and president of Yale, Charles C. Van Hise, progressive president of the University of Wisconsin, and ally of Ely, reformer and influential young Harvard Law professor, Felix Frankfurter, Theodore N. Vail, chairman of AT&T, progressive engineer and businessman, Herbert C. Hoover, and financier R. Fulton Cutting, an officer of the New York Bureau of Municipal Research. Eakins, "Origins of Corporate Liberal Policy Research," pp. 168–69.

[95]On the Commercial Economy Board, see Clarkson, *Industrial America in the World War*, pp. 211ff.

served on the administrative board of Harvard Business School, staffed the board with Harvard Business people; the secretary was Harvard economist Melvin T. Copeland, and other members included Dean Gay. The board, which later became the powerful Conservation Division of the War Industries Board, focused on restricting competition in industry by eliminating the number and variety of products and by imposing compulsory uniformity, all in the name of "conservation" of resources to aid the war effort. For example, garment firms had complained loudly of severe competition because of the number and variety of styles, and so Gay urged the garment firms to form a trade association to work with the government in curbing the surfeit of competition. Gay also tried to organize the bakers so that they would not follow the usual custom of taking back stale and unsold bread from retail outlets. By the end of 1917, Gay was tired of using voluntary persuasion and was urging the government to use compulsory measures.

Gay's major power came in early 1918 when the Shipping Board, which had officially nationalized all ocean shipping, determined to restrict drastically the use of ships for civilian trade and to use the bulk of shipping for transport of American troops to France. Appointed in early January 1918 as merely a "special expert" by the Shipping Board, Gay in a brief time became the key figure in redirecting shipping from civilian to military use. Soon Edwin Gay had become a member of the War Trade Board and head of its statistical department, which issued restrictive licenses for permitted imports, head of the statistical department of the Shipping Board, representative of the Shipping Board on the War Trade Board, head of the statistical committee of the Department of Labor, head of the Division of Planning and Statistics of the War Industries Board (WIB), and, above all, head of the new Central Bureau of Planning and Statistics. The Central Bureau was organized in the fall of 1918, when President Wilson asked WIB chairman Bernard Baruch to produce a monthly survey of all the government's war activities. This "conspectus" evolved into the Central Bureau, responsible directly to the president. The importance of the bureau is noted by a recent historian:

> The new Bureau represented the "peak" statistical division of the mobilization, becoming its "seer and prophet" for the duration, coordinating over a thousand employees engaged in research and, as the agency responsible for giving the president a concise picture of the entire

economy, becoming the closest approximation to a "central statistical commission." During the latter stages of the war it set up a clearinghouse of statistical work, organized liaisons with the statistical staff of all the war boards, and centralized the data production process for the entire war bureaucracy. By the war's end, Wesley Mitchell recalled, "we were in a fair way to develop for the first time a systematic organization of federal statistics."[96]

Within a year, Edwin Gay had risen from a special expert to the unquestioned czar of a giant network of federal statistical agencies, with over a thousand researchers and statisticians working under his direct control. It is no wonder then that Gay, instead of being enthusiastic about the American victory he had worked so hard to secure, saw the Armistice as "almost ... a personal blow" that plunged him "into the slough of despond." All of his empire of statistics and control had just been coming together and developing into a mighty machine when suddenly "came that wretched Armistice."[97] Truly a tragedy of peace.

Gay tried valiantly to keep the war machinery going, continually complaining because many of his aides were leaving and bitterly denouncing the "hungry pack" who, for some odd reason, were clamoring for an immediate end to all wartime controls, including those closest to his heart, foreign trade and shipping. But one by one, despite the best efforts of Baruch and many of the wartime planners, the WIB and other war agencies disappeared.[98] For a while, Gay pinned his hopes on his Central Bureau of Planning and Statistics (CBPS), which, in a fierce bout of bureaucratic infighting, he attempted to make the key economic and statistical group advising the American negotiators at the Versailles peace conference, thereby displacing the team of historians and social scientists assembled by Colonel House in the Inquiry. Despite an official victory, and an eight-volume report of the CBPS delivered to Versailles by the head

---

[96]Alchon, *Invisible Hand of Planning*, p. 29. Mitchell headed the price statistics section of the Price-Fixing Committee of the War Industries Board.

[97]Heaton, *Edwin F. Gay*, p. 129.

[98]See Rothbard, "War Collectivism," pp. 100–12. [Editor's remarks] See Chapter 12, pp. 390–99.

of CBPS European team, John Foster Dulles of the War Trade Board, the bureau had little influence over the final treaty.[99]

Peace having finally and irrevocably arrived, Edwin Gay, backed by Mitchell, tried his best to have the CBPS kept as a permanent, peacetime organization. Gay argued that the agency, with himself of course remaining as its head, could provide continuing data to the League of Nations, and above all could serve as the president's own eyes and ears and mold the sort of executive budget envisioned by the old Taft Commission. CBPS staff member and Harvard economist Edmund E. Day contributed a memorandum outlining specific tasks for the bureau to aid in demobilization and reconstruction, as well as rationale for the bureau becoming a permanent part of government. One thing it could do was to make a "continuing canvass" of business conditions in the United States. As Gay put it to President Wilson, using a favorite organicist analogy, a permanent board would serve "as a nervous system to the vast and complex organization of the government, furnishing to the controlling brain [the president] the information necessary for directing the efficient operation of the various members."[100] Although the President was "very cordial" to Gay's plan, Congress refused to agree, and on June 30, 1919, the Central Bureau of Planning and Statistics was finally terminated, along with the War Trade Board. Edwin Gay would now have to seek employment in, if not the private, at least the quasi-independent, sector.

But Gay and Mitchell were not to be denied. Nor would the Brookings-Willoughby group. Their objective would be met more gradually and by slightly different means. Gay became editor of the *New York Evening Post* under the aegis of its new owner and Gay's friend, J.P. Morgan partner Thomas W. Lamont. Gay also helped to form and become first president of the National Bureau of Economic Research in 1920, with Wesley C. Mitchell as research director. The Institute for Government Research achieved its major objective, establishing a Budget Bureau in the Treasury Department in 1921, with the director of the IGR, William F. Willoughby, helping to draft the bill that established the bureau.[101] The IGR people soon

---

[99]See Heaton, *Edwin F. Gay*, pp. 129ff.; and the excellent book on the Inquiry, Lawrence E. Gelfand, *The Inquiry: American Preparations for Peace, 1917–1919* (New Haven, CT: Yale University Press, 1963), pp. 166–68, 177–78.

[100]Heaton, *Edwin F. Gay*, p. 135. Also see Alchon, *Invisible Hand of Planning*, pp. 35–36.

[101]In 1939 the Bureau of the Budget would be transferred to the Executive Office, thus completing the IGR objective.

expanded their role to include economics, establishing an Institute of Economics headed by Robert Brookings and Arthur T. Hadley of Yale, with economist Harold G. Moulton as director.[102] The institute, funded by the Carnegie Corporation, would be later merged, along with the IGR, into the Brookings Institution. Edwin Gay also moved into the foreign policy field by becoming secretary-treasurer and head of the Research Committee of the new and extremely influential organization, the Council on Foreign Relations (CFR).[103]

And finally, in the field of government statistics, Gay and Mitchell found a more gradual but longer-range route to power via collaboration with Herbert Hoover, soon to be Secretary of Commerce. No sooner had Hoover assumed the post in early 1921 when he expanded the Advisory Committee on the Census to include Gay, Mitchell, and other economists and then launched the monthly *Survey of Current Business*. The *Survey* was designed to supplement the informational activities of cooperating trade associations and, by supplying business information, aid these associations in Hoover's aim of cartelizing their respective industries. Secrecy in business operations is a crucial weapon of competition, and conversely, publicity and sharing of information is an important tool of cartels in policing their members. The *Survey of Current Business* made available the current production, sales, and inventory data supplied by cooperating industries and technical journals. Hoover also hoped that by building on these services, eventually "the statistical program could provide the knowledge and foresight necessary to combat panic or speculative conditions, prevent the development of diseased industries, and guide decision-making so as to iron out rather than accentuate the business cycle."[104]

---

[102]Moulton was a professor of economics at the University of Chicago, and vice president of the Chicago Association of Commerce. See Eakins, "Origins of Corporate Liberal Policy Research," pp. 172–77; Dorfman, *Economic Mind in American Civilization*, vol. 4, pp. 11, 195–97.

[103]Gay had been recommended to the group by one of its founders, Thomas W. Lamont. It was Gay's suggestion that the CFR begin its major project by establishing an "authoritative" journal, *Foreign Affairs*. And it was Gay who selected his Harvard historian colleague Archibald Cary Coolidge as the first editor and the *New York Post* reporter Hamilton Fish Armstrong as assistant editor and executive director of the CFR. See Lawrence H. Shoup and William Minter, *Imperial Brain Trust: The Council on Foreign Relations and United States Foreign Policy* (New York: Monthly Review Press, 1977), pp. 16–19, 105, 110.

[104]Ellis W. Hawley, "Herbert Hoover and Economic Stabilization, 1921–22," in *Herbert Hoover as Secretary of Commerce: Studies in New Era Thought and Practice*, E. Hawley, ed. (Iowa City: University of Iowa Press, 1981), p. 52.

In promoting his cartelization doctrine, Hoover met resistance both from some businessmen who resisted prying questionnaires and sharing competitive secrets and from the Justice Department. But, a formidable empire-builder, Herbert Hoover managed to grab statistical services from the Treasury Department and to establish a "waste elimination division" to organize businesses and trade associations to continue and expand the wartime "conservation" program of compulsory uniformity and restriction of the number and variety of competitive products. As assistant secretary to head up this program, Hoover secured engineer and publicist Frederick Feiker, an associate of Arch Shaw's business publication empire. Hoover also found a top assistant and lifelong disciple in Brigadier General Julius Klein, a protégé of Edwin Gay's, who had headed the Latin American division of the Bureau of Foreign and Domestic Commerce. As the new head of the bureau, Klein organized 17 new export commodity divisions — reminiscent of commodity sections during wartime collectivism — each with "experts" drawn from the respective industries and each organizing regular cooperation with parallel industrial advisory committees. And through it all Herbert Hoover made a series of well-publicized speeches during 1921, spelling out how a well-designed government trade program, as well as a program in the domestic economy, could act both as a stimulant to recovery and as a permanent "stabilizer," while avoiding such unfortunate measures as abolishing tariffs or cutting wage rates. The best weapon, both in foreign and domestic trade, was to "eliminate waste" by a "cooperative mobilization" of government and industry.[105]

A month after the Armistice, the American Economic Association and the American Statistical Association met jointly in Richmond, Virginia. The presidential addresses were delivered by men in the forefront of the exciting new world of government planning, aided by social science, that seemed to loom ahead. In his address to the American Statistical Association, Wesley Clair Mitchell proclaimed that the war had "led to the use of statistics, not only as a record of what had happened, but also as a vital factor in planning what should be done." As he had said in his final lecture in Columbia University the previous spring, the war had shown that when the community desires to attain a great goal "then within a short period far-reaching social changes can be achieved." "The need for scientific planning of social change," he added, "has never been greater, the chance of

---

[105]Hawley, "Herbert Hoover," p. 53. Also see ibid., pp. 42–54. On the continuing collaboration between Hoover, Gay, and Mitchell throughout the 1920s see Alchon, *Invisible Hand of Planning*.

making those changes in an intelligent fashion ... has never been so good." The peace will bring new problems, he opined, but "it seems impossible" that the various countries will "attempt to solve them without utilizing the same sort of centralized directing now employed to kill their enemies abroad for the new purpose of reconstructing their own life at home ..."

But the careful empiricist and statistician also provided a caveat. Broad social planning requires "a precise comprehension of social processes" and that can be provided only by the patient research of social science. As he had written to his wife eight years earlier, Mitchell stressed that what is needed for government intervention and planning is the application of the methods of physical science and industry, particularly precise quantitative research and measurement. In contrast to the quantitative physical sciences, Mitchell told the assembled statisticians, the social sciences are "immature, speculative, filled with controversy" and class struggle. But quantitative knowledge could replace such struggle and conflict by commonly accepted precise knowledge, "objective" knowledge "amenable to mathematical formulation" and "capable of forecasting group phenomena." A statistician, Mitchell opined, is "either right or wrong," and it is easy to demonstrate which. As a result of precise knowledge of facts, Mitchell envisioned, we can achieve "intelligent experimenting and detailed planning rather than ... agitation and class struggle."

To achieve these vital goals, none other than economists and statisticians would provide the crucial element, for we would have to be "relying more and more on trained people to plan changes for us, to follow them up, to suggest alterations."[106]

In a similar vein, the assembled economists in 1918 were regaled with the visionary presidential address of Yale economist Irving Fisher. Fisher looked forward to an economic "world reconstruction" that would provide glorious opportunities for economists to satisfy their constructive impulses. A class struggle, Fisher noted, would surely be continuing over distribution of the nation's wealth. But by devising a mechanism of "readjustment," the nation's economists could occupy an enviable role as the independent and impartial arbiters of the class struggle, these disinterested social scientists making the crucial decisions for the public good.

---

[106]Alchon, *Invisible Hand of Planning*, pp. 39–42; Dorfman, *Economic Mind in American Civilization*, vol. 3, p. 490.

In short, both Mitchell and Fisher were, subtly and perhaps half-consciously, advancing the case for a postwar world in which their own allegedly impartial and scientific professions could levitate above the narrow struggles of classes for the social product, and thus emerge as a commonly accepted, "objective" new ruling class, a 20th-century version of the philosopher-kings.

It might not be amiss to see how these social scientists, prominent in their own fields and spokesmen in different ways for the New Era of the 1920s, fared in their disquisitions and guidance for the society and the economy. Irving Fisher, as we have seen, wrote several works celebrating the alleged success of prohibition and insisted, even after 1929, that since the price level had been kept stable, there could be no depression or stock market crash. For his part, Mitchell culminated a decade of snug alliance with Herbert Hoover by directing, along with Gay and the National Bureau, a massive and hastily written work on the American economy. Published in 1929 on the accession of Hoover to the presidency, with all the resources of scientific and quantitative economics and statistics brought to bear, there is not so much as a hint in *Recent Economic Changes in the United States* that there might be a crash and depression in the offing.

The *Recent Economic Changes* study was originated and organized by Herbert Hoover, and it was Hoover who secured the financing from the Carnegie Corporation. The object was to celebrate the years of prosperity presumably produced by Secretary of Commerce Hoover's corporatist planning and to find out how the possibly future President Hoover could maintain that prosperity by absorbing its lessons and making them a permanent part of the American political structure. The volume duly declared that to maintain the current prosperity, economists, statisticians, engineers, and enlightened managers would have to work out "a technique of balance" to be installed in the economy.

Recent Economic Changes, that monument to "scientific" and political folly, went through three quick printings and was widely publicized and warmly received on all sides.[107] Edward Eyre Hunt, Hoover's long-time aide

---

[107]One exception was the critical review in the *Commercial and Financial Chronicle* (May 18, 1929), which derided the impression given the reader that the capacity of the United States "for continued prosperity is well-nigh unlimited." Quoted in Davis, *World Between the Wars*, p. 144. Also on *Recent Economic Changes* and economists' opinions at the time, see ibid., pp. 136–51, 400–17; Eakins, "The Development of Corporate Liberal Policy Research

in organizing his planning activities, was so enthusiastic that he continued celebrating the book and its paean to American prosperity throughout 1929 and 1930.[108]

It is appropriate to end our section on government and statistics by noting an unsophisticated yet perceptive cry from the heart. In 1945 the Bureau of Labor Statistics approached Congress for yet another in a long line of increases in appropriations for government statistics. In the process of questioning Dr. A. Ford Hinrichs, head of the BLS, Representative Frank B. Keefe, a conservative Republican Congressman from Oshkosh, Wisconsin, put an eternal question that has not yet been fully and satisfactorily answered:

> There is no doubt but what it would be nice to have a whole lot of statistics. ... I am just wondering whether we are not embarking on a program that is dangerous when we keep adding and adding and adding to this thing ...
>
> We have been planning and getting statistics ever since 1932 to try to meet a situation that was domestic in character, but were never able to even meet that question. ... Now we are involved in an international question. ... It looks to me as though we spend a tremendous amount of time with graphs and charts and statistics and planning. What my people are interested in is what is it all about? Where are we going, and where are you going?[109]

---

in the United States, 1885–1965," pp. 166–69, 205; and Edward Angly, comp., *Oh Yeah?* (New York: Viking Press, 1931).

[108]In 1930, Hunt published a book-length, popularizing summary, *An Audit of America*. On *Recent Economic Changes*, also see Alchon, *Invisible Hand*, pp. 129–33, 135–42, 145–51, 213.

[109]*Department of Labor — FSA Appropriation Bill for 1945*. Hearings Before the Subcommittee on Appropriations. 78th Congress, 2nd Session, Part I (Washington, 1945), pp. 258ff, 276ff. Quoted in Rothbard, "Politics of Political Economists," p. 665. On the growth of economists and statisticians in government, especially during wartime, see also Herbert Stein, "The Washington Economics Industry," *American Economic Association Papers and Proceedings* 76 (May, 1986): 2–3.

APPENDIX

TOWARD THE CENTRALIZATION OF SCIENCE:
THE NATIONAL RESEARCH COUNCIL[110]

Scientific research before World War I was free, diffuse, individualistic, and independent, with very little guidance or control exerted by the federal government. Most scientists and Americans in general approved of this system, but there were always one or two visionaries yearning for an alternative. George Ellery Hale, one of the founders of astrophysics, the director of Mt. Wilson Observatory and one of the founders of the California Institute of Technology, was one of those visionaries, particularly after he was named to the National Academy of Sciences (NAS) in 1902. The NAS had been charted in 1863 as a private organization of scientists to consult with the government on scientific and military matters during the Civil War. By the turn of the 20th century, the NAS was moribund, forgotten by all, including the president of the United States. But George Ellery Hale, turning from the joys of science to the rather different joys of bureaucratic empire and power-building, had a different vision. He sought to make the NAS a vibrant, activist organization, and one of his most important visions was that the NAS should, with the aid of government, acquire a dominant, centralizing power over all scientific research in the nation. And sitting at or near the pinnacle of scientific power, of course, would be George Ellery Hale. He delivered a series of lectures and published articles at the NAS to that effect in 1913–14, but the old fuddy-duddies of the Academy weren't listening.

George Hale did not come to his vision purely on this own. As director of the Mt. Wilson Observatory, he had gained a powerful friend and political mentor — one of the most influential men of the Eastern Establishment: Wall Street lawyer, Secretary of War, Secretary of State, U.S. Senator from New York, and personal attorney for J.P. Morgan, Elihu Root. Root, the son of a professor of astronomy, informed Hale upon his election to the unknown NAS of the untapped potential of the agency for advising and coordinating science on behalf of the government. And it was clear that Root would do all he could to further that objective.[111]

---

[110][Editor's footnote] Due to space constraints, Rothbard did not include this section in the final draft of his paper. It is published here for the first time as an appendix.

[111]Noble, *America by Design*, p. 151.

Then, as luck would have it, the World War began in Europe. By the spring of 1916, Hale was champing at the bit to enter the war on the Allied side, averring his deep hatred for Germans, and bitterly attacking the anti-interventionist stance of Henry Ford and William Jennings Bryan. Hale was certainly succinct about what he would do with these dissidents. "They ought to be imprisoned as traitors," he wrote, "or thoroughly chloroformed."[112] Hale pressured the more laggard patriots of the executive council of the NAS to offer the services of the Academy to the federal government in case of war. After the surprised president learned of the existence of the NAS, Wilson accepted the offer.

George Ellery Hale quickly became chairman of the new NAS committee to plan the Academy's services after war came. His most enthusiastic collaborator on the NAS was Robert A. Millikan, a University of Chicago physicist who had become a member in 1915. Hale exulted that war would be "the greatest chance we ever had to advance research in America."[113] By June 1916, Hale and Millikan had decided that the NAS should create a new agency, the National Research Council (NRS), which would have the operating power to coordinate scientific research when war came. Under pressure from Elihu Root, Wilson approved the idea of the NRC in July. The next problem was to secure funding, since the NRC would be a privately-financed agency, and since the NAS had very little spare money of its own. Financial support was obtained from the Engineering Foundation, which committed its entire annual income of $10,000 to the project, in addition to a personal contribution of $5000 put in by the founder and chairman of the Engineering Foundation, the Cleveland machine-tool and telescope manufacturer Ambrose Swasey, an old friend of Hale.

Its financing secured, the National Research Council was launched in September, dedicated to: performing an inventory of all scientific researchers, projects, and equipment in the country, in preparation for war planning; to cooperate with educational institutions and research foundations; and to function as a "clearing house" to coordinate research projects and scientific information. Moreover, the NRC was to encourage research on national defense and resource problems.

112Tobey, *The American Ideology of National Science*, p. 35.

113Ibid., p. 36.

The Board of the Engineering Foundation, launched in 1914, obtained representation of the various national engineering societies. Vice-chairman of the Engineering Foundation, and another old friend of the ubiquitous Hale, was another scientific visionary: the Serbian immigrant, physicist, inventor, and Columbia University professor, Michael Pupin. While recognizing the importance of individualism and freedom in science, Pupin insisted that there was a far more important requisite for the growth and success of science: "creative coordination," which he explicitly defined as cooperation enforced by compulsion. Without coercion binding everything together, Pupin philosophized, all would be anarchy and chaos, including science. And, of course, as Pupin correctly noted, the State is overwhelmingly the most important instrument of coercion. Therefore, there must be centralization of science under State dictation. Pupin's goal is what he termed, probably not ironically, "ideal democracy," which consisted of the "state organism" being ruled and directed by the "trained intellects" guiding the destiny of the people. Of course, scientists were a crucial, if not the most vital, part of the trained intellect serving as brain of the social organism. Michael Pupin of course hailed the NRC as the first step toward the compulsory coordination of America's intellectuals and their organizations.[114]

They were an effective team for a collectivized science: Michael Pupin the theoretician, and George Hale the activist, assisted by Millikan. To ensure the NRC's stellar role in the war effort, Hale lobbied successfully to make the NRC an official department of the Council of National Defense, with sole responsibility for coordinating scientific resources for war. The NRC now happily set up subcommittees in each discipline: Hale's good friend Edwin Conklin as chairman of the biology subcommittee. James McKeen Cattell in charge of the psychology subcommittee, and Pupin and Robert A. Millikan dominating the physics subcommittee.[115] Millikan, who became the major personality and ideological force in American science during the 1920s, was a former student and protégé of Michael Pupin. An

---

[114]Michael Pupin, *The New Reformation* (1927); and Tobey, *American Ideology of National Science*, pp. 38ff.

[115]Cattell was also a long-time advocate of the government-supported and controlled science. His power base was the Committee of One Hundred on Scientific Research of the American Association for the Advancement of Science, of which Cattell was secretary. The Committee was established in 1913 to try to organize a scientific inventory of the nation. When war came, Cattell coordinated the AAAS activities with the NRC.

assistant professor of physics at the University of Chicago, Millikan had floundered in his researches from 1896 on, until finally becoming extremely successful; by 1912, he had embarked on his researches on electron charge that would win him the Nobel Prize. Millikan, was made a member of the organizing committee of the NRC in 1916, and went from there to become a member of the executive committee, and then vice president and chief administrative officers of the NRC, as well as chairman of the physics committee of the Anti-Submarine Council. So dedicated was Millikan to the war effort that he left Chicago to plunge into full-time war work in Washington, with a commission as an army officer.[116] Many of the nation's leading scientists and engineers entered the armed forces. Thus, physicist Ernest Merritt, of Cornell, entered the navy in order to head up the New London, Connecticut anti-submarine warfare naval base staffed by university scientists.

Well before the end of the war, the problem uppermost in the minds of the scientists was to make the NRC permanent. The organized scientists and in particular the scientists connected with industry, from the beginning envisioned the NRC not merely as a wartime agency, but as a permanent government force sponsoring and coordinating the application to science in industry. Thus, George Hale circulated an anonymous, strictly confidential memorandum within the NRC executive council in May 1919, proclaiming the original intent and the future goal of the agency:

> The Academy organized the National Research Council
> ... with a view to stimulating the growth of science and its
> application to industry and particularly with a view to the
> coordination of research agencies for the sake of enabling
> the United States, in spite of its democratic, individualis-
> tic organization, to bend its energies effectively toward a
> common purpose.[117]

As early as eight months before the Armistice, the organized scientists began to agitate for a quick presidential order making the NRC a permanent, peacetime agency. Since the agency, though governmental, had to be financed by private funds, the first step was to demonstrate secure, durable

---

[116]Robert A. Millikan was the son of an Iowa preacher, and attended the Yankee pietist stronghold of Oberlin College. From 1893 to 1895 he was the only graduate student in physics at Columbia, with Pupin one of his teachers. After obtaining his doctorate in 1895, Pupin loaned Millikan the money to do post-doctoral study at the University of Berlin.

[117]Noble, *America by Design*, p. 154; also Tobey, *American Ideology of National Science*, p. 52.

financing. The Carnegie Corporation, headed by none other than Hale's friend and mentor, Elihu Root, happily obliged with a $5 million grant for an NRC building and an operating endowment. Soon, Hale's old friends at the Engineering Foundation assumed continuing financial responsibility for the NRC, and at that point Elihu Root managed to persuade Colonel House to secure President Wilson's approval.[118] Wilson created a permanent National Research Council by executive order on May 11, 1918.

By the time of Wilson's imprimatur, the irrepressible George Hale was already circulating a letter proclaiming a shift in emphasis from military to permanent industrial research. To that end, he informed his colleagues of the NRC, he proceeded to create a new Industrial Relations Division. The Division was composed of six leaders from elite companies engaged in industrial research: Frank Jewett, director of the Western Electric labs, a wholly owned subsidiary of A.T.&T., J.J. Carty, long-time chief engineer at A.T.&T., Arthur D. Little, the nation's engineering consultant, Raymond Bacon, director of the Mellon Institute, Charles E. Skinner, director of research at the Mellon-oriented Westinghouse Electric, and Willis Whitney, director of research at the Morgan-aligned General Electric.

On May 29, George Hale officially launched the Industrial Relations Division with a gala formal banquet at the University Club of New York, a banquet which symbolized and embodied the new, continuing alliance of the federal government with the top brass in industrial science and research. Addressing the banquet, George Hale proclaimed that "Hitherto, the National Research Council activities have been mostly devoted to war, but plans have been under contemplation for industrial research and the time has arrived to put these plans forward." In their banquet speeches, Hale and Elihu Root stressed the need for national coordination of industrial resources.

Perhaps the most exuberant of the speakers was the original financier of the NRC, the industrialist Ambrose Swasey. Americans and other nations might at that moment be fighting and dying in one of the

---

[118]The leading lights of the Engineering Foundation now included Hale's old friend Gano Dunn, of the J.G. White Engineering Company, Frank B. Jewett, head of Bell Labs for the Morgan-oriented A.T.&T. and apostle of organized scientific research; Arthur D. Little, a Boston born chemical engineer and head of the nation's largest engineering consulting firm; and president E. Wilbur Rice of Morgan-oriented General Electric. Jewett, son of a top engineer for the Morgan-dominated Atchison, Topeka & Santa Fe Railroad, received a Ph.D. in physics from the University of Chicago, studying under Millikan, and eventually joined A.T.&T. as an electrical engineer. See Nobel, *America by Design*, pp. 115, 127, 155.

most devastating wars in history, but to Swasey the war was an exhilarating experience. "We who are living in these wonderful times," Swasey exclaimed, "have thrilling opportunities and correspondingly weighty responsibilities." Enumerating the great advances occasioned by the war, Swasey noted that "whereas a year ago this country produced no optical glass, it is now manufacturing this material by the carload." Part of the great progress occasioned by the war, he pointed out, was due to the U.S. seizure of German patents. Swasey concluded with a brief demurrer before exulting over the war's matchless benefits: "While deeply deploring the war," Swasey proclaimed, "the marvelous advances it was bringing in the mental, moral and spiritual realms, with consequent great benefits to mankind ..."[119]

The main harvest of this banquet was the creation of an advisory committee of industrial leaders to the Industrial Research Division, and the publication of a pamphlet on the new division co-authored by some of the most distinguished leaders present at the banquet. Chairman of the advisory committee was the eminent Theodore N. Vail, president of A.T.&T., and other members included Cleveland H. Dodge, vice president of Phelps-Dodge mining and President Wilson's favorite industrialist, George Eastman, head of Eastman Kodak, Andrew Mellon, head of the mighty Mellon banking and industrial family, and soon to become Secretary of the Treasury, Pierre DuPont, Ambrose Swasey, Elihu Root, Judge Elbert H. Gary, head of the Morgan-influenced U.S. Steel, E. Wilbur Rice, president of General Electric, and Henry S. Pritchett, president of the Carnegie Foundation for the Advancement of Teaching.[120]

In the pamphlet, the various distinguished contributors beat the drums for a national coordination of science, a veritable coordinated government-science-industry complex. Thus, President Vail of A.T.&T. declared that

> Organization and coordination of research for industrial
> purpose is urgently necessary. ... Plans should be formu-

---

[119]Noble, *America by Design*, p. 156.

[120]The son of an astronomer, Henry Pritchett was one of the most prominent astronomers in the country, formerly professor at Washington University of St. Louis, superintendent of the U.S. Coast and Geodetic Survey, and then president of M.I.T., before becoming the founder and first president of the Carnegie Foundation. Pritchett had long sought centralized government standardization as part of national industrial competition against Germany. Ibid., pp. 72–73, 156.

lated at once. ... Whatever is done should be national in
its comprehensiveness. ... Industry may be expected to
support generously any organization which promises to
effectively coordinate and correlate efforts for the increase
of knowledge, since it is now generally recognized that
industrial progress and success are chiefly dependent
upon our knowledge.[121]

In the midst of the wartime model, it is not surprising that military-
like "discipline" was a common theme of these industrial, scientific and
political leaders. Thus, Elihu Root in his article, "The Need for Organization in Scientific Research," opined that "scientific men are only recently
realizing ... that the effective power of a great number of scientific men
may be increased by organization just as the effective power of a great
number of laborers may be increased by military discipline." In the war,
Root added, the power of science has "amazingly increased the productive power of mankind." After the war, that same power "will be applied
again and the prizes of industrial and commercial leadership will fall to
the nation which organizes its scientific forces most effectively."

And Henry S. Pritchett, of the Carnegie Foundation, who had long
admired the German model of a national physical laboratory and national
coordination of science, called for post-war America to establish a similar
system. Pritchett insisted that "The research men of a nation are not isolated individuals but an organized and cooperating army."[122]

In early 1919, the NRC was formally structured for the post-war world
into a number of divisions. One of the most active in serving and subsidizing industry was the Industrial Relations Division (later renamed the
Industrial Research Division, and finally the Industrial Extension Division), which established cooperative research programs in various industries and initiated research projects in various areas of metals and electro-
plating. In particular, the Industrial Relations Division created a number
of industrial research institutes in collaboration with various trade associations.[123]

---

[121]Ibid., p. 158.

[122]Ibid., pp. 157–58.

[123]By 1919, the chairman of the Industrial Relations Division was John Johnston, of U.S.
Steel.

Another very active division of the NRC was the Engineering Division, launched during the war in 1918. The Engineering Division was founded under the auspices of the Engineering Foundation which by now had become the research branch of the American Engineering Council, the umbrella organization of all the various engineering associations. Engineering Foundation head Ambrose Swasey also became a member of the new Engineering Division of the NRC. The function of the division was to encourage direct industrial research, the funds often to be supplied by the industry concerned, but the organizing and coordination to be performed by the NRC. The first project of the Engineering Division was a large-scale study of metal fatigue, financed by the Engineering Foundation and by General Electric. On the other hand, a project to study the heat treatment of carbon steel was financed by the federal government, and federal and state governments supported a program of highway research conducted by the division.[124]

Another important post-war arm of the NRC, the Research Information Service, also began during the war as the Research Information Committee, under physicist and Bureau of Standards head Samuel Stratton, to disseminate scientific information between the U.S. and its European allies. After the war, the RIS prepared scientific compilations, source books, abstracts, handbooks, and bibliographies and disseminated them, in George Hale's words, to those who "can use it to advantage." In the words of Charles L. Reese, research and chemical director of Du Pont, the service operated as an "intelligence agency."[125]

The major dispute among the NRC-affiliated and connected scientists was whether or not scientific research in the postwar world should be thoroughly centralized under one governmental research institute and national laboratory, in physics and chemistry. George Vincent, president of the Rockefeller Foundation, and his colleague Edward C. Pickering, head of the Harvard Observatory, had been agitating for the idea of a centralized research institute since 1913, trying to persuade the membership of the American Association for the Advancement of Science. During the war, Vincent, backed by Dr. Simon Flexner, head of the Rockefeller Institute for Medical Research, wrote a letter to the NRC executive proposing the

---

[124]In 1919, chairman of the Engineering Division was electrical engineer Comfort A. Adams, of Harvard, who was succeeded in 1923 by Frank Jewett. See Noble, *America by Design*, pp. 162–66.

[125]Ibid., p. 161.

plan for the postwar world. Hale, Pritchett, and Root were highly enthusiastic, but the more cautious Millikan and Whitney advocated three to
six regional laboratories at existing university facilities. None of the con-
tending parties, of course, had any desire to return to the good old days
of decentralized, free and private scientific research. Finally, all parties
agreed on a compromise plan, which provided for no national or regional
laboratories, but did set up a massive fellowship program in graduate physics and chemistry, administered by the government NRC and financed
entirely by the Rockefeller Foundation. The science centralizers might not
have achieved all of their aims, but they were well on the road.

CHAPTER 14

The Federal Reserve as a Cartelization Device: The Early Years, 1913–1930

To most economists, historians, and lay people, a modern economy without a central bank is simply unthinkable. With that kind of mindset, the creation of the Federal Reserve System in December 1913 can be attributed to a simple, enlightened acceptance of the need to

Originally published in *Money in Crisis: The Federal Reserve, the Economy, and Monetary Reform*, Barry N. Siegel, ed. (San Francisco, CA: Pacific Institute for Public Policy Research, 1984), pp. 89–136.
    [Editor's footnote] It is important to keep in mind that a "bank cartel" is different than a traditional cartel. A traditional cartel restricts output and raises prices. The goal of a bank cartel, on the other hand, is not to restrict credit expansion and raise interest rates, but for banks to engage in credit expansion in unison and lower interest rates, and to maintain this by not calling on other banks' notes and deposits. Just like traditional cartels on the free market fail, bank cartels also fail because of internal and external pressure as banks inside the cartel are faced with the irresistible temptation to call on others' notes and deposits, and the notes and deposits eventually wind up in other banks outside of the cartel (including foreign banks). See Mises, *Human Action*, pp. 441–45; Murray Rothbard, *The Mystery of Banking* (Auburn, AL: Mises Institute, 2008 [1983]), pp. 111–24.
    On the other hand, government can stabilize bank cartels either by restricting entry to stifle the redemption mechanism, or by providing new sources of reserves. The Federal Reserve promoted general monetary expansion, and also empowered New York City banks by increasing their interbank deposits relative to other central reserve cities through the Federal Reserve Bank of New York's liberal discount window policies, and by injecting new reserves there first as they led the monetary expansion in the 1920s. Moreover, the

bring the economy of the United States into the modern world. It is generally held, in addition, that a central bank is necessary to curb the natural instincts of free-market banks to inflate and, as a corollary, to level out economic fluctuations. It has become all too clear in recent years, however, that the Fed has scarcely succeeded in this supposed task. For since the establishment of the Fed, we have suffered the longest and deepest depression in American history, and we have, since World War II, experienced the unique phenomenon of a chronic, accelerating secular inflation. Since instability, inflation, and depressions have been far worse since the inception of the Federal Reserve, many economists have concluded that the Fed has failed in its task and have come up with various suggestions for reform to try to get it on the correct task.

It is possible, however, that the current critics of the Fed have missed the essential point: that the Fed was designed to meet very different goals. In fact, the Fed was largely fashioned by the banks as a cartelizing device. The government interventions of the Progressive era were systemic devices to restrict competition and cartelize industry, stratagems that followed on the previous failure of industry to sustain successful voluntary cartels. Just as other industries turned to the government to impose cartelization that could not be maintained on the market, so the banks turned to government to enable them to expand money and credit without being held back by the demands for redemption by competing banks. In short, rather than hold back the banks from their propensity to inflate credit, the new central banks were created to do precisely the opposite. Indeed, the record of the American economy under the Federal Reserve can be considered a rousing success from the point of view of the actual goals of its founders and of those who continue to sustain its power.

A proper overall judgment on the actual role of the Fed was delivered by the vice-chairman and de facto head of the Federal Trade Commission, Edward N. Hurley. The Federal Trade Commission was Woodrow Wilson's other major Progressive reform, following closely on the passage of the Federal Reserve Act. Hurley was president of the Illinois Manufacturers Association at the time of his appointment, and his selection and subsequent performance in his new job were hailed throughout the business community. Addressing the Association of National Advertisers in December 1915,

---

Fed personnel was heavily dominated by banking interests. In addition to this chapter, see George Selgin, "New York's Bank: The National Monetary Commission and the Founding of the Fed," *Cato Institute Policy Analysis* (June, 2016): 1–38.

Hurley exulted that "through a period of years the government has been gradually extending its machinery of helpfulness to different classes and groups upon whose prosperity depends in a large degree the prosperity of the country." Then came the revealing statement: The railroads and shippers had the ICC, the farmers had the Agriculture Department, and the bankers had the Federal Reserve Board. Hurley concluded that "to do for general business that which these other agencies do for the groups to which I have referred was the thought behind the creation of the trade commission."[1] What, then, did the Federal Reserve do for the nation's bankers?

1. The Origins of the Federal Reserve: The Dissatisfaction of New York Bankers

The Federal Reserve did not replace a system of free banking. On the contrary, an approach to free banking existed in the United States only in the two decades before the Civil War. Under the cover of the wartime emergency, the Republican Party put through changes that had long been proposed by the Republicans' ancestor, the Whig Party. The National Bank Acts of 1863–65 replaced the hard-money free banking of pre–Civil War days with the quasi-centralized regime of the national banking system. By levying a prohibitive federal tax, the national banking system in effect outlawed state bank notes, centralizing the issue of bank notes into the hands of federally chartered national banks. By means of an elaborate set of categories and a structure of fractional reserve requirements, entry into national banking in the big cities was limited to large banks, and bank deposits were encouraged to pyramid on top of a handful of large Wall Street banks. Furthermore, an expansion of any one bank in the pre–Civil War era was severely limited, since the free market would discount the notes of shaky banks, roughly proportionate to the distance of the circulating notes from the home base of the bank.[2] The national banking acts removed that restraint by forcing every national bank to accept the notes and demand deposits of every other national bank at par. Genuine redeemability of notes and deposits was also restrained by the continued legal prohibition of interstate or even intrastate branch banking, which

---

[1]Kolko, *The Triumph of Conservatism*, p. 274.

[2]In contrast, notes of more solid banks circulated at par, even at great distances.

severely hobbled the efficiency of clearing systems where one bank presents the obligations of another for redemption. Redemption was also curtailed by a rigid statutory maximum limit of $3 million per month by which national bank notes could be contracted. Furthermore, although private national bank liabilities were of course not legal tender, the federal government conferred quasi-legal tender status upon them by agreeing to receive all national bank notes and deposits at par in dues or taxes.

The banking system of the United States after 1865 was, therefore, a halfway house between free and central banking. Banking was subsidized, privileged, and quasi-centralized under the aegis of a handful of large Wall Street banks. Even at that, however, the large national banks and their financial colleagues were far from satisfied. There was no governmental central bank to act as the lender of last resort. The banks could inflate more readily and uniformly than before the Civil War, but when they got into trouble and bank-generated booms turned into recessions, they were forced to contract and deflate to save themselves. As we will see further below, the bankers' drive for fundamental change was generally couched in terms of an attack on the "inelasticity" of the national banking system. Translated into plain English, "inelasticity" meant the inability of the banking system to inflate money and credit, especially during recessions.[3]

---

[3]See Milton Friedman and Anna Jacob Schwartz, *A Monetary History of the United States, 1867–1960* (Princeton, NJ: National Bureau of Economic Research, 1963), pp. 168–70. Friedman and Schwartz grant validity to the complaints of inelasticity in at least one sense: that deposits and notes were not easily interconvertible without causing grave problems. If bank clients wished to redeem bank deposits for bank notes, the fractional reserve requirements for deposits but not for notes meant that such simple redemption had a multiple contractionist effect on the supply of money and vice versa, since the exchange of notes for deposits had an expansionist effect. Friedman and Schwartz conclude that this defect justified various centralizing remedies. They fail to point out another alternative: a return to the decentralized banking of pre-Civil War days, which did not suffer from such problems of interconvertibility.

One curiosity of the national banking system is that the notes issued by the national banks were rigidly linked by law to the total holdings of federal government bonds by each bank. This provision, a holdover from various state bank systems imposed by the Whigs before the Civil War, was designed to tie the banks to state deficits and the public debt. See Ron Paul and Lewis Lehrman, *The Case for Gold: A Minority Report of the U.S. Gold Commission* (Washington, D.C.: Cato Institute, 1982), p. 67. The source of "inelasticity," however, could easily have been remedied by abolishing this link without imposing a central bank. Many of the early bank reforms proposed during the 1890s aimed to do just that. See Robert Craig West, *Banking Reform and the Federal Reserve, 1863–1923* (Ithaca, NY: Cornell University Press, 1977), pp. 42ff.

The big banks' turn to the idea of a central bank came after the beginning of the 20th century. The increased dissatisfaction with the status quo was prompted particularly by the rising competition of state banks and private banks outside the direct purview of the national banks of Wall Street. State banks had recovered from their initial shock and, after the 1860s, grew rapidly by pyramiding loans and deposits on top of national bank notes. These state and other non-national banks provided increasingly stiff competition with Wall Street for the banking resources of the nation. State banks were free of the high legal capital requirements for entry into the national banking business, and banking laws, especially in such important states as Michigan, California, and New York, became more lenient during the 1890s. As a result, the proportion of non-national bank deposits to national bank notes and deposits, which had been 67% in 1873, rose to 101% in 1886 and to 145% in 1901. To make things worse for cartelization, New York City lost its monopoly of designated "central reserve city" status — the base of the nation's banking pyramid — to St. Louis and Chicago in 1887. As a result, the total bank deposits of St. Louis and Chicago, which had been only 16% of the combined total of the three major cities in 1880, rose sharply to 33% by 1912. Banking in the smaller reserve cities rose even more rapidly in this period: the bank clearings outside of New York, 24% of the national total in 1882, rose to 43% by 1913.[4]

The major New York banks were understandably perturbed at the rising competition of non-New York and non-national banks. They were upset, too, by the fact that they had to compete with each other for the deposits of the burgeoning state banks. As one New York banker put it: "We love the country bankers, but they are the masters of the situation. We dance at their music and pay the piper."[5]

The New York national bankers were also particularly perturbed at the mushrooming growth of private trust companies in New York, which were gathering the major share of the new and profitable trust business, when national and most state-chartered banks were prohibited by law from handling trust accounts. At the behest of the national banks, the New York Clearing House, a private organization for the clearing of notes and deposits, tried to impose reserve requirements on trust companies to hobble their competition with banks. In reply, 17 of them walked out

---

[4]U.S. Department of Commerce, *Historical Statistics of the United States, Colonial Times to 1957*, pp. 626–29.

[5]Quoted in Kolko, *Triumph of Conservatism*, p. 141.

of the Clearing House for a decade. Finally, the House of Morgan formed the banker-owned Bankers' Trust Company in 1903 to compete with the private trust companies.[6]

J.P. Morgan & Co. was the most powerful financial grouping in Wall Street and hence in the country. An investment bank that came to own or control the bulk of the nation's important railroads, the House of Morgan controlled such leading Wall Street national banks as Guaranty Trust Company, the First National Bank of New York, and, before the 1930s, the Chase National Bank. Despite (or perhaps because of) its mammoth size and influence, Morgan was doing poorly in the gales of competition after 1900. In addition to the factors mentioned above that weakened New York banks, railroads, in which the Morgans had concentrated their forces, began to enter their long secular decline after the turn of the century. Furthermore, virtually all the mergers in the 1898–1902 period that tried to achieve monopoly control and monopoly profits in various industries collapsed with the entry of new firms and suffered major losses. Some of the most egregious failures — including International Harvester, United States Steel, and International Mercantile Marine — were Morgan creations.

J.P. Morgan had long favored corporatism and government cartelization where competition proved inconvenient. After decades of abject failure of Morgan-created railroad cartels, Morgan took the lead in establishing the Interstate Commerce Commission in 1887 to cartelize the railroad industry. Now, after slipping badly in the free market after 1900, Morgan joined other big business interests, such as the Rockefellers and the Belmonts, in calling for the compulsory cartelization of the American economy. This alliance of powerful big business interests, professionals who sought power and place constituted what is now known as the Progressive Era (approximately 1900 to 1918). The Federal Reserve Act was a "progressive" Wilsonian reform that, as Edward Hurley and others pointed out, "did for" the bankers what the other reforms had done for other segments of industry.[7]

---

[6]See Kolko, *Triumph of Conservatism*, p. 141; and Lester V. Chandler, *Benjamin Strong, Central Banker* (Washington, D.C.: Brookings Institution, 1958), pp. 25–26.

[7]The major pressure group calling for "progressive" cartelization was the National Civic Federation (NCF), founded in 1900, an organized coalition of big business and intellectual-technocrat groups as well as a few corporatist labor union leaders. On the importance of the NCF, see Weinstein, *The Corporate Ideal in the Liberal State*. See also Eakins, "The Development of Corporate Liberal Policy Research in the United States," pp. 53–82.

In the past two decades, a massive literature has developed on the Progressive Era

2. THE ROAD TO THE FEDERAL RESERVE[8]

During the McKinley and Roosevelt administrations, treasury secretaries Lyman J. Gage and Leslie M. Shaw respectively tried to operate the Treasury Department as a central bank, pumping in money during recessions by purchasing government bonds on the open market and depositing large funds with commercial banks. In 1900, Gage called for the establishment of regional central banks, and Shaw suggested in his last annual report in 1906 that he be given total power to regulate the nation's banks. Their efforts failed, and these failures helped to spur the big bankers to seek a formal central bank.[9]

Neither Gage nor Shaw was an isolated treasury bureaucrat whose power was suddenly going to his head. Before his appointment, Gage was president of the powerful First National Bank of Chicago, one of the major banks in the Rockefeller orbit. He also served as president of the American Bankers Association. After leaving the Treasury Department, Gage became president of the Rockefeller-controlled U.S. Trust Company, and his hand-picked assistant at the department, Frank A. Vanderlip, left to become a top executive at the Rockefellers' flagship bank, the National City Bank of New York.[10] Gage's appointment as treasury secretary was secured for him by Mark Hanna, close friend, political mastermind, and financial backer of President McKinley. Hanna, a coal magnate and iron

---

from both a cartelizing and a technocratic power-seeking perspective. The best treatments are in Kolko, *Triumph of Conservatism*; Weinstein, *Corporate Ideal in the Liberal State*; and Gilbert, *Designing the Industrial State*. On the railroads and the ICC, see Kolko, *Railroads and Regulation*.

[8][Editor's footnote] For more on the background of the Federal Reserve, see Rothbard, "The Origins of the Federal Reserve," pp. 188–208, 234–59. Here Rothbard describes in much more depth the earlier measures and events, including the 1897 and 1898 Indianapolis Monetary Conventions and the Gold Standard Act of 1900. He also elaborates on the role of bankers, economists, technocrats, and their respective organizations in agitating for a central bank.

[9]On Gage's and Shaw's proposals and actions in office, see Friedman and Schwartz, *Monetary History of the United States,* pp. 148–56; and Kolko, *Triumph of Conservatism*, pp. 149–50.

[10]John D. Rockefeller was the largest stockholder of National City Bank; its president until 1905 was James Stillman, two of whose daughters married sons of Rockefeller's brother William. See Carl P. Parrini, *Heir to Empire: United States Economic Diplomacy, 1916–1923* (Pittsburgh: University of Pittsburgh Press, 1969), pp. 55–65.

manufacturer, was a close business associate as well as an old friend and high school classmate of John D. Rockefeller, Sr.[11]

Leslie Shaw was a small-town Iowa banker who became governor of his state in 1898 and continued as president of the Bank of Denison until the end of his term. He reached his post as governor by being a loyal supporter of the Des Moines Regency, the Republican machine in Iowa, and a close friend of the Regency's leader, the powerful and venerable U.S. senator William Boyd Allison. Allison was the one who secured the treasury position for his friend Shaw and in turn was tied closely to Charles E. Perkins, a close Morgan ally, president of the Chicago, Burlington and Quincy Railroad, and kinsman of the Forbes financial group of Boston, long associated with the Morgans.[12]

After the failure of Shaw's interventions, and particularly after the Panic of 1907, the big bankers turned in earnest to a drive for the establishment of a central bank in the United States. The movement was launched in January 1906 when Jacob H. Schiff, the head of the powerful investment banking firm of Kuhn, Loeb & Co., urged the New York Chamber of Commerce to advocate fundamental banking reform. Heeding the call, the New York chamber immediately established a special committee to study the problem and propose legislation. The committee was comprised of leaders from commercial and investment banking, including Isidor Straus of R.H. Macy's (a close friend of Schiff) and Frank A. Vanderlip of the National City Bank. In March, the special committee report, not surprisingly, called for the creation of a strong central bank "similar to the Bank of Germany."

The New York chamber proved reluctant to endorse this far-reaching scheme, but the big bankers had the bit in their teeth. In mid-1906, the American Bankers Association followed suit by naming a commission of inquiry of leading bankers from the major cities of the country, headed by A. Barton Hepburn, chairman of the board of Chase National Bank. The Hepburn commission was more cautious, and its report of November 1906 called for imperative changes in the existing banking system, including a system of regional clearing houses for the issue of bank notes. The notes

---

[11]On Gage's connections, see Burch, *The Civil War to the New Deal*, vol. 2, pp. 137, 185, 390.

[12]On Shaw's connections, see Burch, *Civil War to the New Deal*, pp. 148, 402. On Allison and Perkins, see ibid., pp. 65, 121, 122, 128, 151.

would be guaranteed by a common pool built up by taxes levied on the notes.[13]

A variant of the Hepburn plan was passed by Congress in May 1908, after the Panic of 1907, in the Aldrich-Vreeland Act. Aldrich-Vreeland provided for the issuance of "emergency" currency by groups of bankers clustered in "National Currency Associations." Although this regional cartel scheme was devised as a stopgap measure, the congressional authorization was to be for seven years, a rather long "temporary" period.[14]

In fact, however, Aldrich-Vreeland provisions were used only once, and that was in 1914, shortly after the launching of the Federal Reserve System. By far the most significant aspect of Aldrich-Vreeland turned out to be its clause setting up a National Monetary Commission to study the American and foreign banking systems and to emerge with a plan of reform. The commission consisted of nine senators and nine representatives and, in standard bureaucratic procedure, the chairman of the commission was Senator Nelson W. Aldrich and the vice-chairman was Representative Edward B. Vreeland.

Representative Vreeland was a banker from the Buffalo area of New York, and little more need be said about him. Far more important was the powerful Senator Nelson W. Aldrich, a Republican from Rhode Island who made millions during his long years of service in the U.S. Senate. One of the prime movers in the creation of the Federal Reserve System, Nelson Aldrich was the father-in-law of John D. Rockefeller, Jr., and may be fairly regarded as Rockefeller's man in the Senate.[15]

From the inception of the National Monetary Commission until the presentation of its Aldrich plan to Congress four years later, Senator Aldrich and the commission were a vitally important nucleus of the drive for a central bank. Particularly influential in the deliberations of the commission were two men who were not official members. Aldrich asked J.P. Morgan to recommend a banking expert, and Morgan happily responded with Henry P. Davison, a Morgan partner; the other unofficial member

---

[13]See Kolko, *Triumph of Conservatism*, p. 152.

[14]On Aldrich-Vreeland, see Friedman and Schwartz, *Monetary History of the United States*, pp. 170–72. On the jockeying for power among various banking and business groups over different provisions of Aldrich-Vreeland, see Kolko, *Triumph of Conservatism*, pp. 156–58.

[15]When the Rockefeller forces gained control of the Chase National Bank from the Morgans in 1930, one of their first actions was to oust Morgan man Albert H. Wiggins and replace him with Nelson Aldrich's son Winthrop W. as chairman of the board.

was George M. Reynolds of Chicago, president of the American Bankers Association.[16]

Aldrich and the National Monetary Commission, however, were by no means the only focus of the movement for a central bank. Another was Paul Moritz Warburg, one of the most vital influences on the creation of the Federal Reserve System. Warburg, scion of the great international banking family and the German investment banking firm of M.M. Warburg and Company, of Hamburg, emigrated to the United States in 1902 to become a partner in the influential New York banking house of Kuhn, Loeb & Co.[17] From the moment he came to the United States, Warburg worked tirelessly, in person and in print, to bring the blessings of European central banking to this monetarily backward land. Sensitive to American political objections to the idea of centralization or of Wall Street control, Warburg always insisted disingenuously that his plan was not *really* a central bank. His first printed banking reform essay came in January 1907 in his "A Plan for a Modified Central Bank." The plan called for centralized reserves and a centralized note issue as a key to assuring economic stability. The most elaborate versions of Warburg's reform plan were presented in two speeches in 1910: "A United Reserve Bank of the United States" and "Principles that Must Underlie Monetary Reform in the United States."

Warburg's United Reserve Bank delineated the major features of the future Federal Reserve System. The key to its power was to be its legal monopoly on all note issue in the United States; to obtain such notes, the banks would have to keep their reserves at the Reserve Bank. Reserves would therefore be centralized at long last. Depositors at the Bank would be strictly limited to the member banks and the federal government. The

---

[16]See West, *Banking Reform and the Federal Reserve*, p. 70. Investment banking houses were — and still are — partnerships rather than corporations, and Morgan activities in politics as well as industrial mergers were conducted by Morgan partners. Particularly conspicuous Morgan partners in both fields were George W. Perkins, Thomas W. Lamont, Henry P. Davison, Dwight Morrow, and Willard Straight.

[17]Or at least *partially* emigrated. Warburg spent half of each year in Germany, serving as a financial liaison between the two great banks, if not between the two countries themselves. Warburg was related to Jacob H. Schiff by marriage. Schiff was a son-in-law of Solomon Loeb, a co-founder of Kuhn, Loeb & Co., and Warburg, husband of Nina Loeb, was another son-in-law of Solomon's by a second wife. The incestuous circle was completed when Schiff's daughter Frieda married another partner, Warburg's brother Felix, which in a sense made Paul his brother's uncle. See Birmingham, *"Our Crowd,"* pp. 21, 209–10, 383, appendix.

Bank was to be governed by a board selected equally by three groups: the member banks, the stockholders of the Reserve Bank, and the federal government. Not surprisingly, Warburg's plan repeated the essential features of the operation of the German Reichsbank, the central bank in his native Germany.[18]

The greatest cheerleader for Warburg's plan, and the man who introduced his banking reform essays to Columbia University's Academy of Political Science, was Warburg's kinsman, the Columbia economist Edwin R.A. Seligman, of the investment banking family of J. & W. Seligman and Company.[19]

The top bankers were clear from the beginning that, to assuage widespread fears of centralized and Wall Street control, they would have to avoid the *appearance* of an orthodox central bank on the lines of England or Germany. The chosen course was a spurious "regionalism" and "decentralization," the appearance of a virtually uncoordinated set of regional central banks. The idea was in the air when Victor Morawetz made his famous speech in November 1909 calling for regional banking districts under the ultimate direction of one central control board. Although reserves and note issue would be *pro forma* decentralized in the hands of the regional reserve banks, all would really be centralized and coordinated by the central control board. This specious decentralization was, of course, the scheme eventually adopted in the Federal Reserve System.

Who was Victor Morawetz? He was a distinguished attorney and banker and in particular the counsel and chairman of the executive committee of the Morgan-controlled Atchison, Topeka and Santa Fe Railroad. In 1908, Morawetz had been, along with J.P. Morgan's personal lawyer, Francis Lynde Stetson, the principal drafter of an unsuccessful Morgan-National Civic Federation bill for a federal incorporation law that would have cartelized and regulated American corporations. Later, Morawetz

---

[18]On Warburg's plan, see West, *Banking Reform and the Federal Reserve*, pp. 54–59. Warburg's plan and essays, as well as his other activities on behalf of central banking in the United States, are collected in his *The Federal Reserve System*, 2 vols. (New York: Macmillan, 1930). See also Warburg, "Essays on Banking Reform in the United States," *Proceedings of the Academy of Political Science* 4 (July, 1914): 387–612.

[19]Professor Seligman's brother Isaac N. was marred to Guta Loeb, sister of Paul Warburg's wife Nina. This made Seligman the brother of Warburg's brother-in-law; see Birmingham, "*Our Crowd*," appendix.

was to be a top consultant to another "progressive" reform of Woodrow Wilson's, the Federal Trade Commission.[20]

In late 1910, someone in the Aldrich circle, probably Henry P. Davison, got the idea of convening a small group of leading advocates of a central bank in a top secret conclave to draft a bill for a central bank. The clandestine meeting was held in November at a duck-shooting retreat for wealthy members, the Jekyll Island Club on Jekyll Island, Georgia. The cover story given to the press was that the conferees were going down for a duck-hunting expedition. Extraordinary measures were taken to ensure secrecy, with the conferees traveling down to Georgia under assumed names in a private railroad car chartered by Aldrich. Some reporters got wind of the meeting, but Davison managed to talk them out of any publicity.[21]

The blue-ribbon participants at the week-long Jekyll Island meeting were:

Senator Nelson W. Aldrich, Rockefeller in-law

Henry P. Davison, Morgan partner

Paul M. Warburg, Kuhn, Loeb & Co. partner[22]

Frank A. Vanderlip, vice-president of Rockefeller's National City Bank

Charles D. Norton, president of Morgan's First National Bank of New York

A. Piatt Andrew, Harvard economist and staff assistant to Aldrich on the Monetary Commission

There is no clearer physical embodiment of the cartelizing coalition of top financial and banking interests that brought the Federal Reserve System

---

[20]On Morawetz, see West, *Banking Reform and the Federal Reserve*, pp. 59–62; and Kolko, *Triumph of Conservatism*, pp. 134, 183–84, 272.

[21]So shrouded in secrecy did the meeting remain that details did not leak out until the publication of the authorized biography of Aldrich 20 years later. It is not even clear which club member arranged the facilities for the meeting, since none of the participants was a member. The best guess on the identity of the helpful Jekyll Island member is J.P. Morgan. See West, *Banking Reform and the Federal Reserve*, p. 71; see also Nathaniel W. Stephenson, *Nelson W. Aldrich* (New York: Scribner's, 1930).

[22]Aldrich was in the audience when Warburg delivered his famous "United Reserve Bank Plan" speech to the Academy of Political Science in 1910. The enthusiastic Aldrich who had been greatly impressed by German central banking views during the Monetary Commission's trip to Europe the previous year, promptly invited Warburg to attend the upcoming Jekyll Island gathering; see Kolko, *Triumph of Conservatism*, p. 184.

into being than the sometimes allied, often clashing Rockefeller-Kuhn, Loeb and Morgan interests, aided by economic technicians.

Using the research of the National Monetary Commission, the Jekyll Island conclave drafted a bill for a central bank. The ideas of this draft, which eventually became the Aldrich Bill, were basically Paul Warburg's, with a decentralized *soupcon* taken from Morawetz. The final writing was contributed by Vanderlip. The main disagreement at the meeting was that Aldrich wanted to hold out for a straightforward central bank on the European model, whereas Warburg and the other banks, oddly enough more politically astute on this issue than the veteran senator, insisted that the reality of central banking be clothed in the palatable garb of decentralization. The Jekyll Island draft was presented by Aldrich to the full National Monetary Commission in January 1911. Slightly revised, it was introduced, together with the commission report, a year later as the Aldrich Bill, which in turn became in all essentials the final Federal Reserve Act passed in December 1913.

In the Aldrich-Jekyll Island plan, the central bank with branches was called the National Reserve Association; the main difference between the draft and the eventual legislation is that in the former, the national board of directors was largely chosen by the banks themselves rather than by the president of the United States. This provision was so blatantly cartelist that it was modified for political reasons to have the president name the board. The economist Henry Parker Willis, who played a large role in the enactment of the Federal Reserve System, lamented this alteration: "Political prejudice proved too strong for the establishment of this form of financial self-government or 'integration.'"[23]

Aldrich and the Monetary Commission took the unusual step of delaying their report to Congress for 12 months, from January 1911 to January 1912. With the Democratic victory in the congressional elections of 1910, it was necessary to spend a year drumming up support for a central bank among Democrats, bankers, and the lay public. Accordingly, at the beginning of February 1911, twenty-two top bankers from 12 cities met for three days behind closed doors in Atlantic City to consider the Aldrich plan; the conference warmly endorsed the plan. In the private deliberation, James B. Forgan, President of the Rockefeller-dominated First National Bank of Chicago, declared outright that everyone there

---

[23]Henry Parker Willis, *The Theory and Practice of Central Banking* (New York: Harper & Bros., 1936), p. 77.

approved of the Aldrich plan and that, as Kolko puts it, "the real purpose of the conference was to discuss winning the banking community over to government control directed by the bankers for their own ends. ... It was generally appreciated that the [Aldrich plan] would increase the power of the big national banks to compete with the rapidly growing state banks, help bring the state banks under control, and strengthen the position of the national banks in foreign banking activities."[24]

In November 1911, Aldrich won support for his plan from the American Bankers Association. In his address to their convention, he declared: "The organization proposed is not a bank, but a cooperative union of all the banks of the country for definite purposes."[25]

The major propaganda organization created for the benefit of the lay public by Aldrich and his colleagues in the spring of 1911 was the National Citizens' League for the Creation of a Sound Banking System. The league grew out of a resolution that Paul Warburg had pushed through a meeting of the National Board of Trade in January 1910, setting aside January 18 of the following year as a "monetary day" devoted to a "Business Men's Monetary Conference." At that January 1911 meeting the conference appointed a committee of seven, headed by Warburg, to organize a business-leaders' monetary reform league. A group of leading Chicago businessmen, headed by John V. Farwell and Harry A. Wheeler, president of the U.S. Chamber of Commerce, established the National Citizens' League, with economist J. Laurence Laughlin of the University of Chicago as operating head.

Warburg and the other New York bankers chose Chicago as the site of the Citizens' League to give the organization a bogus appearance of grass roots populism. In reality, banker control was virtually complete. The stated purpose of the league was to advance the cause of "cooperation, with dominant centralization of all banks by an evolution out of our clearing-house experience"; a decade later, Professor Henry Parker Willis, Laughlin's top assistant at the league as well as former student and long-time disciple, conceded that the Citizens' League had been the propaganda organ of the nation's bankers.[26]

---

[24]Kolko, *Triumph of Conservatism*, p. 186.

[25]West, *Banking Reform and the Federal Reserve*, p. 73. The full text of the Aldrich speech is reprinted in Herman E. Krooss and Paul Samuelson, eds., *Documentary History of Banking and Currency in the United States* (New York: Chelsea House, 1969), vol. 3, p. 1202. See also Kolko, *Triumph of Conservatism*, p. 189.

[26]Henry Parker Willis, *The Federal Reserve System* (New York: Ronald Press, 1923), pp.

There is no need to go into the minutiae of the splits within the Citizens' League or of the shift by the incoming Democrats in 1913 from the dreaded Republican name of Aldrich to a bill named by their own Representative Carter Class. Much of this conflict revolved around the desire by Laughlin and the Democrats, and to some extent by Warburg, to shed the name Aldrich for a more palatable one. Nevertheless, there was very little substantive difference between the Glass bill, which became the Federal Reserve Act, and the original Aldrich plan. Friedman and Schwartz are surely correct in insisting on the "near identity" of the two plans.[27] The important point is that whatever the difference on minor technical points, the nation's bankers, and especially the big bankers, were overwhelmingly in favor of a new central bank. As A. Barton Hepburn of the Chase National exulted at the annual meeting of the American Bankers Association in August 1913, in the course of his successful effort to get the bankers to endorse the Glass bill: "The measure recognized and adopts the principles of a central bank. Indeed, if it works out as the sponsors of the law hope, it will make all incorporated banks together joint owners of a central dominating power."[28] Precisely.

All in all, Professor Kolko sums up the point well:

> The entire banking reform movement, at all crucial stages, was centralized in the hands of a few men who for years were linked, ideologically and personally, with one another. The problem of the origin of the Federal Reserve Act, and the authorship of specific drafts, was later hotly debated by [men] who greatly exaggerated their differences in order that they might each claim responsibility for the guiding lines of the Federal Reserve System. Yet ...

149–50. At the same time, Willis's account conveniently ignores the dominant operating role that both he and his mentor played in the work of the Citizens' League; see West, *Banking Reform and the Federal Reserve*, p. 82.

[27]See Friedman and Schwartz, *Monetary History of the United States*, p. 171n. For similar judgments, see West, *Banking Reform and the Federal Reserve*, pp. 106–07; Kolko, *Triumph of Conservatism*, p. 222. Two decades after the establishment of the Federal Reserve, Paul Warburg demonstrated in detailed parallel columns the near identity of the Aldrich bill and the Federal Reserve Act; see Paul M. Warburg, *The Federal Reserve System: Its Origins and Growth* (New York: Macmillan, 1930), vol. 1, chaps. 8 and 9. There are many sources for examining the minutiae of the various drafts and bills; good places to start are West, *Banking Reform and the Federal Reserve*, pp. 79–135; and Kolko, *Triumph of Conservatism*, pp. 186–89, 217–47.

[28]Quoted in Kolko, *Triumph of Conservatism*, p. 235.

although they may have differed on details they agreed on
major policy lines and general theory. The confusion over
the precise authorship of the Federal Reserve Act should
not obscure the fact that the major function, inspiration,
and direction of the measure was to serve the banking
community in general, and large bankers specifically.[29]

3. The Structure of the Federal Reserve

The structure of the Federal Reserve System — which was enacted in
December 1913 and opened its doors the following November — was at
once cartelizing and inflationary.[30] The cartelizing nature of the Fed can be
seen in its organization: an intimate partnership between the federal government and the nation's banking community. There are 12 regional and
district Federal Reserve Banks, the stock of which is held by the member
banks in the district. Each Bank is governed by nine directors, of whom
three are chosen directly by the banks in the district; three others are supposed to represent commerce, agriculture, or industry, but they too are
chosen by the member banks in the district. That leaves only three directors appointed by the overall Federal Reserve Board in Washington. Furthermore, of the three publicly appointed directors, one — who becomes
the chairman of the district Bank — must be a person of tested banking
experience: in short, an ex-banker.

Not only are six — arguably seven — of each Bank's directors private
bankers, but the chief executive officer of each Bank (originally called the
governor and now the president) is appointed by the Bank directors themselves, not by the central Reserve Board (even though the latter must approve
the choice). The central board has seven members, two of whom must be
former bankers; all are appointed by the president of the United States.

Some critics of the Federal Reserve assert that it is really and simply a
private central bank, since it is owned wholly by its member banks and it

---

[29]Ibid., p. 22.

[30]The terms "inflation" and "inflationary" are used throughout this article according to
their original definition — an expansion of the money supply — rather than in the current
popular sense of a rise in price. The former meaning is precise and illuminating; the latter
is confusing because prices are complex phenomena with various causes, operating from
the sides of both demand and supply. It only muddles the issue to call every supply-side
price rise (say, due to a coffee blight or an OPEC cartel) "inflationary."

makes profits from its policies. But this view ignores the fact that all profits made by the Banks are now taxed away by the treasury. The point of the cartel is not make profits directly as shareholders of each Reserve Bank, but to benefit from the cartelizing and inflationary policies of the entire system.

At the same time, those who maintain that the Federal Reserve System is a wholly government-controlled institution overstate the case. It is true that all members of the Federal Reserve Board are government appointed and that all district Bank officials are instructed to act within the guidelines set by the Board. But every governor (or president) of a Federal Reserve Bank is selected largely by the bankers of the district, and these governors can exert a considerable amount of influence on Fed policy.[31] As we will see below, the banker-elected governor of the Federal Reserve Bank of New York seized the reins of power from the Federal Reserve Board from the inception of the system in 1914 until his death 14 years later.

The Federal Reserve System, like all central banking systems, is inherently inflationary. In the first place, the central bank acts as a lender of last resort, a giant governmentally privileged institution standing ready to bail out banks in trouble. Second, by coordinating bank activities, the central bank can pump in new reserves throughout the system and thereby induce a multiple expansion of bank money and credit. Since the banks can inflate uniformly, individual expanding banks no longer suffer from the constraining redemptions by nonexpanding banks that prevail in a regime of free and decentralized banking. If a bank expands credit on its own, it will soon find that its expanded notes or deposits will be passed on from its own clients to clients of other banks and that in the normal course of business they will be returned to the expanding bank for redemption. Yet the expanding bank will not have the funds to redeem these claims. There is also a third reason, which might not be as evident: Even if legal reserve requirements remain the same, the *centralizing* of reserves into the hands of the Fed by itself permits a considerable inflation of money and credit. In short, if before the establishment of a central bank every bank keeps its own cash reserves, and if afterward most of the cash is deposited in the central bank, the bank can then pyramid its own liabilities on top of its cash, thereby exerting a multiple leverage effect on the previously existing cash.

---

[31]A banker's institution of far less importance is the Federal Advisory Council, composed of bankers selected by the board of directors of their district Bank. The council's recommendations garner considerable publicity, but it has no power within the system.

480 The Progressive Era

In an illuminating book on the Federal Reserve and the Great Depression, Phillips, McManus, and Nelson summarize this process:

> Thus, if the commercial banks prior to the inauguration of a system of bankers' banking are required to hold an average reserve, say, of 10 percent against deposit liabilities, their deposits may be ten times that reserve, or, they may expand credit roughly on a ten-fold basis. With the reserves of the commercial banks transferred to the Federal Reserve Banks, and with the latter required to maintain a reserve of only 35 percent against the deposit liabilities due to the member banks, credit expansion may, at its utmost, proceed to approximately thirty times the amount of the reserves. Thus is seen that the establishment of a central banking system [in the United States] magnified the former expansive power virtually three-fold.[32]

This statement overlooks the fact that the pre-Federal Reserve banking system was not free and decentralized, and it therefore exaggerates the quantitative inflationary effect of the creation of the Fed. But the basic point is correct.

A fourth inflationary effect of the creation of the Fed is inherent not so much in its structure as in the legal power to change the reserve requirement of the banks. Thus, before the enactment of the Fed, the average minimum reserve requirement for the nation's banks was 21.1%. The Federal Reserve Act of 1913 slashed those reserve requirements to an average of 11.6%, a reduction of 45%. Four years later, in June 1917, reserve requirements were further lowered to an average of 9.8% — a cut of 54% since 1913. In short, added to whatever multiple inflation of money and credit was permitted by the centralization inherent in the existence of the Fed, a twofold expansion in four years was permitted by the slash in reserve requirements.[33] Furthermore, in an inflationary move that was

---

[32]C.A. Phillips, T.F. McManus, and R.W. Nelson, *Banking and the Business Cycle: A Study of the Great Depression in the United States* (New York: Macmillan, 1937), pp. 25–26.

[33]The Committee on War Finance of the American Economic Association hailed this development in early 1919: "Recent improvements in our banking system, growing out of the establishment of the Federal Reserve System and its subsequent development, have made our reserve money ... more efficient than it formerly was; in other words, have enabled a dollar in reserve to do more money work than before. This in effect is equivalent to increasing the supply of reserve money." It is indeed, provided that money's "work" is to be

to become highly significant in the 1920s, the Federal Reserve Act drastically lowered the reserve requirements for time deposits in the banks. Previously, there had been no distinction in the legal reserve requirements between demand and time deposits; both had therefore averaged 21.1%. Now, however, the requirement for time deposits was lowered to 5% and then to a negligible 3% in June 1917.[34]

4. The Personnel of the Federal Reserve

The people in positions of power in America's new central bank were at least as important as its structure. The bankers, warmly hailing the enactment of the Federal Reserve, waited eagerly to see who would be running the powerful new institution.[35]

Of the seven members of the Federal Reserve Board, two were (by statute at the time) *ex officio*, the secretary of the treasury and the comptroller of the currency. Before assuming their posts in the Wilson administration, these two men had been close business and financial associates. Secretary of the Treasury William Gibbs McAdoo had been a failing businessman in New York City when he was befriended and bailed out by J.P. Morgan and his associates. The Morgans set McAdoo up as president of New York's Hudson & Manhattan Railroad until his appointment in the Wilson administration. McAdoo spent the rest of his financial and political life securely in the Morgan ambit. When he was president of the Hudson & Manhattan for a decade, McAdoo's fellow officers and board members were virtually all Morgan men. His vice-presidents were Edmund C. Converse, president of the Morgan-run Bankers Trust Company, and Walter G. Oakman, president of Morgan's flagship commercial bank, Guaranty Trust. His fellow directors included Judge Elbert H. Gary, chairman of the board of Morgan's attempted steel monopoly, U.S. Steel, and a director of

---

as inflationary as possible and "efficiency" means producing as much inflation as rapidly as possible. See "Report of the Committee on War Finance of the American Economic Association," *American Economic Review* 9, Supplement no. 2 (March, 1919): 96–97; quoted in Phillips, McManus, and Nelson, *Banking and the Business Cycle*, p. 24n (see also pp. 21–24).

[34]Phillips, McManus, and Nelson, *Banking and the Business Cycle*, p. 29.

[35]See the reference to the proceedings of the conventions of the Kansas and California bankers associations in May 1914, in Kolko, *Triumph of Conservatism*, pp. 247–328. Senator Aldrich wrote to a friend in February: "Whether the bill will work all right or not depends entirely … upon the character and wisdom of the men who will control the various organizations, especially the Federal Reserve Board" (p. 248).

another failed Morgan monopoly attempt, International Harvester, Frederic B. Jennings, partner in the "Morgan" law firm of Stetson, Jennings & Russell (whose senior partner, Francis Lynde Stetson, was J.P.'s personal attorney), and John G. McCullough, a director of the Morgan-controlled Atchison, Topeka & Santa Fe Railroad. Directors of Hudson & Manhattan's parent company, the Hudson Companies, included William C. Lane, a vice-president of Guaranty Trust, and Grant B. Schley, a brother-in-law of one of the country's top Morgan lieutenants, George F. Baker, head of the First National Bank of New York. Shortly after his appointment as secretary of the treasury, William McAdoo cemented his political stature by marrying President Wilson's daughter.[36]

The comptroller of the currency was a long-time associate of McAdoo's. A Virginia banker and president of the Richmond Trust & Safe Deposit Company, John Skelton Williams had been a director of McAdoo's Hudson & Manhattan Railroad and president of the Morgan-oriented Seaboard Airline Railway. When McAdoo became secretary of the treasury, he appointed Williams as one of his two assistant secretaries.

One of President Wilson's five appointees to the Federal Reserve Board was another close associate of McAdoo's, Charles S. Hamlin, whom McAdoo had appointed as his other assistant secretary. Hamlin was a Boston attorney who had married into the wealthy Pruyn family of Albany, a family long connected with the Morgan-dominated New York Central Railroad.

Of the other Wilson appointees to the board, one was none other than Paul M. Warburg. Others were Frederic A. Delano, uncle of Franklin D. Roosevelt and president of the Rockefeller-controlled Wabash Railway, William P.G. Harding, president of the First National Bank of Birmingham, Alabama, and son-in-law of Joseph H. Woodward, head of the Woodward Iron Company, which had several prominent Morgan and Rockefeller men on its board, and finally, Professor Adolph C. Miller, economist at the University of California, Berkeley. Miller had married into the wealthy, Morgan-connected Sprague family of Chicago. His father-in-law, Otho S.A. Sprague, had been a prominent businessman and had served as a director of the Morgan-dominated Pullman Company. Miller's wife's uncle, Albert A. Sprague, was a director of numerous large firms, including

---

[36]See Burch, *Civil War to the New Deal*, pp. 207–09, 214–15, 232–33. On McAdoo, see also John J. Broesamle, *William Gibbs McAdoo: A Passion for Change, 1863–1917* (Port Washington, NY: Kennikat Press, 1973).

the Chicago Telephone Company, a subsidiary of the mighty Morgan-controlled monopoly American Telephone & Telegraph Company.[37]

The Federal Reserve Board thus began its existence with three Morgan men, one person in the Rockefeller ambit, a leader of Kuhn, Loeb & Co. (allied with the Rockefellers), a prominent Alabama banker, and an economist with vague family connections to Morgan interests. No board could have better symbolized the alliance of banking and financial interests, aided by a few economists, that had conceived and successfully driven through a radical transformation of the American banking system.

But more important from the inception of the Fed through the 1920s was the man appointed as governor of the Federal Reserve Bank of New York, who swiftly took control of the policies of the system. Benjamin Strong had spent virtually his entire business and personal life in the circle of top aides of J.P. Morgan. Secretary of several trust companies in New York City, Strong lived in the then wealthy suburb of Englewood, New Jersey, where he became close friends of three top Morgan partners: Henry P. Davison, Thomas W. Lamont, and Dwight Morrow. Davison in particular became Strong's mentor and in 1904 offered him the post of secretary of the new Morgan-created Bankers Trust Company. Strong soon married the daughter of the wealthy Edmund C. Converse, then president of Bankers Trust, and succeeded Thomas W. Lamont as vice-president. Not long after, Strong was acting as virtual president of Bankers Trust under the aging Converse, and in January 1914, he officially became president of the company.

Strong had favored central banking reform at least since 1907, and in August 1911 he participated with Nelson Aldrich in a lengthy meeting on the Aldrich plan with Davison, Vanderlip, and a few other leading bankers on Aldrich's yacht. He also spoke before the American Bankers Association on its behalf. When, at the suggestion of his close friend Warburg, Strong was offered the post of governor of the New York Fed, he at first refused, since he wanted a "real central bank ... run from New York by a board of directors on the ground" — in short, a frankly and openly Wall Street-run cartelized banking system. After a weekend in the country, Davison and Warburg persuaded Strong to change his mind and accept; presumably, he now realized that he could achieve a Wall Street-run cartel on a little less

---

[37]See Burch, *Civil War to the New Deal*, pp. 214–15, 236–37. Wilson also tried to appoint to the board his old friend Thomas D. Jones, a Chicago lawyer and director of the Morgans' International Harvester Company, but the Senate turned down the appointment.

candid basis from his powerful new post at the heart of the nation's money market. Strong became governor of the New York Fed in October 1914.[38]

Strong moved for seizure of commanding power shortly after the organization of the Federal Reserve System. At the organizing convention of the system in October 1914, an extra-legal council of governors was formed. At the first meeting of the council in December, Benjamin Strong became chairman not only of the council but also of its operating executive committee. From then on, Strong acted as chairman of the governors and assumed the dominant powers that the statute had envisioned for the Federal Reserve Board. William P.G. Harding, who became governor (now chairman) of the Federal Reserve Board in Washington in 1916, cracked down on the meetings of the council, but Strong continued as the dominant force in the system, a position ensured by his being named the sole agent for the open-market operations of all the Federal Reserve Banks.[39]

Two years after the establishment of the Federal Reserve and a year before the American entry into World War I, Representative Carter Class, a Democrat from Virginia who had drawn up the final Federal Reserve bill in the House, looked back on his cartelizing handiwork and found it good. He pointed out that his objective was very far from injuring Wall Street financial dominance:

> The proponents of the Federal reserve had no idea of impairing the rightful prestige of New York as the financial metropolis of this hemisphere. They rather expected to confirm its distinction, and even hoped to assist powerfully in wresting this scepter from London and eventually making New York the financial center of the world. ... Indeed, momentarily this has come to pass. And we may point to the amazing contrast between New York under the old system in 1907, shaken to its very foundations because of two bank failures, and New York at the present time, under the new system, serenely secure in its

---

[38]See Chandler, *Benjamin Strong*, pp. 23–41. On the details of the first organization of the Federal Reserve Bank of New York, see Lawrence E. Clark, *Central Banking under the Federal Reserve System* (New York: Macmillan, 1935), pp. 64–82.

[39]On the Strong seizure of power, see Clark, *Central Banking under the Federal Reserve*, pp. 102–5, 161; Chandler, *Benjamin Strong*, pp. 68–78.

> domestic banking operations and confidently financing
> the great enterprises of European nations at war.[40]

However, there was still a problem: the failure of the state-chartered banks to join the Federal Reserve System. All national banks were compelled by law to join the system and to keep their reserves with the Fed, but the eagerness with which they joined is revealed by the fact that virtually no national banks abandoned their national status to seek state charters. State banks were free to join or not, and a bane of the Fed's existence is that virtually none of them did so, preferring the lesser regulation of state law.

In a letter of October 1916, Benjamin Strong lamented the situation, writing: "Frankly, our bankers are more or less an unorganized mob. Until they are educated by experience to the advantages of cooperation through the Reserve System, I believe it is unsafe to rely upon reserves contributed by their voluntary action."[41] In such a vein has every cartelist reacted to the ambitions of individual firms or entrepreneurs to kick over the collective discipline of the cartel. All Fed officials felt the same way, and only political considerations have thus far prevented compulsory membership.

5. The Federal Reserve and World War I

The Federal Reserve System arrived fortuitously for the financing of U.S. entry into World War I, for it is doubtful whether the government would have been politically able to finance the war through taxes, borrowing from the public, or the simple printing of greenbacks. As it was, the Fed was able to engineer the doubling of the money supply from its inception in 1914 until 1919.

World War I also led to a strengthening of the power of the Federal Reserve System and particularly of the dominance of Benjamin Strong and the Federal Reserve Bank. With banking subject to treasury demands for financing the huge deficits, Secretary of the Treasury McAdoo and Benjamin Strong assumed virtual joint control of the Federal Reserve. As Willis wrote, "It was the entry of the United States into the World War that finally cast a decisive vote in favor of a still further degree of high centralization;

---

[40]Quoted in Kolko, *Triumph of Conservatism*, p. 254. Carter Class was a small-town Virginia newspaper editor and banker.

[41]Chandler, *Benjamin Strong*, p. 81; see also Clark, *Central Banking under the Federal Reserve System*, pp. 143–48.

and that practically guaranteed some measure of fulfillment for the ambitions that had centered around the Federal Reserve Bank of New York."[42]

Strong's new dominance was facilitated by the treasury's making the
Federal Reserve its sole fiscal agent. The secretary of the treasury had not
done so before the war arrived, instead continuing the Jacksonian policy of
depositing the disbursing funds from its own sub-treasury branches (the
Independent Treasury System). Under the spur of war, however, McAdoo
fulfilled Strong's long-standing ambition; the Fed was now clothed with
full governmental power. Strong had previously written: "We must, if possible, persuade [McAdoo] to permit the Reserve Banks to become the real,
active, and effective fiscal agents for the Government. If he does that, our
place in the country's banking system will be established for all time."[43]
Strong's biographer summarizes how treasury operations during the war
accelerated the dominance of the New York Fed:

> The war and the delegation of fiscal agency had a special
> effect on the New York Bank and on Strong's position in
> the System. Situated in the nation's great central money
> market, the New York Bank sold and distributed nearly
> half of all securities offered by the Treasury during the war
> and collected and disbursed great sums of money. At the
> country's foreign exchange center and gateway to Europe,
> it handled most of the Treasury's foreign exchange busi-
> ness, made many financial arrangements for the Treasury
> with foreign countries, acted as a central depository of
> funds from the other Reserve Banks as well as the New
> York district for payment to the representatives of for-
> eign countries or to suppliers of munitions to them, and
> was the principal purchaser of acceptances. Thus it was
> only natural that the New York Bank came to enjoy the
> prestige of being the principal bank of the government,
> the Treasury came to use it as a channel for communicat-
> ing with the other Reserve Banks, Strong's counsel was
> given heavy weight by the Treasury, and both the New
> York Bank and Strong emerged from the war with greater

---

[42]Willis, *Theory and Practice of Central Banking*, pp. 90–91.
[43]Chandler, *Benjamin Strong*, p. 105.

prestige, both absolutely and relative to the other Reserve Banks and the Board. [44]

Moreover, Strong had long wished to concentrate the country's gold coin and bullion in the hands of the Federal Reserve and outside the control of the public. In that way, cartelization would be intensified, and the inflationary potential of the Fed, which pyramided its own notes and deposits on top of its gold stock, would greatly increase. In 1917, in view of the war, the law was changed to permit the Federal Reserve to issue notes in exchange for gold (previously it could only issue them for commercial notes) and to require all legal bank reserves to be kept as deposits at the Fed rather than in cash. Furthermore, relaxed federal regulations on state banks in 1917 finally induced a considerable number of state banks to join the system, intensifying the concentration of reserves and of gold still further. Finally, from September 1917 to June 1919, the United States went implicitly, though not formally, off the gold standard — at least for foreigners. Foreign exchange operations were controlled and gold exports prohibited. As a result of all of these measures, gold was virtually nationalized and successfully concentrated at the Fed. At the end of 1916, the gold reserves of the Reserve Banks were only $720 million, or 28% of the country's monetary gold stock. Two years later, gold reserves at the Fed were up to $2.1 billion, or no less than 74% of the nation's gold.

6. INTERNATIONALIZING THE CARTEL

The fortunes of the House of Morgan had been declining since the turn of the century, and so the Morgans saw a glorious opportunity open to them upon the outbreak of the war in Europe. The Morgans had close and long-time financial connections with England. In particular, Edward Grenfell (later Lord St. Just), senior partner of Morgan, Grenfell & Co., the London branch of J.P. Morgan & Co., was also a long-time director of the Bank of England. Grenfell had long been the main informal link between the Bank of England and the New York financial community, and the relationship was formalized when the Morgan Bank became the fiscal agent of the Bank of England.[45] Led by partner Henry P. Davison at the end of 1914, the Morgans got themselves named virtually sole purchasing agent in the United States

---

[44]Ibid., p. 107.

[45]Sir Henry Clay, *Lord Norman* (London: Macmillan, 1957), p. 87; Parrini, *Heir to Empire*, pp. 55–56.

for British and French war goods. To pay for this immense export of arms and other materiel, the British and French were obliged to float immense loans in the United States, and the House of Morgan became the sole underwriter for these Allied bonds in the United States. Not only did Morgan find these monopolies highly profitable, but it prospered relative to its great rival Kuhn, Loeb & Co. — which, being German and connected with German banking and finance, was excluded from Allied war operations. As the Morgans and the bond market geared up to finance massive munitions and other exports to the Allies, Davison's old friend and colleague Benjamin Strong stood ready to inflate money and credit to finance these foreign loans.[46] The

---

[46]On the interconnections among the Morgans, the Allies, foreign loans, and the Federal Reserve, see Tansill, *America Goes to War*, pp. 32–134. [Editor's remarks] Rothbard elsewhere described the motivations of the Morgan ambit in the drive for U.S. involvement in World War I, citing the aforementioned work of Charles Tansill. It is worth quoting his analysis in full:

> The House of Morgan was hip-deep in the Allied cause from 1914 on … Morgan's railroads were in increasingly grave financial trouble, and 1914 saw the collapse of Morgan's $400 million New Haven Railroad. Concentrating on railroads and a bit laggard in moving into industrial finance, Morgan had seen its dominance in investment banking slip since the turn of the century. Now, World War I had come as a godsend to Morgan's fortunes, and Morgan prosperity was intimately wrapped up in the Allied cause.
>
> It is no wonder that Morgan partners took the lead in whipping up pro-British and French propaganda in the United States; and to clamor for the U.S. to enter the war on the Allied side. Henry P. Davison set up the Aerial Coast Patrol in 1915, and Willard D. Straight and Robert Bacon, both Morgan partners, took the lead in organizing the Businessman's Training Camp at Plattsburgh, New York, to urge universal conscription. Elihu Root and Morgan [Jr.] himself were particularly active in pressing for entering the war on the Allied side. Furthermore, President Wilson was surrounded by Morgan people. His son-in-law, Secretary of the Treasury, William G. McAdoo, had been rescued from financial bankruptcy by Morgan. Colonel Edward M. House, Wilson's mysterious and powerful foreign policy adviser, was connected with Morgan railroads in Texas. McAdoo wrote to Wilson that war exports to the Allies would bring "great prosperity" to the United States, so that loans to the Allies to finance such exports had become necessary.

See Rothbard, *The Mystery of Banking*, p. 243. See also Rothbard, *Wall Street, Banks, and American Foreign Policy*, pp. 17–23. The war purchases for Britain and France totaled $3 billion, and the House of Morgan earned a commission of $30 million. Moreover, the Morgans were able to steer British and French war contracts to Morgan affiliated firms,

Wilson administration and the Federal Reserve Board were prepared to do likewise.[47]

Benjamin Strong had scarcely been appointed when he began planning for an international cartel, a regime of "international cooperation" between the leading central banks of the world. In practice, such high-sounding terms could mean only cooperation for world monetary expansion. The classical gold standard, which basically prevailed before World War I, placed a firm restraint on the propensity of national central banks to inflate: The expansion of one country's currency would raise nominal income and prices in that country, cause a deficit in its balance of payments and an outflow of gold, thereby causing a check on inflation and perhaps a compulsion on the central bank to deflate back to its previous position. International central bank "cooperation" (or cartelization) then and now means the establishment of formal and informal mechanisms to prevent pressures for redemption and contraction on an inflating nation's currency. If this were *not* the meaning, there would be no need for international cooperation or indeed for central banking at all, since all any individual bank need do to keep itself afloat is to keep its rate of inflating to a minimum.

In the latter part of 1915, Benjamin Strong worked on international central bank collaboration, and in February 1916, he sailed to Europe to launch the first step: the establishment of the banks of England and France as foreign agents or correspondents for the New York Fed. Strong had long admired the central banking record of the Bank of England, and close collaboration with that leading central bank was to be the keystone of the new regime of inter-central bank cartelization. In England in March, Strong worked out an agreement of close collaboration between the New York Fed and the Bank of England, with both banks maintaining an account with each other and the Bank of England purchasing sterling bills on account for the New York Bank. In his usual high-handed manner, Strong expressed his determination to go ahead with the agreement even if the other Reserve Banks objected or failed to go along. Finally, after

---

including General Electric and U.S. Steel. See Murray Rothbard, "The Gold Exchange Standard in the Interwar Years," in *A History of Money and Banking in the United States*, Joseph Salerno, ed. (Auburn, AL: Ludwig von Mises Institute, 2005), pp. 370–71.

[47]With the exception of the two pro-German members of the Federal Reserve Board. Warburg and Miller, both of German descent, who fought unsuccessfully against bank financing of munitions exports to the Allies. See Tansill, *America Goes to War*, pp. 105–08.

some backing and filling, the Federal Reserve Board endorsed the scheme as well as the initiating of a similar agreement with the Bank of France.[48]

Strong made his agreement with the governor of the Bank of England, Lord Cunliffe, but his most fateful meeting in England was with the then assistant to the deputy governor, Montagu Norman. This meeting proved the beginning of the momentous Strong-Norman collaboration that highlighted the international financial world of the 1920s.[49]

Montagu Collet Norman was born to banking on both sides of his family. His father was a partner in the British banking house of Martin & Co. and was related to the great banking family of Barings. His uncle was indeed a partner of Baring Bros. Norman's mother was the daughter of Mark W. Collet, a partner in the international banking firm of Brown Shipley & Co. Brown Shipley was the London branch of the great Wall Street banking firm of Brown Brothers. Grandfather Mark Collet, furthermore, had been governor of the Bank of England in the 1880s.

At the age of twenty-one, young Norman began his working life at the family bank of Martin & Co., and then at Brown Shipley. In 1895, he went to work at the New York office of Brown Brothers, where he stayed for three years, returning to London to become a partner of Brown Shipley in 1900.

Strong and Norman became close friends as well as collaborators almost immediately, writing a steady stream of correspondence, personal and financial, and visiting each other at length every year from 1919 until Strong's death in 1928. They spent long vacations together, sometimes at Bar Harbor or Saratoga but more often in southern France.

---

[48]Chandler, *Benjamin Strong*, pp. 93–98.

[49][Editor's footnote] The Morgans were also involved in the Strong-Norman connection. Norman's close friends were directors of the aforementioned Morgan, Grenfell & Co. They were also prominent in the Coolidge administration. One of Calvin Coolidge's political mentors was Morgan partner Dwight Morrow. Coolidge first offered the Secretary of State position to Morgan attorney Elihu Root, but after he declined, settled for Frank B. Kellogg, who had Morgan connections, along with his assistant secretary Joseph C. Grew. Dwight Morrow and Henry L. Stimson, a disciple of Root, were also involved in international relations with Mexico and Nicaragua. Secretary of the Treasury was Andrew C. Mellon, who was generally allied to the Morgan interests. Morgan influence continued in the Hoover administration, and Dwight Morrow served as an important unofficial advisor to Herbert Hoover. See Rothbard, "The Gold Exchange Standard," pp. 368–81, 422.

7. BRITAIN AND THE GOLD EXCHANGE STANDARD

Britain, the major gold standard country before World War I, ended the war facing a set of grave, interlocking financial and economic problems, most of its own making. Along with the other warring nations, Britain had inflated sharply to finance the war effort. Each country except the United States (which had *de facto* suspended gold exports) had therefore been obliged to go off the gold standard. At the end of World War I, Britain determined that its own and the world's economic health required a return to the gold standard. And, in a fateful decision, it also determined — with surprisingly little discussion — that the pound sterling would have to be reestablished at the traditional prewar par of approximately $4.86.[50] Because of the greater inflation in Britain than in the United States, the free-market exchange rate of the two currencies was far lower than $4.86. The British government, with the help of J.P. Morgan & Co., succeeded in artificially pegging the pound at $4.75 from early 1916 until March 1919. Finally, the British let the pound float, and it quickly plummeted, reaching a low of $3.21 in February 1920.[51]

Britain's curious insistence on returning to the gold standard at a par overvalued by some 34% meant that the British had to face a massive price deflation. It was particularly important for Britain — dependent as it always has been on exports to purchase large quantities of imports — to keep its export prices competitive, and for that, deflation would be necessary. Although difficult at all times, deflation did not present major problems before World War I, since price and wage rates were flexible downward. But during the war, a massive system of high-benefit unemployment insurance and a strong network of trade unions had developed in Britain, making deflation impossible without the repeal of welfare state measures and the rolling back of trade union power. Britain was not willing to take such heroic measures; in fact it wished to continue permanently the pleasant system of cheap credit and inflation that it had pursued during the war. Yet it continued to insist on an unrealistic $4.86 par in order to regain London's prewar prestige as the world's financial center.

---

[50]On the portentous consequences of the British decision to return to gold at $4.86, see Lionel Robbins, *The Great Depression* (New York: Macmillan, 1934), pp. 77–87.

[51]See Clay, *Lord Norman*, p. 135; Chandler, *Benjamin Strong*, p. 293; and especially Benjamin M. Anderson, *Economics and the Public Welfare: Financial and Economic History of the United States, 1914–1946,* 2nd ed. (Indianapolis: Liberty Press, 1979), pp. 63–64.

Britain, in short, insisted on resting its postwar foreign monetary policy on a pair of inconsistent but fiercely held axioms: (1) a return to gold at the overvalued prewar par and (2) a refusal to permit the deflation needed to make axiom 1 at all viable. In fact, it insisted on continuing an inflationary policy. Britain's entire international financial policy during the 1920s was an attempt to square the circle, to maintain these two inconsistent axioms.

How could it do so? First, Britain would have to force or cajole other countries either to inflate themselves, so that Britain would not lose gold to them, or to return to a peculiar new form of gold standard, which would retain the prestige of gold without the content. Thus, Britain, operating particularly through the Financial Committee of the League of Nations (an organization that it controlled), induced or forced the vanquished or small victor states of postwar Europe (1) to return to gold at overvalued pars, thereby crippling *their* exports and subsidizing British imports, (2) to acquire their own central banks, so that they too could inflate in collaboration with the Bank of England, to discourage exports or gold from flowing from Britain, and (3), and perhaps most important, to return not to a classical gold standard but to a new form of "gold exchange standard." In a genuine gold standard, each currency is backed by gold, and gold flows in or out of the country. In the new form, each European country was expected to keep its reserves not in gold, but in pounds sterling, which would be backed by gold. Then, when Britain inflated, instead of losing gold to other countries, the sterling balances would pile up in London and themselves be used as a base on which to pyramid European currencies.

Britain was further protected from its inflationary policies in the 1920s by pledging to redeem pounds not in gold coin, as before the war, but only in large-denomination gold bullion. This ensured that gold could not circulate within the country and that gold would only be redeemed by large-scale international holders.

Having manipulated most of the European countries into ceasing to become a threat to its inflationary policies, Britain was still faced with the problem of the United States. The danger was that a non-inflating, hard-money, genuinely gold standard country such as the United States would soon drain inflating Britain of its gold and thereby wreck the new jerry-built international monetary system. Britain, therefore, had to persuade the United States to inflate *pari passu* with Great Britain; in particular, U.S. price levels could be no lower than Britain's and its interest rates no higher, so that gold funds would not be attracted out of London and into the United States. To persuade the United States to inflate — ostensibly in order to help Britain return to the gold standard — then became the premier task of Montagu Norman.[52]

Later in the 1920s, Emile Moreau, governor of the Bank of France and a caustic hard-money critic of Britain's international financial policy, recorded in his diary that England had established

> a basis for putting Europe under a virtual financial domination. The Financial Committee [of the League of Nations] at Geneva has been the instrument of that policy. The method consists of forcing every country in monetary difficulty to subject itself to the Committee at Geneva, which the British control. The remedies prescribed always involve the installation in the central bank of a foreign supervisor who is British or designated at the Bank of England, which serves both to support the pound and to fortify British influence. To guarantee against possible failure they are careful to secure the cooperation of the Federal Reserve Bank of New York. Moreover, they pass on to America the task of making some of the foreign loans if they seem too heavy, always retaining the political advantages of these operations.[53]

---

[52]See Murray N. Rothbard, "The New Deal and the International Monetary System," in Leonard P. Liggio and James J. Martin, eds., *Watershed of Empire: Essays on New Deal Foreign Policy* (Colorado Springs: Ralph Myles, 1976), pp. 20–27. See also Rothbard, *America's Great Depression*, pp. 131–32; Chandler, *Benjamin Strong*, pp. 293–94; *Unemployment, a Problem of Industry*, chap. 16; and Frederic Benham, *British Monetary Policy* (London: P. S. King, 1932).

[53]Chandler, *Benjamin Strong*, p. 379. Norman did indeed dominate the Financial Committee of the League, particularly through three close associates, Sir Otto Niemeyer of the treasury, Sir Arthur Salter, and Sir Henry Strakosch. The major theoretician of Norman's imposed gold exchange standard was Ralph Hawtrey, director of financial studies at the treasury. As early as 1913, Hawtrey was advocating international collaboration by central banks to achieve a stable price level, and in 1919, he was one of the first to call for international central bank cooperation in the context of a European gold exchange standard. See Clay, *Lord Norman*, pp. 137–38; Rothbard, *America's Great Depression*, pp. 159–61; Paul Einzig, *Montagu Norman* (London: Kegan Paul, 1932), pp. 67, 78; Palyi, *The Twilight of Gold*, pp. 134, 155–59.

On the gold exchange standard and Britain's inducement of European countries to overvalue their currencies, see H. Parker Willis, "The Breakdown of the Gold Exchange Standard and Its Financial Imperialism," *The Annalist* 33 (16 October 1931): 626ff.; and William Adams Brown, Jr., *The International Gold Standard Reinterpreted, 1914–1934* (New

Moreau also recorded a fascinating report sent by his close aide in 1926 on the intentions of Montagu Norman. The aide reported that the chief objective of Norman and his group was

> the setting up of links between the various Banks of Issue. ... The economic and financial organization of the world appears to the Governor of the Bank of England to be the major task of the Twentieth Century. ... Hence his campaign in favour of completely autonomous central banks, dominating their own financial markets and deriving their power from common agreement among themselves.[54]

Norman succeeded in getting the nations of Europe to agree to adopt the postwar gold exchange standard at the Genoa Conference, called by the Supreme Council of the Allies in April 1922. All of the details of the financial world of the 1920s were agreed on then by the Financial Commission of the Conference. Britain actually adopted this standard in 1925, and the other European nations followed at about the same time. The United States had decided at the last minute not to participate at Genoa because of Soviet participation, but the administration, especially the powerful Secretary of Commerce Herbert Hoover, was enthusiastic about the idea of inter-central bank collaboration of currency stabilization.[55]

8. OPEN-MARKET PURCHASES IN THE 1920S

The Federal Reserve generated a monetary expansion averaging approximately 7% per annum in the great boom years from 1921 to 1929, an expansion propelled by an average annual increase of member bank reserves of

---

York: National Bureau of Economic Research, 1940), vol. 2, p. 732–49.

[54]Palyi, *Twilight of Gold*, pp. 134–35.

[55]On the Genoa Conference, see ibid., pp. 133–40, 148–49 (the latter for a text of the relevant resolutions); Michael J. Hogan, *Informal Entente: The Private Structure of Cooperation in Anglo-American Economic Diplomacy, 1918–1928* (Columbia: University of Missouri Press, 1977), pp. 42–48 (on the administration's position); Stephen V.O. Clarke, *Central Bank Cooperation: 1924–31* (New York: Federal Reserve Bank of New York, 1967), pp. 34–36; and Rothbard, *America's Great Depression*, pp. 161–62.

6% per year.[56] By far the most important factor in generating the increased reserves was open-market purchases by the Federal Reserve Bank of New York. The purchases came in three great bursts: in 1921–22, in 1924, and in the latter half of 1927. In the first surge, the Fed tripled its holding of government securities from $193 million in November 1921 to $603 million in June 1922. This was the Fed's famous "discovery" of the inflationary effect of open-market purchases, a discovery that the authorities were delighted to make. Before the war, there had been little government securities available on the market and almost no short-run floating treasury debt. There was therefore little scope for open-market operations as a deliberate expansionary or restrictive policy even if this method had been discovered. After World War I, however, there was suddenly a large mass of short-term floating debt on the market that needed to be rolled over.[57] The Federal Reserve purchased the massive amounts in 1921–22 largely to acquire income-earning assets during the era of business recession. It then saw to its delight that a new and powerful instrument of monetary expansion and inflation had been discovered.

That this discovery was, to an extent, anticipated by Benjamin Strong is indicated by a letter he wrote on April 18, 1922, to Undersecretary of the Treasury S. Parker Gilbert, who had wondered about the Fed's unusually large purchases of government securities. Strong explained that the policy had been designed not only to add to the Fed's income-earning assets but also "to establish a level of interest rates, or at least to maintain rates at a level, which would facilitate foreign borrowing in this country" and thus would assure "more stable conditions and [would] facilitate business improvement." This indicates that, at least to some degree, Strong bought

---

[56]What would now be considered M-2, all bank deposits and savings and loan shares increased by 6.8% per annum from June 1921 to June 1929, whereas M-2 plus net life insurance policy reserves increased by an average of 7.7% during the same period. The rationale for including the latter is that this completes the figure for all claims redeemable in dollars at par on demand. See Rothbard, *America's Great Depression*, pp. 88–96, 100–01; Board of Governors of the Federal Reserve System, *Banking and Monetary Statistics* (Washington, D.C.: Federal Reserve Board, 1943), p. 34. On time deposits as actually redeemable on demand in the 1920s, see Anderson, *Economics and the Public Welfare*, pp. 139–42; Phillips, McManus, and Nelson, *Banking and the Business Cycle*, pp. 98–101.

[57]See Rothbard, *America's Great Depression*, p. 125; H. Parker Willis, "What Caused the Panic of 1929," *North American Review* 229 (February, 1930): 178; Charles O. Hardy, *Credit Policies of the Federal Reserve System* (Washington, DC: Brookings Institution, 1932), p. 287. See also Esther Rogoff Taus, *Central Banking Functions of the United States Treasury, 1789–1941* (New York: Columbia University Press, 1943), pp. 182–83.

the securities in order to push interest rates lower, to expand money and credit, and to stimulate an economic upturn.[58]

The expanded open-market operations led Governor Strong to reconvene the governors conference on a regular and systematized basis. In May 1922, the conference set up an executive committee that would henceforth centralize and execute open-market operations for the entire system; Benjamin Strong was, not coincidentally, made chairman of this governors committee.[59] From that point on, and particularly from the time of the second committee meeting in October 1922, Strong was conducting open-market purchases and sales for the entire system, instead of merely functioning as an agent and processing orders from other regional Reserve Banks.

Strong fell ill in February 1923 and was out sick until October. Shortly after, in April, the Federal Reserve Board in Washington, prodded by Adolph Miller, took steps to try to take dominance of the system away from the absent Strong. The board dissolved the extralegal governors committee and reconstituted a new one — the Open Market Investment Committee — strictly under the control of the board. With Strong temporarily gone, the board managed to force the New York Fed to sell most of its remaining government securities, for Miller, and the treasury as well, had continued to be uneasy at the large open-market purchases the Fed had made the previous year. Strong was furious both at the loss of his power and at the sale of securities, which he feared would cause a recession. In November, however, Strong came roaring back, seizing control of the Federal Reserve from that point until his final illness in the spring of 1928. Regaining his power over the Open Market Investment Committee, Strong, as chairman, created a Special System Investment Account at the New York Fed into which committee purchases and holdings were put. He also let it be known that he would expand such purchases whenever any economic downturn loomed: "The Reserve System should not hesitate to resume open-market purchases, thereby again reducing bank borrowings and easing money rates, rather than permit an unwarranted state of

---

[58]Chandler, *Benjamin Strong*, p. 211. See also Harold L. Reed, *Federal Reserve Policy, 1921–1930* (New York: McGraw-Hill, 1930), pp. 14–41. Gilbert, who had come to the Treasury Department from the leading Wall Street law firm of Cravath and Henderson (now Cravath, Swaine & Moore), later became a partner of J.P. Morgan & Co. (Burch, *Civil War to the New Deal*, pp. 298–99).

[59]The full name of the committee was highly descriptive: The Committee of Governors on Centralized Execution of Purchases and Sales of Government Securities by Federal Reserve Banks (Chandler, *Benjamin Strong*, p. 215).

mind alone to disturb the even course of the country's production and consumption."[60]

The next big burst of inflationary credit expansion came in 1924. Shortly after Strong's return, he began to purchase securities on a massive scale, buying $492 million from October 1923 through 1924. The overriding reason was the determination to help Britain and Montagu Norman return to gold at its overvalued par. To do so, the United States had to embark on an inflationary, cheap money policy to lower interest rates and raise prices relative to Britain so that Britain would not lose gold to the United States. In 1922, Norman had hailed the easy credit and drop in interest rates to match Britain's credit expansion. During that and the following year, Norman continued to pepper Strong with appeals and demands for further extensions of credit in the United States. But Strong felt that the time was not yet ripe.

Finally, in 1924, with Britain's return to the gold standard looming the following year, Strong felt that the time was ripe, and the massive open-market purchases began. Furthermore, the pound sterling, which had risen to $4.61 by the end of 1922 with news of the impending return to gold, had fallen sharply to $4.34 by mid-1924. Only massive inflationary pressure in the United States could raise the pound to $4.86.

Strong set forth his basic policies in a lengthy letter on May 27, 1924, to Secretary of the Treasury Andrew Mellon:

> There still remains the serious problem of the disparity of price levels in the different countries due to monetary disturbances and currency inflation, the correction of which must be undertaken before a return to actual gold payment will be safe. This may be illustrated by the case of British prices and our own. The pound sterling is, roughly, at 10 percent discount measured in our gold currency ...
>
> At the present time it is probably true that British prices for goods internationally dealt in are as a whole, roughly, in the neighborhood of 10 percent above our prices and one of the preliminaries to the re-establishment of gold payment by Great Britain will be to facilitate a gradual readjustment of these price levels *before* mon-

---

[60]Ibid., pp. 232–33. On Strong's resumption of power, see ibid., pp. 222–34; Clark, *Central Banking under the Federal Reserve*, pp. 162–74.

etary reform is undertaken. In other words, this means some small advance in prices here and possibly some small decline in their prices. ... No one can direct price changes. They will be to a certain extent fortuitous, but can be facilitated by cooperation between the Bank of England and the Federal Reserve System in the maintaining of lower interest rates in this country and higher interest rates in England so that we will become the world's borrowing market to a greater extent, and London to a less extent. The burden of this readjustment must fall more largely upon us than them. It will be difficult politically and socially for the British Government and the Bank of England to force a price liquidation in England beyond what they have already experienced in face of the fact that their trade is poor and they have over a million unemployed people receiving government aid.[61]

The inflationary open-market purchases led to a fall of interest rates in the United States below Britain by mid-1924. Sterling rose again, reaching $4.78 by the spring of 1925. Britain resumed the gold standard at the prewar par by the end of the year. This resumption was further aided by the New York Fed's loan of a line of credit of $200 million to Britain, accompanied by a similar credit of $100 million to Britain by J.P. Morgan & Co.[62]

The final great burst of inflation, and the most intense of the 1920s, came in the latter half of 1927, when the Federal Reserve purchased $225 million of government securities and $220 million of banker's acceptances, adding $445 million to bank reserves from these two sets of purchases alone.[63]

The problem was that Britain's return to the gold standard quickly proved an unhappy one. The sharp rise in the value of sterling put great pressure on Britain's already depressed exports, especially on the coal industry. Britain's chronic depression intensified and rigid wage rates intensified unemployment. A general strike and a lengthy coal mine strike

---

[61]Chandler, *Benjamin Strong*, pp. 282–84.

[62]See Rothbard, *America's Great Depression*, pp. 133–34; Robbins, *Great Depression*, p. 80; Chandler, *Benjamin Strong*, pp. 301–21.

[63]Rothbard, *America's Great Depression*, pp. 102–03, 107. On the significance of the acceptance market, see "Creating the Acceptance Market," below.

in 1926 were the direct consequence of the return to gold at an overvalued par. Instead of deflating, therefore, to validate the $4.86, Britain insisted on inflating in a vain attempt to relieve the depression. Prices rose, the Bank of England lowered its discount rate, and the balance of payment deficit and the resulting gold outflow became much worse. The pressure on the sterling intensified. Unwilling to stop inflating and tighten credit, Montagu Norman turned to Benjamin Strong, his old ally.

Benjamin Strong purchased some sterling bills to reverse the dollar flow from Britain and also sold France $60 million in gold to forestall French demands for redemption of sterling. But these were just temporary expedients. So Strong invited three top central bankers for a highly secret conference in New York in July 1927. So secret was the conclave that Strong, in his usual high-handed fashion prevented Gates W. McGarrah, chairman of the board of the Federal Reserve Bank of New York, from attending the meeting, and the Federal Reserve Board in Washington was also kept in the dark.[64] In addition to Norman, the other European representatives were Professor Charles Rist, deputy governor of the Bank of France, and Hjalmar Schacht, governor of the German Reichsbank. Strong and Norman tried hard to get Rist and Schacht to agree on a concerted and massive four-country cheap credit and inflation, but the Europeans vigorously refused, expressing alarm at the inflationary trend. While Rist and Schacht sailed for home, the Anglo-American combine stayed to weld their pact for inflation, expanded credit, and lower interest rates. Before Rist left, however, Strong told him buoyantly that he was "going to give a little *coup de whiskey* to the stock market."[65]

President Coolidge and Secretary Mellon endorsed the new inflationary policy, the only high-level objectors being Adolph Miller and Herbert Hoover. The Federal Reserve authorities stayed silent about the reasons for their sudden expansion in late 1927, with only Governor W.J. Bailey of the Kansas City Federal Reserve Bank repeating the line that Strong had told him: that the cheap credit policy — including the open-market purchases, the lowering of rediscount rates, and the lowering of Fed buying rates on

---

[64]See Anderson, *Economics and the Public Welfare*, p. 189. Gates McGarrah was a close business associate of Albert H. Wiggin, chairman of the board of Morgan's Chase National Bank (Clark, *Central Banking under the Federal Reserve*, p. 267). See also ibid., pp. 313–14; Chandler, *Benjamin Strong*, pp. 440–54.

[65]Charles Rist, "Notice biographique," *Revue d'économie politique* 65 (November-December, 1955): 1006–008. See also Rothbard, *America's Great Depression*, pp. 141–42.

acceptances — was being pursued to "help the farmers." Helping Britain — not a very popular policy in the American heartland at the time — was kept under wraps as the major reason for the inflationary surge.[66]

The importance of helping Britain in the inflationary policy of the 1920s is seen in Benjamin Strong's comments to Sir Arthur Salter, secretary of the League of Nations and a Norman associate, in Paris in May 1928. Rejecting the idea of a formal meeting of the world's central banks, Strong cited the political hostility in the United States. Then, as an aide summarized:

> To illustrate how dangerous the position might become in the future as a result of the decisions reached at the present time and how inflamed public or political opinion might easily become when the results of past decision became evident, Governor Strong cited the outcry against the speculative excesses now being indulged in on the New York market and the criticism of the Federal Reserve System for its failure to curb or prevent this speculation. He said that very few people indeed realized that we were now paying the penalty for the decision which was reached early in 1924 to help the rest of the world back to a sound financial and monetary basis.[67]

9. Creating the Acceptance Market

Nowadays there are two methods by which the Federal Reserve can add to bank reserves and therefore to the inflating process of pyramiding new money on top of reserves as a base. One is open-market operations; the other is changing the rediscount rate at which the Fed, as the lender of last resort, lends reserves to banks in trouble. But a third method was highly

---

[66]Anderson, *Economics and the Public Welfare*, pp. 189–91. See also Benjamin H. Beckhart, "Federal Reserve Policy and the Money Market, 1923–1931," in *The New York Money Market,* B.H. Beckhart, J.G. Smith, and W.A. Brown, eds. (New York: Columbia University Press, 1931), vol. 4, p. 45.

[67]Chandler, *Benjamin Strong*, pp. 280–81. In the autumn of 1926, a leading banker admitted that bad consequences would follow the cheap money policy but added: "That cannot be helped. It is the price we pay for helping Europe"; see H. Parker Willis, "The Failure of the Federal Reserve," *North American Review* 227 (May, 1929): 553. For lavish praise of Strong by English bankers and politicians, see Clark, *Central Banking under the Federal Reserve*, pp. 315–16.

important in the 1920s: the intense subsidization — indeed, the very creation — of a market in acceptances.

Discount policy was inflationary during the 1920s. In the first place, rates were set below the market instead of a penalty rate above it, thus inducing banks to borrow reserves from the Fed. Second, the Fed decided to lend continuously rather than only in emergencies. As the Federal Reserve Board wrote in its annual report of 1923:

> The Federal Reserve banks are ... the source to which the member banks turn when the demands of the business community have outrun their own unaided resources. The Federal Reserve supplies the needed additions to credit in times of business expansion and takes up the slack in times of business recession.[68]

Presidents Harding and Coolidge repeatedly pledged to lower interest rates and to keep them low during the 1920s, and each did his best to fulfill that pledge. In 1922–23, 1925, and 1928, periods when the Federal Reserve was belatedly trying to stop its inflationary policies, the discounting process, spurred by artificially low rediscount rates, came to the banks' rescue.[69] During the onrushing stock market boom in 1927, President Coolidge and Secretary Mellon stepped in whenever the boom showed signs of flagging and egged it on, predicting lower interest rates and urging higher prices. In one of these statements, Mellon assured the market that "there is an abundant supply of easy money which should take care of any contingencies that might arise."[70] Furthermore, both Harding and Coolidge appointed Federal Reserve members who would implement the low discount rate, low interest rate policy.[71]

The most unusual aspect of the Federal Reserve-generated inflation of the 1920s was its creation and subsidization of the acceptance market in

---

[68]Federal Reserve *Annual Report 1923*, p. 10; cited in Seymour E. Harris, *Twenty Years of Federal Reserve Policy* (Cambridge, MA: Harvard University Press, 1933), vol. 1, p. 109. See also ibid., pp. 3–10, 39–48, 108–09.

[69]Rothbard, *America's Great Depression*, pp. 102–3; see also pp. 110–17.

[70]Ibid., p. 117. See also Anderson, *Economics and the Public Welfare*, p. 190; Oliver M.W. Sprague, "Immediate Advances in the Discount Rate Unlikely," *The Annalist* (1926): 493.

[71]See H. Parker Willis, "Politics and the Federal Reserve System," *Bankers' Magazine* (January, 1925): 13–20; idem, "Will the Racing Stock Market Become a Juggernaut?" *The Annalist* (24 November 1924): 541–42; and *The Annalist* (10 November 1924): 477.

502	The Progressive Era

the United States. Commercial paper in the United States had always been confined to single-name promissory notes, often discounted at commercial banks. By contrast, in Europe and particularly in Britain, foreign trade (not domestic) was habitually financed by the mechanism of an endorsement of the debt, or *acceptance*. The acceptance bank endorsed and purchased the note and then sold it to a "dealer," or bill broker, who in turn sold it to a commercial bank for discount.

From the inception of the system, the Federal Reserve set out to bring a thriving acceptance market into being by massive subsidization. Since there had been virtually no naturally arising acceptance market in the United States, the demand for acceptances by discount banks was extremely slight. The Federal Reserve, therefore, undertook to buy all acceptances offered to it, either by the member banks or by a tiny group of designated dealers, and to buy them at a very low, subsidized rate. Generally, this rate was lower than the discount rate for similar commercial paper. In this way, the Federal Reserve provided reserves in a way unusually favorable to the banks. First, not only was the rate cheap, but acceptances were, like discounts and unlike open-market operations, *always* there to be provided by a passive Federal Reserve. And second, the acceptances never had to be repaid to the Fed and therefore, unlike discounts and like open-market purchases, they constituted a permanent addition to the reserves of the banks.[72]

The dominance of the Federal Reserve in making a market for acceptances can be seen in the proportion of acceptances held by the Fed. On June 30, 1927, over 46% of bankers' acceptances were held by the Federal Reserve, over 26% for its own account and another 20% for foreign central banks.[73]

The subsidizing of acceptances was, from the early years, highly concentrated in New York City. In the first place, the New York Fed seized control of the acceptance policy in 1922 and kept it for the remainder of the decade. Second, the bulk of acceptances were on foreign transactions, and *all* of those acceptances were purchased by the Fed from only nine

---

[72]For a lucid explanation of acceptance and the Federal Reserve's role in the market, see Caroline Whitney, "The Bankers' Acceptance Market," in *The Banking Situation,* H. Parker Willis and John M. Chapman, eds. (New York: Columbia University Press, 1934), pp. 725–36. See also H. Parker Willis, *Theory and Practice of Central Banking,* pp. 201ff.; Rothbard, *America's Great Depression,* pp. 117–23.

[73]The Fed held the same proportion in June 1929; see Hardy, *Credit Policies of the Federal Reserve,* p. 258.

very large acceptance dealers located in New York City. Third, the number of acceptance banks was also quite small: 118 in the entire country in 1932, of which 40 were located in New York City. And three-quarters of all acceptances were executed by banks in New York City. The acceptance banks were generally large commercial banks but also included the huge International Acceptance Bank of New York, the world's largest acceptance bank, which in the 1930s merged with the Kuhn, Loeb-dominated Bank of Manhattan Company.[74]

Fed policy on acceptances played an inflationary role at crucial periods during the 1920s. In late 1922, this policy supplemented the role of discounts by far more than offsetting the open-market sale of securities by the Fed. In the 1924 credit expansion, almost twice as many acceptances as government securities were purchased in the open market. And in the fateful 1927 inflationary surge, acceptances ("bills bought") were equally as powerful in adding to reserves as the Fed's purchase of securities. Furthermore, during the latter half of 1928, when the Fed stopped buying securities in an attempt to get the runaway boom under control, massive purchases of acceptances kept the boom going.

Benjamin Strong was, of course, the man who instituted and maintained the Federal Reserve creation and subsidizing of the acceptance market. Indeed, Strong often took the lead in urging cheaper and cheaper rates to intensify the subsidy. For Strong, this policy was vital for the promotion of foreign trade and for facilitating international central bank collaboration and management of the world financial system.[75]

But by far the most enthusiastic and tireless advocate of ever greater Federal Reserve aid to the acceptance market was Strong's close friend Paul Moritz Warburg. From the very beginning of Warburg's promotion of a central bank in 1907, that bank's subsidization of acceptance paper was crucial to his plan. He scoffed at the prevalence of single-name promissory notes in the United States, a practice, he opined, that left the

---

[74]One of the nine designated acceptance dealers, the Discount Corporation of New York, was itself organized by a group of accepting banks to deal in bankers' acceptances; see Whitney, "Bankers' Acceptance," 727–28, 732–33. See also Beckhart, *Money Market*, 3:319, 333, 410; Clark, *Central Banking*, p. 168; H. Parker Willis, "The Banking Problem in the United States," in H.P. Willis et al., eds., "Report on an Inquiry into Contemporary Banking in the United States," 1925, vol. 1, pp. 31–37 (unpublished); Hardy, *Credit Policies of the Federal Reserve*, pp. 100–101, 256–57; A.S.J. Baster, "The International Acceptance Market," *American Economic Review* 27 (June, 1937): 298.

[75]Chandler, *Benjamin Strong*, pp. 86–93.

backward United States "at about the same point that had been reached by Europe at the time of the Medicis, and by Asia, in all likelihood, at the time of Hammurabi." Warburg envisioned a money supply issued by a central bank based on acceptance paper purchased by that bank.[76]

We have seen that Paul Warburg was one of the most influential founders and shapers of the Federal Reserve System. He was on the board from 1914 to 1918, when he resigned because of his German ancestry, but he continued to be highly influential through the 1920s as chairman of the Fed's Federal Advisory Council. In January 1923, Warburg boasted before the American Acceptance Council, a trade association of acceptance banks and dealers organized four years before, that he had been largely responsible for the Fed's acceptance-buying policy as well as for the repeated statutory widening of eligibility for those purchases. In 1922, Warburg demanded still lower buying rates on acceptances, and in the spring of 1929, when he began to worry about the developing boom, he still called for the Fed to create a wider acceptance market.[77]

It is certainly plausible to hold that Warburg's unremitting zeal for massive Federal subsidy of the acceptance market, as well as its cartelization in the hands of a few New York acceptance bankers and dealers, was connected to his status as a leading acceptance banker. For Paul Warburg was chairman of the board of the world's largest acceptance bank, the International Acceptance Bank of New York, from its inception in 1920. He also became a director of the important Westinghouse Acceptance Bank and of several other acceptance houses and was the chief founder and chairman of the executive committee of the American Acceptance Council. His vaunting speech to that council in early 1923 was his presidential address.[78]

---

[76]Quoted in Elgin Groseclose, *America's Money Machine: The Story of the Federal Reserve* (Westport, CT: Arlington House, 1980), p. 49. See also ibid., pp. 48–51, 93–98; and Warburg, *Federal Reserve System*, vol. 2, pp. 9–25.

[77]See Rothbard, *America's Great Depression*, pp. 119–20; Harris, *Twenty Years*, p. 324; *The Commercial and Financial Chronicle*, 9 March 1929, 1443–44, Warburg's speech before the American Acceptance Council is in Warburg, *Federal Reserve System*, vol. 2, p. 822.

[78]Rothbard, *America's Great Depression*, pp. 120–21; Groseclose, *America's Money Machine*, p. 97. It is fitting that after Benjamin Strong's death, Warburg paid him high tribute by hailing him for "welding the central banks together into an intimate group" and concluding that "members of the American Acceptance Council would cherish his memory" (Warburg, *Federal Reserve System*, vol. 2, p. 870).

10. FROM BOOM TO DEPRESSION

In the spring of 1928, with Benjamin Strong ill and absent after mid-May, the Federal Reserve became alarmed by the now exploding stock market and tried to put an end to the inflationary boom. The Fed managed to contract reserves by selling securities, but its efforts were partially offset by large increases in rediscounting spurred by the Fed's failure to raise rediscount rates sufficiently and by the banks' shifting of credit from demand to time deposits, which required far less reserves. Still, the contraction of reserves took hold from May through July, and as a result, the rate of money growth leveled off sharply.[79] Stock prices rose far more slowly than before, and the gold drain out of the United States began to reverse.

The boom could have ended in mid-1928, and the resulting contraction could have been mild. But this was not to be. Instead, the Fed's massive purchases of acceptances increased reserves in the latter half of the year, and the money supply growth rose again. One reason for the Fed's failure to stay its relatively less inflationary course was the great pressure it received from Europe. The short-run "benefits" of the inflationary injection of 1927 in Europe had already dissipated: The pound was sagging again, gold was flowing out of Britain, and interest rates were again higher in the United States than in Britain. With the exception of France, Europe clamored against any tighter money in the United States, and the Fed's aggravation of inflation in late 1928 eased the flow of gold from Britain.[80] And Benjamin Strong, though ill and traveling in Europe, kept up a stream of pressure for easier money. In mid-July, Strong looked back on his handiwork and found it good. In a letter to S. Parker Gilbert, he wrote that his policy since 1924 had

> enabled monetary reorganization to be completed in Europe, which otherwise would have been impossible. It was undertaken with the well recognized hazard that we were liable to encounter a big speculation and some expansion of credit. ... Six months ago we faced the new year with practically all the European nations in a strong position in monetary matters. ... Our course was perfectly

---

[79]M-2, which had risen at an annual rate of 7.7% in the latter half of 1927 (8.1% if net life insurance policy reserves are included), increased by only 3.2% in the first half of 1928 (4.3% if life insurance is included), see Rothbard, *America's Great Depression*, pp. 102–3.

[80]See Harris, *Twenty Years*, pp. 437–38.

obvious. We had to undertake it. The conditions permitted it, and the possibility of damage resulting abroad were
[sic] at a minimum.[81]

Strong went on to express his concern at the "very high rates" then
prevailing in New York and looked forward to rate reductions in the fall.
On his return to the United States in August, Strong continued to express
concern, not over the inflationary boom and the runaway stock market
but over what he considered excessively high interest rates. He clearly
wished to resume his old inflationary policy.

After Strong's retirement in August, his faithful followers tried to
tread the same path. His successor as governor, George L. Harrison, led
the Open Market Committee to worry about excessively high rates and
asked and obtained the board's permission for the authority to engage in
massive open-market purchases.

The end of Strong's reign (he died in October 1928) led to indecisive
splits and fragmented power within the Federal Reserve System. Although
Harrison attempted to emphasize open-market purchases, the majority
of the board wanted the Fed to buy far more acceptances. Each faction
wanted its own version of inflationary credit expansion.

One reason for the Fed's emphasis on acceptances was the increasing adoption in Washington of the curious theory of "moral suasion,"
which was to plague efforts to end the inflationary boom during the latter half of 1928 and through 1929. Until the end, President Coolidge was
still trying to boost the stock market. But the new President Hoover and
Governor Roy Young of the Federal Reserve Board had a different theory:
that credit could remain cheap and easy for "legitimate" business but be
restrictive toward the stock market. As soon as Hoover assumed office, he
tried moral suasion by intimidation, sending an old banker friend, Henry
M. Robinson of Los Angeles, to New York to try to persuade the banks to
restrict stock loans and calling a meeting of editors and publishers to warn
them of high stock prices.[82] Moral suasion was abandoned by June 1929.
The Federal Reserve, after finally shutting off the acceptance window in
March by raising its buying rate above the discount rate, delayed raising
the rediscount rate under pressure from Hoover. Finally, it raised the rate
in August, but typically the Fed offset this check to the boom by lowering

---

[81]Chandler, *Benjamin Strong*, p. 458; see also pp. 459–63.

[82]See Burner, *Herbert Hoover*, pp. 246–47.

the acceptance rate at the same time. As a result of this unprecedented "straddle," large Fed purchases of acceptances from July to October drove the stock market to new heights. These acceptances were largely sterling bills purchased by the New York Fed once again to help Britain. Great Britain was trying to inflate and pursue cheap credit in the midst of a worsening depression, and the Fed was trying to stem the renewed outflow of gold in the United States.[83]

With all eyes on the stock market, however, the great American boom of the 1920s was already over. For despite, or perhaps because of, the waffling and confusion of the Fed, the money supply remained level from the peak at the end of 1928 through September 1929. A recession was now inevitable.

Unbeknownst to most Americans, the economy started turning downward around July 1929. Three months later, on October 24, the great stock market crash brought the shift from boom to depression to the attention of everyone.

The Federal Reserve did not meet the crash with any idea of *laissez-faire* or of allowing the economy to liquidate the malinvestments of the boom. On the contrary, its inflationist attitude during the boom was matched by a similar and even more aggravated outlook during the depression. In an unprecedented act, the Fed inflated reserves wildly in one week — the week of the crash. In the last week of October, the Fed doubled its holdings of government securities and discounted $200 million for member banks, adding $350 million to total bank reserves. Almost all of these increased reserves were poured into New York in order to prevent liquidation of the stock market and to induce New York City banks to take over the brokers' loans that nonbank lenders were in the process of unloading. As a result,

---

[83]The grave fallacy in the efforts of 1928 and 1929 to keep credit abundant in trade and industry while restricting the stock market was pointed out in an excellent epitaph on this policy by A. Wilfred May: "Once the credit system had become infected with cheap money, it was impossible to cut down particular outlets of this credit without cutting down all credit, because it is impossible to keep different kinds of money in water-tight apartments. It was impossible to make money scarce for stock-market purposes, while simultaneously keeping it cheap for commercial use. ... When Reserve credit was created, there was no possible way that its employment could be directed into specific uses, once it had flowed through the commercial banks into the general credit stream" ("Inflation in Securities," in Willis and Chapman, eds., *Economics of Inflation*, pp. 292–93). See also Hardy, *Credit Policies of the Federal Reserve*, pp. 124–77; and Oskar Morgenstern, "Developments in the Federal Reserve System," *Harvard Business Review* 9 (October, 1930): 2–3.

member banks expanded their deposits during that fateful last week in October by $1.8 billion — a monetary expansion of nearly 10% in one week. Almost all of this amount, totaling $1.6 billion, came from increased deposits in New York City banks. The Federal Reserve at the same time sharply lowered its rediscount and acceptance rates.

By mid-November, the great stock market break was over and, stimulated by artificial credit, began to rise again. Total bank reserves then fell, so that at the end of November they had reached precrash levels. This contraction stemmed from a decline in discounts and acceptances, a gold outflow, and increased money in circulation; the Fed tried to offset this in vain by purchasing more securities. If we compare October 23, the day before the crash, with the situation at the end of 1929, we find that bank reserves *controlled* by the Fed — all government securities — tripled in size. This expansion was offset by such *uncontrolled* factors affecting reserves as a decline in gold and an increase in cash in circulation brought on by falling public confidence in the banks and in the dollar itself. The Fed had done its best to inflate in the last quarter of 1929, but its efforts were thwarted by seasonal cash outflows and the exigencies of the gold standard. The result was that the total money supply remained level in the final quarter of 1929.

President Hoover was proud of his experiment in cheap money and, in a speech to a White House conference of several hundred business leaders in December, hailed the nation's good fortune in possessing the magnificent Federal Reserve System, which had succeeded in saving banks, restoring confidence, and lowering interest rates. Hoover also revealed that he had done his part for the cause by personally urging the banks to rediscount more extensively at the Federal Reserve. Secretary of the Treasury Mellon issued one of his by now traditionally optimistic pronouncements, stating that there was "plenty of credit available." And William Green, head of the American Federation of Labor, hailed the Federal Reserve for its success in ending the depression. On November 22, 1929, Green opined: "All the factors which make for a quick and speedy industrial and economic recovery are present and evident. The Federal Reserve System is operating, serving as a barrier against financial demoralization. Within a few months, industrial conditions will become normal, confidence and stabilization of industry and finance will be restored."[84]

---

[84]*The American Federationist* 37 (March, 1930): 344. See also Rothbard, *America's Great Depression*, pp. 191–93.

Apparently, many leading Federal Reserve officials were disposed, at the end of 1929, to "let the money market 'sweat it out' and reach monetary ease by the wholesome process of liquidation."[85] But this *laissez-faire* policy was not to be. Instead, Governor George L. Harrison, head of the New York Fed, led a policy of massive easy money. Rediscount rates at the Fed, buying rates on acceptances, and the call loan rate all fell drastically. At the end of August 1930, Governor Roy Young of the Federal Reserve Board resigned and was replaced by a thoroughgoing inflationist, Eugene Meyer, Jr.[86] Total bank reserves rose during the year, chiefly through large Fed purchases of government securities. But all this inflationism was to no avail, since a wave of bank failures struck toward the end of the year, and shaky banks had to contract their operations. The net result was that the total money supply remained level throughout the year. For a while stock prices rose again, but they soon fell sharply, and production and employment kept falling steadily.

Meanwhile, the New York Fed continued to lead collaborations with foreign central banks, often against the wishes of the federal administration. Thus, the new "'central bankers' bank," the Bank for International Settlements (BIS), was instigated by Montagu Norman, and much of the American capital for the BIS was put up by J.P. Morgan & Co. The BIS treated the New York Fed as America's central bank, and Governor Harrison made a trip abroad in late 1930 to confer with European central bankers. Chairman of the BIS's first organizing committee was Jackson E. Reynolds, a director of the New York Fed, and the first president of the BIS was Gates W. McGarrah, who resigned as chairman of the board of the New York Fed to assume the post. Yet there was no legislative sanction for U.S. participation in the bank.

Despite the administration's and the Fed's systemic attempts to inflate and provide cheap money, the inflationists were not satisfied with the course of events. In late October, *Business Week* thundered against the

---

[85]Anderson, *Economics and the Public Welfare*, p. 227.

[86]Eugene Meyer, Jr., was the son of a partner in the great international banking firm of Lazard Frères. Like stock speculator and close friend Bernard Baruch, Meyer had made a fortune through financial association with the wealthy Guggenheim family and with the Morgans in mining investments. At the time of Meyer's appointment, his brother-in-law George Blumenthal was a partner at J.P. Morgan and Co. [Editor's remarks] For more on the origins of Eugene Meyer, Jr., see Rothbard, "From Hoover to Roosevelt," pp. 278–86.

supposed "deflationists in the saddle," supposedly inspired by the large commercial and investment banks.[87]

In contrast, in the same month Herbert Hoover apparently felt that the time had come for self-congratulation. In an address to the American Bankers Association, he summed up the multifaceted intervention of the preceding year. He hailed the Federal Reserve System as the great instrument of promoting stability and called for an "ample supply of credit at low interest," which he pointed out was now available "through the cooperation of the banks and the Federal Reserve system." Hoover proceeded to point out that the Federal Reserve was the locus of a vast system of cartelization:

> The reserve system and its member banks and the Treasury participation in fact form a widespread cooperative organization, acting in the broad interest of the whole people. To a large degree it can influence the flow of credit. Bankers themselves are represented at each stage of management. And, in addition, the various boards and advisory committees represent also industry, agriculture, merchandising, and the Government. The reserve system therefore furnished an admirable center for cooperation of the banking business with the production and distribution industries and the Government in the development of broad and detached policies of business stability.[88]

Moreover, these broad and detached policies of cooperation had succeeded in combating the depression:

> We have all been much engaged with measures of relief from the effect of the collapse of a year ago. At that time I determined that it was my duty, even without precedent, to call upon the business of the country for coordinated and constructive action to resist the forces of disintegration. The business community, the bankers, labor, and the Government have cooperated in wider spread measures of mitigation than have ever been attempted before. Our

---

[87]*Business Week*, 22 October 1930. See also Rothbard, *America's Great Depression*, pp. 212–13.

[88]William Starr Myers, ed., *The State Papers and the Public Writings of Herbert Hoover* (Garden City, NY: Doubleday, Doran & Co., 1934), p. 379.

bankers and the reserve system have carried the country through the credit storm without impairment.[89]

The rest is history.

11. SUMMARY

The bleak record of accelerating inflation and recession since the inception of the Federal Reserve in 1913 may be seen in a different light if we reevaluate the purpose that this central bank was intended to serve. For the Federal Reserve was designed not to curb the allegedly inflationary tendencies of freely competing banks but to do precisely the opposite: to enable the banks to inflate uniformly without worrying about calls for redemption by noninflating competitors. In short, the Federal Reserve was designed to act as a government-sponsored and -enforced cartel promoting the income of banks by preventing free competition from doing its constructive work on behalf of the consumer. The Federal Reserve emerged in an era when federal and state governments were embarked on precisely this kind of program in many sectors of industry, and it was designed to do for the banks what the ICC had done for the railroads, the Agriculture Department for the farmers, and the FTC for general industry. These actions of the Progressive era came after widespread attempts, in the late 1890s and earlier, to cartelize or create monopolies voluntarily, attempts that almost all came to swift and resounding failure. Various large business groupings, therefore, came to the conclusion that government would have to play an active and enforcing role if cartelization was to succeed.

This chapter demonstrates the unhappiness of particularly the large Wall Street banks with the "inelasticity" of the pre-Federal Reserve banking system, that is, its inability to create more money and credit. They were unhappy also with the growing decentralization of the nation's banking by the early part of the 20th century. After the failure of attempts by McKinley and Roosevelt's secretaries of the treasury to engage in central banking, and particularly after the Panic of 1907, large banking and financial groups, in particular those of Morgan, Rockefeller, and Kuhn-Loeb, began a drive to establish a central bank in the United States. Despite minor political disagreements, the numerous variants of Federal Reserve proposals, from the Aldrich plan to the final bill in 1913, were essentially the same.

---

[89]Ibid., p. 381.

The structure of the Federal Reserve Act was cartelizing and inflationary, and the personnel of the Federal Reserve Board reflected the dominance of the large banking groups, particularly the Morgans, in the drive for a central bank. The ruling force in the Federal Reserve System from its inception until his death in 1928 was Benjamin Strong, Governor of the Federal Reserve Bank of New York, who all his life had been firmly in the Morgan ambit.

Strong's policies were what one might expect. His willingness to inflate money and credit to purchase government deficits was critical to financing America's entry into World War I. He also moved quickly to internationalize the banking cartel by forming a close tie with the Bank of England, of which the Morgan Bank was fiscal agent. The Morgans were also closely connected with munitions and other war-related exports to Britain and France, and enjoyed the sole privilege of underwriting British and French war bonds in the United States.

Benjamin Strong was obliged to inflate money and credit during the 1920s in order to help Britain return to an inflationary form of the gold standard at a highly overvalued pound. Only by Strong's increasing the supply of dollars could his close collaborator, Montagu Norman, head of the Bank of England, hope to stem the flow of gold from Britain to the United States. Strong performed this inflationary role not only by keeping rediscount rates below the market and buying treasury securities on the open market but also by subsidizing — indeed, virtually creating — a market in bankers' acceptances, which the Fed stood ready to buy in any amount offered at artificially cheap rates. This acceptance policy, designed to promote foreign trade (especially in London), was adopted under the influence of one of the founders of the Federal Reserve, Paul M. Warburg of Kuhn-Loeb & Co. who also became the nation's largest acceptance banker.

When the stock market crash hit, the Federal Reserve and the Hoover administration were scarcely ready to allow free-market processes to bring about recovery. Instead, the Fed, backed strongly by Hoover, inflated reserves wildly, and interest rates fell sharply — all, of course, to no avail.

CHAPTER 15

Herbert Hoover and the Myth of Laissez-Faire

1. Herbert Hoover as Secretary of Commerce

The conventional wisdom, of historian and layman alike, pictures Herbert Hoover as the last stubborn guardian of *laissez-faire* in America. The *laissez-faire* economy, so this wisdom runs, produced the Great Depression in 1929, and Hoover's traditional, do-nothing policies could not stem the tide. Hence, Hoover and his hidebound policies were swept away, and Franklin Roosevelt entered to bring to America a New Deal, a new progressive economy of state regulation and intervention fit for the modern age.

The major theme of this chapter is that this conventional historical view is pure mythology and that the facts are virtually the reverse: that Herbert Hoover, far from being an advocate of *laissez-faire*, was in every way the precursor of Roosevelt and the New Deal, that, in short, he was one of the major leaders of the 20th-century shift from relatively *laissez-faire* capitalism to the modern corporate state. In the terminology of William A. Williams and the New Left, Hoover was a preeminent "corporate liberal."

Originally published in *A History of Leviathan*, Ronald Radosh and Murray N. Rothbard, eds. (New York: E.P. Dutton & Co., 1972), pp. 111–15. Rothbard did not provide subsections to this essay; to keep the format of the chapters uniform subsections have been added by the editor.

When Herbert Hoover returned to the United States in late 1919, fresh from his post as Relief Administrator in Europe, he came armed with a suggested "Reconstruction Program" for America. The program sketched the outlines of a corporate state; there was to be national planning through "voluntary" cooperation among businesses and groups under "central direction."[1] The Federal Reserve System was to allocate capital to essential industries and thereby eliminate the industrial "waste" of free markets. Hoover's plan also included the creation of public dams, the improvement of waterways, a federal home-loan banking system, the promotion of unions and collective bargaining, and governmental regulation of the stock market to eliminate "vicious speculation."[2] It is no wonder that Progressive Republicans as well as such Progressive Democrats as Louis Brandeis, Herbert Croly, and others on the *New Republic*, Edward A. Filene, Colonel Edward M. House, and Franklin D. Roosevelt boomed Hoover for the presidency during the 1920 campaign.

Hoover was appointed Secretary of Commerce by President Harding under pressure by the Progressive wing of the party, and accepted under the condition that he would be consulted on all the economic activities of the federal government. He thereupon set out deliberately to "reconstruct America."[3]

Hoover was only thwarted from breaking the firm American tradition of *laissez-faire* during a depression by the fact that the severe but short-lived depression of 1920–21 was over soon after he took office. He also faced some reluctance on the part of Harding and the Cabinet. As it was, however, Hoover organized a federal committee on unemployment, which supplied unemployment relief through branches and subbranches to every state, and in numerous cities and local communities. Furthermore, Hoover organized the various federal, state, and municipal governments to increase public works, and persuaded the biggest business firms, such as Standard Oil of New Jersey and United States Steel, to increase their expenditure on repairs and construction. He also persuaded employers to spread unemployment by cutting hours for all workers instead of dis-

---

[1]Hoover's earlier career confirms this appraisal of his views; there is no space here, however, to analyze his earlier ideas and activities.

[2]See Dorfman, *The Economic Mind in American Civilization,* vol. 4, pp. 26–28; Hoover, *Memoirs,* vol. 2, pp. 27ff.; and Rothbard, *America's Great Depression,* p. 170 and Part 3.

[3]Hoover to Professor Wesley C. Mitchell, July 29, 1921. Mitchell, *Two Lives,* p. 364.

charging the marginal workers — an action he was to repeat in the 1929 Depression.[4]

Hoover called for these interventionist measures with an analogy from the institutions of wartime planning and collaboration, urging that Americans develop "the same spirit of spontaneous cooperation in every community for reconstruction that we had in war."[5]

An important harbinger for Hoover's later Depression policies was the president's Conference on Unemployment, a gathering of eminent leaders of industry, banking, and labor called by President Harding in the fall of 1921 at the instigation of Hoover. In contrast to Harding's address affirming *laissez-faire* as the proper method of dealing with depressions, Hoover's opening address to the Conference called for active intervention.[6] Furthermore, the Conference's major recommendation — for coordinated federal state expansion of public works to remedy depressions — was prepared by Hoover and his staff in advance of the conference.[7] Of particular importance was the provision that public works and public relief were to be supplied only at the *usual* wage rate — a method of trying to maintain the high wage rates of the preceding boom during a depression.

---

[4]Hoover, *Memoirs*, vol. 2, p. 46; and Joseph H. McMullen, "The President's Unemployment Conference of 1921 and Its Results" (Master's thesis, Columbia University, 1922), p. 33.

[5]On the lasting significance of government economic planning and "war collectivism" during World War I, see Leuchtenburg, "The New Deal and the Analogue of War," pp. 81–143.

[6]See E. Jay Howenstine, Jr., "Public Works Policy in the Twenties," *Social Research* (December, 1946): 479–500.

[7]Playing a crucial role on this staff was Otto Tod Mallery, the nation's leading advocate of public works as a remedy for depressions. Mallery had inspired the nation's first such stabilization program, in Pennsylvania in 1917, and had been a leading official on public works in the Wilson administration. He was also a leader in the American Association for Labor Legislation, an influential group of eminent citizens, businessmen, and economists devoted to government intervention in the fields of labor, employment, and welfare. The AALL, endorsing the Conference, boasted that the Conference's proposals followed the pattern of its own recommendations, which had been formulated as far back as 1915. Apart from Mallery, the Conference employed the services of nine economists who were also officials of the AALL.

The AALL singled out for particular praise Joseph H. Defrees, of the U.S. Chamber of Commerce, who appealed to business organizations to cooperate with the Conference's program, and to accept "business responsibility" for the unemployment problem.

See Dorfman, *Economic Mind in American Civilization*, vol. 4, pp. 7–8; McMullen, "The President's Unemployment Conference," p. 16; and John B. Andrews, "The President's Unemployment Conference–Success or Failure?" *American Labor Legislation Review* (December, 1921): 307–10.

Although these interventions did not have time to take hold in the 1921 depression, a precedent for federal intervention in an economic depression had now been set, as one of Hoover's admiring biographers writes, "rather to the horror of conservatives."[8]

The president's Conference established three permanent research committees, headed overall by Hoover, which continued during the 1920s to publish studies advocating public-works stabilization during depressions. One such book, *Seasonal Operations in the Construction Industry* (Washington, D.C.: Conference on Unemployment, 1921), the foreword to which was written by Hoover, urged seasonal stabilization of construction. This study was in part the result of a period of propaganda emitted by the American Construction Council, a trade association for the construction industry, which of course was enthusiastic about large-scale programs of government contracts for the construction industry. This Council was founded jointly by Herbert Hoover and Franklin D. Roosevelt in the summer of 1922, with the aim of stabilizing and cartelizing the industry, and of planning the entire construction industry through the imposition of various codes of "ethics" and of "fair practice." The codes were the particular idea of Herbert Hoover. Following the path of all would-be cartelists who are hostile to no one more than the individualistic competitor, Franklin D. Roosevelt, president of the American Construction Council, took repeated opportunity to denounce rugged individualism and profit-seeking by individuals.[9]

Throughout the 1920s Hoover supported numerous bills in Congress for public-works programs during depressions. He was backed in these endeavors by the American Federation of Labor, the United States Chamber of Commerce, and the American Engineering Council, of which Hoover was for a time president. It was clear that the engineering profession would also benefit greatly from government subsidization of the construction industry. By the middle twenties, President Coolidge, Secretary Mellon, and the National Democratic Party had been converted to the scheme, but Congress was not yet convinced.

After he was elected president, but before taking office, Hoover allowed his public-works plan (the "Hoover Plan") to be presented to the

---

[8]Eugene Lyons, *Our Unknown Ex-President* (New York: Doubleday and Co., 1948), p. 230.

[9]See Daniel Fusfeld, *The Economic Thought of Franklin D. Roosevelt and the Origins of the New Deal* (New York: Columbia University Press, 1956), pp. 102ff.

Conference of Governors in late 1928 by Governor Ralph Owen Brewster of Maine. Brewster called the plan the "Road to Plenty," a name that Hoover had taken from Foster and Catchings,[10] the popular co-authors of a plan for massive inflation and public works as the way to end depressions. Although seven or eight governors were enthusiastic about the plan, the Governors' Conference tabled the scheme. A large part of the press hailed the plan extravagantly as a "pact to outlaw depression." Leading the applause was William Green, head of the AF of L, who hailed the plan as the most important announcement on wages and employment in a decade, and John P. Frey of the AF of L who announced that Hoover had accepted the AF of L theory that depressions are caused by low wages. The press reported that "labor is jubilant" because the new president's remedy for unemployment is "identical with that of labor."

The close connection between Hoover and the labor leadership was no isolated phenomenon. Hoover had long agitated for industry to encourage and incorporate labor unionism within the framework of the emerging industrial order. Moreover, he played a crucial role in converting the labor leaders themselves to the idea of a corporate state with unions as junior partners in the system, a state that would organize and harmonize labor and capital.

Hoover's pro-union views first achieved prominence when, as chairman of President Wilson's Second Industrial Conference (1919/20), he guided this conference of corporate-liberal industrialists and labor leaders to criticize "company unionism" and to urge the expansion of collective bargaining, government arbitration boards for labor disputes, and a program of national health and old-age insurance. Soon afterward Hoover

---

[10]Waddill Catchings was a prominent investment banker who founded the Pollak Foundation for Economic Research, with Dr. William T. Foster as director, Foster was Brewster's technical advisor at the Governor's Conference. Foster and Catchings had called for a $3 billion public-works program to iron out the business cycle and stabilize the price level. William T. Foster and Waddill Catchings, *The Road to Plenty* (Boston: Houghton Mifflin & Co., 1928), p. 187. Brewster's presentation can be found in Ralph Owen Brewster, "Footprints on the Road to Plenty–A Three Billion Dollar Fund to Stabilize Business," *Commercial and Financial Chronicle* (November 28, 1928), p. 2, 527.

Foster and Catchings reciprocated by praising the "Hoover Plan" a few months later. The Plan, they exulted, would iron out prices and the business cycle; "it is business guided by measurement instead of hunches. It is economics for an age of science–economics worthy of the new President." William T. Foster and Waddill Catchings, "Mr. Hoover's Plan: What It Is and What It Is Not — the New Attack on Poverty," *Review of Reviews* (April, 1929): 77–78.

arranged a meeting of leading industrialists with "advanced views" in an unsuccessful attempt to persuade them to "establish liaison" with the AF of L. In January, 1921, the AF of L journal published a significant address by Hoover, which called for the "definite organization of great national associations" of economic groups and their mutual cooperation. This cooperation would serve to promote efficiency and mitigate labor-management conflict. Above all, workers would be protected from "the unfair competition of the sweatshop." Still more did this mean "protection" of the lower-cost large employers from the competition of their smaller "sweatshop" rivals — a typical instance of monopolizers using humanitarian rhetoric to gain public support for the restriction and suppression of competition. Hoover went so far in this address as to support the closed shop, provided that the closure was to be for the sake of unity of purpose in aiding the employer to increase production and to mold a cooperative labor force. In conclusion, Hoover called for a new economic system, what was in effect a corporate state, that would provide an alternative to old-fashioned *laissez-faire* capitalism on the one hand and Marxian socialism on the other.[11]

In an authoritative study, William English Walling, an intimate of Samuel Gompers, wrote of the crucial influence of Hoover's theories upon Gompers and the AF of L, especially from 1920 on. This influence was particularly strong in persuading the labor leaders to endorse the idea of organizing all the large occupation groups and then effecting their mutual harmony and cooperation under the aegis and control of the federal government. Capital and labor in each industry, organized in collaboration, were to have the role of government of that particular industry.[12] It was indeed appropriate for the French politician Edouard Herriot to praise Hoover in

---

[11]Herbert Hoover, "A Plea for Cooperation," *The American Federationist* (January, 1921). Also see the important work by Ronald Radosh, "The Development of the Corporate Ideology of American Labor Leaders, 1914–1933" (Doctoral dissertation in history, University of Wisconsin, 1967), pp. 82ff.

[12]William English Walling, *American Labor and American Democracy* (New York: Harper & Bros., 1926), vol. 2: *Labor and Government*, cited in Radosh, "The Development of Corporate Ideology," pp. 85ff. Addressing the International Association of Technical Engineers, Architects and Draftsmen in May, 1921, Gompers spoke enthusiastically of the close "entente" that had developed between engineering groups and the AF of L. It was Gompers, furthermore, who persuaded Hoover to accept the presidency of the American Engineering Council.

1920 for his idea of fusing the "economic trinity" of labor, capital, and government into one system, thus putting an end to the class struggle.[13]

Another reason for Hoover's pro-union attitude was that he had adopted the increasingly popular thesis that high wage rates were a major cause of prosperity. It then followed that wage rates must not be lowered during depressions. In contrast to all prior depressions, including 1920–21, when wage rates were cut sharply, wage-cutting was considered by Hoover to be impermissible and as leading to a failure in purchasing power and the perpetuation of depression. These views were to prove a fateful harbinger of the policies used during the Great Depression.

One of Hoover's most important labor interventions during the 1920s came in the steel industry. He persuaded Harding to hold a conference of steel manufacturers in May, 1922, after which he and Harding called upon the steel magnates to bow to the workers' demand to shift from a 12-hour to an eight-hour day. In doing so, Hoover was siding with the liberal wing of the steel industry, led by Charles R. Hook and Alexander Legge, whose plants had already instituted the shorter workday, and who of course were anxious to impose higher costs on their lagging competitors. When Judge Gary of United States Steel and other leading steelmen refused to go along, Hoover acted to mobilize public opinion against them. Thus, he induced the national engineering societies to endorse the eight-hour day, and himself wrote the introduction to the endorsement. Finally, Hoover wrote a stern letter of rebuke for President Harding, which Harding sent to Gary on June 18, 1923, forcing Gary to capitulate.

Herbert Hoover also played a leading role in collectivizing labor relations in the railroad industry, thereby cartelizing that industry still further than before and incorporating railway unions within the cartel framework. After repeated and largely unsuccessful interventions to try to gain pro-union concessions during the railroad strike of 1922, Hoover became a major author — along with union lawyers Donald Richberg and David E. Lilienthal — of the Railway Labor Act of 1926, by which the railway unions got themselves established in the industry. The ancestor of the New Deal's Wagner Act, the Railway Labor Act, imposed collective bargaining upon the industry; in return, the unions agreed to give up the strike

---

[13]Radosh, "The Development of the Corporate Ideology of American Labor Leaders," p. 88n.

weapon. The great majority of the railroads warmly supported this new departure in American labor relations.[14]

In a major address before the United States Chamber of Commerce, on May 7, 1924, Hoover spelled out his corporatist views in some detail. He called for the self-regulation of industry by way of trade associations, farm groups, and unions. In a vein strongly reminiscent of English Guild Socialism, Hoover harked back to the Middle Ages for his model: the guilds, he asserted, obtained "more stability through collective action." The job of the associations was to strengthen "ethical standards" in industry by eliminating "waste" and "destructive competition." In short, Hoover was calling for the national cartelization of industry under the aegis of government.[15] Samuel Gompers hailed the address and considered this "new economic policy" to be the same as the newly forged position of the AF of L.[16]

Herbert Hoover's entire program of activities as Secretary of Commerce was designed to advance the subsidization of industry and the interpenetration of government and business. As Hoover's admirer and former head of the United States Chamber of Commerce put it, Hoover had advanced the "teamplay of government with the leaders of character in the various industries."[17] Thus, Hoover expanded the Bureau of Foreign and Domestic Commerce fivefold, opening numerous offices at home and abroad. His trade commissioners and attachés aided American exports in numerous ways. He also reorganized the Bureau along commodity lines, with each commodity division headed by someone chosen by the particular trade or

---

[14]For a pro-union account of the affair by a leading participant, see Donald R. Richberg, *Labor Union Monopoly* (Chicago: Henry Regnery, 1957), pp. 3–28.

[15]In his book *American Individualism*, Hoover had hailed the growing "cooperation" and "associational activities" of American industry and the consequent reduction of "great wastes of over-reckless competition." Hoover, *American Individualism* (New York: Doubleday, 1922).

[16]Samuel Gompers, "The Road to Industrial Democracy," *American Federationist* (June, 1921). Also see Ronald Radosh, "The Corporate Ideology of American Labor Leaders from Gompers to Hillman," *Studies on the Left* (November–December, 1966): 70. After Gompers' death in 1924, his successor, William Green, continued the close AF of L collaboration with Hoover. See Radosh, *The Development of Corporate Ideology*, pp. 201ff.

[17]Julius H. Barnes, "Herbert Hoover's Priceless Work in Washington," *Industrial Management* (April, 1926), pp. 196–197. Also see Brandes, *Herbert Hoover and Economic Diplomacy*, p. 3.

industry, from the trade "he knows and represents."[18] Furthermore, Hoover promoted the cartelization of each industry by inducing each trade to create a committee to cooperate with the Department of Commerce, and to select the industry's choice for head of the commodity division. Officials in the Department were systematically recruited from business to stay in the Department for a few years and then to return to private business at higher-paying jobs.

One favorite method of Hoover's for subsidizing as well as cartelizing exports was to foster the creation of export-trade associations. Thus, in 1926, Hoover repeatedly urged the coffee trade to band together and create a National Coffee Council, so that all American coffee buyers could join together to lower buying prices. Hoover and his aides craftily suggested to the coffee trade that one union leader and one woman consumer be named to the proposed Coffee Council as a public-relations device to relieve public fears of a cartel.[19]

The difficulties of forming a coffee cartel proved insurmountable; but Hoover had more luck with the rubber industry, organizing it to fight British cartel restrictions on Asian rubber production that had been imposed in 1922. Hoover led the rubber industry in a drive to induce Americans to buy less rubber and hence to lower the price, as well as to promote American-owned sources of supply, by such means as government subsidies to new United States-owned rubber plantations in the Philippines.[20] An American rubber-buying pool was established in 1926 and lasted until the end of British restrictions two years later.[21]

As soon as he assumed office, Hoover induced President Harding to pressure investment bankers to require that the proceeds of their loans abroad be used to purchase American exports. When little came of this

---

[18]Brandes, *Herbert Hoover and Economic Diplomacy*, p. 5.

[19]Ibid., pp. 17–18, 132–139.

[20]On Hoover's repeated urging of American oil companies to join in the development of petroleum in Mesopotamia, see Nash, *United States Oil Policy*, pp. 56–57.

[21]Harvey Firestone was the most enthusiastic rubber user backing the Hoover program, and also in organizing American owned rubber plantations in Liberia. The mighty U.S. Rubber Co., on the other hand, already owned large rubber plantations in the Dutch East Indies, which were not subject to British restrictions. U.S. Rubber was therefore the rubber user least enthusiastic about the buying pool. Brandes, *Herbert Hoover and Economic Diplomacy*, pp. 84–128. On Firestone's acquisition of Liberian land, see Frank Chalk, "The Anatomy of an Investment: Firestone's 1927 Loan to Liberia," *Canadian Journal of African Studies* (March, 1967): 12–32.

pressure, Hoover began to threaten congressional action if the banks did not agree. For Hoover, the aim of subsidizing exports was so important that even unsound foreign loans that could serve this purpose were considered worthwhile.[22]

Hoover's opposition to foreign "monopoly" did not of course prevent him from supporting a protective tariff in the United States, thus providing privilege to American domestic as well as export firms. During the 1920s, Hoover was also active in promoting the cartelization of the domestic oil industry. As an active member of President Coolidge's Federal Oil Conservation Board since its inception in 1924, Hoover worked in collaboration with a growing majority of the oil industry in behalf of restrictions on oil production in the name of "conservation." This was a "conservation," by the way, that was urged regardless of whether American oil resources seemed to be scarce or superabundant. Hoover was particularly interested in removing antitrust limitations on industrial cooperation in such restrictive measures.[23]

In the field of coal, Hoover sponsored repeated attempts at cartelization. The first attempt was a bill in 1921 to establish a federal coal commission to gather and publish statistics of the coal industry, so as to publicize price data and thereby facilitate industry-wide price-fixing. Failing a commission, the Department of Commerce was eager to take on the task. However, this and a later scheme by Hoover to encourage marketing cooperatives in coal by exemption from antitrust laws, were defeated by the opposition of competitive low-cost Southern coal operators. Undaunted, Hoover, in 1922, prepared a full-fledged cartelizing plan. The idea was to establish unemployment insurance in the coal industry, so designed as to penalize in the cost of the plan the part-time and seasonal coal mines, and thereby to drive these higher-cost mines out of business. The coal industry would then form cooperatives, which would fix and allocate quotas on production, putting more mines out of operation, the owners to be compensated out of the increased cartel profits made by the rest of the industry. The district coal cooperatives were to market all the

---

[22]See Jacob Viner, "Political Aspects of International Finance, Part II," *Journal of Business* (July, 1928): 339; Hoover, *Memoirs*, vol. 2, p. 90. Also see Brandes, *Herbert Hoover and Economic Diplomacy*, pp. 170–91. Hoover also clashed with banks that made foreign loans to Germany, since he was worried about the loans building up competitors to American firms, especially chemical manufacturers. Ibid., pp. 192–95.

[23]Nash, *United States Oil Policy*, pp. 81–97.

coal and then divide the revenues proportionately. But once again Hoover could not command the needed support from the coal industry and the public.[24]

Hoover played a similar role in cartelizing the cotton textile industry. Favoring the "open-price" plan for stimulating price agreements, Hoover used his Department of Commerce to provide the price publicity that might be illegal for a trade association. Hoover also played a role in forcing the cotton textile industry to establish a nationwide rather than a regional trade association, to the delight of the bulk of the industry. Hoover repeatedly urged the many reluctant firms to join this Cotton Textile Institute, which gave promise of stabilizing the industry and eliminating "waste" in production. Hoover went so far as to endorse, in 1927, the CTFs plan to urge each of the member firms to cut production by a certain definite amount.[25]

One of the clearest indications of how far removed Hoover was from *laissez-faire* was his leading role in nationalizing the airwaves of the fledgling radio industry. Hoover put through the nationalizing Radio Act in 1927 as a substitute for the courts' increasing application of the common law, granting private ownership of the airwaves to the first radio stations that put them into use.[26]

One of the most pervasive and least studied methods by which Hoover helped to monopolize industry during the 1920s was to impose standardization and "simplification" of materials and products. In this way, Hoover managed to eliminate the "least necessary" varieties of a myriad of products, greatly reducing the number of competitive sizes, for example, of automobile wheels and tires, and threads for nuts and bolts. All in all, about three thousand articles were thus "simplified."

[24]See Hawley, "Secretary Hoover and the Bituminous Coal Problem, 1921–1928," pp. 247–70. Also see Hoover, *Memoirs*, vol. 2, p. 70. During the coal strike in the spring of 1922, Hoover organized an emergency system of rationing and price controls. Harking back to his wartime experience, he established a network of district committees to hold down coal prices. After the typically Hooverian "voluntary" controls failed to work, Hoover called for governmental price-fixing, and by late September, Congress had passed a law appointing a Federal Fuel Distributor to enforce "fair prices."

[25]Galambos, *Competition and Cooperation*, pp. 78–83, 102–03, 108, 114–15, 123, 128–29. The cotton textile industry urged Secretary Hoover to become the first president of their new Institute; as it was, the president was a man recommended by Hoover.

[26]See in particular Ronald H. Coase, "The Federal Communications Commission," *Journal of Law and Economics* (October, 1959): 30ff. Also see Hoover, *Memoirs*, vol. 2, pp. 139–42.

The recommendations for simplification were worked out by the Department of Commerce with the aid of the eager committees representing each trade.[27]

Hoover's approach to the farm question was consistent: a repeated emphasis on the cartelization of agriculture.[28] At first, the favored means was the subsidizing by government of farm cooperatives. Hoover helped write the act of August, 1921, which expanded the funds allotted to the War Finance Corporation and permitted it to lend directly to the farm co-ops. He also supported the farm-bloc bill for an extensive system of Federal Intermediate Credit Banks and a Federal Farm Loan Board, which were to lend federal funds to farm co-ops. In the Department of Commerce, he was able to help farm co-ops with marketing programs and with aid in finding export markets.

Hoover soon enlarged his ideas of farm intervention; he was one of the earliest proponents of a Federal Farm Board, designed to raise and support farm prices by creating federal stabilization corporations that were to purchase farm products and to lend money to farm co-ops for such purchases. And to this end, in 1924, Hoover helped write the unsuccessful Capper-Williams Bill. As a presidential candidate in 1928 he promised the farm bloc that he would promptly institute a farm price-support program.[29] It was a promise that he hastened to keep, for as soon as he became president, Hoover drove through the Agricultural Marketing Act of 1929. This Act created a Federal Farm Board with a revolving fund of $500 million to raise and support farm prices and to aid farm co-ops; the Board was to conduct its price-raising operations through stabilization corporations for the various commodities, with the corporations also serving as

---

[27]Hoover, *Memoirs*, vol. 2, pp. 66–68.

[28]In the case of salmon fishing, Hoover called for federal regulations from 1922 on. In that year he induced Harding to create salmon reservations in Alaska, thus cutting salmon production and raising prices. See Donald C. Swain, *Federal Conservation Policy, 1921–1933* (Berkeley: University of California Press, 1963), pp. 25ff.

[29]It was not only the farm bloc that wanted a nationally cartelized agriculture. Two of the fathers of the agitation for farm price support were George N. Peek and General Hugh S. Johnson, heads of the Moline Plow Company, one of the largest farm-equipment manufacturers. As such they were directly interested in the subsidizing of farmers. Big business in general was also enthusiastic, the farm price-support plan being warmly supported by the Business Men's Commission on Agriculture, established jointly by the U.S. Chamber of Commerce and the National Industrial Conference Board. See Dorfman, *The Economic Mind in American Civilization*, vol. 4, pp. 79–80.

marketing agencies for the coops. Furthermore, Hoover appointed to the Board representatives of the various agricultural and farm co-op interests: a cartelization operated by the cartelists themselves.[30]

2. HERBERT HOOVER FIGHTS THE GREAT DEPRESSION

Mobilizer and economic planner of World War I; persistent advocate of cartelization and government-business partnership in stabilizing industry; pioneer in promoting a pro-union outlook in industry as a method of insuring the cooperation of labor; booster of high wages as a sustainer of purchasing power and business prosperity; ardent proponent of massive public-works schemes during depressions; advocate of government programs to boost farm prices and farm co-ops; no one could have been as ideally suited as Herbert Clark Hoover to be president at the onset of a Great Depression and to react with a radical program of statism to be trumpeted as a "New Deal." And that is precisely what Herbert Hoover did. It is one of the great ironies of historiography that the founder of every single one of the features of Franklin Roosevelt's New Deal was to become enshrined among historians and the general public as the last stalwart defender of *laissez-faire*.

Let us consider the New Deal — a rapid intensification of government intervention that began in response to a severe depression, and featured: cartelization of industry through government-and-business planning; bolstering of prices and wage rates, expansion of credit, massive unemployment relief and public-works programs, support of farm prices, and propping up of weak and unsound business positions. Every one of these features was founded, and consciously so, by President Hoover. Hoover consciously and deliberately broke sharply and rapidly with the whole American tradition of a *laissez-faire* response to depression. As Hoover himself proclaimed during his presidential campaign of 1932:

> ... we might have done nothing. That would have been
> utter ruin. Instead we met the situation with proposals

---

[30]Chairman of the eight-man FFB was Alexander Legge, president of International Harvester Co., one of the major farm machinery manufacturers, and like Peek and Johnson, a protege of financier Bernard M. Baruch since the days of the economic planning of World War I. Others represented on the Board were the tobacco co-ops, the livestock co-ops, the Midwest grain interests, and the fruit growers. See Theodore Saloutos and John D. Hicks, *Agricultural Discontent in the Middle West* (Madison: University of Wisconsin Press, 1951), pp. 407–12.

to private business and to Congress of the most gigantic program of economic defense and counterattack ever evolved in the history of the Republic. We put it into action. ... No government in Washington has hitherto considered that it held so broad a responsibility for leadership in such times. ... For the first time in the history of depressions, dividends, profits and the cost of living, have been reduced before wages have suffered. ... They were maintained until the cost of living had decreased and the profits had practically vanished. They are now the highest real wages in the world.[31]

Hoover began his "gigantic" program as soon as the stock market crashed on October 24, 1929. His most fateful act was to call a series of White House Conferences with the nation's leading financiers and industrialists and induce them to pledge that wage rates would not be lowered and that they would expand their investments. Hoover explained the general aim of these conferences to be the coordination of business and government agencies in concerted action. Industrial group after group pledged that wage rates would be maintained. Hoover insisted that, contrary to previous depressions when wage rates fell promptly and rapidly (and, we might add, the depression was then soon over), wage rates must now be the last to fall, in order to prop up mass purchasing power. The entire burden of the recession, then, must fall upon business profits. The most important of these conferences occurred on November 21, when such great industrial leaders as Henry Ford, Julius Rosenwald, Walter Teagle, Owen D. Young, Alfred P. Sloan, Jr., and Pierre du Pont pledged their cooperation to the Hoover program. These agreements were made public,

---

[31]Rothbard, *America's Great Depression*, pp. 169–86. One of the first observers who saw that the radical break with the past came with Hoover and not with F.D.R. was Walter Lippmann, who wrote in 1935 that the "policy initiated by President Hoover in the autumn of 1929 was something utterly unprecedented in American history. The national government undertook to make the whole economic order operate prosperously. ... The state attempted to direct by the public wisdom a recovery in the business cycle which had hitherto been left with as little interference as possible to individual exertion." Walter Lippmann, "The Permanent New Deal," reprinted in *The Shaping of Twentieth-Century America*, R.M. Abrams and L.W. Levine, eds. (Boston: Little, Brown & Co., 1965), p. 430. Similarly, the perceptive term "Hoover New Deal" was coined by the contemporary observer and economist Benjamin M. Anderson. See "The Road Back to Full Employment," in *Financing American Prosperity*, P. Homan and F. Machlup, eds. (New York: Twentieth Century Fund, 1945), pp. 9–70; and Anderson, *Economics and the Public Welfare*.

and Hoover hailed them at a White House conference on December 5, as an "advance in the whole conception of the relationship of business to public welfare ... a far cry from the arbitrary and dog-eat-dog attitude of ... the business world of some thirty or forty years ago." The AF of L lauded this new development; never before, it proclaimed, have the industrial leaders "been called upon to act together ..."[32] By the following March, the AF of L was reporting that the big corporations were indeed keeping their agreement to maintain wage rates.[33]

In September, 1930, Hoover took another step to relieve unemployment and, by the way, to prop up wage rates. By administrative decree, Hoover in effect barred almost all further immigration into the country. In keeping with this policy of curing unemployment by forcing people out of the labor force, he deliberately accelerated the deportation of "undesirable" aliens, the deportation level reaching 20,000 per year.

The wage agreement held firm in the midst of a cataclysmic Depression and unprecedented and prolonged mass unemployment.[34] In fact, since prices were falling rapidly, this meant that the *real* wage rates of those lucky enough to remain employed were increasing sharply. The economist Leo Wolman noted at the time that it "is indeed impossible to recall any past depression of similar intensity and duration in which the wages of prosperity were maintained as long as they have been in the depression of 1930–31."[35] It was a record hailed by liberals from the AF of L to John Maynard Keynes. It was only by 1932, after several years of severe depression and catastrophic unemployment, that businesses could keep up wage rates no longer. When, in the fall of 1931, the United States Steel Corporation finally summoned up the courage to cut wage rates, it did so over the opposition of its own president and to the accusation of William Green that its 1929 pledge to the White House was being violated.[36] The large

---

[32] *The American Federationist* (January, 1930). On the White House Conferences, see Robert P. Lamont, "The White House Conferences," *The Journal of Business* (July, 1930): 269.

[33] *The American Federationist* (March, 1930): 344.

[34] Particularly active in keeping industry in line was the President's Emergency Committee for Employment; see E.P. Hayes, *Activities of the President's Emergency Committee for Employment, October 17, 1930–August 19, 1931* (Printed by the author, 1936).

[35] Leo Wolman, *Wages in Relation to Economic Recovery* (Chicago: University of Chicago Press, 1931).

[36] See Fred R. Fairchild, "Government Saves Us from Depression," *Yale Review* (Summer 1932): 667ff; and Dorfman, *The Economic Mind in American Civilization,* vol. 5, p. 620.

firms were particularly slow to break the agreement, and even then many of the cuts were made in executive salaries where the unemployment problem was at a minimum. Even with the cuts in wages, wage rates fell by only 23% from 1929 to 1933 — less than the decline of prices. Thus, *real* wage rates actually rose over the period, by over 8% in the leading manufacturing industries. The drop in wage rates had been far more prompt and extensive in the far milder 1921 depression. In the face of this record of wage maintenance, the unemployment rate rose to 25% of the labor force by 1933, and to a phenomenal 46% in the leading manufacturing industries. There were, unfortunately, only a few observers and economists who understood the causal connection between these events: that maintenance of wage rates was precisely the major factor in deepening and prolonging mass unemployment and the Depression.[37]

Hoover did his best, furthermore, to engineer a massive inflation of money and credit. In the crucial figure of government securities owned by the Federal Reserve Banks, Federal Reserve holdings rose from $300 million in September, 1929, to $1,840 million in March, 1933 — a sixfold increase. Ordinarily this would have led to a sixfold expansion of bank reserves and an enormous inflation of the money supply. But the Hoover drive for inflation was thwarted by the forces of the economy. Federal Reserve rediscounts fell by half a billion due to sluggish business demand, despite a sharp drop in the Federal Reserve's discount rate, cash in circulation increased by one and a half billion due to the public's growing distrust of the shaky and inflated banking system, and the banks began to pile up excess reserves because of their fear of making investments amidst the sea of business failures. The Hoover administration grew livid with the banks, and Hoover denounced the "lack of cooperation of the commercial banks … in the credit expansion drive." Atlee Pomerene, head of the Reconstruction Finance Corporation, went so far as to declare that any bank that is liquid and doesn't extend its loans is a "parasite on the country."[38] Hoover told Secretary of the Treasury Ogden Mills to form a committee of lead-

---

[37]See the unfortunately neglected study by Sol Shaviro, "Wages and Payroll in the Depression, 1929–1933" (Master's essay, Columbia University, 1947). Also see Rothbard, *America's Great Depression*, pp. 236–39, 290–94; Phillips, McManus, and Nelson, *Banking and the Business Cycle*, pp. 231–32; National Industrial Conference Board, *Salary and Wage Policy in the Depression* (New York: Conference Board, 1933), pp. 31–38; and Dale Yoder and George R. Davies, *Depression and Recovery* (New York: McGraw-Hill, 1934), p. 89.

[38]*New York Times*, May 20, 1932.

ing industrialists and bankers to pressure the banks into extending their credit.[39] By the end of his term and the abject failure of his inflationist program, Hoover was proposing what are surely typical New Deal measures: bank holidays and at least temporary federal "insurance" of bank deposits.

In fact, Hoover seriously considered invoking a forgotten wartime law making the "hoarding" of gold (that is, redemption of dollars into gold) a criminal offense.[40] Although he did not go that far, he did try his best to hamper the workings of the gold standard by condemning and blackening the names of people who lawfully redeemed their dollars in gold or their bank deposits into cash. In February, 1932, Hoover established the Citizens' Reconstruction Organization under Colonel Frank Knox of Chicago, dedicated to condemning "hoarders" and unpatriotic "traitors." Leading industrialists and labor leaders joined the CRO. Hoover also secretly tried to stop the American press from printing the full truth about the banking crisis and about the rising public criticism of his administration.[41]

Neither was Hoover lax in increasing the expenditures of the federal government. Federal expenditures rose from $3.3 billion in fiscal 1929 to $4.6 billion in fiscal 1932 and 1933, a rise of 40%. Meanwhile, federal budget receipts fell in half, from $4 billion to less than $2 billion, demonstrating that Hoover was so much of a proto-Keynesian that he was willing to incur a deficit of nearly 60% of the budget. This was, to that moment, the largest peacetime federal deficit in American history.

Part of this massive rise of federal expenditures went, as one might expect, into public works. So promptly did Hoover act to expand public works (proposing a $600 million increase by December, 1929) that by the end of 1929 the economist J.M. Clark was already hailing Hoover's

---

[39]Chairman of the committee was Owen D. Young of General Electric. Included in the committee were Walter S. Gifford of AT&T, Charles E. Mitchell of National City Bank, and Walter C. Teagle of Standard Oil of New Jersey. For more on Hoover's, threats against the banks, see Herbert Stein, "Pre-Revolutionary Fiscal Policy: The Regime of Herbert Hoover," *Journal of Law and Economics* (October, 1966): 197n.

[40]Jesse H. Jones and Edward Angly, *Fifty Billion Dollars* (New York: Macmillan, 1951), p. 18. Also see H. Parker Willis and John M. Chapman, *The Banking Situation* (New York: Columbia University Press, 1934), pp. 9 ff. Furthermore, Hoover's Secretary and Undersecretary of the Treasury had decided, by the end of their terms, that the gold standard should be abolished. *New York Herald Tribune*, May 5, 1958, p. 18.

[41]Kent Cooper, *Kent Cooper and the Associated Press* (New York: Random House, 1959), p. 157.

"great experiment in constructive industrial statesmanship."[42] In February, 1931, Hoover's Emergency Committee for Employment was instrumental in pushing through Congress Senator Wagner's (D., N.Y.) Employment Stabilization Act, which established an Employment Stabilization Board to expand public works in a depression, and a fund of $150 million to put the plan into effect. In happily signing the measure, Hoover gave a large amount of credit to the veteran public-works agitator, Otto Tod Mallery.[43] In his memoirs, Hoover recalled with pride that his administration had constructed more public works than had the federal government over the previous thirty years, and that he personally had induced state and local governments to expand their public-works programs by $1.5 billion. He also launched the Boulder, Grand Coulee, and California Central Valley dams, and, after agitating for the project since 1921, Hoover signed a treaty with Canada to build a St. Lawrence Seaway, a treaty rejected by the Senate.[44] Furthermore, the Boulder project was the first example of large-scale, federal, multipurpose river basin planning.[45]

It must be noted, however, that in the last year of his term, Hoover, the veteran pioneer of public-works stabilization, began to find the accelerating movement toward ever greater public works going beyond him. As writers, economists, politicians, businessmen, and the construction industry called loudly for many billions in public works, Hoover began to draw back. He began to see public works as costly, and as bringing relief to a selected group only. He came to favor a relatively greater emphasis on federal grants-in-aid and on public works that would be self-liquidating. As a result, federal public-works spending increased only slightly during 1932. As we shall see, Hoover's growing doubts on public works were symptomatic of a more general process of being left behind by the accel-

---

[42]John Maurice Clark, "Public Works and Unemployment," *American Economic Review, Papers and Proceedings* (May, 1930): 15ff.

[43]See Irving Bernstein, *The Lean Years* (Boston: Houghton Mifflin, 1960), p. 272; Dorfman, *The Economic Mind in American Civilization*, vol. 5, p. 7n.

[44]It is instructive to note the attitude of private electrical companies toward the government-built Boulder Dam. They looked forward to purchasing cheap, subsidized governmental power, which they would then resell to their customers. The private-power companies also saw Boulder Dam as a risky, submarginal project, the costs of which they were happy to see shouldered by the taxpayers. See Harris Gaylord Warren, *Herbert Hoover and the Great Depression* (New York: Oxford University Press, 1959), p. 64.

[45]See Swain, *Federal Conservation Policy*, pp. 25ff, 161ff.

erating onrush toward collectivist thinking that developed during his final year as president.[46]

Another massive dose of government intervention was President Hoover's Home Loan Bank System, established in the Federal Home Loan Act of July, 1932. Supported enthusiastically by the building and loan associations, the act paralleled the Federal Reserve Act in relation to these associations. Twelve district banks were established under a Federal Home Loan Bank Board, with a $25 million capital supplied by the Treasury, as a compulsory, central mortgage-discount bank for the building and loan industry. Hoover had originally proposed a grandiose national mortgage-discount system that would also include savings banks and insurance companies, but the latter refused to agree to the scheme. As it was, Hoover complained that Congress had placed excessively rigorous limits on the amount of discounting that could be made by the Board; but he did his best to spur use of the new system.

One of Mr. Hoover's clearest harbingers of the New Deal was his creation in January, 1932, of the Reconstruction Finance Corporation. The RFC was clearly inspired by and modelled after the old wartime War Finance Corporation, which had extended emergency loans to business. One of the leading originators of the RFC was Eugene Meyer, Jr., Governor of the Federal Reserve Board and former Managing Director of the WFC; most of the old WFC staff were employed by the new organization.[47]

The RFC began in the fall of 1931 as the National Credit Corporation, through which leading banks were persuaded, at a secret conference with Hoover and his aides, to extend credit to shaky banks, with Federal Reserve assistance. When the banks balked at this scheme, Hoover threatened legislation to compel their cooperation; in return for their agreement to the NCC, the administration agreed that it would be strictly temporary, to be replaced soon by an RFC.

The RFC bill was passed hurriedly by Congress in January, 1932. The Treasury furnished it with half a billion dollars, and it was empowered to issue debentures up to $1.5 billion. Meyer was chosen to be chairman

---

[46]See Vladimir D. Kazakevich, "Inflation and Public Works," in H. Parker Willis and John M. Chapman, eds., *The Economics of Inflation* (New York: Columbia University Press, 1935), pp. 344–49.

[47]Leuchtenburg, "The New Deal and the Analogue of War," pp. 98–100. Also see Gerald D. Nash, "Herbert Hoover and the Origins of the Reconstruction Finance Corporation," *Mississippi Valley Historical Review* (December, 1959): 455–68.

of the new organization. In the first half of 1932, the RFC extended, in the deepest secrecy, $1 billion of loans, largely to banks and railroads.[48] The railroads received nearly $50 million simply to repay debts to the large banks, notably J.P. Morgan & Co. and Kuhn, Loeb and Co. One of the important enthusiasts for this policy was Eugene Meyer, Jr., on the grounds of "promoting recovery" and frankly, of "putting more money into the banks." Meyer's enthusiasm might well have been bolstered by the fact that his brother-in-law, George Blumenthal, was an officer of J.P. Morgan & Co., and that he himself had served as an officer of the Morgan bank.

But Hoover wasn't satisfied with the massiveness of the RFC program. He insisted that RFC be able to lend more widely to industry and to agriculture, and that it be able to make capital loans. This amendment — the Emergency Relief and Construction Act — passed Congress in July, 1932; the Act nearly doubled total RFC capital from $2 billion to $3.8 billion and greatly widened the scope of RFC lending.[49] During 1932, the RFC extended loans totaling $2.3 billion.

Herbert Hoover's enthusiasm for government aid to industry and banking was not matched in the area of Depression relief to the poor; here his instincts were much more voluntarist. Hoover steadfastly maintained his voluntary relief position until mid-1932. As early as 1930/31, he had been pressured on behalf of federal relief by Colonel Arthur Woods, the Chairman of Hoover's Emergency Committee for Employment, who had previously been a member of Rockefeller's General Education Board. But in mid-1932 a group of leading Chicago industrialists was instrumental in persuading Hoover to change his mind and establish a federal relief program. In addition to widening the powers of the RFC loans to industry, Hoover's Emergency Relief and Construction Act was the nation's first federal relief legislation. The RFC was authorized to lend $300 million to the states for poor relief.[50]

---

[48]Many large loans were made by the RFC to banks that were in the ambit of RFC directors themselves, or of others high up in the Hoover administration. Thus, shortly after General Charles Dawes resigned as President of the RFC, the bank that he headed, the Central Republic Bank and Trust Co., received a large RFC loan. See John T. Flynn, "Inside the RFC," *Harpers' Magazine* (1933): 161–69.

[49]See J. Franklin Ebersole, "One Year of the Reconstruction Finance Corporation," *Quarterly Journal of Economics* (May, 1933): 464–87.

[50]Bernstein, *The Lean Years*, p. 467.

Throughout the Depression, Herbert Hoover gave vent to his long-standing dislike of speculation and the stock market. In the fall of 1930, Hoover threatened federal regulation of the New York Stock Exchange, *hitherto* thought to be constitutionally subject only to state regulation. Hoover forced the Exchange to agree "voluntarily" to withhold loans for purposes of short selling. Hoover returned to the attack during 1932, threatening federal action against short selling. He also induced the Senate to investigate "sinister ... bear raids" on the Exchange. Hoover seemed to find it sinful and vaguely traitorous for the stock market to judge stock values on the basis of current (low) earnings. Hoover went on to propose what later came to pass as the New Deal's SEC, a regulation that Hoover openly applauded.

Hoover's Federal Farm Board was ready to move when the Depression arrived and the FFB proceeded on its proto-New Deal farm policy of attempting to raise and support farm prices.

The FFB's first big operation was in wheat. The Board advised the receptive wheat farmers to act like cartelists: in short, to hold wheat off the market and wait for higher prices. Soon it began to lend $100 million to wheat co-ops to withhold wheat stocks, and thereby raise prices; and it established a central grain corporation to centralize and coordinate the wheat cooperatives. When the loans to coops failed to stem the tide of falling wheat prices, the grain corporation began to buy wheat on its own. The FFB loans and purchases managed to sustain wheat prices for a time; but by the spring of 1930 this had only aggravated the wheat surplus by inducing farmers to expand their production, and the only result was further declines in price.

It became clear to the Hoover administration that the cartelizing and price-raising policy could not work unless wheat production was reduced. A typical Hooverian round of attempted voluntary persuasion ensued, led by the Secretary of Agriculture and the FFB; a group of economists was sent from Washington to urge the marginal Northwestern wheat farmers — the original agitators for wheat price supports — to shift from wheat into some other crop. Secretary of Agriculture Arthur M. Hyde and the FFB's Alexander Legge toured the Middle West, urging farmers to lower their wheat acreage. But, as could have been foreseen, none of this moral exhortation was effective, and wheat surpluses continued to pile up and prices to fall. By November, the government's Grain Stabilization Corporation had purchased over 65 million bushels of wheat to hold off the market, but to no avail. Then, in November, 1930, Hoover authorized the

GSC to purchase as much wheat as might be necessary to stop any further fall in wheat prices. But economic forces could not be defeated so easily, and wheat prices continued to fall. Finally, the FFB conceded defeat and dumped its accumulated wheat stocks, further intensifying the fall in wheat prices.

Similar price-support programs were tried in cotton, but with similar disastrous results. Chairman James C. Stone of the Federal Farm Board even tried to mobilize the state governors to plow under every third row of cotton, but still to no avail. Similar calamitous attempts at cartelization occurred in wool, butter, grapes, and tobacco.

It was becoming clear that the cartelizing program could not work unless there were compulsory restrictions on production; there were simply too many farmers for voluntary exhortations to have any effect. President Hoover began to move down that road, recommending at least that productive land be withdrawn from cultivation, that crops be plowed under, and that immature farm animals be slaughtered — all to reduce the very surpluses that Hoover's price supports had accumulated.[51]

Meanwhile, President Hoover pursued cartelization in other fields with more success. In May, 1931, he ordered the cessation of new leases in the federal forests for purposes of lumbering. He also withdrew over two million acres of forest land from production and into "national forests," and increased the area of national parks by 40%.[52]

Hoover put through the McNary-Watres Act of April, 1930, which deliberately used postal air-mail subsidies and regulation to bring commercial airlines under federal organization and control. Hoover's admiring biographers wrote that as a result of this law, "The routes were consolidated into a carefully planned national system of commercial airways. ...

---

[51]It was left for the conservative Senator Arthur H. Vandenberg (R., Mich.) to propose the final link in the chain that was to form the New Deal's AAA: compelling farmers to cut production. Gilbert N. Fite, "Farmer Opinion and the Agricultural Adjustment Act, 1933," *Mississippi Valley Historical Review* (March, 1962): 663.

[52]Warren, *Herbert Hoover and the Great Depression*, p. 65. Hoover also endorsed the privately financed Timber Conservation Board, formed to encourage cooperation in the lumber industry. Ellis W. Hawley, "Herbert Hoover and the Economic Planners, 1931–32" (Unpublished manuscript, 1968), p. 9.

In a prefiguration of the New Deal's CCC, Hoover's Forestry Service put through a large-scale program of work relief for the unemployed in public-works construction in the national forests. Swain, *Federal Conservation Policy*, p. 25.

The Nation was saved from a hodgepodge of airways similar to the tangle that had grown up in rail transportation."[53]

Hoover also urged upon Congress what would have been the first federal regulation of electric power companies. Hoover's original proposal was to give the Federal Power Commission the power to set interstate power rates in collaboration with state power commissions. But Congress refused to go that far, and the FPC, although expanded, continued to exercise power only over water power in rivers.

In the coal industry, Hoover sympathized with the Appalachian Coal combine, which marketed three-quarters of Appalachian bituminous coal, in an attempt to raise coal prices and allocate production quotas to the various coal mines. Hoover also called for the reduction of "destructive competition" reigning in the coal industry.[54]

Hoover was more specific in helping to cartelize the oil industry. Hoover and his Secretary of the Interior Ray Lyman Wilbur stimulated such states as Texas and Oklahoma to pass oil proration laws in the name of "conservation" to curtail crude oil production and thereby raise prices and to establish an interstate compact to collaborate in the proration program. Hoover also aided these laws by suspending all further oil leases on public lands and by pressuring oil operators near the public domain to agree to restrict oil production.

In sponsoring and encouraging proration laws particularly, Hoover was taking his stand with the large oil companies. Hoover and Wilbur's suggestion of general Sunday shutdowns of oil production was approved by the large companies, but defeated by the opposition of the smaller producers. The smaller firms particularly urged a protective tariff on imported crude and petroleum products, which Hoover finally agreed to in 1932. The tariff served to make the domestic cartel and proration laws more generally effective. In its restriction of imports, the tariff demonstrated that the drive for proration laws had little to do with simply conserving domestic oil reserves, but was rather aimed at cutting the supply of oil available to the domestic market.

[53]William Starr Myers and Walter H. Newton, *The Hoover Administration* (New York: Charles Scribners, 1936), p. 430.

[54]Myers and Newton, *The Hoover Administration*, p. 50; Waldo E. Fisher and Charles M. James, *Minimum Price Fixing in the Bituminous Coal Industry* (Princeton, NJ: Princeton University Press, 1955), pp. 21–27.

Despite these services by Hoover, the oil industry was still restive; the industry wanted more, it wanted federal legislation in outright support of restricting production and raising prices. Here, too, President Hoover was beginning to lose the leadership of the accelerating cartelization movement in American industry.[55]

In the cotton textile industry, the trade association, the Cotton Textile Institute, which had long been close to Hoover, cunningly decided to press for monopolistic curtailment of production under the guise of "humanitarianism." The device was to call for the abolition of night work for women and children; such a drive was neatly calculated to appeal both to Hoover's (and to the industry's) monopoloid convictions, as well as to his humanitarian rhetoric. CTI's campaign of 1930/31 to pressure the various mills to abolish night work for women and children was substantially aided by Hoover and his Department of Commerce, who actively "helped to whip the non-cooperators into line." Hoover publicized his firm support, and Secretary of Commerce Lamont sent personal letters to cotton textile operators, urging their adherence to the plan.[56] Intense administration pressure continued throughout 1931 and 1932. Lamont called a special conference to which he brought several leading bankers and the endorsement of Hoover to pressure the holdouts into line.

But this cartel scheme also failed, for cotton textile prices continued to fall. As a result, compliance with the curtailment of production began to crack. The cartel failed for reasons similar to the failure of the FFB: despite the intense administration pressure, the production cuts remained only voluntary. So long as there was no outright governmental compulsion on the textile firms to obey the production quotas, prices could not be raised. By 1932, the cotton textile industry, too, was becoming impatient with its old friend Hoover; the industry was rapidly beginning to agitate for governmental coercion to make cartelization work.[57]

This attitude of the cotton textile, petroleum, and agricultural industries spread rapidly throughout American industry during 1931 and 1932: an impatience with the pace of America's movement toward the corporate state. Under the impact of the Great Depression, American industry, along

---

[55]See George W. Stocking, "Stabilization of the Oil Industry: Its Economic and Legal Aspects," *American Economic Review, Papers and Proceedings* (May, 1933): 59–70.

[56]Galambos, *Competition and Cooperation*, pp. 153–57, 165–69.

[57]Ibid., pp. 176–84.

with the nation's intellectuals and labor leaders, began to clamor for the outright collectivism of a corporate state — for federal organization of trade associations into compulsory cartels for restricting production and raising prices. In short, a general clamor arose for an economy of fascism.

The most important call for the compulsory cartelization of a corporate state was sounded by Gerard Swope, the veteran corporate liberal who headed General Electric. Swope delivered his famous "Swope Plan" before the National Electrical Manufacturers Association in the fall of 1931, and it was endorsed by the United States Chamber of Commerce in December.[58] Particularly enthusiastic was Henry I. Harriman, president of the Chamber, who declared that any dissenting businessmen would be "treated like any maverick. ... They'll be roped and branded, and made to run with the herd."[59] Charles F. Abbott of the American Institute of Steel Construction hailed the Swope Plan as "a measure of public safety" to crack down on "the blustering individual who claims the right to do as he pleases."[60] The AF of L endorsed a similar program, with a slightly greater share to go to the unions in overall control; particularly enthusiastic were John L. Lewis and Sidney Hillman, later to form the New Deal-oriented CIO.[61]

Dr. Virgil Jordan, economist for the National Industrial Conference Board, summed up the state of business opinion when he concluded, approvingly, that businessmen were ready for an "economic Mussolini."[62]

In the light of Herbert Hoover's lengthy corporatist career, the business leaders naturally expected him to agree wholeheartedly with the new drive toward business collectivism.[63] Hence they were greatly surprised and chagrined to find Hoover sharply drawing back from the abyss, from pursuing the very logic toward which his entire career had been leading.

---

[58]The text of the Swope address can be found in *Monthly Labor Review* 32 (1931): 834ff. Also see David Loth, *Swope of GE* (New York: Simon and Schuster, 1958), pp. 202ff.

[59]Quoted in Arthur M. Schlesinger, Jr., *The Crisis of the Old Order, 1919–1933* (Boston: Houghton Mifflin Co., 1957), pp. 182–83.

[60]J. George Frederick, *Readings in Economic Planning* (New York: The Business Course, 1932), pp. 333–34.

[61]See Rothbard, *America's Great Depression*, pp. 245–49; Rothbard, "The Hoover Myth: Review of Albert U. Romasco, *The Poverty of Abundance*," in James Weinstein and David W. Eakins, eds., *For a New America* (New York: Random House, 1970), pp. 162–79; and Hawley, "Herbert Hoover and the Economic Planners," pp. 4ff.

[62]Schlesinger, *Crisis of the Old Order*, p. 268.

[63]Hawley, "Herbert Hoover and the Economic Planners," pp. 4–11.

It is not unusual for revolutions to devour their fathers and pioneers. As a revolutionary process accelerates, the early leaders begin to draw back from the implicit logic of their own life work and to leap off the accelerating bandwagon that they themselves had helped to launch. So it was with Herbert Hoover. All his life he had been a dedicated corporatist; but all his life he had also liked to cloak his corporate-state coercion in cloudy voluntarist generalities. All his life he had sought and employed the mailed fist of coercion inside the velvet glove of traditional voluntarist rhetoric. But now his old friends and associates — men like his longtime aide and Chamber of Commerce leader Julius Barnes, railroad magnate Daniel Willard, and industrialist Gerard Swope — were in effect urging him to throw off the voluntarist cloak and to adopt the naked economy of fascism. This Herbert Hoover could not do; and as he saw the new trend he began to fight it, without at all abandoning any of his previous positions. Herbert Hoover was being polarized completely out of the accelerating drive toward statism; by merely advancing at a far slower pace, the former "progressive" corporatist was now becoming a timid moderate in relation to the swift rush of the ideological current. The former leader and molder of opinion was becoming passé.[64]

Hoover began to fight back, and to insist that a certain proportion of individualism, a certain degree of the old "American system," must be preserved. The Swope and similar plans, he charged, would result in a complete monopolization of industry, would establish a vast governmental bureaucracy, and would regiment society. In short, as Hoover told Henry Harriman in exasperation, the Swope-Chamber of Commerce Plan was, simply, "fascism."[65] Herbert Hoover had finally seen the abyss of fascism and was having none of it.

Franklin Roosevelt was to have no such scruples. Hoover's decision had vital political consequences: for Harriman told him bluntly at the start of the 1932 campaign that Franklin Roosevelt had accepted the Swope

[64]Hoover had done his best to further corporatism in more moderate and gradual ways. In addition to the measures described above, Hoover sponsored the highly protectionist Smoot-Hawley Tariff in 1929/30, and he signed the Norris-LaGuardia Act of 1932, which sponsored labor unionism by outlawing contractual agreements not to join unions and greatly curtailing the use of injunctions in labor disputes.

[65]See Hawley "Herbert Hoover and the Economic Planners," p. 21n. Hoover also resisted corporate-collectivist pressure from within his own administration, notably from such men as Frederick Feiker, head of the Bureau of Foreign and Domestic Commerce, and his old friend Secretary of the Interior Ray Lyman Wilbur.

Plan — as he was to prove amply with the NRA and AAA. If Hoover persisted in being stubborn, Harriman warned, the business world, and especially big business, would back Roosevelt. Hoover's brusque dismissal led to big business carrying out its threat. It was Herbert Hoover's finest hour.[66] America's legion of corporate liberals, who found their Holy Grail with the advent of Franklin Roosevelt's New Deal, never forgave or forgot Herbert Hoover's hanging back from America's entry into the Promised Land. To the angry liberals, Hoover's caution looked very much like old-fashioned *laissez-faire*. Hence Herbert Hoover's pervasive entry into the public mind as a doughty champion of *laissez-faire* individualism.[67] It was an ironic ending to the career of one of the great pioneers of American state corporatism.

---

[66]Hoover, *Memoirs*, vol. 3, pp. 334–35. Also see Loth, *Swope of GE*, pp. 208–10; Eugene Lyons, *Herbert Hoover* (Garden City, N.Y.: Doubleday & Co., 1964), pp. 293–94; Myers and Newton, *The Hoover Administration*, pp. 245–56, 488–89.

[67]For a penetrating exception to this common view, see William Appleman Williams, *The Contours of American History* (Cleveland: World Publishing Co., 1961), pp. 385, 415, 425–38.

Bibliography

Abramovitz, Moses, and Vera F. Eliasberg. *The Growth of Public Employment in Great Britain.* Princeton, NJ: National Bureau of Economic Research, 1957.

Abrams, Ray H. *Preachers Present Arms.* New York: Round Table Press, 1933.

Adams, George P., Jr. *Wartime Price Control.* Washington, DC: American Council on Public Affairs, 1942.

Alchon, Guy. *The Invisible Hand of Planning: Capitalism, Social Science, and the State in the 1920's.* Princeton, NJ: Princeton University Press, 1985.

Allen, Howard W., and Jerome Clubb. "Progressive Reform and the Political System." *Pacific Northwest Quarterly* (July, 1974).

Amenta, Edwin, Elisabeth Clemens, Jefren Olsen, Sunita Parikh, and Theda Skocpol. "The Political Origins of Unemployment Insurance in Five American States." *Studies in American Political Development* 2 (1987).

Anderson, Benjamin M. *Economics and the Public Welfare: Financial and Economic History of the United States, 1914–1946.* Indianapolis, IN: Liberty Press, 1979 [1949].

——. "The Road Back to Full Employment." In P. Homan and F. Machlup, eds., *Financing American Prosperity.* New York: Twentieth Century Fund, 1945.

Anderson, Oscar E., Jr. *The Health of a Nation: Harvey W. Wiley and the Fight for Pure Food.* Chicago: University of Chicago Press, 1958.

Anderson, William L., and David Kiriazis. "Rents and Race: Legacies of Progressive Policies." *Independent Review* (Summer 2013).

Andreano, Ralph, ed. *The Economic Impact of the American Civil War*, 2nd ed. Cambridge, MA: Schenkman, 1967.

Andrews, John B. "The President's Unemployment Conference–Success or Failure?" *American Labor Legislation Review* (December, 1921).

Angly, Edward, comp. *Oh Yeah?* New York: Viking Press, 1931.

Anthony, Susan B., and Ida H. Harper. *The History of Woman Suffrage.* Rochester, NY: Susan B. Anthony, 1902.

Armentano, Dominick T. *Antitrust and Monopoly: Anatomy of a Policy Failure,* 2nd ed. Oakland, CA: Independent Institute, 1990.

Baack, Ben, and Edward John Ray. "The Political Economy of the Origin and Development of the Federal Income Tax." In *Emergence of Modern Political Economy,* ed. Robert Higgs. JAI Press Inc., 1985.

Barnes, Julius H. "Herbert Hoover's Priceless Work in Washington." *Industrial Management* (April, 1926).

Barron, Clarence W. *More They Told Barron.* New York: Harper & Bros., 1931.

Baruch, Bernard M. *American Industry in the War.* New York: Prentice-Hall, 1941.

Baster, A.S.J. "The International Acceptance Market." *American Economic Review* 27 (June, 1937).

Beaver, Daniel R. *Newton D. Baker and the American War Effort, 1917–1919.* Lincoln: University of Nebraska Press, 1966.

Beckhart, Benjamin H. "Federal Reserve Policy and the Money Market, 1923–1931." In *The New York Money Market,* eds. B.H. Beckhart, J.G. Smith, and W.A. Brown. New York: Columbia University Press, 1931.

Benham, Frederic. *British Monetary Policy.* London: P. S. King, 1932.

Beito, David T., and Linda Royster Beito. "Gold Democrats and the Decline of Classical Liberalism, 1896–1900." *Independent Review* (Spring 2000).

——. "The 'Lodger Evil' and the Transformation of Progressive Housing Reform, 1890–1930." *Independent Review* 20, no. 4 (2016).

Bensel, Richard Franklin. *The Political Economy of American Industrialization, 1877–1900.* Cambridge: Cambridge University Press, 2000.

Benson, Lee. *Merchants, Farmers, and Railroads: Railroad Regulation and New York Politics, 1850–1887.* Cambridge, MA: Harvard University Press, 1955.

Bernstein, Irving. *The Lean Years.* Boston: Houghton Mifflin, 1960.

Bethell, Tom. *George Lewis: A Jazzman from New Orleans.* Berkeley: University of California Press, 1977.

Beveridge, William. *Unemployment, a Problem of Industry.* London: Macmillan, 1930.

Birmingham, Stephen. *"Our Crowd": The Great Jewish Families of New York.* New York: Pocket Books, 1977.

Bishop, Theodore. *Theodore Roosevelt and His Time.* New York, 1920. Vol. I.

Blakey, George T. *Historians on the Homefront: American Propagandists for the Great War.* Lexington: University Press of Kentucky, 1970.

Blewett, John, S.J. "Democracy as Religion: Unity in Human Relations." In *John Dewey: His Thought and Influence,* ed. John Blewett. New York: Fordham University Press, 1960.

Blumberg, Dorothy Rose. *Florence Kelley: The Making of A Social Pioneer.* New York: Augustus M. Kelley, 1966.

Bordin, Ruth. *Woman and Temperance: the Quest for Power and Liberty, 1873–1900.* Philadelphia: Temple University Press, 1981.

Board of Governors of the Federal Reserve System. *Banking and Monetary Statistics.* Washington, DC: Federal Reserve Board, 1943.

Boudreaux, Donald J., and Thomas J. Dilorenzo. "The Protectionist Roots of Antitrust." *Review of Austrian Economics* 6 no. 2 (1993).

Boyer, Paul. *Urban Masses and Moral Order in America, 1820–1920.* Cambridge: Harvard University Press, 1978.

Bradley, Robert L., Jr. *Capitalism at Work.* Salem, MA: M&M Scrivener Press, 2009.

——. *Edison to Enron: Energy Markets and Political Strategies.* Salem, MA: M&M Scrivener Press, 2011.

——. *Oil, Gas, and Government: The U.S. Experience.* Lanham, MD & Washington, DC: Rowman and Littlefield Publishers and the Cato Institute, 1995. Vol. 1.

——. "On the Origins of the Sherman Antitrust Act." *Cato Journal* 9, no. 3 (Winter 1990).

Bradley, Robert L., Jr. and Roger Donway. "Reconsidering Gabriel Kolko: A Half-Century Perspective." *Independent Review* (Spring 2013).

Brandes, Joseph. *Herbert Hoover and Economic Diplomacy.* Pittsburgh, PA: University of Pittsburgh Press, 1962.

Brewster, Ralph Owen. "Footprints on the Road to Plenty—— A Three Billion Dollar Fund to Stabilize Business." *Commercial and Financial Chronicle.* November 28, 1928.

Broesamle, John J. *William Gibbs McAdoo: A Passion for Change, 1863–1917.* Port Washington, NY: Kennikat Press, 1973.

Brown, William Adams, Jr. *The International Gold Standard Reinterpreted, 1914–1934.* New York: National Bureau of Economic Research, 1940.

Burch, Philip H., Jr. *Elites in American History: The Civil War to the New Deal.* New York: Holmes & Meier Publishers, Inc., 1981.

Burner, David. *Herbert Hoover: A Public Life.* New York: Alfred A. Knopf, 1979.

Burnham, John C. "Medical Specialists and Movements Toward Social Control in the Progressive Era: Three Examples." In *Building the Organizational Society: Essays in Associational Activities in Modern America,* ed. J. Israel. New York: Free Press, 1972.

——. "The Progressive Era Revolution in American Attitudes Toward Sex." *Journal of American History* 59 (March, 1973).

Burnham, Walter Dean. *Critical Elections and the Mainsprings of American Politics.* New York: W.W. Norton, 1970.

——. "Rejoinder." *American Political Science Review* (September, 1974).

——. "Theory and Voting Research: Some Reflections on Converse's Change in the American Electorate." *American Political Science Review* (September, 1974).

Burran, James A. "Prohibition in New Mexico, 1917." *New Mexico Historical Quarterly* 48 (April, 1973).

Burt, William D. "Gabriel Kolko's *Railroads and Regulation* at Fifty." *Railroad History* (Spring-Summer 2016).

Camhi, Jane Jerome. "Women Against Women: American Antisuffragism 1880–1920." Unpublished doctoral dissertation in history, Tufts University, 1973.

Casey, Gerard. *Murray Rothbard: Major Conservative and Libertarian Thinkers.* New York: Continuum, 2010.

Chalk, Frank. "The Anatomy of an Investment: Firestone's 1927 Loan to Liberia." *Canadian Journal of African Studies* (March, 1967).

Chambers, John W., II. "Conscripting for Colossus: The Adoption of the Draft in the United States in World War I." Ph.D. dissertation, Columbia University, 1973.

Chandler, Alfred D., Jr., ed. *The Railroads: The Nation's First Big Business.* New York: Harcourt, Brace & World, 1965.

———. "The Beginnings of Big Business in American Industry." *Business History Review* (Spring 1959).

———. *The Visible Hand: The Managerial Revolution in American Business.* Cambridge, MA: The Belknap Press of Harvard University Press, 1977.

Chandler, Lester V. *Benjamin Strong, Central Banker.* Washington, DC: Brookings Institution, 1958.

Chernow, Ron. *The House of Morgan: An American Banking Dynasty and the Rise of Modern Finance.* New York: Touchstone, 1990.

Chessman, G. Wallace. *Governor Theodore Roosevelt: The Albany Apprenticeship, 1898–1900.* Cambridge, MA: Harvard University Press, 1965.

Clark, John Maurice. "Public Works and Unemployment." *American Economic Review, Papers and Proceedings* (May, 1930).

Clark, Lawrence E. *Central Banking Under the Federal Reserve System.* New York: Macmillan, 1935.

Clarke, Ida Clyde. *American Women and the World War.* New York: D. Appleton and Co., 1918.

Clarke, Stephen V.O. *Central Bank Cooperation: 1924–31.* New York: Federal Reserve Bank of New York, 1967.

Clarkson, Grosvenor B. *Industrial America in the World War.* Boston: Houghton Mifflin Co., 1923.

Clay, Sir Henry. *Lord Norman.* London: Macmillan, 1957.

Clifford, John Garry. *The Citizen Soldiers: The Plattsburg Training Camp Movement.* Lexington: University Press of Kentucky, 1972.

Coase, Ronald H. "The Federal Communications Commission." *Journal of Law and Economics* (October, 1959).

Coit, Margaret L. *Mr. Baruch.* Boston: Houghton Mifflin Co., 1957.

Coletta, Paolo E. *William Jennings Bryan, I: Political Evangelist, 1860–1908.* Lincoln: University of Nebraska Press, 1960.

Collier, Peter, and David Horowitz. *The Rockefellers: An American Dynasty*. New York: New American Library, 1976.

Comegna, Anthony. "'The Dupes of Hope Forever:' The Loco-Foco or Equal Rights Movement, 1820s–1870s." Ph.D dissertation in history, University of Pittsburgh, 2016.

Commons, John R. *Myself*. Madison: University of Wisconsin Press, 1964 [1934].

Conner, Valerie I. "'The Mothers of the Race' in World War I: The National War Labor Board and Women in Industry." *Labor History* 21 (Winter 1979–80).

Cooper, Kent. *Kent Cooper and the Associated Press*. New York: Random House, 1959.

Coppin, Clayton A., and Jack High. *The Politics of Purity: Harvey Washington Wiley and the Origins of Federal Food Policy*. Ann Arbor: University of Michigan Press, 1999.

Cramer, C.H. *Newton D. Baker: A Biography*. Cleveland, OH: World Publishing, 1961.

Croly, Herbert D. *Marcus Alonzo Hanna*. New York: MacMillan Company, 1912.

Cross, Whitney R. *The Burned-Over District: The Social and Intellectual History of Enthusiastic Religion in Western New York, 1800–1850*. New York: Harper Torchbooks, 1950.

Crunden, Robert M. *Ministers of Reform: The Progressives Achievement in American Civilization, 1889–1920*. New York: Basic Books, 1982.

Cubberley, Ellwood P. *Changing Conceptions of Education in America*. Boston: Houghton Mifflin, 1909.

Cuff, Robert D. "A 'Dollar-a-Year Man' in Government: George N. Peek and the War Industries Board." *Business History Review* (Winter 1967).

———. "Bernard Baruch: Symbol and Myth in Industrial Mobilization." *Business History Review* (Summer 1969).

———. "Business, Government, and the War Industries Board." Doctoral dissertation in history, Princeton University, 1966.

Cuff, Robert D., and Melvin I. Urofsky. "The Steel Industry and Price-Fixing During World War I." *Business History Review* (Autumn 1970).

Cullen, M.I. *The Statistical Movement in Early Victorian Britain: The Foundations of Empirical Social Research*. New York: Barnes & Noble, 1975.

Davis, Allen F. *American Heroine: The Life and Legend of Jane Addams.* New York: Oxford University Press, 1973.

———. *Spearhead for Reform: the Social Settlements and the Progressive Movement, 1890–1914.* New York: Oxford University Press, 1967.

Davis, Joseph S. *The World Between the Wars, 1919–39, An Economist's View.* Baltimore, MD: Johns Hopkins University Press, 1975.

DeCanio, Samuel. *Democracy and the Origins of the American Regulatory State.* New Haven, CT: Yale University Press, 2015.

Dewey, John. *John Dewey: The Early Works, 1882–1889.* In John Dewey: The Early Works, 1882–1889, eds. Jo Ann Boydstan and George E. Axetell. Carbondale: Southern Illinois University Press, 1969–71.

Dewing, Arthur S. "A Statistical Test of the Success of Consolidations." *Quarterly Journal of Economics* (1921).

———. *Corporate Promotions and Reorganizations.* Cambridge, MA: Harvard University Press, 1914.

———. *The Financial Policy of Corporations.* New York: Ronald Press, 1953. 5th ed. 2 Vols.

Diggins, John P. "Flirtation with Fascism: American Pragmatic Liberals and Mussolini's Italy." *American Historical Review* (January, 1966).

———. "Mussolini's Italy: The View from America." Ph.D. dissertation, University of Southern California, 1964.

DiLorenzo, Thomas J. "The Myth of Natural Monopoly." *Review of Austrian Economics* 9, no. 2 (1996).

———. "The Origins of Antitrust: An Interest-Group Perspective." *International Review of Law and Economics* 5 (1985).

Dodds, Gordon B. "The Stream-Flow Controversy: A Conservation Turning Point." *Journal of American History* (June, 1969).

Doherty, Brian. *Radicals for Capitalism: A Freewheeling History of the Modern American Libertarian Movement.* New York: PublicAffairs, 2007.

Domhoff, William G. *The Power Elite and the State: How Policy is Made in America.* New York: Aldine de Gruyter, 1990.

Dorfman, Joseph. *The Economic Mind in American Civilization, III, 1865–1918.* New York: Viking Press, 1949.

——. *The Economic Mind in American Civilization, 1918–1933.* New York: Viking Press, 1959. Vol. 4.

——. *The Economic Mind in American Civilization, 1918–1933.* New York: Viking Press, 1959. Vol. 5.

——. "The Role of the German Historical School in American Economic Thought." *American Economic Review, Papers and Proceedings* 45 (May, 1955).

Eakins, David W. "The Origins of Corporate Liberal Policy Research, 1916–1922: The Political-Economic Expert and the Decline of Public Debate." In *Building the Organizational Society: Essays in Associational Activities in Modern America*, ed. J. Israel. New York: Free Press, 1972.

——. "The Development of Corporate Liberal Policy Research in the United States, 1885–1965." Ph.D. dissertation in history, University of Wisconsin, 1966.

Ebersole, J. Franklin. "One Year of the Reconstruction Finance Corporation." *Quarterly Journal of Economics* (May, 1933).

Einzig, Paul. *Montagu Norman.* London: Kegan Paul, 1932.

Ekirch, Arthur A., Jr. *The Decline of American Liberalism.* Oakland, CA: Independent Institute, 2009 [1955].

——. "The Reform Mentality, War, Peace, and the National State: From the Progressives to Vietnam." *Journal of Libertarian Studies* (Spring 1979).

Everhart, Robert B. ed. *The Public School Monopoly: A Critical Analysis of Education and the State in American Society.* San Francisco: Pacific Institute for Public Policy Research, 1982.

Fabricant, Solomon. *The Trend of Government Activity in the United States since 1900.* New York: National Bureau of Economic Research, 1952.

Fairchild, Fred R. "Government Saves Us from Depression." *Yale Review* (Summer 1932).

Ferguson, Thomas. "Industrial Conflict and the Coming of the New Deal: The Triumph of Multinational Liberalism in America." In *The Rise and Fall of the New Deal Order, 1930–1980*, eds. S. Fraser and G. Gerstle. Princeton, NJ: Princeton University Press, 1989.

Fine, Sidney. *Laissez Faire and the General-Welfare State: A Study of Conflict in American Thought, 1865–1901.* Ann Arbor: University of Michigan Press, 1956.

Finnegan, John Patrick. *Against the Specter of a Dragon: the Campaign for American Military Preparedness*, 1914–1917. Westport, CT: Greenwood Press, 1974.

Fishback, Price. "The Progressive Era." In *Government and the American Economy*. Chicago: University of Chicago Press, 2007.

Fishback, Price, and Shawn Kantor. *A Prelude to the Welfare State: The Origins of Workers' Compensation*. Chicago: University of Chicago Press, 2000.

Fischer, David Hackett. *Albion's Seed: Four British Folkways in America*. New York: Oxford University Press, 1989.

Fisher, Irving. *Stabilised Money*. London: Allen & Unwin, 1935.

Fisher, Irving Norton. *My Father Irving Fisher*. New York: Comet Press, 1956.

Fisher, Muriel Olivi. "The Evolution of the Conservation Cartel and its Effect on Forest Resource Policy." Unpublished MA essay in history, University of San Diego, 1979.

Fisher, Waldo E., and Charles M. James. *Minimum Price Fixing in the Bituminous Coal Industry*. Princeton, NJ: Princeton University Press, 1955.

Fishlow, Albert. "Productivity and Technological Change in the Railroad Sector, 1840–1910." In National Bureau of Economic Research, *Output, Employment and Productivity in the United States After 1800*. New York, 1966.

Fite, Gilbert N. "Farmer Opinion and the Agricultural Adjustment Act, 1933." *Mississippi Valley Historical Review* (March, 1962).

Flexner, Eleanor. *Century of Struggle: The Woman's Rights Movement in the United States*. New York: Atheneum, 1970.

Flora, Peter, and Jens Alber. "Modernization, Democratization, and the Development of Welfare States in Western Europe." In *The Development of Welfare States in Europe and America*, eds. Peter Flora and Arnold Heidenheimer. New Brunswick, NJ: Transaction Press, 1981.

Folsom, Burton, Jr. *The Myth of the Robber Barons: A New Look at the Rise of Big Business in America*. Herndon, VA: Young America's Foundation, 2007 [1987].

Forcey, Charles. *The Crossroads of Liberalism: Croly, Weyl, Lippmann and the Progressive Era, 1900–1925*. New York: Oxford University Press, 1961.

Fosdick, Raymond B. *Chronicle of a Generation: An Autobiography*. New York: Harper & Bros., 1958.

Foster, William T., and Waddill Catchings. "Mr. Hoover's Plan: What It Is and What It Is Not —— the New Attack on Poverty." *Review of Reviews* (April, 1929).

——. *The Road to Plenty.* Boston: Houghton Mifflin & Co., 1928.

Frederick, J. George. *Readings in Economic Planning.* New York: The Business Course, 1932.

Friedman, Milton, and Anna Jacob Schwartz. *A Monetary History of the United States, 1867–1960.* Princeton: National Bureau of Economic Research, 1963.

Furner, Mary O. *Advocacy and Objectivity: A Crisis in the Professionalization of American Social Science, 1865–1905.* Lexington: University Press of Kentucky, 1975.

Furniss, Edgar S. *The Position of the Laborer in a System of Nationalism.* New York: Kelley & Millman, 1957.

Fusfeld, Daniel. *The Economic Thought of Franklin D. Roosevelt and the Origins of the New Deal.* New York: Columbia University Press, 1956.

Flynn, John T. *God's Gold: The Story of Rockefeller and His Times.* New York: Harcourt, Brace and Company, 1932.

——. "Inside the RFC." *Harpers' Magazine* (1933).

Gable, John Allen. *The Bull Moose Years: Theodore Roosevelt and the Progressive Party.* Port Washington, N.Y.: Kennikat Press, 1978.

Galambos, Louis. *Competition and Cooperation.* Baltimore: Johns Hopkins Press, 1966.

Garraty, John A. *Right-Hand Man: The Life of George W. Perkins.* New York: Harper & Bros., 1960.

Garrett, Paul Willard. *Government Control Over Prices.* Washington, DC: Government Printing Office, 1920.

Gates, Paul W. "The Homestead Law in an Incongruous Land System." *American Historical Review* (July, 1936).

Gelfand, Lawrence E. *The Inquiry: American Preparations for Peace, 1917–1919.* New Haven, CT: Yale University Press, 1963.

Gienapp, William E. "Nativism and the Creation of a Republican Majority in the North before the Civil War." *Journal of American History* 72 (December, 1985).

Gilbert, James. *Designing the Industrial State: The Intellectual Pursuit of Collectivism in America, 1880–1940.* Chicago: Quadrangle Books, 1972.

Gilchrist, D.T. "Albert Fink and the Pooling System." *Business History Review* (Spring 1960).

Goldin, Claudia. "Labor Markets in the Twentieth Century." In *The Cambridge Economic History of the United States,* eds. Stanley Engerman and Robert Gallman. Cambridge: Cambridge University Press, 2000. Vol. 3.

Gompers, Samuel. "The Road to Industrial Democracy." *American Federationist* (June, 1921).

Gordon, David. *The Essential Rothbard.* Auburn, AL: Mises Institute, 2007.

Gould, Lewis L. *Progressives and Prohibitionists: Texas Democrats in the Wilson Era.* Austin: University of Texas Press, 1973.

Graham, Otis L., Jr. ed. *From Roosevelt to Roosevelt: American Politics and Diplomacy, 1901–1941.* New York, 1971.

Granitz, Elizabeth, and Benjamin Klein. "Monopolization by 'Raising Rivals' Costs': The Standard Oil Case." *Journal of Law and Economics* (April, 1996).

Grattan, C. Hartley. "The Historians Cut Loose." *American Mercury,* August 1927, reprinted in Harry Elmer Barnes, *In Quest of Truth and Justice.* Colorado Springs: Ralph Myles Publisher, 1972. 2nd ed.

——. *Why We Fought.* New York Vanguard Press, 1929.

Griffin, G. Edward. *The Creature from Jekyll Island: A Second Look at the Federal Reserve.* Westlake Village, CA: American Media, 1994.

Grimes, Alan P. *The Puritan Ethic and Woman Suffrage.* New York: Oxford University Press, 1967.

Grodinsky, Julius. *Jay Gould: His Business Career, 1867–1892.* Philadelphia: University of Pennsylvania Press, 1957.

——. *The Iowa Pool: A Study in Railroad Competition, 1870–1884.* Chicago: University of Chicago Press, 1950.

——. *Transcontinental Railway Strategy, 1869–1893: A Study of Businessmen.* Philadelphia: University of Pennsylvania Press, 1962.

Groseclose, Elgin. *America's Money Machine: The Story of the Federal Reserve.* Westport, CT: Arlington House, 1980.

Grossman, David M. "American Foundations and the Support of Economic Research, 1913–29." *Minerva* 22 (Spring–Summer 1982).

Gruber, Carol S. *Mars and Minerva: World War I and the Uses of the Higher Learning in America.* Baton Rouge: Louisiana State University Press, 1975.

Haber, Samuel. *Efficiency and Uplift: Scientific Management in the Progressive Era, 1890–1920.* Chicago: University of Chicago Press, 1964.

Hamowy, Ronald. "Medicine and the Crimination of Sin: 'Self-Abuse' in 19th Century America." *Journal of Libertarian Studies* I (Summer 1972).

Hansbrough, H.C. *The Wreck: An Historical and Critical Study of the Administrations of Theodore Roosevelt and William Howard Taft,* 1913.

Harbaugh, William Henry. *Power and Responsibility: The Life and Times of Theodore Roosevelt.* New York: Farrar, Straus and Cudahy, 1961.

Harbeson, Robert. "Railroads and Regulation, 1877–1916, Conspiracy or Public Interest?" *Journal of Economic History* (June, 1967).

Hardy, Charles O. *Credit Policies of the Federal Reserve System.* Washington, DC: Brookings Institution, 1932.

Harris, Seymour E. *Twenty Years of Federal Reserve Policy.* Cambridge, MA: Harvard University Press, 1933.

Hawley, Ellis W. "Herbert Hoover and the Economic Planners, 1931–32." Unpublished manuscript, 1968.

——. "Herbert Hoover and Economic Stabilization, 1921–22." In *Herbert Hoover as Secretary of Commerce: Studies in New Era Thought and Practice,* ed. E. Hawley. Iowa City: University of Iowa Press, 1981.

——. "Secretary Hoover and the Bituminous Coal Problem, 1921–1928." *Business History Review* (Autumn 1968).

Hayek, F.A. "The Intellectuals and Socialism." In *Studies in Philosophy, Politics and Economics.* Chicago: University of Chicago Press, 1967.

Hayes, E.P. *Activities of the President's Emergency Committee for Employment, October 17, 1930 – August 19, 1931.* Printed by the author, 1936.

Hays, Samuel P. *Conservation and the Gospel of Efficiency: The Progressive Conservation Movement, 1890–1920.* Cambridge, MA: Harvard University Press, 1959.

——. "The Politics of Reform in Municipal Government in the Progressive Era." *Pacific Northwest Quarterly* 55, no. 4 (1964).

Hazlett, Thomas W. "The Legislative History of the Sherman Act Re-examined." *Economic Inquiry* 30 (April, 1992).

Heaton, Herbert. *Edwin F. Gay, A Scholar in Action.* Cambridge, MA: Harvard University Press, 1952.

Hidy, Ralph W., and Muriel E. Hidy. *Pioneering in Big Business, 1882–1911.* New York: Harper & Bros., 1955.

Higgs, Robert. *Crisis and Leviathan: Critical Episodes in the Growth of American Government.* New York: Oxford University Press, 1987.

——. *Murray N. Rothbard: In Memoriam,* ed. Llewellyn H. Rockwell, Jr. Auburn, AL: Mises Institute, 1995.

——. "Regulatory Harmonization: A Sweet-Sounding, Dangerous Development." In *Against Leviathan: Government Power and a Free Society.* Oakland, CA: The Independent Institute 2004 [2000].

High, Jack, ed. "Introduction: A Tale of Two Disciplines." In *Regulation: Economic Theory and History.* Ann Arbor: University of Michigan Press, 1991.

Higham, John. *Strangers in the Land: Patterns of American Nativism, 1860–1925.* New Brunswick, NJ: Rutgers University Press, 1955.

Hildebrand, George H. "International Flow of Economic Ideas-Discussion." *American Economic Review, Papers and Proceedings* 45 (May, 1955).

Hilton, George W. "Review of Albro Martin, *Enterprise Denied.*" *Bell Journal of Economics and Management Science* (Autumn, 1972).

——. "The Consistency of the Interstate Commerce Act." *Journal of Law and Economics* (October, 1966).

Himmelberg, Robert F. "Business, Antitrust Policy, and the Industrial Board of the Department of Commerce, 1919." *Business History Review* (Spring 1968).

——. "The War Industries Board and the Antitrust Question in November 1918." *Journal of American History* (June, 1965).

Hirschfeld, Charles. "Nationalist Progressivism and World War I." *Mid-America* 45 (July, 1963).

Hofstadter, Richard. *The American Political Tradition and the Men Who Made It.* New York: Vintage Books, 1961.

Hogan, Michael J. *Informal Entente: The Private Structure of Cooperation in Anglo-American Economic Diplomacy, 1918–1928.* Columbia: University of Missouri Press, 1977.

Hoover, Hoover. "A Plea for Cooperation." *The American Federationist* (January, 1921).

———. *American Individualism.* New York: Doubleday, 1922.

———. *Memoirs.* New York: Macmillan, 1952.

Howenstine, E. Jay, Jr. "Public Works Policy in the Twenties." *Social Research* (December, 1946).

Hummel, Jeffrey. *Emancipating Slaves, Enslaving Free Men: A History of the American Civil War.* Chicago: Open Court, 1996.

Hutchison, T.W. *A Review of Economic Doctrines, 1870–1929.* Oxford: Clarendon Press, 1953.

Israel, Jerry. *Progressivism and the Open Door: America and China, 1905–1921.* Pittsburgh: University of Pittsburgh Press, 1971.

Jenkins, J. Craig, and Barbara G. Brents. "Social Protest, Hegemonic Competition, and Social Reform: A Political Struggle Interpretation of the American Welfare State." *American Sociological Review* 54 (December, 1989).

———. "Capitalists and Social Security: What Did They Really Want?" *American Sociological Review* 56 (February, 1991).

Jenks, Jeremiah W. *The Trust Problem.* New York: McClure, Phillips & Co., 1903. 3rd ed.

Jenks, Jeremiah W., and Walter E. Clark. *The Trust Problem.* Garden City, NY: Doubleday, Doran and Co., 1929. 5th ed.

Jensen, Richard J. *The Winning of the Midwest: Social and Political Conflict, 1888–1896.* Chicago: University of Chicago Press, 1971.

Johnson, Arthur M. "Theodore Roosevelt and the Bureau of Corporations." *Mississippi Valley Historical Review* 45 (March, 1959).

Jones, Jesse H., and Edward Angly. *Fifty Billion Dollars.* New York: Macmillan, 1951.

Josephson, Matthew. *The Politicos, 1865–1896.* New York: Harcourt, Brace & World, 1964 [1938].

———. *The President Makers: The Culture of Politics and Leadership in an Age of Enlightenment, 1896–1919.* New York: Harcourt, Brace and Company, 1940.

———. *The Robber Barons: The Great American Capitalists, 1861–1901.* New York: Harcourt, Brace & World, 1962 [1934].

Kazakevich, Vladimir D. "Inflation and Public Works." In *The Economics of Inflation,* eds. H. Parker Willis and John M. Chapman. New York: Columbia University Press, 1935.

Kennan, George. *E.H. Harriman.* Boston: Houghton Mifflin, 1922. Vol. 2.

Kenneally, James J. "Catholicism and Woman Suffrage in Massachusetts." *Catholic Historical Review* (April, 1967).

Kerr, K. Austin. *American Railroad Politics, 1914–1920: Rates, Wages, and Efficiency.* Pittsburgh, PA: University of Pittsburgh Press, 1968.

Kleppner, Paul. "From Ethnoreligious Conflict to 'Social Harmony': Coalitional and Party Transformations in the 1890s." In *Emerging Coalitions in American Politics,* ed. S.M. Lipset. San Francisco: Institute for Contemporary Studies, 1978.

———. "Religion, Politics, and the American Polity: A Dynamic View of Relationships." *Journal of Libertarian Studies* (Summer/Fall 1982).

———. *The Cross of Culture: A Social Analysis of Midwestern Politics, 1850–1900.* New York: The Free Press, 1970.

———. "The Demise of Ethnoreligious Politics, 1900–1920." In "The Demise of Ethnocultural Politics: Parties and Voters, 1896–1920." Unpublished paper delivered at the 1980 annual meetings of the Organization of American Historians, San Francisco, April, 1980. Vol. 3.

———. *The Third Electoral System, 1852–1892: Parties, Voters, and Political Cultures.* Chapel Hill: University of North Carolina Press, 1979.

Kirkland, Edward C. *Industry Comes of Age: Business, Labor, and Public Policy, 1860–1897.* New York: Holt, Rinehart, and Winston, 1961.

Koistinen, Paul A.C. "The 'Industrial-Military Complex' in Historical Perspective: World War I." *Business History Review* (Winter 1967).

Kolko, Gabriel. *Railroads and Regulation: 1877–1916.* Princeton, NJ: Princeton University Press, 1965.

———. *The Triumph of Conservatism.* Glencoe, IL: The Free Press, 1963.

Kousser, J. Morgan. *The Shaping of Southern Politics: Suffrage Restrictions and the Establishment of the One-Party South, 1880–1910.* New Haven, CT: Yale University Press, 1974.

Kraditor, Aileen S. *The Ideas of the Woman Suffrage Movement, 1890–1920.* New York: Columbia University Press, 1965.

Krooss, Herman E., and Paul Samuelson, eds. *Documentary History of Banking and Currency in the United States.* New York: Chelsea House, 1969.

Kyvig, David E. *Repealing National Prohibition.* Chicago: University of Chicago Press, 1979.

La Follette, Belle Case, and Fola La Follette. *Robert M. La-Follette.* New York: Macmillan, 1953. Vol. 2.

Lamont, Robert P. "The White House Conferences." *Journal of Business* (July, 1930).

Lamoreaux, Naomi. *The Great Merger Movement in American Business, 1895–1904.* New York: Cambridge University Press, 1985.

Lasch, Christopher. *The New Radicalism in America, 1889–1963: The Intellectual as a Social Type.* New York: Random House, 1965.

Lee, Susan Previant, and Peter Passell. *A New Economic View of American History.* New York: W.W. Norton & Co, 1979.

Leonard, Thomas C. *Illiberal Reformers: Race, Eugenics & American Economics in the Progressive Era.* Princeton, NJ: Princeton University Press, 2016.

Letwin, William. *Law and Economic Policy in America: The Evolution of the Sherman Antitrust Act.* New York: Random House, 1965.

———. "The Origins of Antitrust Policy." *Journal of Political Economy* (April, 1956).

Leuchtenburg, William E. "The New Deal and the Analogue of War." In *Change and Continuity in Twentieth-Century America,* ed. John Braeman et al. New York: Harper & Row, 1967.

Levy, David W. *Herbert Croly of the New Republic.* Princeton, NJ: Princeton University Press, 1985.

Libecap, Gary D. "The Rise of the Chicago Packers and the Origins of Meat Inspection and Antitrust." *Economic Inquiry* 30 (April, 1992).

Liggio, Leonard P. "A Classical Liberal Life." In *I Chose Liberty: Autobiographies of Contemporary Libertarians*, ed. Walter Block. Auburn, AL: Mises Institute, 2010.

——. "Murray Rothbard and Jacksonian Banking." In *The Contributions of Murray Rothbard to Monetary Economics*. Winchester, VA: Durell Institute, 1996.

Lippmann, Walter. "The Permanent New Deal." In *The Shaping of Twentieth-Century America*, eds. R.M. Abrams and L.W. Levine. Boston: Little, Brown, 1965.

Loth, David. *Swope of GE*. New York: Simon and Schuster, 1958.

Lundberg, Ferdinand. *America's 60 Families*. New York: Vanguard Press, 1938.

Lyons, Eugene. *Herbert Hoover*. Garden City, NY: Doubleday and Co., 1964.

——. *Our Unknown Ex-President*. New York: Doubleday and Co., 1948.

MacAvoy, Paul W. *The Economic Effects of Regulation: The Trunk-Line Railroad Cartels and the Interstate Commerce Commission Before 1900*. Cambridge, MA: The MIT Press, 1965.

Markowitz, Gerald Edward. "Progressive Imperialism: Consensus and Conflict in the Progressive Movement on Foreign Policy, 1898–1917." Ph.D. dissertation, University of Wisconsin, 1971.

Marina, William. "From Opponent of Empire to Career Opportunist: William Howard Taft as Conservative Bureaucrat in the Evolution of the American Imperial System." In *Reassessing the Presidency: The Rise of the Executive State and the Decline of Freedom*, John Denson, ed. Auburn, AL: Mises Institute, 1999.

Martin, Albro. *Enterprise Denied: The Origins of the Decline of the American Railroads, 1897–1917*. New York: Columbia University Press, 1971.

Martin, George Whitney. *Madame Secretary: Frances Perkins*. Boston: Houghton Mifflin, 1976.

May, A. Wilfred. "Inflation in Securities." In *The Banking Situation*, eds. H. Parker Willis and John M. Chapman. New York: Columbia University Press, 1934.

McCraw, Thomas K. "Regulation in America: A Review Article." *Business History Review* (Summer 1975).

McDonald, Forrest. *Insull*. Chicago: University of Chicago Press, 1962.

McGee, John S. "Predatory Price Cutting: The Standard Oil (N.J.) Case." *Journal of Law and Economics* (October, 1958).

McMullen, Joseph H. "The President's Unemployment Conference of 1921 and Its Results." Master's thesis, Columbia University, 1922.

McSeveney, Samuel T. *The Politics of Depression: Political Behavior in the Northeast, 1893–1896*. Oxford: Oxford University Press, 1972.

Mencken, H.L. "An American Bonaparte." *A Mencken Chrestomathy*. New York: Knopf, 1949.

——. "Professor Veblen." In *A Mencken Chrestomathy*. New York: Knopf, 1949.

Merk, Lois Bannister. "Boston's Historic Public School Crisis." *New England Quarterly* 31 (June, 1958).

Mitchell, Lucy Sprague. *Two Lives*. New York: Simon and Schuster, 1953.

Mises, Ludwig von. *Human Action*. Auburn, AL: Mises Institute, 2008 [1949].

——. *Theory and History: An Interpretation of Social and Economic Evolution*. New Haven, CT: Yale University Press, 1957.

Mock, James R., and Cedric Larson. *Words that Won the War*. Princeton, NJ: Princeton University Press, 1939.

Mooney, Chase C., and Martha E. Layman. "Some Phases of the Compulsory Military Training Movement, 1914–1920." *Mississippi Historical Review* 38 (March, 1952).

Moorhead, James H. "The Erosion of Postmillennialism in American Religious Thought, 1865–1925." *Church History* 53 (March, 1984).

Morgenstern, Oskar. "Developments in the Federal Reserve System." *Harvard Business Review* 9 (October, 1930).

Morris, Charles. *The Tycoons*. New York: Owl Books, 2005.

Murphy, Paul. *World War I and the Origin of Civil Liberties in the United States*. New York: W.W. Norton, 1979.

Myers, William Starr, ed. *The State Papers and the Public Writings of Herbert Hoover*. Garden City, N.Y.: Doubleday, Doran & Co., 1934.

Myers, William Starr, and Walter H. Newton. *The Hoover Administration*. New York: Charles Scribner's, 1936.

Nash, Gerald D. "Herbert Hoover and the Origins of the Reconstruction Finance Corporation." *Mississippi Valley Historical Review* (December, 1959).

——. *United States Oil Policy, 1890–1964.* Pittsburgh, PA: University of Pittsburgh Press, 1968.

National Industrial Conference Board. *Salary and Wage Policy in the Depression.* New York: Conference Board, 1933.

Newman, Patrick. "Origins of the National Banking System: The Chase-Cooke Connection and the New York City Banks." *Independent Review* (Winter 2018).

——. "The Depression of 1873–1879: An Austrian Perspective." *Quarterly Journal of Austrian Economics* (Winter 2014).

Nevins, Allan. *Grover Cleveland: A Study in Courage.* New York: Dodd, Mead, 1932.

——. *Study in Power: John D. Rockefeller, Industrialist and Philanthropist.* New York: Charles Scribner's Sons, 1953. 2 Vols.

Noble, David F. *America By Design: Science, Technology and the Rise of Corporate Capitalism.* New York: Oxford University Press, 1977.

Noble, David W. "The *New Republic* and the Idea of Progress, 1914–1920." *Mississippi Valley Historical Review* 38 (December, 1951).

North, Gary. "Millennialism and the Progressive Movement." *Journal of Libertarian Studies* 12 (Spring 1996).

O'Connor, Harvey. *World Crisis in Oil.* New York: Monthly Review Press, 1962.

Palyi, Melchior. *The Twilight of Gold, 1914–1936: Myth and Realities.* Chicago: Henry Regnery, 1972.

Parrini, Carl P. *Heir to Empire: United States Economic Diplomacy, 1916–1923.* Pittsburgh, PA: University of Pittsburgh Press, 1969.

Paul, Ron, and Lewis Lehrman, *The Case for Gold: A Minority Report of the U.S. Gold Commission.* Washington, DC: Cato Institute, 1982.

Payne, Elizabeth Ann. *Reform, Labor, and Feminism: Margaret Dreier Robins and the Women's Trade Union League.* Urbana: University of Illinois Press, 1988.

Pearlman, Michael. *To Make Democracy Safe for America: Patricians and Preparedness in the Progressive Era.* Urbana: University of Illinois Press, 1984.

Peffer, E. Louise. *The Closing of the Public Domain: Disposal and Reservation Policies, 1900–50.* Stanford, CA: Stanford University Press, 1951.

Penick, James, Jr. *Progressive Politics and Conservation: The Ballinger-Pinchot Affair.* Chicago: University of Chicago Press, 1968.

Perlman, Selig. *A History of Trade Unionism in the United States.* New York: Macmillan, 1922.

——. *A Theory of the Labor Movement.* New York: Augustus M. Kelley, 1949.

Peterson H.C., and Gilbert C. Fite. *Opponents of War: 1917–1918.* Madison: University of Wisconsin Press, 1957.

Petro, Sylvester. "Injunctions and Labor Disputes, 1880–1932, Part I." *Wake Forest Law Review* 14 (June, 1978).

Phillips, C.A., T.F. McManus, and R.W. Nelson. *Banking and the Business Cycle: A Study of the Great Depression in the United States.* New York: Macmillan, 1937.

Pickens, Donald K. *Eugenics and the Progressives.* Nashville, TN: Vanderbilt University Press, 1968.

Porter, Robert H. "A study of cartel stability: the Joint Executive Committee, 1880–1886." *Bell Journal of Economics* (Autumn, 1983).

Potter, David M. "The Historical Development of Eastern-Southern Freight Relationships." *Law and Contemporary Problems* (Summer 1947).

Powell, Jim. *Bully Boy: The Truth about Theodore Roosevelt's Legacy.* New York: Crown Forum, 2006.

Previts, Gary John, and Barbara Dubis Merino. *A History of Accounting in America.* New York: Ronald Press, 1979.

Pringle, Henry F. *Theodore Roosevelt, A Biography.* New York: Harcourt, Brace and Co., 1931.

Purcell, Edward A., Jr. "Ideas and Interests: Businessmen and the Interstate Commerce Act." *Journal of American History* (December, 1967).

Quadagno, Jill. *The Transformation of Old Age Security: Class and Politics in the American Welfare State.* Chicago: University of Chicago Press, 1988.

——. "Welfare Capitalism and the Social Security Act of 1935." *American Sociological Review* 49 (October, 1984).

Quandt, Jean B. "Religion and Social Thought: The Secularizing of Postmillenialism." *American Quarterly* 25 (October, 1973).

Rader, Benjamin G. *The Academic Mind and Reform: the Influence of Richard T. Ely on American Life.* Lexington: University of Kentucky Press, 1966.

Radosh, Ronald. *American Labor and United States Foreign Policy.* New York: Random House, 1969.

——. "The Corporate Ideology of American Labor Leaders from Gompers to Hillman." *Studies on the Left* (November–December, 1966).

——. "The Development of the Corporate Ideology of American Labor Leaders, 1914–1933." Ph.D. dissertation in history, University of Wisconsin, 1967.

Raimondo, Justin. *An Enemy of the State: The Life of Murray N. Rothbard.* Amherst, NY: Prometheus Books, 2000.

Reed, Harold L. *Federal Reserve Policy, 1921–1930.* New York: McGraw-Hill, 1930.

Richberg, Donald R. *Labor Union Monopoly.* Chicago: Henry Regnery, 1957.

Richman, Sheldon. "Commentator on Our Times: A Quest for the Historical Rothbard." In *Man, Economy, & Liberty: Essays in Honor of Murray N. Rothbard*, eds. Walter Block and Llewellyn H. Rockwell, Jr. Auburn, AL: Mises Institute, 1988.

Riesman, David. *Thorstein Veblen: A Critical Interpretation.* New York: Charles Scribner's Sons, 1960.

Rist, Charles. "Notice biographique." *Revue d'economie politique* 65 (November-December, 1955).

Ritter, Gretchen. *Goldbugs and Greenbacks: The Antimonopoly Tradition and the Politics of Finance in America, 1865–1896.* Cambridge: Cambridge University Press, 1997.

Robbins, Lionel. *The Great Depression.* New York: Macmillan, 1934.

Rose, Al. *Storyville, New Orleans.* Montgomery: University of Alabama Press, 1974.

Rothbard, Murray. "A Conversation with Murray N. Rothbard." In *Austrian Economics Newsletter* 11, no. 2 (Summer 1990).

——. "A History of Money and Banking in the United States Before the Twentieth Century." In *A History of Money and Banking in the United States: The Colonial*

Era to World War II, ed. Joseph Salerno. Auburn, AL: Mises Institute, 2005 [1982].

——. *America's Great Depression*. 4th ed. New York: Richardson & Snyder, 1983 [1963].

——. *An Austrian Perspective on the History of Economic Thought: Classical Economics*. Vol. 2. Auburn, AL: Mises Institute, 2006 [1995].

——. *An Austrian Perspective on the History of Economic Thought: Economic Thought Before Adam Smith*. Vol. 1. Auburn, AL: Mises Institute, 2006 [1995].

——. "Beginning the Welfare State: Civil War Veterans' Pensions." N.d.

——. "Bureaucracy and the Civil Service in the United States." *Journal of Libertarian Studies* (Summer 1995).

——. *Conceived in Liberty*. Auburn, AL: Mises Institute, 2011 [1975, 1975, 1976, 1979].

——. "Compulsory Education in the United States." In *Education, Free & Compulsory*. Auburn, AL: Mises Institute, 1999 [1971].

——. "Economic Determinism, Ideology, and the American Revolution." *Libertarian Forum* (November, 1974).

——. "Egalitarianism and the Elites." *Review of Austrian Economics* 8, no. 2 (1995).

——. *For a New Liberty: The Libertarian Manifesto*. 2nd ed. Auburn, AL: Mises Institute, 2011 [1978].

——. "From Hoover to Roosevelt: The Federal Reserve and the Financial Elites." In *A History of Money and Banking in the United States: The Colonial Era to World War II*, ed. Joseph Salerno. Auburn, AL: Mises Institute, 2005.

——. "Government Medical Insurance." In *Making Economic Sense*. Auburn, AL: Mises Institute, 1995.

——. "H.L. Mencken: The Joyous Libertarian." *New Individualist Review* (Summer 1962).

——. "Herbert Hoover and the Myth of Laissez Faire." *A New History of Leviathan*, eds. Ronald Radosh and Murray Rothbard. New York: E.P. Dutton, 1972.

——. "Historical Origins." In *The Twelve Year Sentence*, ed. William F. Rickenbacker. San Francisco, CA: Fox & Wilkes, 1999 [1974].

——. "Introduction." In *Lysander Spooner: Libertarian Pietist, Vices Are Not Crimes*. Cupertino, CA: Tanstaafl, 1977.

——. "Left and Right: The Prospects for Liberty." In *Egalitarianism as a Revolt Against Nature and Other Essays*. Auburn, AL: Mises Institute, 2000 [1965].

——. *Man, Economy, and State with Power and Market*. Auburn, AL: Mises Institute 2009 [1962].

——. "Only One Heartbeat Away." *Libertarian Forum* (September, 1974).

——. "Origins of the Welfare State in America." *Journal of Libertarian Studies* 12, no. 2 (1996).

——. *Power and Market: Government and the Economy*. Menlo Park, CA: Institute for Humane Studies, 1970.

——. "Recommended Reading." *Libertarian Forum* (December, 1972).

——. "Report on George B. DeHuszar and Thomas Hulbert Stevenson, *A History of the American Republic*, 2 vols." In *Strictly Confidential: The Private Volker Fund Memos of Murray N. Rothbard*, ed. David Gordon. Auburn, AL: Mises Institute, 2010 [1961].

——. "Roots of the American Corporate State: 1890's–1920's." N.d.

——. "Roots of the Modern State: The Progressive Era." N.d.

——. "Selected Bibliographical Essay." N.d.

——. *Strictly Confidential: The Private Volker Fund Memos of Murray N. Rothbard*, ed. David Gordon. Auburn, AL: Mises Institute, 2010.

——. "The Anatomy of the State." In *Egalitarianism as a Revolt Against Nature and Other Essays*. Auburn, AL: Mises Institute, 2000 [1965].

——. *The Case Against the Fed*. Auburn, AL: Mises Institute, 1994.

——. "The Conspiracy Theory of History Revisited." *Reason* (April, 1974).

——. "The End of Socialism and the Calculation Debate Revisited." In *Economic Controversies*. Auburn, AL: Mises Institute, 2010 [1991].

——. *The Ethics of Liberty*. New York: New York University Press, 2002 [1982].

——. "The Federal Reserve as a Cartelization Device, The Early Years: 1913–1930." In *Money in Crisis: The Federal Reserve, the Economy, and Monetary Reform*, ed. Barry N. Siegel. San Francisco, CA: Pacific Institute for Public Policy Research, 1984.

——. "The Gold-Exchange Standard in the Interwar Years." In *A History of Money and Banking in the United States*, ed. Joseph Salerno. Auburn, AL: Ludwig von Mises Institute, 2005 [1998].

———. "The Hoover Myth: Review of Albert U. Romasco, The Poverty of Abundance." In *For a New America,* eds. James Weinstein and David W. Eakins. New York: Random House, 1970.

———. *The Mystery of Banking.* Auburn, AL: Mises Institute, 2008 [1983].

———. "The New Deal and the International Monetary System." In *Watershed of Empire: Essays on New Deal Foreign Policy,* eds. Leonard Liggio and James Martin. Colorado Springs, CO: Ralph Myles, 1976.

———. "The Origins of the Federal Reserve." In *A History of Money and Banking in the United States: From the Colonial Era to World War II,* ed. Joseph Salerno. Auburn, AL: Mises Institute, 2005 [1999].

———. *The Panic of 1819: Reactions and Policies.* New York: Columbia University Press, 1962.

———. "The Politics of Political Economists: Comment." *Quarterly Journal of Economics* 74 (November, 1960).

———. "The Progressive Era and the Family." In *The American Family and the State,* eds. Joseph R. Peden and Fred R. Glahe. San Francisco, CA: Pacific Research Institute, 1986.

———. "The Railroading of the American People." In *The American Economy and the End of Laissez-Faire: 1870 to World War II.* 1986 audio lecture.

———. *Wall Street, Banks, and American Foreign Policy.* Auburn, AL: Mises Institute, 2011 [1984].

———. "War Collectivism in World War I." In *A New History of Leviathan,* eds. Ronald Radosh and Murray Rothbard. New York: E.P. Dutton, 1972.

———. "World War I as Fulfillment: Power and the Intellectuals." *Journal of Libertarian Studies* 9, no. 1 (1989).

Rushdoony, Rousas John. "John Swett: The Self-Preservation of the State." In *The Messianic Character of American Education: Studies in the History of the Philosophy of Education.* Nutley, NJ: Craig Press, 1963.

Rusk, Jerrold G., and John J. Stucker. "The Effect of the Southern System of Election Laws on Voting Participation: A Reply to V.O. Key, Jr." In *The History of American Electoral Behavior,* eds. J. Sibley, A. Bogue, and W. Flanigan. Princeton, NJ: Princeton University Press, 1978.

Salerno, Joseph T. "Introduction." In Murray Rothbard, *A History of Money and Banking in the United States: The Colonial Era to World War II,* ed. Joseph Salerno. Auburn, AL: Mises Institute, 2005.

Saloutos, Theodore, and John D. Hicks, *Agricultural Discontent in the Middle West.* Madison: University of Wisconsin Press, 1951.

Sanders, Heywood. "Paying for the 'Bloody Shirt': The Politics of Civil War Pensions." In *Political Benefits*, ed. Barry Rundquist. Lexington, MA: D.C. Heath, 1980.

Schlesinger, Arthur M., Jr. *The Crisis of the Old Order, 1919–1933.* Boston: Houghton Mifflin Co., 1957.

Sears, Marian V. "The American Businessman at the Turn of the Century." *Business History Review* (December, 1956).

Selgin, George. "New York's Bank: The National Monetary Commission and the Founding of the Fed." *Cato Institute Policy Analysis* (June, 2016).

Shaffer, Butler. *In Restraint of Trade: The Business Campaign Against Competition, 1918–1938.* Cranbury, NJ: Associated University Presses, 1997.

Shalev, Michael. "The Social Democratic Model and Beyond: Two Generations of Comparative Research on the Welfare State." *Comparative Social Research* 6 (1983).

Shaviro, Sol. "Wages and Payroll in the Depression, 1929–1933." Master's essay, Columbia University, 1947.

Shoup, Lawrence H., and William Minter. *Imperial Brain Trust: The Council on Foreign Relations and United States Foreign Policy.* New York: Monthly Review Press, 1977.

Shradar, Victor L. "Ethnic Politics, Religion, and the Public Schools of San Francisco, 1849–1933." Ph.D. dissertation, School of Education, Stanford University, 1974.

Sklar, Kathryn Kish. "Hull House —— the 1890s: A Community of Women Reformers." *Signs* 10, no. 4 (Summer 1985).

Skocpol, Theda. *Protecting Soldiers and Mothers: The Political Origins of Social Policy in the United States.* Cambridge, MA: Belknap Press of Harvard University Press, 1992.

Skowronek, Stephen. *Building a New American State: The Expansion of the National Administrative Capacities, 1877–1920.* Cambridge: Cambridge University Press, 1982.

Smith, Robert F. *The United States and Cuba.* New York: Bookman Assoc., 1960.

Smith-Rosenberg, Carroll. *Disorderly Conduct.* New York: Alfred A. Knopf, 1985.

Sprague, Oliver M.W. "Immediate Advances in the Discount Rate Unlikely." *The Annalist* (1926).

Steel, Ronald. *Walter Lippmann and the American Century.* New York: Random House, 1981.

Stein, Herbert. "Pre-Revolutionary Fiscal Policy: The Regime of Herbert Hoover." *Journal of Law and Economics* (October, 1966)

——. "The Washington Economics Industry." *American Economic Association Papers and Proceedings* 76 (May, 1986).

Steinreich, Dale. "100 Years of Medical Fascism." *Mises Daily* (April, 2010).

Stephens, John. *The Transition from Capitalism to Socialism.* London: Macmillan, 1979.

Stephenson, Nathaniel W. *Nelson W. Aldrich.* New York: Scribner's, 1930.

Stigler, George. "Can Government Protect the Consumer?" In *The Citizen and the State.* Chicago: University of Chicago Press, 1975 [1971].

——. "The Theory of Economic Regulation." *Bell Journal of Economics and Management* (Spring 1971).

Stigler, George, and James Kindahl. *The Behavior of Industrial Prices.* New York: NBER, 1970.

Stocking, George W. "Stabilization of the Oil Industry: Its Economic and Legal Aspects." *American Economic Review, Papers and Proceedings* (May, 1933).

Stromberg, Joseph. "Introduction." In Murray Rothbard, *Man, Economy, and State, with Power and Market.* Auburn, AL: Mises Institute, 2004. First ed.

——. "The Spanish-American War as Trial Run, or Empire as its Own Justification." In *The Costs of War: America's Pyrrhic Victories*, ed. John Denson. Auburn, AL: Mises Institute, 1999.

——. "William McKinley: Architect of the American Empire." In *Reassessing the Presidency: The Rise of the Executive State and the Decline of Freedom*, ed. John Denson. Auburn, AL: Mises Institute, 1999.

Swain, Donald C. *Federal Conservation Policy, 1921–1933.* Berkeley: University of California Press, 1963.

Tabarrok, Alexander. "The Separation of Commercial and Investment Banking: The Morgans vs. The Rockefellers." *Quarterly Journal of Austrian Economics* 1, no. 1 (1998).

Tansill, Charles Callan. *America Goes to War.* Boston: Little, Brown & Co., 1938.

Tariello, Frank. Jr., *The Reconstruction of American Political Ideology, 1865–1917.* Charlottesville: University Press of Virginia, 1981.

Taus, Esther Rogoff. *Central Banking Functions of the United States Treasury, 1789–1941.* New York: Columbia University Press, 1943.

Thorelli, Hans B. *The Federal Antitrust Policy: The Origination of an American Tradition.* Baltimore: Johns Hopkins Press, 1955.

Tobey, Ronald C. *The American Ideology of National Science, 1919–1930.* Pittsburgh: University of Pittsburgh Press, 1971.

Thornton, Mark. *The Economics of Prohibition.* Salt Lake City: University of Utah Press, 1991.

———. "The Fall and Rise of Puritanical Policy in America." *Journal of Libertarian Studies* 12 (Spring 1996).

Timberlake, James H. *Prohibition and the Progressive Movement, 1900–1920.* New York: Atheneum, 1970.

Troesken, Werner. *Why Regulate Utilities? The New Institutional Economics and the Chicago Gas Industry, 1849–1924.* Ann Arbor: University of Michigan Press, 1996.

Tyack, David B. *The One Best System: A History of American Urban Education.* Cambridge: Harvard University Press, 1974.

U.S. Department of Commerce. *Historical Statistics of the United States, Colonial Times to 1957.* Washington, DC: Government Printing Office, 1960.

Ulman, Lloyd. *The Rise of the National Trade Union.* Cambridge, MA: Harvard University Press, 1955.

Urofsky, Melvin I. *Big Steel and the Wilson Administration.* Columbus: Ohio State University Press, 1969.

Valelly, Richard M. *Radicalism in the States: the Minnesota Farmer-Labor Party and the American Political Economy.* Chicago: University of Chicago Press, 1989.

Vietor, Richard H.K. "Businessmen and the Political Economy: The Railroad Rate Controversy of 1905." *Journal of American History* (June, 1977).

Viner, Jacob. "Political Aspects of International Finance, Part II." *Journal of Business* (July, 1928).

Violas, Paul C. "Jane Addams and the New Liberalism." In *Roots of Crisis: American Education in the 20ᵗʰ Century,* eds. C.J. Karier, P.C. Violas, and J. Spring. Chicago: Rand McNally, 1973.

——. "Progressive Social Philosophy: Charles Horton Cooley and Edward Alsworth Ross." In *Roots of Crisis: American Education in the 20ᵗʰ Century,* eds. C.J. Karier, P.C. Violas, and J. Spring. Chicago: Rand McNally, 1973.

Wagner, Ronald R. "Virtue Against Vice: A Study of Moral Reformers and Prostitution in the Progressive Era." Ph.D. dissertation, University of Wisconsin, 1971.

Walton, Gary M., and Hugh Rockoff. *History of the American Economy.* New York: Harcourt Brace & Company, 1998. 8th ed.

Warburg, Paul. "Essays on Banking Reform in the United States." *Proceedings of the Academy of Political Science* 4 (July, 1914).

——. *The Federal Reserve System.* 2 vols. New York: Macmillan, 1930.

Ward, Robert D. "The Origin and Activities of the National Security League, 1914–1919." *Mississippi Valley Historical Review* 47 (June, 1960).

Warren, Harris Gaylord. *Herbert Hoover and the Great Depression.* New York: Oxford University Press, 1959.

Weinstein, James. *The Corporate Ideal in the Liberal State, 1900–1918.* Boston: Beacon Press, 1968.

Weisberger, Bernard A. *They Gathered at the River: The Story of the Great Revivalists and their Impact Upon Religion in America.* Boston: Little, Brown, 1958.

West, Robert Craig. *Banking Reform and the Federal Reserve, 1863–1923.* Ithaca, NY: Cornell University Press, 1977.

White, Lawrence. "Foreword." In William Leggett, *Democratik Editorials: Essays in Jacksonian Political Economy.* Indianapolis, IN: Liberty Fund, 1984.

——. "William Leggett: Jacksonian editorialist as classical liberal political economist." *History of Political Economy* 18 (1986).

Whitney, Simon N. *Antitrust Policies: The American Experience in Twenty Industries.* New York: The Twentieth Century Fund, 1958.

Whitney, Caroline. "The Bankers' Acceptance Market." In *The Banking Situation,* eds. H. Parker Willis and John M. Chapman. New York: Columbia University Press, 1934.

Wiebe, Robert H. *Businessmen and Reform: A Study of the Progressive Movement.* Cambridge: Harvard University Press, 1962.

Wilensky, Harold. *The Welfare State and Equality.* Berkeley: University of California Press, 1975.

Williams, William Appleman. *The Contours of American History.* Cleveland, OH: World Publishing Co., 1961.

Williamson, Harold F. and Arnold R. Daum. *The American Petroleum Industry: The Age of Illumination 1859–1899.* Evanston, IL: Northwestern University Press, 1959.

Willis, H. Parker. "Politics and the Federal Reserve System." *Bankers' Magazine* (January, 1925).

——. "The Banking Problem in the United States." In "Report on an Inquiry into Contemporary Banking in the United States," ed. H.P. Willis. Unpublished, 1925.

——. "The Breakdown of the Gold Exchange Standard and Its Financial Imperialism." *The Annalist* 33 (16 October 1931).

——. "The Failure of the Federal Reserve." *North American Review* 227 (May, 1929).

——. *The Federal Reserve System.* New York: Ronald Press, 1923.

——. *The Theory and Practice of Central Banking.* New York: Harper & Bros., 1936.

——. "Untitled." *The Annalist* (10 November 1924).

——. "What Caused the Panic of 1929." *North American Review* 229 (February, 1930).

——. "Will the Racing Stock Market Become a Juggernaut?" *The Annalist* (24 November 1924).

Willis, H. Parker, and John M. Chapman. *The Banking Situation.* New York: Columbia University Press, 1934.

Wolman, Leo. *Ebb and Flow in Trade Unionism.* New York: National Bureau of Economic Research, 1936.

———. *The Growth of American Trade Unions, 1880–1923*. New York: National Bureau of Economic Research, 1924.

———. *Wages in Relation to Economic Recovery*. Chicago: University of Chicago Press, 1931.

Woods, Eleanor H. *Robert A. Woods; Champion of Democracy*. Boston: Houghton Mifflin, 1929.

Woods, Thomas, Jr. "Theodore Roosevelt and the Modern Presidency." In *Reassessing the Presidency: The Rise of the Executive State and the Decline of Freedom*, ed. John Denson. Auburn, AL: Mises Institute, 1999.

Wunsch, James. "Prostitution and Public Policy: From Regulation to Suppression, 1858–1920." Ph.D. dissertation, University of Chicago, 1976.

Yellowitz, Irwin. *Labor and the Progressive Movement in New York State, 1897–1916*. Ithaca, NY: Cornell University Press, 1965.

Yoder, Dale, and George R. Davies. *Depression and Recovery*. New York: McGraw-Hill, 1934.

Young, James Harvey. *Pure Food: Securing the Federal Food and Drugs Act of 1906*. Princeton, NJ: Princeton University Press, 1989.

Zerbe, Richard. "Monopoly, The Emergence of Oligopoly and the Case of Sugar Refining." *Journal of Law and Economics* (October, 1970).

———. "The American Sugar Refinery Company, 1887–1914: The Story of a Monopoly." *Journal of Law and Economics* 12 (October, 1969).

Index of Names

Compiled by Patrick Newman

Index of Subjects

Compiled by Patrick Newman

Hickey Freeman Co., 443
High-License League of Indianapolis,
141
Home Owners Loan Corporation, 354
Homestead Law, 267
Hopkins Bill, 69–70
Hudson and Manhattan Railroad,
365–66, 481–82
Hudson Companies, 482
Hudson Motor Co., 264
Hull House, 341–42, 344–48, 351, 354

Illinois Manufacturing Association,
359, 464
Illinois Staats-Zeitung, 177
Illinois State Board of Charities, 343
Immigration, 31, 38, 40, 110–11,
116–21, 123, 127, 129–30, 136, 138,
143–44, 151–56, 158–60, 190, 292,
299, 301–309, 311, 314–15, 330, 409,
411–13, 527
Immigration Act, 315
Immigration Protective League, 190
Immigration Restriction League, 155
Independent Treasury System, 486
Indianapolis Monetary Convention,
469
Industrial Board, 392–93
Industrial Conference, 517
Industrial Relations Councilors, 357–58
Industrial Revolution, 55, 91–93, 97–98
Ingersoll-Rand, 281
Inland Waterways Commission, 270–71
Institute for Christian Sociology, 336,
432
Institute for Government Research,
443–44, 447–48
Institute for Humane Studies, 24
Intellectuals
court, 20, 25–27, 30, 39, 107,
196–97, 206, 210–12, 215–17, 234,
251–53, 260, 262, 270–94, 302,
308, 327, 350, 362, 381, 383–88,

397–99, 402, 420–36, 468, 474–75,
483, 515
pietist, 37, 40, 316–18, 333–40, 356,
398–99, 414, 421, 430–31, 438–39,
456
revolutionary, 20
secularization of, 26, 32, 316,
333–50, 356, 399, 421, 432
turn to empiricism, 26, 32, 428–31,
436–52
Inter-Church Federation of Vermont,
317
Inter-State Commerce Railway Association, 77–80
Interborough Rapid Transit Company,
278
Intercollegiate Socialist Society, 420
International Acceptance Bank of New
York, 503–04
International Association for Labor
Legislation, 292
International Association of Technical
Engineers, Architects, and Draftsmen, 518
International Harvester, 33–34,
100–01, 218, 220–21, 227, 234, 278,
280, 283, 353, 367, 384, 468, 482–83,
524
International Labor Bureau, 292
International Ladies Garment Workers Union, 352
International Mercantile Marine, 468
International Oil War, 230–34
International Statistical Congress, 437
International Sugar Committee, 377
Interstate Commerce Act, Commission, 26, 34, 69, 73–80, 211, 214–15,
291, 380–82, 395, 438, 464, 468–69,
511
Iowa Pool, 59–61
Irish, 118, 128–32, 136, 151, 166, 174,
176–78, 180, 186, 299, 301, 303–309,
330, 345

THE MISES INSTITUTE

The Mises Institute, founded in 1982, is a teaching and research center for the study of Austrian economics, libertarian and classical liberal political theory, and peaceful international relations. In support of the school of thought represented by Ludwig von Mises, Murray N. Rothbard, Henry Hazlitt, and F.A. Hayek, we publish books and journals, sponsor student and professional conferences, and provide online education. Mises.org is a vast resource of free material for anyone in the world interested in these ideas. The Mises Institute is funded entirely by voluntary contributions. We do not accept government funding and never will.

Made in the USA
Middletown, DE
30 January 2024

48602161R00335